I0878713

happiness by design

JUSTUS NIELAND

happiness by design

MODERNISM AND MEDIA IN THE EAMES ERA

UNIVERSITY OF MINNESOTA PRESS
MINNEAPOLIS LONDON

Portions of chapter 2 were previously published in "Midcentury Futurisms: Expanded Cinema, Design, and the Modernist Sensorium," *Affirmations: Of the Modern* 2, no. 1 (December 2014): 46–84; and "Making Happy, Happy-making: The Eameses and Communication by Design," *Modernism and Affect*, ed. Julie Taylor (Edinburgh: Edinburgh University Press, 2015). Portions of chapter 3 were previously published as "Conference Technique: The Goldsholls and the Aspen Idea," *Up Is Down: Mid-Century Experiments in Advertising and Film at the Goldsholl Studio*, ed. Amy Beste and Corinne Granof (Evanston, Ill.: The Block Museum of Art, Northwestern University, 2018).

Funding that contributed to the production of this book was made possible through the generosity of the MSU Foundation of Michigan State University.

Copyright 2020 by Justus Nieland

All rights reserved. No part of this publication may be reproduced, stored in a retrieval system, or transmitted, in any form or by any means, electronic, mechanical, photocopying, recording, or otherwise, without the prior written permission of the publisher.

Published by the University of Minnesota Press
111 Third Avenue South, Suite 290
Minneapolis, MN 55401-2520
http://www.upress.umn.edu

Designed and typeset in Eames Century Modern and Trade Gothic Condensed by Elizabeth Elsas Mandel.

Printed in Canada on acid-free paper.
The University of Minnesota is an equal-opportunity educator and employer.

26 25 24 23 22 21 20   10 9 8 7 6 5 4 3 2 1

LIBRARY OF CONGRESS CATALOGING-IN-PUBLICATION DATA
Nieland, Justus, author.
Happiness by design : modernism and media in the Eames era / Justus Nieland.
Minneapolis : University of Minnesota Press, [2020] | Includes bibliographical references and index. |
Identifiers: LCCN 2019001520 (print) | ISBN 978-1-5179-0204-9 (hc) | ISBN 978-1-5179-0205-6 (pb)
Subjects: LCSH: Motion pictures—Art direction. | Motion pictures—Setting and scenery. | Eames, Charles—Influence. | Eames, Ray—Influence. | Modernism (Art)—United States. | United States—Civilization—20th century.
Classification: LCC PN1995.9.A74 N54 2020 (print) | DDC 791.4302/5—dc23
LC record available at https://lccn.loc.gov/2019001520

for my parents

contents

introduction

AMONG THE PERSONAL PAPERS of architect and designer Eero Saarinen is a curious chart of the marriages of his friends, ranking their relative happiness on a scale from 0 to 100 percent.[1] At the top of the chart—with a whopping 90 percent happiness rating—are Saarinen's dear friends Charles and Ray Eames. Saarinen's diagrammatic approach to the happiness of his intimates may strike us as rather technical, perhaps overly quantitative or schematic. Theodor Adorno would have been horrified. By what empirical method does one measure something as unquantifiable or resistant to calculation as happiness—the notoriously fuzzy affective complex of well-being, contentment, and pleasure that has long been at the center of the philosophical question of what counts as the "good life"?[2] Even as his chart gestures to midcentury happiness as a product of calculation and technique, Saarinen's choice of the Eameses as almost completely happy was entirely in keeping with the couple's public image at midcentury. Arguably the most influential American designers of the postwar period, the Eameses were a model happy couple whose iconic designed objects and design practice would be globally exported as the promise of the cheery lifestyle afforded by U.S.-style democratic liberalism (Plate 1). As a mode of creative production across media forms and disciplinary boundaries, the Eamesian *homo faber* needed film, and reinvented the medium's midcentury usefulness for a world of new needs, capacities, and satisfactions.

Taking the Eameses as its presiding figures, *Happiness by Design* explores the transformations of modernism at midcentury through the film and media experiments of the designer, a profession with a new cultural prestige and world-historical mission in the Cold War period. The midcentury has been often viewed as the moment of modernism's institutionalization and the domestication of its utopian demands on the senses.[3] This book, by contrast, traces a vital midcentury modernism that used film and moving-image technologies as the defining media of postwar happiness. For the designers at the heart of this book—experts in the stuff and style of the postwar "good life"—happiness was both a technical and an ideological problem central to the future of liberal democracy. Being happy demanded new things, but also vanguard approaches to work and play, consumption and pedagogy, knowledge production and its horizon of dissemination—namely, *communication*, a crucial Cold War shibboleth. Happiness, in short, required technique and fueled designers' media experimentation. Assuming public roles worldwide as the face of the American Century's exuberant material culture, Cold War designers increasingly engaged in creative activity that spanned disciplines, crossed art and technoscience, and reckoned with the environmental reach of media at the dawn of the information age. Designers became the master communicators in an era that understood multimedia communication—rational, efficient, transparent—as the very lifeblood of happiness.

I call this the "Eames era," a periodizing term perhaps more familiar as a baggy descriptor for alluring midcentury design objects, tastefully consumed on eBay and elsewhere. In this book, it captures the extent to which this happy couple's film and media practice exemplified the postwar paradigms and institutional sites that remade modernism's sensory politics and its designs on happiness at midcentury. Influenced by communications theory and cybernetics, theories of corporate management, notions of democratic perception and creative activity, debates about postwar educational reform, and nascent ecological thought, the Eameses and designers in their orbit found new worlds for film at midcentury. In the process, they brought a modernist tradition of media experimentation and sensory training into a Cold War period marked by pervasive concerns about postwar technoscience's threat to the human scale, proliferating humanisms, and debates about the value of the humanities and the parameters of humane disciplinarity as such. The Eameses' human-scale modernism helped teach postwar citizens how to be happy in media by organizing and disciplining the sensorium, preparing it for life in the culture of informatic abundance that defines our present.

In making a claim to a transformed modernist media practice in something called "the Eames era," I imagine that literary modernists, hip to Hugh Kenner's landmark 1971 study of Ezra Pound, might remember that its follow-up was *Bucky: A Guided Tour of Buckminster Fuller* (1973), one of the first studies of the architect and "comprehensive designer," and a hero and friend of the Eameses. In his introduction,

Figure I.1. Charles and Ray Eames pose with steel frame during construction of Case Study House No. 8, 1949. Copyright 2017 Eames Office LLC (eamesoffice.com).

Kenner recalled his undergraduate encounter with the glossy visual culture of abundance that the Eameses helped to furnish in its postwar maturation, when he cut from the pages of a March 1943 *Life* magazine the pieces of Fuller's Dymaxion World map. Its color patterns demarcated not nation-states in the throes of a devastating total war but the temperatures regulating a peaceful postwar climate of global air travel. For the Eameses, too, 1943 marked a decisive moment in a broader shift from wartime production to the anticipation of the postwar good life, and their famous innovations in living's constitutive materials and technologies—plywood chief among them. Having moved from the Cranbrook Academy of Art in Bloomfield, Michigan, to Los Angeles to

Life Presents

R. BUCKMINSTER FULLER'S

DYMAXION WORLD

Printed on one side only of the two heavy center sheets of this issue of LIFE is a new kind of world map. It is a projection of the round earth on 14 flat segments, eight triangles and six squares. The map may be removed from the magazine and, in accordance with instructions on pages 44 and 53, cut out and assembled as a three-dimensional approximation of a globe or laid out as a flat map, with which the world may be fitted together and rearranged to illuminate special aspects of its geography.

As the Dymaxion World, this map bears the hallmark of R. Buckminster Fuller (*above*), engineer, who is now on the staff of the Board of Economic Warfare. Fuller's Dymaxion house (1927) and Dymaxion car (1933) figure in every constructive discussion of post-war shelter and transport. Fuller's Dymaxion World embodies his effort to resolve the dilemma of cartography: how to depict as a flat surface this spherical world, with true scale, true direction and correct configuration at one and the same time (LIFE, Aug. 3).

Orthodox cartography demands that the world be projected correctly in at least one of these aspects, even to the sacrifice of the other by distortion. This is a reasonable requirement in maps that are to be used for navigation, statistical work and other precise purposes. On his map, Mr. Fuller adjusts the requirements of scale, direction and shape in a compromise which distributes distortions evenly between them and around the globe. For the layman, engrossed in belated, war-taught lessons in geography, the Dymaxion World map is a means by which he can see the whole world fairly and all at once.

CONTINUED ON NEXT PAGE

Figure I.2. Buckminster Fuller's Dymaxion World map, *Life* magazine, 1943.

develop their molded-plywood chair prototypes, their newly hatched Plyformed Wood Company had that year significantly upped production of the manufacture of plywood splints for the U.S. Navy to two hundred units per day, and had begun developing parts for various aircraft manufacturers, including the nose section of an experimental military glider designed to transport bodies and materiel "between home and battleground" (Plate 2).[4] *Between home and battleground.* The phrase nicely describes the terrain of Eames-era happiness, much of it defined by media experimentation within a postwar visual and technical culture indelibly marked by war, the deadly engine of so much design innovation.[5] For Fuller, the conceptual and programmatic transition from "weaponry to livingry" was the basic challenge of humanity, and would be met by a global "design science revolution" predicated on the rational, technocratic management of global resources, and the supersession of politics itself as the sphere of constitutive antagonism.

For Kenner, Fuller's design philosophy portended a broader ontology of nature and technology capable of overcoming the "generic twentieth-century problem, discontinuity," and uniting "the airplane and the horse, 'artifice' and 'nature.'"[6] He read Fuller's *Ideas and Integrities* (1963) and *No More Secondhand God* (1963), and finally, in 1967, he heard the seventy-two-year-old Fuller lecture on "Whole Systems" and the abiding persistence of patterns that ecologically united art and technics, nature and second nature. The encounter was decisive: Kenner credited the designer with "solving" for him, "that week, a book called *The Pound Era* I had been trying to think out for years and was suddenly able to start writing."[7] In the final, elegiac paragraphs of that study, in fact, Kenner saw fit to narrate Pound's eventual meeting with Fuller, during his 1970 lectures in Venice at the International University of Art. One of the subjects of Fuller's four lectures was Pound. The two met and talked, and a "copy of Fuller's Nehru Memorial Lecture changed hands; Pound listened to it, sitting up late at night. Men are impoverished, it says, by an accounting system 'anchored exclusively to the value of metals.' But all wealth comes 'from the wealth of the minds of world man.'"[8]

Kenner's explanation for the genesis of *The Pound Era* reminds us that one of modernism's landmark studies of poetic technique and mediation was born in design theory and practice's pronounced ecological turn in the late 1960s, much of its plummy rhetoric of "world man" influenced by Fuller's utopian and technocratic approach to the abiding continuity of physical systems.[9] But it also bears witness to the penumbra of influence of the midcentury's most publicly visible media theorist, Marshall McLuhan, who first introduced Kenner, his University of Toronto student, to a then-disgraced Pound in 1948, and got him thinking ecologically about poetics and communications media. By 1967 McLuhan and Fuller had become regular interlocutors in a range of high-profile interdisciplinary conferences and symposia on the arts and sciences of "communication," including—as I discuss in more detail later—designer Will Burtin's Vision 67 conference in New York City, where they were featured as keynote speakers. As Mark Goble has argued in his essential study of modernism's "mediated life," the Kenner/McLuhan nexus at midcentury connects "modernism's culture and aesthetics to a faith in communication."[10] As such, it serves as a powerful reminder of how "the study of both modernism and communications . . . emerged almost simultaneously as twentieth-century preoccupations and flourished as conglomerating triumphs of the postwar university in the United States."[11]

One of this book's abiding convictions is that these intersecting midcentury preoccupations—faith in communication and media experimentation, ecological practice and the challenges of Fuller's "world man," the fate of Cold War modernism and the power of postwar institutions, including the university—can't be completely understood without a full reckoning with designer film and media practice and its Eames-era modernism.[12] As we'll see, conceptualized as a vanguard communicative strategy, the media practices of designers like the Eameses and Burtin found their way directly into the classrooms of the postwar university. Designers were key players in far-flung debates about postwar education reform and the role of film and visual media in the operation and bureaucratic extension of the research university as a "media system."[13] These practices overlapped at various junctures with progressive and technophilic pedagogical institutions in the postwar period, from the New Bauhaus in Chicago and Black Mountain College in North Carolina (where Fuller and his students erected his first geodesic dome), to the Aspen Institute and the Hochschule für Gestaltung (school of design) in Ulm, Germany. The full extent of designers' communicative zeal becomes clear only by embedding their film and media experiments in the fitful terrain of media theory and practice that would, at midcentury, transfigure modernism, as Kenner himself sensed. Investigating the work of these postwar prophets of communication at the moment of modernism's own institutionalization, this book explores how designers remade the utopian aspirations of modernism through various modes and sites of media experimentation and inquiry.

Eames-era designer media practice was a vital mode of modernist interdisciplinarity, abetted by the rise of communication as mode of working, making, and thinking between and across conventional boundaries of knowledge. By featuring designers who worked across media and disciplines, I hope to revise accounts of modernist periodization and familiar assessments of the consolidation of a modernist doctrine of medium specificity at midcentury. Because there were no perceived medial limits to their instrumental, problem-solving ambitions, designers' media practice helps us see how, at midcentury, Greenbergian and New Critical sensory idioms—bureaucratic and ascetic—were at once institutionalized and immediately beset by "communication" and "environmental" paradigms for understanding the life of the senses—paradigms that refused medium specificity. Crucially, the midcentury designers discussed in this book were thinking hard about disciplinarity: its functions and its limits, its institutional sites, and its various and competing claims to expertise. Designers were drawn to transdisciplinary universalism and aspired to holistic, integral, humanistic knowledge as an antidote to specialization and the fragmentation of knowledge regimes. This book's own interdisciplinary method is meant to address the expanded medial and cultural terrain that design sought to manage by thinking at environmental and ecological levels.

My approach here is animated by a spate of superb recent work at the intersection of modernism and media studies, and in the so-called medial turn that has helped us resee modernism as itself an event in the longer history of media change. Literary modernisms of the interwar period, for example, have lately been recast (by Goble, Kate Marshall, Julian Murphet, David Trotter, Mark Wollaeger, and others) as ways of resisting and accommodating the technical media's challenge to the prestige of the human.[14] *Happiness by Design* extends such revisionist histories of modernist media practice into the informatic thicket of the midcentury period, and into the high humanism of Eames-era designers—prophets of communication whose modernism helped make media a lifestyle. They also designed to reckon with a media environment defined by flows of information, and its abiding technologies and theories of communication; they strived *to be happy and make happy* by scaling this media environment to human needs and capacities; and they, too, anxiously faced nature grown unnatural, permeated by technics, and demanding a new kind of organic design.

I also draw on recent film and media scholarship attentive to the role of institutions in shaping the heterogeneity of the cinematic apparatus at midcentury, and respond to calls for thicker histories of avant-garde practice within—and not merely against—the operations and administrative practices of institutional life.[15] Film's position within a capacious, intermedial design practice was not unique to the midcentury, even though it would abet period-specific programs of happiness. Designers had long been drawn to film as a medium, as a technology within a new landscape of modern technics, and as a component of a broader apparatus serving a range of imperatives: corporate and state, industrial and aesthetic. This history of fascination and intermedial experimentation extends significantly back into both the heady terrain of the interwar avant-gardes—especially as they intersected with the techno-utopian agendas of the Bauhaus—and the more quotidian, instrumental practices of industrial and educational film and other modes of what Charles Acland and Haidee Wasson call "useful cinema."[16]

For this reason, design—as an expansive and at times unruly domain of intermedial production with its own rich disciplinary histories—has begun to emerge in film and media studies as a key category for scholars pursuing a richer and more nuanced historiography of modernist and avant-garde practices.[17] World's Fairs of the kind consuming much of the Eameses' time and energy at midcentury, like the tradition of interwar exhibition design's appeals to the "cinematic model," have allowed scholars to embed film historiography in a broader media history of display, exhibition, what Wasson dubs practices of "industrial showmanship."[18] At the fairs, whose pavilions were orchestrated by designers, industrial films were "ontologically complex events": cameras, screens, and projectors coalesced with a host of display practices and exhibitionary traditions, including the travelogue and diorama, and intersected with changing idioms of corporate expression and communication. Variously incorporated into exhibition design, film and specifically cinematic perception yielded what Bauhausler Herbert Bayer theorized as "a new discipline, as an apex of all media and powers of communication and collective efforts and effects."[19] Beginning in the late 1930s, escalating through the war with the rise of state- and foundation-funded communications research, and abetted in the postwar period by the prestige of cybernetics and a technical discourse of information, designers' film and media practice was one of the period's most powerful manifestations of a modernism remade through a sweeping communications paradigm. In the process, a familiar modernism of formal difficulty and communicative intransigence was challenged and reconfigured by a program of communicative clarity and transparency, information processing, and a humane problem solving as ambitious as it was anxious.

How Modernism Communicates

With the simultaneous postwar institutionalization of modernist aesthetics and communication studies, we have been told, a once-transgressive, "bad" modernism becomes "good." By this, critics have named an avant-garde modernism defanged and banalized, smuggled into the disreputable domain of middlebrow taste as "good design," and often conscripted in the ideological melodrama of the Cold War and its state and corporate imperatives.[20] Manifested in the centrifugal domain of "communication" (which is to say, information handling, propaganda, the winning of hearts and minds), such imperatives reflect the postwar influence of empirical research into the effects of mass media, and their role in the shaping of public opinion and strategies of democratic governance.

Perhaps the most consequential of these projects, organized in the late 1930s, was the Rockefeller Foundation–funded "Communications Group," whose aims and key personnel also intersected, fitfully at times, with the Frankfurt School, then in exile in the United States.[21] An important collaboration among the academy, the state, and private foundations, the Communications Group's explorations of the problems of "mass influence," the dynamics of fascist propaganda, and the possibility of "genuinely democratic propaganda" joined humanists, critical theorists, and social scientists in "the common goal of understanding cultural and mass communication in the age of totalitarianism."[22]

After the war, the success and influence of the group led to the consolidation of mass communications research as a social scientific discipline and the entrenchment of Harold Laswell's model for understanding communications systems and media effects: who says what to whom in which channel with what effect? But it also marked a technocratic revision of traditional democratic theory insofar as its media research seemed to confirm the need for a democracy guided by experts. These more illiberal inclinations deepened in the first decade of communications studies as a newborn academic discipline after the war, when "U.S. military, propaganda, and intelligence agencies provided the large majority of all project funding for the field."[23] For these reasons, and buoyed by the publication of Claude Shannon's revision of Laswell's linear model in *A Mathematical Theory of Communication* (1948), the late 1940s became what John Durham Peters has called "probably the single grandest moment in the century's confrontation with communication," a postwar vogue marked by two dominant discourses: "a technical one about information theory and a therapeutic one about communication as cure and disease."[24]

What did the communication boom, with its positivist roots and soft behaviorist Cold War ambitions, mean for modernism at midcentury? As a reliable synonym for propaganda, as the mandate of a corporate idiom of global capital that designers helped craft and display, and the anxious salve of a Cold War détente between nuclear powers whose feared capacity for mutual annihilation was the most catastrophic sign of communicative breakdown, communication could easily become a prime culprit in the domestication of modernism's unruly and negative aesthetic politics. Death by happiness.

Herbert Marcuse surely thought so. "Contradiction," he insisted in *One-Dimensional Man* (1964), must "have a medium of communication."[25] In a not-so-distant past, contradiction had found that medium in Brechtian modernism, what he called "literature's own answer to the threat of total behaviorism" (*ODM*, 67). By the mid-1960s, however, modernist antagonism had been lost in the domain of "everyday living," where the "alien and alienating oeuvres of intellectual culture become familiar goods and services" (*ODM,* 61). The modernist communicative project he artfully reverse engineered out of the jumble of literary history was the key preserve of Hegel's "unhappy consciousness," joining strategies of alienation, decadence, and avant-garde irrationality. As it did for Adorno and other members of the Frankfurt School, this melancholy modernism bore formal witness to a "divided world," stained by suffering, fragmented and discontinuous, and therefore testimony to the "defeated possibilities, the hopes unfulfilled, and the promises betrayed" of capitalist modernity (*ODM,* 61). Drawing on Roland Barthes's *Le degré zéro de l'écriture* (1953; translated into English as *Writing Degree Zero),* Marcuse insisted that "the truly avant-garde works of literature"—the poetics of Arthur Rimbaud, Dada, and surrealism—"communicate the break with communication," exploding "pre-established structure[s] of meaning," and becoming their own kinds of mute and intolerable objects (*ODM,* 68–69). Against this modernism of communicative opacity, linguistic difficulty, and utopian unhappiness, he positioned a happy, repressive functionalism evident both in language—the linguistic theory of operational philosophy—and new, "more 'integrated'" architecture linking cultural centers, shopping centers, and government centers. "Domination," he observed, "has its own aesthetics, and democratic domination has its democratic aesthetics" (*ODM,* 65).

Marcuse thus extended into Cold War debates about technical rationality and its hostility to autonomy (that keyword of New Left happiness) what Mark Wollaeger has described as interwar modernism's abiding desire "to clear a space for more *authentic* forms of communication."[26] Such modernist authenticity is bureaucracy's other, what Sven Spieker calls the "giant paper jam based on the exponential increase of stored data" in the wake of the control revolution.[27] Enshrined institutionally at midcentury by the New Critics and the New York Intellectuals, high modernism's aesthetic of communicative ambivalence, difficulty, and authenticity squares off against an expansive, technocratic postwar control paradigm that desires communicative efficiency and transparency, and understands human expression as integrated within communication networks that service and regulate organisms and information-processing machines alike. In the process, human communication is rethought within a new paradigm of organization—a "networked, systems-based, feedback-driven" organicism.[28] Writing in 1957 in the wake of the influence of these new communicative paradigms on the postwar avant-garde, cresting in the first wave of conceptual and systems-based art, Meyer Schapiro made a similar plea for a modernist formalism of "non-communication."[29] For him, postwar communication theory typified a world of "social relationships which is impersonal, calculating, and controlled," and art that followed from it expressed the pathos of a culture "increasingly organized through industry, economy, and the state."[30]

Marcuse's and Schapiro's claims about an unruly, negative modernism's fate at the hands of Cold War institutionalization and the organizational power of the corporate communications paradigm are powerful. Their threnody of modernism is also more than a bit misleading, and not always helpful for understanding the stakes and ambitions of the designer film and media practices I discuss in this book. It suggests that modernism's materialities of communication can be somehow isolated from a messier terrain of competitive media practices in which they were honed. It downplays the role of modernism in the midcentury administration of culture, a complex endeavor indeed, linking philanthropic organizations, the postwar university, and the state in surprising new partnerships and alliances.[31] It forgets the bevy of media-savvy, pragmatic, and rationalist variants of interwar modernism fueling designers, from constructivist utopianism or the logical positivism of the Vienna Circle, with its desire for a purified language, to the quest of general semantics for kinds of linguistic clarity hostile to propagandistic abuse.[32] These strains, as they weave throughout designer film and media practices in a postwar period newly sensitive to media's role in liberal governance and the shaping of a democratic polity, affirm in different ways Kenneth Burke's midcentury insistence on the modernist artist as primarily a rhetorician, embedded in public culture of communication and all its competing media forms.[33]

The death-by-communication thesis also overlooks how the extension of the postwar communications paradigm allows us to glimpse robust varieties of interdisciplinary media practices precisely at the moment when modernism, we are told, became less interesting, and less worthy of our critical attention. It's not that versions of modernism weren't institutionalized at midcentury, or often weaponized as a form of soft power in the Cold War. They were, and Eames-era designers often helped in decisive ways. Rather, it's that the process of institutionalization was itself livelier, and its sites and administrative agendas stranger, and therefore more compelling as media-historiographic objects, than we have fully realized. As modernism confronted, and often abetted, the communicative capacities of the postwar corporation, it repositioned the designer as a manager of epochal change, a culture administrator, and an experimental media practitioner across familiar forms and tidy disciplinary boundaries. With this aspiration toward interdisciplinarity, designers positioned themselves as the creative types most needed in the modern world, what George Nelson called "a strange and explosive place where accelerating change seems to be the only remaining constant, where intangible relationships are more concrete than tangible things and where cooperation has replaced competition as the one possible technique for survival."[34] As change managers, designers grappled with postwar media's seemingly new nature, gauged the sensorium and world awareness that media technologies would extend and organize, and assessed the mass media's increasingly powerful role in the postwar management of citizenship, culture, and lifestyle. Buoyed by the prospect of a bold midcentury world for the making, the designers' expansive liberal optimism incarnated what Reyner Banham called "the problem of affluent democracy," and brought a modernist tradition of media experimentation and sensory utopianism into the institutional operations of what art historian Pamela Lee has dubbed the "Cold War semiosphere."[35] Instead of framing the rise of communications as the demise of any modernism worth caring about, I argue that designers' film and media practices played essential roles both in an overlooked interdisciplinary genealogy of Anglo-American media theory and in the administration of postwar happiness itself as a modernist technique.

A Communications Primer; or, Happiness by Design

Eamesian happiness, circulating through both images and objects, comprised a particular midcentury product that linked the "goodness" of the American good life, secured through the United States' booming consumer economy and global hegemony at the dawn of the Cold War, to the "goodness" of so-called good design. In the postwar United States, the Eameses' designed objects and lifestyle were exhibited within a broader revolution in American architecture, design, and the booming housing market that Mark Jarzombek has dubbed "Good-Life Modernism," a massive effort to "integrate the house once and for all into the realm of consumer goods."[36] Formally an architectural merger of the modernist aesthetics of the European International Style and the American ranch style, the new, airy domesticity of good-life modernism was theorized in key manifestos for postwar living, such as George Nelson and Henry Wright's *Tomorrow's House: A Complete Guide for the Homebuilder* (1946). And it was promulgated through "a nexus of interests of unparalleled dimension": influential lifestyle magazines like *House & Home*, architectural schools, banking establishments, construction industries, and museums. Properly administered, modern design's "goodness" would become indispensable equipment for everyday life.

Figure I.3. Interior, Case Study House No. 8. Photograph by Julius Shulman. Copyright J. Paul Getty Trust. Getty Research Institute, Los Angeles (2004.R.10).

The Cold War museum, of course, played a powerful role in the cultural apparatus of good-life modernism. Spearheaded in 1948 by MoMA's director of industrial design, Edgar Kaufmann Jr., the museum's "Good Design" program was a landmark merger of art and commerce—a partnership with the largest wholesale marketer in the United States, the Chicago Merchandise Mart. The program selected the best, most innovatively designed American consumer goods for display in a series of semiannual exhibitions in Chicago and New York under the aegis of MoMA, and reflected the museum's interest in design as a way of fusing modern art and domestic everydayness.[37] Kaufmann was not just an engineer of new corporate synergies between modern art and business; he was also a true believer in the political significance—indeed, the democratic vitality—of modernist household objects, whose intent, as he put it in his 1950 manifesto *What Is Modern Design?*, was *"to implement the lives of free individuals."*[38] The domestic and international success of the exhibitions convinced Kaufmann of the role of design in presenting "the best and most progressive side of our life to the European public," and spurred him to bring good design into the realm of cultural diplomacy in projects like the Marshall Plan exhibition, *Design for Use, U.S.A.* Jointly sponsored by the State Department and the European Cooperation Administration, *Design for Use* was the first of three European exhibitions prepared by MoMA between 1951 and 1955 dedicated to American-designed objects, and starring, among other goods, the happy things of Eamesian making.

Attentive to the contexts of such Cold War exhibitions, and other sites of modernism's institutionalization at midcentury, design historians have recently cast "good design"—with its promise of happiness through consumption and democratic futurity in the American model —as a form of "soft power." This mode of propaganda and information handling persuades by attraction and enticement rather than coercion, "enlisting support through intangibles like culture, values, belief systems, and perceived moral authority."[39] Model homes, like model families or model couples such as the Eameses, thus become normalizing instruments, implementing, to borrow Kaufmann's instrumental language, "the lives of free individuals" in a Cold War pedagogy of democratic lifestyle and its abiding promise of happiness. If happiness, as Sara Ahmed has argued, can be understood as a general phenomenological "orientation toward something as being 'good,'" a broad "horizon of likes" with a more complex intentionality than other emotions, it is also, powerfully, a normative promise.[40] Our orientation toward objects deemed "happy," or potentially happy making, dovetails with the operations of habit and taste—taste as "a very specific bodily orientation that is shaped by 'what' is already desired to be a good or a higher good."[41] Ahmed continues: "To become oriented means to be directed towards specific objects that are already attributed as being tasteful."[42] In this way, she argues, happiness becomes temporalized and grafted onto specific images of tasteful futurity that, once put into circulation, accrue affective value and create communities as forms of shared orientation toward "the good." Eamesian happiness can thus be described as one of the midcentury's more powerful normative horizons for orienting audiences and consumers at home and abroad toward designed objects and "ways of life" deemed "good," or that might circulate—as did images *of* the Eameses and *by* the Eameses—as signs of the postwar good life.

I take a different tack, arguing in this book's first two chapters that Eamesian happiness is ultimately more instructive as a model of production. For Eames-era designers, happiness was a medial and technical process of working with objects and images, and should be seen as a midcentury multimedia pedagogy, rather than the reified promise of any particular good. Such happiness requires relentless making, and making in media. It is both a *media effect* and a way of being at home in mediation, including what seems *least natural* about media. This making natural of media is part of what is meant by the so-called organic design of the midcentury.[43] The intermedial production and media pedagogy informing the Eameses' design practice require a more fine-grained account of the technological, medial, and scientific environments of the postwar period in which they worked. These environments radically transformed what seemed taken for granted or "natural" in the unfolding of the good life and in the status of its exemplary image objects like Eames chairs. As Douglas Mao has observed, a certain strain of modernist aesthetic production found in the solid object—neither a Good nor a God—a kind of fragile happiness as respite from the violence of instrumental reason.[44] But in the postwar terrain of production presided over by the new cultural prestige of designers like the Eameses, the midcentury object is thrown into further crisis: its solidity fissured, catastrophically, by atomic science; its materiality flattened in a postindustrial society driven by the circulation and consumption of images; its capacity to function as an autonomous fragment of nonself challenged by expanding informatic networks that force it into scenes of communicative transparency. In this horizon of production, there will be no relief from ideology, but rather an enthusiastic functionalism, an insistence on usefulness and service, and a seriousness of purpose regarding the range of human problems that might be solved by good design.

The new global prestige of designers like the Eameses was anxiously observed by any number of midcentury cultural critics suddenly overcome by a culture of abundance. Its surfeit of goods often outstripped consumer desires, which then had to be created anew in the postwar period's robust, and for many, pernicious human science of market research and attention management. But C. Wright Mills had the acuity to link the designer's centrality in the production of "the good" to a new postwar matrix of communications practices and what Adorno, in 1960, indicted as "an age of integral organization"—a historical conjuncture defined by "the present-day proximity of the concepts 'culture' and 'administration.'"[45] In a searing address delivered in the summer of 1958 at the International Design Conference in Aspen (IDCA), and published in revised form that November in *Industrial Design* magazine, Mills decried the neutralization of culture by its proximity to organization and capital in the operation of what he called "the cultural apparatus," and he specifically identified the designer as the crucial exemplar of the declining autonomy of "cultural workman."[46] At its core, Mills's essay is a theory of mediation, one that diagnoses the designer's role in a primarily "second-hand world" of images: "Between the human consciousness and material existence stand communications and designs, patterns and values which influence decisively such consciousness as [people] have" ("MM," 375). As a technician of the communications "so decisive to experience itself," the designer's practice embodies the process of mediation at the core of the cultural apparatus—"those organizations and *milieux* in which artistic, intellectual and scientific work goes on," and that stand "between men and events, the meanings and images, the values and slogans that define all the worlds men know" ("MM," 376). The designer's work is the labor of world making, shaping the truths and values that constitute the worlds it is possible to believe in. This conspicuous new power, Mills insists, is a specific symptom of an "overdeveloped society" in the midst of two epochal developments: a postindustrial shift from an economic system of production and consumption to distribution, public relations, and "the ethos of advertisement"; and "the bringing of art, science and learning into a subordinate relation with the dominant institutions of the capitalist economy and the nationalist state" ("MM," 374). As a worker trapped in a distributor's culture, the designer's middling position can be remedied, Mills argues, only through a reconsideration of the designer's fundamental values, and by reclaiming an ethos of craftsmanship, "common denominator of art, science and learning, and also the very root of human development" ("MM," 383).

The terms of Mills's critique help us better understand designers' interest in mediation itself, as a process in which they served as key cultural workers with widened spheres of influence. Mills's terms also suggest designers' commitment to thinking carefully about the forms of media in which they worked, which would be approached at the IDCA from a range of disciplinary positions. Part of what is so striking about the postwar design conference was its way of boldly arrogating such far-flung disciplinary territory seemingly beyond designers' scope of expertise. As I demonstrate in chapters 3 and 4, the design conference became an important site for midcentury film and media theory, and functioned as an overlooked midcentury technical and managerial form in its own right. Seen from the perspective of Eames-era designers (and midcentury management theorists), what Mills laments as the cultural

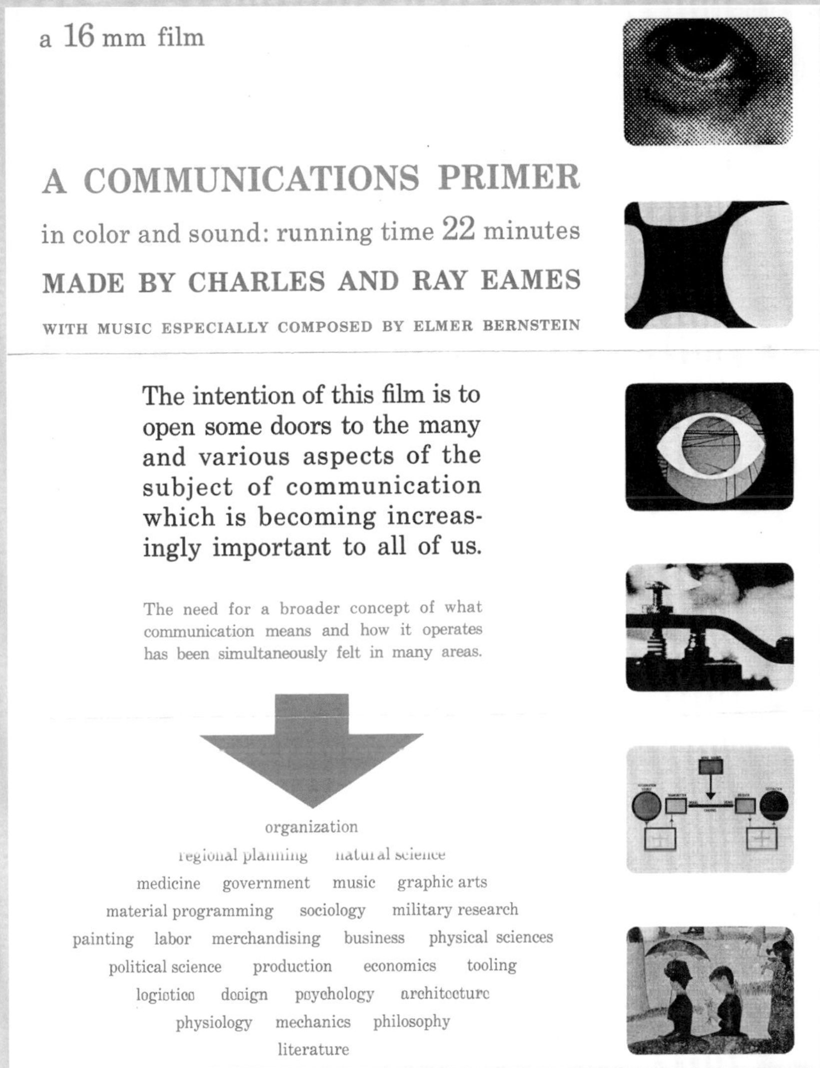

Figure I.4. Brochure for *A Communications Primer,* 1953. Copyright 2017 Eames Office LLC (eamesoffice.com).

apparatus's production of consciousness through its monopoly on communication, and the merging of mass, public, and design arts, might be viewed as precisely the kind of boundary-breaking, flexible thinking urgently required of creative management. Such vanguard thinking would be modeled formally in the design conference itself as a space of interdisciplinary knowledge production.

In the Eameses' case, the conceptual ground zero of their expansive media practice in the postwar period was *A Communications Primer*

(1953). As I explain in chapter 2, the film began as a node or module in a boundary-breaking, multimedia experiment in humanistic education called, alternatively, "Art-X" or "A Rough Sketch for a Sample Lesson for a Hypothetical Course," first at the University of Georgia in January 1953, and then at UCLA in May. With their friend Alexander Girard, the Eameses participated in this Rockefeller Foundation–funded attempt to reform Georgia's staid art curriculum at the invitation of George Nelson, then director of design at the Herman Miller Furniture Company in Zeeland, Michigan, the distributor of the Eameses' furniture as of 1946. By 1953 the Eameses had begun to rethink design as a kind of postindustrial knowledge work in which filmmaking was embedded in the communicative self-organization of a postwar information society. Like the Eameses' films and furniture, Charles's "work at the university" would be explained in their appearance on the TV program *Discovery* as "the logical continuation of the design program."[47] This audacious claim epitomizes how design for the Eameses constituted what John Harwood has described as "a generalized problem-solving technique, a practice that could be itself redesigned—along with every other human endeavour—into a pure, formal logical system."[48]

Such indifference to medium specificity or disciplinary propriety is evident in the galley proofs of a curious ad for the film *A Communications Primer* in the Eames archive at the Library of Congress that cross-promotes the film with the plywood furniture group: "low-cost chairs designed by Charles Eames will quickly turn your selling floor into a center for universal modern seating." Presumably targeted to furniture dealers, the advertisement for *A Communications Primer* betrays the inkling that the stuff of modern furniture and au courant theories of information processing might share a similar logic, or partake of the same aspiration toward universality, or boundary-crossing interdisciplinarity.

Of all the Eameses' early works, *A Communications Primer* best exemplifies the couple's overlapping scales of production and their worldly ambit, their way of spiraling from micro to macro. This curious work—whose basic conceptual ambitions would be upscaled in the Eameses' better-known multiscreen exhibitions *Glimpses of the U.S.A.* (1959), displayed at the U.S. National Exhibition in Moscow, and *Think* (1964–65), their contribution to the I.B.M. Pavilion at the New York World's Fair—became a 16mm film distributed in 1954 by the MoMA Film Library. MoMA, we should note, began distributing the Eameses' films *Blacktop* and *Parade* in 1953, at a moment when the museum's role in disseminating American propaganda during the Cold War was firmly established. One can readily sense the appeal of the Eameses' early films for MoMA at midcentury. On the one hand, they exemplified the artistic range of

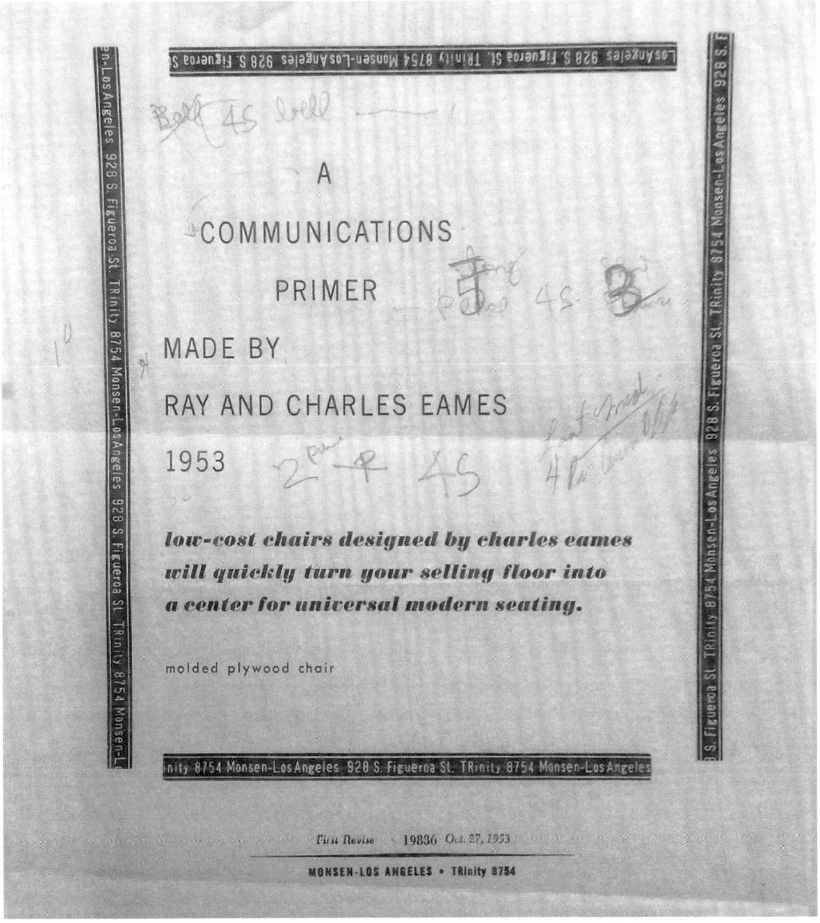

Figure I.5. Galley of advertisement for *A Communications Primer* and Eames molded plywood seating. II: 114, Charles and Ray Eames Papers, Manuscripts Division, Library of Congress, Washington, D.C. Copyright 2017 Eames Office LLC (eamesoffice.com).

designers whose reputation the museum had helped consolidate in its *Good Design* shows, and precisely when the Film Library itself was shifting from a sociological investment in film to a focus on the medium—especially Hollywood movies—as a site of a popular American art and artistry. *Blacktop*'s bubbling poetics of a schoolyard's everyday wonder, and *Parade*'s display of the "unselfconscious" beauty of animated toys, were scaled-down versions of vital, amateur, American "art film" whose authenticity the Film Library would also champion in the professional, commercial work of D. W. Griffith, Charlie Chaplin, and John Ford. On the other hand, a film like *A Communications Primer,* an illustration of communications theory that would decisively shape how the Eameses understood the sensory pedagogy of their later corporate and state-sponsored work, harkened back to the institutional origins of the

Film Library itself, and sought to extend its communicative mission into the Cold War period. Established by the Rockefeller Foundation to aid in its empirical research into the effects of propaganda and the understanding of visual communication, the Film Library, as Peter Decherney as shown, was born "at the crossroads of modern corporate public relations techniques and a growing theory of film sociology."[49] It became "the nucleus of the U.S. film propaganda machine" from the 1930s through World War II, working under contract from the "communication research wing of the Rockefeller Foundation and later for government intelligence agencies, making the world safe for democracy and Hollywood."[50] In this sense, the Eameses' films carried many of the wartime theoretical activities of the "Communications Group" into the postwar period.

A good portion of Charles Eames's voice-over in the film is based on Warren Weaver's introduction to Shannon's *A Mathematical Theory of Communication* (1949), and the film's credits acknowledge not just Shannon and Weaver but other cybernetic luminaries such as Norbert Wiener himself, as well as Oskar Morgenstern and John von Neumann, with whom the Eameses later consulted on several other projects. The voice-over begins by hazarding a characterization of the present era as "the age of communications," and reproduces Shannon's diagrammatic approach to communication, before defining its constituent elements and terminology—information source, transmitter, message, signal, receiver, destination, noise, redundancy—through a series of far-flung examples illustrated by what would become the couple's typical combination of live-action footage and animation, and with periodic returns to Shannon's schema. As promotional material for the film has it, formally *A Communications Primer* works to present "the basic steps of communications theory" in "the warm terms of everyday experience," a domesticating operation typical of the Eameses' films, which often work by means of charming analogies between abstract mathematical or scientific principles and the near sphere of quotidian experience.[51]

Beginning with the familiar communicative scenario of "reading" (a book; words read from a typewriter), the film quickly moves to telegraphy; human speech (the human brain is the "information source," the message is the thought "I love you," and the transmitter is the voice); and then to painting. Here, as elsewhere, the ideal is communicative transparency, the goal a smooth passage from the "mind and experience" of painter as information source, to the "concept" of painting as message, to the artist's "technique and talent" as transmitter, to the "receiver"—its destination in the minds and experiences of the painting's beholders. Noise, of course, is as undesirable as it is omnipresent, and can come "in many forms," from the flickering exterior light that breaks the reading of the train's passenger to the less mechanical noisiness of cultural or linguistic difference itself. Charles notes, in his painting example, that the background and experiences of a receiver may so differ as to make the message impossible to decode, and then summons the familiar modernist example of Chinese script as the very limit of communicative transparency. Thankfully, this geopolitically telling example of the difficulty in decoding across difference is mitigated by other nonverbal codes—and here we cut to the smiling face of a Chinese girl—that are presumably universal symbols, like fire or colored flags, capable of transcending "the barriers of language and custom."

Summoning these examples, the Eameses insist on communication as the stuff of social organization, of happy integration that joins human society and nonhuman processes across the evolutionary scales of deep time, as symbols change and evolve, pass into obscurity, and "become readable only by the anthropologist." One long shot observes a flock of birds, wheeling in constantly reaggregating patterns in the sky, as the voice-over asks, "What holds such birds together in their flight?," and answers, "Communication is that which links any organism together. It is what keeps society together." We cut to a busy city sidewalk, our view just above street level, where strollers stream in opposing directions, silently navigating their urban habitus, enmeshed in a kinetic flow of social communication that allows them to go about their business, if not with avian grace, then at least without collisions.

As the film builds to its conclusion, it begins to link more tightly the flows of communication to questions of agency, choice, and responsibility through the informatic work of specifically binary decisions, from the dot/dash of the telegraph, or the stop-and-go firing of neural activity, to the dots of halftone image reproduction and—perhaps most significantly for the Eameses' later work—the cards "punched or not punched" by the electronic calculator. As in the Eameses' many later films and exhibitions about computers for IBM, their rhetorical goal here is twofold: to assert an analogy between the "prodigious," and potentially threatening, number of decisions, calculations, and information-storage capacities of electronic machines, and the familiar scale of human life and human cognition; and to subject the machine, as "one great tool," to the control, and ultimate responsibility, of its human user. In *A Communications Primer,* Charles pauses his narration for several seconds to listen in fascination to the strange "sounds that are the functioning of an actual calculator," its "pulse," before insisting on far greater, indeed "innumerable," stop-and-go decisions required in even the smallest human movements, whose quotidian flow, for the Eameses, conceals a version of the neuromathematical sublime. Sometimes, the Eameses conclude, human decisions seem vague, but even those "things we accept as undecided vagaries would be, if we could bring our focus in sharp, decisive individual units." This scalar oscillation between micro and macro, individual unit and organized whole, has been the visual strategy of much of the film, moving, in one recurring example, from tight close-ups of halftone dots as geometric abstractions out to the total figure of a young girl that the dots constitute, building a pattern through abiding, singular decisions. The film's concluding emphasis on the inescapability of individual choices returns to this pattern in its editing, which links images of a mosaic (first close-ups of loose tiles, then the completed pattern), and Georges Seurat's pointillist technique in *A Sunday on La Grande Jatte,* to the organized communication between an airplane during landing, its instrument panel, and the control tower. "It is," Charles concludes, "the responsibility of selecting and relating parts which makes possible a whole which itself has unity. . . . The communication of the total message contains the responsibility of innumerable decisions made again and again, always checking through a constant feedback system. . . . Communication means responsibility of decision, all the way down the line."

In these ways, the Eameses' first filmic experiment in voice-over joins human cognition, aesthetic making, and modern technological feedback systems in a vision of systemic self-organization secured by liberal choice making and responsibility. Synopses of the film written later by the Eames Office for distribution purposes describe it thus: "Our first organized picture at [*sic*] which we attempted to put together all of our ideas on communication theory and present them to the world of architecture. Architects turned a deaf ear, but many agencies in our government, and in England gave it a lot of attention."[52]

Embedded in an expanded terrain of creative media production linking experiments in furniture, filmmaking, pedagogy, and vanguard communications theory, *A Communications Primer* enacts a theory of what this book calls "happiness by design." I've claimed that such happiness is a media effect, a technical matter of organization and economy, and an ideological problem. If Eamesian happiness involves happiness *in media,* and its abiding communication technologies, this is a response to the scale and power of postwar technics—and to the sheer pressure those brought to bear on concepts of human agency in the Eames era, which was also what Mark Greif has called "the age of the crisis of man."[53] The domain of technology included both technical objects like airplanes, bombs, and films, but also what Greif, following Lewis Mumford and others, calls "human techniques," "especially the forms and techniques that organize men and women," whether in discourses of planning, machine control, or technical efficiency.[54] Within the pervasive humanist discourse at midcentury that arose in the historical shadow of fascism and totalitarianism, designers viewed the postwar human condition as both set in and beset by a world of technological saturation that demanded managerial technique, and that fueled their media experimentation and pedagogy. When asked, in 1956, to appear on CBS's prestige program *Omnibus*, for example, Eames explained that any program about him would "make little reference to the *things* we have done, but explore a few of the great *variety* of things we have done to help shape a real, human-scale environment of the future." The show would thus feature the wide-ranging objects of Eamesian interest, "from toys & kites to electronic calculators and games of strategies."[55]

Shaping a "human-scale environment," Eames clarifies, demands both products—new things—and vanguard processes, a wide-ranging domain of creative production scaling vertiginously from toys to game theory, 16mm films and kites to the emerging computational infrastructure of postindustrial society. In his 1961 essay "Design by Choice," British architecture and design critic Reyner Banham marveled at precisely the Eameses' capacious terrain of making: after the first Eames chair, there followed "in a bewildering succession, toys, films scientific researches, lecture tours, special exhibits, three further generations of chairs, the celebrated *Ahmedabad Report* on design in development [*sic*] countries, and a great number of awards and citations."[56] For Banham, the designers' ever-new environments for creative production epitomized a broader midcentury shift in architectural practice from total design to a more pervasive influence over mass taste and choice in the domain of consumer goods, objects often designed by others. In this novel "world of the visually sophisticated consumer," Banham reasons, the responsibilities of designers have only increased, with their aim now "to exercise choice and background control over the choice of others, to advise, suggest and demand on the basis of knowledge and understanding."[57] As good-life advisers, and indeed, as models of new ways of choosing and valuing explored in *A Communications Primer,* the Eameses' counterparts were not just other designers but what Banham calls "new men" doing design thinking by other names, and indeed, from other disciplines. They were mathematicians and experimental psychologists, pop artists like Banham's friend Richard Hamilton, and in the United States, "liberal sociologists like David Riesman and Eric Larrabee."[58]

As an upscalable category of creative making, the Eamesian model of happiness by design was poised to tackle the same basic question that nagged at Riesman and his contemporaries about postwar affluence and the crisis of legitimacy it posed for liberalism. "Abundance for what?" Reisman famously asked in 1957. He observed a historically unprecedented condition in which capitalism's excessive productive capacity, after an initial "stockpiling" of desires for stuff, was now met with a vexing new "wantlessness": a broad weariness about the good of consumer goods alone, and a distressing absence of "plans for substitute goals," or the political or economic channels to develop them.[59] Missing amidst a postwar boom driven by a "sub rosa military Keynesianism" were clearly identified values and collective aspirations whose institutionalization constituted, for Riesman, "the fundamental economic and meta-economic task" of the midcentury.[60] From a different vantage, Hannah Arendt observed a homologous trajectory in *The Human Condition* (1957), her own crucial contribution to postwar design thinking. As Arendt argued, the productive power of midcentury technics, rather than freeing humans to explore and develop their inherent capacities in work or leisure, locked consumers in an unending cycle of *labor*: namely, the labor to maintain spurious standards of living dictated by false needs. For Arendt, both the "transformation of the whole of society into a laboring society," a hallmark of what is most inhuman about modernity, and the contemporaneous rise of automation, imperiled that other crucial basic category of human activity she called *work,* which creates permanent physical objects that constitute the shared material fabric of the human-built world.[61]

Riesman's and Arendt's fears help us appreciate the high stakes of the Eameses' clear-eyed optimism about designing "a human-scale environment of the future." Manifested in promiscuous making, the couple's design thinking positioned itself to intervene on the terrain of value and meaning, aiming at once to identify, to perform, and to teach the liberal values at the core of postwar goodness. Work for the Eameses was one such exemplary value, but it was a particular kind of happy, creative work undertaken in the thick of what Riesman called the postwar period's "sudden onrush of leisure."[62] Like many architects and designers in the postwar period, the Eameses intertwined their aspirations for democratic freedom with a ludic impulse, a freedom to play that gained traction in architectural circles with the publication of Dutch philosopher Johan Huizinga's book *Homo Ludens* (1938), translated into English in 1949. Indeed, Riesman may well have grouped the couple alongside those privileged artists and intellectuals "who regard their work as play and their play as work," people for whom "work frequently provides the central focus of life without necessarily being compartmentalized from the rest of life either by its drudgery and severity or by its precariousness."[63]

But Riesman might also have seen in their expanded media practice the urgent proof of the "possibility of making work in modern society more meaningful," and a harbinger of his wished-for "new arrangement of work and leisure."[64] For the Eameses' productive ethos, what the couple called "taking their pleasure seriously," everywhere blurred boundaries between work, play, and knowledge work—that new category of labor simultaneously coined by Peter Drucker and Fritz Machlup in 1962. The Eameses understood that education, as a process of inculcating value, taste, and choice, was itself a crucial postwar product, necessary to human and democratic flourishing, albeit what Riesman called "one of the intangibles for which the demand curve is nearly completely flexible."[65] As Rockefeller Foundation–funded knowledge work at a moment when knowledge was increasingly a problem of the nation-state, and installed in the managerial heart of the postwar "communications complex," the Eameses' explicit interventions in the classroom extended a pedagogical program that began in and around furniture design.[66] This technical program required media (chairs *and* film), and sought to perform and secure the conditions of happiness in it. As I argue in chapter 1, the series of sponsored chair films the Eames Office made for Herman Miller constituted a kind of ergonomic film curriculum in the times, speeds, and technologies of postindustrial society that would also be explored in the couple's sequence of overtly pedagogical experiments in networked "relationship seeing" around *A Communications Primer* discussed in chapter 2.

As an optimistic experiment in human-scale environmental design, then, *A Communications Primer* marks an early intersection in the Eameses' work of what we might called the ludic-productivist happy, the communicative-therapeutic happy, and the cybernetic happy. I've begun to describe the first, which urges us to understand a film like *A Communications Primer* within an environmental practice of creative, multimedia making at a moment when creativity itself became the object of social scientific research, and designers such as the Eameses would themselves become the subjects of vanguard psychological studies of creative minds, processes, and situations.[67] But for Charles Eames, it was the technical shaping of that environment through a cybernetic logic of communication, control, calculation, and strategic decision making that the film perhaps best exemplified. Sending a print of *A Communications Primer* to Ian McCallum, editor of the London-based *Architectural Review*, in 1953, Eames described its "background thinking" as "the greatest tool ever to have fallen into the hands of the architects and planners" because it allows architects to maximize their capacity to calculate and predict often unfathomably complex "relationships of factors" that emerge in any human problem-solving endeavor.[68] He cited von Neumann and Morgenstern's *Theory of Games and Economic Behavior* (1944) as an example of how their mathematical "method of treating human actions and needs" could be extended from economics to the domains of planning and design. At a time, Eames noted anxiously, when "numbers and complications seem about to obliterate the human scale," game theory's programmatic logic "would seem actually to use large numbers and unlimited relationships to help us return to the human scale and the richness of the townscape in the terms of our times."

In this way, the Eameses' cybernetic investments and their connection to a calculable theory of needs affirmed a wider midcentury commitment to what Howard Mumford Jones dubbed "techniques of happiness" in the concluding chapter of his contemporaneous study *The Pursuits of Happiness* (1953). Jones had in his sights the movement of happiness as a contemporary practice from the spheres of law, political economy, and liberal government into the increasingly all-encompassing "sphere of psychology."[69] He cast this as the "steady transplanting of the roots of happiness" from the "world of Jefferson and Adam Smith" to the "world of Adler, Jung, and Freud"—of "the doctor, the psychiatrist, the personnel director, and the social psychologist" (*PH,* 146, 149). The psychoanalytic keyword for this tendency, Jones insisted, was "adjustment," a sweeping project joining the midcentury psychologist, the sociologist, and the cultural anthropologist in instructing "not only individuals but groups, cities, and even the nation in modes of behavior" (*PH,* 150). The practical aim of their overlapping domains of professional work is "to induce what is known as 'adjustment,' or a harmonious (and therefore happy) relation between the inner world of the psyche and the outer world of reality, whether the clinical problem arise out of maldevelopment, domestic tension, or the strain upon the personality of the whole social order" (*PH,* 150). Carried out simultaneously on the scientific and popular level, these various projects of adjustment joined behaviorist psychology and Freudian psychoanalytic therapy to notions of "mental hygiene." Their common assumption, Jones asserted, was that "life in the United States appears to be a problem of insecurity," one best treated through techniques of happiness (PH, 150).

While Jones's study doesn't acknowledge it directly, the discourse of "mental hygiene," psychological adjustment, and pervasive postwar insecurity was also lodged at the feedback-driven heart of the contemporary Macy Conferences on Cybernetics (1946–53; 1954–60), the famous series of interdisciplinary conferences sponsored by the Josiah Macy Jr.

Foundation—an organization founded in 1930 to fund new methods in "psychobiological and sociological" approaches to heath care.[70] As Steve Heims has shown, a decade before cyberneticians like Wiener began drawing analogies between human and servomechanical behavior, the Macy Foundation had laid out an "organismic" approach to biological health, endorsing concepts such as homeostasis and mental hygiene. Reviewing the foundation's activities in 1955, its president, Willard C. Rappleye, asserted, in a typical psychologizing gesture, that "social conflicts are actually symptoms of underlying causes" whose elucidation and treatment required the expertise of precisely those technicians of happiness described by Jones.[71] Macy conferees, Heims notes, readily accepted "knowledge of techniques, pharmacological or psychological, that influence human behavior and affect states of mind in more or less predictable directions," and tended to "reduce human affairs to positive science" of technical and technological operations.[72]

This was evident in the wide-ranging knowledge work of the Macy conferences, and also in the 1948 formation of the World Federation for Mental Health, organized by the cybernetics group regulars Lawrence Frank, neurologist Frank Freemont-Smith, and anthropologist Margaret Mead. In the summer of 1948, the WFMH group held a UNESCO-sponsored conference in Paris that provided a forum for various approaches to "the tensions that cause wars," as the conference proceedings were later titled. These approaches included what we might call the liberal-therapeutic model of happiness, secured by techniques of global mental health as laid out, for example, in psychiatrist Henry Stack Sullivan's essay "Tensions Interpersonal and International: A Psychiatrist's View"; the Marxist-Leninist position that sourced global unhappiness in the form of wars and oppression to monopoly capitalism's exploitative nature; and the more Freudian, Frankfurt School account of human need and character, represented at the Paris conference by Max Horkheimer. The latter, in an analysis of the origins of German and Italian fascism then being extrapolated into a full-blown theory of the "authoritarian personality," noted that "the main task" for alleviating "international tensions" consists "in the removal of the objective causes for such anxieties, which are far from purely psychogenic in nature."[73] Happiness, for Horkheimer, was not a psychological issue but a materialist fact of political economy.

In their personnel and their range of interdisciplinary investments, the midcentury design meetings such as the International Design Conference in Aspen (chapter 3) and the Vision conferences (chapter 4) overlapped significantly with the therapeutic, technical ambitions of the Macy conferences, the liberal-democratic outlook of UNESCO, and

Figure I.6. Cover of brochure, *Vision 65: New Challenges for Human Communication,* designed by Will Burtin. Will Burtin Papers, RIT Libraries: Graphic Design Archives, Rochester Institute of Technology.

various strands of the cybernetic happy running through the Eameses' own media practice. Such conferences, I argue, themselves constituted techniques of happiness at a moment when the international, interdisciplinary conference—as a form of communication within a broader landscape of communications media—became the object of theoretical investigation. Margaret Mead, for example, long preoccupied with group dynamics and their capacity to be upscaled to the level of international relations, was a ubiquitous figure in the domain of midcentury metacommunication I call "midcentury conference theory." Mead's theory of the conference as a holistic technique of multimodal communication appealed to a range of midcentury designers, and their conferences assumed a managerial definition of this vital communicative form similar to Mead's: *"The new institution of an expanding body of knowledge in a shrinking world."*[74]

Figure I.7. Audience at Vision 65 conference, Southern Illinois University. Courtesy of Southern Illinois University Libraries.

The far-flung retinue of experts assembled at design conferences would repeatedly frame their interdisciplinary, international technique as a way of managing the pace and global scale of change—and thus a reckoning with postwar happiness as a volatile, unpredictable landscape of human needs and satisfactions. This was clear even at the first IDCA conference, "Design as a Function of Management," where Eames laid out what Edgar J. Kaufmann Jr. called the goal of "responsible" designers: "the full development and wide distribution of human satisfactions, both spiritual and physical."[75] To be fair, in Aspen Eames spoke less of spirit than of the "facets of performance" of any designed product, and the integrated goodness of the product, from its production to its life of service to consumers ("DD," 98). By this systemic goodness, what Eames called "goodness all the way down the line," he imagined an "integrated design program" stretching from materials, packages, delivery, and office to the plant morale: if "the intention is really to make the life of the employee on the job a happy one, the steps are clear, and the relation of morale to goodness of product will take care of itself" ("DD," 98). For Eames, the foundational aim of design—discerning the good and prescribing the service of human needs—requires a scrutiny of objectives on levels big and small. This far-reaching, indeed visionary perspective toward production standards was embodied, for Eames, by Buckminster Fuller. Fuller was committed to the designer's capacity to provide "security in change," the "great advantage that education can provide to a student" ("DD," 99). This is a telling turn in the drift of Eameses' IDCA lecture: from the moral lesson of the "good" object to an overtly pedagogical agenda of change management that anticipates the Eameses own work in the classroom training of students. Its abiding version of *happiness as security in change* unites the design of objects and the perceptual training of subjects. Both face the possibility of a future "with a higher standard of living and more leisure than ever before," and the pressing realities of living in a world where one's "only real security will lie in the knowledge that he can deal with the new and unexpected."[76]

The Eameses' media pedagogy aimed at the production of a similar kind of liberal-democratic happiness. Feelings of security in change would be made in the classroom as a space of knowledge production and transmission, and modeled in the couple's relentless creative activity that combined work and play in the times, speeds, and technical environments increasingly constitutive of postindustrial society. The phrase "happiness by design" insists, in an Eamesian way, on subjective well-being and security as established within necessary limits or rational constraints. But it also captures the designers' aspirations toward the domestication of "contingency" itself—chance, the radically unforeseen change, the "hap" in the etymological root of *happiness.* As we've begun to see, such happiness was thus often wedded to period-specific discourses of control like cybernetics, and to contemporary techniques and technologies of speculation and prediction. Such expert techniques, Daniel Bell clarified, were wielded by the dominant figures of the emerging postindustrial society ("the scientists, the mathematicians, the economists, and the engineers of the new computer technology") and honed in that society's newly powerful "intellectual institutions": research corporations, laboratories, "experimental stations," and the universities.[77] Noting the ever-increasing speed and diffusion of technical innovation in the first six decades of the twentieth century, Bell speculated that the "most important social change of our time is the emergence of a process of direct and deliberate contrivance of change itself. Men now seek to anticipate change, measure the course of its direction and impact, control it, and even shape it for predetermined ends."[78] The Eameses' early pedagogical experiments in "security in change" need to be understood as related endeavors in change management.

I'll discuss the Eameses' interest in a curriculum of "rationally organized speculation" in more detail in chapter 2, and contextualize it within debates about postwar educational reform. For now I want to note how—as *security in change*—much of the happiness to follow, technically, the media-pedagogical work of midcentury designers like the Eameses, assumes a technophilic managerial logic enacted at design conferences and elsewhere. As the well-being engineered by planners and experts in the future of the good life, "happiness by design" thus captures the extension into postwar U.S. liberalism of some of the technocratic ambitions of the New Deal. These linkages were quite direct in Fuller's case, and apparent in his lifelong faith in the optimization of human welfare through efficient industrial methods and the probabilistic modeling and managing of the world's resources—superabundant, in Fuller's rosy view. Much of the designer film and media practice I discuss in this book evinces the kind of worldly confidence associated with a less obviously authoritarian strand of midcentury modernization theory that Nils Gilman has dubbed "technocosmopolitanism."[79] In the late 1950s, as Cold War sociologists borrowed the mantle of "modernity" from vanguard aesthetic discourse, using it to intervene in older policy debates about "development" by defining a "singular path of progressive change" (the capitalist West's, naturally), modernism itself was redefined to name a "social and political practice in which history, society, economy, culture, and nature itself were all to be the object of technical transformation."[80] In this sense, midcentury modernization theory continued the legacy of New Deal social engineering and technocratic experiments, but now practiced them abroad, with undeveloped postcolonial states as the "third-world analog to the welfare state."[81] As I will show, the media experiments and technical ambitions of Eames-era modernism often overlapped with the rationalist geopolitical agenda of modernization theory. It often tacitly assumed or overtly endorsed postwar modernizers' specious assumptions about a universal human subject with constant needs and desires, and affirmed what Pheng Cheah calls global capitalism's concept of "world" as a category of spatial circulation and market exchange.[82] At midcentury, these notions of world building were shaped by period-specific theories about the role of communication and the "free flow" of information in a global modernizing agenda whose terms were established by the United States and its geopolitical allies in the Cold War. Part of the work of chapters 2, 3, and 4 is to explain how Cold War cosmopolitanism and projects of corporate *Bildung* or "environmental management" intersected with, abetted, and were occasionally contested by the film and media practice and theory of midcentury designers, and shaped by the enabling institutions of such "world men."

If at times functioning in this book as a homology for security—a hedge against too-rapid change or environmental maldevelopment in the mode of "information overload"—at others, the problem of happiness shades more directly into an urgent idiom of global survival. This is perhaps clearest in the title of Will Burtin's Vision conference, "V67: Survival and Growth," the second of the two conferences on the "arts and sciences of communication" orchestrated by the designer in the 1960s. Born from a more discrete set of circumstances and institutions than Aspen's agenda of corporate humanism, the Vision conferences nevertheless extended the IDCA's organizational agenda and brought Burtin's technocosmopolitan managerial ambitions into bracing contact with the energies of the postwar avant-garde and the counterculture. At stake were the conflicting—and occasionally overlapping—utopian ideals of both the New Left and liberal theorists of postindustrial society, as well as the pressures exerted on those dreams of happiness by the accelerated development of a novel "technological milieu" and its abiding information and communication technologies. The explosive growth and uneven global development of that changing environment demanded the knowledge work of the conference, begging expert assessment and the technocratic planning of its futures.

At such conferences, as design's purview and scale expanded at midcentury, its claims on human happiness threatened to merge with the imperatives of a coercive, postwar technocracy—the subsensible, networked "control" system of the Cold War's "closed world."[83] Indeed, for many of technocracy's most strident postwar critics, advanced industrial society needed to be assessed, on some fundamental level, as a process of what Marcuse called "the containment of change" in *One-Dimensional Man* (1964). This infamous diagnosis of technical rationality by the former Office of Strategic Services employee and erstwhile State Department functionary also hinges on a theory of systemic and compulsory happiness by design. It's Marcuse's Frankfurt School riposte to the Fullerian tonic of security in change. Acknowledging his debt to the work of Mills, as well as to the best-selling pop sociology of Vance Packard and William F. Whyte, Marcuse critiqued the totalitarian dimensions of the excessive productive apparatus of the United States in its tight political control of the domain of "false needs." These prevailing needs produced, for Marcuse, a repressive satisfaction through the ever more technically savvy administration of the good life, a monstrous well-being incapable of critique or the conceptualization of radical change (*ODM,* 5). Marcuse characterized the postwar "image of the Welfare State" set forth in his polemic, with the happy individual at its center, as "a historical freak between organized capitalism and socialism, servitude and freedom, totalitarianism and happiness" (*ODM,* 52). And he insisted that "happy consciousness," the welfare/warfare state's chief ideological product and the auspicious "token of declining autonomy and comprehension," was also a potent media effect evident in the widespread functionalization of language and the "systematic promotion of positive thinking and doing" (*ODM,* 76, 85). This "sort of well-being, the productive superstructure over the unhappy base of society," he argued, "permeates the 'media' which mediate between the masters and their dependents. Its publicity agents shape the universe of communication in which the one-dimensional behavior expresses itself" (*ODM,* 85).

As a media effect, what Marcuse identified in the mid-1960s as the repressive well-being of a one-dimensional society was a relatively late entry into what I call "designer film theory" and describe in chapters 5 and 6. These linked chapters explore designers' overtly conceptual reckonings with the medium of film as a technique of human happiness. They begin in the interdisciplinary man of the Bauhaus, with its pedagogical hostility to the specialization and the fragmentation of knowledge

Figure I.8. László Moholy-Nagy at the Institute of Design, Chicago, 1946. Copyright 2018 Estate of László Moholy-Nagy/ Artists Rights Society (ARS), New York.

regimes, and in the theory and practice of László Moholy-Nagy and György Kepes at the Institute of Design in Chicago, founded at the New Bauhaus in Chicago in 1937 following the shuttering of Ludwig Mies van der Rohe's Berlin school by the Nazis in 1933. Spanning Moholy's tenure at the ID, and ending in the late 1960s at the Hochschule für Gestaltung in Ulm, Germany, these chapters track a series of conversations between designers and classical film theorists about film as a redemptive and therapeutic medium: for developing human creativity, for reckoning with a postwar domain of nature transfigured by technicity (a reliable, anxious example of creative manipulation), and for producing forms of democratic rehabilitation. This largely overlooked realm of designer film theory and its abiding technophilic humanism allows me to narrate a series of intersections between "classical film theory proper" (of Rudolf Arnheim, Maya Deren, and Siegfried Kracauer) and the interdisciplinary domain of postwar communications and information theory, cybernetics, and semiotics, prior to the consolidation of film studies as a humanist, liberal arts discipline in the early 1960s. In the process, the institutionalization of film studies comes into view within the broader "universe of communication" in which designers conceptualized the medium from the 1940s through the 1960s. The story I tell of designers' therapeutic investments in film also allows me to unfold a shadow history of the emergence of so-called political modernism in the late 1960s and early 1970s, itself a Brechtian refusal of the closure of the universe of discourse in the one dimension of happy functionalism.

Marcuse's despairing sense that midcentury communications media had made themselves "immune against the expression of protest and refusal" by absorbing contradictions, suppressing historicity, and dissolving the political contestation, would also be expressed by a range of countercultural media theory and practice taken up at midcentury design conferences such as the IDCA and Vision conferences (*ODM*, 90). The eruptions of heterodox practices of pleasure and pursuits of happiness signaled the fracturing of a universalizable "goodness" pursued across the demarcations of class, race, gender, and nation, and announced the demise of the communicative and cosmopolitan ideals that had long buoyed these venues' favored modes of happy talk. In this sense, the institutional and medial lives of such design conferences witnessed the undercutting of the interlocking technocratic assumptions about happiness enumerated (and ruthlessly mocked) by Theodore Roszak in his groundbreaking study of the counterculture: that human needs "are purely . . . technical in character"; that their formal, systemic analysis is nearly complete; and that "wherever social friction appears in the technocracy, it must be due to what is called a 'breakdown in communication.' For where human happiness has been so precisely calibrated and where the powers that be are so utterly well intentioned, controversy could not possibly derive from a substantive issue, but only from misunderstanding."[84]

Modernity's so-called goods had become its bads. And this badness was all the worse perceived, as it was at midcentury design conferences, by the very ambassadors of its goodness. Especially at the 1970 IDCA meeting, "Environment by Design," designers were confronted with a dynamic familiar to theorists of "reflexive modernization," whereby the forces unleashed by advanced industrial societies and capitalist development worldwide snowball, spawning a series of unintended side effects: pollution, resource depletion, and other forms of ecological devastation; the threat of nuclear annihilation; and widespread political disenfranchisement, with the collapse of "the unstable unity of shared life experiences mediated by the market and shaped by status" and the rise of new social movements.[85] In the process, a first modernity defined by wealth distribution cedes to a managerial modernity of risk distribution, reflexively preoccupied with containing the ambivalent side effects of the good life, "discovering, administering, acknowledging, avoiding or concealing . . . hazards."[86] The Eameses' colleague George Nelson sensed this boomerang effect as early as 1962, calling "the pursuit of comfort . . . a very deadly kind of thing."[87] As Nelson spun it out, the desire for, say, more comfortable chairs leads you first to "a chair you can fall asleep in," then to "a bed with a nice mattress," where—again, you can fall asleep: "And this, finally, takes you to the notion that maybe the most comfortable thing there is . . . is a fur-lined coffin." Indeed, it becomes clear that, in Nelson's eyes, the United States' future is deathbound, and further, that this is a broader failure of Cold War modernity itself, dominated by the form of the corporation and its organizational logic stretching, for Nelson, from the local automobile dealership, to the bureaucracies of Soviet Russia, to Brasilia's proliferation of ministries. "It is as if," Nelson posits, "a modern industrial state can only organize on corporate lines no matter what [its ideology]." Like all modern societies, the United States is simply a "disciplining instrument," with no objective, Nelson asserts, "beyond survival." Now, having "exhausted the potency of organization," our period—what Nelson calls the "age of materialism"—is, he observes, "coming to an end," "cracking up."

Nelson's canny appraisal of modernity's midcentury crack-up reminds us that Eames-era technicians of happiness were also astute observers of the limits, and potentially catastrophic telos, of good-life modernism and its sunny dream of anthropocentric environmental design. Today, of course, the reflexive dynamics of risk modernity at midcentury appear as effects of the so-called great acceleration yielding that most obvious sign of modernity's bads—the Anthropocene.[88] We could call this newly minted epoch the ironic geological achievement of the Eamesian desire to shape "a human-scale environment of the future." In this sense, this book's return to Eames-era designs on happiness, and its analysis of the film practice and the media theory abetting them, acknowledges the persistence of postwar dreams about democratic access to goods into ourneo-liberal present. In her influential account, Lauren Berlant has dubbed this contemporary affective structure "cruel optimism," when what we desire most in that "moral-intimate-economic thing called 'the good life'" becomes an impediment to human flourishing.[89] Today, she reminds us, we witness the "fraying relation between post–Second World War state/economic practices and fantasies of the good life endemic to liberal, social democratic, or relatively wealthy regions."[90] Further, the contemporary attrition of postwar, good-life fantasies—about couples and families, about upward mobility and job security, political institutions and markets—has produced a new set of aesthetic conventions derived from "embodied, affective rhythms of survival."[91] Because Eames-era happiness sought to deliver on the promises of these democratic fantasies, it offers a crucial prologue to the affective contours of the neoliberal present. However, rather than see the midcentury period as the domain of happy, unsustainable fantasy against which the optimism of the present is suffered, and seems ever more cruel, this book insists that the production of the good life was always a high-stakes process marked by a premonition of risk, the metrics and technics of survival, and the regulative idiom of emotional adjustment. The Eames era was a modernist achievement of technique, media, and their transdisciplinary conceptual glue—communication—whose scenes of administration and management we have yet to appreciate fully.

As a communicative practice spanning the global economy's postwar boom and eventual bust in the late 1960s and early 1970s—and with it, with the demise of a collective vision of the welfare state and the rise of personalized lifestyle media—the midcentury designer film and media experimentation I discuss in this book is a prehistory of our communicative present. Linking the promise of U.S.-style democracy to increasingly globally interconnected communication and information technologies, midcentury happiness by design anticipated the contemporary condition Jodi Dean has called "communicative capitalism," for her the "technological infrastructure of neoliberalism."[92] Secured by the ideological rhetorics of access, participation, and wholeness, today's networked environment of "expanded and intensified communicativity" affirms the protocols of a lifeworld in which the constitutive antagonism of the political has been subsumed into consumption, personalization, and the commodification of lifestyles, which we display and perform through the circulation of messages in a nonstop data stream.[93] If this condition has mistakenly been called postpolitical, it reminds us of one present terminus of Fuller's wished-for transcendence of politics as glimpsed in the Dymaxion World map, and perused by a young Hugh Kenner in the midst of the war. Mounting a similarly persuasive critique of the "compulsory functionality of communication that is inherently and inescapably 24/7," Jonathan Crary has sourced the contemporary colonization of the private realm in the overlapping temporalities of labor, consumption, and marketing in the midcentury media environment.[94] Its hallmark was the "intensifying occupation of everyday life by consumption, organized leisure, and spectacle," a trend increasingly contested in the 1950s and 1960s in the thought of Henri Lefebvre, Guy Debord, and others, and anxiously apprehended in Arendt's diagnosis of the period's surfeit of "artificial life" in *The Human Condition*.[95] Following World War II, in what Crary calls the "crucible in which new paradigms of communication, information, and control were forged," the fragile fiction of everyday life as "*unadministered* life" would begin to collapse.[96]

Formed in the heat of this same crucible, designers' film and media practices at midcentury should compel our attention today. Within a postindustrial reorganization of the boundaries of work and leisure, designers turned to film and other technical media to model versions of creative, happy making. They worked to find pleasure in an everydayness newly saturated by technics and revolutionary technologies. They sought a human-scale environment of the future in a new world demanding relentless communication, and they intervened in the building and management of that environment at various scales, including in the production of knowledge and the training of citizens as future knowledge workers. *Happiness by Design* thus explores how the Cold War's expanded media environments, and seemingly entropic culture of information, fueled novel techniques of culture administration and spawned new partnerships among cultural institutions, the federal government, and the postwar corporation. To be sure, these styles of management raised the specter of more subtle forms of totalitarianism in the guise of technocracy, an expanding military-industrial complex, and in sciences of communication and control such as cybernetics, with its claims to disciplinary universalism. But they also led to a surprising terrain of interdisciplinary media experimentation that produced unlikely alliances among humanists and social scientists, film theorists and propaganda analysts, midcentury designers and communications theorists.

This book thus alerts us to the forms of administered culture that define our current disciplinary "crises" about the use and value of the humanities, and shape our present moment of informatic abundance and media transformation. So much depends upon what it means to domesticate media, to make it a lifestyle. In the Eames era, these lessons begin with the revolutionary medium of the chair.

1

happy furniture

On the Media Environments of the Eames Chair

THE PROMISE OF THE HAPPY LIFE in the Eameses' work is indicated in a delightful photograph of the couple on the cover of *Architectural Design* magazine, their arms and legs spread wide in a nod to Vitruvian perfection, a humanist ideal supplemented by the metal forms that pin the cheery, hand-holding couple to the ground. These inhuman supports are the thin, bent-metal bases of the couple's famous molded plywood chairs. A visual pun about anthropomorphic furniture, the image brings the tubular legs of machined metal into whimsical proximity with the malleable appendages of the human body, whose limbs are reorganized by good design. The chairs and cabinets eventually licensed and sold by the Herman Miller Furniture Company were produced with a sophisticated plywood molding process requiring a synthetic plastic resin first developed for military prosthetics, as well as trainer aircrafts and gliders.[1] In this iconic image from 1947, happy humanity is bound to thingly harbingers of the changed substance of postwar matter that seem not to bother the couple a bit.

An early lesson in the art of humanizing postwar technics, the image anticipates the abiding relationship between the Eameses' furniture and its media environments. In this chapter, I approach the problem of happy making in the postwar period through several of the Eameses' furniture films. These are films *about* the transfigured materiality and new technologies of the postwar period, and films that use furniture to allegorize the conditions of happy, democratic life: chiefly, its new media environments and the forms of humane, technophilic production they seemed to call for. Like the Eameses' furniture, the films offer a kind of pedagogy of midcentury lifestyle. In teaching spectators and consumers about the postwar arts of living and their systemic operations, these

Figure 1.1. Charles and Ray Eames posing with metal chair bases, 1947. Photograph by Don Albinson. Copyright 2017 Eames Office LLC (eamesoffice.com).

films estrange the matter of sitting. Much like the chairs' famously novel stuff and their marvels of engineering, the chair films materialize the new in postwar lifestyle. Their alien terrain of experience, for sitters and spectators alike, is the environment within and about which the furniture films communicate.

Transformed in the postwar period by the conceptual rigor of cybernetics, semiotics, and structuralism, design was increasingly understood as a species of communication, and its happy objects were said to speak their technical and social environments. The designed object became communicative. From a semiotic vantage, the object held a sign value beyond its use and a functionalist capacity to transmit a message, from object to user. But this talky world of things was also assessed in a broader, specifically structuralist sense: the collective ensemble of objects in the world was structured like a language—a syntactical field or a differential "system of objects," in Jean Baudrillard's terms. This range of midcentury design discourses, which coalesced under the rubric of "metadesign," attempted to conceptualize design's communicative potential, what Larry Busbea calls "the will to a network, to a world in which all aspects of the post-industrial environment were connected at a deep technological and structural level."[2]

The Eameses' work everywhere manifests this will. The chair films embed furniture's materiality—plywood, fiberglass, steel, aluminum—in expansive technical environments that include filmmaking itself as a mode of participation in the communicative, systems-oriented work of a nascent information society. The happy furniture these films take as their subject receives less attention for its objecthood than for the networks of relentlessly expanding "relationships" in which the stuff finds itself (the Eameses' preferred term for this is "connections"). This shift of aesthetic priorities comports with contemporary tendencies in the visual arts, and marks a salient realignment in design practice from the making of objects to "the crafting of situations," from the designer as an autonomous author to the designer as node in a "sprawling web of individuals, corporations, institutions, and events."[3]

Self-aware technologies of postwar modernity, the Eameses' furniture films show the designers' orientation toward what seemed newly immaterial in the scenes of production of the postwar period, and promote filmmaking as a tool for exploring the midcentury's technical environments of happy making. Like the iconic chairs, the couple's filmmaking became the global sign of a lifestyle linking technophilia and democracy, of a modernist comfort in the brave new object world of the midcentury, and expressed across the range of their design practice. As "useful cinema," these films put the couple's nontheatrical, sponsored work in dialogue with the global ambitions and international reach of their furniture designs and toys, and their overlapping experiments in television, pedagogy, and multiscreen performances.[4] But these short, generally unknown films are also conversant with a capacious range of better-recognized tendencies in the visual and plastic arts at midcentury. These modernist idioms were similarly animated by an environmental language of mobility and image saturation, information processing and systemic functionality, and with putatively democratic ambitions: from sculpture, collage, and exhibition design, to kineticism, pop, and minimalism. By renewing these conversations across the remarkable sweep of Eamesian making, this chapter charts the media environments of the Eames chair and explains the stakes of finding happiness there.

The New Subscape

Icons of midcentury technics, Eames chairs are strange kinds of things. How might their promise of postwar happiness extend beyond the chairs' commodity status and into their function as something like a medium? Consider how the organic qualities of the Eameses' furniture were initially characterized when it first garnered international attention through MoMA's famous "Organic Design in Home Furnishings" competition and resulting exhibition in 1940–41. Conceived by Eliot F. Noyes, MoMA's first curator of industrial design and later the "consultant director of design" at IBM, the "Organic Design" event was at once exhibition and business opportunity, its winners to be awarded large-scale manufacturing and distribution contracts. At the time, Charles Eames, having arrived at the Cranbrook Academy of Art in 1938 on a fellowship offered by Director Eliel Saarinen, was head of the Design Department and working in the architectural firm of Eliel and his son Eero. One of several important collaborations between Eames and Eero Saarinen at Cranbrook, their MoMA furniture entries won in the categories of living room seating and chair design, and exemplified, for Noyes, the definition of "organic design" that frames his exhibition catalog: "A design may be called organic when there is an harmonious organization of the parts within the whole, according to structure, material, and purpose."[5] Yet Noyes's definition is followed by two passages from Lewis Mumford's *Technics and Civilization* (1934), which clarify that this is a *compensatory* organicism, with large stakes:

> Our capacity to go beyond the machine rests in our power to assimilate the machine. Until we have absorbed the lessons of objectivity, impersonality, neutrality, the lessons of the mechanical realm, we cannot go further in our development toward the more richly organic, the more profoundly human.
>
> The economic: the objective: and finally the integration of these principles in a new conception of the organic—these are the marks, already discernible, of our assimilation of the machine not merely as an instrument of practical action but as a valuable mode of life.

These observations, drawn from the "Assimilation of the Machine" chapter of Mumford's landmark history of technology, articulate what architectural and design historian John Harwood has called "the central problems of design," as Noyes saw them in 1940: "The chair and the living room were points of interface between the human and the machine. The success of that interaction hinged on the development of a newly organic—that is, newly organized, relationship between human being and machine" (*TI,* 25).

The Eames chair—not a thing but an interface. Harwood reminds us of the new valence given to the word "interface" in the late 1940s in the nascent discipline of ergonomics: the "site at which the human body interacts with a complex mechanical apparatus" (*TI*, 25). To think about the Eames chair as an interface, a "coordination between two or more agents in a singular system," is to consider its modernity as part of the midcentury's system of objects, as a node in a media system whose

Figure 1.2. Eliot Noyes, *Organic Design in Home Furnishings* (New York: Museum of Modern Art, 1941). Cover design by Edward McKnight Kauffer.

operations are part of what Mumford hails as a "new conception of the organic" (*TI*, 10). What was revolutionary about Eames and Saarinen's chair designs was their way of "anthropomorphically" bending plywood, and thus bringing the inhuman object and human body into relation as the "meeting of two identically shaped surfaces," in which "subject and object comfortably inhabit and identify themselves with each other" (*TI*, 125). In this sense, the organic qualities of happy, modern furniture play a role analogous to what Mumford's contemporary Walter Benjamin famously described as the special capacity of film—"*to train human beings in the apperceptions and reactions needed to deal with a vast apparatus whose role in their lives is expanding almost daily.*"[6] Midcentury furniture as revolutionary media: its organic design allows for adaptations to the new, technological environments of the postwar period.

The Cranbrook context in which these celebrated designs emerged is crucial. Most obviously, Eames encountered there the young artist Ray Kaiser, who enrolled in 1940 after studying painting in New York with German emigré abstractionist Hans Hofmann. It has been said that Charles Eames was less of a modernist than Ray when they met, and he was certainly less of a cinephile than his future (second) wife. Affiliated with the American Abstract Artists group, a devotee of modern dance, and an avid reader of modernist literature, Ray Eames was also a passionate moviegoer in New York. Consider this representative list from Ray's assiduous accounting of her daily budget in the mid- to late 1930s: "trolley, subway, subway, movie, dinner, ink, drugs, cream"; or ".05 subway, .35 dinner, .30 Joan d'Arc, .25 magazines."[7] Her filmgoing was equally compulsive. She stockpiled dozens of film programs and kept a list of star sightings in New York in 1935: Merle Oberon (Fifty-Seventh Street), Louise Brooks (Waldorf), Katharine Hepburn (Fifty-Seventh and Fifth Avenue).[8] She was not just a fan but also attentive to MoMA's efforts to enshrine film as a modern art, saving the MoMA Film Library's announcement for "A Cycle of Seventy Films, 1895–1935," as part of MoMA's summer exhibition *Art in Our Time*. By 1951 Charlie Chaplin, whom Ray had seen in *Modern Times* (1936) at the Plaza Theatre in New York, would be a guest in a tea ceremony at her then-famous home with Charles in Pacific Palisades. By 1953 the MoMA Film Library would begin to distribute the couple's own films, including one about their shared life in their famously modern home, *House: After Five Years of Living* (1955). Between their first meeting at Cranbrook in 1940 and 1955, then, the Eameses had become media celebrities. As the subjects of high-profile features in *Life* magazine and, as we'll see, on television, they were the happy protagonists of midcentury lifestyle media. Chaplin, for Benjamin, was one famous allegory for life under the productive conditions of Fordist modernity. The Eames chair, and its designers, offered another, as industrial manufacture shifted to postindustrial production and distribution, pedagogy, and knowledge work.

Titles from the MoMA Film Library were also regularly screened at Cranbrook beginning in the mid-1930s, but more importantly, another kind of *communicative* filmic modernity was on display and at work at the school.[9] At Cranbrook the Eameses were first encouraged to think about filmmaking within an intermedial design practice, a lifestyle blurring boundaries between work and play, happy making and exhibition, pedagogy and promotion. Charles worked there in furniture design, film, and exhibition design simultaneously, but also collaboratively, and within the broader communicative agendas of the esteemed educational institution that employed him, and had quickly learned the lessons of the PR revolution.

Eames referred to the administrative unit he led at Cranbrook as the department of "experimental design," and he made repeated trips to Moholy-Nagy's Institute of Design in Chicago to consult with the Bauhaus master on the scope of a vanguard pedagogical practice. At the ID, this included film, and so too at Cranbrook. In 1939 Charles produced *Academy Film,* his first work of useful cinema and, effectively, his first sponsored film, designed to promote and publicize the educational activities and aesthetic aspirations of the Academy of Art. He followed this with footage assembled as *New Academy Movie* (1941).[10] These were not Cranbrook's first forays into promotional film. The school had contracted the New York–based public relations firm, Tamblyn and Tamblyn, to produce a series of films on the educational community's various schools beginning in 1935, as part of an ambitious campaign to boost enrollments and promote "not just a good school, but a good school *plus,*" including radio spots and a series of glossy bulletins.[11] A paean to Cranbook's value added, *New Academy Movie*'s footage lavishes considerable attention on the campus—its remarkable buildings, including its new library and museum, its sculptures and fountains—and social life at the academy, including students' leisure activities: sunbathing, tobogganing, even some comic roughhousing with Eero Saarinen. It documents visiting speakers such as Frank Lloyd Wright and esteemed faculty like ceramicist Maija Grotell, whose process of happy making is shown in admiring close-ups of the shaping and firing of a series of vases. The film's subjects are design objects and practices, from Grotell's ceramics or Eliel Saarinen's tea urn to Eames and Saarinen's chair prototypes, which students hop on at one point. This preoccupation with process extends, of course, to Cranbrook itself—its campus an object of total design, and its educational mission and abiding lifestyle overlapping design processes demanding communication.

The film concludes with a sequence featuring an exhibition of student work across media: textiles, painting, sculpture, photography, and photocollage. Eames and Saarinen, we should note, had collaborated on the design of a faculty exhibition in 1939, its style indebted to the Bauhaus designs of Herbert Bayer, whose influence is also apparent in the later student exhibition featured in Eames's film. But it's unlikely that Charles Eames shot all this exhibition footage. The framings of several of the shots are nearly identical to those in photographs of the exhibition taken by members of the Photography Department (which did not include Eames). This uncertainty about authorship is precisely to the point, underscoring the widespread use of film and photography at Cranbrook as a communicative, rhetorical form. This is what *New Academy Movie* enacts as what we might call a Cranbrook metaexhibitionary film rather

Figure 1.3. Charles Eames (behind camera), Eero Saarinen to the left of Eliel Saarinen (center with hat), and architecture students on peristyle steps of the Cranbrook Art Museum, May 1941. Copyright Cranbrook Archives, 5699-3.

than an "Eames" film per se. It was designed to circulate and promote the intermedial design work of an educational institution keenly aware of its need to engage a complex media landscape and compete for audiences and enrollments alike.

If Cranbrook's multimedia exhibitionary practice acknowledged a recent Bauhaus past, and its promotional use of film dovetailed with Moholy-Nagy's New Bauhaus present, notice how a photograph of Charles Eames at Cranbrook, taken by its Photography Department, acknowledged a Bauhaus medial wish. The image depicts Eames seated on an armchair prototype for the MoMA competition. It insists on the experimental proximity of mechanical recording media and furniture through a superimposition dissolving, organically, human into technological form. The photograph echoes Noyes's theory of organic chair design, and the pronounced trend he and others noted in modern furniture toward lightness, flexibility, and dematerialization in systems, as it had been predicted by his teacher and friend at the Bauhaus, Marcel Breuer. In 1926 Breuer presented a playful theoretical manifesto on chairs in the form of a poster—*ein bauhaus-film, fünf jahre lang* (a Bauhaus film, five years long)—that used the graphic form of the filmstrip to chart a historical progression of his own chair designs of the 1920s. The series ended in a sixth, hypothetical "chair" marked "19??" in which no chair was visible, only the figure of a seated woman, her body floating in air, Marx's ur-medium of the modern into which all solid things melt. The image is accompanied by the caption: "It gets better and better every year. In the end, we will all sit upon an elastic column of air."

In casting dematerialized furniture in a speculative, sci-fi scenario from the heyday of the historical avant-garde, Breuer anticipated the midcentury observations of designer and critic George Nelson, who would soon hire the Eameses in his capacity as Herman Miller's director of design. In "Notes on the New Subscape," a witty essay first published in *Interiors* magazine in 1950, Nelson recounted the "manifold wonders in a zone of nearly total invisibility" that he once encountered when, relaxing from the "mighty labors of a designer's day" on a low-slung modern couch, the stuff of his magazine's inner fold spilled to the floor, sending Nelson to the ground after them.[12] Brought low, and through "Alice's looking glass," Nelson gazed upon his living room with a "mouse-eye view" and was as "bemused by it as a visitor from Mars. On all sides, as far as the eye could reach, were the elements, structures, and symbols of the contemporary subscape": a "slender steel shaft supporting a light plywood tray"; "eight more steel rods, this time holding up two seats of molded plywood"; "a couch leg crudely shaped like an over-scaled bent hairpin" ("NS," 195, 197). The defamiliarizing view thus allows one "to see with devastating clarity" the subscape's displacement of wood supports with metal, which Nelson links to the interwar progenitors of tubular furniture like Breuer's, and its corresponding openness, "like a young forest without underbrush" ("NS," 197, 199). Indeed, for Nelson the subscape seems interwar in more ways than one, not just

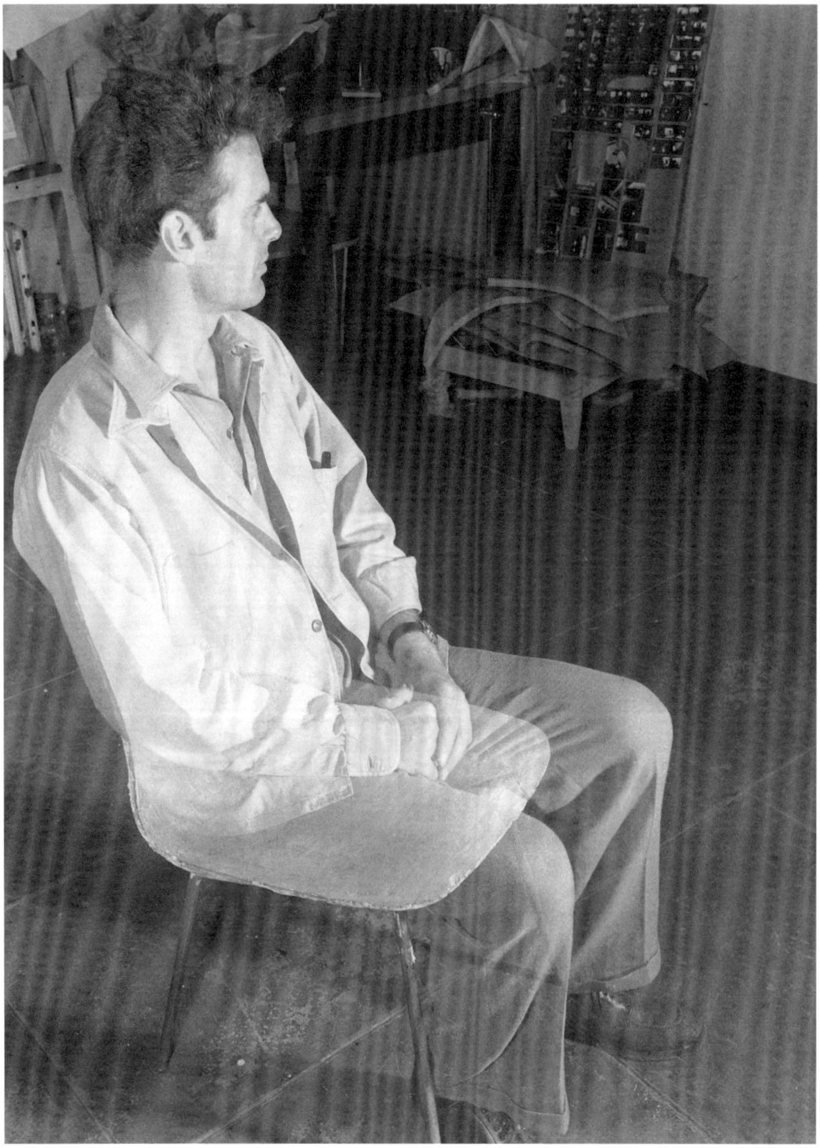

Figure 1.4. Charles Eames superimposed on armchair prototype, June 1941. Courtesy Cranbrook Archives. 5702-1.

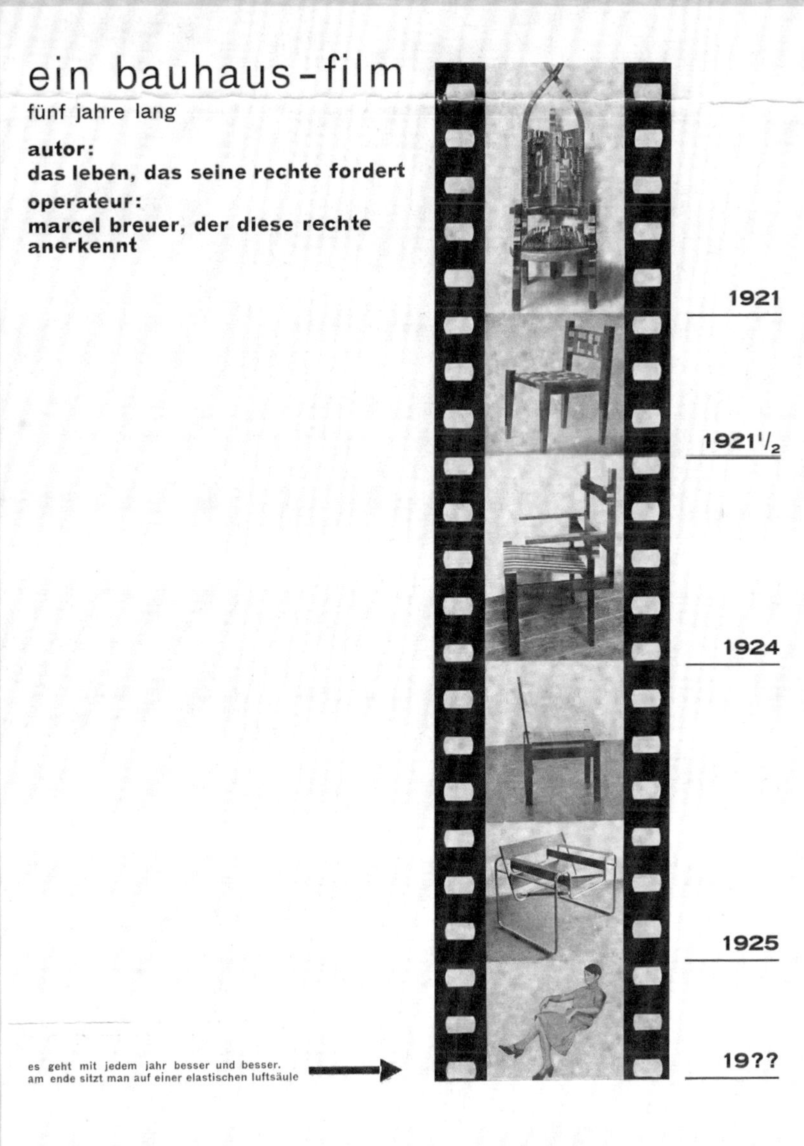

Figure 1.5. Marcel Breuer, photomontage, *ein bauhaus-film, fünf jahre lang* (a Bauhaus film, five years long). Bauhaus-Archiv Berlin.

Most characteristic of the new subscape are its wide open spaces. Vast reaches of unencumbered floor extend in all directions, interrupted only by stems of metal. The terrain is ideal for the movement of infants, toys, vacuum cleaners, cats, dogs and inquiring photographers. The silhouetted object in the foreground is one of the steel underpinnings of a couch. It seems appropriate, somehow, that the gateway to the modern subscape should be an arch turned upside down.

141

Figure 1.6.
A view from below. Interior page of George Nelson's "Problems of Design: Notes on the New Subscape," *Interiors* 110 (November 1950): 140–43. Photographer unknown.

in its style of worked metal but also in terms of the historical forces that materialize it, making the metal available—at hand—for human design: "whether one likes it or not, [the subscape] is at any rate here. I'd say here to stay for a while were it not for Korea and Korea's possible successors. Perhaps it will become a gently nostalgic reminder of the brief breathing spell between metal shortages" ("NS," 200). Yet the subscape cannot be easily contained in the terrain of the ludic and cute—what Nelson calls the "vastly increased *lebensraum*" of domestic animals, children, and vacuum cleaners ("NS," 200). Capable of disappearing again in the seemingly inevitable event of the *next* war, it extends beyond the domain of the intimate and small to various scales of human production at midcentury, from architecture, infrastructure, and modern art to atomic physics:

> The new subscape also has a great many relatives in the modern world, some of them quite imposing. These include the new skyscrapers, heavy blocks set on a base of thin stilts; they include Calder's mobiles, in which large shapes are held up by the thinnest of supports; the doodles of Joan Miro which exhibit the same characteristics, the newest elevated highways, the Horton spheroid found in the vicinity of refineries and chemical plants, diagrams of molecular structure—the list is a long one, and remarkably varied to boot. ("NS," 200)

For Nelson, the airy underside of an Eames chair opens onto the many design miracles of the subscape's "zone of invisibility"—their shared feats of structural engineering, their seeming defiance of natural laws or the visible properties of matter. Such invisibility, Nelson will later make clear, is an abiding quality of the transformed nature of the postwar. The following year, in an essay titled "The Enlargement of Vision," Nelson cast the curious materiality of furniture within a sweeping account of a new, modern environment whose defining trait was its dematerialization and insensibility—specifically, its invisibility, its being "a world we scarcely see at all."[13] This atmosphere, Nelson argued, privileged increasingly abstract networks over individual, atomistic consciousness and autonomous, bounded entities. Drawing alternatively on Mumford's *Technics and Civilization*, Sigfried Giedion's *Mechanization Takes Command* (1948), and John Dewey's *Art and Experience* (1932), Nelson argued that parallel developments in physics and in psychology tended to substitute a "picture of the world" that privileges "transparency . . . for solidity, relationships for dissociated entities, and tensions or energy, for mass" ("EV," 71). Modern physics had demonstrated that "other material 'entities'—say, solid objects such as tables or chairs—were really complicated series of electrical tensions" ("EV," 71). Across the domains of the fine arts, the natural sciences, architecture, and furniture design, these "remarkable developments" yield, for Nelson and others, nothing short of a new theory of production itself newly oriented toward "expanding networks" of relationships, and the conditioning of a sensorium shaped by postwar communications theory and cybernetics: "building is becoming less of a traditional art and more an integrated, sheltered network of 'nervous systems' for communication." Anticipating the systemic, communicative work of the Eameses' furniture films, Nelson concluded, "Furniture very naturally tends to find its organic place in this highly organized complex" ("EV," 71).

Medial Furniture

Networks of organization and postwar nature transfigured are the consistent subjects of the Eameses' furniture designs. This was true from the start. The Eameses left Cranbrook for Los Angeles in 1941 with a plan to mass-produce their award-winning furniture designs. They followed the promise of plywood, an experimental material whose demand soared during the metal shortages of a global war. Upon moving to L.A., Charles took a job as a set designer at MGM, but quit this for good after the United States' entry into the conflict, when the navy ordered 150,000 molded plywood splints, and the Eameses, alongside architect Gregory Ain and two of Charles's associates at MGM, architect Griswald Raetze and set designer Margaret Harris, established the Plyformed Wood Company in late 1942. The following year, to help scale up production, that company became the Molded Plywood Division of the Evans Products Company, and moved into a space at 901 Washington Boulevard in Venice. When the Eames Office opened in 1943, it occupied only a part of the property at 901—an old garage of twelve thousand square feet. The rest, including its reception area, was shared with Evans Products' plywood division, the first manufacturer of the Eameses' plywood furniture before Herman Miller began distributing it and eventually took over its manufacture in 1946.

The Eames Office's film work began in the brave new object world of plywood, the stuff at the center of the studio's expansive, intermedial technical environment. Plywood's world was not limited to the machine shop, but overlapped significantly with the media-savvy environment of wartime and postwar Los Angeles, with the personnel of film industry, and with liberal, technophilic visions of a happy, postwar future. Plywood experimentation was always part of 901's broader terrain of media practice. This was also true at Moholy-Nagy's Institute of Design. A syllabus for "Product Design" from 1943–44, for example, asks students to read

Wood Technology alongside Moholy's *The New Vision* and John Dewey's *Art and Experience.* Take one week's work in the Basic Workshop: "a. Movie, b. Execute Machine Sculpture, c. Read *Modern Plywood.*"[14]

In the Eameses' case, the proximity in L.A. of machined wood and modernist media experimentation in a visionary program of arts integration was most evident in the 1940s in the pages of *Arts & Architecture* magazine. Formerly a "genteel regional publisher of homes, gardens and theatre reviews," *California Arts & Architecture* was bought, revamped, and relaunched by editor John Entenza in 1943.[15] A committed liberal, Entenza had worked in an experimental film production unit at MGM under Paul Bern and eventual blacklist victim Irving Pichel. Under Entenza's editorship, *Arts & Architecture* played a pivotal role in the articulation of a California modernism with speculative designs on the future, and on the abiding technologies of the postwar good life, most famously in its sponsorship of the Case Study House Program. Given Entenza's background in the film industry, it's no surprise that his magazine regularly featured film reviews and criticism, industry news, and writing by left-oriented industry professionals. In many respects, *Arts & Architecture*'s merger of integrated aesthetics and a social scientific investment in communication across media extended into midcentury architecture and design the same utopian, liberal commitment to a peaceful postwar order evident in an important film and media publication such as *Hollywood Quarterly,* founded in 1945, and whose editorial board included Pichel, Entenza's former MGM collaborator. Prior to the consolidation of film studies as a humanities discipline in the late 1950s, these contemporaneous publications were invested in a "politicized, socially responsible cinema," and keenly attentive to film's capacity to "influence and indoctrinate."[16]

In *Arts & Architecture*'s September 1943 issue, Ray Eames made her own pitch for plywood's centrality in the integrated technoaesthetic terrain Nelson later dubbed the "new subscape." Preceded by an ad for the George E. Ream Company promoting "Plywood For War . . . Later For Peace," Ray's photomontage depicts an Eames chair in an expansive terrain of production including works of painting (Picasso's *Guernica*) and sculpture, but also oil derricks, military helmets, contemporary skyscrapers, airplanes, and the reels of a film-editing table.[17] The collage is accompanied by a short prose manifesto that announces a contemporary aesthetics "influenced by the world in which we live and by the synthesis of the experiences of the world by all creators," including "the engineer mathematician physicist chemist architect doctor musician writer dancer teacher baker actor editor the man on the job the woman at home and painters." In the September 1946 issue, the Eameses own

Figure 1.7. "Kazam Machine" in the Eameses' Los Angeles apartment, 1941. Copyright 2017 Eames Office LLC (eamesoffice.com).

Figure 1.8. Ray Eames collage, *Arts & Architecture,* September 1943, letterpress on paper. Copyright 2017 Eames Office LLC (eamesoffice.com).

plywood furniture designs, some of them prototyped in the storied Kazam Machine housed in the couple's L.A. apartment, designed by *Arts & Architecture* board member Richard Neutra, were treated to a lavishly illustrated twenty-page feature written by Eliot Noyes.[18] It contained a number of stunning illustrations by Swiss photographer and designer Herbert Matter, then a member of the Plyformed Wood Company and the Eames Office staff (Plate 3). Within the magazine's liberal editorial vision of integrated arts, its readers could learn of the democratic promise of plywood and also take in Robert Joseph's "Cinema" column—here about the U.S. Office of Military Government's recently finished concentration camp documentary, *Todesmühlen* (released with the English title *Death Mills*). We might think of them together as signs of the Janus-faced power of wartime technics and contrary harbingers of the future of so-called modern man. Joseph's praise for this landmark work of German political reeducation, much of it done by Billy Wilder at the Film Section of the Information Control Division, summons the power of U.S. propaganda in "all mediums of communication—radio, theater, newspapers, magazines, books and motion picture films" to "acquaint the German people with the horror of these terrible murder factories."[19] Its communicative aspirations lodged between technologies of mass death and postwar happiness, the media culture of Eames-era plywood in the 1946 was capacious indeed.

As 901's plywood objects moved from wartime to postwar environments, the function of the designer expanded from the making of consumer goods to participation in the creative, knowledge-based, information-saturated operations of a nascent postindustrial society. This change placed 901—and the more than one hundred films the Eameses made there—at the heart of the Eames Office's postwar investigations in education, experiments in the communication of information and ideas, and what John Harwood has called "sustained interdisciplinary research conducted in tandem with the central scientific institutions of the postwar period, public and private."[20] In this way, 901's intermedial plywood R & D was also implicated in what Caroline Jones and Peter Galison have identified as a broad shift in the postwar studio from the centralized, "aggregative and social mode of production" of work of the wartime factory to a decentralized dispersal of production "among multiple authors at multiple sites," and in "the spectacular and discursive realms of print, film, and photographic media."[21]

When Herman Miller moved the tooling of the Eameses' furniture to Michigan in the 1950s, the Eames Office expanded at 901. But the word "expansion" is too mild—it doesn't capture the explosion of experimental activity within what Catherine Ince has described as the office's dual "condition as both shop (in the American sense of the word) and studio set."[22] While Charles Eames happily wrote of being able to leave MGM to focus on the work of furniture design, he wasn't so much leaving the film studio as he was beginning to reconceptualize its Fordism within a culture of postindustrial image production and consumption. Film—like photography—was at the heart of 901's wide-ranging design activities across media from the 1950s through the 1970s. As a creative environment in a historical moment in which the Eameses became exemplary of the so-called creative personality then undergoing systematic social scientific study, their furniture design and interdisciplinary R & D at 901 was always aided by photography and film *as research technologies* and modes of communication. In addition to its furniture workshop, office spaces, and kitchen, 901's quasi-utopian space included "full-color and black-and-white photo labs," a film-editing area, and a conference room for meeting clients that doubled as an impromptu screening room.[23]

As the September 1946 *Arts & Architecture* feature affirms, Eames chairs from early on lived conspicuously medial lives as the inhuman protagonists of the couple's varied terrain of happy making. Material avatars of a utopian future and instrumental forms of corporate mass media, the furniture designs were conceived and produced at 901 in zones of intermedial experimentation that fueled the Eameses' engagement with moving-image technology and pedagogy. Photography, filmmaking, and furniture design were understood by the designers as related species of communication, expressing the Eameses' flexible, curious, and to some observers, quintessentially American lifestyle.

The molded-fiberglass shell chairs that the Eameses first successfully mass-produced in 1950 for Herman Miller, and that would come to exemplify the postwar tendency to define U.S.-style democracy on the model of material abundance and consumer choice, began in another experimental medium, plastic, and the extravagantly suggestive futurity of La Chaise (1948). Its surreal airiness the product of a foam rubber and Styrofoam core sandwiched by two layers of the then-novel material "fiberglass" (glass-reinforced polyester), La Chaise's playful form, the Eameses acknowledged, "did not 'anticipate the variety of needs it is to fill' because those needs remained 'indefinite.'"[24] Later mass-produced in a spectrum of colors, the fiberglass shell chairs were available for purchase with a variety of bases (Plate 4). Together, fiberglass chairs, the plywood chairs, the wire mesh chairs, and the Eames Storage Units—a lightweight, modular storage system—all embodied the same basic concept: "that mass-produced, standardized parts could be combined in different ways to meet the unique needs of each consumer."[25]

This was, in part, the Fordist promise of the Eameses' furniture. A revealing anecdote: in 1954, Charles Eames wrote directly to Henry Ford Jr., the president of the automobile giant, noting he had "been driving Ford's continuously since 1929. . . . We believe in standard production models."[26] The Eameses were in the market for a new convertible. And they were advised by their friend Alexander Girard to write Ford Jr. directly with a request speccing an "acceptable, anonymous model": exterior, black; top, "natural," and with a "minimum of advertising symbols attached—preferably none"; interior, "simple neutral tan color or good neutral synthetic material—*no two tones*." Ray's handwritten notes add a political edge to their discerning consumer choices: "We find the forced, no alternative garish décor dictatorship-like."

The request aligns Fordist standardization practices with the Eameses' own furniture work for Herman Miller, and enacts its promise of customization and individuation *within* mass-produced anonymity. Similarly, the Eames chairs—moving from dreamy prototype to the mass-produced present—rapidly became a symbol of the postwar ideal of lightweight, mobile, endlessly recombinant furniture often packaged and sold as fragments of easily transportable, knock-down kits. "The Eames idea of design," Beatriz Colomina explains, "turns on the continuous arrangement and rearrangement of a limited kit of parts. Almost everything they produced can be rearranged; no layout is ever fixed."[27] It was this Eamesian sense of the midcentury interior as an "unrestricted combinatorial system"—one whose objects are valued less for intimacy than as information or code, one in which "everything intercommunicates"—that Jean Baudrillard, writing in *The System of Objects,* saw as the rebirth of modern man as cybernetician, obsessed with "the perfect circulation of messages."[28]

We can observe a similar communicative flexibility, a modular or recombinant quality, in the Eameses' media experimentation concerning the furniture itself and within its distribution networks, often allegorized in the films. The Eameses, in other words, were not only engaging in principles of mass production as "one of the many positive things that bear the name of Ford."[29] They were also enacting a Fordist medial lesson about what Lee Grieveson has called film's role as a "communicative, rhetorical, and pedagogical form" and a technology deeply intertwined with systems of production, mass distribution, and mass communication.[30] In films like *The Road to Happiness* (1924), for example, the Ford Motion Picture Department situated the ur-modern technology of film in a story of well-being guaranteed by "efficient distribution and productivity," where film is "imagined as one aspect of a wider networked infrastructure, helping facilitate and mediate the mobility of goods and capital."[31] The Eameses' Herman Miller films also framed film as a postwar medium of happiness: a networked technology of speed, efficient distribution, and time-space compression that required the flexible media experimentation the designers performed, through media, and as a postindustrial lifestyle.

In fact, the Eameses' inaugural furniture film was made for the occasion of another medial first—their debut television appearance on *Discovery,* a public-service program sponsored by the San Francisco Museum of Art, and broadcast on station KPIX in December 1953. As producer Allon Schoener proposed the notion to Charles, the series, whose theme was "Creative Arts Today," aimed to be "one of the nation's outstanding cultural programs," featuring, among others, photographer Ansel Adams, the San Francisco Opera Company, Frank Lloyd Wright, and director Fred Zinnemann. Schoener pitched a program on furniture design, apparently, in which Eames would "explain the evolution of some of [his] designs, demonstrate their uses, and possibly include a film section showing how they were made in the factory." With "no experience with television," Eames warmed to the notion of using prefabricated filmed modules as stand-alone "answers" to questions posed to him on-air by the program's emcee: "from what I hear," he wrote, "it might be best to get a certain amount on film and avoid studio panic." Sending Eames a rough outline of the program, Schoener insisted that the filmed material—however much it allowed the Eameses control over the show's content—not betray television's essence as "carefully planned and rehearsed spontaneity." He thus cast the show as both an experiment and a kind of summation of Eamesian R & D: the program, Schoener insisted, would be "much more interesting if you felt it could be your own presentation and the result of your experiments."[32]

Schoener's initial request for a film about the making of the Herman Miller furniture—a short, lost film about the molded plywood chair titled *Chair Story* in the program's drafted script—led Charles to propose several filmed modules: an animated sequence illustrating some principles of design evolution; a two-minute film labeled *Toys, Other Designs* in the script's final version; and two filmed sequences of stills shot in and around the couple's already-famous home in Pacific Palisades—material later recombined into *House: After Five Years of Living* (1955).[33] Ostensibly about furniture design as a creative art, the TV program effectively showcased, while expanding, the terrain of the Eameses' media experimentation. Within it, the processes of making a toy or a chair, filming its manufacture, or broadcasting that activity on television connote the same mobile, happy lifestyle enacted in the couple's modern home. This kind of promiscuous productivity is everywhere acknowledged in the correspondence about the *Discovery* show's planning. Schoener, for example, asks after the Eameses' film *Blacktop* (distributed, like *Parade,* by MoMA beginning in 1953), explaining his desire to include it in a "history of art film series" on a program to be devoted to "the topic of abstractions" the following March. He also remarks on the sheer difficulty of scheduling Eames on his show owing to conflicts with Charles's "spectacular" lectures running concurrently in the fall of 1953 and continuing through the spring semester of 1954 at the University of California–Berkeley. Putatively an introduction-to-architecture course, this idiosyncratic class, as chapter 2 explains, also relied on the use of films, slides, and other forms of audiovisual risk taking.

Chair Story, then, is both a film about the revolutionary processes of molded-plywood manufacturing and a testing ground—like the TV appearance itself—for the Eameses' ongoing, overtly communicative experiments. It is one part of a flexible media kit that had to include TV. Like *A Communications Primer* (1953), on which the Eameses were simultaneously working, *Chair Story* betrays their fascination with communication theory, and with the abstraction and distillation of informatic essence. Charles described the film as "the condensed form of the outline of a synopsis of a kind of minimum digest of what actually went on" in the making of the famous chair. The formulation links the film, as a work of abbreviation and compression, directly to the couple's contemporaneous pedagogical experiments such as "Art-X." In the same year as the *Discovery* show and the "Sample Course," the Eameses collaborated with their friends Eero and Aline Saarinen on a proposal, funded by the Ford Foundation, to conceptualize ways of portraying art on educational television.[34] Admirers of Edward R. Murrow's groundbreaking work in television, and Walter Cronkite's historical education program *You Are There,* the Eameses were taken with the pedagogical power of the new medium. Charles Eames's secretary wrote to CBS requesting permission to use the 16mm kinescope of the "Vindication of Savonarola" episode in Charles's Berkeley architecture course, explaining that "a most important part of this course involves the use of film and slide material" as "a way of helping the spectator identify with the period."[35] Eames insisted that the kinescope of *You Are There,* deployed in his architecture class, "would be invaluable in helping students break down the barriers which exist in their minds between various areas of learning." While the *Discovery* program may have featured furniture designs, those designs were, within the context of the Eameses' contemporaneous interests in television, already folded into a broader, multimedia pedagogical practice. In it, their films, like Charles's work at the university, would be explained to the TV audience as "the logical continuation of the design program."[36]

A midcentury episode in convergence media, the *Discovery* program's basic format—a toy box of flexible film modules and loosely scripted talk—was repeated in May 1956, and the *Chair Story* module repurposed, when Charles Eames was invited to appear on CBS's "prestige" public-affairs program *Omnibus.* Then occupied with second-unit location shooting for his friend Billy Wilder's film *Spirit of St. Louis* (1957), for which he filmed and edited a snappy montage of the iconic plane's own manufacturing process, Eames notes his and Ray's admiration for this experimental program:

> Perhaps a painless way of doing a program about "myself" would make little reference to *things* we have done but explore a few of a great *variety* of things that will help shape a real human scale environment of the future—this would include many of the things in which we have been interested, from toys and kites to electronic calculators and games of strategy. . . . Inasmuch as this is for a television *workshop* I would not feel right unless we could give special attention to the "production"—some things we would have to shoot, cut, and score here. . . . I doubt we would want to use much of our existing films.[37] (Eames's emphasis)

Nodding to his familiarity with *Omnibus*'s something-for-everyone format, Eames insists not on autonomous things but on their sheer variety and networked relations; not on himself as expressive maker but rather on scenes of experimental production. Such happy making is especially suited to a TV workshop, as *Omnibus* fashioned its "overall atmosphere of cultural uplift and education."[38] As its modular schema clarifies, the *Omnibus* program reused some films from the *Discovery* broadcast, including *Chair Story* and *Toys* (which, from the script, appears to consist of images and sound from what would become *Toccata for Toy Trains*) and presented alternate versions of others. Portions of *House* now included Elmer Bernstein's bright score, and helped introduce both the designers and their credo that "everything is architecture." The schema also includes films labeled *Kite Film, Feedback Film,* and *ABC.* In the first draft of the script, however, the Eameses proposed an alternate final section, which would follow the six-minute *Chair Story* and a station break.[39] Here, *Feedback,* a working version of *Introduction to Feedback* (1960), the IBM-commissioned sequel to *A Communications Primer,* would be "replaced with some film and short (twenty second) pertinent statements by Eero Saarinen, Billy Wilder, and Norbert Wiener."

What is an appropriate showbiz segue from the production of plywood chairs to cybernetic thought? The goal of the third part was to model just such connections—to move from the problems involved in chair design to the expanding ground of Eamesian production, to "point out that what was shown in the chair film marked just the beginning of designers' responsibilities." That this terrain might appear disconnected, or seemingly unrelated to the stuff of furniture, is indicated by notes penciled on the proposed conclusion of the *Omnibus* script: "somehow should end up with a chair if it's about a chair."[40] Indeed, the chair's "aboutness" is at stake. Is it an isolated thing or systemically defined? The filmed statements from the unlikely trio of Saarinen, Wilder, and Wiener provide the conceptual logic that would explain to *Omnibus*'s TV audience why the program about a chair is not *just* about a chair—why the designers' thinking ranges so widely across media and seemingly disparate zones of inquiry, a scalar flexibility provided through the disciplinary solvent of communications theory and the universal aspirations of cybernetics. Saarinen's oft-cited quip about the designer's centrifugal expansion of attention to "The Next Larger Thing" (from a chair, to its room, to the building that houses it, to its site, etc.), the script explains, "leads to communication through graphics and through film." Wilder, it seems, would explain "the help that comes through communication theory and how this is often at a very human scale." And Wiener, finally, would offer a caveat about "the danger of abandoning the seemingly unimportant outposts of thinking." The dispersed sites of the Eameses' happy making, the program will argue, are so many "ways of keeping these outposts alive." Ray Eames's planning notes acknowledge the far-flung domains of creative production that the show will enact and explain, in a specifically pedagogical register hostile to specialization. "What is it," she asks, that "these things have in common?"[41] She offers an answer by describing the *Omnibus* program's basic strategy, a list of four "tacks": "1. The attacking of the design problem/The realm of design. 2. The whole man—the miraculous solution. 3. The creative climate. 4. Communication."[42]

The furniture communicated, but the Eameses also communicated about and through it—for Herman Miller, on television, and in graphics and film. In 1950 the Eames Office began producing print advertisements for its furniture designs that appeared in trade periodicals and in magazines such as *Interiors, Architectural Forum,* and *Arts & Architecture,* as well as brochures, instruction booklets, packaging, and point-of-sale promotional pieces. And in 1954 the Eameses made *S-73 (Sofa Compact),* their first surviving film about a furniture design, and one of eight works of nontheatrical, useful cinema made for Herman Miller between 1954 and 1973.[43] The film, which gets its numeric name from the sofa's listing in the Herman Miller catalog, was made to explain the design and function of the Eames Sofa Compact to Herman Miller's sales force, dealers, and merchants.[44]

If useful cinema, as Wasson and Acland have argued, is a "disposition, an outlook, an approach toward a medium on the part of institutions and institutional agents," then *S-73* exemplified how the Eameses *thought film* at Herman Miller.[45] Beginning with a seemingly modest film like *S-73*, the Eames Office was not only teaching its client—and its client's clients—how to use this piece of furniture, but in fact, enacting how the filmic apparatus itself might be put to corporate use as a flexible communicative device, its technological mobility basically of a piece with the film's ostensible subject. From the start, *S-73*'s future life of exhibition is conceptualized as a kind of metapedagogy in a corporate circuit extending from Herman Miller's production and distribution networks

Figure 1.9. S-73 Sofa Compact advertisement for the Herman Miller Furniture Company. Courtesy of Herman Miller.

Figure 1.10. A model couple beginning to assemble a compact sofa in *S-73,* 1954, directed by Charles and Ray Eames.

(manufacturers, sellers, dealers) to their own clients, who can show the film to their sales staffs. *S-73*, in this way, is fashioned as a visual aid to be bundled, boxed, and shipped alongside the sofa. The film travels with, and like, the couch whose systemic workings it communicates.

The film's opening montage frames the sofa's compact design as the materialization of the solution to a problem in and of modern systems—the problem of shipping as both the manufacturer's responsibility and the "designer's problem." Following a distribution parable about shipped goods' vulnerability to damage in transit, we get our first glimpse of the S-73, as Eames explains how the size of sofas exacerbates the difficulty of shipping furniture—a problem solved by this unit's compact design, as we see in an animated sequence. Capable of being shipped more cheaply, at one-third the volume of its standing size, the S-73 is introduced here in a complex *logistical* drama involving not just the management of transportation infrastructures that stretch from dollies to airplanes but the commodification of abstract, volumetric space. Capitalizing on the compact is a way of rationalizing air that fuels the genre of low-cost modern furniture design, delivering on the Eamesian design mantra—namely, to "get the most of the best to the most for the least." The film's graphic play with boxes of various kinds—trucks, trains, cubes, packages, and grids stretching from floor tiles to living room drapes—announces its exhibition catalog while a man behind her gazes silently at the abstract works on the wall behind her. The elegant, segmented profile of this sofa's steel frame, like its chrome-plated steel legs, is a designed thing of beauty of the same order as nature itself. It is nature transfigured: an exemplary "subscape." Eames clarifies this in the next cut: a close-up of an abstract metal sculpture against a background of diffuse yellow. As the camera racks focus, the sculpture blurs in the foreground, revealing the sharp yellow fabric of an S-73, now located in some modern living room. The camera pulls back from the sculpture, and we realize that it sits atop a television faced by the S-73, now positioned in another site of distractibility. A woman enters from frame right and lies on the sofa, her back to us. Cut to a reverse angle of the sofa in a tastefully appointed interior. For two beats, there is no movement, until a young boy—her son, we assume—enters from frame left, and attempts to wake his mother by shaking her head and rousing her to duties she has momentarily forgotten, or escaped from. We cut to the camera drifting from the top of the sofa to the checkerboard drapes, and fade to black. In the next, final, shot, we see a close-up of the female half of the average couple, who smiles directly at the camera as Eames's voiceover concludes, "Thank you, Molly. We hope your new sofa will bring you many years of service and pleasure."

The film ends with the wish for a kind of long-lived happiness of the sort the S-73 can provide, but it has labored to show us that this temporal continuity of "service and pleasure" exists alongside the other, more vulnerable times of midcentury media environments materialized by the sofa: the abstract time in which it is boxed and shipped; the habit-forming time of domestication it takes to incorporate this new technology into one's lifestyle; the time of labor that produces it; the downtimes between what counts as eventful in one's day; even the press of contingency (the event of a spilled jelly sandwich) that only synthetic upholstery can accommodate. "There is no predicting what may happen in the life of a sofa," Eames's voiceover observes. Carving out any time for leisure, and the designed spaces of restive repose that allow us to take pleasure in it—this, *S-73* clarifies, takes work: it calls for logistical control, discipline, and predictive capacities. When does the life of service begin and end? Do designers ever sleep? In asking these questions, *S-73* is less a chair or a film than a plea for systematicity, for better modes of time management. Beginning with the box, the grid, and the shipping container, it is a film about a sofa, and about that broader, and largely neglected category that John Durham Peters has called "logistical media"—media that "arrange people and property into time and space"; it attests to the place of flexible sofas and speedy film production at 901 within what media historian Alexander Klose calls the ascendancy of the "container principle."[46]

The Eameses would, of course, make a lounge chair sufficiently soft and comfortable enough for you to actually fall asleep in (Plate 5). And how. The celebrated 1956 Eames Lounge Chair was, Charles later explained, conceived "as a present for a friend, Billy Wilder," himself a devotee of modern art and design who was forced to abandon—among other things—a prized Mies chair when he fled Hitler's Germany for the United States in 1933.[47] The lounger was the second of three Eames designs developed with their pal Wilder's forms of repose in mind. The first was the molded plywood "TV chair" of 1946. A 1950 *Life* magazine piece on the Eames house pictures Wilder in the chair in a striking multiple-exposure photograph by Peter Stackpole; the caption reads, "Eames designed this special chair in which the restless Wilder can easily jump around while watching television."[48] This image of a recumbent Wilder rocking back and forth in a state of medial distraction brings together photographic, here protocinematic, time, the forms

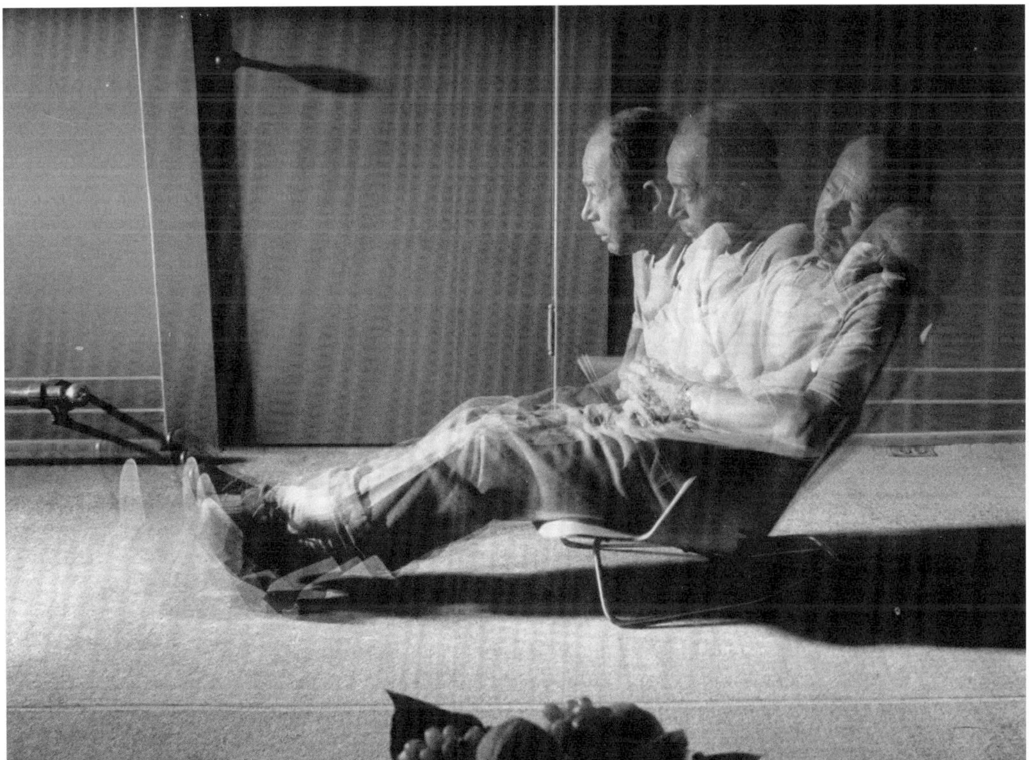

Figure 1.12. Multiple exposures of Billy Wilder in Eames "TV chair." Photographed by Peter Stackpole for *Life* magazine. The Life Picture Collection/Getty Images.

of attention called for by television, and the viewing protocols materialized by modern furniture. The image, like the concluding vignette of *S-73*, demonstrates that the Eameses had begun to think hard about the relationship between modern furniture, filmic and photographic time, and the postwar incursion of television into the domestic interior that prompted the broadcast of their first furniture film. No surprise, then, that *S-73* finds itself in a living room reoriented around a television set that it faces. The momentary pleasure it offers to the mother who tries to catch a nap on it seems to depend on both mom and TV being, for a time, turned off, removed from broadcast television's ongoing space of abstract flows.

Two years later, the Eameses unveiled their lounger in a charming two-minute promotional film, *Eames Lounge Chair*, broadcast on April 14, 1956, as part of a lengthy spot on NBC's show *Home*, hosted by Arlene Francis. It was the mission of domestic programming such as *Home* to train its audience in regimes of postwar consumption, promoting new signs of taste and sophistication like Eames chairs, and the show went to some lengths to stage the Eameses' latest work in a broader design history of revolutionary modern furniture.[49] When Francis asked Charles about the "basic theory of design for [his] chairs," he responded with a

Figure 1.13. A recumbent male fantasy in *Eames Lounge Chair*, 1956, directed by Charles and Ray Eames.

negative definition: that they never design for fashion, nor has Herman Miller ever asked them to design for a market. The way the Eameses work, Charles explains, the "timing is more or less our own. Sometimes it is too slow, but we're allowed to follow it through." The comment causes Francis to marvel: "You say it's too slow, and yet you've done so much and so many and so much sooner than most people." It's a telling exchange: although the chair—and the history of its design—was a labored, time-consuming production, the film about it was a rushed job. In fact, the couple was invited on the show just before Herman Miller was to formally unveil the chair at a press conference at its New York City showroom, and they hatched the idea to make the short film to communicate the chair's design and assembly for Francis's largely female audience. Shot over a weekend in the Eames Office's Venice, California, studio, with an improvised score by Elmer Bernstein, the film would become one of Charles's favorite examples of what he called "spontaneous production"—a project designed to fill a pressing need, "produced and delivered without the luxury of a long deliberation time."[50]

When the curtain finally rises on the chair, Francis asks Charles to tell her audience something about it. He responds that a better idea would be to "build it for you right here," and we dissolve to the film proper—or better, to another site of media convergence: chair, television, film. Part by part, segment by segment, built by hand from the base up, the Eames Lounge Chair comes into being in accelerated motion, and through a stop-motion technique using time-lapse photography first employed by the Eameses in their early toy films, *Parade* and the unfinished *Traveling Boy* (1950). When the chair is finally assembled, the assembler sits in it and closes his eyes. A woman emerges from frame left. Carrying a Herman Miller brochure for the chair, she crosses in front of the lounging man, gliding unnaturally across the floor, by virtue of the Eameses' pixilation technique. When she exits the frame, the ottoman materializes in front of the man, and he puts his feet up. A cut inserts lounging into the temporality of male fantasy, which is clarified in two dissolves: first, when the still-lounging man, dressed as a modest laborer in jeans, sneakers, and a T-shirt, transforms into a suited gentleman of leisure, with black leather dress shoes and reading a paper; then, a blonde woman in an evening gown emerges, for just a second or two, and perches at his feet on the ottoman. She vanishes first, then goes the man's classy outfit. As Bernstein's piano jumps into overdrive, the original assembler wakes up, rapidly disassembles chair and ottoman, and boxes them separately. Two people lift the filled box toward the camera, and the film ends.

Eames Lounge Chair is, of course, a pedagogical film about a chair and an advertisement. Like *S-73*, it teaches us how to assemble the chair, and how it gives its users pleasure. But one communicative lesson of the Eameses' chair films is to deny their status as autonomous objects, and to visualize instead their environmental, systemic functioning. Instead of asking us to see this systematicity through the chair's manufacture, as the Eameses do by historicizing the labor of chair design in *S-73*, or by documenting factory production in their later film *The Fiberglass Chairs: Something of How They Get the Way They Are* (1970), here we are asked to see and learn something about media, time, and the systems in which these chairs live and are consumed. A film about a chair made quickly, "spontaneously," to be broadcast on network television, *Eames Lounge Chair* epitomizes Charles Eames's tendency to collapse medial differences in the service of conceptual rigor. The dispersed medial condition of commercial TV broadcasting itself seems an analogy for the Eameses' professed desire to democratize design. Its broadcast context draws connections between the transmissibility and transit of chair, film, and televisual image, underscoring the major functions of media: transmission across space and time, storage, logistics. By thinking about the chair's transportation toward the space-time of its owner (boxing); the image's transmission toward Arlene Francis's audience of potential buyers (sending); and, through its specifically filmic capacities for accelerated motion and stop-motion animation (compressing), the film also seems to have an idea about the time of media superimposed on it.

Not just the accelerated time in which segments of chairs or celluloid are assembled or disassembled, or the slow temporalities of labor, leisure, and fantasy, but also the temporality of logistics.[51] Not lounge time but logistical time, organizational time—because the human sitter, even in this lavish seat, just doesn't lounge for very long, positioned as he is as a node in a flexible network of production, consumption, and distribution across various medial forms. What Eames is asking us to see—on TV, on film, in this chair's very materiality—is not just a happy human but a human at home in a corporate system of organized complexity incarnated in the chair's transmissibility as both object and image.

The pedagogical vision that the Eameses rely on in this TV spot, and with which they experimented again on *Omnibus* the following month, champions communication as a way of seeing processes of organization, of visualizing postwar modernity as a technocratically integrated system, a dynamic network of relations of thickening complexity and scalar fluidity.[52] The Eameses' understanding of the link between perception and organization—what their friend György Kepes called "the language of vision"—owed a strong debt to the Hungarian designer and visual artist, as chapter 2 explores in more detail. The Eameses' enthusiastic embrace of television in and around the production of these furniture films in the postwar period echoes the integrative, humanist visuality that Kepes consistently stumped for, first in *The Language of Vision* (1944), and later in the multivolume Vision + Value series that Kepes edited at MIT. As Reinhold Martin has shown, this model of an organizing vision, shaped by Kepes's encounters with Gestalt psychology and cybernetics, entailed the aesthetic proposition that the "organized image is not the carrier of the message; it *is* the message." Organization is, as Martin has it, "a media effect."[53] In his groundbreaking book *The New Landscape in Art and Science* (1956), for example, Kepes compares the magnetic core memory inside an MIT computer and the patterns of experimental ceiling lighting to the modular components of the Eames chairs. Hardware and houseware: as Charles insisted to Arlene Francis, everything is architecture. As an aesthetic ideology at work in the Eameses' furniture films and multiscreen experiments, the language of vision aims to train the viewer in the integrative, organizational work of information processing.

The Eameses' faith in an abiding language of perceptual organization, and its enabling technologies, is all the more evident the more rapidly the objects of vision speed by, or are multiplied across screens, or are chopped up into bits, like modular furniture, and playfully reassembled. Especially instructive in this regard are the Eameses' experiments in kaleidoscopic vision, their 1959 film *Kaleidoscope Shop,* and their 1960 companion piece, *Kaleidoscope Jazz Chair.* The first film was produced, in fact, as a visual surrogate for the very experimentalism of the Eameses' own productive activity. By the late 1950s, 901 had become, as had the couple, internationally famous. So when Charles was invited to give a lecture at the Royal College of Art in London, and asked to give an illustrated tour of this famous workshop, he responded with a four-minute film that displays an iconic site of organized production by dissolving it into play and sensation, asking the tourist-spectators to see *work* by looking through a toy. Graphic layout rooms, film production spaces, offices, the furniture shop—all the spaces of the Eameses' media practice are presented to the viewer as part of a relentlessly active visual field in which the eye, like these designers, never rests.

Charles described the choice of the kaleidoscopic camera—which he developed in the office with collaborators Parke Meek and Jeremy Lepard—as both a way to liven up a possibly boring lecture and a strategy to preserve a sense of privacy about 901's inner workings. The two films knowingly mobilize the kaleidoscope's long-standing connections to the intimate, protocinematic pleasures of peeping and the technology's capacity to produce variegated patterns of sensual effects around elusive visual objects never fully present. Oriented toward sensory pleasure rather than information, the films recall the centrality of this kaleidoscopic perception to the nineteenth century's standardization of "modern" observers themselves, their submission to the dictates of rationalization and serial production. Jonathan Crary, for example, has argued that the device's inventor, Sir David Brewster, justified the fashioning of the kaleidoscope in 1815 by the "productivity and efficiency" of its image making. "He saw it as a mechanical means for the reformation of art according to an industrial paradigm."[54] *Kaleidoscope Jazz Chair,* a film occasionally used for publicity purposes by Herman Miller, acknowledges this by linking the merger of art and industry effected by its enabling optical device to the happy seriality of the Eameses' furniture (Plate 6).

This seven-minute film, in fact, has two segments: the first, as does *Kaleidoscope Shop,* involves the fast-moving kaleidoscopic transformation of stuff in Eames Office, including its iconic chairs. In the second, the fragmented images produced by the kaleidoscope's radial technique give way to a compensatory form of serial organization. This happens through a sequence of stop-motion shots in which the Eameses' multicolored fiberglass chairs emerge into organized rows, stack themselves in endless variations of color, and in one case, speed one after another in single file toward the camera. At one moment in this otherwise inhuman serial landscape of the film, the couple appears briefly on the chairs, only to vanish before the infinite variety of their work. In another sequence, the seat colors change in time with the syncopated score; they appear to be keys on a Herman Miller color organ, synesthetically blending jazz and color to provoke warm feelings through color's sensory-affective potential and capacity for visual music. Brewster, it is worth recalling, had high hopes for expanding the kaleidoscope's affective power beyond the single, private viewer and toward a public spectacle projected on a screen through an "electric lime ball" magic lantern, a kind of kaleidoscopic phantasmagoria. If Brewster was dreaming of the kaleidoscope's future in a more hallucinogenic domain of sensorial play that we tend to associate with the expanded cinema spectacles of the 1960s, such as Warhol's Exploding Plastic Inevitable multiscreen events, perhaps it is no surprise that the art students who saw *Kaleidoscope Shop* during Eames's lecture would later describe the experience as feeling "more like the beginning of the 'swinging sixties' than a presentation by the world's most 'serious' industrial designer."[55]

In asking us to view their kind of experimentalism through kaleidoscopic views of a famous office-turned-playground, the Eameses announce their filmmaking practice as a *lifestyle*. Filmic experimentation is perceptual experimentation, and both are embedded in the times, speeds, and sensations of serial, industrialized production and its transformations of the spaces of private life, its reworking of the boundary between leisure and work. That boundary vanishes in this film—indeed, it is everywhere collapsed by the Eameses' way of working and playing—and yet the Eameses still summon a space of privacy that the spectacle of chairs kaleidoscopically fragmented, then serially paraded as abstract sensation, would seek to preserve. The Eameses' furniture films are not merely advertisements, or uncritical mirrors of a material culture of commodified everydayness; rather they are midcentury "allegories of production," forms of small-format, domestic production that materialize their own location in the new nature of industrial, and postindustrial, image making.[56]

The most striking filmic allegory of Eamesian technoliving and image production, however, is their 1955 *House: After Five Years of Living*, a ten-minute film composed entirely of a sequence of three hundred still images of the Eameses' own home. The images are of the house's interior and immediate environs, and its dazzling surfeit of carefully arranged objects (furniture, collectibles, knickknacks)—rapidly edited in what would become the Eameses' trademark style of "fast cutting," and scored again by Bernstein. British architect Peter Smithson would

Figure 1.14. *House: After Five Years of Living*, 1955, directed by Charles and Ray Eames.

later cast the house's technoairiness as the definitive expression of the "Eames aesthetic," their way of selecting, arranging, and juxtaposing objects in surprising domestic combinations that is everywhere modeled in the conspicuous arrangements and combinations of their film *House*.[57] But he was also commenting on the Eameses' way of mobilizing wonder through various media and technologies: "This sounds like whimsy, but the basic vehicle—the steel lattice frame in the case of the house, the colour film and colour processing in the graphics work, the pressing and moulding in the case of the furniture—are ordinary to

Figure 1.15. Exterior, Case Study House No. 8. Photograph by Julius Shulman. J. Paul Getty Trust. Getty Research Institute, Los Angeles (2004.R.10).

Figure 1.16. Charles Eames, drawing for Eames, John Entenza, and Herbert Matter, "What Is a House?" *Arts & Architecture,* July 1944. Copyright Travers Family Trust. Reprinted with permission.

the culture."[58] In short, Charles Eames is happy in a variety of media, modeling a way of living and working in the becoming ordinary of postwar technologies that is, literally, the stuff of his house, and his film about it, *House.*

The so-called Eames House that served as the couple's home and studio for many years was conceived as part of the Case Study House Program, launched in 1945 through the sponsorship of John Entenza's *Arts & Architecture* magazine, and publicized in its pages. Constructed in the traumatic shadow of World War II, the Case homes imagined their future occupants reoriented by the war; they assumed, in Beatriz Colomina's words, that "the solider returning from war had become a 'modern man,' a figure who would prefer to live in a modern environment utilizing the most advanced technology rather than return to live in the 'old-fashioned houses with enclosed rooms.'"[59]

What was "modern" about the environment of the Case houses was not just their use of standardized, prefab building materials but also, as Smithson would later argue, their enactment of a postwar lifestyle in which domesticity was at home in the spaces and times of modern image-making technologies such as photography and newly mobile 16mm cameras. The July 1944 issue of *Arts & Architecture,* for example, featured a manifesto titled "What Is a House?," cowritten by Entenza,

Charles Eames, Fuller, and Herbert Matter. Setting the conceptual terms for the Case Study House Program to begin the following year, they defined the house as "the basis for the environment that conditions us; the envelope which encases the most important of our life's functions."[60] Those postwar lives and their vital capacities would only "break through into the future" when their environment—the home—acknowledged its degree of technological saturation.[61] A drawing by Eames positions these ways of assimilating machines in an array of "family functions," including film-viewing, kite-flying, card-playing, listening to records, the shaking of cocktails, painting, and, naturally, lounging on modern furniture.[62] Domestic filmmaking and film viewing were cast within a broad vital continuum of postwar lifestyle to be performed while enveloped in technology. Eames and Saarinen's accompanying briefs for Case Study Houses 8 and 9 (the Eames house and the Entenza house, respectively) extended this logic of efficient modern spaces in which one lives and produces in time and media: " 'House' in these cases means center of productive activities" (Plate 7).[63] The Eameses are here described anonymously as "a married couple both occupied professionally with mechanical experiment and graphic presentation."[64] They require an environment in which "work and recreation are involved in general activities: Day and night, work and play, concentration, relaxation with friend and foe, all intermingled personally and professionally with mutual interest."[65] In the Eames house, play dissolves into work, work is the stuff of enjoyment, and professional and personal investments blur in the domain of serious pleasure. As a "background for life in work," the house itself becomes an unobtrusive stage or frame for productive lifestyle.[66]

As the early public versions of *House* on TV made clear, this was a photogenic dwelling, whose airy interior everywhere opened to the gaze of the camera.[67] When the Eameses made the film *House,* they had begun to explore film and TV as pedagogical media of temporal and informatic compression, drawing analogies between film's technical mobility and their furniture designs. As elements in a broader experiment in the delivery and sensory processing of information *in time,* the fast-cut stills of *House* anticipated the speedy, Emmy Award–winning montage the Eameses prepared for CBS in *The Fabulous Fifties* (1960), as well as the elaborate, multiscreen slide shows to come. As an experiment in quantity or the accumulation of materiality, the three hundred–plus stills of *House* incarnate filmically the principle of "object overload" that the Eameses wrote into their brief for the house in 1945, which specified a "large, unbroken area of pure enjoyment of space in which objects can be placed and taken away—driftwood, sculpture, mobiles, plants, constructions, etc."[68] The principle carried over into the excrescence of text, illustration, and objects in exhibition designs such as the IBM-sponsored *Mathematica* (1961)—exercises in spectatorial data sampling from a "very broad menu of options" that were occasionally criticized for their cluttered too-much-ness.[69]

By beginning to ask—in *House*—just how much information their viewers could handle, or how quickly they could handle it, the Eameses' experiments in information overload aimed to cultivate a specifically *democratic* sensorium. The furnishings inside the Eames house, or the dream of postwar mass production that the structure itself is, were read as the stuff of the American "good life," and beyond that, signs of a hegemonic American-style democracy on the model of what Victoria de Grazia has dubbed the "Market Empire."[70] Such homologies between the sheer *scale* of American affluence and the speed or size of images of abundance, or between the vital multiplicity of American pluralism and the multiplication of screens, are important and would animate the design of *Glimpses of the U.S.A.*, the Eameses' famous multiscreen exercise in global communication at the 1959 American National Exhibition in Moscow. But these experiments unfolded in the context of what Fred Turner has called a "Cold War politics of attention" and its preoccupation with the crafting of multimedia, "democratic surrounds."[71] By this Turner means a midcentury intellectual climate that understood the perceptual and psychological labor of choosing from among, and drawing relationships between, a complex, speedy array of images as, in fact, the enactment of democratic perception. In his revisionist analysis of the infamous *Family of Man* photographic exhibition of 1955, Turner reminds us that Edward Steichen's way of linking democracy to imagistic excess was influenced by the display aesthetics of former Bauhaus instructor Herbert Bayer. His exhibition designs in the 1930s mobilized a Gestaltist theory of visual perception that held that viewers "should be surrounded, even overwhelmed by materials" and images—a notion of spectatorship that also shaped the Eameses' exhibition designs as well as *Think* and their other multiscreen works.[72]

Turner's inspired genealogy of the "democratic surround" helps explain the curious logic behind Eamesian experiments in information overload—for example, *House,* which the Eames Office called "an exercise in looking at architecture through the medium of film."[73] In its carefully paced images of domestic life, the Eameses allow spectators to synthesize from these various details their own webs of significant "relationships" or "connections." *House* is therefore a key furniture film precisely *because* the Eames chair—as a singular object—is not privileged, but rather assumes its semiotic and syntactical function in the film's broader communicative universe. Intercut in a montage of the

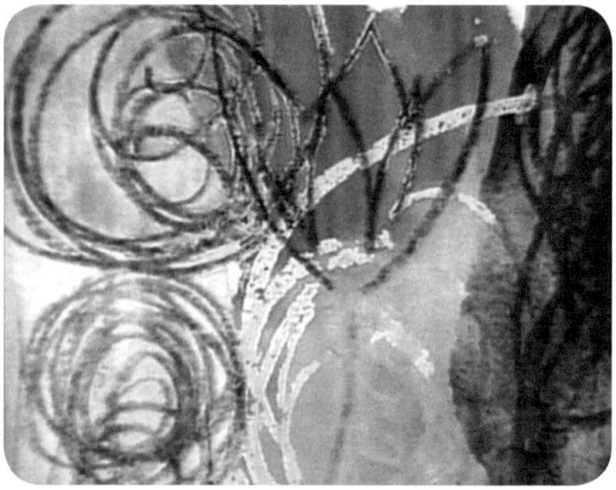

couple's domain of making, for example, we glimpse two images of a black Eames chair between images of a bowl of stones, the leaves of a houseplant, the florid strokes of an abstract watercolor, a camera tripod, a folk art toy, and various images of the slumbering studio and signs of work in progress: stacked film cans, lights, empty reels, a 16mm camera, and reels of film in the process of being edited. The status of the chairs within the film—in and around this home studio—is consistent with their framing in the broader context of media experimentation in which *House* emerged, as a film. The 1953 *Discovery* program opened with shots of the molded plywood chair before showing a module of the film *House* as a means of introducing the Eameses and their terrain of happy making. The couple's famous house was adduced as a reflection of its own natural environment, and beyond that, of the Eameses' attitudes toward design, work, and collaboration.[74] To talk of these designers is to talk of their chairs, which is to speak of their house, which is to say something of the things in it, which is to marvel at their curious assemblages and thus work to make connections. To speak of the Eameses is to enact a cascading logic of interrelatedness and connectivity. As Charles explained in showing portions of *House* in his 1953 introduction-to-architecture class at Berkeley, many of whose students were baffled by its surfeit of arranged stuff, "the point is that everything is in relation with every other thing in the room, all of which is architecture."[75]

In the mid-1950s, the anthropological business of reading the imprint of human design through the seemingly mute assemblages of the object world had begun to be understood as part of a cybernetic structure of communication. Consider a work the Eameses were likely aware of, for example, *Non-Verbal Communication: Notes on the Visual Perception of Human Relations* (1956).[76] Cowritten by the psychiatrist Jurgen Ruesch and the artist Weldon Kees, and with the assistance of Reusch's collaborator, anthropologist and linguist Gregory Bateson, the book explored

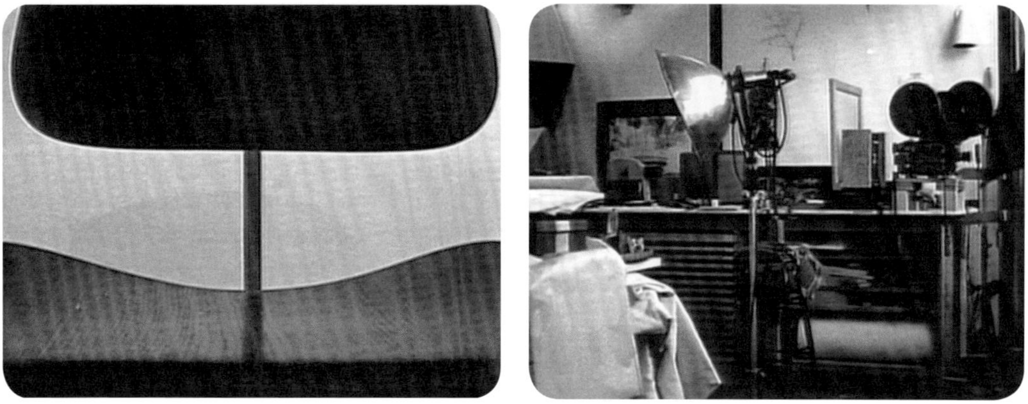

Figure 1.17. Eames Lounge Chair Wood (LCW), in a life of happy making. *House: After Five Years of Living* (1955), directed by Charles and Ray Eames.

nonverbal communication within the framework of modern communications theory. Its section "Message through Object and Picture" analyzes the "material environment" of various midcentury homes as both a mode of "personal expression" through atmosphere and as a "syntax of object language." To move through a home, Ruesch and Kees argue, is to be given "a sense of the prevailing atmosphere" that announces personhood, sensibility, and an abiding organization *without* human presence, and through "the sensory appeal of object language."[77] And this perceptible quality of human capacity increases "in the course of time"—after, for example, five years of living. This is so, Ruesch and Kees say, because the more "man accumulates a variety of things that threaten to clutter the home," the more distinctively he expresses himself in his manner of coping with accumulation and the entropic drift of stuff over time.[78]

House's subtitle—*After Five Years of Living*—is especially significant, joining the film's architectural, organizational, and anthropological ambitions in a study of the impress of human living, which becomes legible in time. *House* is an archive of human encounters with, and production in, an inhuman technical environment. As an experiment in nonverbal communication that runs on the principle of information overload and perceptual storage, *House* thus operates with a crucial difference from that of Steichen's *The Family of Man* or *Glimpses of the U.S.A.*, since it is conspicuously devoid of humans—those fleshy beings whose faces and activities, in being gazed upon, would set into motion acts of "mutual recognition" and "empathy," the "core perceptual and affective skills on which democracy depended."[79] *House*'s structuring paradox is its happy impersonality, its joyful anonymity: it is often described as a deeply personal film, filled with the stuff of the Eameses' shared life together, but it has no people in it. Instead, it offers a curiously abstract domesticity in which the couple's traces appear only in what Robert Venturi once described as the "eclectic assemblages" of their things.[80]

What signs of happiness can be found in a dwelling without humans? What marks of intimacy or personality are left in this network of gabby things? Here, the home of *House* seems to borrow a biomorphic lesson from the organic furniture—its way of gesturing toward its human users despite their absence. One of the more striking and oft-remarked features of the Eameses' mass-produced furniture designs is the way their sensuous curves conjure the intimate presence of the human body. Even without sitters, the molded plywood or fiberglass seems touched by a body, evoking a history or future of embodied contact through negative space. Such is the personality of the mass-produced. Explaining the design process of the molded plywood chair to the viewers of the *Discovery* show, for example, Eames argued for the terrain of similitude and shared comfort incarnated in the very abstraction of the mass-produced object—the ergonomic commons, as it were—while he stressed its embeddedness in the time and history of its human facture.[81] On the same show, remember, Eames offered a film, *Chair Story,* to exemplify the compression of that human-scale time of labor and process. *House: After Five Years of Living* performs a similar feat of filmic compression. Its subject is the life of another famously mass-produced model—both the locus of domestic experience and the product of studio-made artifice, over time. *House* defines productive life as the building of a shared world, one made through a vast continuum of activities (working, creating, collecting, selecting, arranging, photographing, filming) that transpire while being "enveloped" in technologies that have become second nature. The stilled world revealed by the camera in this anthropological film only seems "without us," ghostly and spectral. Instead, *House* is the technical reanimation of a world fabricated and organized by humans, and the logical enactment of Charles's contemporary definition of architecture "not in terms of buildings but as the world and the extension of man and his environment."

Solar Do-Nothings

House is a story of human happiness without humans, an allegory of their lives with things and lives in technology. But stories about postwar happy making can also be told in films about a functionless technical object, like the Eameses' *Solar Do-Nothing Machine* (1957). An automated thing, the machine's ontology exists somewhere between the stuff of a toy box, the "eccentric technicity or gratuitous formalism" of the gadget, and the nameless, "empty functionalism" of the gizmo.[82] Although not a piece of furniture, this quasi-sculptural hybrid echoes the environmental preoccupations of the Eameses' furniture films, connecting kinetic, ludic matter (here, aluminum), moving-image technologies, and democratic lifestyles (Plate 8).

An advertisement for Alcoa and the product of considerable work, the Do-Nothing Machine flaunts its own uselessness. It models the time of leisure, open and unstructured, just as the machine is a thing unmoored from teleology. It's a playful response, in the key of Rube Goldberg, to the instrumental operations of the sponsored films with which the Eameses were accustomed by 1957. Its solar-powered kinesis is energetically efficient, but in the service of getting nothing done. Conspicuously aesthetic, its sculptural dynamism is embedded in a vanguard genealogy of kinetic art, and period-specific crossings between art and design, between the airiness of modern furniture and the environmental aspirations of modern sculpture. And its scale is intimate and cosmic at once. As Nelson's musings on the "new subscape" remind us, acts of human production within the new natures and atmospheres of the midcentury tend to precipitate often dizzying scalar movements between registers of smallness and bigness. Such fluidity of movement between microcosm and macrocosm is the central conceit of the Eameses' best-known film, *Powers of Ten* (1968, 1977).[83] But it is also evident in *Solar Do-Nothing Machine,* a curious film/object that works to convert the specter of sublime human interventionism in the postwar atmosphere into the jejune energies of a delightful aluminum toy-thing.

"The key to Eames' world," art critic Lawrence Alloway observed, "is his toys."[84] And the Eameses were fascinated with toys as special kinds of material objects conveying the beauty, order, and creative possibilities within "everyday acts of play."[85] In 1945 they fashioned a trial run of five thousand plywood chairs and stools for children, as well as molded plywood animals intended as both furniture and objects of play. In 1950 they mass-produced the Toy, a kite-like play-kit of brightly colored triangular and square panels that could be assembled into a flexible variety of different environments by happy adults and children alike. The Toy's packaging proclaimed it was "Large • Colorful • Easy to Assemble • For Creating a Light, Bright Expandable World."[86] In the same period, the couple also developed a number of recombinant paper playthings, including the House of Cards (1952), the Giant House of Cards (1953), and the Coloring Toy (1955). As simple kits that invited design-minded children to participate in the joys of "construction, arrangement, and building," the Eameses' toys joined what Amy F. Ogata called a postwar "vogue for 'creativity'" among educators, psychologists, and child-development experts, who were critical of educational toys that had become "mindlessly didactic tools of social competition rather than open-ended objects that might stimulate original thinking."[87] By 1957 the Eameses had also made a series of charming, well-crafted short films with trains, puppets, and mechanical toys as protagonists, including *Traveling Boy* (1950), *Parade, or Here They Come Down Our Street* (1952), and *Toccata for Toy Trains* (1957). Thus, the Eameses were perhaps the natural choice as designers to produce a toy as part of an advertising campaign for Alcoa—the Aluminum Company of America—whose explosive wartime production of aluminum for military aircraft made the lightweight, malleable metal virtually synonymous with the United States' heroic World War II airplanes. In 1957 and '58 a recession sent aluminum prices down. Alcoa sought to solve the problem of decreased demand, and its production surplus, through its so-called Forecast Program, an insistently futural advertising campaign whose goal was to promote aluminum by commissioning top designers to fashion new aluminum products. The designs weren't things so much as concepts, metallic metaphors for the bold, domestic future of aluminum; and they were built to circulate as images, photographed for magazine advertisements.

The Eameses were commissioned to design an aluminum toy, and they built the Solar Do-Nothing Machine, a whimsical, redundant contraption that deployed freestanding aluminum reflector screens to capture sunlight and reflect it into panels of photovoltaic cells. The cells turned sunlight into electrical energy that set into motion ten revolving displays of brightly colored pinwheels and stars. This is the sunny future of aluminum: a happy atmosphere in which natural energy is harnessed in the production of an utterly gratuitous spectacle of movement and color. As a feature on the Eameses' gadget in *Life* magazine put it, the Solar Do-Nothing Machine is "a bit of scientific and artistic whimsy now," but it was being "sent on tour as an enchanting harbinger of more useful sun-machines in the future."[88] The mobile gizmo gestured toward a utopian environment to come.

In 1957 the Eameses were not alone in scanning the unseen energies in the air above for signals of the future of the *homo faber*. Hannah Arendt opened *The Human Condition* (1958) with a prologue starring an aerial, technical wonder—Sputnik.[89] For Arendt, this feat of technological prowess exemplified "modern world alienation, its twofold flight from the earth into the universe and from the world into the self" (*HC*, 3, 6). Sputnik is part of the broader realm of human artifice that Arendt terms "world," produced by the distinctively human activity of "work" (*HC*, 2). What Sputnik augurs, for Arendt, is the hypertrophy of human design, and the dangerous attempt to transcend human's earthly existence. If Sputnik bespeaks a new, alienated midcentury domain of "artificial life," a "no less threatening event" is the "advent of automation," which sucked humans into an accelerating process of production and consumption (*HC,* 4). Automation, for Arendt, crystallizes a situation in which technical know-how outstrips the political capacity for thinking and speaking, leaving us "at the mercy of every gadget which is technically possible, no matter how murderous it is" (*HC,* 5). Faced with this "new and yet unknown age" of design—the airborne, automatic gadgets that have conspired to transform the foundational activities of humans—Arendt offers her study as an attempt "to think what we are doing" (5, 6).

Arendt, to be fair, was likely unaware of the Solar Do-Nothing Machine. But the gadget stages the discrepancy *The Human Condition* anxiously examines between midcentury technical know-how and utility, between human "work" and the final yield of human purposiveness. It is a knowing thingamajig that knows it solves no problem, beyond the spectacular promotion of aluminum. The Solar Do-Nothing Machine film is similarly self-reflexive, joining the excesses of its visible superfluity to the miraculous but invisible energetic transfers transpiring atmospherically. Like many of the Eameses' toys/films, it betrays a fascination with how things work. Its editing segments and analyzes the machine in a jazzy sequence of charming close-ups of mobile, sun-powered aluminum, shots that alternately foreground the substance's materiality, and seek to dissolve it entirely into airy, abstract biomorphic patterns or the hazy atmosphere of sunlight that animates it. Such animation, and our optical delight in it, the film seems to claim, could go on infinitely, in an endless temporal loop; its energy source only cuts out, abruptly, with the film's own conclusion. Thus, the Solar Do-Nothing Machine recasts the Toy's promise of a "light, bright, expandable world" as a green wish for clean air and infinitely renewable natural energy. Less a tool for present-day problem solving than a medium of speculation, the machine offers what Daniel Barber has called a "concise expression of the place solar power occupied in the expansion of energy infrastructures right after WWII," when "solar energy was able to do, if not exactly nothing, then very little."[90]

In its efforts to visualize unseen energies in the air through kinesis, the Solar Do-Nothing Machine is not just a premature ecotechnology but also a conspicuously modernist machine. Its dream of mobile aluminum and infinitely renewable energy summons an avant-garde genealogy joining fantasies about kinetic matter to utopian designs on the moving image. As Andrew Uroskie has argued, the interwar dialogue that Marcel Duchamp's ludic optics established between modernist sculpture and the temporality and kinetics of the moving image was reactivated by a postwar generation of artists and filmmakers in exhibitions like 1955's *Movement,* held in the Parisian gallery of Denise René.

This show included kinetic works by Duchamp, Victor Vasarely, Jean Tinguely, Robert Breer, and of course, Alexander Calder. Film was seen as an ideal medium for reproducing Calder's airy sculpture, and the Eameses were surely aware of *Works of Calder* (1951), a short film made by their friend Herbert Matter, with the help of Jackson Pollock. Like the medial inconstancy of the Solar Do-Nothing Machine—object, advertisement, film—the materiality of Duchamp's toys and Calder's

Figure 1.18. László Moholy-Nagy, *Lightplay: Black White Gray* (*Ein Lichtspiel: schwarz weiss grau*), ca. 1926. Digital image copyright The Museum of Modern Art/Licensed by SCALA/Art Resource, NY.

filmic mobiles embodies both "the obdurate solidity of the sculptural object and the uncanny immateriality of a purely optical experience of movement and transformation."[91]

The Solar Do-Nothing Machine's fantasy of a technological overcoming of traditional sculpture's massiveness in a future of luminous, energetic movement also has a political horizon, recalling the materialism of constructivist works like Moholy-Nagy's *Light Prop for an Electric Stage* (1922–30). Later referred to as the "Light-Space Modulator," *Light Prop* was not properly an object but a utopian, multimedial construction, enacting Moholy's belief, expressed in *Vision in Motion* (1947), that sculpture "has tactile existence but may be changed to visual grasp [*sic*]; from static to kinetic; from mass to space-time relationships."[92] Built for a Werkbund installation—a model communal apartment devised by Walter Gropius for the annual exposition of the Société des artistes décorateurs in Paris in 1930—*Light Prop* materialized the Bauhauslers' own experiments in living. It was the spectacular accoutrement to the exhibition's featured designs for new domestic spaces, furniture, and lighting by Bayer, Breuer, and Gropius himself. And it was the star of Moholy's

Figure 1.19. Installation views of the German section of the annual salon of the Société des artistes décorateurs, Paris, 1930. Moholy-Nagy's Light Prop to the left, and Schlemmer's costumes for Triadic Ballet to the right. Bauhaus-Archiv, Berlin.

short abstract film *Lightplay: Black White Gray,* the generator of that film's dazzling play of light and shadow. Like *Light Prop,* the Solar Do-Nothing Machine's dynamism enacts—and advertises—a revolutionary, democratic lifestyle forecast by the energetic lightness of its constitutive materials. In Moholy's case, this dream of sculptural dematerialization has been read as a displacement of the materialism of Vladimir Tatlin and Alexander Rodchenko for the spiritual idealism of Naum Gabo and Antoine Pevsner, anticipating the domestication of a Bauhaus "new vision" as it was remade in postwar, corporate America.[93]

The Eameses' whirring Alcoa advertisement is better understood as a thingly allegory of a tech-savvy lifestyle with environmental designs. Like the furniture films, it links mobile, ludic technologies and democratic environments much as the contemporaneous movement consolidated as "kinetic art." At stake in kinetic art's rhetorical movement from autotelic autonomy to the idiom of "environment" was the artwork's activation of a more participatory, interactive—indeed democratic—sensorium, where meaning was contingent on the equally mobile eye and body of the spectator. Kineticism's very raison d'être was, as Larry Busbea puts it, "the highly charged spaces of the modern environment," and it was activated "as a kind of tool to modify existing spaces and environments" that had grown habitual—the spatial encrustation of gestures constituting a "way of life."[94] Because kineticism's "environment" sought to bring together, and mutually transform, various kinds of space—optical, architectural, experiential—it marked the politicized turn of an earlier modernist investment in abstract optical space (the domain of spirit or the absolute) toward particular, contingent, embodied spaces. Indeed, for many artists in the 1960s, such spaces would be the very terrain of dereification, the space of participatory politics—what Arendt would celebrate as the human capacity for "action."

In the same year that saw Sputnik shot into orbit, and the Solar Do-Nothing Machine set into motion, Guy Habasque hailed the "spatiodynamic" idiom of Hungarian-born Frenchman Nicolas Schöffer, designer of the first cybernetic sculpture—*CYSP 1*—in 1956.[95] The name is a portmanteau combining the first two letters of "cybernetics" and "spatiodynamism." Built with the aid of engineers from the Philips Company, Schöffer's *CYSP 1* was composed of right-angled black steel, sixteen plates of polychrome aluminum, and an "electronic brain" that allowed it to move in response to ambient feedback.[96] The Eameses' contemporaneous Solar Do-Nothing Machine is not a properly cybernetic work, of course. Its electrical assemblage of lightweight aluminum is less responsive than *CYSP 1* to information fed back into its processors from its ambient surround. Nor can it correct, modulate, or otherwise adjust its unidirectional movement in response either to changes in its environment or to the contingent, embodied situation of its spectator. At the same time, the manner in which its objecthood orients itself to an environment whose energies inform, and recursively shape, its own movement dovetails with the midcentury cybernetic principles in which the Eameses were steeped, and that informed their chair design and films alike. When they built the Solar Do-Nothing Machine and made the film in 1957, they had already made *A Communications Primer* (1953), and had temporarily shelved its IBM-commissioned sequel, *Introduction to Feedback* (1960) to complete their related film *The Information Machine: Creative Man and the Data Processor* (1957), in time for its exhibition at the IBM Pavilion at the 1958 Brussels World's Fair. Like these films, whose rhetoric everywhere hinges on the same abiding analogies between the behavior of humans and machines at the core of first-order cybernetics, *Solar Do-Nothing Machine* proposes that we think the productive activity of humans and machines together, bound here in a similarly unknown future of adaptations to technical environments surging with unseen, energetic potential.

What's more, the film insists that its imagined future of freedom from entropy, loss, and waste is fully compatible with the most extravagant, most useless human interventions in matter and energy. The Solar Do-Nothing Machine is a toy whose scale is the world. Its abiding design dream of human technology as at once infinitely large and infinitely small, excessively powerful and doing nothing at all, redounds to a post-atomic world that can imagine such intensely utopias of energy because it has witnessed the scale of nuclear annihilation. Although humans are not present in the film, it nonetheless makes a spectacle of the Eameses' modernist faith in human ingenuity and humane design. Its compensatory wish is for a decisive human manipulation of matter and nature that would leave no human trace. As an Arendtian fable of the extremes of human "worldliness" or a cyberautomated future, *The Solar Do-Nothing Machine* gives no inkling of a mission or end. It asks after the future of human making—what are we doing?—with an anxious eye toward the technoscientific environments in which Eamesian happiness was made.

Art Chairs

Eamesian allegories of production were part of a design pedagogy with a global reach. Within it, the designed object heralded a new, consumer-oriented sensorium, and modular furniture came to signify, for others, the sign of postwar sociability abstracted into "atmosphere." This was Baudrillard's term for the postwar's functionalist discourse of systemic relationships devoid of "rough edges" (antagonism and desire). And he heard its cybernetic communications spoken from the depths of mobile modern furniture.[97] In closing, let's follow Baudrillard's suspicion and observe a few salient affinities between the media environments allegorized in the Eameses' furniture films and contemporaneous tendencies in postwar visual art, from the seriality of pop and minimalism to conceptualism's aesthetics of administration.[98] Postwar art told its own stories of medial furniture.

As an extension of *S-73*'s graphic idiom of logistically organized grids and boxes, the designed world of universal modularity promulgated by the Eameses often echoed the visual vocabulary of administration evident in 1960s visual art. This idiom joined the work of sculptor (and furniture designer) Donald Judd, such as *Untitled (DS 85)*, from 1966, or *Untitled (DS204)*, from 1969; to postwar international-style architecture such as Skidmore, Owings & Merrill's Union Carbide Building (1955–60), modular outside and in; or to the related modularity of new information technologies like IBM's computer System/360, designed by the Eameses' friend and collaborator Eliot F. Noyes, who had turned from the interface of organic chairs to that of the computer.[99] In his introduction to *Connections: The Work of Charles and Ray Eames,* Ralph Caplan linked the revolutionary airiness of the Eameses' furniture technology and the "semiconductors it anticipated," noting that this particular sort of lightness "made mass-produced objects personal not by 'personalizing' them but by incorporating free individual use into their design."[100] Such objects are fashioned to be open ended for their users. Freedom is an effect of modular design.

These aesthetic and conceptual affinities between the informatic cool of systems-based art and the impersonality and putative universality of design had already begun to be drawn in the 1960s. Kynaston McShine, curator of the landmark *Primary Structures* exhibition of 1966, linked the "white cube framework" of Sol LeWitt's work to the aesthetics, logic, and modular structures in the "comprehensive design" of Buckminster Fuller. Lucy Lippard and John Chandler, who produced perhaps the best-known assessment of these tendencies in the visual arts in 1968, also had reviewed designer György Kepes's Vision + Value book series the previous year, placing its attempts to bridge art and science into conversation with "some of the younger 'structural artists' (Judd, Morris, LeWitt, Smithson, Andre, to name a few)."[101] Titled "Visual Art and the Invisible World," the ambivalent review linked these artists' manifest attraction to "modular concepts" to a transformed notion of the natural order and a reconsideration of "the organic" itself: "The organic structure of Tony Smith's sculptures and Buckminster Fuller's geodesic domes may be difficult to discern, yet both find the source of their tetrahedral structure in nature."[102] Smith and Fuller's shared interest in modularity, for Lippard and Chandler, is just one instance of a broader attunement to networked systems, a "general concern in all disciplines to visualize phenomena in terms of whole structures, patterns and configurations rather than individual parts."[103] Famously, in Michael Fried's landmark "Art and Objecthood" essay of the same year, Smith's work exemplified the suspension of modernist objecthood in the objectionable "theatricality" of contemporary sculpture: its quality of endlessness, experiential inexhaustibility, and temporal ongoingness. For Fried the "repetition of identical" units in Smith's work required the beholder to complete the work. Such seriality spelled for him the end of the self-sufficient presentness of modernist art in an endless temporality of the beholder's phenomenological experience, in which, devoid of value, everything is "merely interesting."[104]

In the domain of design, Caplan had sensed something similar in describing the Eames chairs' central democratic paradox: their serial abstraction, anonymous or functionally indifferent at their mass-produced core, is precisely what liberates them, allowing them to be put to use differently by the sheer variety of their postwar sitters. Peter Smithson described it this way: "Eames chairs are the first chairs which can be put in any position in an empty room. They look as if they alighted there. . . . The chairs belong to the occupants, not to the building."[105] Their democratic nature, in other words, cannot be easily separated from a kind of valueless, abstract leveling. In the environments in which the chairs might choose to alight, everything is potentially of interest and nothing is necessarily more interesting than anything else. For the Eameses, this did not signal abandoning the terrain of value. Instead, as we'll see, it sparked a rigorous technical program of happiness demanding decisions and the shaping of consumers' tastes—a program secured, they believed, by communication and vanguard techniques of information processing.

The Eameses were not alone in linking stories about the materiality of modern furniture to canny reflections on the environmental aspirations of postwar aesthetic production. Nor were they unique in positioning the chair itself as a node in technical networks or as a protagonist in a midcentury aesthetics of information. Consider the becoming informatic of chairs in the Eameses' films—their oscillation between sensuous, tactile objecthood and image—alongside some of the more famous, medially reflective chairs of the 1960s. In *Three Chair Events* (1961), Fluxus artist George Brecht sought to transform the prosaic chair, as inert object, into a dynamic, participatory event, inserting it into an ongoing temporality of process and duration. Working with the post-Cagean form of the "event score," an idea or template—here, for the banal act of sitting—that would generate multiple, site-specific realizations, Brecht conceived a "chair event" that moved from conceptual proposition to object to performance.[106] Like Brecht, Claes Oldenburg was rethinking aesthetic experience on the model of participatory performance, creating Kaprow-esque "environments" such as *Bedroom Ensemble* (1964).[107] This kitschy modern furniture suite, installed at the Sidney Janis Gallery, examined the space of the gallery itself as both business office and curiously private interior, blurring the institutional site of art's display and commodification with the domestic, bourgeois site where art goes when it is bought and displayed, as so much good design.

In the same year, Joseph Beuys explored the tactile quality of furniture in *Fat Chair* (1964), a quasi-sculptural work located on the cusp of medium-based and postmedium conceptions of art. The chair's haptic solicitation is ambiguous: at once everyday, immediate, and embodied, yet ungraspable, unstructured, and seemingly removed from our ability to readily access it as a familiar consumer object, in the manner of Oldenburg's art furniture, whose ironic edge cut on its being made for bourgeois consumption. As Alex Potts has shown, *Fat Chair*'s perplexing materiality was of a piece with a broader split in 1960s sculptural practice between a fetishization of materials and a desire to be liberated from the material formal constraints attending a Greenbergian notion of medium specificity. Crucially, this split mirrored a historical bifurcation in the chair's economic horizon of production: between the tangibility of industrial materials and artisanal production, on the one hand, and a "focus on consumption and on the more intangible operations of information and image circulation" specific to a postindustrial, postproductivist age, on the other.[108] This focus culminated in the conceptual art practices anthologized in Lippard's influential *Six Years: The Dematerialization of the Art Object from 1966 to 1972*. And the conceptualist suppression of things by recourse to the putative abstractions of language and image—what Benjamin Buchloh described as the desire "to replace the object of spatial and perceptual experience by linguistic definition alone"—had its own canonical chair gag: Joseph Kosuth's *One and Three Chairs* (1965).[109] Kosuth's systematic substitutions and tautologies between actual chair (object), photograph of a chair (image), and a dictionary definition as wall statement (language) re-presented the chair across medial forms, while they dissolved the chair-object into what Liz Kotz calls an "ascending spiral of abstraction."[110] In his 1967 essay "The Recentness of Sculpture," Clement Greenberg surveyed a number of such "far out" postsculptural tendencies toward the ideational and phenomenal, "as opposed to the aesthetic or the artistic." Lamenting the way "minimal works are readable as art, as almost anything is today—including a door, a table, or a blank sheet of paper," Greenberg dismissed minimalist sculptural practice as a kind of middlebrow pop furniture. In its quest for novelty and surprise, Greenberg huffed, "Minimal followed too much where Pop, Op, Assemblage, and the rest have led"—namely, "the realm of Good Design," and its "continuing infiltration . . . into what purports to be advanced and highbrow art."[111]

At the same moment, however, that the stuff of Eamesian "Good Design" would become something like a Greenbergian diss—shorthand for any affront to his fetish of medium specificity—it energized the practice of artists more receptive to the postwar "infiltration" of design and technology into art. In 1964, for example, British Independent Group artist Richard Hamilton included the Eames Office's La Fonda chair (1961)—manufactured for the La Fonda del Sol restaurant in New York's Time & Life Building—in his mixed-media painting *Interior II* (Plate 9). One of the work's key foci, the chair, as image-object, has quite literally become media—collage material, in a nod to cubist experiments like Picasso's *Still-Life with Chair Caning* (1912). Positioned in front of an image of actor Patricia Knight, the chair sits in the center of the scene's carefully orchestrated nexus of gazes, perspectives, and display techniques. By what cultural logic has an Eames chair, in the early 1960s, found itself a protagonist in Hamilton's hypermediated pop interior?

As Peter Smithson's admiring appraisal, quoted earlier, attests, the Eameses enjoyed close ties with many of Hamilton's colleagues in the Independent Group, the association of iconoclastic young artists, architects, and critics whose meetings at London's fledging Institute of Contemporary Arts in the early 1950s helped shape an insurgent, anti-authoritarian "aesthetics of plenty." In his landmark 1961 essay, Reyner Banham—the chief spokesman for the IG—took stock of a broad transformation of design values at midcentury brought about by the increasing mechanization of Western households, new rates of obsolescence, product miniaturization, and the introduction of "a degree of mechanization into the creative work" of painters, sculptors, and designers alike.[112] This shift, Banham argued, recast the purview of the modern architect. No longer the "absolute master of the visual environment," the architect was now a tastemaker or selector, whose goal was to "exercise choice and background control over the choice of others."[113] For Banham, no figure in the world of design "has made so great an impact on the world, both by his products and personality," as Charles Eames.[114]

If Eames's output epitomized "design by choice," and the "problem of affluent democracy" driving postwar technological change, part of what was so striking about Eamesian production was the way it embodied the happy promise of the postwar American good life through a disarming sense of comfort in the power of technology itself, from mobile plywood to 16mm. As I show in chapter 2, for IG architects and critics like the Smithsons, Banham, and Alloway, and for artists like Hamilton and John McHale, the Eameses were the apotheosis of an attitude toward technology itself that would shape the IG's pop sensibility. In short, the IG learned from the Eameses how to be happy in technology's horizon of obsolescence and ephemerality, in its modes of packaging and visual display, and in the antihierarchical drift of its image sphere. In this climate, Alison Smithson declared, "the Eames chair was like a message of hope from another planet."[115]

By giving the La Fonda chair the visual prominence it does, Hamilton's painting inserts the chair into its portrait of technology, while insisting on the medial process of collage itself—on Hamilton's own imaging technologies (photography and screen printing), which bring chair, TV, and film image (Patricia Knight) into the same pictorial space.[116] The painting's subject is not just a mediated interior but also the expanded field of art itself, in whose context "a Rietveldt or Eames chair serves the same purpose as a reproduction of a Fra Angelico or an ancestral portrait . . . : they are souvenirs."[117] Hamilton famously described the logic of his collage images as "tabular," a term critics have taken to describe the processes of composition as a kind of tabulation, the "graphic form of a list," in which what accrues in the collage's pictorial space remains unhierarchized.[118] As the Eameses did with their own furniture, so too Hamilton's *Interior II* deploys La Fonda in a midcentury aesthetics of information. The chair's technology is celebrated even as it is tabulated as cultural data, as an advertising image with transatlantic reach. Appropriately enough, it sits among other cultural technologies of display that have converted the space of the interior—much like the Eameses' film *House*—into a system of mobile views.

As object and image, harbinger of postwar technics and commodity fetish, design technology and display technology, Hamilton's La Fonda finds itself in the same informatic networks in which the Eameses themselves would increasingly chart the future of their design work. These, Hamilton's *Interior II* observes, are the technological, imagistic, and semiotic environments of an Eames chair. Indeed, as the Eameses' design practice expanded in the 1950s from its initial focus on product and graphic design toward filmmaking and exhibition design, it became, in Charles's words, "more and more concerned with the way information is handled."[119] This preoccupation is evident in the sensual pedagogy of the furniture films, and as chapter 2 argues, it extends to the couple's more overtly global pedagogical exercises in the context of so-called expanded cinema, and a media practice with newly environmental, immersive, and global aspirations.[120]

Figure 1.20. Nigel Henderson, Eduardo Paolozzi, Alice Smithson, and Peter Smithson, seated in unidentified street, for the cover of the *What Is Tomorrow?* exhibition catalog, Whitechapel Gallery, London. Copyright 2017 Tate London.

2

the scale is the world

Designer Pedagogy and Expanded Cinema

PROMOTED INTERNATIONALLY BY MOMA as the democratic future of "good design," Eamesian design aspired to the universal. With an exuberant futurity typical of an early Cold War period shaped by the cultural hegemony of the United States, midcentury designers like the Eameses laid claim to a sweeping transformation of lifestyle, which they would refashion in the new natures, image environments, and scenes of production of the postwar. Herman Miller was quick to capitalize on the world-historical prestige of its designers, and cross-promoted its mutually beneficial partnership with MoMA, in advertisements like one from 1954 that casts its director of design, George Nelson, alongside his colleagues Charles Eames and Alexander Girard, as "traveling men," chic emissaries of the jet age.

Introducing this famous triumvirate by announcing the globe-trotting ambit of the designer's profession, the advertisement suggests the fluid registers on which the cosmopolitan problem solving of the Eameses and George Nelson operated in the postwar period, moving from revolutionary chair design to blueprints for postcolonial nationhood. For we see that Eames and Nelson (alongside Robert Motherwell and Richard Neutra) are off to Germany "under the auspices of the German Foreign Office." Eames, the text notes, has also been "invited to visit Japan by the Japanese Government," and Girard (with Edgar Kaufmann Jr.) is embarking on another far-flung mission, set to "leave for India to collect material for a new show" at MoMA—namely, *Textiles and Ornamental Arts of India* (1955), the first large-scale exhibition of Indian art in the United States. The installation featured a short film by the Eameses and an accompanying music, dance, and film program that culminated in the world premiere of Satyajit Ray's *Pather Panchali.* Staged in the same year as the Bandung Conference, the MoMA exhibition—a governmental effort to improve relations between the United States and a geopolitically vital, nonaligned country—brought the Eameses into contact with a range of experts on Indian art, including Pupul Jayakar, who recommended that the Eameses visit the country to advise Nehru, a champion of modern design, on the modernizing agenda of his postcolonial

Figure 2.1. George Nelson, Charles Eames, and Alexander Girard, "traveling men" advertisement for the Herman Miller Furniture Company, Zeeland, Michigan. Courtesy of Herman Miller.

nation-state. After five months of travel in India, funded by the Ford Foundation, the Eameses produced the so-called *India Report,* an analysis of Nehruvian modernization's effects on the qualities of the Indian good life and a statement on "design as a value system." The report's recommendations led directly to the founding of India's National Institute of Design in 1961, the "first attempt by a developing country to use design principles inherited from the Bauhaus as a tool for national regeneration."[1]

Part of what was so striking about Eamesian production was its dizzying scalar movement between the domestic and the geopolitical, its swift expansion from the everyday thing to the wider world-to-be-designed. The expansive liberal optimism that swells the democratic scenes of Eamesian design informed a multimedia pedagogy with global ambitions: its terrain of experimentation extended from furniture, toys, and Solar Do-Nothing Machines to Nehruvian modernization schemes and World's Fairs. As a less well-known example of this global prestige, consider the appearance of the Eameses' multiscreen works *Think* and *House of Science* in the Iranian arts and culture weekly *Ferdowsi* published in Tehran in February 1969. The works are discussed in an essay titled "After Avant-Garde, Experimental, and Underground Cinema:

پس از سینمای پیشرو ـ تجربی ـ زیرزمینی،
«سینمای توسعه یافته»

Figure 2.2. "After Avant-Garde, Experimental, and Underground Cinema: Expanded Cinema," *Ferdowsi,* Tehran, 1969. Library of the House of Cinema (Khaneh Cinema). Courtesy of Kaveh Askari.

Figure 2.3. Cover of Eames Office brochure for A Rough Sketch for a Sample Lesson for a Hypothetical Course (Art-X), 1953, design by Jerome Gould. Copyright 2017 Eames Office LLC (eamesoffice.com).

Expanded Cinema," a summary of Sheldon Renan's *An Introduction to the American Underground Film* (1967), and written on the occasion of a festival of American experimental films in the capital. Traveling men, indeed.

These internationally famous works of multimedia pedagogy began in the ideologically charged space of the postwar U.S. classroom. If you happened to be on the UCLA campus in May 1953, for example, you might have encountered a brochure promoting a "sample lesson" advertised as a public service by the Department of Engineering and University Extension.[2] The brochure's smart cover brings camera lens, designer lamp, and globe into graphic likeness. The text entices with the frisson of disciplinary transgression: "Something new is happening . . . a normal progression perhaps, toward breaking down the barriers between fields of learning . . . toward making people a little more intuitive . . . toward increasing communication between people and things." And because, the breathless language continues, the lesson "is more of an emotion than an action . . . it is difficult to explain. . . . A *sample lesson* must be seen and heard and felt and smelled." This novel experience in intuition and sensation will take shape as a class about art—but from men who "know that art is not paint and a frame, or stone and a base. . . . Art is a building, a house, a machine, art is a chair, a test tube, a loaf of bread." These purveyors of an expansive aesthetic vision and a vanguard

Figure 2.4. Interior of Eames Office brochure for A Rough Sketch for a Sample Lesson for a Hypothetical Course (Art-X), 1953, design by Jerome Gould. Copyright 2017 Eames Office LLC (eamesoffice.com).

pedagogy are none other than Eames, Nelson, and Girard, and their "sample lesson" was a multimedia experiment in communication and attention, information processing and networked visuality that came to be called "Art-X."

When "everything is architecture," problems of postwar building quickly become problems of postwar *Bildung*. Designers are reborn as educators; pedagogy is rethought as communication. But how did the Eameses and Nelson ever find themselves in this spot in the first place: as instructional reformers tasked with remaking a putatively staid art curriculum? What pedagogical logics and traditions, and what assumptions about moving-image media, connect their work as makers of postwar things to makers of postwar citizens, guides to life in a world of superabundant data?[3] And what is the place of film in the work of training students and audiences in the perceptual and cognitive skills necessary to function responsibly within what Nelson called "a new picture of the world"? As designers widened the scope of their own responsibilities, scaling up design and media experimentation to the level of social practice, how did they press cinema itself to expand in a Cold War pedagogy of the senses?

To answer such questions, this chapter draws on recent scholarship on the history of modern design education (especially concerning the Bauhaus), as well as resurgent interest within film studies in the rich

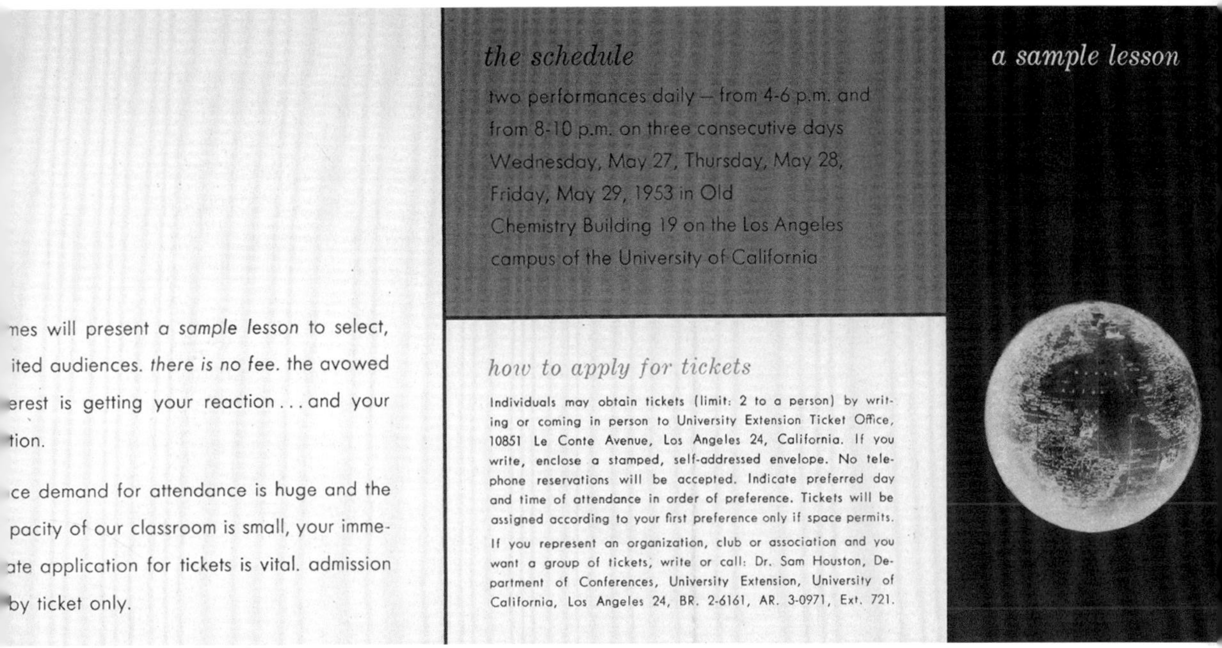

history of film and moving-image media's usefulness within the media architecture of the classroom.[4] Challenging our understanding of the cinematic apparatus by opening it to more flexible deployments and configurations, this work has demonstrated film's embeddedness in a striking range of efforts to inculcate forms of selfhood and citizenship, and to discipline subjects—and long before the disciplinary invention of film studies proper. Such scholarship has also renewed our attention to the university classroom as a primary site of mediation, vanguard technologies, and techniques, while also inserting the institution of the university within modernity's competitive media culture. This climate demanded deft PR, canny bids for the attention of audiences, and designs on the liberal management of populations.

Building on such work, this chapter argues that the scalar fluidity of the Eameses' media practice is not just a Cold War dynamic, specific to the technoscientific environments of the postwar period, but a perceptual and sensual problem central to a broad range of modernist moving-image practices at midcentury, including the Eameses' pioneering multiscreen works. As Art-X attests, such experiments began as pedagogical endeavors in a midcentury ferment of educational reform, and a new humanist attentiveness to the creative, open mind as the perceptual training ground of democratic citizenship, and indeed, of national wealth. This modernism sought to recalibrate, and expand, the sensorium of liberal-humanist citizenship to parameters, communicative scenarios, and forms of awareness understood as "worldly," even ecological.

At midcentury, the often-universalizing pedagogy of designers like the Eameses and Nelson was shaped by a slate of related, occasionally overlapping educational philosophies with global ambitions. In the domain of design, there was, of course, the propagandistic "soft power" of MoMA-sponsored good design shows and their "democratic" values. But designers were also influenced by the interdisciplinary, holistic, and pragmatic pedagogy of the Bauhaus. Eames first came to this, and the Arts and Crafts tradition that animated the Bauhaus's workshop ethos, at the Cranbrook Academy of Art, where he experimented with a range of forms and materials, techniques and technologies, including film. At the Bauhaus, this pedagogy of practice, process, and patterns was exemplified in the school's non-medium-specific investment in the potential

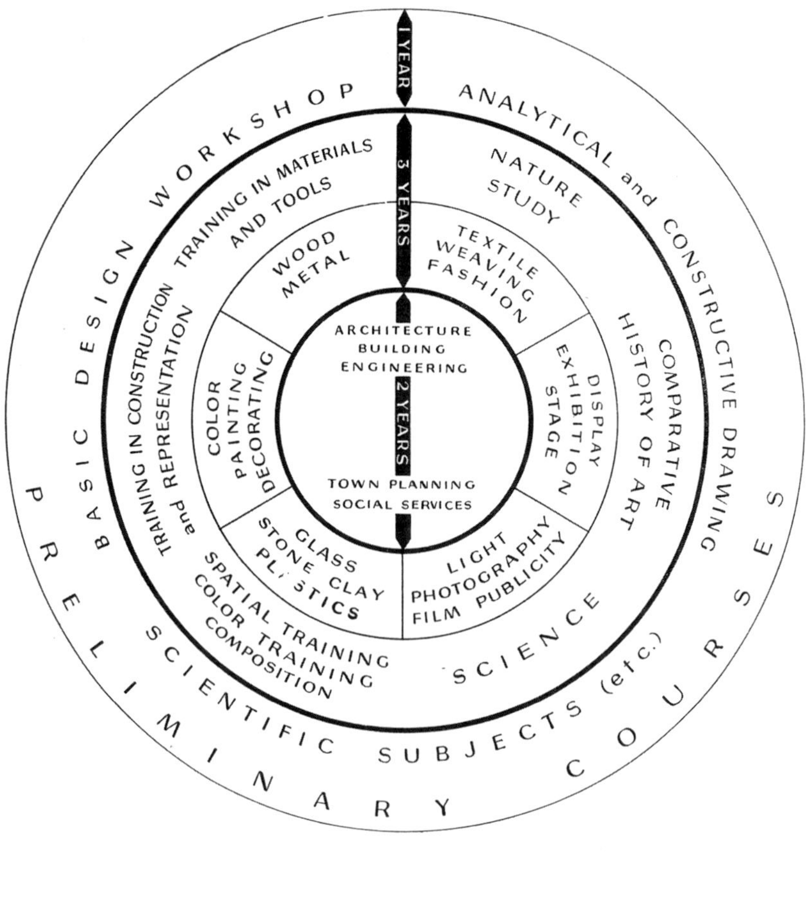

Figure 2.5. Preliminary course diagram, New Bauhaus catalog, 1938–39. Institute of Design Collection, box 3, folder 54, IDR_0003_0054_pg4, Special Collections and University Archives, University Library, University of Illinois at Chicago.

of materials and the inculcation of multisensory awareness—principles incarnated in its famous Preliminary Course, which László Moholy-Nagy would export to the United States in 1937 after the Nazis shuttered the Berlin Bauhaus, and restore to the core of the Institute of Design's curriculum in Chicago. And it was also evident in György Kepes's and Moholy's interest in the training of visual perception beyond the observation of static things, toward a kind of systems-oriented, networked "pattern seeing" in which the designer-artist participated in the business of representing information and visualizing data.[5]

Here and elsewhere, the Eameses' and Nelson's design pedagogy could not escape the technophilic and technocratic ambitions of their friend Buckminster Fuller. His vision of the "comprehensive designer," presiding over a global utopia of efficiently managed resources, was also incarnated in the worldly stuff of organic mass production and modularity—not chairs but the "universal" forms of the geodesic dome. Kepes included images of both Fuller's domes and Eames's chairs in his visual anthology of the postwar physis, *The New Landscape in Art and Science* (1956). Fuller reportedly coined the term "comprehensive design" as the title of a course he taught in the summer of 1948 at Black Mountain College, where he first erected a geodesic dome; he would teach it again shortly thereafter at the Institute of Design. Less well known is that Charles Eames, alongside Kepes, Marcel Breuer, Josep Lluís Sert, and Ralph Rapson, was on the short list to succeed Moholy as the ID's director following his death in 1946. In fact, in 1953, the same year he was embroiled in Art-X and a series of multimedia lectures at UC Berkeley, Charles Eames was invited by Dan Rice to head up the "workshop institute" at Black Mountain. Under the aegis of its soon-to-be-new rector Charles Olson, the school was to revamp its regular sessions through an "institute plan." In this model, the so-called twin of the Institute for Advanced Study at Princeton, the college would sponsor four or five institutes during the academic year, and employ as guest faculty men who, in Olson's terms, "in the present are pushing knowledge forward at the edge of the unknown."[6] Rice's letter of invitation to Eames began by noting Black Mountain's "interest in experiments," and its faculty's way of "applying the democratic process to education" in the way they "live and work."[7] The letter also indicates how design pedagogy—on the frontier of the unknown—would begin to lose its disciplinary boundaries. Ultimately unsuccessful, Rice's pitch to entice Eames to North Carolina appealed to a principle "essential to Black Mountain College & American education": namely, "that real knowledge does not exist as abstract or boxed into labeled areas; rather, that its real life seems an organic existence between or inter these areas."

As I argue in chapter 1, the Eameses' domain of happy production around their furniture performed this organic existence—at home "between or inter" disciplines and domains of knowledge, but also in media technologies. As the embodied lessons of their medial furniture increasingly overlapped with the overtly pedagogical space of the classroom, these designers expanded film beyond its routine commercial functioning and theatrical sites. They found new worlds for the medium, and they modeled this worldedness in their very facility with the new nature of the built environment, what Hannah Arendt called the midcentury's preponderance of "artificial life." By "world," I mean both a historically situated idea of the world, a "world concept" like Arendt's own, and the actual, material substrate of a world situation.[8] At midcentury, these worlds were glimpsed with a new acuity of vision by designers whose spatial sense of "worldliness" was part and parcel of the postwar globalization of the economy, and the geopolitical hegemony of the United States. Designer pedagogy was, in this fashion, an expression of what historian Nils Gilman has dubbed modernist "technocosmopolitanism."[9] Gilman uses the term to characterize postwar modernization theorists' liberal confidence in U.S.–style democratic modernity as a model or blueprint for the world. Technocosmopolitans exuded a universalist faith that history, society, economy, culture, and nature were all "to be the object of technical transformation," especially in postcolonial societies—so-called developmental states such as the India of the Eameses' *India Report*.[10] Undeniably, the Eameses and Nelson shared in the promise of this enlightened, rationalist modernism—one wedded, for a time, to postwar liberalism's confidence in the power of the state, and of the designer, to bring about utopian changes to patterns and habits of living and worldviews around the globe.

Buoyed by the prospect of a bold midcentury world for the making, designers thus brought a modernist tradition of media experimentation and sensory utopianism into the institutional operations of the Cold War "semiosphere." Scaled to the world, this sensory pedagogy turned enthusiastically to moving-image technologies to experiment with forms of global communication. Informed by an evolutionary idiom of the senses, designer pedagogy positioned the human organism within an unstable and uncertain environment of technological transformation and change, requiring perceptual acclimation to, and security within, the new nature of the postwar. If cinema expanded in the process, this is only because so, it seemed, had the world.

In this chapter, I narrate the tactics and scenes of the sensorium's perceived transformation at midcentury, and its cultural administration in the mode of designer pedagogy. I turn first to the contested status of the Eameses in recent critical assessments of the sensory politics of "expanded cinema," before offering an alternative genealogy of expanded cinema discourses through the theory of designers, artists, and critics like the Eameses, Nelson, John McHale, and Gene Youngblood, as well as Fuller, their shared interlocutor. That genealogy begins with a few of the Eameses' overtly pedagogical media experiments in the early 1950s at the University of Georgia, UCLA, and UC Berkeley. I traverse a number of the discourses and institutional sites that have been lost or underexamined in scholarly reckonings with the designers' multiscreen work, including Cold War educational reform and its vision of the humanities' role in the world, the worldly ambitions of a Bauhaus sensory pedagogy, postwar communications theory and cybernetics, and the cultural and governmental institutions whose global agendas shaped the very heterogeneity of the cinematic, as these designers understood it. The chapter reframes expanded cinema discourses as a terrain of modernist thought about the very worldliness of media—its baffling spatial and geographic extensiveness across the globe; its seemingly new times, speeds, and natures; and the forms of belonging, community, and citizenship it might offer in proposing a human sensorium scaled to the world. In the process, it begins to provide an account of the status of modernism's sensory utopianism at midcentury, remade by the new prestige of communication theory and wielded by designers who positioned themselves as communication's postwar prophets and global emissaries.

Relationship Seeing as Cold War Communication

Consider the extravagant futurism of the so-called Information Machine at the IBM pavilion for the 1964–65 World's Fair in New York. The pavilion's goal was "to tell the story of modern information handling devices in an interesting, informative and educational manner."[11] The pavilion, designed by Eero Saarinen and Associates, consisted of a "grove of 45 man-made steel trees" providing a canopy for exhibitions in which probability displays and data-processing systems were framed by charming puppet theater. The centerpiece of the exhibition was the "Information Machine"—a giant, hollow egg made of a concrete shell whose white surface was covered over with the IBM logo (Plate 10). Inside the egg was a multimedia theater that presented, on fifteen screens of various sizes, the Eameses' film and slideshow *Think*. An experiment in the new quantities and speeds of information, and their demands on the human sensorium, *Think*'s enveloping, "total environment" extended a Bauhaus tradition of exhibition design exemplified by the work of Herbert Bayer, while continuing the Eameses' long-standing interest in communication that began with *A Communications Primer*. In that film IBM saw a

Figure 2.6. Installation view of *Think* multiscreen presentation, IBM Pavilion, New York World's Fair, 1964–65. Copyright 2017 Eames Office LLC (eamesoffice.com).

vision of postwar technology's future firmly in line with the reinvention of its own corporate image in the 1950s and 1960s presided over by Eliot F. Noyes, the first curator of design at MoMA. For IBM the Eameses produced both *Introduction to Feedback* (1960), conceived as a "sequel" to *A Communications Primer,* as well as *The Information Machine: Creative Man and the Data Processor* (1957), an animated film made for the IBM pavilion at the 1958 Brussels World's Fair. As in *The Information Machine,* the aim of *Think* was, in part, to demystify and domesticate computers, showing, through a welter of audiovisual information, how these machines "help solve the most complex problems with the same principles of logic, similar to those we all use in making decisions everyday [*sic*]."[12] The audience experienced *Think*'s technospectacle by taking seats on a five-hundred-person "People Wall," which was then lifted hydraulically fifty feet into the egg's interior, all while suspended over a pool of water.

Think has not fared well in many of the more persuasive reassessments of the sensory-affective politics of expanded cinema, though it appears in many of the canonical articulations of that category, including Fluxus artist George Maciunas's "Expanded Arts Diagram" for the special "Expanded Arts" issue of Jonas Mekas's *Film Culture.* Alongside the Eameses' landmark multiscreen *Glimpses of the U.S.A.,* shown in 1959 at the American National Exhibition in Moscow (site of the infamous Nixon-Khrushchev "kitchen debates"), *Think*'s now-ironic optimism is generally recalled to position the Eameses as critical bad objects. They exemplify a midcentury paradigm of sensory normalization and discipline over and against the liberatory sensorial regimes of the counterculture.

For example, in Andrew Uroskie's compelling recent history, *Between the Black Box and the White Cube,* the 1964–65 New York World's Fair appears as a crucial foil for distinguishing between two modes of cinematic "expansion."[13] One entails a properly "conceptual" concern with the "institutional qualities of the cinematic situation" also emerging in the fall of 1965, and best exemplified by the Expanded Cinema Festival held that winter at the Film-Makers' Cinematheque in New York (an event covered at length in the *Film Culture* special issue). The other involves a merely "formal" expansion of cinema evident in faddish multiscreen spectacles featured at the fair, including the Eameses' *Think,* for IBM.[14] This latter, expanded cinema manqué, for Uroskie, is maximalist rather than minimalist, following Maciunas's framing of the Eameses alongside the circus, fairs, international expos, and the "pseudotechnology" of "Walt Disney spectacles." It is concerned with quantity (size and number of screens), speed (the pace of images), and sensory intensity ("the efficiency of sensory bombardment"). From Raoul Grimoin-Sanson's Cinéorama of 1900 to the Cinerama of the 1950s, multiscreen experimentation proceeds "with a singular aim": the "enfolding of the spectator in an immersive, diegetic world through the overwhelming sensory conditions of display. . . . By immersing the subject within an overwhelming accumulation of visual data, they sought to produce a heightened experience of reality without too great a concern for realism."[15]

Uroskie's study exemplifies a persistent way of understanding the sensory-affective politics of midcentury designers like the Eameses.[16] Such work has noted, first, that all departures from mainstream norms of cinematic exhibition—as in the *Think* presentation—are neither necessarily liberatory nor disruptive, but rather proximate to the forms of corporate propaganda of mainstream display culture or to military-scientific technologies and their ideological work. It has further posited that the Eameses' apparent attentiveness to the disjunctive and dislocating effects of electronic media, modeled in *Think*'s very imagistic excess, might actually constitute a "more active form of suture, and identification with and subjection to the electronic image."[17] This, then, is how the media pedagogy of the Information Machine has been recently understood: a corporate plot to "immerse the audience in images and overwhelm them with sensation" fully complicit with the logic of advanced

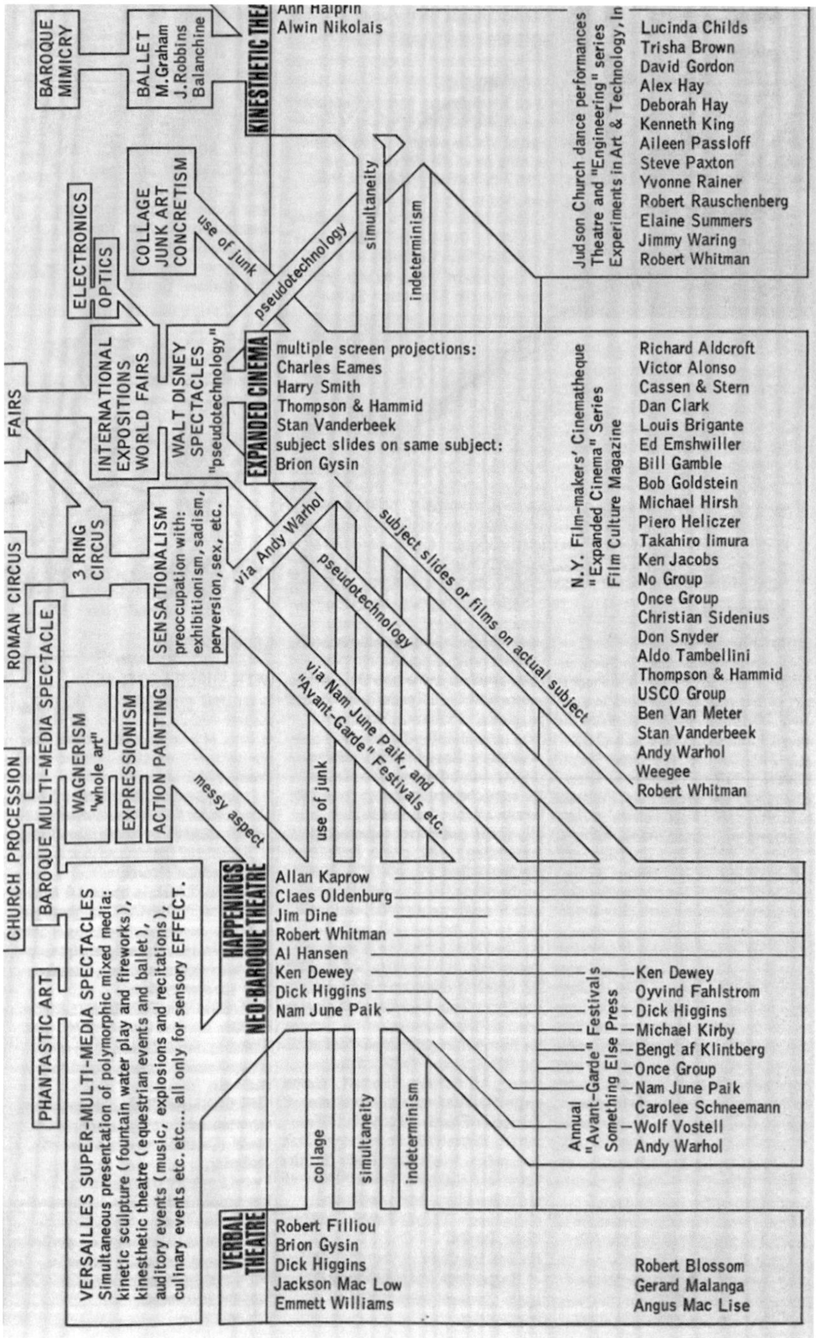

Figure 2.7. Detail, George Maciunas, "Expanded Arts Diagram," *Film Culture* special issue "Expanded Arts," 1966.

capital; a phantasmagoric forgetting of the lived body in a virtual environment of mystification; or as a nefarious form of perceptual distraction—one that not only naturalizes the speeds of a new information economy but also allows for more subtle forms of social control in which subjection to the electronic image masquerades as active human participation.[18]

Such readings' central dialectics between absorption and disjunction, or active and passive spectatorship, assume a familiar model for conceptualizing the sensory-affective politics of cinematic attention and visual spectacle. It has a clear modernist pedigree, hinging on a critique of the faux "nature" of bourgeois illusionism, and a preference for defamiliarization that runs from Russian formalism and the Soviet montage theory of Sergei Eisenstein and Dziga Vertov, through Bertolt Brecht and Walter Benjamin's materialist critiques of fascist aesthetic spectacle—anesthetized against historicity—to the resurgence of Brechtian reflexivity and anti-illusionism in the 1970s discourse of "political modernism" that fueled the consolidation of a powerful theory of the cinematic apparatus.[19] Such binaries (immersion/disjunction, sutured/alienated, active/passive) have led scholars to underestimate the nature of the Eameses' technical interest in sensory "discipline," and to misrecognize its intellectual sources, its institutional contexts, and the reach of its midcentury utopianism—its worldly ambitions. As I argue in chapter 1, this utopianism, like the images of Eamesian happiness through which it circulated worldwide, is best understood not solely through consumption and spectatorship, but as a model of technophilic production, a process or technical manner of working with objects and images in their midcentury technoscientific environments. The Eameses' terrain of happy making is indebted to their modernist self-understanding as inheritors of a Bauhaus genealogy in which promiscuous aesthetic production across media is the therapeutic expression of an integrated personality—a "whole man" in an era whose modernity is synonymous with debilitating overspecialization. The Eameses, for their part, repeatedly called their vast range of production ways of "taking their pleasure seriously." The phrase typifies a quasi-ascetic modernist approach to pleasure as a way of making unfamiliar demands on the senses, one necessarily involving a regime of discipline, difficulty, or unpleasure.[20] It also signals the designers' preference for modes of constraint-based production that worked not with autonomous things in isolation but, as I describe in chapter 1, things perceived in relationships, and whose networked functioning it was the work of multiscreen presentations such as *Think* to model. And it anticipates their hostility to any model of agency predicated on total freedom, spontaneity, or the will to original self-expression.[21] Allergic to such expressive models of unfettered aesthetic production, the Eameses' mode of expanded cinema—like the midcentury world of happiness to be designed—requires calculation and decision, a tooling of feeling and sensation.

The Eameses first pressed cinema to expand in the ideologically contested space of the postwar classroom itself; in that context, the Eameses produced the film *A Communications Primer,* the conceptual heart of their designs on happiness. The film's vision of human-scale environmental design, secured by happy talk, was of interest to, and circulated among, viewers and institutions at home and abroad. Equally important, though, is where and how the film began: as a node or module in a boundary-breaking, multimedia experiment in humanistic education in which Eames participated at the invitation of George Nelson. In the summer of 1952, Nelson was invited to Athens, Georgia, by Lamar Dodd, head of the Department of Fine Arts at the University of Georgia, to observe his faculty in the classroom and studio, and consult on the reform of the university's art curriculum. With a grant from the Rockefeller Foundation, Dodd had evidently decided to shake things up a bit, importing Nelson to energize his department.[22] Nelson was a disciplinary outsider; he had never taught painting or sculpture, nor had he any specific expertise in educational policy. Indeed, in 1952, after serving as associate editor at *Architectural Forum* and *Fortune,* Nelson was then most visible in his capacity as director of design at Herman Miller, where he was reinventing the spaces, textures, and constitutive stuff of the midcentury American good life. Nelson, to be fair, acknowledged his ill fit for the task and professed his ignorance about educational policy. But Dodd was not dissuaded. He had found in the designer a potential reformer. Nelson rounded out his advisory committee with the other members of Herman Miller's design trio—Eames, whom Nelson had hired in 1946, and Girard.

After visiting classes in Athens in the fall of 1952, and after more conversations with Dodd and his faculty, Nelson and Eames eventually decided to focus not on adding courses or requirements to the fine arts curriculum, as they had initially discussed, but rather on exploring pedagogic *method* and *process.* What they noticed in their classroom observations was, first, a distressing disciplinary *segmentation*—"Education," as Nelson put it, was "like the thinking of the man in the street, sealed off into too many compartments"—and second, a disturbing wasting of time in the faculty's communication of concepts. In proposing a counter-pedagogy intended to combat inefficiency and the atomization of knowledge regimes, the designers purported to train students in what Nelson called "an awareness of *relationships.* . . . The idea was to develop high-speed techniques for exposing relationships between

Figure 2.8. Herman Miller advertisement, design by Irving Harper. Courtesy of Herman Miller.

seemingly unrelated phenomena. This meant films, slides, sounds, music, narration—the familiar world of audio-visual aids."[23] Nelson's contemporaneous essays on design theorize film as a medium tailor-made for what Nelson called "the development of the individual's capacity to establish connections between isolated phenomena" because, as he put it, "film *is* a relationship—the picture strips of which it is composed have no meaning by themselves."[24] And this emphasis on seeing relationships in vast informatic fields, for Nelson and Eames, was all the more pressing for a program like Georgia's, whose graduates rarely pursued careers as professional artists and so would be better served with training that fostered understanding and creative capacity. This kind of flexible humanistic training, as Nelson hoped, "could be employed in any situation," and conveyed by impersonal, indeed, explicitly mass-produced methods—what he cheekily called "canned education" or "the teacher-on-film."[25] As Nelson put it, if "a girl wanted to know something about decorating her future home and what she got was a class in painting, this might make perfectly good sense, but perhaps it was up to the school to build a bridge between the two so that she might see how they were related. Whether this was accomplished by personal or impersonal methods seemed of little consequence."[26]

In Art-X, then, the designers rejected arid proscription or mere telling, opting for something considerably showier and, in a peculiar way, *impersonal*—specifically, a multimedia, multisensory performance of technique in the form of a one-hour sample lesson for an imaginary art course to come, and presented six times in Athens in January 1953, and then three more times at UCLA the following May. Dodd prepared the university community for the event by presenting a display of the three designers' now-iconic furniture and products, no doubt prompting faculty and students alike to wonder what in the "good design" of lovely postwar consumables like molded plywood chairs and bubble lamps would qualify their makers as art educators. "Art-X," Nelson's preferred name for the exemplary experiment, gestures nicely toward the designers' insistent formalism, their seeming indifference to content.[27] Eventually, though, Nelson and Eames did settle on a subject for the "sample lesson," namely, "Communication."

Nelson's pedagogical aspirations for this communicative experiment—his emphasis on nonspecialized liberal understanding, the holistic seeing of "relationships," and flexible creative capacity that would bridge seemingly discrete activities (here, painting and interior decoration)—echo a number of the buzzwords of postwar educational reform in the United States. The Cold War fascination with "open-mindedness," as an ideal of national and intellectual character, grew out of wartime concerns with morale and perceived threats to national unity. This crisis overlapped with a broad (and long-standing) critique of modernity as an engine of the fragmentation of knowledge into increasingly disparate domains of specialization and expertise. For many, this fracturing erected barriers to communication and learning across insular disciplines, and testified to the loss of a "common" national culture.[28] A series of sweeping curricular reforms emerged to remedy the problem, solutions offered by proponents of both "liberal" and "general" education movements. The former camp, championed by the likes of Mark Van Doren at Columbia University, or Mortimer Adler and Robert Maynard Hutchins at the University of Chicago, laid the loss of the common culture at the door of technoscientific habits of thought; they turned to the classics of the Western canon—the "Great Books"—for synthetic, humanistic cultivation in the domains of religion, philosophy, and literature. The latter, more pragmatically oriented camp, thought of culture ethnographically—as a set of common, democratic values, a unified way of life imperiled by modernity, science, and technology—and envisioned its therapeutic synthesis through a curriculum geared not toward the cultural past but rooted in matters of contemporary relevance and "real life," which would, perforce, include science and technology. At midcentury, this movement's pedagogical philosophy was exemplified in *General Education in a Free Society* (1945), the publication Geoffrey Galt Harpham has described as the "single most important document in the history of the 'humanities.'" The so-called Harvard Red Book was developed by a committee chaired by Harvard University president James Bryant Conant, who turned to the problem of education while serving on the National Defense Research Committee, a group that aided in the development and use of the atomic bomb.[29] Anxious about a crisis in

Figure 2.9. Second presentation of A Rough Sketch for a Sample Lesson for a Hypothetical Course (Art-X), UCLA, May 1953. Copyright 2017 Eames Office LLC (eamesoffice.com).

which "the various fields of college study . . . have become a kind of higher vocational training," the Red Book argued that education should "prepare an individual to become an expert both in some particular vocation or art and in the general education of the free man and citizen."[30]

The Red Book's central conclusion was that postwar democratic education would be achieved not through a set curriculum or common core of knowledge, since this would betray the diversity seen as central to American society, but by a "flexible," methods-based one. This humanist flexibility sought to train a specific mentality—a set of basic intellectual tools including "effective thinking, judgment, communication, and the ability 'to discriminate among values' "—rather than particular works.[31] Given the burgeoning complexity of modern society, and its surfeit of specialized knowledge, in which "everyone was either an expert or layman according to context," the "aim of general education," the authors of the Red Book argued, was to provide "the broadest critical sense by which to recognize competence in any field."[32] The Red Book thus sought democratic unity in interdisciplinarity, and imagined a future "technocracy in which each citizen was educated in how to appreciate, judge, and defer to expertise."[33] This free society "would flourish because its citizens would have cultivated universal standards of judgment as well as faith in and commitment to the mental virtues of rationality, creativity, tolerance, communication, and open-minded inquiry."[34]

Surely, the Red Book's vision of general education erected now-familiar, perhaps romantic distinctions between the humanities and commercial values, or between the unifying power of literature and art and the domain of "mass communications" (especially advertisements) that are challenged by Nelson's enthusiastic, technocratic embrace of an "industrial approach to education" in Art-X. After all, he styled himself as an iconoclast set to shake up an intransigent humanist professoriate, and cut through their "tweedy ramblings" with modern production techniques. By the same token, though, Nelson's contemporaneous writings on pedagogy, design, and the challenges of the modern world are animated by general education discourse's foundational orientation toward the "whole man" and citizen, whose learning would equip him to grasp "the complexities of life as a whole"; its hostility to the centrifugal forces of specialization; and its promise of protection from "the ill effects of overrapid change," the ballyhooed restoration of the students' "equilibrium."[35] This climate, for Nelson and the Eameses, called for new modes of specifically worldly perceptual reorientation, a kind of networked visuality for postwar citizenship that would, necessarily, be enabled by the very media technologies that instantiated the pace and scale of postwar change, and might help to manage it.

In his 1951 essay "The Enlargement of Vision," for example, Nelson took stock of the place of the designer in a postwar society "undergoing a transformation of extraordinary dimensions," a "change so drastic it tends to assume more and more the appearance of a crack-up: physical, economic, moral, and esthetic."[36] Dominated by materialistic values, and pervaded by a post-Hiroshima fear of sudden annihilation, postwar society possessed a "new sense of intellectual mastery over the physical world" that made us "acutely aware of the world over which seemingly we have no mastery at all" ("EV," 63). The designer's role, Nelson continued, was to teach citizens to see this new "picture of the world"—dematerialized, often invisible, and increasingly privileging "relationships for dissociated entities, and tension or energy for mass" ("EV," 71). This meant combating habitual, "atomistic" ways of seeing and thinking, "the result not only of schooling but of our total education," and supplanting this vision—which sees everything as a "static object or idea, not related in any important way to anything else"—with a sensual pedagogy that assumes a modern, dynamic vision ("EV," 65).

Evident across the varied domains of physics, architecture, modern painting and sculpture, psychoanalysis, and, as we saw in chapter 1, the "new subscape" of modern furniture, this way of seeing modern worldliness is, for Nelson, closer to the "truth about things" because it starts by assuming that things exist not in themselves but in "expanding networks" of relationships. Nelson pits this kind of modern, interconnected visuality, and the "dissolving transformations" it both follows from and ministers to, against a broader story of alienated subjectivity within industrial modernity, and its "destruction-creation cycle."[37] This dynamic, Nelson admits, produces alienated labor, overspecialization, and widespread unhappiness; it splits thinking and feeling, scientific and artistic temperaments, separating, as John Dewey put it, "imagination from executive doing" ("EV," 73). Detached from the purposiveness of work, the modern subject succumbs to a potentially "totalitarian" dependence on mass-produced entertainment. A strange cocktail of Dewey, Joseph Schumpeter, and Sigfried Giedion, and infused with the Frankfurt School's skepticism about authoritarian personalities, Nelson's narrative pictures a postwar subject "degenerating badly in many respects" ("EV," 73–74). But with destruction, creation: here, in the outline of a newly integrated social being, one who is "noncompetitive" and potentially "non-national," and who is beginning to understand what is a "myth" about his so-called individuality: "He accepts his role as a member of a synchronized, cooperative group and one of these days he will arrive at a new comprehension of the many possible relationships between the individual and the group" ("EV," 74).

Nelson spelled out the pedagogical techniques for combating modern alienation, and producing new forms of worldly integration and organization, in two related essays, "High Time to Experiment" (1955) and "The Designer in the Modern World" (1957). The former hinges on the distinction between "training," a procedure for "developing special competence," and education, whose aim "is no less than the total integration" of the individual ("HT," 79). The educated person, Nelson continues, "collects information primarily for the purpose of establishing new relationships," both with society and with the past, and requires a concept of morality, a creative orientation, and the capacity for critique, for occasionally going against society ("HT," 80). In "High Time to Experiment," Nelson thus reconciles a number of the values common among advocates for general education, still considered "a handicraft activity," with the methods and technical procedures of an industrial society—namely, mass production ("HT," 79). In this way the good teacher is turned into a "production tool" by being put on film, thereby "multiplying his effectiveness," while the outdated "mass production tool" that education has long relied on—the book—is updated by deploying all the available devices to "increase the speed and accuracy of communication," including "photography, printing methods, records, radio, magnetic tape, television, and movies" ("HT," 81).

In "The Designer in the Modern World," Nelson reiterates his claim that the modern world is "a complex" of present and past worlds, and "a constantly developing sense of worlds still in the making." Education is defined by this incipient worldliness, a process of allowing us to cope with being "enmeshed in a tangle of phenomena."[38] It does so by imposing "something resembling a common order on this mass of events" ("DM," 75). In this activity, the industrial designer has an advantage over the more familiar painter or sculptor, mythically seen as socially isolated, for the designer "is far more commonly an *organization* than an individual" ("DM," 76). In this sense, the designer-educator is not just shaping order but enacting—by virtue of his corporate personhood, as it were—"the existence of the organization as a dominant social form," a social form that itself arose as a response to a "social problem . . . how to cope effectively with increasingly quantities of information" ("DM," 76). This problem of information overload, Nelson continues, has prompted a crisis in education: the crisis of consensus, of a terrain of shared values and common texts. Since it is possible that "agreement on a basic curriculum will never again be reached," the "common ground will be found in *methods* of organizing and transmitting information" ("DM," 76).

The conceptual terms of this suite of essays reveal that Nelson, like the Eameses, was keenly attentive to the ways general education's aims overlapped with the broader demands of a nascent "postindustrial society." In fact, as Anna Vallye has observed, Daniel Bell arrived at his canonical formulation of the term while working on a faculty report on general education for Columbia College. In it Bell stumped for a curriculum that deprivileged "subject matter" so as to "make fundamental the nature of conceptual innovation and the processes of conceptual thought."[39] Indeed, postwar hallmarks of the general education philosophy such as the Harvard Red Book, Vallye argues, might best be read as an attempt to train "both liberal democratic political man and the postindustrial knowledge worker," restructuring his mental apparatus by equipping him "with a capacity to confront—and more than that—to embrace and advance the unexpected."[40] This feeling of "security in change," remember, was what Eames, invoking Fuller, called the greatest good an education can offer, alongside an awareness of "value and relationships."[41]

In its attempts to manage, and restore equilibrium to, a changing world, education was of pressing concern to the postwar corporation, which also turned to liberal arts curricula as a hedge against the perceived technical superiority of the Soviets and a palliative to the threat of overspecialized managers, prey to conformist groupthink.[42] The corporation's new, experimental investments in humanistic pedagogy informed the Art-X project and allowed professional avatars of organization such as designers to lay claim to the classroom and its media, and to become players in a midcentury administration of culture that challenged easy distinctions between art and industry, literature and mass communications. In fact, just a few months before journeying to Georgia in 1952 to visit Lamar Dodd, Nelson, and Eames, alongside Fuller and Bayer, were invited by Walter Paepcke, visionary chairman of the Container Corporation of America, to design a striking home in Aspen, Colorado, that might attract people to his nascent Aspen Institute for Humanistic Studies.[43] As I explain in chapter 3, the same corporate *Bildungsideal* that inspired the founding of the Aspen Institute led to the inaugural International Design Conference in Aspen in 1951, "Design as a Function of Management," attended by Nelson and Eames, as well as MoMA director René d'Harnoncourt and Edgar Kaufmann Jr. Consider also that Nelson's "High Time to Experiment," referring to the pressing social need for "broad vision and independent thinking" at the management level, retrospectively compares Art-X's production techniques and training in the seeing of relationships to "the experiment of Pennsylvania Bell Telephone and the University of Pennsylvania" ("HT," 83). Also conceptualized in the fall of 1952, the Bell Institute for Humanistic Education for Business Executives was a one-year course in general education for middle managers at Bell Telephone. Designed by Penn English professor Morse Peckham, the curriculum in art, philosophy, and the sciences—which culminated in an eight-week seminar on James Joyce's *Ulysses* (1922)—sought to train future business leaders in an "experimental attitude" and the habits of mind ("perspective, a technique of learning, self-awareness, flexibility, growth") essential to the postwar's "new world, stretching away in an endless and challenging vista of a multitude of new questions and answers."[44] This new world, presided over by the corporation, and the new prestige of designers like the Eameses and Nelson, required leaders who "can rise above the immediate day-to-day problems of national life and can see them as a whole. They try to understand the infinite relations among people and institutions at work in their country," and to understand "other countries, their principles . . . in order to comprehend their own nation's environment which is formed by other nations and peoples."[45] This groundbreaking corporate-university partnership received a lengthy write-up in *Harper's* in 1955, and a copy of it is included in the Eames pre-1960 research file, alongside a series of columns from *Time* magazine's recurring "Education" column, which chronicled postwar experiments like this one, as well as those of Hutchins and Adler.[46]

The designers' form of integral, holistic seeing also drew specifically on a Bauhaus pedagogy of the senses, and the interdisciplinarity modeled in its famous Preliminary course. However seemingly indifferent to content, Art-X purported to be *some* kind of art class, after all. Reflecting on the experiment in a 1974 address to the American Academy of Arts and Sciences (AAAS), Charles Eames explained its intention as an attempt "to demonstrate the importance of using the language of vision at the university."[47] Art-X's lessons in integration, interdisciplinarity, and world communication, Eames continued, were all the more relevant for today's universities, which "are becoming discontinuity headquarters, with each department avoiding communication with others and the rest of the world. Used as it could be, the language of vision is a real threat to this discontinuity, and so it is avoided at all costs."[48]

In its title and content, Eames's lecture to the AAAS summoned the seminal work of his friend György Kepes, *The Language of Vision* (1944), a highly influential work of design theory in the postwar period and the conceptual culmination of Kepes's efforts in developing a visual design curriculum at Moholy's Institute of Design in Chicago. Eames thus located Art-X in a broad genealogy of interdisciplinary endeavor with which its audience was sympathetic. Art-X extended the critique at the core of the Bauhaus's communalist, therapeutic, multimedial curriculum, itself designed as a corrective to the overspecialization of design professions within industrial modernity, and the fracturing of sensation, emotion, and reason it produced in the modern individual, to concerns about the overcompartmentalized knowledge of the postwar classroom, familiar in general education reform discourse of the period. Kepes himself, as Vallye demonstrates, was invested in bridging the gap between the "language of vision," and the integrative "form thinking" at its core, to the problem of general education—namely, "how to articulate a link between vision and socially-mediated character formation."[49] In fact, the AAAS, a Boston-based interdisciplinary learned society, which Kepes and Eames both joined in the 1950s, was affiliated with the American Unity of Science movement (which enjoyed historical ties to the Bauhaus) and was engaged in the problem of general education in the postwar period, bringing its concerns with linguistic integration and unifying precepts of knowledge into the postwar problem of the whole, humanistically integrated curriculum, and the democratic world citizen it sought to train.[50]

For Kepes, the language of vision fulfilled a broader Bauhaus pedagogical ideal, ministering to what Moholy called "the whole man" in an era of debilitating overspecialization. Influenced, like Moholy, by the Gestalt school of perceptual psychology, Kepes understood the organized plastic image—the patterned visual unit—as itself a kind of organism, formed "through an organizing process in which the individual parts were determined by the dynamics of an encompassing, integrated 'system.'"[51] As such, the image—and modern media of "optical communication" such as movies and television, or scientific imaging technologies—could function as a tool of psychic integration and an agent of social equilibrium within a midcentury environment defined, for Kepes and others, by a baffling new nature, an inability to "keep pace with events," and a disorienting "crisis of scale."[52]

In Kepes's compensatory narrative, midcentury technoscience had "disrupted the atom, and speared the moon," conspiring to produce only "nature that is alien": "The man-made world has extended so explosively in so many directions that we seem unable to grasp its dimensions or assert authority over its dynamics" ("VA," 7). This new nature, and new scale of events in the "expanded world" it augurs, Kepes insisted, should not be recoiled from, but rather demands "new levels of sensibility, a new capacity for unification," and the unification of the domains of science and art to "bring our sensations, feelings, and attitudes into harmonious correspondence with the broad movements of nature and society" ("VA," 12). Kepes's "language of vision" thus extended Moholy-Nagy's own celebration—in *The New Vision* and elsewhere—of photography's and film's capacity to extend the human senses: to reveal more of the world's complexity and integrate it into an expansive worldview.[53] Here and throughout his work, Kepes embraced various forms of technologically enhanced visuality for their ability to lay bare an abiding integrity, producing not anxiety in the new scale of events but rather "joy in new vistas of what life can be": "Motion picture, television and related techniques have now given us the flexibility we need to mark the time flow of images, the growth, succession, rhythm, and orderly continuity of vision" ("VA," 7).[54] An ideal of perceptual integration, Kepes's language of vision would bring humans into equilibrium with the new, "total environment" of the postwar period, now scaled to the "fantastic expanse of cosmological pattern, from ultramicroscopic, to superastronomical, unrolling from the looms of science." And it "takes courage," Kepes adds, to "see this whole as a whole" ("VA," 11).

So, too, in Art-X's multimedia "language of vision," the specificity of film *as film* is minimized, subordinated to the experiential, affective, and organizational dimensions of communication. As a performance, this vanguard pedagogy was conceived as modular in structure, as a sequence of what Eames and Nelson alternatively referred to in their correspondence in the planning of Art-X as "packages" or "capsules," each prepared individually by the designers. The modularity was, in a sense, pragmatic, allowing the designers, located separately in New York, Venice, and Michigan, to work independently on their capsules. But it was also a formal and ideological principle. The packages themselves were composed of short films, shown with a single 16mm projector, and thematically arranged slide shows, which displayed images across three screens in varying patterns. The visual content was accompanied by tape-recorded soundtracks and narrations, and in some cases, by smells in the form of synthetic bottled odors that Girard pumped through the auditorium's air ducts during the performance. A color-coded schema gives some indication of the complexity and logistical coordination required for this experiment. Some of the films—a documentary film about Egypt; *La lettre*, a French film about the emergence of writing and the invention of printing; excerpts from a UPA (United Productions of America) cartoon titled *The Animated Calligraphy of Sound*—were selected by Charles Eames through consultation with his contacts on the UCLA film faculty.[55] But others, such as Nelson's opening film *Art-X*, and two films made by the Eameses that would be combined and refined later that year into *A Communications Primer*, were original works made specifically for the Georgia events. The Art-X lesson at Athens concluded with Eames's slide show *Bread*, complete with Girard's simulated aroma of baking bread, as the teaser for the hypothetical next day's equally hypothetical next lesson, which would take up the multiplicity of bread's functioning, both in nutrition and art, politics and symbolism, and which would later, when Art-X went to UCLA, be shown as a film—a paean to the universality and variety of bread, and of its human makers.

The class opened with Nelson's module, the short film *Guys and Dolls*. The film selects an exemplary message, here, the song "Paul Revere" from the titular Broadway musical. Nelson plays the song as its lyrics scroll for viewers, and briefs the class in music history, noting that the song is a fugue, which he quickly defines and whose temporal patterning he diagrams visually. Having established the complexity of the message,

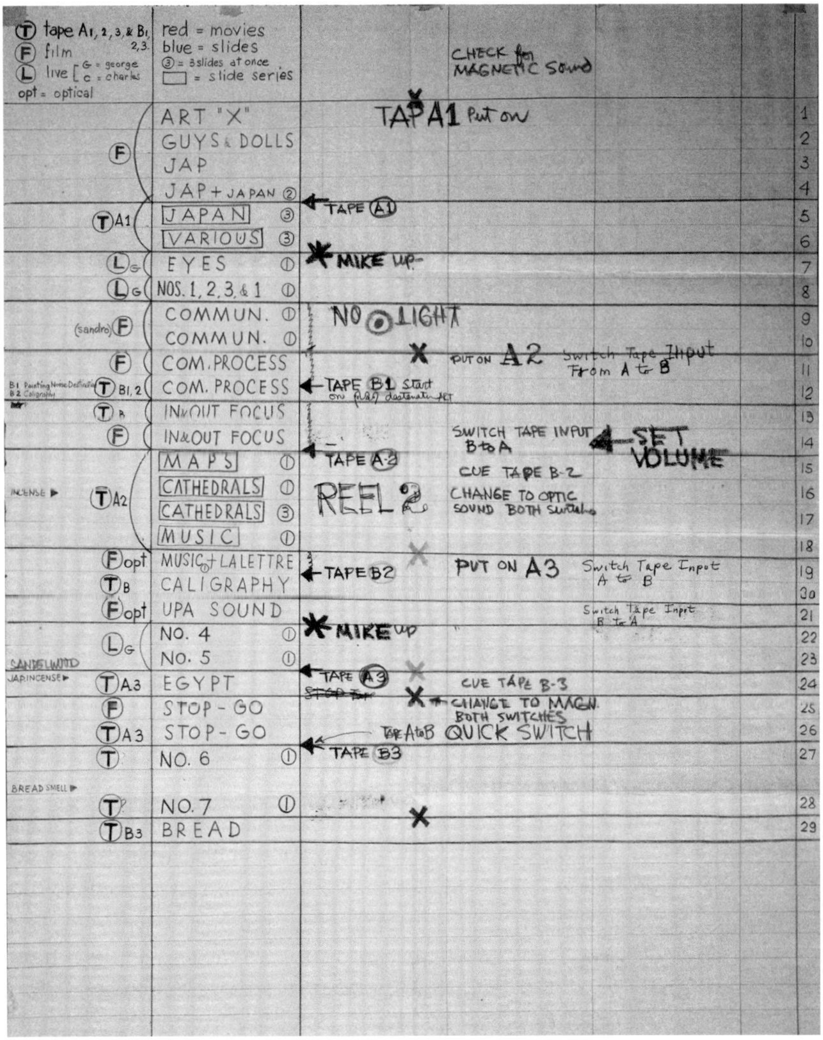

Figure 2.10. "Score" for A Rough Sketch for a Sample Lesson for a Hypothetical Course (Art-X), 1952–53. Copyright 2017 Eames Office LLC (eamesoffice.com).

Nelson summons three human "receivers"—a bookie (an expert in horses who is also a connoisseur of cheesecake but is ignorant about fugues and musicals); a master's degree student in American history (who studied Paul Revere the man, not the horse); and last, at the limits of communication, a visitor from Japan. "One communication," the voice-over continues, "one transmitter, but all different kinds of receiving sets." We hear the final "receiver" speak in untranslated Japanese. Nelson explains: "This receiver is turned into a transmitter, and I don't happen to have the equipment for tuning in. Can you even imagine what happens when you put together *Guys and Dolls* and the totally different background of this man?"

Of Art-X's organizing topic, communication, Nelson later remarked that "if you asked me how we picked so impossibly difficult a theme I can only answer that at the time we did everything the hard way. As we went from one possible subject to another, what we were most interested in finding was something which would permit the exploration of relationships, and if it offered nothing else, 'Communication' certainly did that."[56] But communication also became the impossibly vast content fleshing out Art-X's experiment in a transdisciplinary poetics of happiness because it was the central category in the Cold War semiosphere. As I argue in the introduction, "communication" united a range of competing meanings, technocratic dreams, and fantasies about the therapeutic overcoming of national, geopolitical, and disciplinary divides, and it enjoyed a privileged status within the putatively "universal" discipline of cybernetics, whose prestige had been ratified by the first Macy Conference in New York, which would have its tenth meeting in 1953, the year of Art-X and *A Communications Primer.* Indebted to cybernetics' claims to disciplinary universalism, *A Communications Primer*'s capacious thinking, which, as its promotional materials stated, "discourages thinking of communication in a limited way" and "aspired to the breaking down of barriers between areas of learning," was also touted as the yield of Art-X's pedagogical experiment.[57] The Eameses and Nelson were well aware of first-order cybernetics theories of communication and control, and were actively seeking to popularize cybernetic concepts, swayed by their application as models for comprehending the complexity of modern society, and as tools of a properly democratic social order. Such models, of course, were first developed during the new wartime collaborations between the military-industrial complex and academic institutions, and were exemplified in mathematical research such as Norbert Wiener's study of antiaircraft weaponry.[58] Human and machinic behavior, thought of as analogous processors of information within self-correcting, self-organizing systems, could, Wiener suggested, be subjected to probabilistic analysis, prediction, and control.

As many historians of science and Cold War cultural historians have argued, what made these cybernetic models striking was their universalizing vision of communication, and the rapidity with which they were assembled as an apparatus, both an "instrument" and a "strategic convention of heterogeneous actors."[59] Cybernetics' vision of the systemic self-organization of organisms and machines alike, and its investment in message circulation as a form of governance, guidance, and control, were extrapolated willy-nilly across the disciplinary boundaries of biology, physics, mathematics, sociology, anthropology, and linguistics, and toward a global vision of analogous, self-regulating systems (biological, mechanical, informational). The cybernetic world was organized into systems composed of signals and messages requiring recognition and interpretation. Because cybernetics thought of information as pattern within noise, and therefore "a model of material and social order," it saw feedback as order maintaining, and information systems as moral goods, potentially happy making.[60]

What lesson is to be gleaned from this kind of informatic happiness? When Wiener invokes the word "happiness," or brings it into alignment with "things" and "goods," as in the "Progress and Entropy" chapter of *The Human Use of Human Beings* (1950), a work the Eameses and Nelson knew well, it is severely qualified, and modulated by tragedy. Because the "archenemy" of the scientist seeking the order and organization of the universe is entropic disorganization, what draws Wiener to the likeness between machines and living organisms in the first place is the way their feedback-driven, self-organizing decisions "seem to resist the general tendency for the increase of entropy."[61] And so, even though "in a very real sense we are shipwrecked passengers on a doomed planet," the theory of entropy need not plunge us into despair, or invalidate moral purpose, provided we refuse what Wiener indicted as an American fallacy of progress (*HU,* 58). This, "the unlimited and quasi-spontaneous process of change as a *Good Thing,*" flies in the face of the citizenry's own religious traditions, for none of which is "the world a *good* place in which an enduring happiness is to be expected" (*HU,* 59, 60). Instead, Wiener opts for what he dubs a "reduced" notion of progress. One hopes, at best, for the "relatively happy outcome" that might come from "the irreversible movement into a contingent future which is the true condition of human life," or perhaps that "this limited vision of progress in the face of overwhelming necessity may have the purging terror of Greek tragedy" (*HU,* 71, 58).

CARDBOARD TOWERS ARCH 1N

Figure 2.11.
Cardboard towers exercise, Arch 1N, University of California, Berkeley, from Ark Annual, Berkeley Lectures. Copyright 2017 Eames Office LLC (eamesoffice.com).

With *A Communications Primer* at its heart, Art-X is an early Eamesian effort in their pedagogy of cybernetic happiness. Like Wiener's own sense of the "relatively happy," the Eameses and Nelson are anxious about human production in the unhappy shadow of catastrophe and war, and their sense of liberal well-being is marked by an acute sense of the contingency of progress. In his contemporaneous essay "Design as Communication," Nelson redefined the designer as a "purveyor, not of comforts . . . but of truths."[62] He would model a particularly "total awareness of the modern world" that integrates the "outlook of the scientist, the mathematician," first to "comprehend," and then, if possible, to "control" a "strange and explosive world where accelerating change seems to be the only remaining constant, where intangible relationships are more concrete than tangible things and where cooperation has replaced competition as the only possible technique for survival."[63] The Eameses called this ineluctable web of relationality the work of "connections," and like Nelson, they installed it at the conceptual center of their design practice at the same time a similar fidelity to internally differential systems energized the postwar convergence of cybernetic communications theory, anti-Soviet political agendas, and "second-wave" structural linguistics in the work of Roman Jakobson and Claude Lévi-Strauss.[64]

Shortly after Art-X, the Eameses would again have a chance to train the sensorium of aspiring students—now, architects—in modes of perceptual-affective "awareness" again framed in cybernetic terms, and conceptualized within Cold War scenarios of choice and decision making, prediction and speculation. Late in 1953 Charles Eames accepted the invitation of Dean William Wurster to restructure a first-year design course for beginning students at UC Berkeley's School of Architecture. From December 1953 to April 1954, he delivered to a 125-student class a series of monthly lectures, the bulk of which were taken up by a rather astonishing swath of multimedia experimentation spawned by the Eameses' interests in communication theory: slideshows, films (the Eameses' and those of others), and lengthy readings from divergent sources ranging from rational-choice economic theory to editorials on information theory from *Astounding Science Fiction*.[65] The experiments called for, and performed, not just the flexible, open habits of mind typical of Cold War educational reform but also a sensory pedagogy of worldliness and citizenship in precisely the terms laid out elsewhere by the Eameses' friends and collaborators Nelson and Kepes.

The concept of architecture, Eames explained in his Berkeley lectures, would be taught not in terms of buildings but architecture "as the world, and the extension of man and his environment." The capacity for human beings' architectural "extension" was not just physical but cognitive and perceptual: such architecture required worldly, integral seeing as embodied in the Eameses' own famous Case Study House No. 8, modeled in its mediated forms. In the ninth lecture, the slideshow of the Eames house that would later become the film *House: After Five Years of Living* (1955) was shown as a living example of architecture as an "art of relationships," and the slides of the couple's carefully arranged domestic items marshaled as evidence of networked visuality. To see a succession of such arrangements flit by as slides is to observe how "everything in the room is in relation to every other thing in the room, all of which is architecture," an architecture perpetually scaled to the "next largest thing."

Four multiscreen slideshows or "scapes" comprised the most insistent technology of the Berkeley lectures, and were at the center of this strategy of visualizing "relationships": *Townscape*, *Seascape*, *Roadrace* (portions of which reappeared in *Think*), and *Railroad,* also called *Trainscape.* Eames referred to these as "awareness shows," and he described their manipulation of sight and sound as ways of developing "emotional relationships" between images, cultivating the students' attitude of "involvement" in problems and overcoming boredom. Photography was cast as a medium of involvement, storage, and retrieval: a mode of "intensive looking" and defamiliarization, as well as a tool for building a "storehouse of experience" in the "post-office of the mind." In *Townscape,* nonsynced soundtracks including city and traffic noises, "nickelodeon, Oriental, march and jazz music," and even a recording of Gertrude Stein reading a section of *The Making of Americans* were played alongside slides of "scenes around town," their variety of attendant associations—produced by the students—constituting what Charles called "sight-sound poems." Stein's writing was summoned as both the limit of sense and the sheer potential of human sense making. Juxtaposed with images of road signs, telephone lines, store fronts, Stein's prose offers "a good example in sound of how seemingly meaningless words can suggest meaning by association." For Eames, even the most intransigent modernist language communicates.

To get a better understanding of this sensory pedagogy, consider how *Seascape* operated in the lecture context. Eames's third lecture begins with a discussion of the importance of decisions and the necessity of adjudicating quality, despite—or perhaps because of—the absence of absolute values. *Seascape,* adduced as an experiment in "audible and visible associations," is projected to train the students' repertoire of "built-in" experiences necessary in decision making and judgment. Eames proceeds by a disjunctive montage of sound and vision: images of people at the beach, and then elements of the beach itself and marine life shown in rapid succession alongside a tape recording that mixes the continuous breaking of surf along the beach with snatches of French, American, and Italian songs, and the ambient sounds of the seascape: seagulls, barking dogs, and airplanes. After the show, the students were asked what they best remembered, and whether it affected them negatively or positively. Several complained that the scenes were too "busy" and that "noise filled the brain"; others, that the slides went by too quickly, producing a confusing discrepancy between sound and image. Eames's comments on the students' "associations" are revealing. For the handful of students repulsed by the "slimy" or "stagnant" aspects of marine life, Eames responded that this is but a personal, relative view, an arbitrary moralizing of forms of life that are, in themselves, neither good nor bad. Indeed, the student consensus about the "horrors of the sea" was surprising enough to Eames that he returned to it at the start of the next lecture, remarking that he was "unable to conceive a form that was in itself ugly," but rather only so "relative to its surroundings." He then reran a series of *Seascape* slides, especially shellfish in states of deterioration, but without sound, to ask whether they seemed "less horrible in themselves at second sight."

By insisting on this sensual pedagogy of pragmatic relativism, Eames's Berkeley lectures acknowledged their debt to the work and thought of Buckminster Fuller, and his claim that the kind of happiness that education could instill in students is "the feeling of security in change." Fuller protégé and Fuller Research Institute member Geoffrey Lindsay gave the one guest lecture in the course—on the achievements of his mentor in the area of low-cost housing, from firecracker tents and trailer-packed houses to Fuller's experiments with geodesic domes of various sizes and scales of complexity. For Eames, Fuller's brand of ecological awareness exemplified "relationship" thinking and teaching as compensatory modes of achieving "security in change," a mode of happiness abetted by information and communication technologies. In the Berkeley lectures, Eames screened *A Communications Primer* in this context, immediately following Lindsay's lecture, and prefaced the film by returning to Fuller, noting that one way of "building up the feeling of security in change is to concentrate on the relationships of things to each other and the value of relationships rather than valuing the idea of the thing in itself." He followed this with another discussion of the contextual determination of morality, value, and convention (in the Crusades, he noted, both sides cried "Kill the infidel!"), but now turned this to a new, related problem—the emergence of novelty and difference, and the management of the unexpected or improbable within any given "environment." How, in sum, does "security in change" happen? Here, Eames remarks on the double standards that emerge to challenge binary distinctions between friend and enemy: if "our team" retreats, it is "courage," but if the opposition does, it is "weakness"; our rule breaking is "originality," theirs is "taboo." In fact, the following year, Charles proposed to Edgar Kaufmann Jr. that the scapes (transferred to 16mm film) be used to communicate a "human-scale" image of the United States to Japan—formerly an enemy, and now, newly, a friend.[66] In the Berkeley lectures, Eames's point about relationship thinking is that the new and "true" is often *the illogical*—indeed, that truth includes "improbable data, or peripheral truths." If the truth-value is high, its degree of probability is correspondingly low. He's linking "truth," in the way of communications theory, to the quantity of "information." What Fuller would call "security in change" thus requires training in "knowing the nature of [any given] opposition," in "seeing the relationship between the familiar and the unfamiliar" in order to integrate the new. This is change you can feel secure in.

Much like *A Communications Primer,* the "awareness shows" would school their viewers in forms of sensory integration that sought to speculate about, and better manage, the new and eventful. In the Cold War context, this discursive horizon of security in the unforeseen was decisively shaped by the event of the bomb. Eames makes this point directly following his discussion of *Seascapes,* arguing for the importance of science fiction literature as one of the few arenas today in which the "art of speculation is practiced," and he suggests that such a course be taught in public schools. Better practiced in speculating about the future, students will avoid the disasters that come when they wish "harder" rather than wisely: "Had we been collectively trained in an art of speculation," he reasons, we might not have wished so hard for "a weapon that could destroy whole cities." Thus he proposes a curriculum of "rationally organized speculation," offering the example of MIT's program in creative engineering, which asks students to envision an existing planet and its inhabitants, and to design products for it in a way that requires their conceptual "points of reference be changed from that of earth."[67] But speculation also entails historical thinking, involvement in "the situations and conditions under which people solved problems in their own society," and so he tasks students with a design exercise in the reconstruction of a historical environment, and screens films that exemplify acute historical awareness.

For Eames speculative thought demands of students both conceptual flexibility—the capacity to imagine radically other scenarios or environments, whether in unearthly space or historical time—and mobile forms of collective production and problem solving that challenge ideas about individual expression and creativity. One of the more striking moments in the lectures comes when Eames recalls one of Fuller's many exercises in catastrophic speculation: imagine Chicago as a city to be destroyed in fourteen days, and design an evacuation strategy. Fuller's solution, Eames explains enthusiastically, was a series of mobile units that would house 10,000 people, serve 5,000 meals per day, and be capable of moving every twenty-four hours to points within a 200-mile radius.[68] Eames calls this exercise in mobile planning a "circus community," and proceeds to develop an analogy between this kind of flexibility and that of the Ringling Bros. circus, whose forms of mobility (tents, ropes, pulleys, pegs, canvas, fasteners) constitute an "architecture of tension," which he illustrates with a slideshow and accompanying soundtrack. The community and its architectural forms, Eames insists, is a model of efficient communal production across large swaths of time. You can sense, he notes, the presence of individual innovations and improvements, but they are subordinated to a supervening organizational structure, an abiding, integral whole. This kind of making, he continues, in which tremendous variety, modifications, and refinements are domesticated within a larger unit of production, and its abiding limits, is best exemplified by the making of bread, and the Eameses' film *Bread* is screened as a paean to just this kind of disciplined, communal making.

In the context of the Berkeley lectures, then, we can read *Bread* not just as a carb-heavy reminder of the Eameses' liberal humanism in the film's documentation of the sheer democratic *varieties* of bread across cultures and times, but also as an allegory of largely anonymous, corporate making in which the individual is integrated into a community, and freedom of expression is tempered by long-standing limits and constraints that produce "the feeling of security in change." Indeed, of all of the arguments Eames makes in the lectures, he is perhaps most insistent about this one—the necessity of working within limitations, the critique of originality for its own sake, and the need for modes of creative discipline. In the lectures' various examples of the Eameses' interest in the structure of theme and variations, Eames stresses that the variations have meaning "in relation to the one before it," which of course is the sensual and semantic lesson of the awareness shows broadly speaking. He makes the same points about writing itself as an expressive technology that developed in the scale of deep, evolutionary time: 250,000 years of human history elapsed before the first cave paintings; another 15,000 until the emergence of Egyptian hieroglyphics; 5,000 more until the first "nonphonetic" letter, and then, relatively rapid development of Greek and Roman systems of writing. The fetish of originality, he insists, is overrated. In fact, it is one of the major hurdles for designers to overcome. Better to set limitations, often dictated by the medium in which one works: take granite, which allows for control over the terrain of possible decisions, and allows one to avoid the "horrible freedom in a completely plastic medium."

Eames's students, we should point out, were largely unreceptive to these efforts to redefine freedom and creativity as "knowing an objective and working within restraints," and had a chance to critique the pedagogy in the penultimate lecture, when Eames solicited oral feedback on the semester. To his surprise, one student expressed frustration with the limitations of the exercises, which kept them from being free, and expressed a desire to explore the "impractical." Another wished for a problem that asked them to do the "most fantastic thing utterly without discipline," and that would encourage them to design "so that the expression of the architect is in the building." Eames's response was that the desire to do the impractical would require a great deal of discipline (in noticing and deciding what *not* to do) and that architects, and the environments they construct, are always embedded in time and history: "Our economy is all around us and we build with what we have." More striking, however, was his related claim about freedom itself: "All freedom is too big."

In making the claim, Eames again displayed his conceptual affinity for what Anna Vallye has called the "imbrication of economic and political imperatives driving the training of the mind" in the broader discourse of general education of the period and its vision of Cold War global citizenship.[69] Indeed, the Harvard Red Book would make a similar point about the too-bigness of freedom, and its implications for the role of humanistic education within democracy: "We are apt sometimes to stress freedom, the power of individual choice, and the right to think for oneself—without taking sufficient account of our obligation to cooperate with our fellow men: democracy means an adjustment between the values of freedom and social living."[70] For the Eameses' friend Kepes, this attempt to reconcile a postwar demand for economic growth with the Fulleresque feeling of order and "security in change" fueled an agenda to align the individual scale of visual perception—the "dynamic equilibrium" between "order-security" and "freedom-growth"—to a sociopolitical scale, the "political relationship between freedom and community."[71]

Like the Art-X experiments before them, the Berkeley lectures demonstrate that the "language of vision" that designers like the Eameses began to test out in the media-pedagogical classroom experiments that developed in and around *A Communications Primer*—and would culminate in multiscreen extravaganzas such as *Think*—should be considered as a related series of perceptual-affective techniques of happiness.[72] In them, designers sought not sensory "immersion" or absorption" but the reconciliation of order and growth, security and change, novelty and relationship. They would achieve it, technically, through the cognitive and perceptual training that saw individuals and individual units in broader webs of "relationships," and that allowed for the kinds of networked communications and decisions upon which, as they saw it, nothing less than the future of the world depended. If the Eameses inherit such instrumentality from the utopian modernist tradition of the Bauhaus, and Fuller's homeostatic desire for security in change, they and other designers put it differently to work for the conditions of capitalist democracy in a postwar geopolitical order presided over by the United States and its technoscientific hegemony. Within this context, the senses cannot *not* be administered, managed, or otherwise designed. If the scale of this regime of sensory discipline is now "the world," this is not so because that world should everywhere be made one, necessarily, with spectators' sutured or absorbed into its most normative operations, but because the technological and scientific environments of the postwar period have so radically transformed what seemed normative, or "natural" in the midcentury world as given to the senses, and in the object world thought to exemplify the good life. These designers aren't reifying a world, but reckoning with its unnaturalness, what Kepes called its strange "new nature."

Design as Environmental Communication

Across the Atlantic, for the artists John McHale and Richard Hamilton, then members of the London-based insurgent Independent Group, the media practices of U.S. designers were understood in just this way. For them, the Eameses' experiments epitomized a sustained investigation into the expanded scales of sensory experience afforded by postwar technologies, and an exemplary encounter with significant changes in the scope, speed, and nature of media now understood as an "environment" that made quasi-evolutionary demands on the future of the human organism. An association of iconoclastic young artists, architects, and critics—including McHale and Hamilton, but also Lawrence Alloway, Reyner Banham, Peter Smithson and Alison Smithson, Toni del Renzio, and Eduardo Paolozzi—the IG emerged in the early 1950s around the fledgling Institute for Contemporary Arts to account for what David Mellor has called "the massive postwar proliferation of scientific and technical discourses, perceived as originating mainly in the United States."[73] But the IG, by virtue of its encounter with postwar technoscience in various American guises, was also a key site of nascent expanded cinema discourses, although it has never been credited for that. A recognizably expanded cinematic idiom—the language of sensory and medial extension, an evolutionary understanding of organism and its technological "total environment," attention to the communicative and informatic processes regulating humans and machines—pervaded the IG in theory and practice, especially in the work of McHale and Hamilton. McHale's career, in fact, provides a crucial link between Gene Youngblood's canonical countercultural theory of expanded cinema in 1970 and the design practice of the Eameses. These seemingly disparate sensory worlds, as we will see, come together through a shared investment in the utopian globalism of Fuller.

By the early 1950s the Eameses' films and design practice were in the discursive thick of the IG's typically wide-ranging conversations about technology, design, and postwar art and culture, taken up for discussion alongside, say, the architectural writing of Sigfried Giedion, the art of Jean Dubuffet and Francis Bacon, the cultural force of horror comics and movie starlets, the films of Kenneth Anger, developments in probability and information theory, and the ubiquity of advertising, so-called sociology in the popular arts.[74] In 1955 the Eameses' *A Communications Primer* was shown at the ICA, just a few months before the London premiere of Hamilton's landmark exhibition *Man, Machine, and Motion,* which aimed to consider "as the essential material of history," machines that "extend the powers of the human body" and "the range of the senses."[75] The theories of information and communication explicated in the Eameses' film, like Norbert Wiener's thought specifically, informed Hamilton's early art and exhibition designs, and Hamilton would later fold a discussion of the Eameses' early cybernetic experiments in multiscreen sensory pedagogy into his lecture on Hollywood's widescreen technologies, "Glorious Technicolor, Breathtaking Cinemascope and Stereophonic Sound."[76] For the IG, the couple's work epitomized a media practice whose terrain was a sensorium remade through the "general field of visual communication," in which cultural value hierarchies collapse, and art and advertising, the designed object and industrial film are viewed equally as data-rich sign systems, organized by the choices and decisions of individual users.[77]

In 1956, for example, IG critic Lawrence Alloway chaired an IG discussion about the toys and films of the Eameses, and his brief essay, "Eames World," appeared in the *Architectural Association Journal.* Surveying the range of Eamesian production, Alloway argued that image-based toys such as House of Cards, a kit made up of photos collected by the Eameses from around the world, were the conceptual key to this universe because of their specific orientation toward the user or spectator. "Common to all Eames toys is a large margin of permissiveness regarding usage and interpretation by the spectator," Alloway observed, and yet "Eames retains a sort of remote control" over the user by "the given structure of his six slotted cards and by his initial choice of images."[78] This mixture of recombinant, user-driven, democratic choice and designer-fashioned control, for Alloway, hinged on the modular principle uniting the toys, "his own house in Venice, his storage units, and in the Herman Miller Furniture Company showrooms." "By leaving the use of his designs to the spectator," Alloway suggested, Eames exemplifies a pragmatic "approach to design defined by the conditions of use by and people's basic, symbol-making capacity."[79]

As heralded by the IG, then, the Eameses' design activity was nothing short of world making: it served as the hallmark of the technological saturation of postwar life in the American century, and as the apotheosis of an attitude toward technology and postwar Americanization on the continent that would shape the IG's pop sensibility. As for the Eameses, so too for IG artists such as Hamilton, Paolozzi, and McHale did the display technologies engaged in their art fuel a modernist collage practice that, at midcentury, achieved newly environmental and global aspirations: "In the '50s," Hamilton would later write, "we became aware of the possibility of seeing the whole world, at once through the great visual matrix that surrounds us; a synthetic, 'instant' view. Cinema, television, magazines, newspapers immersed the audience in a total environment and this new visual ambiance was photographic."[80]

One crucial midcentury enunciation of such global futurism was the IG's *This Is Tomorrow* exhibition of 1956, specifically the most popular of the show's twelve exhibits: a sensory environment designed and planned chiefly by McHale and Hamilton, and built by architect John Voelcker. No surprise, perhaps, that in the poster promoting *This Is Tomorrow,* IG artist Nigel Henderson chose to photograph the Group Six members in and around four seats plopped in the middle of a drab London street, including two Eiffel Tower–based fiberglass Eames chairs—the mise-en-scène of the exhibition's technofuturity. The show opened at the Whitechapel Art Gallery in August of that year with the help of a full-sized model of Robby the Robot, star of MGM's sci-fi film *Forbidden Planet.* A sweating human operator inside Robby, on loan from the studio, read text written by art critic Lawrence Alloway: "This is the first time a robot has opened an art exhibition," Robby explained. "Formerly, people were used."[81] No mournful lament of incipient automation's displacement of the human, it is a gag about a new midcentury attitude toward technics and pleasure, and its sci-fi iconography, that extended into the Group 2 exhibit of McHale and Hamilton. Here visitors would again encounter Robby, now flattened as a sixteen-foot-high color image, and with his inhuman hands full of the sensory blandishments of industrial art: one metallic arm cradles the ample bosom of a swooning blonde, on top of the other is collaged an image of Marilyn Monroe and her gravity-defying skirt from *The Seven Year Itch.* At the nexus of Hollywood cinema and science fiction, Robby, and the domain of expendable popular imagery he represents, would inspire Group 2's exploration of the new worlds of midcentury perception and sensation. It would play out within a designed environment that also included an inhabitable Möbius strip, part of the period-specific fascination with topology; a giant Guinness bottle; a jukebox; a massive "Cinemascope panel" that amassed the dazzling products of Hollywood's new scalar experiments in wide screen into an equally encompassing collage; a spongy floor that emitted strawberry air freshener when stepped on; and a disorienting fun house composed of optical illusions—Duchampian roto reliefs and an optical illusion "corridor"—that constituted kind of a mini-archive of two traditions of vanguard perceptual experimentation fueling Group 2's sense of "environment": the Bauhaus and Dada.

The show's environmental awareness was spawned, in part, by McHale's visit to the United States in 1955, where he had a yearlong fellowship at the Yale School of Fine Art. There, he would continue to work with Fuller as he studied under former Bauhaus painter Josef Albers. He also amassed the trunk of American ephemera (advertisements from newspapers and magazines, Elvis Presley records, and *Mad* magazines) whose contents made their way into Group 2's environment and served as a visual archive for Richard Hamilton's collage, *Just What Is It That Makes Today's Homes So Different, So Appealing . . . ?,* one of the defining works of British pop art, which appeared in Group 2's contribution to the *This Is Tomorrow* exhibition catalog. As he planned the Group 2 exhibition from the United States, in correspondence with Hamilton and others, McHale expressed his preoccupation with issues of perception, visual illusion, and science fiction: "Main kick now is perception via [Adelbert] Ames etc. coupled with Joe's [Albers] field of color vibration."[82] His notes and mock-up for the catalog layout, set forth in his correspondence, suggest "a largely visual-scientific" attitude, proposing "pictorial use of the equality E = MC, and also the standard diagram of 'sense extension,' derived from a book by E. W. Meyers," a British cybernetician who had addressed the IG in March 1955 in a lecture titled "Probability and Information Theory and Their Application to the Visual Arts."[83]

McHale's perceptual investments and their sources informed Group 2's catalog statement, which asserted that "tomorrow can only extend the range of the present body of visual experiences" and called for "the development of our perceptual potentialities to accept and utilize the

Figure 2.12. *This Is Tomorrow* exhibition, Whitechapel Art Gallery, 1956, London: Group 2 exhibit-c. Royal Institute of British Architects.

continual enrichment of visual material" (*IG*, 154). Crucially, the cata log continued, because we exist "at a point in human affairs where the actual nature of [practical accepted] reality as traditionally evidenced by the senses is under question," the exhibition will not reify or stabilize the nature of that reality but rather underline the very "discrepancy between physical fact and perception of the fact, and the way this discrepancy may be so magnified by traditional attitudes and assumptions as to obscure the significance of the factual reality" (*IG*, 154). Thus, the exhibition's sensory inducements, and its particular preference for optical illusion, are cast as a perceptual training ground for reckoning with a changed ratio among human organism, environment, and sensorium: "Any change in man's environment is indicative of a change in man's relationship to it, in his actual mode of perceiving and symbolizing his interaction with it" (*IG*, 154). This language allows for a way of thinking about the idiom of scale taken up in the exhibition, and indeed in the catalog's language of extension and magnification. The fun house, we might say, is an environment of an environment, about which it seeks to provide knowledge and information: it is a "complex of sense experience which is so organized, or disorganized, as to provide acute awareness of our sensory function in an environmental situation" (*IG*, 154).

The preoccupations of Group 2's catalog constitute a kind of rough draft of McHale's landmark essay, "The Expendable Ikon," published in two parts in *Architectural Design* in 1959. The essay defines the work of the architect and designer as "participants in the process of mass communications," and offers an inquiry into the "ikonic content" of the mass media, both in its visuality and within a communications network.[84] McHale argues that the goal of the ikon in human evolution, from totems and masks, or poetry and cathedrals, to contemporary science fiction and stars such as Monroe and Presley, is to *communicate environmentally*: "Aside from conveying simple messages about the disposition of perceptual reality in the everyday world, there is the more complex communication by sign, symbol or 'loaded image,' of statements about man's total environmental situation" (*ER*, 48). What *has* changed the quality of the ikon's communicability—as an "array of symbolic images" of the human condition—is its own environment, the second machine age, and its newly scaled sensorium: "Culturally a period of enormous expansion and exploration; the whole range of the sensory spectrum has been extended—man can see more, hear more, travel faster—experience more than ever before. His environment extensions, movie, TV, picture magazine, bring to his awareness an unprecedented scope" (*ER*, 49). With these "changes in the human condition" comes the demand for "symbolic images" of humanness on pace with "the requirements of constant change, fleeting impressions and a high rate of obsolescence. A replaceable, expendable series of ikons" (*ER*, 49). McHale's logic is that the second machine age's extension of the regular operations of the human sensorium has, in its very defamiliarization of the human condition, produced a new, compensatory preoccupation with man at "the centre of the picture" (*ER*, 52). The expendable ikon is thus an "anthropocentric ikon" (*ER*, 52) whose historically contingent forms circulate in the repetition of images of "man" in various environmental relations. As examples of these image environments, McHale suggested various categories: robots, mutants, and mecanomorphs; outer space as a frontier of science and technology; industrial design's modes of commodifying "tomorrow"; the quiz show; Elvis Presley; and the rivalry between television and Hollywood over the locations and scales of the screen, what he called the "alchemy of the moving image in the rectangle" (*ER*, 59).

In sum, McHale's expendable ikon is at the center of an image ecology and a worldly midcentury sensorium shaped by the economic horizon of Americanization and the "democracy" of consumption within Britain's postwar boom. It is a "world" characterized by a new temporality of obsolescence, repetition, and expendability (rather than permanency and uniqueness). It is a world preoccupied with the status of the image, and "imageability," for its capacity to communicate about, and within, a "total environment." And it is a world marked by a specifically environmental idiom and practice whose aspirations toward aesthetic wholeness underscored the world concept's long-standing relationship to "problems of totality, self-enclosure, and spatiotemporal relations," and thereby resuscitated a modernist investment in the *Gesamtkunstwerk* in the process.[85] Because the worldly sensorium seeks to gauge the space-times of the new nature and its putative changes to the human condition, it not only relied on a scalar language to do so but also was supplemented by image technologies whose powers of scalar manipulation revealed new worlds. This last point of emphasis, on the capacity of images and image technologies to reveal worlds *beyond* the human senses, was a consistent point of fascination in the IG exhibitions, as it was for Kepes's *New Landscape*.[86]

In McHale's case, this preoccupation with the worldliness of the midcentury image ecology deepened and expanded in ambition through his transformative encounter with Buckminster Fuller, whose relationship to technology he discussed at length in an overview of the designer's work in 1956. In the early 1960s, McHale would join Fuller at Southern Illinois University. There he wrote the first biography of Fuller, received his Ph.D. in sociology on the concept of the future in social thought, and served as executive director of Fuller's Inventory of World Resources, Human Trends, and Needs. The collaboration joined McHale's long-standing preoccupation with the total environment of midcentury information and image ecologies, begun in the context of the Independent Group, with a Fulleresque approach to worldliness. McHale shared his mentor Fuller's concern with natural ecologies, the problem of global resources and their equitable distribution, the search for humane, sustainable modes of "world dwelling," and his quasi-perfectionist belief in the power of science and technology as tools of human betterment within a broader philosophy of "comprehensive design science."[87]

The appeal and the problem of Fuller's worldliness have received sustained scholarly attention of late from a new generation of artists, as well as architectural and design historians. At stake in the most recent Fuller vogue is the contemporary relevance of his consistent ecological mandate to "think world."[88] During the heyday of the last Fuller vogue in the 1960s and 1970s, the terms of this worldliness made him a kind of hero to the counterculture, and a key figure in a number of strains of neo-avant-garde and postformalist aesthetic practice.[89] Today, Fuller's consistent preoccupations with the global management of populations and resources have found a new appeal for contemporary architects, designers, and planners invested in sustainable design and development practices, and yet critically sensitive to the potential complicity between Fuller's technocratic leanings and the operation of contemporary biopolitics.[90] Simultaneously, scholars have cast Fuller as a prophet of the information age, and an influential artist who brought the practice of design and architecture into dialogue with image-making technologies, media infrastructures, and communication networks.[91] This Fuller is less an architect than a data visualization strategist, preoccupied with coping with massive flows of information whose gathering, management, and processing through ever-vaster global databases would be the linchpin of any just, equitable distribution of the world's finite resources—the very guarantor of future human survival on "Spaceship Earth."

Perhaps the most telling design project in this vein was Fuller's Geoscope, which linked resource and data management in a futurist quest for a global view of the world *as* information system, and thus joined a range of Fuller's attempts at worldly visualization. Fuller began the project in 1952 with John McHale. Working with architecture students at Cornell University, the University of Minnesota, and Princeton University, Fuller and McHale developed a series of prototypes for an enormous globe, two hundred feet in diameter, whose goal was "to afford the viewer a swift and comprehensive awareness of man in the universe, to provide a World View."[92] Composed of triangular panels that recalled Fuller's Dymaxion Air-Ocean World Map (1943), the Geoscope's glowing surface—dotted with millions of lightbulbs whose display patterns and varying intensity would be controlled by a computer—would "graphically display the inventory and patterns of the world's resources and needs, in real time, slowed down, or speeded up, simultaneously or separately, for study and comparison—from stock trading and voting trends to weather patterns, tourist routes to military movements."[93] Fuller promoted the Geoscope as a gambit to render the totality of the earth's resources for view: "to satisfy the same need of humanity—to comprehend the total planetary, all-evolutionary historical significance of each day's development."[94] Over the course of the 1960s, he proposed a number of properly worldly venues for the Geoscope: a rotating installation in cities hosting the Olympic Games; permanently installed in the East River, suspended by cables across from the United Nations building; or displayed at the U.S. Pavilion at Expo 67 in Montreal. There, the Geoscope would serve as a database for Fuller's World Game, in which players equipped with information about the world's conditions, events, and resources would construct competing speculative scenarios about various planetary futures, and thus be trained in the art of steering "Spaceship Earth."

For Fuller, too, this was homeostatic art yoking cybernetic principles of feedback and governance to a vision of "global humanity liberated from nation-based constraints, a humanity comprising 'nomadic citizens of the world.'"[95]

An unrealized artifact of midcentury world making, the Geoscope project of Fuller and McHale dovetails with the worldly pedagogies of perceptual training and exercises in global awareness and communication at the center of the Eameses' multiscreen experiments from the early 1950s through the mid-1960s, for example, *Think*. IG members such as Alloway recognized in the design practice of Fuller and the Eameses a similar fluidity of scale in which the "world" of an Eames toy (e.g., House of Cards) announced the same pedagogical dialectic of user freedom and designer control that would play out in their multiscreen experiments and the worldly citizenship they sought to inculcate.[96] McHale, for his part, connected an Eamesian ethos of "catalogue building" to the global reach of Fuller's own approach to mass production, most evident in the geodesic domes and their increasingly global locations (*ER*, 134–35). For McHale, such "catalogue building" transpires within the midcentury's image ecologies and distribution networks. In the Eameses'

Figure 2.13. Mini-Earth above the East River, drawing by Winslow Wedin, 1955. R. Buckminster Fuller Papers, M 1090, Department of Special Collections, Stanford University Libraries, Stanford, California. Courtesy, The Estate of R. Buckminster Fuller.

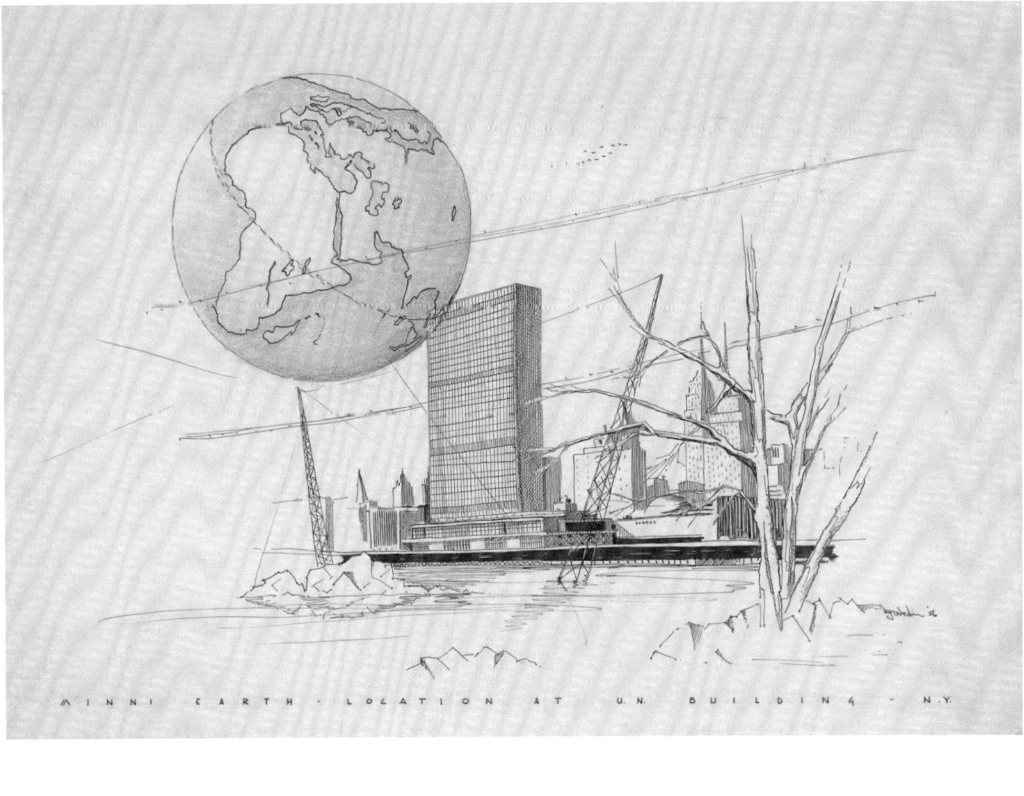

case, "catalogue building," as a "mecano aesthetics," joins the toy to their famous Case Study house (built of prefabricated parts customized by a user) and to their extension of "the designer's attitude into other management areas," such as filmmaking and consulting for IBM (*ER*, 135). The Eameses build through a collage-like process of receiving, extracting, and distributing images: "extracting components from catalogues, and seeing their own designs get into catalogues" (*ER*, 134). Fuller, relatedly, builds by exploiting fits between the scalability of the geodesic dome and other midcentury exercises in expansion: "Fuller domes grow more geographically widespread: radomes in the Artic, a concert hall in the South Seas and the recent one in Kabul, Afghanistan," for the U.S. Pavilion in the International Trade Fair, where it "housed, among other items, an 80-ft. Cinemascope screen" (*ER*, 135–36).

Scalar fluidity in the work of Fuller, the Eameses, and the IG itself animated a design practice with worldly ambitions, and pressed cinema and other moving-image technologies to expand beyond their normal institutional operations and sites. Understood this way, the Geoscope is itself a site of medial expansion: the technical failures of its prototypes to deliver on a dream of a total world picture fueled Fuller and McHale's own intermedial experimentation with a range of state-of-the-art image-making technologies, including multiscreen "projection devices, flat-screen data displays, triangular-faced television tubes, new kinds of photography, multi-slide machines, microfilm, eight-millimeter cinema units, videotape mechanisms for film and data storage, and so on."[97] For McHale and Fuller, the dream of the Geoscope would be linked to its thinking brain—a networked computer fed by the "embryonic" networks of various libraries, universities, and international agencies, constituting a buildingless "global university orchestrated by communications satellites, transistor radios, television sets."[98] The product of this networked, mass-mediated university would be a newly postnational world citizen, one who thinks not in binaries (us–them), but ecologically, in dynamic "relationships." In his 1965 keynote address at the Vision 65 conference in Carbondale, Illinois, Fuller would adduce the Geoscope as a device for the dynamic apprehension of a transfigured universe itself—as a "nonsimultaneous complex of unique motions and transformations," in which world society operates "almost exclusively in the inaudible nonvisible area of the physical universe."[99] Frustrated "by all of our local, static organizations of an obsolete yesterday," Fuller's Geoscope would thus augur the emergence of a new "world man"—one who would conceive vision, communication, and the senses within new, experimental, intermedial configurations that reflect just such a mobile universe.[100] One such world man was Gene Youngblood, and his name for these dynamic configurations was "expanded cinema."

Expanded Cinema as Design Science

Youngblood's canonical study, *Expanded Cinema* (1970), is everywhere announced as groundbreaking, but nowhere taken very seriously. Andrew Uroskie, for example, acknowledges the debt of Youngblood's "world historical visions" to the work of Fuller, Marshall McLuhan, and Norman O. Brown.[101] Yet Uroskie also seeks to separate Youngblood's rhetoric of "expanded consciousness" from another idea of expanded cinema that emerged in New York between 1964 and 1966, one imbued with a postminimalist sense of cinematic site specificity and institutional self-awareness. But this approach misunderstands the Eameses' work as preoccupied with "mere" scalar expansion as a strategy of sensory immersion, rather than as the fluid terrain of a design practice preoccupied with the vexing new nature of the postwar and seeking to apprehend the contours of a worldly sensorium spawned in its wake. Approached through the design genealogy sketched earlier in this chapter, Youngblood's *Expanded Cinema* appears less as a "tour de force of parascholarly speculation" than as the conceptual formalization of many of the assumptions behind the media practice of the Eameses, McHale, and Fuller.[102] The landmark study codifies, in a countercultural idiom, the designers' long-standing preoccupation with the evolutionary recalibration of the human sensorium to the new worlds of the midcentury, and their commitment to forms of speculative futurism. On the heels of *Expanded Cinema*'s publication, in fact, Youngblood would appear in 1971 at the International Design Conference in Aspen—a key venue for conceptualizing the worldly humane mission of the designer, as I'll explain in the next chapter.

As a final example of the tangled aesthetic and intellectual genealogies of designer pedagogy, I will return briefly to Youngblood's study, specifically the chapter titled "The Artist as Design Scientist," and Susan Sontag's canonical "One Culture and the New Sensibility" (1964). The pairing is less capricious than it may seem: Youngblood explicitly takes up the essays from Sontag's *Against Interpretation* (1966) in *Expanded Cinema* as part of his eclectic bibliography. In this breathless four-page chapter, Youngblood includes not just Sontag herself ("On Style," in this instance) but also Jacob Bronowski, Arthur Eddington, Herbert Read, A. N. Whitehead, Ludwig Wittgenstein, Rudolf Arnheim, and John Cage. It is the culminating chapter of the first part of the book, titled "The Audience and the Myth of Entertainment," whose goal, broadly

Figure 2.14.
Cover, Gene Youngblood, *Expanded Cinema* (Dutton, 1970).

speaking, is to critique the operations of industrial-commercial entertainment as ill suited to the "experiential needs of an aesthetically impoverished culture," and fundamentally out of step with the radical coevolution of the human condition and the contemporary "intermedia" environment (what Youngblood calls, following Fluxus artist Dick Higgins, the "intermedia network").[103]

Locating the terms of this radical coevolution within the transition between the industrial and postindustrial age, Youngblood proposes the term "Paleocybernetic" as a conceptual tool best suited to comprehend "the significance of our present environment" (*EC,* 41). The term captures the "practical utopianism" he associates with cybernetic thought, and the primitive potential of humankind that realizes "there is no such thing as human nature." Instead, the human is "relative to its past and present conditioning," and so can be improved, its capacities "expanded" through control of its environment, whose media and technologies share and transmit our "symbolic needs and their expression on a world scale" (*EC,* 55). Although expanded cinema, Youngblood insists, means "expanded consciousness," industrial-commercial cinema perpetuates a manipulative "system of conditioned response to formula," circulating redundant and entropic messages and thus "increasing our degree of ignorance about" the human condition (*EC,* 62). Youngblood's application of cybernetics and communications theory—as in, for example, Norbert Wiener's definition of information—is rather loose, resulting in formulations such as the following:

> From the cinema, we receive conceptual information (ideas) and design information (experiences). In concert, they become one phenomenon, which I've described as the experiential information of aesthetic conceptual design. This information is either useful (additive) or redundant. Useful information accelerates change. Redundant information restricts change. If sustained long enough, redundant information becomes misinformation, which results in negative change. (*EC,* 62)

Not quite gobbledygook, nor entirely lucid, this passage is symptomatic of Youngblood's desire here and elsewhere to overlap a modernist and countercultural commitment to experience (perceptual novelty, change, the interruption of routine and habit) with an idiom of design, and to draw on cybernetic concepts (information, feedback, communication, negentropy) in doing so. In this way, Youngblood's *Expanded Cinema* is fully in keeping with an important strain of experimental art practice in the 1960s informed by Fuller and McHale, as well as McLuhan, that brought ecological art into the domain of an information aesthetics that would unfold in open systems and planetary networks.[104]

This impulse comes to a head in the chapter titled "Artist as Design Scientist," where Youngblood observes that art and science are united by a desire to "order the facts of experience," and then redefines the work of the artist through an etymology of design:

> The word "design" is composed of "de" and "sign," indicating that it means "to remove the symbol of." In this context "symbol" signifies ideas distinct from experiences. As design scientist the artist discovers

> and perfects language that corresponds more directly to experience; he develops hardware that embodies its own software as a conceptual tool for coping with reality. He separates the image from its official symbolic meaning and reveals its hidden potential, its process, its actual reality, the experience of the thing. (*EC,* 71)

As etymology, this is pretty thin. But it attests to the influence of the design metaphor as a way of confronting the midcentury's new sense of worldliness, and clarifies its anxious location at the dawn of the posthuman. What Youngblood wants in "aesthetic conceptual design information" is, he makes clear, liberation from official or "ordinary" vision. Such vision's ordering and conditioning of experience through symbols works with old ideas and old information, and within an old-world picture with an outmoded conception of the human organism at its center: "The historical preoccupation with finding the one idea that is Man will give way to the idea that earth is, and then to the idea of other earths" (*EC,* 49). Youngblood's call for properly ecological consciousness entails the "end of archetypal Man" and consequently, the redefinition of some of the central markers of the human: intelligence and morality, man and environment, progress and creativity: "What happens to our definition of 'man' when our next door neighbor is a cyborg (a human with inorganic parts)? . . . What happens to our definition of 'environment' when our video extensions bring us the reality of the solar system daily? What do we mean by 'nature' under these circumstances?" (*EC,* 52). As a result of such shifts, Youngblood continues, humans now live in another "world." And this inability to recalibrate humans to worlds, to provide them with nonredundant information about their condition sufficient to the complexity of the new environments in which they find themselves, is for Youngblood the chief problem with popular commercial cinema: its idiom "speaks to a world that no longer exists"; "for one thing," as he explains, " 'world' now includes the microcosm of the atom and the macrocosm of the universe in one spectrum" (*EC,* 54). Youngblood's ecological call for expanded consciousness—its mandate for "a new cinema that takes us to another world entirely"—thus deploys the idiom of art as a "design science" because design, in the technocosmopolitan tradition of Eames, Nelson, Kepes, Fuller, and McHale that Youngblood takes up and extends, had already firmly established its own concern with the transfigured physis of the midcentury. And the force of this tradition is evident in Fuller's lengthy introduction to *Expanded Cinema,* which casts the book as a coping strategy—a way of providing "worldaround man with the most effective communication techniques for speaking universal language to universal man"—and in Youngblood's dependence on McHale himself as his primary theorist of the status of "expendability and impermanence in radical evolution" (*EC*, 51).[105]

While Susan Sontag's mandarin cool and controlled style of intellectual history seem a world apart from the loose West Coast sensibility of Youngblood, her canonical essay, "One Culture and the New Sensibility," exemplifies how the aspirations at the heart of the designer pedagogy sketched here make for strange bedfellows. In fact, the essay anticipates a number of the tropes and preoccupations of Youngblood's study, especially the premium he places on transformed experience and consciousness, with the radically extended media that deliver it, and the new scales and worlds through which they operate. The essay is motivated by a challenge to a "facile humanism" that would, in the model of C. P. Snow's "two cultures" formulation, set the values of art and science into opposition. To do so, Sontag observes a sweeping redefinition, and expansion, of the aesthetic: "Art today is a new kind of instrument, an instrument for modifying consciousness and organizing new modes of sensibility. And the means for practicing art have been radically extended" ("OC," 296). Crucially, for Sontag, the primary feature of the new sensibility is "that its model product is not the literary work, above all, the novel," but rather expresses a new "non-literary culture" that includes "certain painters, sculptors, architects, social planners, filmmakers, TV technicians, neurologists, musicians, electronics engineers, dancers, philosophers, and sociologists" ("OC," 298). Her list of authors of the key texts of this new cultural alignment includes not just Nietzsche, Wittgenstein, Artaud, Breton, Barthes, and Lévi-Strauss, but also a number of crucial figures in the history and theory of modern architecture and design: Giedion, McLuhan, Kepes, and, of course, Fuller.

While it is often credited as a foundational enunciation of a postmodern sensibility, "One Culture" is better understood as an essay that bears the traces of the postwar displacement of humanist literary value by the informatic "cool" of design. By this, I mean design's midcentury vogue and prestige and its nonsentimental dispensation toward a sensorium transfigured by postwar technoscience, and administered by Eames-era "technicians" and "specialists" (Sontag's terms). Such technicians tend to think of art as "problem solving," and their instrumental approach to "the analysis and extension of sensation" operates irrespective of media, and across cultural value hierarchies. Thus, for Sontag the "coolness" of this nonliterary culture, where the "artist's work is only his idea, his concept," becomes at once the hallmark of an incipient conceptualism in the arts, and the echo of "a familiar practice in architecture" ("OC," 297). Because the sensibility conceives art as the "disciplining of the feelings and programming of sensations," it rejects the dichotomy between a "morally neutral science and technology" and "morally committed, human-scale art" ("OC," 300). Instead, advanced art's "unclosing" of the senses requires an attunement to unprecedented changes in a sensory environment now rescaled, Sontag observes, toward the "infra" or "ultra" sensorial, an "environment which cannot be grasped fully by the senses" ("OC," 300–302). Sontag's guide to the infrasensorial is, perhaps unsurprisingly, Fuller himself, one of the central inspirations of Youngblood's self-understanding as "a child of the New Age, for whom 'nature' is the solar system, and 'reality' is an invisible environment of messages" (*EC*, 45).

As Sontag sees it, midcentury designers expanded exponentially the range of what counted as meaningful communicative situations and environments for human sensation, attending to the senses' remaking in built environments and technical networks that now exceed humans, and urge them to rescale the human domains of perception, attention, and awareness. This design-centric genealogy of expanded cinema practices is concerned less with repudiating the Greenbergian fetishes of aesthetic reflexivity and autonomy than with carving out an anxious, "human-scale" modernism that begins with a Fullerian aim: to live well at the dawn of the posthuman, and within an unstable climate of bewildering technological change and a transformed physis. This designer pedagogy, and its modernism, traversed a midcentury moment defined by the sheer multiplicity of worlds, times, and natures, often on the thresholds of sensation, and thus fueled new, decidedly uncertain formal experiments. Designers sought to train postwar citizens to sense themselves as embedded in worldly relationships; to think beyond disciplinary boundaries; to cope with vast amounts of information; to anticipate the new and contingent; to adjudicate value, and to decide. Designer pedagogy responded to such changes in worldedness with new strategies of sensory management and discipline, and new models of speculative futurism. As a pedagogical technique of security in change, such happiness was forged in an educational climate marked by a sweeping rethinking of the needs, capacities, and skills of what would be known as the postindustrial knowledge worker.

Designer pedagogy thus demands keener attention to the implication of the sensorium in debates about how screen cultures and their institutional sites abet forms of governmentality, and to the sensation of democracy itself in the designed environments of postwar life, including expanded cinema. Within this modernism, the sensible conditions of democratic life blurred with the tactile solicitations of a strange new object horizon. Democratic perception, like democratic citizenship, was enabled by postwar technologies of freedom and control that operated under the expansive rubric of "communications," and fueled an aesthetics of information in which designers, as artists and experts, played essential roles.[106] As I'll argue in the next chapter, one key site for this emergent aesthetics of communication, information, and interdisciplinary knowledge production was the postwar design conference. From Aspen, Colorado, to Carbondale, Illinois, film and moving-image media's prominence as managerial technologies brought the domains of filmmaking and design, modernism and corporate aesthetics, into a broader Cold War administration of culture and *Bildung.* In conferencing, an urgent occasion for modernist media practice, designers conceptualized a powerful communicative form in its own right and explored a key technique in their world-making activities.

3

management cinema

Film, Communication, and Postwar World Making in Aspen

TO MY KNOWLEDGE, the name Rhodes Patterson appears in none of the standard studies of documentary, amateur, or industrial filmmaking in the postwar era. Nor is it indexed in design histories of the Cold War period in the United States, which gravitate, with good reason, toward star designers like the Eameses, George Nelson, or Saul Bass during the period in which the design profession's new, global visibility was tightly bound to the productive capacity and affluence of the West in the throes of the "great acceleration."[1] Yet Patterson's work, which crossed the domains of filmmaking and design, was situated at the heart of an ambitious campaign to bring modern design—and with it, shards of a modernist utopianism—into the ambit of a corporate aesthetics.

His utility film, *International Design Conference in Aspen: The First Decade* (ca. 1961), sponsored by the Container Corporation of America, is an especially good example. By the early 1960s, as we will see, the IDCA had established itself as a crucial institution for the midcentury merger of the corporation, the designer, and a late-Bauhaus aesthetic retooled for American-style democratic liberalism. Taking stock of the IDCA's inaugural decade, Patterson's twenty-minute film captures a key moment in the consolidation of the conference; it memorializes its institutional emergence, reifies its organization, and promotes the significance of its future iterations for what the film's voice-over calls "our total culture"—a telling phrase. Generically, it is a kind of industrial "process" film, only here what is documented is not the production and functionality of a product or commodity but the making of the conference as a space of postwar knowledge production, spawned from its founder

Walter Paepcke's inspired conception. The fruits of the conferees' immaterial labor—panels, speeches, keynotes, seminars—are documented through film and audio recordings. The film is largely composed of highlights from the first decade of the conference proceedings, reassembled through Patterson's editing, and organized by a voice-over. Structured according to the IDCA's typical five-day conference schedule, Patterson's film is a kind of metacommunicative work. It talkily performs the surfeit of communication that sustains, and thus organizes, Aspen as a "creatively oriented conclave," stressing that even the seemingly extracurricular conference moments—impromptu poolside chats—are "sites of significant conversation." One can't *escape* communication at Aspen. At postwar conferences like this, all talk is meaningful, and all space is space *for talk.* Fed back into the organization, conversation sustains the IDCA as its discursive lifeblood. In this way, *IDCA: The First Decade* exemplifies the midcentury designer's way of thinking film itself: as a "communicative" medium, a mode of organization, and thus, a technology of postwar management.[2]

Patterson's film earned an unofficial riposte a decade later in *IDCA 1970,* a vérité-influenced film codirected by Claudia Weill and Eli Noyes, the son of Eliot F. Noyes, the industrial designer and architect responsible for reinventing IBM's corporate image in the 1950s and 1960s. Noyes Sr. had served as the chairman of the IDCA's board of directors until resigning, exhausted and disillusioned, on the heels of the tumultuous events of the 1970 conference, Environment by Design, documented arrestingly in his son's film. That summer, the generally sunny proceedings of this then-mainstream design institution were clouded over by the protests of a number of environmental action groups invited to the conference, including the activist multimedia collective Ant Farm and a "French delegation" headed by Jean Aubert and Jean Baudrillard of the Utopie

Figure 3.1. Leisure and communication in Aspen, featuring Morton Goldsholl and Herber Bayer. *IDCA: The First Decade,* ca. 1961, directed by Rhodes Patterson. Courtesy of the Chicago Film Archive.

group. Indeed, two important media-theoretical essays by Baudrillard, "Requiem for the Media" (1971) and "Design and Environment" (1972), would follow directly from the turmoil of IDCA '70. From a variety of positions, the student activists attacked the modernist orthodoxies of the conference and the media theory abetting it. Critiquing the IDCA's eschewal of politics from questions of ecology, they took issue with the nonparticipatory, one-way communication of the conference itself, which one so-called dissident mocked as a "fourteenth-century lecture system in the age of media, film, etc."[3] In effect, the protesters upended the IDCA's long-standing ideals of communicative clarity and transparency across disciplinary boundaries, jamming the IDCA corporate message with the noise of dissensus. George Nelson, convinced like other attendees that the conference would never recover, stepped down as IDCA president, saying, "I feel after this conference battered, bruised, stale, and weary, and I am of the impression we have come to the end of the line."

IDCA 1970 documents the confrontation of conference technique with the emergence of potentially inassimilable ideas and values. Throughout, Noyes Jr. and Weill's camera seeks to capture moments of ideological contestation or discursive impasse, and to document seeming breaches in conference form, many coming from conference outsiders. Such communicative breakdowns challenge what Saul Bass calls the "enlightened self-interest" of the IDCA's board of directors and its own visions of totality, throwing the designers of the interface into a state of profound, soul-searching unhappiness. As a kind of unhappy cinema vérité, *IDCA 1970*'s technique never quite rises to an undermining of its own formal powers of depiction, but neither does it work in an idealist sphere of nonmediation. Its style has learned the medial lessons of this noisy conference. Every gesture recorded, every change of

Figure 3.2. Scenes from the contentious IDCA 1970 meeting, Environment by Design, in *IDCA 1970*, 1970, directed by Eliot Noyes Jr. and Claudia Weill.

posture, every conference table, every amphitheater has been ideologically "imprinted."[4] The charged media of the IDCA's messages are ripe for antagonistic exchange, their communications semantically unstable and primarily political.

IDCA 1970 clarifies how the conference, two decades in, had become a lightning rod for midcentury debates about communication, design, and their mutual implication in a modernist aesthetics transformed by the media environments and politics of the Cold War. But the postwar design conference had long been a site for exploring film and moving-image media from various domains of expertise and disciplinary knowledge, and it remains an unexplored location for the historiography of modernist designs on film in the postwar period. What kind of knowledge about film, or new approaches to moving images, would be produced at locations like this, in an era of "groupthink" and think tanks with their own designs on the Cold War semiosphere?[5] What would a modernist film theory look like if it were hatched—at midcentury—in the mountains of Aspen, Colorado, then in the process of being redeveloped not just for postwar leisure (skiing, naturally) but also as the cultural ground zero of a corporate-sponsored humanism?

This chapter approaches these questions by discussing the role of film at the IDCA from its inception in the early 1950s in the context of a wide-ranging experiment in corporate *Bildung*, through the 1959 conference, Communication: The Image Speaks, the first explicitly devoted to conceptualizing film *as communication*, and within a competitive terrain of media evolution. Typical of the IDCA's wide-ranging constituencies, this conference was not only attended by TV executives, educators, and social scientists but also played host to major figures of modernist filmmaking at midcentury, including Norman McLaren and Len Lye. The presence of vanguard artists such as these, and also, later, John Cage,

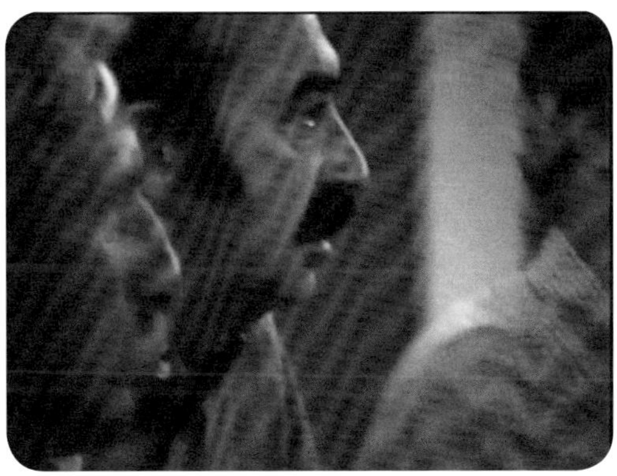

Figure 3.3. Brochure for Communication: The Image Speaks, Ninth International Design Conference in Aspen, 1959. Will Burtin Papers, RIT Libraries: Graphic Design Archive, Rochester Institute of Technology.

John Whitney, Stan VanDerBeek, Archigram, Allan Kaprow, Nam June Paik, and Gene Youngblood, would be a fairly regular feature at IDCA in its first two decades.[6] On the one hand, this is a testament to the competing and contradictory media practices and aesthetic politics given a platform at a conference that began by proposing to consider design "as a function of management." But it is also a provocation to consider film's own role and conceptualization as a managerial technology in an age when, as Theodor Adorno put it, "whoever speaks about culture speaks of administration as well."[7] This chapter and the following one approach the international design conference as an important midcentury form, and a genre of knowledge work in its own right. As these two IDCA documentaries clarify, at this moment, the so-called technique of the conference—*as* communication and *among* other media and technologies of communication—was subjected to heightened scrutiny across disciplinary boundaries. Chapter 4 homes in on two other landmark design conferences of the postwar period: Vision 65 and Vision 67. Chaired by the German émigré designer Will Burtin, a founding member of the IDCA and an Aspen regular, the Vision conferences shared many of the conceptual and political aspirations of the IDCA, featured a number of

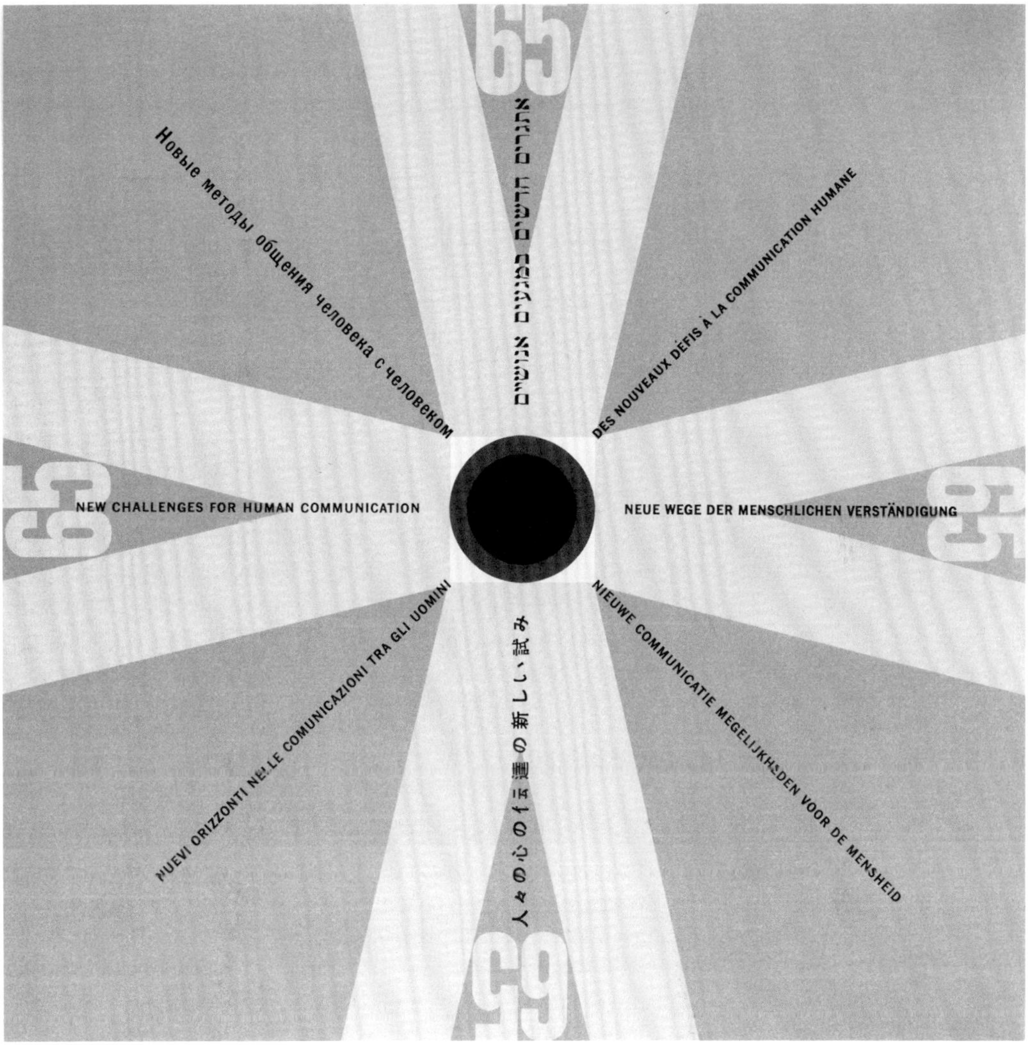

the same speakers, and were organized and supported by some of the key players and institutions that buoyed the so-called Aspen phenomenon. Together, these chapters argue that the IDCA and Vision conferences constitute part of a larger organizational *dispositif*—a broad constellation of knowledge, discourse, and material practices—that emerged to meet the challenges of the postwar world order over which the designer would now preside. There, conferees would think film as they came to grips with the broader role of communication—its media, its technologies, its global infrastructures—in organizing and administering the future of that world. As indicated in the ambitious full title of Vision 65—World Congress on New Challenges for Human Communication—new

Figure 3.4. Brochure for Vision 65: New Challenges for Human Communication, designed by Will Burtin. Will Burtin Papers, RIT Libraries: Graphic Design Archive, Rochester Institute of Technology.

techniques and technologies of management would be hashed out in this crucial space of midcentury knowledge production: the conference. By conferencing, technicians of international communication engaged in a novel, ritualistic form of postwar discursivity. Drawing out the competing variety of film theories staged at IDCA, and the range of institutional locations abetting them, this chapter allows us to begin to resee the midcentury as a similarly promiscuous terrain of media experimentation—one that made strange bedfellows of humanists, social scientists, corporate interests, and government agencies, who competed and collaborated on projects to "manage populations by managing media."[8]

Conferencing

Patterson's minor IDCA film underscores how the conference as a form and a technique achieved new visibility and political significance in a geopolitical era in which the aftermath of totalitarian nationalism, total war, and atomic annihilation had proved to many observers the catastrophic failures of communication. Always conference! So, we might say, is E. M. Forster's humanist injunction ("Only connect!") recast at midcentury within what John Durham Peters has called the "therapeutic project"—a crucial site of the "postwar buoyancy about communication."[9] UNESCO, founded in 1945, would wed its global projects of visual education and its groundbreaking studies of national media infrastructures to the UN's foundational ideals of a peaceful postwar order marked by the free and democratic flow of information. In its famous "Tensions" project, UNESCO convened in Paris in 1948 an international conference of social scientists to explore the psychological dynamics of nations that led to tension, hostility, and the outbreak of war. Understanding the globe as a single psychological system, the "Tensions" group assumed, in Fred Turner's words, that "international relations between nations too could be modeled as if they were small-group interpersonal relations taking place on a global scale."[10] In UNESCO's therapeutic understanding of communication as "global enlightenment," the international conference was enshrined for its capacity to operationalize the healing powers of universal humanism.[11] So, while the knowledge work of the "Tensions" conferees yielded studies such as *The Tensions That Cause Wars* (1950), UNESCO also convened in Paris in 1948 a "meeting of experts for the preliminary study of the technique of international conferences" themselves, and, in 1951, published *The Technique of International Conferences: A Progress Report on Research Problems and Methods.*

One expert who regularly attended these and other UNESCO conferences was the ubiquitous anthropologist Margaret Mead. In 1968 Mead coauthored with Columbia University's Paul Byers a fascinating study, *The Small Conference: An Innovation in Communication,* in which she made the argument for the "small substantive conference" as "new social invention."[12] A key text in the domain of metacommunication constitutive of what we might call midcentury conference theory, Mead's slim volume was the fruit of her decades-long experience with the conference form as both theorist and participant. This included a spate of conferences convened by UNESCO, the UN, and the World Health Organization, but also, importantly, the Macy Conferences (1941–60), described by Mead as formally exemplifying "the newly realized principles of feedback and error correction"; the American Academy of Arts and Sciences Conferences (1962, 1965); the Delos Symposia (1963, 1964, 1965), a floating conference in the Greek islands meant to model its founder's abiding interest in "networking operations" through the interactions of the far-flung experts brought on board; and the 1956 "conference on conferences," held in Eastbourne, England, in 1956 (*SC*, 10).[13] The proceedings of this last, cosponsored by the Josiah Macy Jr. Foundation and the World Federation of Mental Health, were published in book form in 1960 as *Communication or Conflict: Conferences; Their Nature, Dynamics, and Planning,* but received extensive coverage in a 1957 special issue of the journal *ETC: A Review of General Semantics,* edited by S. I. Hayakawa, including Mead's own report "A Meta-Conference." There, Mead explained one tangible result of the proceedings' immaterial labor as having arrived at a definition of their own object and occasion, the conference: *"The new institution of an expanding body of knowledge in a shrinking world."*[14]

For Mead, to participate in the knowledge work of a conference is to be sensually involved in a special kind of boundary-breaking, organized process—one fit to meet the "new hardships on the scholar and scientist" posed by "the information explosion" (*SC*, 11). At its therapeutic best, conference communication is multimodal and nonlinear, requiring "continuous participation" and consistent, self-correcting "systemic appraisal" of the behavior of others (*SC*, 108, 7). To participate in the "conference situation" is to experience a dynamic form of "organization and process" at once protoecological and explicitly cybernetic (*SC*, 108).[15] The "situation" is structured to "permit the participants to act as whole individuals, using all of their senses as they seldom do in the narrower, more specialized contexts of other forms of professional and academic life" (*SC*, 108, 29). To think together with others *across* disciplines and generations—as this special form allows—is both to act as a whole individual and to participate, sensually, in a "group of minds" that can manage informatic excess, that can "tap large stores of knowledge quickly as a means of developing new ideas and new knowledge" (*SC*, 57).

As organized occasions for communication, the IDCA and Vision conferences emerged with similar midcentury aspirations toward a

Figure 3.5.
Cover, Margaret Mead and Paul Byers, *The Small Conference* (1968).

kind of boundary-breaking interdisciplinarity Mead championed. The design conference was one such management technique during the mid-century period presided over by the postwar corporation, the geopolitical hegemony of the West, and the designer—one of the Cold War's more fetishized figures of anthropogenesis. At the postwar design conference, a kind of industrial common sense was forged, and eventually contested, regarding film and moving-image technologies as instruments of organization, as strategies of humane world making, and as compensation for the seemingly unnatural or dissensual worlds of postwar life. Mead herself, as we will see, was invited to the IDCA for its 1955 meeting, Crossroads: What Is the Common Basis for the Arts?, where, with general semanticist S. I. Hayakawa, Charles Eames, and Herbert Bayer, she was invited to speak on the "Communications" panel. Mead would be invited again to IDCA '59, and based on her essay "The Information Explosion," she was an eagerly pursued speaker for Will Burtin's Vision 65. While Mead attended neither conference, her approach to the ideal conference form was everywhere apparent at the IDCA—most obviously in Hayakawa's 1955 address, "How to Attend a Conference." Hayakawa's paper aimed to ameliorate the potentially clashing professional jargons deployed by the range of experts assembled at Aspen, and to set linguistic norms to unify their various disciplinary locations and thus "ensure the maximum flow of information and ideas from one person to another."[16] Hayakawa's address would become recommended reading for all IDCA attendees at future conferences well into the 1960s. This makes sense for a few reasons. There were strong historical connections among general semanticist ideals of communicative clarity and transparency, the logical positivism of the Vienna Circle, and Bauhaus rationalism. And general semanticist principles would, at midcentury, find their way into the behavioral sciences, and their specific application to management theory then in the throes of the human relations revolution.[17] But Hayakawa's "basic conversational traffic rules" for Aspen talk also echo Mead's allegiance to conference technique as a mode of humane, therapeutic internationalism and as a powerful communicative genre among other postwar communications media. Through such media—verbal and nonverbal, and at multiple scales—Aspenites ascertained and managed the contours of the postwar global order, and the forms of internationalism it required, while also giving voice to anxieties about human agency and explosive, potentially catastrophic productivity.

Culture and Administration in Aspen's Happy World

Rhodes Patterson's camera arrived in postwar Aspen under the auspices of Walter Paepcke's "humane" corporatism, the expansive cultural vision of the Container Corporation of America, where Patterson worked for over twenty-five years. A legendary champion and sponsor of modernism in the arts, Paepcke had remade the CCA's corporate image in the 1930s and '40s by commissioning the work of famous modern artists and graphic designers (Herbert Bayer, A. M. Cassandre, György Kepes, Willem de Kooning, Fernand Léger, and Herbert Matter), creating a vanguard corporate image for a cardboard box manufacturer. In the early 1950s, Paepcke—whose father was a Prussian immigrant—was in the throes of a capital-intensive effort to transform the moribund mining town of Aspen, Colorado, into a thriving cultural and intellectual center.[18] His aim, in short, was to resuscitate an eighteenth-century *Bildungsideal*—a belief in humane culture as a response to modernity's putative overspecialization, vocational training, and positivism. This overtly therapeutic pedagogical discourse, oriented to the sensory training of "the whole human," sparked Paepcke's sponsorship of Moholy-Nagy's New Bauhaus in Chicago, later the Institute of Design. After Moholy's death in 1946, Paepcke's investments in Bauhaus pedagogy led to the development of postwar Aspen itself as a center of adult education. This project began with the twenty-day Goethe Bicentennial Festival in 1949, followed the next year by the founding of the Aspen Institute for Humanistic Studies, a summer program that aimed to unite the burgeoning general education movement with the experimental, "hairshirt" pedagogical ethos of Black Mountain College and Reed College. With the aid of educational reformers such as the University of Chicago's Mortimer Adler and Robert Maynard Hutchins, as well as the conservative Spanish philosopher José Ortega y Gasset, Paepcke's Aspen Institute would, he hoped, be a site for humane midcentury world making. Ortega himself called the institute an attempt "to create in the Aspen summer a 'world.' A 'world,' however, is not a fortuitous gathering of individuals. It is a living together *informed* by unity."[19]

The institute's lofty cosmopolitan aims were buoyed also by the specific ideal of a world government promulgated at Aspen and elsewhere by Hutchins and his university colleagues Adler and Giuseppe Antonio Borgese, and joined to the visions of world literature (*Weltliteratur*) and humanitarianism (*Humanität*) they advocated at the Goethe Festival. Part of the celebration's ideological work was to promote Goethe as a "one-worlder," his multidisciplinary interests the embodiment of what Bayer called "the Universal Man," a fully integrated, whole human—a proto-Bauhausler.[20] Thus, Goethe's concept of world literature was framed as an ideal for the kind of humane cosmopolitanism and postnational thinking underpinning the constitutions for world government then being drafted by Hutchins and his collaborators, and circulated in the pages of their journal *Common Cause*.[21] For Goethe, as Pheng Cheah has argued, the "world" of world literature meant not mere geospatial extension (the globe) and global circulation, but rather the teleological end of "revealing universal humanity across particular differences, even as those differences were valued."[22] World-literary intercourse was the horizon of humanity's spiritual unity, as a form of "relating, belonging, and being with."[23] The language of spirit was very much in the festival's thin Aspen air and wafted from the pages of the souvenir program: "The difficulty of our time is a world difficulty, and the spirit of Goethe

Figure 3.6. Herbert Bayer, *Weakness into Strength,* from the Early Series. 1941. Gelatin silver print and gouache on paperboard sheet, 17 x 14 inches (43.2 x 35.3 cm). Gift of Container Corporation of America. Smithsonian Art Museum, Washington, D.C./Art Resource, New York. Copyright 2017 Artists Rights Society (ARS), New York/VG Bild-Kunst, Bonn.

is a world spirit. . . . What can we find in Goethe's grand plan of world literature that would serve us?"[24] But as Hutchins's concluding lecture for the festival made clear, the spiritual telos of Goethean worldiness was secured through "communication," the "theme of Goethe's life," and moreover, this "communication and transportation would be used not to send bombs, spies, propaganda of tribal self-adulation, and messengers of misguided self-interest from one country to another, but to exchange students, professors, ideas, and books, and to develop a supranational community founded on the humanity of the whole human race."[25] It was as if Hayakawa had cribbed the rules of good conferencing from what Hutchins, in 1949, praised as the heart of *Weltliteratur*: "The essence of the civilization of the dialogue is communication."[26]

With the founding of the Aspen Institute, Paepcke and company sought to extend the cultural work of the Goethe Festival into Cold War pedagogy. Despite its high-minded aims, the Aspen Institute's inaugural summer program of 1950, The Essence of Humanism, was poorly attended and lost money. At the urging of Paepcke's friends, especially media magnate Henry Luce and his wife Clare Booth Luce, the institute was quickly retooled to cater specifically to businessmen, members of the new professional managerial class, and future actors in the echelon of political, economic, and military influence that C. Wright Mills would shortly dub "the power elite."[27] Now marketed as the "Aspen Program for Business Leadership," and later the "Aspen Executives Program," the institute would not forsake humanist questions entirely but rather attempt to tackle head-on the "human problems" facing midcentury corporate capitalism, training executives (including many future members of the Kennedy administration) for their widened scope of responsibilities and domains of expertise in the postwar world.

In Paepcke's Aspen, Goethean cosmopolitanism, pedagogical reform schemes, and the very future of the humanities were part of a sweeping administrative program of postwar well-being. Paepcke and his Aspen collaborators were in the happiness business, and they cast Aspen's postwar development as ground zero of a happy postwar lifestyle in an unlikely cultural mecca. Hailed as the "Aspen way" in Patterson's film, this visionary form of life united enlightened leisure, humane and ethically self-aware business practices, and a full-throated defense of humanities values. In his 1951 speech titled "Industry in the Arts," Paepcke embraced a recent headline calling him "a Boxmaker Interested in Philosophy," and outlined a grand administrative vision joining what his notes called "lasting values—ideas, philosophy, culture," and "lasting happiness—creative work, enjoyment of art."[28] Following Charles Eames's account of the artist-designer's role in providing "security in change," Paepcke's talk seconded Eames's commitment to design as a way of intervening in, and adjudicating, values on a human scale. Paepcke took pains to distinguish such immaterial "lasting happinesses" from "the attainment of a certain amount of wealth, or a certain amount of power or prestige."[29] And he quoted at length a letter from Ortega explaining that the postwar pursuit of comfort in the United States became "excessive" when it hindered man's ability to "live his own intimate person, [to] give himself fully to thinking, imagining, willing, feeling."

"Man is inwardness," Ortega pronounced. But Paepcke's happy humanities program of liberal self-management at Aspen scaled up and outward, from the individual—too preoccupied with daily life for introspection or philosophizing—to the national level, where "ethics, morals, religion" are "the only methods we have for human control" and for defense against the "Frankenstein which science has produced and which we fear could wipe us out."[30] And the vision extended to the globe in the moment of the American Century. Paepcke observed critically the global influence of his country in sending out "to so-called backward people" money and devices, including television and radio. Rather, the United States should look to Gandhi's model in the battle for hearts and minds, intervening less through "gadgets" and more through the nation's capacity to cultivate, shape, and model universal human values. Paepcke thus pitched his ambitious Aspen agenda as a plan to "bring together leaders of labor, business, education, and government and attempt to discuss some of the basic philosophies of our American heritage, or freedom, or justice, or happiness, rather than attempting to dwell on purely contemporary matters, such as what to do with the Taft-Hartley Labor Law, the situation in Korea, or the unbalanced budget." The contemporary, he explained elsewhere, was transient. It could only hobble Aspen's universal aspirations toward an enduring happiness.[31]

By providing venues for the cross-fertilization between various specialists and disciplines at Aspen, Paepcke brought the humanities themselves—their inherent value and potential to yield happiness—into the sphere of cultural administration. Their centrality at the Aspen Institute, and in the Executive Seminars, extended what I describe in the previous chapter as a wider postwar investment in the humanities' role in liberal and general education and the making of flexible, open-minded citizens. Postwar educational reformers like Hutchins and Adler, with deep ties to Paepcke, laid the loss of the common at the door of technoscientific habits of thought, and turned to the classics of the Western canon—the "Great Books"—for synthetic, humanistic cultivation in the domains of religion, philosophy, and literature. With Paepcke's financial support, Hutchins and Adler followed up their controversial curricular revisions at the University of Chicago in the 1930s with an ambitious, multimedia program of adult education through books and educational film and television. This began with the creation of a Great Books evening class for prominent Chicago executives (the "Fat Man's Great Books Class") in 1943, and then, when the University of Chicago acquired the Encyclopedia Britannica that same year, led to the famous *Great Books of the Western World* publications.

Culminating in fifty-four volumes published in 1952, this project was, in Hutchins's terms, "more than a set of books. It is a liberal education" on which the "fate of our country and hence the world depends."[32] This humanities program was then systematized with the establishment of the Great Books Foundation, which promoted a national network of reading groups in libraries, schools, colleges, and places of worship. The program had what Reinhold Martin has called its own kind of bureaucratic "operating manual," Adler and coeditor William Gorman's two-volume guide to the Great Books set, *The Syntopicon of Great Books of the Western World.*[33] Collaborating regularly on the Aspen Institute programming and one of the institute's most ubiquitous lecturers, Adler would insist to Paepcke that a good reading list was "a work of art." And the *Syntopicon* was a "list of lists."[34] It indexed the 102 "great ideas"

Meetings and round-table discussions were held in the tented [illegible]phitheatre, designed by Eero [illegible]arinen, here sketched by architect Richard Neutra of California.

ASPEN CONFERENCE ON DESIGN

Welcoming address to the conference, which he instigated last year, was given by Walter Paepcke, chairman of the board of Container Corp., founder of the intellectual and sport center at Aspen. Paepcke, long a proponent of integrated design in industry, hammered hard at the need for "cross-fertilization of ideas" between management and industrial designers. Several presidents of small companies came and a dozen big corporations sent their art directors or designers. Leo Lionni, art director of FORTUNE, was elected to serve as chairman of the 1953 conference.

High in the Rockies, at Aspen, Colorado, a group of designers, architects, art teachers, art directors, and businessmen met this summer in a second annual conference on design. The theme for this year was "Design as a Function of Management." The meeting was one of a series of conferences at Aspen called by Walter Paepcke (left) of the Container Corp. of America to provide cultural stimulation and physical relaxation in an informal, pleasant atmosphere. Four main speeches, by Buckminster Fuller, Alfred Knopf, Walter Dorwin Teague, and Richard Gump, were amplified by round-table discussions and casual talks around the breakfast table, at the swimming pool, or in the bar of the Jerome Hotel. These talks, perhaps more than the formal meetings and seminars, gave the conference its unique quality—an opportunity for free and frank exchange of ideas beyond the inevitable semantic merry-go-round of, Is there such a thing as good design? What is good design? and What is design?

There was no attempt to touch off a revolution in industrial design at Aspen, but many of the designers and businessmen found new ways of approaching their problems. A manufacturer of oil-exploration equipment, S. T. Harris of Texas Instruments, Inc., in Dallas, was convinced that, even in his unlikely business, design was an important tool in merchandising, and more than one businessman was moved to call the meeting "inspirational."

FORTUNE September 1952 113

Figure 3.7. "Aspen Conference on Design," *Fortune,* 1953. Walter P. Paepcke Papers, Special Collections Research Center, University of Chicago Library.

organizing the unity of the fifty-four-volume set, including "Art" and "Man," "Government" and "World," but also "Happiness." Each essay summarized the idea's robust development across the set, and concluded with an "outline of topics" and internal references to those topics in the system as a whole. For "Happiness," this included "the desire for happiness: its naturalness and universality"; the "understanding of happiness: definitions and myths"; "the pursuit of happiness"; the "social aspects of happiness"; the "happiness of men in relation to the gods or the afterlife"; and the "distinction between temporary and eternal happiness."[35]

Wedded to these Chicago-based pedagogical schemes to bind the liberal arts to postwar ideals of the liberal-democratic happy, the IDCA, like Paepcke's Aspen Institute, emerged in a postwar constellation of thought about the value of the humanities in a midcentury world dominated by technoscience and the explosive growth of information. This context raised questions about the scope of the humanities' worldliness, and about their capacity to inculcate the kinds of humane, nonspecialized, broad-based thinking that would improve management. And design. For at roughly the same moment the Aspen Institute was created, CCA designer Egbert Jacobson proposed that an annual design seminar become a part of Aspen's summer offerings, alongside the recently founded Aspen Music Festival. "I'm sure you will agree," Jacobson wrote to Paepcke, that "questions of design are as vital to humanism as music, literature, and philosophy."[36] Thus was born the International Design Conference in Aspen, a then-unprecedented conference in the United States, whose goal was to explore "the importance of design in the life of American communities" and to "establish once and for all the relation of design to business." Its inaugural meeting in 1951, and the following two meetings, were titled Design: A Function of Management. The IDCA quickly established itself as one of the world's most important design conferences, assembling a roster of design heavyweights, artists, educators, corporate executives, and scholars from a diverse range of disciplines for an annual, weeklong series of conversations around a predetermined theme. In many ways, the IDCA was symptomatic both of the new professional legitimacy, cultural prestige, and cosmopolitan ambition of the designer at midcentury. By 1961 Reyner Banham could claim that "Aspen has, to some extent, replaced the [Milan] Triennale as a world center of opinion and debate."[37]

As designers warmed to the prospect of a bold midcentury world-to-be-engineered, they brought a modernist tradition of media experimentation and sensory utopianism into a curious range of disciplines, knowledge regimes, and institutional sites that would administer culture in the Cold War period. The postwar corporation, as the formation of Paepcke's Aspen attests, had its own dreams of a world to be administered by humanities-trained, future-oriented managers. Such individuals, corporate persons who created in groups sustained by communications and their media, would be trained to think beyond conventional disciplinary boundaries, and equipped for the challenges of what Peter Drucker, no stranger to Aspen, described as a dynamic "new world-view" in *Landmarks of Tomorrow* (1959).[38] By this, the hallmark of what he calls the "post-modern world," Drucker imagined organized processes that proceeded horizontally, by sustained patterning and modulation, and by continuous feedback loops between organism and environment.[39] "We are beginning to move," he noted, "from the old mechanical concept of discipline as determined by the static properties of the subject matter, to new disciplines dealing with such universal configurations and processes as 'growth,' 'information' or 'ecology.'"[40] Freed from disciplinary rigidity in the multimodal techniques of the conference, the medium of film was approached at IDCA through such varied and competing domains of expertise, and at a time when film's own disciplinary identity vis-à-vis the humanities was still being forged.

Film and *Bildung* in Aspen

The ninth annual IDCA meeting in 1959 was the first explicitly devoted to exploring the role of film and moving-image technologies. But film had played a key role at the conference since its early days, and followed from the institute's cultural programming ambitions across media. The 1951 institute, themed by Adler as "Our American Heritage," offered a film membership at the Wheeler Opera House, which screened selections from the MoMA film library twice a week. A program for the institute publicized not just the inaugural IDCA that summer but also a range of concerts, lectures, and films, as well as a special photography seminar featuring MoMA's head of photography, Edward Steichen, the photo historian Beaumont Newhall, photographers Berenice Abbott, Ansel Adams, Dorothea Lange, Bayer, and the Hungarian-born filmmaker and photographer Ferenc Berko, a friend of Walter Gropius and Moholy-Nagy with roots in the Bauhaus. Following Moholy's death in 1947, Berko taught film and photography at the Institute of Design before relocating to Aspen at Paepcke's invitation to work on retainer as the primary photographic chronicler of Aspen's cultural activities. Based on his film classes at the ID, Berko compiled his own list of seminal films in the medium's evolution, which launched the institute's long-running Screen Classics program in 1950. As that program grew in popularity in the late 1950s and early 1960s, it spun off the Aspen Film Conference in 1963. Devoted to "The American Film: Its Makers and its Audience,"

Program

Aspen Institute

Summer 1951

Lectures — Forums
Wheeler Opera House

Museum of Modern Art Films
Wheeler Opera House

Concerts
Aspen Amphitheater

Prices

Tickets for Concerts in the Amphitheater	
Unreserved	$1.00
	$1.50
Reserved Box Seats	$2.50
Lectures and Forums at Wheeler Opera House	
Main Floor	$1.00 and .75
Balcony	.75
Reserved Box Seats	$2.00
Film Membership	
8 Performances	$4.00
16 Performances	$8.00

All Prices Plus Tax

All Programs Subject To Change

Figure 3.8. Aspen Institute brochure, 1951. Walter P. Paepcke Papers, Special Collections Research Center, University of Chicago Library.

and featuring a keynote address by Lionel Trilling, the inaugural film conference "advanced the view that the Aspen Institute might be to the American motion picture what the BFI and *Cahiers du cinéma* were to their respective countries."[41]

As the Aspen Institute's website describes this odd genealogy, Berko's postwar program celebrating "the art of film" continues today in the independent Aspen Filmfest.[42] This way of drawing a direct line connecting the Hungarian avant-garde, the American Bauhaus, and the contemporary indie scene through a shared devotion to film art obscures the intermedial, interdisciplinary approach that makes Aspen's institutional context so compelling. Rather, as reported in *Business Screen* in 1962, the film conferences embodied the "essence of the 'Aspen idea,'" allowing American filmmakers an "equal voice" in an urgently needed forum that refused to divide the film community "into separate camps, loosely designated as 'industrial,' 'educational,' 'television,' 'Hollywood,' and so on."[43] In Aspen, film was thought of holistically, allowing artists at various scales of production to discuss "problems common to all these fields without the usual blind spots encountered when specialists confer among themselves."[44] And this approach was contagious, spawning more conferences and occasions to talk across disciplinary boundaries. When the Aspen Institute stopped funding the film conference in the late 1960s, for example, it was taken over by the new University of Southern California Film Conference (many of the Aspen Film Conference speakers were based in Los Angeles). Writing on the USC film conferences as an "outgrowth" of the Aspen Institute for Humanistic Studies, Arthur Knight similarly extolled the Aspen idea in terms that Paepcke or Moholy or Bayer or Eames would admire. Aspen entailed primarily a hostility to specialization, a salutary "cross-fertilization of the arts" that produces "what the people at the Aspen Institute like to [call] the 'ripple effect' of their conferences," spreading knowledge to distant disciplinary shores.[45]

So, a culture-hungry guest at the 1951 institute could, for example, watch Erich von Stroheim's *Greed* at the Wheeler, and the next day attend a seminar titled "The Labor Movement in the History of American Economic Reform"; or see a screening of Robert Flaherty's *Moana* and hear a lecture by Hutchins (as of that year, the associate director of the Ford Foundation), "The Conditions of Peace." Robert Wiene's *The Cabinet of Dr. Caligari,* René Clair's *Le million,* Buster Keaton's *Sherlock Jr.,* George Marshall's *Destry Rides Again* (starring Marlene Dietrich and James Stewart), and a program on "theatrical and social dancing on film" appeared on the same cultural uplift agenda that included roundtable discussions of *The Federalist Papers, Huckleberry*

Finn, Moby-Dick, John Dewey's *Democracy in Education,* and William James's pragmatism; as well as lectures on topics such as "The First New Deal," Thorstein Veblen's *The Theory of the Leisure Class,* and Mark Van Doren's "American Poetry as Poetry."

This schedule reminds us that the IDCA, while semiautonomous and drawing guests and speakers not directly connected to the institute, was very much part of Aspen's humanist mission, and the film programming in Aspen often intersected with the institute's Great Books/Great Ideas initiatives, personnel, and multimedia brand. The clichéd opposition between "great books" and the upstart discipline of film studies, as Dana Polan has shown, was undermined by even the most indefatigable proponents of the liberal-humanist literary canon. Adler himself penned a lengthy ode to the mass art of cinema, *Art and Prudence* (1937), and saw movies as a means "both to test the verities of great ideas . . . and to make those ideas live in the everyday context of present-day modernity."[46] And Scott Buchanan, architect of the landmark Great Books curriculum at St. John's College in Annapolis, had proposed an "Institute of Cinematics" as a graduate research center where films could be studied theoretically and practically, and as a means of elaborating a great books philosophy. Inspired by reading Mumford's *Technics and Civilization,* Buchanan viewed movies—with their vast technical infrastructure—as a pragmatic synthesis of the "useful, liberal, and fine arts," unifying domains of liberal knowledge.[47] While Polan has observed that the Great Books intellectuals had largely given up on cinema as a site of liberal education by the end of the 1930s, Paepcke's Aspen-based humanities program extended these aspirations into the Cold War period, aligning them with the interdisciplinary, communicative sphere of design.

Both the 1956 and 1957 institutes were titled The Great Ideas of Western Man, and the respective design conferences for those years—Ideas on the Future of Man and Design, and Design and Human Values—were conceptualized as part of the institute's broader program, as the titles suggest. The 1956 institute opened with a screening of the Italian film *Maddalena* (1951), and movies like *Cry, the Beloved Country; The Golden Coach; Nanook of the North; Topaze;* and *Battleship Potemkin* were interspersed with no fewer than five lectures by Adler ("The Idea of Beauty," "The Idea of Truth," "The Idea of God," "The Idea of Controversy," and "The Idea of the Teacher"), panel discussions of topics such as "Does Original Thought Operate in Contemporary American Democracy?," and additional promising lectures titled "A Fresh Look at the Idea of Disarmament" and "Freedom and the Idea of Historical Inevitability." Adler also delivered a talk at the IDCA that summer called "Some Philosophical Questions about Design." In it he distinguished between a liberal arts education, which produced learning for the sake of leisure and "living well," and their degraded other—not "technical" or "vocational" training but "servile" arts and education, designed for labor and the mere production of "serviceable things."[48] He might well have called it "The Idea of Design." And he was deeply ambivalent about it. He asked conferees, polemically, whether design and design education aimed for the servile ends of mere biological utility, or liberal, biologically useless beauty. The 1957 institute's program also brought film, "Great Books" liberal education ideals, and debates about the future of leisure together in intriguing ways. The opening night's film, *Gold of Naples,* was followed the next evening by Adler's address "Liberal Education in an Industrial Democracy," and, in the weeks to follow, "The Pursuit of Happiness," "Knowledge and Opinion," and "Revolution in Our Times." Scott Buchanan delivered a "Great Books lecture" that summer, and the Film Classics series included adaptations of prestige dramas such as *Oedipus Rex* and *Richard III,* but also contemporary European art cinema, for example, Federico Fellini's *La Strada,* Jean Cocteau's *Orpheus,* Victor Sjöström's silent-era masterpiece *The Phantom Carriage,* and Jules Dassin's jewelry-heist caper *Rififi.* As an art newly canonized by MoMA, as a mass medium, and as a vexing barometer of the U.S. good life, film also infiltrated the panel discussions: one was titled "Will Science Spoil Rock Hunter?," another "Communication, Conscience, and the Mass Media," and King Vidor himself appeared on a concluding panel and seminar discussion, "'The New Leisure,' America, 1957: Renaissance, Myth or Madison Avenue?"

The film and media work of the Eameses was central to Aspen's nexus of humane communication from its early years, and representative of some of the larger concerns and ideological ambitions of IDCA attendees. A promotional brochure for the Aspen Institute includes a photo of Eames's lecture at the Wheeler Opera House for the inaugural IDCA in 1951. It folds Eamesian communication into an urgent narrative of the institute's philosophical commitment to the "command of ourselves, our management of our human interrelationships, and the enrichment of life through the arts"—a managerial prowess that would match the human being's demonstrable war-making capacity and expanded "control of the sub-human."[49] Promoting the 1952 institute, devoted to "Human Freedom," a photo of Eames is paired with a quotation from Benjamin Franklin on "freedom and security." The Eameses would return to Aspen in 1953, and were eagerly courted by program chairman Leo Lionni (then art director of *Fortune*), who expressed his excitement about the possibility, apparently floated by George Nelson, that they might "do your three-dimensional lecture act in Aspen."[50] Following up

ASPEN INSTITUTE

PROGRAM

The Great Ideas of Western Man

SUMMER 1956

Lectures

Seminar Building

Single — $2.00
Weekly — $6.00
2 Weeks — $11.00

Music Associates of Aspen

Concerts

Amphitheater

adults $3.00; children $1.50

Lecture-Recitals

Opera House

adults $2; children under 16 $1

Film Classics

Opera House

adults 75c; children 50c

Figure 3.9. Aspen Institute brochure, 1956. Walter P. Paepcke Papers, Special Collections Research Center, University of Chicago Library.

Evening lecture by Charles Eames in the recently redecorated Wheeler Opera House, Charles H. Sawyer presiding.

BENJAMIN FRANKLIN on freedom and security
They that can give up essential liberty
to obtain a little temporary safety
deserve neither liberty nor safety.

(Historical Review of Pennsylvania, 1759)

Figure 3.10. Charles Eames, IDCA lecture, 1952, Wheeler Opera House, Aspen Institute brochure. Walter P. Paepcke Papers, Special Collections Research Center, University of Chicago Library.

on his initial invitation, Lionni proposed that Charles "introduce one of our panel discussions 'Idea and Form', on which [György] Kepes, Max Bill, and Bucky [Fuller] will speak," adding, "Also: could you bring movies?" Lionni was likely referring to the "Art-X"/"Sample Lesson" experiment in moving-image pedagogy that, as chapter 2 explains, sought to train students in an integral, networked visuality—a foundational habit of mind of postwar liberal-democratic citizenship. While the Eameses did not ultimately use IDCA 1953 as a trial run for that fall's Art-X, they did screen parts of *A Communications Primer* there, and their films and slides were publicized and shown alongside the work of their friend Kepes, whose "language of vision" motivated Art-X's high-speed experiments in informatic compression.

In fact, the Eameses' films were billed as part of a series of multimedia entertainments, exhibitions, and spectacles at IDCA 1953, including the conference's opening act: the site-specific construction of one of Fuller's geodesic domes by students from the University of Minnesota.[51] The couple's films were featured on a Thursday evening session at the Wheeler alongside the multimedial investigations of Kepes and the Bauhaus artist Xanti Schawinsky. The program lists their "Films-Slides-Comments" alongside Schawinsky's "Spectodrama," an experiment in total theater that the artist, and former Bauhaus student, had first developed at Black Mountain College. A June 25 issue of the *Aspen Flyer*, previewing the week's events, breathlessly describes Eames as "a nice guy who designs everything from kites to movies and a member of the 'exploratory playful' field of design."[52] The Hungarian-born Kepes, then at MIT and previously at Moholy's ID in Chicago, is touted as a "notable addition to our internationalism." Like Schawinsky, Kepes is included in the Thursday evening session with the Eameses, and the two are promoted together under the rubric "Three Ring Circus": "Thursday night sounds like fun. Mr. Kepes will finally have his chance to talk on the 'New Landscape,' and Xanti Schawinsky will bring you the amazing new type of entertainment, SPECTODRAMA!" The conference's "prop department," the *Flyer* continues, "has been in a frenzy since Wednesday morning—on the run for Xanti. A tennis ball, a pistol, a beautiful girl, a false nose with a mustache attached, a complete set of scenery, special lighting, numerous projectors—all this for SPECTODRAMA!!!!!!!!!"[53]

Kepes, for his part, presented work from his book in progress, *The New Landscape in Art and Science* (1956), a project that stemmed from his ongoing efforts to link the "language of vision" to the kinds of overall cognitive faculties necessary for the training of social subjectivity in the postwar period.[54] The *New Landscape* exhibition, and later the book, emerged from Kepes's encounter with the advanced

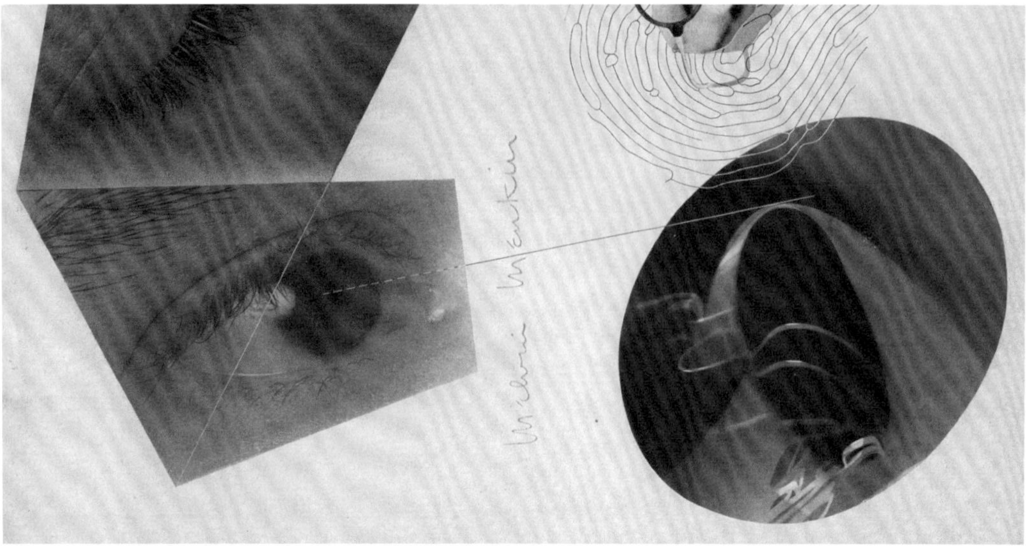

Figure 3.11. Interior, School of Design catalog, 1941–42, "The Eye Opens," design by György Kepes. Institute of Design Collection, box 3, folder 63, IDC_0003_063_P15. Special Collections and University Archives, University Library, University of Illinois at Chicago.

imaging technologies then deployed in MIT's various laboratories, and the broader military-industrial complex of which they were a part. This new generation of scientific images, Kepes argued, opened up a novel landscape of a radically transformed postwar nature—nature "as a medium of transformation and manipulation," existing beyond the threshold of human vision.[55] Through the powers of the oscilloscope, stroboscope, interferometer, radar, and radiograph, Kepes saw what he called "images of the new scale," and with them, new tools for the education of vision: "Leading us away from the system of fixed things, and toward the system of spatio-temporal patterns, the newly revealed visible world brings us to the threshold of a new vision."[56] Kepes's *New Landscape* thus cast the new imaging technologies of science as aesthetic compensation for entropic degeneration and formlessness. For Kepes, all media, insofar as they received and transmitted organizational patterns, were basically interchangeable management technologies for grappling with the potentially chaotic energies unleashed by postwar technoscience.

IDCA 1953 established a pattern for the strikingly broad range of categories through which film and moving-image technologies were conceived at the conference, and the porous boundaries between them: "entertainment," lecture, multimedia spectacle, total theater, corporate promotion, exhibition design, art film, modern art, cultural diplomacy, "the exploratory playful field of design," and a "new landscape of art and science." Underpinning all of them was communication, that master category of the Cold War semiosphere.

As the IDCA increasingly brought social science methodologies to bear on questions of design, the problem of communication and the category's fluidity across disciplinary and medial boundaries would decisively shape Aspen's programming in the 1950s and '60s, as well as its various attempts to theorize film and its media environments. Consider how labile that category was in the evolution of the conference program for the 1955 meeting. With it, the IDCA would now stake an institutional claim to being a leader in the management of the visual arts, with its administrators possessing a humane and increasingly global or cosmopolitan self-awareness. Titled Crossroads: What Are the Directions of Arts?, the program, chaired by Burtin, would

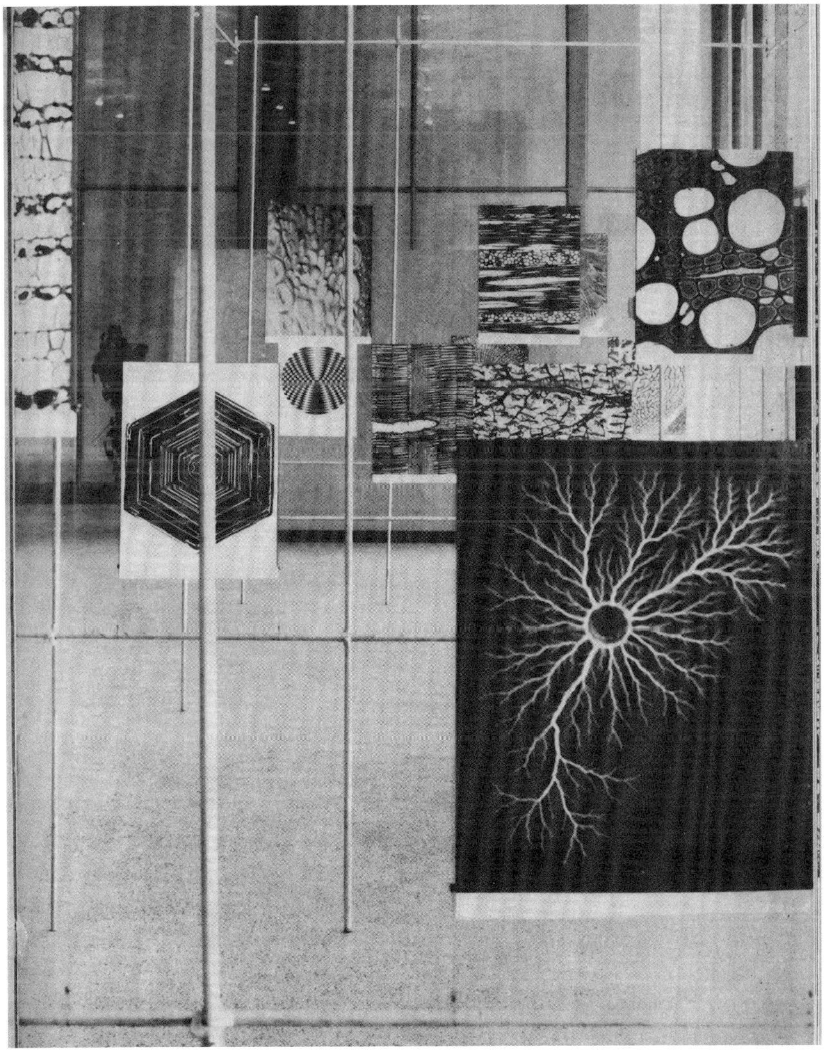

Figure 3.12. György Kepes, *The New Landscape,* installation view, Massachusetts Institute of Technology, 1951. Courtesy of Juliet Kepes Stone.

again feature a "Communication" panel, in addition to others on education, light, structure, cityscape and landscape, and pleasure. In the early stages of planning, the "Communication" panel would feature Charles Eames, the surrealist painter Hans Arp, graphic designer Albe Steiner, and British biologist and mathematician Lancelot Hogben, author of *From Cave Painting to the Comic Strip: A Kaleidoscope of Human Communication* (1949).[57] Burtin's "tentative program schedule" changes the lineup. "Communication" still leads off the proceedings on Monday, but the panel features, in addition to Hogben, designer Herbert Bayer, general semanticist S. I. Hayakawa, Margaret Mead herself, and modernist painter Ben Shahn. Eames has been bumped to the concluding day's session, "Leisure," now alongside Kepes again, cartoonist Robert Osborn, and Japanese film director Teinosuke Kinugasa.[58] In the accompanying program outline, Burtin poses the conference's three animating questions: Are "new social experiences, and new technological means, new scientific thoughts" indicating "new directions in the arts"? What is "at the basis of our changing position and what are the potentialities of a better order?" And finally, "Are we moving toward a world art?"[59] In the final version of the program, though, the Eameses would bow out entirely, as did Mead and Shahn, and the "Communication" panelists actually assembled were Bayer, Hayakawa, Sol Cornberg (a communication systems designer who worked in NBC's first color TV studio and a now-forgotten pioneer of educational media), and actor John Houseman, the former Orson Welles collaborator and Mercury Theatre stalwart, and then an important Hollywood producer.[60]

This bit of IDCA musical chairs around the 1955 "Communication" panel is surely to be expected given the logistical complexity of conference planning, but it also underscores the IDCA's need for that category's very capaciousness. A strategically expansive category, "communication" would allow IDCA conferees to grasp the common basis or future order of the various professions and aesthetic practices transformed by the postwar growth of science, knowledge production, and rapid technological change. "Communication," as the IDCA would approach it, had to cut a wide conceptual swath because it was part of a transdisciplinary attempt to describe and to reckon with the very scale of the mass media and of the new "means" of postwar science and technology as makers and destroyers of a common world. As the designers assembled at Aspen saw it, that scale was defined by a new worldliness and thus, a new responsibility for the world, a fact the IDCA greeted with considerable ambivalence, and would temper with a humanist cosmopolitanism. Designers were invested in film—as a means of communication, as a mass medium, as part of a broader domain of a shared world culture—not just for its capacity to manage the organizations for which they worked, but for its function as a pedagogical tool for the self-fashioning, and self-government of citizens.

This seems especially clear in an IDCA internal memorandum taking stock of the relative successes and failures of the 1955 proceedings, with an eye to the future of the organization. Mass media, the memo explains, tend to abet the fragmentation of knowledge and deepen the perils of specialization, and it is against this narrowcasting that the IDCA needs to define its broad purview of responsibilities. At a historical moment in which "time and space are shrinking," and thus transforming what is local and national in culture, IDCA conferees need to ready themselves for the "challenge of world culture or world chaos"; "find the solution to problems of deeper and wider human understanding"; and reject the "harmful position that they are not morally involved and not co-responsible for our environment." There are three key groups of experts for pursuing this engaged, cosmopolitan mission: the "managerial professions" (small and large business corporations and the government), the "formulating professions" (artists, poets, designers, architects, and scientists), and "the educating professions," from kindergarten to the university. In concluding, then, the memo casts this new institutional mandate as the movement from "Man at the Crossroads," which, it suggests, is how the 1955 conference should be remembered, to "The Condition of Man." Strikingly, the memo explicitly charts the IDCA's future operations in the wake of Edward Steichen's landmark *Family of Man* exhibition of 1955, which "in its humane aspects, is symptomatic of the general need for a big perspective toward which we intend to move."[61]

In light of these remarks, in fact, John Houseman's talk delivered at the 1955 conference, "How Does a Movie Communicate?," emerges as a key text in the consolidation of the IDCA's organizational self-understanding, and the role of film in it.[62] Perhaps with Steichen in mind, Houseman opens by claiming that the "most compelling instrument yet devised for communication between human beings is the image of man himself" ("MC," 23). While Houseman makes an auteurist argument for film as an "unpredictable miracle of individual energy . . . at the core of a movie's essential communication," he is especially interested in film's total effect around the world ("MC," 28).[63] Overseas, Houseman explains, films "follow those laws of energy which relate to the attraction of the greater mass," and have become inevitably linked with the United States as "the world's most rapidly growing unit of political and economic power" ("MC," 29). In sum, Houseman's argument about filmic communication is a somewhat ambivalent assessment of film as an instrument of ideology and cultural diplomacy, a medium that communicates the "pervasive" presence of the United States to "the peoples of the world," who approach the superpower's presence with curiosity and concern ("MC," 29).[64] And his hope is that what is communicated is something beyond dreams of "luxury and energy," a "residue of something more" having to do with "goodwill and with those rights of man mentioned in our Declaration of Independence" ("MC," 30).

During the panel's Q-and-A session, Burtin asked Houseman about the tension between the auteurist model of filmmaking and a corporate ethos of production "based on work and collaboration."[65] Cornberg asked Houseman to clarify his comments about the "immediacy" of television and the nature of the "participation" it allows. In doing so, Cornberg underscored the problematic ways television "permits its audience to participate in its environment," and its generation of desire for products "with a disconcerting degree of 'speed and saturation.'" And yet, for Cornberg, "this plus of communication dictates the very flow of the life's blood of the world community." Hayakawa asked Houseman to elaborate on the specific "kind of movie" capable of functioning as a global language of goodwill. Houseman gave the example of John Ford's *Grapes of Wrath* (1940), and he used it to illuminate the way author John Steinbeck's message could be perceived so differently in different contexts: behind the Iron Curtain the film was shown as an example of "how fallacious American propaganda was," how specious its "continuous picture of material well-being," while elsewhere around the world, it was read as a sign of freedom in the United States, the nation's allowing a critique of capitalism from within. The upshot, for Houseman, was that "there are no absolute statements in any movie," a claim that extended to film as a medium of international communication what Hayakawa had himself underscored as the communicative principle of semantics. "No word or group of words can be said to have meaning or be meaningless in themselves."[66] The communication panelists thus raised fundamental questions about film's and television's various horizons of intelligibility, the extent to which these media enacted individual visions or group dynamics, and the scale and scope of their ambivalent messaging and ways of targeting the attention of populations. These were questions about medium specificity then, but they were also managerial questions that would be explored most fully in the landmark 1959 conference, Communication: The Image Speaks. Now, though, they would be put in fitful dialogue with filmic modernism, and its own designs on communication.

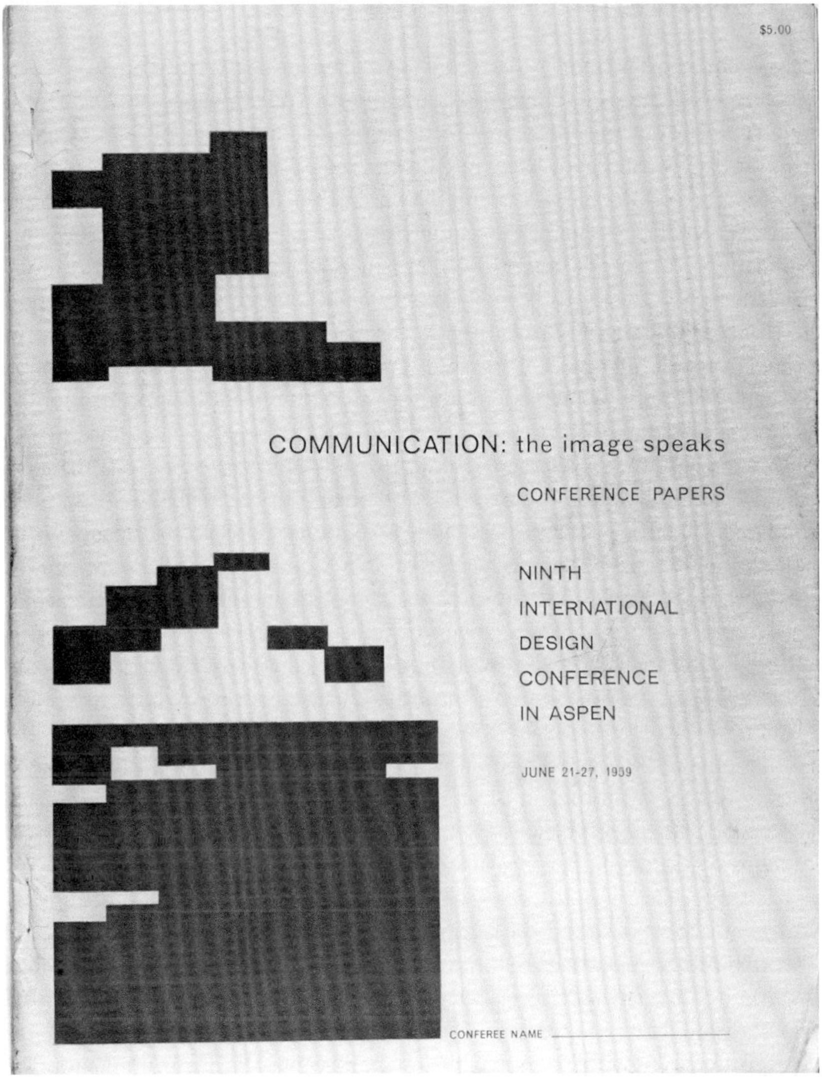

Figure 3.13. Susan Jackson Keig, booklet, *Communication: The Image Speaks.* Conference Papers, Ninth International Design Conference, Aspen, 1959. Will Burtin Papers, RIT Libraries: Graphic Design Archive, Rochester Institute of Technology.

Communication: The Image Speaks

The 1959 program was conceived by two Chicago-based designers, Morton Goldsholl, that year's program committee chairman, and his design partner and wife, Millie Goldsholl, who curated a nightly series of film screenings, an ambitious and wide-ranging program of some seventy films keyed to conference talks and spread over the five-day conference (Plate 11). Trained at Moholy-Nagy's Institute of Design in Chicago, where filmmaking was a central part of the curriculum, the couple established their design firm Goldsholl & Associates in 1955.[67] The couple's work in the medium for clients such as Standard Oil,

Motorola, and Kimberly-Clark was featured in the trade journals *Print, Graphis,* and *Business Screen,* among others, and was screened on trade-show floors and in conference rooms as Chicago itself became known as "the Hollywood of industrial filmmaking." In one of several articles written by an admiring Rhodes Patterson on the couple's filmmaking, Morton Goldsholl described their practice as stemming from a long-standing interest, as "social beings," in "the problems of communication forms."[68] While the Goldsholls insisted, as Millie put it, that "film is the most powerful communication form," they also acknowledged, as Houseman did at IDCA 1955, that "making films is a great responsibility proportionate to the size of audiences they reach and the influences they wield."[69]

The 1959 IDCA meeting was a natural fit for "designers in film" such as the Goldsholls, who believed in the possibility of a socially responsible corporation and even used words such as "Utopic" to describe the aspirations of their design practice.[70] In a piece on the couple's new design studio in 1962, Patterson described its occupants as "philosophically oriented practitioners," and noted that even "casual conversation with the Goldsholls is reminiscent of IDCA sessions."[71] For readers of *Communication Arts,* Aspen's "creatively organized conclave" was synonymous with high-minded ideas, and moreover, it mattered that the Goldsholls walked the Aspen talk. Patterson notes, in fact, that Morton "lamented the inclination of so many designers to leave the ideas generated or re-dedicated at Aspen—in Aspen," and reminded readers of Morton's role as the program chairman for the 1959 Communication conference. There, in his opening remarks, Goldsholl cast contemporary image makers as faced with "a new set of proportions, a new scale of responsibility," because they have been "catapulted by communications technology into an active involvement with all mankind." Summoning the Bauhauslers' hostility to specialization, and the Meadian faith in conference activity as a multisensory participation in humane capacity, he would address his fellow conferees as "whole people."[72]

The 1959 IDCA—in its planning, its talks, and its film programming—was everywhere preoccupied with "human communication" as a universal horizon for understanding the possibilities and limits of human agency, the new scale of the mass media, and the relationship between film's communicative power and various "worlds" of humanist internationalism. Looking to broaden the IDCA's audience by perhaps hosting it overseas, Morton Goldsholl had in fact proposed the theme of "Design and Film" in the first place as the second of two possible topics for the 1959 meeting. The other topic, "Design and Obsolescence," would be of such a "critical nature" that it would have to be held domestically since,

Goldsholl reasoned, if it were held "in Japan or elsewhere it might look like a " 'foreign plot' to discredit American business and might alienate our corporate members." "The Design and Film" program, on the other hand, would be worldly and humane, and good for business. He pitched it as "a complete study of film from the designer's point of view," noting to his colleagues that if "we look to better relationships, internationally, communications designers will have to work in the film and television medium, enrich and design them to be the poster, magazine . . . and book of the future." "The film itself," Goldsholl wrote, "is a fascinating subject, and becomes more so to designers today. The advent of television created a real revolution, a qualitative change in the means of communication into every home in our country." For Goldsholl, it was film's putative internationalism, its capacity to function as a "universal language," that might allow IDCA, for the first time, to appeal to "film production people, animators, artists in film, photographers, [all] over the world," and perhaps be held "overseas, Japan or somewhere."[73]

The stakes of the Communication conference in 1959 were thus unusually high, with film summoned as a universal language at a moment when the nature of the IDCA's internationalism was compromised following a contentious executive board vote against a proposal—supported by Goldsholl and Will Burtin—to hold the 1959 meeting in Japan.[74] It is in this context that we should approach Millie's film program. This was easily the most celebrated feature of the conference, and became an IDCA programming staple thereafter.[75] In Morton's preliminary outline, the film program is pitched as the conference's signature event: "A film festival to end all film festivals."[76] In her summary report on the program to the IDCA executive board, Millie clarified the festival's objective: "to screen best available communication and experimental films. International reputation. Variety of subject matter. Intended to convey the power of film as a communication form."[77] To acquire the films, she wrote directly to fellow entrants in the 1958 Brussels Experimental Film Festival (where her and Morton's *Night Driving* was awarded a bronze medal), held that year in conjunction with the Brussels World's Fair, and visited the American Film Festival in New York City.[78] She also wrote to foreign consulates, whose offerings she dismissed as "too self-gratifying and propagandistic"; to companies "who have reputations for subsidizing good films (ex: Ford, Shell Oil, Standard Oil, Air France, etc.)"; to film producers "we knew or who had been favorably mentioned by reliable film reviewers in Saturday Review, New York Times, Sight and Sound, etc."; to the National Film Board of Canada (who had, she added, "a wealth of terrific film material") and the Canadian Broadcasting Company; and to a number of "commercial distributors" with particular

Figure 3.14. Panelists, Communication: The Image Speaks, 1959 sketch by Ted Rand. Walter P. Paepcke Papers, Special Collections Research Center, University of Chicago Library.

interests in experimental film: Amos Vogel's Cinema 16; Maya Deren's Creative Film Society, and the Museum of Modern Art, among others.[79]

What world, or what picture of midcentury worldliness, might be produced or plausibly reconstructed from the networks of distribution and geopolitical situation of the inaugural IDCA festival? What role would experimental film play in shaping, or challenging, this vision of the world? The Goldsholls' programming choices obviously resonate with the plummy, humanist sensibilities of the international film festival at midcentury and its abiding problematic of "world cinema." As Dudley Andrew explains, film festivals at Cannes, Venice, Locarno, and Berlin, in effect, "promoted UNESCO's humanitarian goals," extending the terrain of therapeutic communication and, we might add, the universalizing "technique" of the midcentury conference itself: festivals "claimed to be utopias where the appreciation of difference and similarity would contribute to tolerance, coexistence, and of course, a richer cinema."[80]

While this kind of lofty rhetoric defined the talks of the 1959 IDCA conferees, the films screened at the festival came from a fairly small number of countries (nine), largely Western and overwhelmingly North American. The screening program lists thirty-six U.S. films, fourteen Canadian films, six French films, six British films, one Swedish film, one Danish film, one Israeli film, one Czech film, and one Romanian film.[81] That a number of Millie Goldsholl's programming choices were routed through the Brussels World Fair is especially telling. As the first such fair since World War II, and a key ideological battleground in the Cold War, the Brussels spectacle had a specific mission, conceptualized in response to what its secretary identified as the increasing isolation and dehumanization of human beings, and the threat of midcentury technoscience. Exhibiting nations and their pavilions were charged with showing "the methods [each] advocates for the 're-humanization of the modern world.'"[82] Film, of course, played a central part in this project, at various scales and formats, from the "Cavalcade of Great American Films" and Disney-designed Circarama spectacles (*The USA in Circarama*), to small loop films of everyday life made by Shirley Clarke and D. A. Pennebaker—films designed to play, as decor, alongside the commodities constitutive of the U.S. good life. The IDCA "experimental" film choices reflect the fair programming, featuring films from the fair at large (the Eameses' *The Information Machine* [1958], an IBM-sponsored paean to computation *as* environmental control, and Shirley Clarke's *Bridges Go Round* [1958]), as well as selected works from the experimental portion of the Brussels Film Festival, held that year within the fairgrounds proper. This section featured 133 films, including works by Stan Brakhage, Agnès Varda, Robert Breer, Kenneth Anger, Len Lye, Norman McLaren, Maya Deren, Stan VanDerBeek, Peter Kubelka, and Roman Polanksi. Reporting on the festival in *Sight and Sound,* British "free cinema" director Karel Reisz observed, with considerable ambivalence, that "no one could claim that Brussels did not bring us face-to-face with the avant-garde."[83] From among these entries, Goldsholl included Deren's *At Land* (1944), Breer's *Cats* (1956), VanDerBeek's *What, Who, How* (1957), and multiple works by McLaren and Lye.

As Pheng Cheah reminds us, debates over the phenomenon of "world cinema" often concern a politics of representation, a giving of visibility and audibility to cultural difference from underrepresented regions of the globe. In these terms, the "world" produced by IDCA 1959's programming—and filtered through the distribution networks of a geopolitically overdetermined site like the Brussels World's Fair—would be overwhelmingly oriented toward the geopolitical center rather than the Global Southern periphery: no Latin American cinema, no African cinema, no Asian cinema. No surprises here.[84]

Things get more complicated, and more interesting, if we approach the version of the world at the Goldsholls' IDCA not only through a politics of representation but also through the liberal managerial logics and traditions revealed by the films screened at the conference, and the theories of film given voice there. In this regard, one might make the case that the presiding conceptual figure at IDCA 1959 was not, for example, Charles Eames, despite the advanced billing of his films in the trade press, or indeed any of individual speakers actually invited to speak, but rather a largely absent presence: John Grierson, the legendary champion of documentary film. Grierson appears on an early list of film panelists "to be invited" for the 1959 conference.[85] And while there is no evidence that he attended, many of the films screened at the festival, and a number of conference speakers, operated within a Griersonian ambit, or what has recently been dubbed "the Grierson effect," which cut an increasingly global swath at midcentury and buttressed competing internationalisms.[86] Some festival films were produced by venerable Griersonian institutions: the General Post Office (GPO) Film Unit, represented in a classic documentary like *Nightmail* (1936); the British Council of Information (formerly the Ministry of Information), which sponsored the Grierson production *Man Alive*; and the National Film Board of Canada, which Grierson helped establish and directed from 1939 to 1945), and which was represented in the work of conference speakers McLaren and Lye, who had also worked with Grierson at the GPO. UNESCO, too, was well represented at the conference. By 1959 McLaren himself had accepted two UNESCO assignments, first in western China, and then in India, where he taught filmmaking under the aegis of the organization's fidelity to film and visual technologies as instruments of mass education and universal literacy. From 1947 to 1948, of course, Grierson had served as the first director of UNESCO's mass communications division; its model of educational film was influenced by a number of documentary filmmakers in Grierson's circle, including Arthur Elton, Basil Wright, and Paul Rotha, who remained involved in UNESCO until the 1960s. Indeed, the Goldsholls' list of recommended readings for all conference attendees—divided into "Art and Design" and "Film"—includes, on the film list, both *Grierson on Documentary* (1947) and the second edition of Paul Rotha's *The Film Till Now: A Survey of World Cinema* (1951).

The Goldsholls would likely have studied the work of Grierson and his collaborators under Moholy-Nagy at the Institute of Design. Moholy had worked for Grierson's GPO Film Unit during his time in London in the 1930s, and included Grierson's work in his "New Vision in Photography" seminar at the ID in 1946.[87] In *Vision in Motion* (included in the Goldsholls' "Art and Design" reading list for IDCA 1959), Moholy notes approvingly Grierson's GPO productions, lauding the role of film as "an educational and propaganda medium of first importance" in "our epoch of political and economic struggle."[88] The Goldsholls' vision of world cinema at IDCA 1959 could be described as Griersonian because many films screened there updated for the postwar liberal world order the essentially managerial and technocratic ambitions of Grierson's social scientific approach to film as a communications medium.[89] Through institutions like UNESCO, and at locations like the IDCA, Grierson's interwar, nationalist ideal of corporate subjecthood—working citizens brought into harmonious interconnection with each other and the state, as in *Nightmail*'s swift journey of the Postal Special train from London to Aberdeen—was being remade in a vision of therapeutic mid-century internationalism and global liberal citizenship. Film historian Lee Grieveson has demonstrated the crucial role of Griersonian documentary in the political economy of capitalist imperialism in interwar Britain. Interwar documentary "flourished in the space shared by state and corporate entities," visualizing the global flow of "raw materials and manufactured goods" within the Commonwealth and "shaping the attitudes and conduct of populations."[90] Significant portions of Millie Goldsholl's film program, with nods to the work of the GPO, Canada's National Film Board, and UNESCO, were made possible by a similar, postwar alignment of state and corporate interests. Like Grierson, such efforts sought to harness the communicative power of film, especially its role in "that central liberal problematic—the question of how individuals were bound to the social order."[91] As we'll see, the ideological power of cinema was taken up and debated at IDCA 1959 in the "Film Image" cycle as a central concern of enlightened liberal experts.

This managerial approach to the challenge of world culture helps us account for the fitful generic overlapping of "communication" and "experimental" categories at IDCA 1959, which shaped the kinds of modernist or avant-garde practice that might emerge there. The interwar Grierson argued for liberal world making as managerial control rather than revolutionary upheaval.[92] As in the interwar period, so too in the Goldsholls' program were the communicative imperatives of documentary, education, and sponsored films met with forms of communicative intransigence. Similarly, the Griersonian version of national, corporate subjectivity, secured by film's unrivaled power of "suggestion," was confronted by the affective maladjustment of various filmic modernisms. The cross section of specifically avant-garde and modernist work screened at Brussels, and partially imported to Aspen that summer through the auspices of Amos Vogel's Cinema 16, Maya Deren, and the MoMA Film Library, testified to the emergence in the 1950s of a vital experimental film culture in the United States.[93] Its novel aesthetic strategies were brilliantly analyzed in Vogel's review of the Brussels Experimental Film Festival, which appeared in the pages of the *Evergreen Review* late in 1958.[94] Vogel juxtaposes the "huge, glimmering, high-priced, chromium-plated concoction of artificialities" of the United States' pavilion and the "massive mediocrity" of the Russian effort with the "visual and aural attacks" of 130 entries in the fair's experimental film competition—"poverty-stricken little films" marked by the "last-ditch sincerity of the step-children and outcasts, with nothing to lose and hence a willingness to say it all" ("AYFM," 336, 337). Noting approvingly the state funding of experimental production in Poland, Germany, and Great Britain, he decries the absence of such financing in the United States, where "any production of surrealist films under Mr. Eisenhower's aegis would be considered 'creeping socialism'" ("AYFM," 344). This way of linking the intimate and the social, the future of the avant-garde and the benighted priorities of governmental agencies (for Vogel, so absurdly on display in the misguided pavilions), extends to his insistence on the politics of the intimate and the validity of the thematics of the self. This seeming inwardness, he insists, is "'relevant' to the social situation: Problems of alienation and atomization of the individual, problems of sex and love, problems of adjustment and conformity are eminently social in character" ("AYFM," 343).

Surveying the range of experimental production, Vogel draws out a consistent "concern with the body politic," and beyond that, an abiding anger, evident not just in the overtly "ideological films" at the festival, like VanDerBeek's *What Who How* or Polanski's *Two Men and a Wardrobe,* but expressed in the "vocabularies and often oblique techniques" of modern art. Such anger, Vogel insists, "remains on the sub-political plane; it is an expression of generalized anguish and tension vis-à-vis organized society, not a call to action" ("AYFM," 343). For Vogel, to be "experimental" in 1958 was in part to insist on aesthetic strategies of what art historian Meyer Schapiro would, that same year, describe as a modernist formalism of "non-communication."[95] Schapiro had in his sights the postwar prestige of a "theory and practice of communication" that abetted a world of "social relationships which is impersonal, calculating, and controlled," and art that followed from it indexed the pathos of "the reduction or fragility of the self within a culture that becomes increasingly organized through industry, economy, and the state."[96] His ideologically fraught counterexample, of course, was Jackson Pollock, whose strategies of automatism testified to the "power of the organism to produce interesting unforeseen effects," bringing into the function of aesthetic ordering its "necessary counterpart, the element of randomness and accident." In the wake of landmark accounts of how abstract expressionism was instrumentalized in the Cold War as a manifestation of a quintessentially American freedom, its humane spontaneity co-opted in propagandistic feats of cultural diplomacy like the Brussels World's Fair, we have become rightly suspicious of this jargon of expressive authenticity. This makes the terms of Vogel's essay on experimental practice, which everywhere insists on the relationship between artistic production and the managerial imperatives of the state, all the more striking. Instead of a manifesto for uninhibited artistic freedom, we get an argument for more enlightened arts management in the United States. His story about the expressive self, we might say, eschews Schapiro's contemporaneous language of radical contingency for a rhetoric of environmental mastery and control, a kind of liberal self-discipline. "The exploration and documentation of the soul," Vogel writes, "is every whit as valid as that of the outer world. It is only through the understanding and mastery of both inner and outer realities that we can hope to control our environment and thereby our own fates" ("AYFM," 343).

A similar scalar language of environmental control and the synchronous comanagement of inner and outer worlds runs throughout the IDCA panel on the humane medium of film. Instead of a comprehensive conference on "Design and Film," the IDCA program actually offered folded filmic specificity under the more expansive, medially indifferent rubrics of "Communication" and "The Image," and sectioned the conference proceedings into three cycles: "The Image Evolves," "The Printed Image," and the culminating "The Film Image," whose international examples—both the films screened and the filmmakers selected as speakers—would, the program notes, "help us to understand the significance and universality of an art which encompasses all other arts and leads men to the status of 'knowing each other' through art."[97] This cycle was chaired by IDCA regular Saul Bass, whose credit sequence for *The Man with the Golden Arm* was featured in the film program, and included talks by five speakers: French filmologist Gilbert Cohen-Séat; the

Figure 3.15.
James C. W. Lunde, front cover of *Report: Ninth International Design Conference in Aspen,* 1959. International Design Conference in Aspen Papers, Special Collections and University Archives, University Library, University of Illinois at Chicago.

Russian-born science photographer and microcinematographer Roman Vishniac; the American Jerry Schnitzler, a pioneer in the filmed television commercial; and two giants of experimental cinema: the Scottish-born Norman McLaren and the New Zealand native Len Lye, then a U.S. citizen. Lye did not attend in person, but his talk, "Is Film a Fine Art?," was distributed with the conference papers under discussion. In that packet, Lye's biography lists, as his profession, "aesthetic kinesthesia," and as his hobby, "utopia."[98]

Lye's cheeky responses are striking, underscoring how the particular sensory demands of this midcentury world in motion would fuel—at Aspen—conflicting aspirations toward the worldly, and relatedly, the universe and the universal, that were legible as both utopian designs and management strategies. While film's inherent universality is, of course, one of the medium's most notoriously unkillable myths, it found renewed prestige within the IDCA's discursive horizon, built as it was on Paepcke's postwar ideal of a Goethean *Humanität* and *Weltliteratur*. With these institutional aspirations in mind, it is perhaps no surprise that IDCA 1959 would rather anxiously position film's capacities for world making or worldly communication—its capacity to concentrate populations on a global scale—as a bulwark against the often baffling variety of worlds, with their conspicuously new movements, speeds, technologies, and natures, that IDCA panelists observed as having opened up at midcentury, and demanding better forms of management. Cast as a protagonist in a postwar "crisis of scale," and of nature transfigured, film was a tool of world making, consensus building, and pattern seeing, but it was also a harbinger of the imperiled universal, and of new or unfamiliar worlds in motion.

The conference's first keynote address, delivered by Bruce MacKenzie, a science writer and editor for IBM, warned the audience of the menacing revolution of new computational technologies, and framed the plight of the designer in his confrontation with an "infinitely expanding, progressively less concrete physical and physic world"—the "disintegration of the apparent solidity of nature."[99] Facing this future, the design profession would function on the frontier of knowledge work, the bridge between aesthetics and science, the humanities and the inhuman power of technology. At the same time, IDCA's conferees conceptualized the utility of film—as a technology, an art, a mode of communication, an informatic medium—within an expansive range of institutional contexts, subjecting it to scrutiny from a range of disciplinary vantages and regimes of expertise. The speakers were finding new worlds for film, expanding its communicative potential within the new media environments and competing knowledge regimes of the Cold War, even as they counted on film's humane universality—its organic or biological dimensions—as compensation for the inhuman, unnatural, or communicatively dissensual in postwar life.

We can see this most urgently in the film panelists' recurring *evolutionary* idiom—their tropism toward the language of organism and visual environment. This allowed them at once to describe and to naturalize what seemed unnatural, untimely, or chaotic in the new worlds these designers sought to manage, and to wed film to a variety of management strategies. Complicating matters was the fact that film itself was both symptomatic of what seemed less human in these worlds, and the inhuman therapy. Vishniac, for example, argued that cinemicroscopy, by giving us the "means to see the last unknown part of this globe," both opens up a new universe and returns humans to the "basic unity and interdependence of the biological universe." Lye's paper mounted a medium-specific argument for film as a kinesthetic art form, one uniting light and motion, and one best suited for the "increasingly pronounced kinetic quality of twentieth-century art," which "evokes a sensory rather than a conceptual involvement." But Lye's enthusiasm for film as a domain of what he called "bodily empathy" was also bound to his claim that every great art object transmits a "biologically founded and psychologically transposed content of evolutionary individuality." Casting the aesthetic as both the engine of humane, corporeal empathy and the carrier of the "evolutionary gene-pattern of individuality," Lye asserted

Figure 3.16. Morton Goldsholl and Dr. Roman Vishniac at the Ninth International Design Conference in Aspen, 1959. Courtesy of Harry Goldsholl.

film art's capacity to supplement technoscience's claims to factual truths and short-lived discoveries with "emotional symbols that convey the depth and greatness of our common evolutionary drives." Indeed, the persistent interest in forms of unalienated somatic experience in Lye's films, and his sense of the dynamic film screen as space for a kinesthetic innervation of technology, consistently operated in a therapeutic register, posited against the sensory depredations of rationally administered modernity. Given his own commissioned, state-sponsored work, most famously for the GPO, Lye was surely attuned to the potential threat to the sovereignty of the individual lurking in his paper's claims for postwar film and television as "the most empathic mediums of communication for inducing an immediate psychological involvement."[100]

The panelist most anxious about the psychological force of mass media and its implications for liberal democracy in a new landscape of Cold War propaganda was Cohen-Séat. During his presentation, he explained his long-standing interest in the unique perceptual dynamics of the "cinematic situation," and described the fruits of one experiment to underscore the power of film as a "calculated inducer of responses."[101] Explaining his technique to the audience, he noted, "I tried at first to get the largest variety of interpretation—then I started changing the film to get *one* answer." Updating Lev Kuleshov, Cohen-Séat's experiments rebooted Soviet behaviorism to manage the baffling contours of what his paper dubbed the contemporary "iconosphere." In it the ancestral human "biosphere" had been supplanted by a new quantity of information signals exceeding individual powers of absorption. Cohen-Séat was extending filmology's interest in establishing film as an object of positivist science, and its interdisciplinary investment in the psychophysiological testing of spectators, into a Cold War domain marked by the "direct aggression of organisms by visual techniques," what he ominously called "the disturbing impregnation of the perceived world." In his *Essay on the Principles of a Philosophy of Cinema,* written in 1946, Cohen-Séat had insisted that the power of film lay both in its humanistic, universal dimensions, what he called its "quality of humanity," and in its democratic potential as a *mass* medium, its "*quantity* of humanity."[102] "It is," he wrote, "first around the human—ordered, individual, and universal—that a progressive concentration of populations ideally occurs by means of the cinema, and on a level and scale previously unknown."[103] Cohen-Séat thus shared a foundational Griersonian investment in the affective power of cinema to bind citizens to the organizational, propagandistic aims of state and corporate entities.[104] In sum, the conference's evolutionary idiom for envisioning the communicative dimensions of the image had clear implications for understanding film's ideological power, and it provided the "philosophical" background for Millie Goldsholl's contemporaneous claim to Patterson that "making films is a great responsibility proportionate to the size of audiences they reach and the influences they yield."

On this, the transfigured scale and power of the midcentury media environment, the panelists could agree. In his precirculated paper, György Kepes included the last chapter of *The New Landscape in Art and Science* (1956), "Continuity, Discontinuity, Rhythm, Scale." The essay, like the larger collection from which it was drawn, was shaped by Kepes's encounters with Gestalt psychology and cybernetics, and his Bauhaus sensory pedagogy. It links biological and social growth to levels of internal organization with an appropriate hierarchy of scale; but the midcentury, as Kepes saw it, was marked by a crisis of scale, a mismatch between the human and "the entire horizon of nature that we can now sense," with technological help. His solution was another kind of sensory management that would harness television, motion pictures, and photography to visualize a dynamic, patterned, organized nature operating at all levels—micro and macro—but often insensible to the naked human eye.

In sum, the conference's scalar and evolutionary idiom for thinking the communicative dimensions of the image had clear implications both for understanding film's capacity to "concentrate populations" (in Cohen-Séat's terms) and the designer's power and responsibility to manage them through moving-images technologies. In his contribution to "The Printed Image" cycle, one of the conference's most contentious sessions, for example, William Capitman drew on the social psychological basis of market research analysis to deny the universality of all communications, and to embed them instead in the messy contingencies of audiences, history, and culture—all of which could be managed by more subtle acts of persuasion. James Real responded by savaging this social scientific targeting of a dependable consumption unit for its collusion with the systemic, cybernetic management of a weapons system whose efficiency is threatened by "failures of the biomechanical link"—the vagaries of human desire. The conference—even when not taking up film specifically—thus raised questions about which versions of democracy or universality would accompany the new powers of designers and the new media of technical administration.

Perhaps the most telling speaker in this regard was the esteemed British physiologist turned medical statistician Lancelot Hogben (Plate 12). A leftist biologist in J. H. Huxley's London circle in the 1930s, by the late 1950s Hogben had authored a number of best-selling popular works on the interrelations of science, communications, education, and media, including *From Cave Painting to Comic Strip: A Kaleidoscope of Human Communication* (1949), which joined Eisenstein, Rotha, Grierson, Arnheim, and Kepes on the Goldsholls' recommended reading list. Hogben was both included as an IDCA 1959 speaker on the "Printed Image" cycle and given the honor of providing a summary address of all of the papers on the conference's final day. In the 1930s Hogben enjoyed strong connections to the British documentary film movement, which, with many in the scientific community, turned to the social relations of science in the 1930s, and he was an important figure in articulating the relationship between documentary, citizenship discourse, applied science, and the conditions of technological modernity.[105]

In many ways, Hogben's addresses and his precirculated paper extended the conceptual thrust of his *From Cave Painting to Comic Strip*. A curious work of high-scientific humanism and quirky media archaeology, the book concerns the supposed "uniqueness of man" as a "picture-making animal." But the book's real preoccupation is global communication—specifically, "the liquidation of illiteracy on a world scale as a prelude to the unification of mankind."[106] Film is thought in Griersonian fashion as a pedagogical tool for world citizenship, but also in Meadian and Eamesian terms as a time-saving tool for managing a glut of information, communicating existing knowledge efficiently, and making visible both temporal concepts and "*the dynamical content of modern science*" (*FCP*, 237). As a way of "serving time, saving time, and showing time," film is conscripted in the urgent task of democratic world government, namely, "speeding up humanistic education for citizenship" and "accelerating the tempo for assimilating knowledge" (*FCP*, 237, 277, 275).[107] Despite his critiques of UNESCO's operational inefficiencies, Hogben insisted on film's vital role in a system of world government on a mission of international communication, even naming admiringly the worldly thought of Robert Maynard Hutchins that had helped bring Paepcke's humane Aspen into being in the first place (*FCP*, 276).

At IDCA 1959, Hogben described the "challenge" of modern science as "the unification of mankind in a world of potential plenty."[108] This requires "the re-orientation of educational procedures to affect a new DESIGN for human communications at every level, linguistic and mathematical, with the fullest exploitation of the new visual aids at our disposal." Hogben's summation returned to MacKenzie's disconcerting opening keynote on the potential threat of the electronic brain and the frenetic pace of knowledge production and information. But he welcomed the knowledge explosion as an opportunity for conferees to think boldly about visual communications technologies such as film and television, and their potential to "speak the language of the eye," transcending "local preoccupations and local prejudices to address a global audience."[109] But he also mocked the conference's moral debates about the designer's obeisance to corporate capitalism and its new social scientific marketing techniques that had defined the contentious early sessions of the conference. This was wasteful hand-wringing, and in bad faith to boot. Hogben's point was not that designers should refuse an instrumental relationship to the image or eschew the Griersonian link between communication, film, and propaganda, but rather that they should rethink the kind of freedom such instrumentality would serve in the first place. Arguing for the unparalleled power of education films for creating a "unified world culture on whatever side of the Iron Curtain they happen to be making them," he chastised fellow conferees for promoting a version of freedom bound to the "vast multiplicity of scarcely identifiably different objects." "Is this the sort of freedom," he asked, "that would appeal to the poverty-stricken and as yet uncommitted peoples of Africa and Asia?" Would this promote the good life or serve the "unification of world culture"? Hardly.

How, we should ask, does this instrumental approach to world communication square with the range of experimental practices voiced at Aspen? Norman McLaren's paper, for example, took up the specificity of music in relationship to the global distribution of film, arguing that film music is a stumbling block to "universal intelligibility," stubbornly regional, before arguing that the variegated "musical susceptibilities" of worldwide populations might be overcome; he called for analysis of a "new kind of 'basic music,'" with an emotional "common denominator."[110] His interest—fueled in part by his UNESCO assignments—in the question of whether it was possible to use "the fundamental ingredients of tempo, dynamics, rhythm, meter, stress and pitch" so that they might "speak a really universal language" extends a long-standing modernist interest in reduction and elementarization. But in the discursive climate of IDCA 1959, it would likely be heard as an echo of Hogben's calls for a common world language, remaking the visual aspirations of Otto Neurath's Isotype on the level of sound.[111] Hogben had himself devised a universal language called "Interglossa," an auxiliary language for a "democratic world order" whose reduced vocabulary (around nine hundred words) was based in the international lexicon of science and technology and their Greek and Latin roots. The achievements of Western technoscience, by remaking the grammar of elemental nature, would provide "the bricks of a minimum vocabulary of world-wide communication," overcoming the "babel of tongues." This new nature, further, was wedded to Hogben's aim of universal world literacy and the developmental model of modernization underpinning it (*FCP*, 280).

The "animated picture," Hogben insisted, allowed for the seeing and sensing of the "dynamical content of modern science" (*FCP,* 237). He might as well have been describing Lye's animated film *Free Radicals,* which was screened at the conference. A five-minute film made by painstakingly hand-scratching through black emulsion, Lye's film had won second prize at Brussels, and was inspired by an article he read in the *New York Times* science section about so-called free radicals—highly reactive and unstable atoms or molecules with unpaired electrons. Movement itself was singled out by moderator Saul Bass as the unifying concern of the "Film Image" panel, and the conferees' various, often competing approaches to film itself were articulated as ways of exploring and managing both the medium's inherent dynamism and its relationship to the scale and pace of postwar change that institutions and experts gathered at Aspen would administer. Like many of the conference's speakers, a number of the experimental films screened at the conference, including *Free Radicals,* placed the medium as an agent in a story of explosive postwar development and technoscientific dynamism. Film at IDCA 1959 was thus embedded in conferees' broader reckoning with the "the great acceleration." The medium became a conceptual hinge between the domain of the fully human, witness to the sheer scale and power of anthropogenesis, and the threat of inhuman technicity.

We might speculate briefly about the competing messages communicated in the Goldsholls' film program about human agency, its relationship to the technoscientific control of environments, and the status of postwar "nature" transfigured within those developmental narratives. The ideological stakes of the dynamism syncopating the experimental films at the conference become much clearer over and against the paeans to the anthropogenic control of nature in some of the communication films. Many of the latter, in fact, are marked by the same evolutionary confidence in postwar technological development expressed by the panelists, and the same wish to harness technology and nature in cheery stories of managed growth and change, and controlled and teleological movement, rather than disruptive or nonlinear dynamism.

The Eameses' IBM-sponsored *The Information Machine* proceeds from caveman to mainframe in an animated, relentlessly teleological story of the development of the computer in a long history of human tool making dedicated to the "mastery and control of the environment." It argues for the threefold potential of the computer: as a control mechanism to ensure the smooth management of public utilities and infrastructure; as a function of design, programmable by tech-savvy creatives to perform various tasks; and for its capacity to simulate and model possible scenarios, predicting the effects of "various courses of action." In

Figure 3.17. Naturalizing the computer as a control technology in *The Information Machine: Creative Man and the Data Processor*, 1957, directed by Charles and Ray Eames.

typical Eamesian fashion, this large-scale power (and its potential inhumanity) is domesticated as the narrator proclaims the computer's "real miracle"—the way it frees us for the "smallest details that have been the basis for man's most rewarding riches." Inner and outer environments are harmonized. Or consider the animated film *Energetically Yours* (1957), with illustrations by the legendary British artist Ronald Searle. Produced by Transfilm for Standard Oil, and directed by UPA (United Productions of America) cofounder David Hilberman, the film offers a history of human evolution as the discovery and exploitation of evermore-powerful energy sources. Beginning in outer space, the animation zooms in on terrestrial man, and the voice-over narration begins: "Who is the most powerful creature on the face of the earth? Man! Man alone is master on land, on sea, and in the air. No other creature moves mountains and rivers, controlling the forces of energy, shaping them to his own designs." The chest-thumping tale of human mastery, abetted by comic counterfactual scenarios of oxen strapping humans to the plow, and fish yanking men out of the sea, hinges on the unique power of human beings, which begins with their large brains and their capacity to harness increasingly more potent energy sources—from animal power to steam to fossil fuels. The thirteen-minute film's swift and unrepentant movement from the industrial era to the contemporary "age of gasoline," in which "hundreds of energy servants" are at our beck and call as tiny butlers managing the energy infrastructure of everyday life, situates Shell's (nonatomic) energy business at the center of increasing demands for energy worldwide.

In this context, one might well wonder what the conferees made of a film like Norman McLaren's *A Chairy Tale* (1957), a stunning allegory of the human's exploitation of things through one's man's vexed attempt to domesticate an ordinary chair by the act of sitting on it. McLaren's animation technique—its interventions into the speeds and times of embodied movement—was situated precisely in the interface between the human and the technological. While the aggressive dance between man and chair is eventually reconciled at the film's conclusion ("and they sat happily ever after"), the film is in many ways a challenge to the human's instrumental relationship to the object world. It enshrines instead a kind of enchanted materialism in which the chair becomes vital, transcending its thingliness, and the human body escapes its habitual movements, coming to experience itself in processes of change and chance, and thereby becoming other to itself.

Or, we might ask how the spatiotemporal manipulations of Maya Deren's *At Land* (1944), and its experimental dynamism, might respond to the dramas of nature, energy, and human control in industrial films

Figure 3.18. Happy endings, in *A Chairy Tale*, 1957, directed by Norman McLaren.

Figure 3.19. Filmmaker Maya Deren and designer Alvin Lustig, *At Land,* 1944, directed by Maya Deren.

such as *Energetically Yours.* In her landmark essay "An Anagram of Ideas on Art, Form, and Film" (1946), Deren made a medium-specific argument for the modernism of film that hinged on an analogy between the transfigurations of nature achieved by postwar technoscience, the result of the "violation of natural integrity," and art's own violence to nature—its capacity to "renounce the natural frame of reference."[112] The "task of creating forms as dynamic as the relationships in natural phenomena is the central problem of both the scientist and the artist," she argued, and this would require a strategic *unnaturalness* ("A," 46). Refusing what she would later identify as "the familiar concept of matter as a static solid anchored in a stable cosmos," film would model instead a new nature, producing a "dynamic living whole in which the interaction of the parts produces more than the sum of the parts."[113] In this way, films like *At Land* are designed to surge with energies as "mysterious and miraculous" as the atomic miracle—a key exemplar, for Deren, of the production of new nature ("A," 46, 47).

Here and elsewhere in Deren's film theory and practice, we see the influence of Gestalt psychology on her notions of the organized image as a new, living whole that also appears contemporaneously in the work of Kepes and Arnheim, both on the recommended reading list for the 1959 conference. Like them, Deren defines the very modernism of film and moving-image technologies in their production of dynamic, artificial, but no less *living* aesthetic unities whose "value derives from the integrated whole of which they are a part, and this whole is not familiar, but a new experience" ("A," 65). In fact, in her 1960 "Cinematography" essay, which refines the theory of filmic "nature" first advanced in "Anagram," Deren cast the disoriented journey of *At Land*'s protagonist as a kind of atomic-age *Odyssey* whose energies reverse the agential drama of Homer's original. Rather than dynamically acting within a static landscape, bending it to her designs, her protagonist finds "that the universe itself has usurped the dynamic action which was once the prerogative of human will, and confronts her with a volatile and relentless metamorphosis."[114] The claim, like the essay, appeared in a special issue of *Dœdalus* titled "The Visual Arts Today," edited by Kepes himself. Acting within the new, transfigured nature, which has now become an agential force threatening her very existence, *At Land* seems to augur the drama of the incipient Anthropocene, puncturing the fantasies of environmental control and mastery screened elsewhere at the conference.[115]

Communications or Film, Circa 1959

In arguing for the International Design Conference in Aspen as a crucial site for understanding the administration of culture in the postwar period, and for exploring film and its worldly aspirations, this chapter has explored the technique of the conference as a mode of knowledge work and an instrument of organization at the dawn of the information age. In Paepcke's Aspen, the power of film was understood not just as spatially coextensive with the postwar geopolitical order presided over by the United States, or a global emissary of ideas and ideologies in the American Century, but also as a uniquely humane, even universal medium of international communication and understanding. Film was part of a managerial enterprise of humane liberal-democratic world making. In conceptualizing the power and influence of moving images, the Goldsholls and the various experts assembled at the IDCA grappled with the contours of the postwar world and assessed the terms of their own heightened responsibility for it.

Although the far-ranging conversations about film within the "communications" paradigm at the IDCA may seem unfamiliar today, subjected to scrutiny from experts whose disciplinary positions and managerial ambitions have been largely ignored in accounts of what Haidee Wasson and Charles R. Acland have dubbed the overlooked "middle period" in film history, we should recall in closing that in 1959, film studies—as a discipline—had not yet been invented.[116] In 1957 and 1958, the Museum of Modern Art gathered a group of university educators to "discuss the teaching of film as an art form," and the place of film in the university. From those meetings, the fledging Society for Cinematologists (SoC), later the Society for Cinema Studies and now the Society for Cinema and Media Studies, was organized in 1959.[117] Thus would a professional organization, and shortly an academic publication, the *Journal of the Society of Cinematologists,* abet film studies' incipient institutionalization. "Cinematology" owed its name to French filmology, and recalled Cohen-Séat's positivist dream of a "science" of cinema, but it would stake its claim for "cinema study as an autonomous discipline" by drawing on the formalist methodology of the New Critics. This meant turning away from social scientific methodologies and arguing instead for the specificity of film studies as part of the liberal arts, with a role to play in the inculcation of liberal-humanist subjects. In the process, film studies began to cleave from the communication studies programs that flourished in the Cold War university, beginning a disciplinary divide that persists today.

The IDCA of the 1950s approached film in the thick of these disciplinary and institutional struggles, which, as Lee Grieveson has argued, eventually produced a "common ground" about the "political efficacy of the liberal arts in the shaping of liberal populations" that would be severely tested over the course of the 1960s, as universities, and their disciplinary imperatives and distinctions, became the object of sustained ideological critique.[118] So too would the liberal-humanist politics of mainstream design institutions like the IDCA, and adjacent ventures like the Vision 65 and 67 conferences, come under attack, despite (or because of) their concerted efforts to bring the energies of the avant-garde and counterculture on board. Perhaps *because* the IDCA's designs on film were more ambitious in their managerial scope than those of the fledgling SoC (wedded as the IDCA's were to programs of global capitalist modernization *as* development), and indeed because the IDCA had long rejected the distinction between the autonomous vitality of the liberal arts and the instrumentality of design as a function of management, this august institution would feel the pressure of "the 1960s" especially acutely, faced with what that decade's great communications theorist Jacques Derrida would, in 1968, call "the ends of man."[119] Amidst the rise (and fall) of structuralism and its posthuman, systems-oriented thinking, this managerial approach to communication—with its attendant attitudes toward the category of the environment, toward the limits of human agency and productivity, and toward the discourse of development itself—would be decisively confronted by new media practices and theorists that continued to find institutional platforms at design conferences (Plate 13). As the universality of the IDCA's designs on world culture splintered into a multiplicity of worlds and competing gambits of utopian world making, these strategies of modernist noncommunication at IDCA 1959, which Vogel had diagnosed as a species of "subpolitical anger," found overt political articulation. Along the way, a new generation of media theory was born.

4

memories of overdevelopment

The Vision Conferences and the Fate of Environmental Design

WRITING TO VISION 67'S DAZZLING ARRAY of potential attendees, Will Burtin described the conference as a "forum of free interdisciplinary debates" intended to "bridge a widening worldwide chasm between human needs and technology."[1] Burtin believed fervently in film's role in closing this divide. For him film was a medium of managed growth: a pedagogical technology for visualizing order in times of rapid economic development and social transformation. He was thus keen to invite speakers to address film's place in projects of education and enculturation. One such speaker was Jerzy Toeplitz, the Polish film critic and director of the famed Polish Film School in Łódź, that year on a visiting appointment at UCLA. Toeplitz would answer Burtin's call for wide-ranging "evaluation of the East and West European film scene"; the critic proposed to describe the pedagogical role of visual media in the "cultural development of humanity" and to discuss "the role of the avant-garde and experimentation."[2] Burtin's reply was enthusiastic, and he politely requested Toeplitz's views on "the moral aspect of movie-making," noting that "McLuhan avoids this consistently." But he did have one question: "Is there," he asked, an " 'avant-garde'? Having seen a great deal of underground movies I am somewhat skeptical. Aside from a certain delight with the effects of brutalization, with sex and strobe sensations, to which I should add multiple projections that are often quite confusing, there is something here that needs a good analytical review. Fine."[3]

Burtin may not have known it, but one of his own exhibition designs had, just a few years earlier, provided the ironic mise-en-scène of maldevelopment in a landmark underground film, Ron Rice's *The Queen*

Figure 4.1. Will Burtin, Union Carbide exhibition, New York. Photograph by Ezra Stoller. Copyright Esto. All rights reserved.

of Sheba Meets the Atom Man (1963). It features Warhol superstar Taylor Mead, who appears in the film consistently stoned and erratic. Early on, having raided a giant carton of heroin, he decamps his grungy pad for a comic, Beckettian stroll in the city. He unlocks a door and finds himself in Burtin's *World of the Future* exhibition, a paean to atomic energy commissioned by Union Carbide to celebrate the opening of the firm's new Park Avenue skyscraper, designed by Gordon Bunshaft of Skidmore, Owings & Merrill. Burtin's interactive educational exhibit, complete with a massive model of a uranium-92 atom, was designed to educate and inform about an environmental future. It placed Union Carbide's uranium-enrichment efforts, and the corporation's promise of cheap nuclear energy, in a deep history of "man's changing concept of the atom over 2,500 years."[4] Approaching the atom's core as its moving lights simulate a chain reaction, Mead jerks and twitches with his own manic, parodic energy. Nearly touching the pulsing nucleus, he mimes a series of frantic licks. Novelist Alberto Moravia called the film's knowing counterpoint of underground and corporate media practices "a protest which is violent, childish, and sincere—a protest against an industrial world based on the cycle of production and consumption."[5] Mead and Rice are messing with Burtin's happy model of environmental futurity and proposing a countermodel of their own design.

From Burtin's vantage, the avant-garde was neither to be dismissed nor ignored at Vision 67, but rather subjected to analysis through the communicative regime of the international conference and its happy, therapeutic talk. Burtin may have had on the brain his prior program for Vision 65: World Congress on New Challenges to Human Communications, held at Southern Illinois University (Plate 14). There, American underground filmmaking was represented by Stan VanDerBeek, experimental filmmaker and multimedia savant, who gave a talk titled "Re:Vision" on the panel "A Visionary Outlook: As Seen from Three Communication Areas," interspersed with screenings of several of his films.[6] He also curated an evening program of avant-garde film. VanDerBeek was perhaps strong tea for Burtin, but his enthusiastic account of Vision 65

Figure 4.2. Taylor Mead at Will Burtin's *World of the Future* exhibition, in *The Queen of Sheba Meets the Atom Man,* 1963, directed by Ron Rice.

Figure 4.3. Will Burtin, working with a model of the *Visual Communications* exhibition, Kalamazoo Arts Center, 1957. Will Burtin Papers, RIT Libraries: Graphic Design Archives, Rochester Institute of Technology.

prompted Amos Vogel to write the designer requesting copies of the conference records and proceedings.[7] For Vision 67, Burtin would extend an invitation to Vogel himself, requesting an "evaluation of the American scene." From both sides of the Iron Curtain, Toeplitz and Vogel would assess "the motion picture's potential value as a communication tool for survival and growth."[8]

However skeptical Burtin may have been about *The Queen of Sheba* and the so-called avant-garde in 1967, he insisted that it be widely represented at the Vision conferences. For Vision 65, this included VanDerBeek, Marshall McLuhan, and Buckminster Fuller (who gave both the opening keynote and the closing summary address); but also Dr. Vera Horvat-Pintarić, a prominent Yugoslavian art critic and promulgator of that country's various socialist modernisms; Max Bill, rector at the legendary Hochschule für Gestaltung (Institute of Design) in Ulm, Germany; Italian painter, sculptor, and graphic designer Eugenio Carmi; Dutch experimental composer and electronic music theorist Gottfried Michael Koenig; American experimental sound designer Tony Schwartz, who played a series of sound collages; and Roger L. Stevens, special adviser for the arts to President Johnson. An emissary of the Great Society, Stevens was on hand to explain the aims of the recently passed bill to establish the National Endowment for the Arts and Humanities, and LBJ's broader designs on the future of state-sponsored arts and humanities education as a technical program of national enrichment in a time of increased leisure. Compared with the modernism that Stevens and his colleagues at the NEA's Visual Arts Program supported in the 1960s, Burtin's assembly of vanguard practice at Vision 67 seems especially ambitious.[9] Burtin included several seminal figures at the intersection of art and technology in the 1960s: mathematician Max Bense, the influential German theorist of "information aesthetics"; writer, theorist, and semiotician Umberto Eco; Hungarian-French op art sculptor Victor Vasarely; and the mischievous Swiss painter and sculptor Jean Tinguely, whose neo-Dada provocation

Figure 4.4. Sculptor Jean Tinguely and Will Burtin, at Vision 67: Survival and Growth, New York. Will Burtin Papers, RIT Libraries: Graphic Design Archives, Rochester Institute of Technology.

at Vision 67 included a site-specific construction of an absurd machine for pulverizing beer bottles.

By extending Burtin's post-1955 IDCA mandate to approach communication through the agglomerated expertise of the managerial, formulating, and educating professions, the Vision conferences made clear the porosity of these disciplinary distinctions, and their mutual implication in the postwar period. In conferencing, bleeding-edge artists, like social scientists, betrayed programmatic and even managerial ambitions. Agents of the state—from Western, socialist, and nonaligned nations alike—variously claimed renewed responsibility for the future of the arts. And designers such as Burtin framed their work as an overtly pedagogical enterprise, a high-stakes reckoning with the shape of the future itself, and the transformed environment of the postwar period.

Indeed, "environment" itself became a privileged term at the Vision conferences—their most potent disciplinary solvent. It was variously invoked as the locus of far-reaching but often invisible transformations in the present and future, and the prized object of knowledge and control, conceptualization and liberatory aesthetic intervention. Burtin put it bluntly in his opening address at Vision 65: "Our environment is destroyed rapidly by the effects of uncontrolled growth which is guided apparently by no other motivations than opportunism, profit, and expansion."[10] To stave off "free fall"—the "wholesale destruction of cities, landscapes, rivers, seashores, and national cultures"—Burtin exhorted speakers to produce a "new plan through exposure to the entire horizon of communications" (*65*, 9). Survey, plan, survive. Communications media, Burtin reasoned, would provide "social, economic, and psychological adjustments" on both "a national and a world scale" (*65*, 8–9).

As Burtin's vanguard project of growth management, the Vision conferences convened at a moment in which architecture and design had assumed new disciplinary identities within what Felicity D. Scott has diagnosed as a broad "discourse of environment" shaped by the postwar confluence of systems theory, cybernetics, information theory, and semiology.[11] As such, "environmental design" became an aspect of media practice and theory; and communications infrastructures—as the engines of social and technological change—were understood as part of the fabric of "the environment" as such. Fuller's opening address at Vision 65, for example, began at the level of the subsensible environment, hailing "the invisible evolution" in which today "world society is operating almost exclusively in the inaudible and nonvisible area of the physical universe" (*65*, 11). McLuhan's concluding keynote, "The Role of the Anti-Environment in Creating Environmental Awareness," drew on Jacques Ellul's recently translated *Propaganda* to describe media change

Figure 4.5. Buckminster Fuller, keynote lecture at Vision 65: New Challenges for Human Communication, Southern Illinois University. Courtesy of Southern Illinois University Libraries.

as an evolutionary, "environmental" process. Through it, each succeeding "new" media environment, "invisible" in its incipience, serves "to make very visible the preceding environment" (*65*, 213).[12] An outline for the hardcover publication of Vision 65's conference proceedings gives the title of VanDerBeek's talk as "The Environmental Film."[13] And while Burtin may not have quite *gotten* VanDerBeek, the artist would later describe Vision 65 as a "glorious conference that talked about trying to make a difference in the world, and trying to make sense of the work and deal with communication."[14] On the back of his Vision 65 conference program, VanDerBeek sketched a prototype of his own, yet-to-be-built Movie-Drome, a now-legendary multimedia environment that VanDerBeek constructed later that year at the Gate Hill Co-op in Stony Point, New York.[15] Within the next year, he would publish four versions of his best-known manifesto, "Culture: Intercom and Expanded

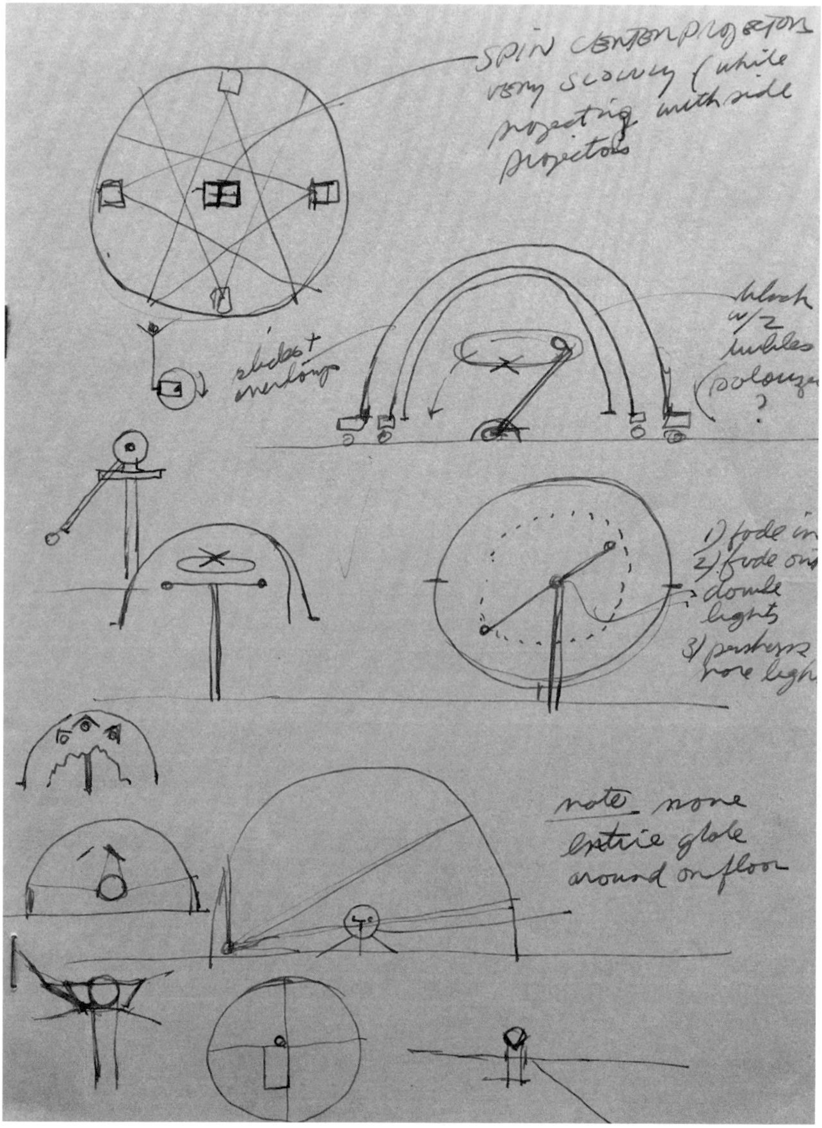

Cinema," a quasi-utopian work of midcentury communications theory that, he acknowledged, "came out of a big international conference at Carbondale called Vision '65."[16]

At the Vision conferences, moreover, this environmental idiom was aligned with a broader developmentalist discourse and its humanist and humanitarian impulses. This language, at the core of liberal midcentury modernization theory and some of its most powerful institutions,

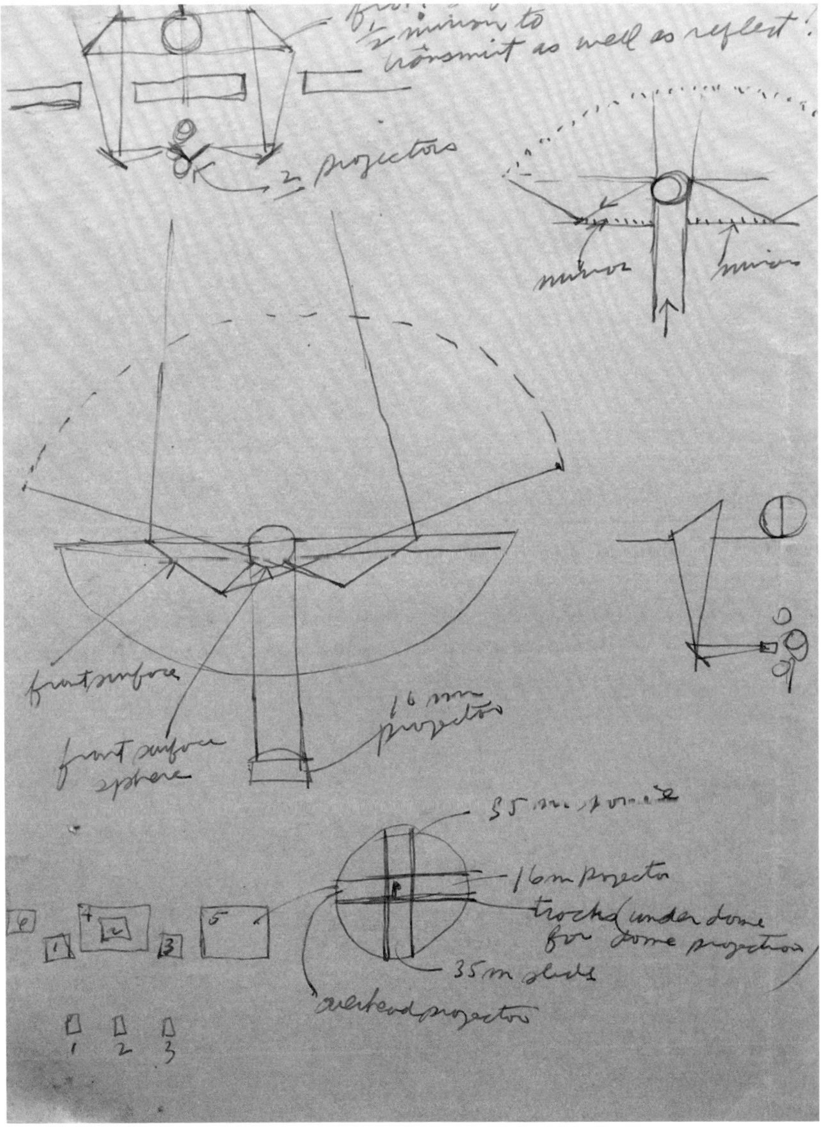

Figure 4.6. Front and rear covers of VanDerBeek's copy of the Vision 65 conference program, including projection schemes for the interior of Movie-Drome. Photo courtesy of Gloria Sutton and the Stan VanDerBeek Estate.

underwrote the competing theories of human progress and evolutionary change—technological, social, and political—offered at the conferences. Like his friend Kepes, and in the avant-garde tradition of Moholy-Nagy, Burtin shared what Reinhold Martin has called the "techno-biologically inflected hypothesis of aesthetic and social change as developmental, or more precisely, as evolutionary."[17] As conceptualized by biologists such as Julian Huxley (a desired speaker for Vision 65), this "second-order evolutionism" held that humanity could, by rational use of communications media, actively intervene in the evolutionary processes, staving off disaster and helping to chart the course for what Kepes called "a sounder evolutionary future."[18] Burtin understood the knowledge work of the Vision conferences—international and interdisciplinary—as just such a *technical* intervention in the course of the future. The aim was to domesticate—through managed environmental growth and control—the explosive development of the West and rapid technoscientific change at a moment of evolutionary transition for global humanity. As Burtin saw it, this political project of forecasting required both surveys of the communication needs of "underdeveloped" nations and the visionary media strategies of the avant-garde.

We hear a similar anxiety about imbalanced or hypertrophic development in the rhetorical urgency of VanDerBeek's "Culture: Intercom" manifesto:

> It is imperative that we quickly find some way for the entire level of world human understanding to rise to a new human scale.
>
> This scale is the world. . . .
>
> Technological research, development and involvement of the world community has almost completely out-distanced the emotional-sociological (socio-"logical") comprehension of this technology.[19]

"Culture: Intercom" offers a vision of global technical development whose title could easily have been swapped with Vision 67's own, "Survival and Growth," so anxious is its author about the threat posed to human survival and the "human scale" in the moment of the Great Acceleration, or what VanDerBeek calls the "technique-power and culture-over-reach that is just beginning to explode in many parts of the earth" ("CI," 15–16).

Such managerial talk, joining the discordant aspirations of VanDerBeek and Burtin, was the lingua franca of the Vision conferences. Following Burtin's lead as program chairman, the conferences sought to lay the conceptual groundwork for the conditions of human happiness through rationally managed growth. For Burtin, this was a futural, technocratic project, inspired in part by French political

Figure 4.7. VanDerBeek in front of the Movie-Drome, 1965. Photograph courtesy of Lenny Lipton and the Stan VanDerBeek Estate.

philosopher Bertrand de Jouvenel's visionary call for what he dubbed "surmising" forums—gatherings of far-flung experts in the vanguard knowledge work of anticipation, speculation, and the planning of national futures.[20] As a forum for prophecy, the conceptual work of the Vision conferences was brought by Burtin into the domain of the new interdisciplinary science of so-called futurology, then in its Cold War heyday.[21] For Burtin these futures were inescapably global. As he put in his crucial essay "Live and Learn," published in 1968 on the heels of Vision 67, "planning for growth" would require a foundation of universal human rights, benevolent scientific knowledge, and the innovative educational uses of efficiently controlled communications media.[22] Once properly "allied with an equally universal and new scientific attitude," Burtin predicted, "the first human culture of a world-range has thus a chance to come about" ("LL," 6).

The prediction, to put it mildly, was wrong, and wrongheaded. But it demonstrates how Aspenite visions of a humane internationalism articulated by the Goldsholls at IDCA 1959 would remain the increasingly imperiled Esperanto of the design conferences, which continued to braid together theories of international communication, aspirations toward interdisciplinarity, and the managerial imperatives of corporations, artists, and agents of the state. It also helps explain the principles of selection for many of the conferees, especially the emissaries of the avant-garde such as VanDerBeek. "Culture: Intercom," we might say, is the media theory for which the Movie-Drome is the countercultural practice. And that theory was not just shaped by McLuhan or Fuller, as Sutton has recently acknowledged, but by the interdisciplinary, internationalist technique of the Vision conferences.[23] In fact, approached in the context of the Vision conferences, "Culture: Intercom" appears as a thoroughly *unoriginal* modernism. It condenses and distills many of the axioms about "visual communication" and its transformed postwar environments voiced by Vision 65's speakers. From various disciplinary backgrounds, geopolitical locations, and political orientations, conference delegates seemed to answer VanDerBeek's own proto-CFP—his call for "a complete examination of all audio-visual devices and procedures, with the idea in mind to find the best combination of such machines for non-verbal interchange" ("CI," 16). In their planning, their internal insistence on planning, and their own medial conditions, the Vision conferences were Burtin's own "Culture: Intercom."

This chapter reverse engineers VanDerBeek's "Culture: Intercom" manifesto, embedding it in the expansive knowledge work of the Vision conferences, and in Burtin's theory and practice of visual communication. However transformative the conference proved to be for VanBerBeek, he got to Carbondale almost by chance, as a last-minute addition to the roster, and his talk was one of several other "visionary" approaches to communication given a hearing.[24] Considering VanDerBeek in this company, this chapter explains what it would mean for Burtin to "review" the range of vanguard aesthetic practices at these conferences, focusing specifically on the theories of film and media accompanying them, and the stories of aesthetic innovation, survival, and future growth told by their expert interpreters. It seeks to unspool and historicize the knotted stories about development and environmental design at the heart of these experimental practices—at once modernist and managerial.

Over the course of the Vision conferences, the competing theories of environment and the coevolutionary progress of humans and technology given voice there yielded an increasingly stark picture of capitalist modernity's unevenly developed communications environments, and its manifest failures to lay the conditions for something like equitable, managed growth. With this dawning "world-ecological" knowledge came increasingly fractious debates at the conferences—debates about the status of "nature" and the enlightened management of cultural, natural, economic resources, but also those resources' iniquitous distribution, both within the United States and worldwide.[25]

Visualization and Postwar Knowledge Production: Propaganda, Planning, Pedagogy

The Vision conferences extended Burtin's long-standing interest in what Johanna Drucker calls "visual forms of knowledge production" and their epistemological and pedagogical value in a world of both material abundance and informatic density.[26] Like the work of other postwar graphic designers, Burtin's various experiments in what today is called "visualization" were increasingly understood under the broader interdisciplinary category of "visual communications." Under this term, invoked by the speakers at Vision 65 as a kind of design buzzword or shibboleth, Burtin organized media practices ranging from typography, exhibition design, and the production of models of complex scientific and technical processes, to the mass media of television and film.[27] The term's impossible broadness suited the expanded social role Burtin attributed to the "communication designer" of the future, whose "essential function" was "to enhance and cultivate communications toward: 1. easier understanding of ideas and complex problems, in the shortest possible time and 2. higher visual and auditory retention of data."[28] The interdisciplinary practice of visual communication aligned Burtin's

Figure 4.8. Will Burtin, Federal Works Agency exhibition, New York World's Fair. Photograph by Ezra Stoller. Copyright Esto. All rights reserved.

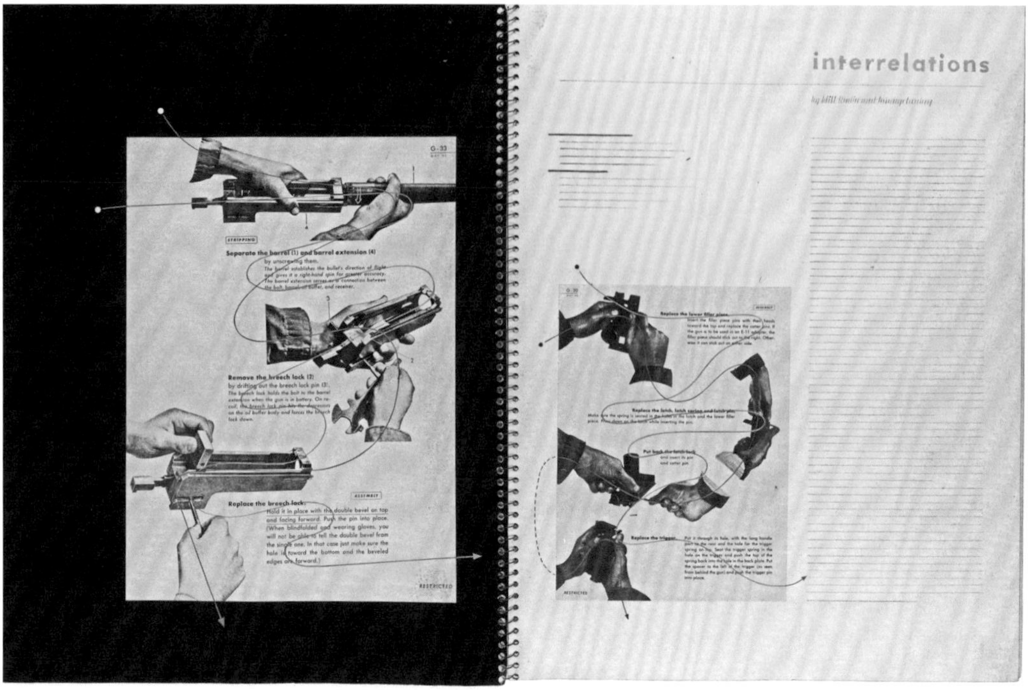

Figure 4.9. Gunnery training manual, and visual flow, as described in "Interrelations." Designed by Will Burtin. Will Burtin Papers, RIT Libraries: Graphic Design Archives, Rochester Institute of Technology.

investments in planning, propaganda, and pedagogy, and blossomed in the postwar period into a survivalist media theory proper—it wedded the visualization of order to projects of growth management and environmental control.

Burtin's own work in film for Upjohn, IBM, and other corporate clients in the 1950s and 1960s began in the context of his Cologne-based exhibition design studio in the 1920s and 1930s, whose sponsored work for corporate clients in Germany and France crossed and combined media.[29] Arriving in the United States after narrowly escaping Joseph Goebbels's plan for him to serve as design director for the Nazi Propaganda Ministry, Burtin accepted a commission for FDR's Federal Works Agency exhibition at the World's Fair in 1939, produced visual education aids for the FWA's adult education program, and began teaching advertising design and psychology at the Pratt Institute in the same year. Like other high-profile designers, Burtin's interwar experience in the overlapping domains of exhibition design, advertising, and government propaganda would be put to use by the U.S. military during World War II, when he was drafted by the army in 1943, and joined the Office of Strategic Services' Visual Presentation Branch, and its interdisciplinary Visual Presentation Unit.[30] Underlying the branch's far-flung work in "the new art of envisioning information" as it developed under Chief Hubert Barton, a New Deal economist, was what Barry Katz has described as a medially indifferent theory of efficient presentation.[31] In the Training Aids Division, for example, Burtin prepared an Army Air Forces training manual "designed to make aerial gunners out of American high-school boys."[32] Writing for the Swiss design journal *Graphis* in 1948, from his demobilized post as art director for *Fortune* magazine, Burtin explained that the pedagogical work of the manual was to train the novice gunner "to learn his gun's mechanism inside out in the shortest possible time." Initially considering a film for the task, Burtin and his collaborator, Lawrence Lessing, opted instead for a "loose-leaf manual" that would retain "cinematic techniques." By connecting visual clarity to visual pedagogy, optical coherence to pictures and texts composed graphically in an "accentuated, almost cinematic flow," the manual embodied a form of "visual reasoning whose purpose is to heighten and clarify man's understanding of a changing world" ("I," 108). As visual communication, the gunner's manual is equally equipment for war and equipment for *change*—for getting green pilots up to speed with the new, technoscientifically enhanced environments whose contours would be learned, and *survived,* by design (Plate 15).

These novel environments, rife with peril, would be navigated and lived through by better modes of visual communication. They extended from theaters of war to the new nature of the postwar period with which much of Burtin's postwar design practice would be preoccupied prior to the Vision conferences—both at *Fortune* and for the Michigan-based pharmaceutical giant, Upjohn. In 1949 Burtin published a design manifesto, "Integration: The New Discipline in Design," which narrated the coevolution of the design profession, the developmental flexibility of the human being, and postwar technoscience (Plate 16). In designing for the continuously changing "reality of man," the designer must himself adjust to "steadily changing conditions"—a milieu of constant transformation powerfully determined by "the extra-sensatory reality of science."[33] Expanding the dimensions of human experience itself, science has also "improved our ability to define and organize data coherently into new visual presentations."[34] The "social responsibility" of the designer, Burtin claims, is "to enlarge and define this vocabulary of visual relations, and thereby contribute toward the integration of our culture."[35]

In these crucial postwar essays, Burtin frames the designer as a guide to the unknown in postwar modernity, playing a "key role in extending human vision by demonstrating a new reality to which the uninitiated as yet have no key" ("I," 111). His task is to "compress a whole field of reality into a single, powerful image, instantly recognized by its composite, associative, impressionistic elements" ("I," 111). In this work of education, clarification, and compression, he must be medially promiscuous, drawing on any means necessary: "abstract paintings, imaginative drawings, movies, X-rays, microscopical studies, all forms of photography, printing techniques, or three-dimensional exhibits" ("I," 111). For Burtin, visual communication through graphic formats was at once a response to the new nature of the midcentury revealed by scientific progress, and a way of understanding and domesticating its strange dimensions, and managing the pace of change. As such, even a brief essay like "Interrelations" can move swiftly from battlefield to lab: from the visual flow of the gunnery manual and the graphic handling of "the space-time relationships" involved in teaching a pilot how to "measure off gun deflections against a fighter plane attacking his own bomber" to a discussion of his twelve-page spread in *Fortune* on the "modern science of astrophysics" and his cover for Upjohn's medical magazine *Scope,* evoking the "warmth of life" through a charming test-tube baby. These seemingly disparate examples are joined by their "projection and organization of space," which "underlines all design problems" ("I," 111). To be in the vanguard of design meant keeping abreast of science, whose innovative visualization techniques—Burtin insisted—were quickly outpacing artistic experimentation.

By the 1950s, Burtin began to conceptualize the technically fitful terrain of aesthetic modernism, and its demands on the spectator, within an evolutionary narrative of visual communication. This narrative of the avant-garde, of a piece with a broader managerial account of technoscientific progress and change at midcentury that earned a hearing at the Vision conferences, is perhaps best exemplified by Burtin's 1957 address at the *Visual Communications* exhibition at the Kalamazoo Art Center, a review of Upjohn's design program, then headed by Burtin and Garrard Macleod. Illustrated by slides of masterpieces of modernist art, Burtin's talk framed advertising as an experimental art of vision in a competitive climate of public information, explosive knowledge production, and the movement into "a world culture instead of the former local or national cultures."[36] Burtin narrated seventy years of art history as the aggregation of visual answers to the same problem faced by a corporate graphic designer in the midcentury's competitive media environment: how "to direct our means of communication with greater accuracy to an increasingly large group of people so we can get back a precise reaction to what we are saying." The explosion of modernist techniques of vision in the avant-gardes of "impressionism, futurism, cubism, pointillism, neoclassicism, constructivism, surrealism, [and] social realism" indicated the "increasing dexterity in the minds of our contemporaries" about vision and understanding. Burtin's proposition is that "we look at the development of the visual arts over the last fifty to seventy years as

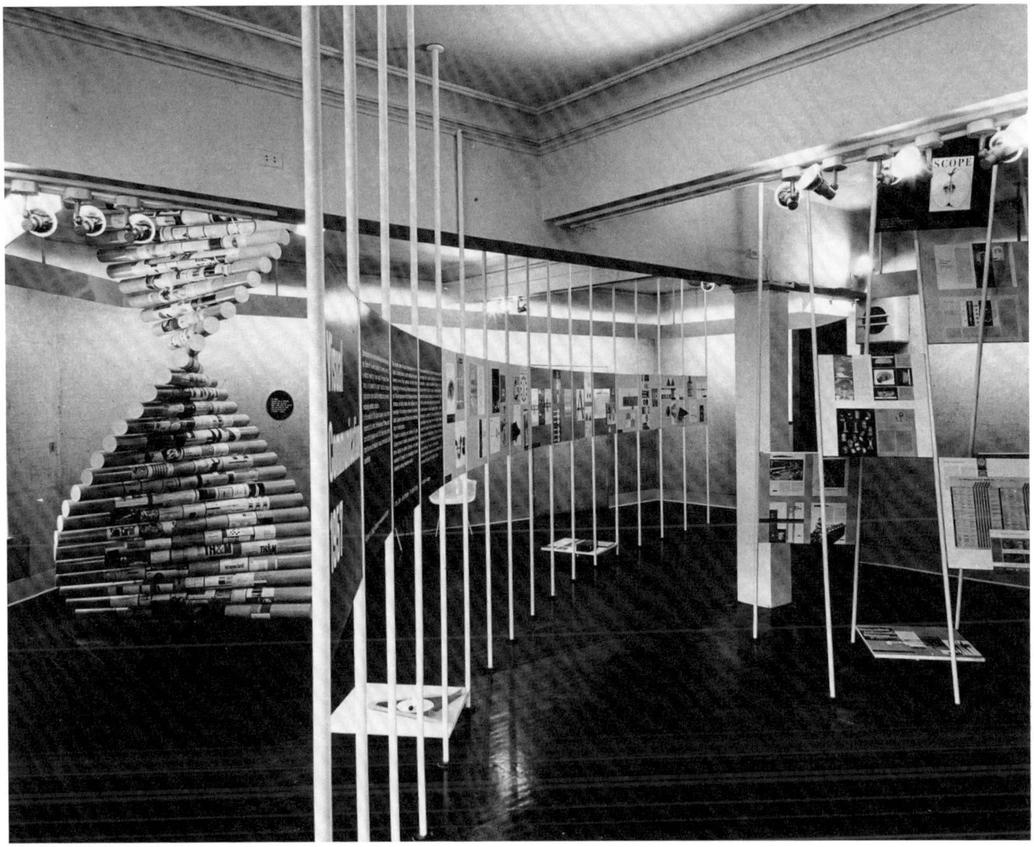

Figure 4.10.
Visual Communications exhibition, Kalamazoo Art Center, 1957, designed by Will Burtin. Will Burtin Papers, RIT Libraries: Graphic Design Archives, Rochester Institute of Technology.

a big research project," one whose "final goal is the utilization of whatever technical scientific phenomena have been developed, with the utilization of such phenomena towards the best good for the most people." This is aesthetic modernism as technoscientific R and D for postwar corporate advertising, a kind of utilitarian knowledge production yielding "more tools to meet new situations which may develop." The avant-garde and Big Pharma are allied in happiness as a project of postwar problem solving, maximizing "the best good."

Looked at retrospectively, as Burtin does in a slideshow, the novel aesthetic and technical work of "each of these various isms" was necessary, indeed, "unavoidable," regardless of whether their abiding theories of perception had demonstrable validity. Burtin's work for Upjohn (the subject of the exhibition, after all) is thus the beneficiary of modernism's visual research projects: its experiments in organizing visual information, in isolating particular aspects of communication, and its ways of testing the psychological effects of "directed impressions." As art history, this is all a bit thin, and it avoids any mention of the radical politics of the avant-garde. At the same time, Burtin strikingly frames modernism's perceptual experiments as a particular kind of sensory pedagogy or discipline—a way of testing various formal strategies for producing directed "impressions" in an embodied observer alongside (and against) the epistemic authority of science and technology, and incorporating those technologies into its own "apparatus of vision."

Burtin's groundbreaking exhibition *The Cell,* produced for Upjohn the following year, is a good example of this apparatus at work (Plate 17). A walk-through educational model of a generalized human red blood cell fashioned of modern plastics and over a mile of electric wiring, *The Cell* allowed Burtin and his team of engineers to realize the dream of visual organization announced in "Integration." This also included *The Cell*'s various medial lives. It was photographed for lavish spreads in *Scientific American, Industrial Design,* and *Life* by Ezra Stoller, sent to Disneyland, and then shipped to London as the mise-en-scène of two BBC TV science specials dealing with the origins of life: one on living cells and the other treating cancer research. The programs combined studio-based

Figure 4.11. The Upjohn *Cell,* BBC, "What Is Life?" and "The Last Scourge," 1959, Will Burtin Papers, RIT Libraries: Graphic Design Archives, Rochester Institute of Technology.

hosts who sat in *The Cell* and prefilmed interviews with science experts, and they were watched by an estimated eleven to fifteen million Britons. While in London, the Shell Oil Film Unit made a color film about *The Cell* that was shown around the world. Upjohn estimated the multimedia apparatus of vision assembled by Burtin's *Cell* to have been viewed, on TV and film, by forty million people, with a publicity value of $10 million in 1959 dollars.[37] As visual communication, *The Cell* confirmed the thrust of Burtin's lecture. As he saw it, vanguard art and advertising alike participate in capitalist modernity's cultures of consumption that demand the making of attentive observers—the production and targeting of attention within a competitive environment of distraction and excessive information. Burtin is not Jonathan Crary, of course, but his now-forgotten talk in Kalamazoo everywhere confirms the drift of Crary's well-known account of modernist technique honed within modernity's regimes of attention and perceptual discipline: namely, that once vision becomes embodied and subjectivized in the nineteenth century, it can be instrumentalized—subject to discipline, quantification, and management.

If attention, as Crary argues, "is the space where new models of subjectivity originated, and in which effects of power circulated," for Burtin the capacity of visualization to concentrate attention and model subjectivity in times of epochal change was most obvious in the field of education. His 1968 essay "Live and Learn" laid out the pedagogical challenge of the vexing environmental conditions he would convene the Vision conferences to address—the environment of a "runaway" world: "We are aware of our loneliness and isolation in the midst of vast accumulations of images and sounds of violence, of wondrous devices and race conflicts, of suburban sprawls and amazing new vistas of our physical world, of adolescent rebellions and super weapons, of corruption and incredible insights into the structures and potentialities of basic matter" ("LL," 5).

The urgency of these conditions, exacerbated by the failure of "modern mass communication techniques," was sharpened by the new social movements of the 1960s—especially in youth culture's "state of revolt against what we have perhaps optimistically assumed to be desirable for us and them to achieve" ("LL," 5). It is a revolution, Burtin insists, on the terrain of value itself: a debate about what *counts* as the good life for the generation that Theodore Roszak had just dubbed "technocracy's children."[38] Yet Burtin draws a curious conclusion from the New Left's exuberant refusal of reification and the threat to autonomy by the deprivations of institutional life. The "deeper message from them to us" is that it is "not only technology and nature which are still uncontrolled" but that "we, as working professionals, educators, and parents, have not succeeded in establishing adequate social controls that would guide 'them' and 'us' through this time of transition and realignment of values" ("LL," 6). He hears a plea for happiness not through social transformation, or the abandonment of economic values that have produced a series of interlocked social crises, but through more enlightened management of nature, technology, and the mind. This entails the thoughtful husbanding of natural and technological resources, as well as the administration of the intellectual and human resources of the "electronic generation" ("LL," 6). The challenges facing educators are legion: not just the moral rebellion and social experimentation of the young but also the task of endowing them with "the new perspectives of the cybernetic revolution" and what he calls the "new world sense"—the concern with "non-Western cultures whose existence and significance have been brought into mass consciousness through communication and transportation technology during the last two decades" ("LL," 6). Such a liberal, new-world education demands "*rational* systems by which the arts and especially the sciences define *universal* and not mere class or racial rights. These universal rights are the foundation of our physical survival and cultural growth and must protect and guide all men—us; the adolescent; a Stokely Carmichael; Africans; one billion Asians—everybody" ("LL," 6).

The essay defines education as the multimedia practice of responding to the condition of "transition" as a "permanent process"—security in change as *an evolutionary fact* ("LL," 6). This happens, first, by making society aware of its condition, and then aiming at "the increased human perfection and *the perfection of the means which serve the former*"—namely, visual communication ("LL," 6). The human mind, Burtin asserts, is "constitutionally imperfect" and capable of "continuous evolution." Because the "product of education is order, established in the composition of data and laid down in human memory," what is needed in this unruly environment of informatic abundance are better strategies of data management. And the key technique in creative art education is the construction of "verbal or visual patterns or models from data bits through which the relationship of individual bit to a larger order, and the logic of such order in relationship to all bits being part of it, become understandable and memorizable" ("LL," 7). Such "dynamic transmitters of knowledge" can be physical or conceptual models, and medially promiscuous. His examples range from television to "film projections and three-dimensional exhibits" to his own 3-D multimedia models for Upjohn: both *The Brain,* his model of the "typical functioning of the brain during the process of developing a thought," and *The Structure of a Chromosome,* a model of a chromosomal section meant to teach basic

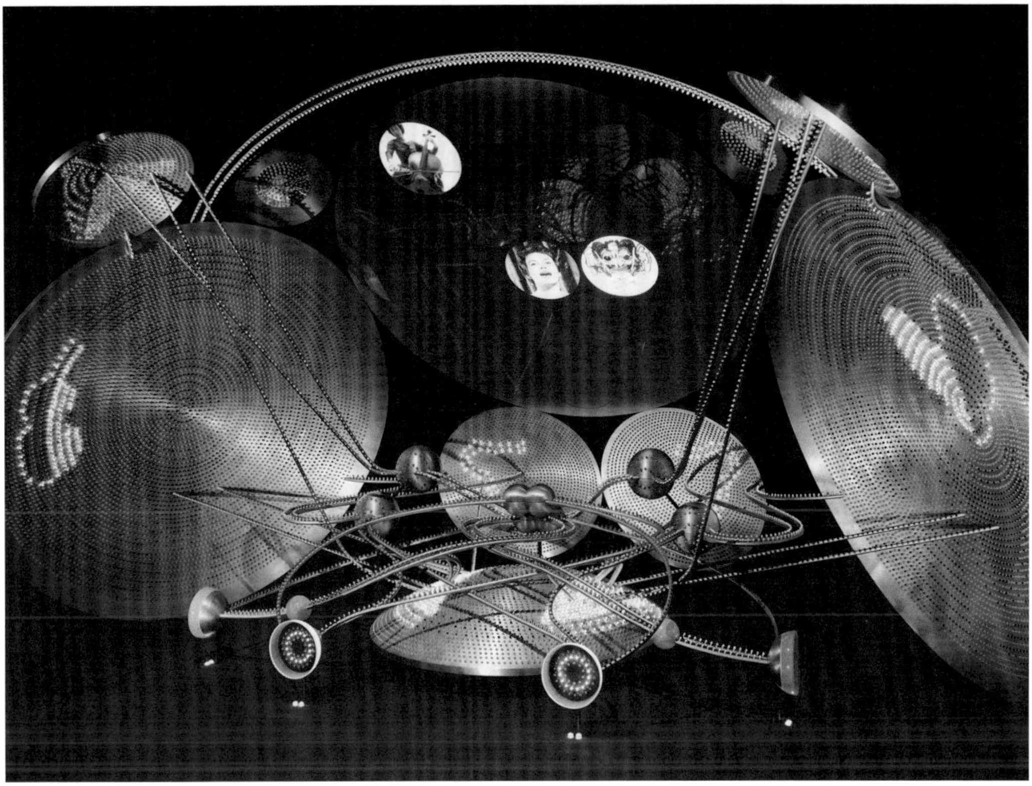

Figure 4.12. Will Burtin, *The Brain*, photograph by Bill Maris. Copyright Esto. All rights reserved.

genetic processes ("LL," 8, 5). By equipping students with the "moral and universal imperatives by which our mutual destiny is shaped," every "thought and image that we project on the screen of a student's mind appears as a related part of a steadily enlarging entity of our reality, instead of disjointed bits of information" ("LL," 6). The metaphor of projection crystallizes Burtin's strategies of visualization, recalling their origins in the quasi-cinematic "flow" of wartime training manuals: attention is now concentrated with the student's mind as a target.

Vision 65's "Culture: Intercom"

Sponsored by the International Center for the Typographic Arts, the Vision conferences took stock of a range of pedagogical strategies for visualizing order, and were themselves conceptualized by Burtin as what he called "geographies" of order: models of dynamic knowledge production and vanguard medial transmission ("LL," 7). With Burtin as Vision 65 program chair, the ICTA's disciplinary specificity would cede to an expansive, interdisciplinary conference technique whose global object was the unruly pace of change itself: uneven economic growth, technological transformation, and the postwar explosion of information and knowledge. Planning for Vision 65 began with Burtin's proposal for a "great analytical review" of communications media and their "new technology in an international environment of new nations, and new social requirements, of who needs them and to what end, and what the shifting value requirement in the various fields will demand."[39] The many existing conferences and professional organizations in the graphic design industry, with their "post-war, boom attitude and anti-intellectual, arty parochialisms," just weren't up to the seriousness of purpose or expansive viewpoint required to meet change on this scale.[40] Global interdisciplinarity would be Vision 65's mark of professional distinction and the technique of its knowledge work, aimed at examining "the social effects and implications of the entire kaleidoscope of communications—in all the media and forms noted above—as they impinge on people in various stages of development, various states of need."[41]

Burtin's conference planning hewed closely to UNESCO's therapeutic ideal of a peaceful globe united by the sort of communicative exchanges modeled on the conference form itself, and it tacitly affirmed the United Nations' "free flow of information" doctrine: its way of linking a New International Economic Order to a New World Information and Communication Order. Through this doctrine, which "dominated international communications and cultural relations" from World War II to the early 1970s, the UN enshrined freedom of information—across cultural and national boundaries—as "a fundamental human right" and "a touchstone of all the freedoms to which the United Nations is consecrated."[42] As a humanitarian ideal positioned against fascist propaganda and the totalitarian control of media, the free-flow doctrine tightly linked global exchanges of information and the spread of universal literacy to modern liberal democracy. And yet as ideology, it was a fundamental weapon in the growth of American corporate power and the imperial ascendency of the United States in the American Century, allowing its corporations coveted monopolies of communications infrastructure and unfettered access to new global markets, opening the floodgates of American media products, and swelling a new wave of cultural imperialism. As the UN's member nations expanded in the 1960s and '70s, including newly independent nations committed to cultural sovereignty, UNESCO witnessed increasing dissent about the free-flow doctrine. Its benevolent neutrality, seemingly outside the sphere of politics, was belied by—and in fact, seemed designed to reinforce—vast disparities of wealth, geopolitical power, and access to media infrastructure between member nations, inequities that were glaringly obvious to the West's former colonies, now diagnosed with chronic "underdevelopment."[43]

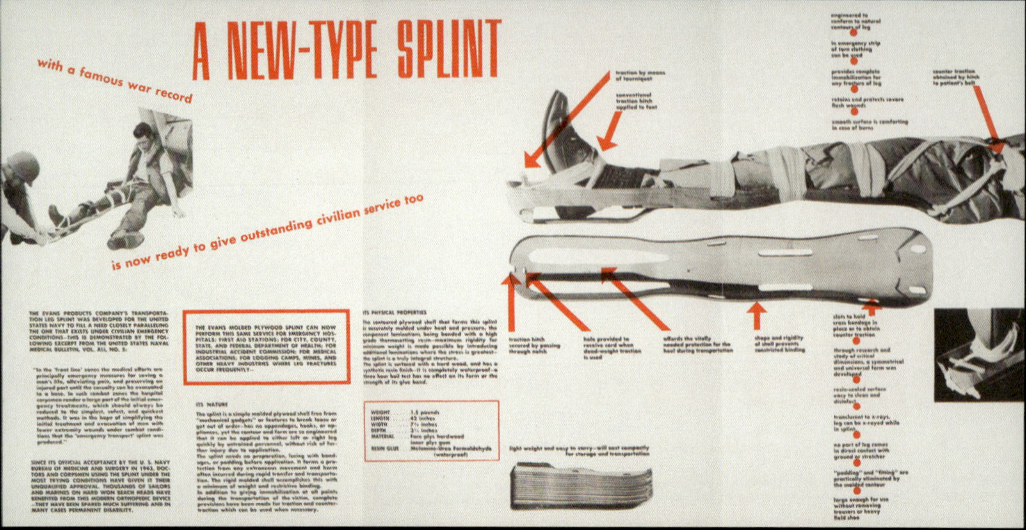

Plate 2.
Charles and Ray Eames for the Molded Plywood Division, Evans Products Company, “From War to Peace” brochure for transportation leg splint, circa 1945 (interior trifold). Copyright 2017 Eames Office, LLC, eamesoffice.com.

Plate 1.
(previous page)
Charles and Ray Eames. Julius Shulman, Job 2717: Eames House (Los Angeles, California), 1958. J. Paul Getty Trust. Getty Research

Plate 3.
Arts & Architecture, September 1946, cover designed by Herbert Matter. Courtesy of Vitra Design Museum, *Arts & Architecture,* and the Travers Family Trust.

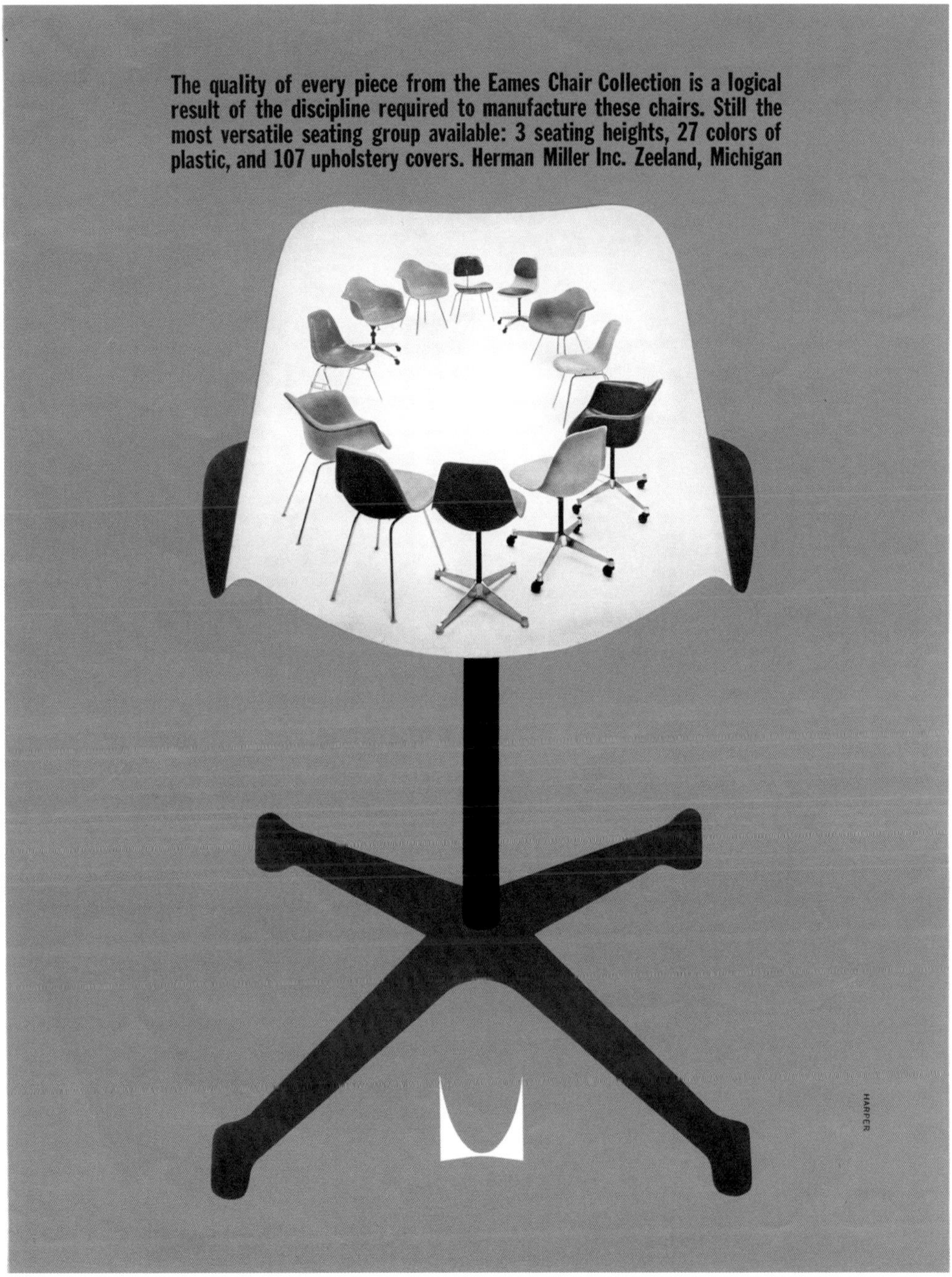

Plate 4.

Herman Miller advertisement for Eames Chair Collection, *Arts & Architecture,* 1961–62. Courtesy of Herman Miller.

Plate 5.

Herman Miller advertisement for Eames Lounge Chair, *Sunset* magazine, October 1959. Courtesy of Herman Miller.

Plate 6.
Kaleidoscope Jazz Chair, 1960, directed by Charles and Ray Eames.

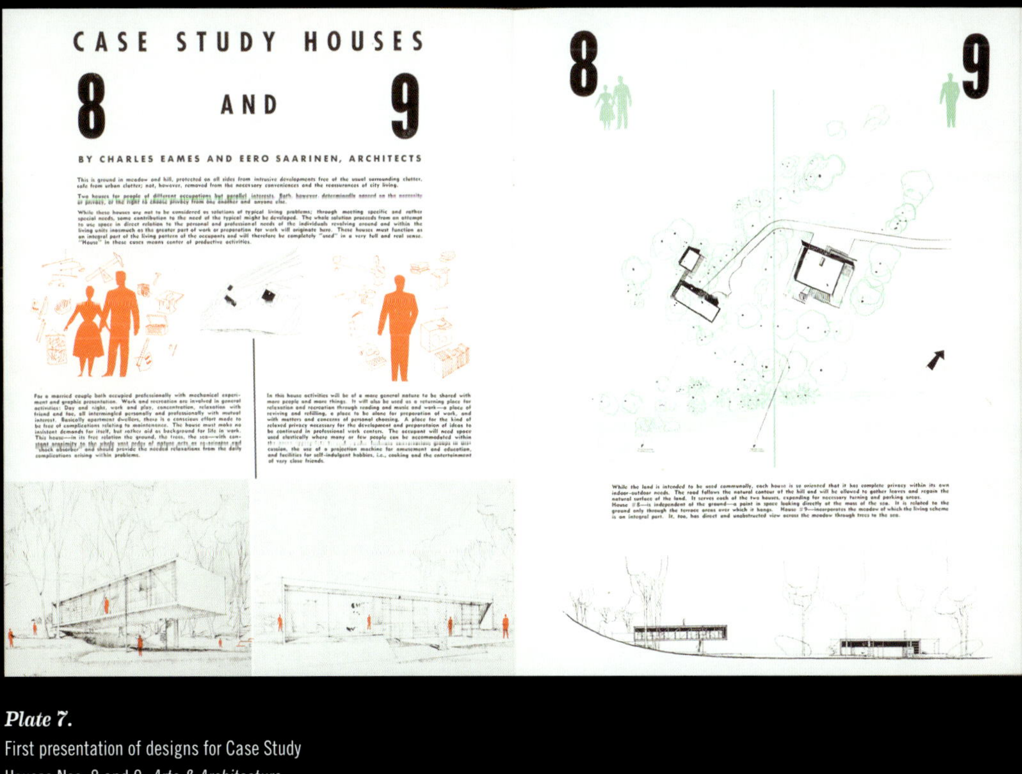

CASE STUDY HOUSES 8 AND 9

BY CHARLES EAMES AND EERO SAARINEN, ARCHITECTS

This is ground in meadow and hill, protected on all sides from intrusive developments free of the usual surrounding clutter, safe from urban clutter; not, however, removed from the necessary conveniences and the reassurances of city living.

Two houses for people of different occupations but parallel interests. Both, however, determinedly agreed on the necessity of privacy, of the right to choose privacy from one another and anyone else.

While these houses are not to be considered as solutions of typical living problems; through meeting specific and rather special needs, some contribution to the need of the typical might be developed. The whole solution proceeds from an attempt to use space in direct relation to the personal and professional needs of the individuals revolving around and within the living units inasmuch as the greater part of work or preparation for work will originate here. These houses must function as an integral part of the living pattern of the occupants and will therefore be completely "used" in a very full and real sense. "House" in these cases means center of productive activities.

For a married couple both occupied professionally with mechanical experiment and graphic presentation. Work and recreation are involved in general activities: Day and night, work and play, concentration, relaxation with friend and foe, all intermingled personally and professionally with mutual interest. Basically apartment dwellers, there is a conscious effort made to be free of complications relating to maintenance. The house must make no insistent demands for itself, but rather aid as background for life in work. This house—in its free relation the ground, the trees, the sea—with constant proximity to the whole vast order of nature acts as re-orienter and "shock absorber" and should provide the needed relaxations from the daily complications arising within problems.

In this house activities will be of a more general nature to be shared with more people and more things. It will also be used as a returning place for relaxation and recreation through reading and music and work—a place of reviving and refilling, a place to be alone for preparation of work, and with matters and concerns of personal choosing. A place for the kind of relaxed privacy necessary for the development and preparation of ideas to be continued in professional work centers. The occupant will need space used elastically where many or few people can be accommodated within [illegible] conversation groups in discussion, the use of a projection machine for amusement and education, and facilities for self-indulgent hobbies, i.e., cooking and the entertainment of very close friends.

8 9

While the land is intended to be used communally, each house is so oriented that it has complete privacy within its own indoor-outdoor needs. The road follows the natural contour of the hill and will be allowed to gather leaves and regain the natural surface of the land. It serves each of the two houses, expanding for necessary turning and parking areas.
House #8—is independent of the ground—a point in space looking directly at the mass of the sea. It is related to the ground only through the terrace areas over which it hangs. House #9—incorporates the meadow of which the living scheme is an integral part. It, too, has direct and unobstructed view across the meadow through trees to the sea.

Plate 7.
First presentation of designs for Case Study Houses Nos. 8 and 9, *Arts & Architecture,* December 1945. Letterpress on paper. Courtesy of Vitra Design Museum, *Arts & Architecture,* and the Travers Family Trust. Copyright the Travers

Plate 8.

Solar Do-Nothing Machine, designed by Charles Eames for the Alcoa Forecast ad campaign.

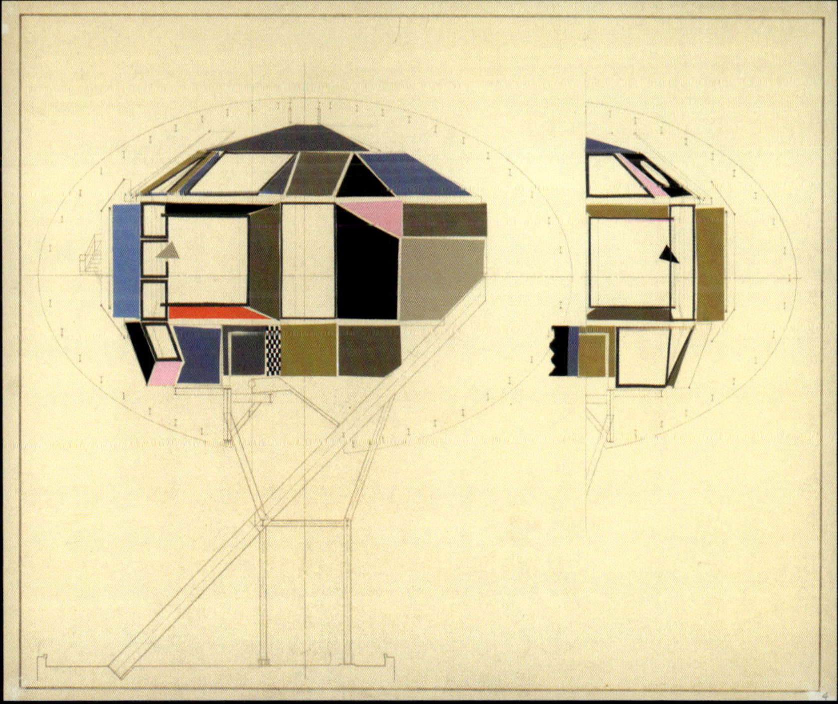

Plate 9. *(above)*
Richard Hamilton, *Interior II,* 1964. Oil, cellulose, collage, and metal relief on panel. 48 x 64 inches. Copyright 2017 Tate, London.

Plate 10. *(below)*
Section of the Ovoid Theater for the IBM Pavilion, New York World's Fair, 1963. Collage on diazotype. Copyright 2017 Eames Office, LLC, eamesoffice.com.

Plate 11.
Bruce Beck, poster for Communication: The Image Speaks, Ninth International Design Conference, Aspen, 1959. Walter P. Paepcke

Plate 12.

Ted Rand, illustration in *Report: Ninth International Design Conference in Aspen,* 1959. University of Illinois at Chicago Library, Special Collections.

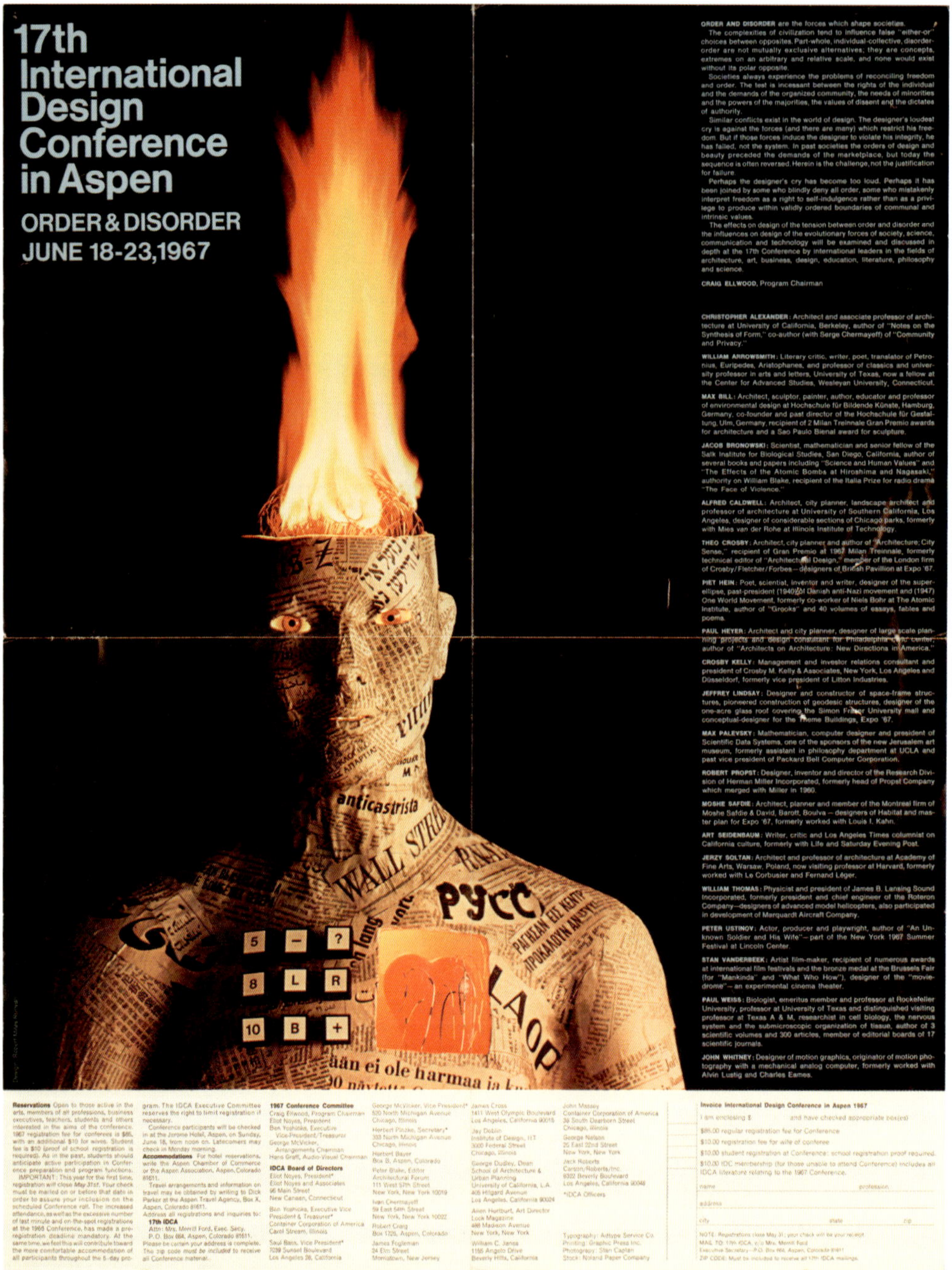

Plate 13.

Robert Miles Runyan, brochure, IDCA 1967: Order and Disorder. International Design Conference in Aspen Collection, box 17, folder 759, IDCA_0017_0759_001. University of Illinois at Chicago Library, Special Collections.

Plate 14.

Will Burtin, cover, Vision 65 brochure. Will Burtin Papers, RIT Libraries: Graphic Design Archives, Rochester Institute of Technology.

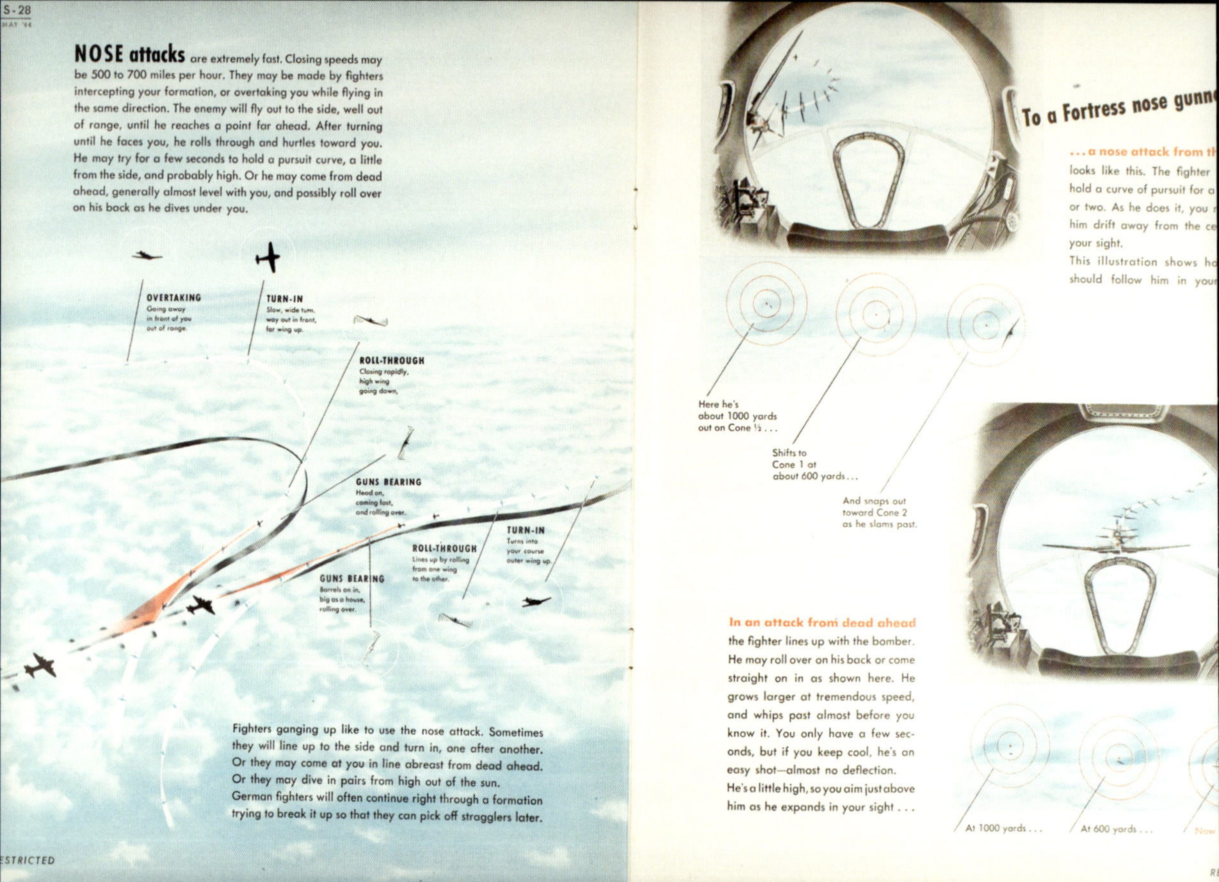
S-28
MAY '44

NOSE attacks are extremely fast. Closing speeds may be 500 to 700 miles per hour. They may be made by fighters intercepting your formation, or overtaking you while flying in the same direction. The enemy will fly out to the side, well out of range, until he reaches a point far ahead. After turning until he faces you, he rolls through and hurtles toward you. He may try for a few seconds to hold a pursuit curve, a little from the side, and probably high. Or he may come from dead ahead, generally almost level with you, and possibly roll over on his back as he dives under you.

Fighters ganging up like to use the nose attack. Sometimes they will line up to the side and turn in, one after another. Or they may come at you in line abreast from dead ahead. Or they may dive in pairs from high out of the sun. German fighters will often continue right through a formation trying to break it up so that they can pick off stragglers later.

ESTRICTED

To a Fortress nose gunn

... a nose attack from th
looks like this. The fighter
hold a curve of pursuit for a
or two. As he does it, you
him drift away from the ce
your sight.
This illustration shows ho
should follow him in your

In an attack from dead ahead the fighter lines up with the bomber. He may roll over on his back or come straight on in as shown here. He grows larger at tremendous speed, and whips past almost before you know it. You only have a few seconds, but if you keep cool, he's an easy shot—almost no deflection. He's a little high, so you aim just above him as he expands in your sight . . .

RE

Plate 15.

Will Burtin, interior, Gunner's Information File,

Plate 16.

Will Burtin, *Integration* exhibition. Photograph by Ezra Stoller. Copyright Ezra Stoller/Esto. All rights reserved.

Plate 18.

Will Burtin, model of Eastman Kodak exhibition. Photograph by Ezra Stoller. Copyright Ezra Stoller/Esto. All rights reserved.

Plate 17.

Will Burtin, model of *The Cell* exhibition. Photograph by Ezra Stoller. Copyright Ezra Stoller/Esto. All rights reserved.

Plate 19.

György Kepes, interior of Institute of Design catalog. Institute of Design Collection, box 6, folder 172, IDC_0006_072_P2. University of Illinois at Chicago Library, Special Collections.

Plate 20.

Cover of catalog for *War Art* exhibition, Renaissance Society at the University of Chicago, 1942. Institute of Design Collection, box 3, folder 84, IDC_0003_0084_cover1. University of Illinois at Chicago Library, Special Collections.

Burtin had read a bit about the high stakes of these vexing geopolitical disparities in Margaret Mead's short essay "The Information Explosion," which appeared in a special supplement to the *New York Times* in May 1965 to promote a meeting of the International Federation for Information Processing, a nongovernmental organization created through UNESCO in the late 1950s.[44] Mead was concerned with how "various components" of the electronic revolution are related to each other in regions, populations, and through living "users" representing "every form of information storage and retrieval known to man," from ancient to modern.[45] These are pressing questions, Mead insisted, with "extraordinary triggering possibilities, in a world that is politically vulnerable at all points to small perturbations at any one point" ("IE," 18). In Mead's fissile world, each user of information is at once a potential advocate—dreaming of a "form of life which will be increasingly permeated by the new technology," and be nevertheless "human and desirable"—and a potential rejector, a Luddite embittered or frustrated, fearful or enraged by the new technology, and therefore prone to "blind reactionary behavior" ("IE," 20). For Mead, managing the consequences of the information explosion in a world of unevenly developed users thus requires the thoughtful design of the interface. New technologies were to be domesticated through strategies of technical simplification and miniaturization in the form of a "household tool or a child's toy," which increase the likelihood of the whole technology being welcomed ("IE," 20). And one such "interim method" for reducing the frustration with which users anticipate the coming of new technology is the conference form itself, especially "conferences which are trans-national and cross-disciplinary," in which specialists "can communicate with each other in multi-sensory modalities" ("IE," 20). Indeed, Mead concludes, "face-to-face contact whenever possible may be the wisest thing we can do while we are preparing to use lasers" ("IE," 20).

Burtin refers approvingly to Mead's essay in his letter inviting her to speak at Vision 65, and he shared her sense of conference technique as a way of managing—and surviving—a world of explosive information.[46] He spelled out this technique in several drafts of the conference call, what Burtin titled a "manifesto" for Vision 64. We are used to the genre in rhetorical annunciations of aesthetic and political radicalism; less so as a design conference CFP. Yet the term conveys the hortatory quality of the proceedings and Burtin's convictions about the conference's significance as a landmark event of avant-garde knowledge production. "Communications," the manifesto begins, "have become world-wide. Geographic, national, and language environments have lost their traditional barriers, and people of all walks of life, in every country, find it now a daily occurrence to be exposed to visual and auditory communications from abroad, to the evidence of other cultures, to the many different levels and problems of a developing world civilization."[47] These changes, another draft argues, "may affect the human perspective and the political structure of entire continents for centuries to come." Because it sought "to know the requirements of new nations," the conference would not only appeal "to governments and individual citizens, be they in politics, education, science, industry, art or business, around the entire world," but *"especially . . . those from the new African, Asian and East European countries"*—capitalist modernity's underdeveloped others.[48]

As pedagogical and managerial technologies for visualization in times of crisis and evolutionary change, film and other media of visual communication were essential to the conference's internationalist vision and technique from the outset. In the initial program draft of Vision 64, the inaugural "Human Perspectives" panel would begin with a multiscreen film presentation and panel discussion of "what the specific needs of communication are, country by country":

> The film is to be produced by
> a) a film designer and producer
> (Francis Thompson, New York City)
> b) a social scientist and neurologist
> (Dr. Magoun, University of California, Los Angeles)
> c) a linguist-semanticist
> (Dr. Hayakawa, Stanford University, Palo Alto, Cal.)[49]

Thompson had just codirected (with Alexander Hammid) *To Be Alive!*, a multiscreen documentary film produced for the Johnson Wax pavilion at the 1964 New York World's Fair, and a humanist paean to the commonalities in child development across the world. And Burtin wanted a big interdisciplinary opening to Vision 65—spectacular but sober, and environmental in dimension. Burtin himself had designed the Kodak Pavilion at the fair, and approached the inaugural Vision conference keen to surpass the fair's narrowly commercial and nationalistic imperatives (Plate 18).

It is unclear just what a multiscreen film coproduced by Thompson, Magoun, and Hayakawa might have looked like (this plan was scrapped), although we can imagine it would exemplify the kind of knowledge work that Burtin demanded. Burtin had collaborated with Magoun on his multimedia visualizations of brain functions for Upjohn, and was fully conversant in cutting-edge brain science, including the contributions of cybernetics to models of neural functioning. Burtin invited Norbert

Wiener and Warren McCullough to Vision 65, and Gordon Pask to Vision 67; he was actively reading the work of Wiener's protégé Alice Mary Hilton, a logician and scientist responsible for coining the term "cyberculture" in 1963 while head of New York's Institute for Cybercultural Research. As in the Eameses' contemporaneous multiscreen exhibition *Think* at the New York World's Fair, an outgrowth of the couple's long-standing interest in communications theory, Burtin's knowledge of vanguard communications environments was everywhere connected to what Bernard Geoghegan calls the "cybernetic apparatus," including not just its connections to UNESCO but also its multiple intersections with avant-garde artistic practice and media theory in the 1960s.[50] Like the Eameses, Burtin sought to align the universalizing "human perspectives" on display in Thompson's film, cybernetic principles of homeostatic social organization, and other rationalist models of communication. Interdisciplinary and multiscreen, the proposed Thompson-Magoun-Hayakawa film would function as a "diagram" or "geography of order," the conference's first model of what Burtin called the conference "method," by which speakers "will propose solutions and plans by means of visual exhibits, visual demonstrations, and discussions."[51]

A reader of McLuhan, Burtin also knew that the media were the message, and central to the conference's knowledge work.[52] He planned for the film recording and distribution of conference speeches across media, and wished for a worldwide satellite television broadcast of the proceedings—the medial enactment of the utopian possibilities of the new global communication environments analyzed by conferees. Conference technique would span the history of communications media, from typography, "one of the oldest and most traditional methods of communication," to the latest developments: the "simultaneous dissemination of broadcast material throughout the world by means of satellites."[53] Inviting his friend and BBC collaborator Aubrey Singer to "talk on the consequences of world-wide television," he expressed confidence that the congress's knowledge work would be put to use: "televised as well as published in the form of a motion picture. Both telecast recording and film are to be sent to many institutions of government, education, and commerce."[54] In what became his boilerplate letter of invitation in the fall of 1964, Burtin noted that UNESCO and the U.S. government had been "instrumental" in plans for a worldwide television broadcast, "especially if our intention to have important writers, film makers, and scientists from Eastern European countries, is materialized."[55] And he consistently promoted the conference's "facilities for multiple film projection, television performances, and multi-lingual translation."[56] Even as the conference venue moved from Manhattan to the less-cosmopolitan

Carbondale, potential speakers were encouraged, "whenever possible," to "utilize visual means to help the international audience in following your ideas. Southern Illinois University is particularly well-equipped for single and multiple projections, film projections, etc."[57] As plans for the global satellite broadcast fell through, Burtin noted that National Educational Television had expressed interest in airing parts of the conference in the United States, and that "the BBC wanted to use a film of the proceedings later on."[58] As of July 1965, Burtin was still hoping for TV coverage, with Southern Illinois University approaching NET, NBC, ABC, and CBS for "pre-congress taping of special 'Conversations' and of live coverage (or video-taped) of congress in session."[59] Plans were also hatched to disseminate congressional proceedings in a "publication package incorporating verbal, visual, etc." Following the conference, a Vision 65 "trailer" was cut—apparently a highlight reel assembled from film footage of various speakers.[60]

Burtin's liberal internationalism was inspired not just by the communicative and educational ideals of UNESCO but also by Fuller's cosmopolitan "world man" and McLuhan's utopian brand of typographic internationalism. His fawning letter inviting Fuller to deliver the conference keynote address described his admiration of *Education Automation* and *No More Secondhand God,* and noted being "moved by [his] tireless, graceful and really monumental efforts aimed at building a unified basis on which a world culture can develop."[61] To sell Fuller, who had appeared on the cover of *Time* a few months earlier, he described the support of the conference from "professional organizations, philanthropic institutions, and the U.S. Government," and name-checked former UNESCO director Julian Huxley as a potential speaker, as well as Lancelot Hogben, Robert Oppenheimer, and Swedish economist Gunnar Myrdal. He also promised a roster of speakers from "Africa and Eastern Europe, as well as India, Japan, Italy, England, Germany, Sweden and France." As a sign of its global import, Burtin added that "the Congress will probably open at the United Nations" and move from there to an auditorium provided by the New York Board of Education. To bring McLuhan on board, he described having read *The Gutenberg Galaxy,* and noted the "problems and opportunities arising from our growth into a world society," as well as the threat of a "rampant and multi-faceted technology" that "disturbs many cultural values on a worldwide scale."[62] McLuhan's presence, Burtin observed, would "contribute decisively toward a unified and progressive approach to communication design." The Toronto English professor was on the brink of publishing *Understanding Media* (1964), which launched his career as a celebrity the same year he came to Carbondale.[63]

As an avant-garde of interdisciplinary knowledge work, Vision 65 crossed the domains of art and science, design and the mass media of film and television, new computational technologies and the techno-political aspirations of postcolonial nations. In an early draft of the conference program, Burtin insisted that one of the four speakers on a proposed panel called "New Horizons?" be "a government leader of a new nation," and he had planned on "Dr. Nkrumah, President of the Republic of Ghana, Africa."[64] The postcolonial perspective would be joined by the communications expertise of "television planner and producer" Aubrey Singer, director of worldwide television for the BBC; "cybernetics specialist" Dr. Norbert Wiener; "museum director and typographer" Willem Sandberg, a Dutch designer who was at that time the director of the Israel Museum; and "social critic" James Baldwin. But a Global South vantage would also be offered, Burtin hoped, on the "Need for Progress" panel. Here, Burtin had invited Gira Sarabhai of India's National Institute of Design, established by Nehru in 1961 as a direct result of *The Eames Report*'s (1958) recommendation that Bauhaus design principles be extended to a program of natural regeneration. An education adviser to the Indian government, Sarabhai declined the invitation but suggested instead former art director, now film director Satyajit Ray.[65]

The yield of this "progressive approach" to communications at Vision 65 was a bevy of competing cultural universalisms propped up by discrepant visions of globally shared knowledge and resources. Some were structured ideologically by developmentalist logics; others by their questioning and critique. The independent African republic finally represented at Vision 65 was not Ghana but Senegal, whose UN ambassador, the Honorable Ousmane Socé Diop, offered "the Senegalese vision of the world of 65" in a fascinating address—the conference opener.[66] Diop's lecture explained Senegal's need to expand communications media infrastructures on both national and international levels, and in a way that asserted the postcolonial specificity of Senegal while proclaiming the ideal of a universal culture in terms that resonated with the contemporaneous manifestos of Burtin and VanDerBeek alike. For Senegal, Diop argued, the condition of political independence was merely a means to the improved "living conditions of our masses." This demanded "a complete network of all communication media: roads, telecommunication, radio, films, educational television, as well as lectures by rural extension agents and technical assistance experts" (65, 1). "No means of communication," Diop explained, would "reach all the layers of our population" without education—"universal primary instruction," especially for the rural masses. And there would be no development, no "putting to good use all the material factors of progress," without "elementary

Figure 4.13. The Honorable Ousmane Socé Diop, Senegal's ambassador to the United Nations, and Will Burtin, at Vision 65: New Challenges for Human Communication, Southern Illinois University. Courtesy of Southern Illinois University Libraries.

knowledge." To this end, Diop called for a planetary archive of cultural production worldwide and its conservation and global circulation: "We should, without delay, proceed to take an exhaustive inventory of the artistic and cultural stock of all peoples in order to conserve it so it may become part of the universal civilization."

While Diop did not propose a new medial form for this process of "becoming acquainted with all civilizations and all original cultures of all the races," he noted the "increasingly overwhelming pressure towards the international standardization of man." And he explained and defended Africa's means of both resisting Western hegemony and contributing to the formation of a universal culture—namely, Léopold Sédar Senghor's Negritude movement. He cast this political aesthetic as a refusal of colonial mimicry, of the "canons and models" of Western civilization, and as a way to locate the "authentic sources of our own civilization" (65, 3). And he opened its diasporic promise, as did Senghor, to African Americans, even while acknowledging the need to guard against Negritude's potential danger—a "narrow sectarianism," or "racism in reverse." Diop closed by noting that the precarious contemporary imbalance between scientific progress and moral consciousness would best be combated by heeding the advice of Henri Bergson: "The overgrown body awaits an extra measure of soul, and materialism is in need of mystique" (65, 4). The vastly extended communications media, for Diop, would be the conduit of soul. Its mystique would entail "spiritual values," less in the abstract service of some fantastic, McLuhanite global village, than as the spur toward "a more equitable distribution of the world's wealth." In the wake of what he critiqued as the demonstrable impasse following the 1964 United Nations Conference on Trade and Development, Diop prophesied that the "apocalyptic consequences" of growth governed only by the "law of profit" would be combated only by "the mystique of justice, mutual assistance, and universal peace for the general welfare of mankind" (65, 5).

Speakers who followed Diop on the program referenced his address repeatedly. Max Bill admired its brilliance, especially Diop's "idea of conserving original culture" in a world of "accelerating development" that demanded, Bill insisted, "a program in Ethics, not one of technical change or so-called progress" (65, 25, 27). But the ethico-political terms of Diop's critique of Western capitalism's hypertrophic, profit-driven growth were imperfectly heard. IBM World Trade director of communications Bruce MacKenzie, who had proposed Senghor as a potential speaker to Burtin, returned to the infrastructural and educational needs of postcolonial Senegal in his address, "Programming Mass Communications to Meet Individual Needs." In its own way, the talk was a manifesto whose overarching burden was "the mission of destroying mass communications," to MacKenzie's mind an anachronistic way of misunderstanding the subtle, feedback-driven flows of information and their enabling infrastructural systems as a crude means of "hitting a very large number of people with one, or several messages" (65, 119). Instead, MacKenzie proposed that his audience understand communication as a matter of understanding—and targeting—what he called "changing patterns of interest," real and imagined (65, 119). In this climate, the software specialist "is coming into his own." By "software," MacKenzie meant not just computer programs but also the expanded domain of the "soft scientist, the behavioral scientist who is interested in people first and things second" (65, 121). These specialists are now poised to "incorporate" IBM's products "into some kind of human system connected by other machines in other communications links so that this machine can then face problems that are really on the avant-garde of human welfare today" (65, 122). The vanguard of welfare includes "economic planning in developing countries" such as Senegal, and the problems faced by econometricians (a "new word," MacKenzie notes) at the University of Dakar, whose applications of hard science could be softened through a better understanding of "the psyche of the people." "What," they should learn to ask, "are their current patterns of interest?" To answer it, they will be assisted by computers now equipped to face not only "business patterns of behavior" but "patterns of human, real-life activity": situations unfolding in real time, from the movement of spaceships, to matters of "life and death" in a hospital, to "real-life situations in city planning."

MacKenzie thus positioned the computer in a global network in which knowledge is locally produced according to "patterns of interest," and then commodified and traded based on the needs of those same interest patterns through a global "information stock exchange" (*65*, 122). Through the exchange, knowledge-producing organizations of various sizes—from publishers, businesses, or a university like Southern Illinois, to international organizations like UNESCO (his examples)—buy and sell "shares of information," collected by "telecommunications links and satellites" and distributed on a global market managed by computers. Each organization develops a "pattern of information it feels reasonably competent to communicate," packages that would be "designed for a number of audiences." A developing country, MacKenzie acknowledges, would want to "buy a share of information . . . different from what a highly industrial country would want" (*65*, 122). From each, according to his pattern of interest; to each, according to the market value of his "knowledge packet." All of this information "has a dollar value," MacKenzie insists, and yes, he admits, the "marketing of information" can be propaganda. But with "honest brokers," MacKenzie remained optimistic that information will flow to the people who need it most. The talk ended by joining this neoliberal vision of the economization of all information and knowledge to the bright future of efficient "computer-assisted instruction" and knowledge compression in the field of global education. Here, communication designers have the chance to play a crucial role in the "visual and graphic aspects" of information processing, introducing novel "patterns of recognition" into the intellectual systems now at their disposition, so that consumers of education might "see an old friend when they see a new way of presenting a textbook or a new way of presenting a play or a novel" (*65*, 125).

Visionary proposals for the transmission of knowledge and information proliferated at Vision 65. British designer Michael Farr, for example, extended this computational model of feedback links between individual and world, organism and environment, to a call for a new "user-inspired" model of design sensitive to locality and cultural particularity—what MacKenzie called "patterns of interest." It would, Farr argued, "enable people to enhance their individualities rather than suppress them" (*65*, 210). Rather than "designing for a world society," Farr argued, we should be designing for "a cohabiting system of different regions, each with its indigenous culture" (*65*, 204). The job of the designer, assisted by

Figure 4.14. Stan VanDerBeek, lecturing as part of the "Visionary Approach to Communications" panel, Vision 65: New Challenges for Human Communication, Southern Illinois University. Courtesy of Southern Illinois University Libraries.

computers, is now to "write good programmes" and provide people with "self-organizing systems." As a programmer, the designer plans with human beings in mind, and conceives means of "enabling living environments to be reconstructed in ways hitherto inconceivable," allowing for the user's "random creativity" (65, 209).

As the watchwords of a new communicative order, feedback and creative participation would stave off catastrophe in the era of what Aubrey Singer dubbed "*homo cyberneticus*." The producer's talk began by aligning the growth of television itself with humans' transformation of their environment, whose four "archetypes"—earth, air, fire, and water—are held in contempt, dominated and controlled at will. Television, he argued, must share in our attempt "to live in a homeostatic relationship with society as well as environment," since the medium "is one of the main contributors to the stream of information which makes up the feedback" (65, 90). He ended with a hypothetical research agenda, exhorting conferees to undertake a "design study of a television system in present-day terms" (65, 96). In it, "communication can occur between all levels our audience and all levels of the culture represented by that audience," such that this "window on culture could become a two-way affair. TV "receivers would become communicators," not just receiving local network or international programs but also using "small cameras and cheap video recorders" to link viewers and their "personal world" to "the library, the bank, the office, the shops, and of course, the Government."

Those familiar with VanDerBeek's "Culture: Intercom" manifesto will hear many of its technoutopian ideas floated in the proposals of

Diop, MacKenzie, Farr, and Singer, however ideologically contradictory they may be. Diop's appeal to the notion of a worldwide, shareable archive of cultural production as the basis of a "universal civilization," or MacKenzie's global "information stock exchange" sourced from local "patterns of interest" are, we might say, conceptual prototypes of VanDerBeek's Movie-Drome, which shortly gave a vanguard medial form to these global aspirations. Such "audio-visual research centers . . . preferably on an international scale," would—VanDerBeek proposed—combine existing and new audiovisual devices "into an educational tool," and train a host of artists in such pedagogical techniques of "non-verbal interchange" ("CI," 16). The history of cultural achievements and productions from around the globe would be first condensed, then shared. One might, for example, depict "the course of western civilization since the time of the Egyptians to the present. . . . It would be possible to compress the last three thousand years of western life into an aspect ratio so that we, the audience, can grasp the flow of man, time, and forms of life that have led us *up to the very moment*" ("CI," 17). Endless variations on this idea would be taken on by "*each* culture group and nationality," presented "in turn to each other cultural group . . . (by telstar, film exchange, 'film mobiles,' traveling shows, etc.)" ("CI," 17). Like Diop's proposed culture archive, the "Culture: Intercom" ideal aims at the universal " 'emotional denominator' of all men" through the culturally particular, and understands communications media as the conduit of meliorative soul. "My concern," VanDerBeek explains, is for the "over-developing technology of part of the world to help the under-developed emotional sociology of all of the world to catch up to the twentieth century . . . to counterbalance technique and logic" ("CI," 17). And, like MacKenzie's information exchange, which would be medially promiscuous, deploying "films, live television, training courses, textbooks, news summaries," the Movie-Drome's communicative network of "image libraries" would also unfold in the computer-aided immediacy of real time: "by satellite, each dome could receive its image from a world wide library source, store them, and program a feedback presentation to the local community that lived near the center, this newsreel feedback, could authentically review the total world image 'reality' in an hour long show that gave each member of the audience a sense of the entire world picture" ("CI," 17). "As what Burtin might call a "geography" of order, the Movie-Drome was a model of informatic compression and the networked exchange of knowledge production in the service of bringing "anyone on earth up to the 20th century," and quickly, and its abiding tool was "an international picture language" ("CI," 18).

It is unclear whether Burtin ever read VanDerBeek's "Culture: Intercom" manifesto when it was published in 1966, but of course he didn't need to.[67] Its central tenets were declared and debated by Vision 65 speakers in some fashion or another: the scale and pace of change, knowledge production, and technoscientific development that conspired to produce a qualitatively new "environment"; the imbalance between the debatable "goods" of accelerated technical progress and the moral, ethical, or emotional impoverishment of humanity that spurred calls for a new "human scale"; the vexing dynamism of a world in motion; the anxious acknowledgment of the West's underdeveloped others; the various appeals to a world community and an international language, including Japanese designer Masaru Katsumi's overview of the international symbol system he designed for the 1964 Tokyo Olympics. Such was the pervasiveness at Vision 65 of the abiding communications dream of

Figure 4.15. Tokyo Olympics display at Vision 65: New Challenges for Human Communication, Southern Illinois University. Design by Masaru Katsumi. Courtesy of Southern Illinois University Libraries.

"Culture: Intercom." If VanDerBeek did not exist, Vision 65 would have had to invent him.

Transition, Abundance, and Arts Management

Burtin was keenly aware of how these lofty ideals of efficient, networked flows of communication, information, and knowledge, like dreams of international goodwill, came down to earth in the cruel realities of growth and change: unjust resource distribution, uneven development, and the messy claims of politics on both national and global scales. This fact, it seemed, only sharpened the urgent need for more enlightened management, and led Burtin to include on the Vision 65 program various experts in cultural and arts administration, either at the state level, or through the aegis of international organizations, or via more radical visions of planned futures—liberal-humanist, socialist, or radically democratic. Managing abundance and explosive change was not just a political-economic project but a pedagogical, knowledge-based one that demanded innovations in communications media as well as systematic, rational investigations of art as the domain of planning, sponsorship, and visual research.

Burtin's insistence on "transition" as an evolutionary fact was also a keyword in the New Left's contemporaneous assessment of overdevelopment in the so-called Triple Revolution manifesto, a copy of which is included in Burtin's Vision 65 planning documents.[68] Issued as an open memo to President Lyndon Johnson in March 1964 by a committee including Myrdal, Tom Hayden, Irving Howe, and Todd Gitlin, and antiracism activists James Boggs and Bayard Rustin, the manifesto declared a historic conjuncture of the cybernation revolution and its fundamental "reordering of man's relationship to his environment"; the weaponry revolution; and the human rights revolution, a "world-wide movement" whose "local manifestation" was the civil rights movement in the United States.[69]

While never using the phrase "postindustrial society," the manifesto linked computational technologies to a radically new era of production. Its massive gains in productivity threatened to make human labor superfluous, a problem especially acute for African Americans demanding both "freedom and jobs," but increasingly "exiled from the economy by cybernation." Explosive postwar development and abundance in the United States disguised a "historic paradox: that a growing portion of the population is subsisting on minimal incomes, often below the poverty line, at a time when sufficient productive potential is available to supply the needs of everyone in the United States." And this dilemma, the "Triple Revolution" group argued, would only be accommodated by a new society that abandoned the principle of scarcity undergirding the industrial economic system, broke the link it postulated between jobs and income, and rethought human work to include social services: "socially valuable but non-productive tasks" that "related people to people rather than people to things." These drastic changes to the nation's way of life ushered in by technology could not be left to the forces of the market. They required instead putting into action what the authors called "the historic discovery of the post–World War II years"—namely, that "change must be managed" by the state, that "the essence of management is planning," and that the "democratic requirement is planning by public bodies for the general welfare." Managing "the transition" to the new society, the manifesto stipulated, would include massive programs of public education, public works, low-cost housing, infrastructure investments, and revisions of the tax structure to redistribute wealth, as well as a host of new planning institutions. "The aim throughout" this process of transition "will be the conscious and rational direction of economic life by planning institutions under democratic control."

We can readily imagine the manifesto's appeal to Burtin. Its story about overdevelopment and its mode of forecasting a just future of abundance, for example, overlapped with the speculative mode adopted in Fuller's own summary address, a familiar call for a comprehensive design revolution. Malthus was dead wrong; a utopian distribution of the world's resources for all *was* possible—but only through the supersession of extant political systems. Fuller protégé H. F. William Perk framed his talk as a hypothetical scenario in the mode of military game theory: set in 1985, it cast a retrospective glance *back* at 1965 as the start of the period of "Great Transformation" brought about by the cybercultural era, whose productive force and unprecedented concentration of political power were together capable of "achieving abundance on a worldwide scale" (65, 139). Beyond Myrdal, whom Burtin had hoped would attend, a few other "Triple Revolution" signatories shaped Vision 65's knowledge work, including Alice Mary Hilton, whose Institute for Cybercultural Research helped to fund Vision 65, and W. H. Ferry, then vice president of the Center for the Study of Democratic Institutions, an influential think tank founded by Robert M. Hutchins in 1959 and an offshoot of the Fund for the Republic, a civil rights foundation.[70] In his invitation to Ferry, Burtin noted admiringly that "The Triple Revolution" manifesto affirms the "basic premise of our endeavor: the need for an inter-disciplinary analysis of where we are, and for an inter-disciplinary action plan to determine where we are going."[71]

Far from the equitable, postpolitical futures conjured by Fuller or Perk, Ferry's screed laid out an approach to communications media that linked their pedagogical function to the New Left's vision of rationally planned democratic life. Part of the panel devoted to the "social and cultural responsibility of mass communications," it brought the conference proceedings fully into the storm of recent political upheavals in the United States, including the Watts riots in Los Angeles two months earlier, the Berkeley Free Speech movement, and the antiwar movement. Titled "Masscomm as Educator," the talk was a full-throated attack on the "masscomm-industrial-military-government axis," and an indictment of mass communications as "rich, white, and privileged" (*65*, 111, 113). For Ferry, the failures of democratic education were most evident in masscomm's inability to inform the public about the dire conditions of economic injustice defining black life in the nation, to say nothing of its capacity to convert American atrocities in Vietnam into a "great patriotic exercise" by manufacturing a common enemy, communism, and thereby consolidating military-industrial power. The talk concluded by proposing sweeping governmental reforms of mass communications and a reining in of private interests through tax incentives that would encourage communications media to advance the work of "liberal education," and through increased foundation support of educational television.

By appealing to the political significance of enlightened media pedagogy in a liberal democracy, a role strengthened by increased public funding for the "intellectual and cultural education" of citizens, Ferry's talk was one of several to take up the role of the state in the management of the arts and cultural production. Indeed, it was largely in this context that the media of film and television specifically were discussed at the Vision conferences. At Vision 65, Burtin was especially excited about the presence of Roger L. Stevens, Lyndon Johnson's special adviser for the arts, who attended on the heels of the recent act of Congress establishing the National Foundation on the Arts and the Humanities, and joined the panel on the social and cultural responsibility of mass communications with Ferry and the BBC's Singer. Reading aloud passages from the act, which states that democracy must "foster and support a form of education designed to make men masters of technology and not its unthinking servants," Stevens described the scope of the NEA and NEH endowments, including the NEA's plans for the American Film Institute (AFI), and harked back to the successes of the WPA, "one of the government's most successful investments" (*65*, 83).

Beyond VanDerBeek, the speakers who directly theorized the vanguard of film and TV did so at Vision 65 in quasi-managerial capacities as present or former representatives of the state or international organizations, in keeping with Burtin's broader concern with problems of media education and development. Besides Singer, this group included the celebrated British director, screenwriter, and producer Thorold Dickinson, who possessed what Burtin called "a truly world grasp of our problems," and Vera Horvat-Pintarić—the conference's sole representative from Eastern Europe.[72] Intertwining narratives of aesthetic, social, and economic development, these speakers explored postwar media's environmental dimensions, and tracked the emergence of a "democratic" spectator cultivated by modernist tendencies in film and the visual arts.

Perhaps best known for directing the celebrated British fiction films *Gaslight* (1940) and *The Queen of Spades* (1949), Dickinson also made wartime propaganda films, films for the new state of Israel, and in the late 1950s served as the chief of film services for the United Nations Department of Public Information. In 1960 he founded the UK's first film studies department at the Slade School of Fine Art. Committed to a range of internationalist agendas over his long and varied career, Dickinson worked from the 1930s through the '60s for a series of institutions in which "visual communication" entailed the efficient control of information, the rhetorical work of propaganda in the service of democratic antifascism, and the overlapping of managerial and pedagogical imperatives in the postwar effort to secure an international peace presided over by the United States and its allies. In short, he was Burtin's kind of communicator.

Dickinson's talk described film itself as a potentially wayward medium in need of discipline and noble, forceful management. His example was the Moscow Film School's correspondence courses, taken by scientists and teachers across the Soviet Union, a competing model of state-sponsored knowledge work he hoped would be taken up by the future AFI. But ensuring that "the assets of cinema can be properly exploited" also requires an "encyclopedic view" of the history of cinema itself—namely, a film archive assembled not in the "totalitarian way" but in the "democratic way, using the word democratic in the Western and not communist sense of the word" (65, 42). He noted UNESCO's underfunded efforts in such acts of central collation and assessment through its catalogs of films on the fine arts, and he proposed an archive of films on world history, an ambitious act of global visualization and distant reading:

> Personally, I see it all in the form of charts. One would make a chart of the last hundred years of world history, for example. Then one would lay over the chart a sheet of tracing paper and black in, film by film, television program by television program, the audio-visual coverage

> of the events and their consequences that are recorded on the chart beneath. . . . In some cases the coverage would be found to have been done over and over again from different points of view. The more the better. (*65*, 48)

Through this database, a better, more democratic future might be better planned.

Dickinson supplemented this proposal with his own brief narrative of the growth and development of "true cinema," one that deployed an explicitly environmental idiom (*65*, 23). Dickinson cribs a bit here from the evolutionary tale of cinematic *Bildung* and survival he had just set forth in his essay "The Maturing Cinema," published in the nascent *Journal of the Society of Cinematologists* (*Journal of Cinema and Media Studies* today). There, he called cinema a "developing art" whose "capacity to survive" depended on one singular element: "the revelation of human character developing in an environment."[73] His developmental world history of film culminated in the soul-probing internationalism of postwar art cinema and its own claims to psychologically acute realism. He thus positioned the modern telos of film history as the realization of a global aesthetics of democratic humanism.[74] This expansive modern worldview of art cinema's young audiences was "vitalized by the growth of internationalism, the outmoding of frontiers, and the concept that . . . patriotism is not enough."[75]

At Vision 65, Dickinson sought to link his "encyclopedic view" of film history, its humanist idiom honed by his work at UNESCO, to the role of film in education—namely, its capacity to "demonstrate," to "introduce a subject or concept so that the student can quickly have the means of choice, of acceptance or rejection" (*65*, 46). Film's pedagogical mode of offering its subject to the democratic capacities of students thus extended the faculties of active spectatorship enabled by new widescreen formats, or deep focus, or the environmental nuances of the "true cinema" and its newly "sophisticated audiences." Tellingly, Dickinson marshaled the example of "the problem of backwardness" to an audience "conditioned to believe we are not backward" (*65*, 46). On the screen, "we can be shown backwardness, poverty, ignorance," see these problems traced to the realities of hunger, and poverty, and solved by nourishment and education. For Dickinson, in sum, film's role is "to prove to us that none of us is wholly developed or wholly under-developed. The trouble with all of us is that we are unevenly developed. And the hope is that in working to level up our own development we can best achieve our aim by helping to balance up the development of the rest of humanity" (*65*, 47).

It fell to Horvat-Pintarić, a Croatian-born art historian and art educator, then a professor at the University of Zagreb, to provide an account of the state sponsorship of advanced visual art outside the putatively "encyclopedic" vantage of the capitalist West. She did so from her position at the center of various developments in Yugloslavia's exuberant postwar modernisms through her affiliation with the Zagreb Gallery of Contemporary Art. Committed to an expansive world perspective, Burtin was keen to have a speaker from Eastern Europe, and Horvat-Pintarić fit the bill especially well. Delivering a survey of arts administration

Figure 4.16. Vera Horvat-Pintarić, lecturing on the "Visionary Approach to Communications" panel, Vision 65: New Challenges for Human Communication, Southern Illinois University. Courtesy of Southern Illinois University Libraries.

and "visual communication" in a nonaligned socialist nation, Horvat-Pintarić was an obvious counterpoint to Stevens at the NEH, but she was placed to give her talk, "The Avant-Garde in a Socialist Culture," as part of the "Visionary Approaches" panel with VanDerBeek, a testament to her vanguard credentials. She described the range of federal grants and subsidies for the arts in Yugoslavia, the work of state institutions like the Working People University (devoted to the aesthetic education of adults), and the freedom of Yugoslav film directors, as proof of the state's broad effort to democratize culture, liberating artists from "the immediate dictates of the market and commercialization" (*65*, 59, 60). And she insisted that the "socialization of goods and the means of production" was inherently connected to the problem of the "socialization of art."

As a narrative of aesthetic development, Horvat-Pintarić's talk hinged on the central influence of the ideological aspirations of Russian avant-gardes of the 1920s in charting the course for the most vital trends in contemporary art. Whereas Dickinson credited the Russians for demonstrating, via montage, cinema's capacities for the "interpretation of fact and opinion," Horvat-Pintarić's survey of visual communication sought to rescue the utopian agenda of constructivist abstraction, whose promises had been foreclosed under the doctrine of socialist realism. Extolling the value of the Russian avant-gardes "in the area of architecture, of graphical and industrial design, and visual research," she brought the constructivist past into alignment with two postwar, Yugoslav-centered modernist formations, crossing the domains of art and science: a Croatian-based group of architects, painters, and designers known as the EXAT 51 group (Experimental Atelier 1951); and the New Tendencies movement (*65*, 61). The latter was an umbrella term for a series of exhibitions, starting in 1961, at the Zagreb Gallery of Contemporary Art, which convened an international range of neoconstructivist practices in concrete art, kinetic art, op art, *arte programmata,* and the nascent computer arts. The geometric abstraction of EXAT 51, Horvat-Pintarić explained, was inspired by the post-October avant-garde, the Bauhaus, and De Stijl, and sought a "synthesis in plastic arts as the basis of their program, together with a need for the study of problems in the field of visual communications" (*65*, 94).[76] The New Tendencies sought to distinguish itself from trends in abstract art (abstract expressionism and tachism) that enshrined irrational, spontaneous, individual creativity, privileging instead a rationally based, collective artistic practice modeled on scientific methods and overtly framed as "visual research."[77]

On the one hand, Horvat-Pintarić explained, Yugoslavia was underdeveloped in the area of visual communication, having only recently founded an International Biennale of Industrial Design in Ljubljana, and with still no institutions of higher education to train industrial designers, and no "serious scientific, sociological, or esthetic research" in the field of mass communications (65, 69). For this reason, the country underappreciated graphic design's capacity to intervene "on a mass scale in everyday life," promoting the sales of industrial products and contributing to the "estheticization and humanization of an urban environment" (65, 64). But on the other hand, in the domain of the plastic arts, the aesthetic return to constructivist principles had positioned Yugoslavia on the cutting edge of knowledge production and, indeed, of environmental transformation. For Horvat-Pintarić, the key link between the environmental sensibilities of these postwar avant-gardes was the Croatian architect and former EXAT 51 member Vjenceslav Richter. Moving fluidly between sculptural and architectural scales, Richter's serially produced "reliefometers" were "open works" bridging the active spectator of kinetic art and the "user" of a newly ludic and participatory architecture. In dialogue with the work of Vasarely and Nicolas Schöffer, Richter contributed to what Horvat-Pintarić called the "democratization and de-mystification of art," indicating the various "problems of new visual research" taken up by the New Tendencies movement (65, 65).

In this way, Horvat-Pintarić brought Carbondale conferees up to speed on the vanguard democratic aspirations of kinetic and op art and the work of some of its key players, who had been featured earlier in the year in William Seitz's *The Responsive Eye* blockbuster exhibition at MoMA—the first U.S. show including work from the New Tendencies. And she did so in the service of a more expansive conceptualization of democratic spectatorship across media—the domain of what she called the "activated image" (65, 66). What European art theory still lacked, Horvat-Pintarić argued, was an account of the relationship between the widespread public interest in kinetic art and "the impact of the new mass techniques of visual communication, television and film, on the average modern person" (65, 66). This spectator—whom she calls a "pure observer" or "televiewer"—has an appetite for "dynamic visual metamorphoses" because he or she is already "accustomed to a continued, active, kinetic image of film and television, to a dynamic visual communication of events or phenomena" (65, 66). As such, this viewer, hungry for "direct emotional participation," is also addressed in the internationally celebrated products of Zagreb's animation studio, another state-sponsored domain of artistic innovation in the "cultivation of plastic values," whose cinematic achievements Horvat-Pintarić described in some detail (65, 68).

Horvat-Pintarić's genealogy of modernist media practice, uniting interwar and postwar avant-gardes in an expansive, technophilic program of visual communications and rational, systematic "visual research," would surely find receptive ears at Vision 65. The first New Tendencies exhibition was the brainchild of Brazilian artist and designer Almir Mavignier, a student of Max Bill's at the Hochschule für Gestaltung in Ulm. It obviously resonated with Burtin, for whom the vanguard of aesthetic visualization must keep pace with scientific development, serving as a pedagogical guide to its new natures. In fact, as an example of his own media pedagogy, Burtin sent Horvat-Pintarić a copy of *Visual Aspects of Science,* a glossy brochure highlighting his exhibition work for Upjohn and his "total communications environment" in the Kodak Pavilion at the World's Fair.[78] Such crossings between design, science, and art also comported with the professional self-understanding of VanDerBeek, her "visionary" copanelist. VanDerBeek's own Vision 65 talk, "Re:Vision," a poetic meditation interspersed with screenings of his own film work, much of it experiments in "the animated image," began with a paean to kinetic vision: "Motion pictures: / pictures in motion—seem most suited to the meta-physics of change / to life in motion." He described himself less as a filmmaker than as a "film worker," a specialist dealing with "the laws of sight" in ways "that seem similar to the laws of physics," and framed his labor as an "art-city planning of the mind, a form of research that is just beginning in motion images" (*65,* 72). And, like Burtin, VanDerBeek turned to the recent example of the World's Fair as a communicative failure, which he would redeem in an act of counterfactual design thinking—another hypothetical research project for his audience of communication designers. What if, he asked, the fair itself was designed not as a static museum object, but as a mobile, mass-produced "kit of communication tools"? Its contents would be delivered in boxes to individual citizens—a "stimulus" to "give each of us continuous research pleasure and stimulation of international ideas," and which could be continuously exchanged, "like books from a world library." VanDerBeek's kinetic idiom, like Horvat-Pintarić's and so many other Vision 65 speakers, was overtly cybernetic, blurring the domains of knowledge work and therapy: "Motion, meta-motion, kinetic identity, body-motor response, homeostasis . . . to relieve the tensions of change (doubt)—of the movement of life itself—by studying it" (*65,* 75). The Movie-Drome, of course, would be VanDerBeek's own "motion-picture research laboratory," testing the theory he floated in "Re:Vision" of motion pictures as an "international decompression chamber," tasked with burning up "international and natural 'toxic' attitudes." Its account of happiness as future survival and growth secured through visual research, and visual forms of knowledge production, was the desideratum of Vision 65 conference technique.

Limits to Growth: Burtin's Cultural Studies at Vision 67

The avant-garde Burtin assembled at Vision 67, held at New York University October 19–21, was embedded in the heady terrain of aesthetic practice surveyed by Horvat-Pintarić two years before. Vision 67 included kinetic artists such as Vasarely and Tinguely, and featured two speakers—Max Bense and Umberto Eco—connected with the New Tendencies and whose understanding of advanced art brought information and communication into the domain of rational, scientistic "programming."[79] But Vision 67 speakers such as Eco, alongside the Polish film critic Jerzy Toeplitz and French filmologist Gilbert Cohen-Séat, also extended questions about the environmental reach of visual communications media firmly into the domain of ideology and cultural contestation. Their talks comprised a survey of various media pedagogies, each with different assumptions about spectatorship, and each with conflicting agendas of cultural programming. They exposed Burtin and fellow Vision 67 conferees to culture itself as a domain of mediation and political technique; and to culture's communications media as potentially revolutionary objects demanding systematic interdisciplinary study.

A revision of McLuhan's work, Eco's talk, "Man Is the Message," offered a theory of the uneven global development of mass communication's conditions of reception and their revolutionary and countercultural possibilities.[80] His call for "communication guerillas," wedded to the more urgent phenomena of contemporary mass dissent ("hippies, beatniks, New Bohemians, and student movements"), assumed an active spectator, capable of counterprogramming in the mode of ideology critique. Cohen Séat was more anxious about cinema as a mass medium with unpredictable psychological effects, susceptible to irrationalism and propaganda. Like Burtin, though, he remained convinced that its menace could be controlled through scientific study and in visionary pedagogical applications.[81] At Vision 67, he laid out such a program of modern visual literacy in his proposal for an international scientific and technical center for the utilization of modern visual techniques. The proposed center aimed to solve the problem of global economic underdevelopment, and UNESCO's outmoded allegiance to "book knowledge," through a sweeping curriculum of visual education. For Cohen-Séat, film and visual communications media, like the vanguard cadre of instructors using them, would model a "set of behaviors and ways of doing things in keeping with [Western] industrial society and its apparatus."[82] The filmologist thus imagined a kind of late-behaviorist spectator as a tractable vessel of efficient liberal-internationalist technique, speedily acquiring the habits of modern, fully developed *homo oeconomicus*.[83] And from his vantage as rector of the Polish Film School,

Figure 4.17. Program, Vision 67: Survival and Growth, designed by Will Burtin. Will Burtin Papers, RIT Libraries: Graphic Design Archives, Rochester Institute of Technology.

Toeplitz also limned the pedagogical role of visual media in the "cultural development of humanity."[84] His talk, "Creative Artists and Active Spectators," argued that systematic training of artists and professionals in film schools—whether in Łódź behind the Iron Curtain, or at USC, UCLA, NYU, or the nascent AFI—would produce a culture of informed media spectators and producers. Such enculturation required thriving film societies and well-funded archives, robust film research at the university level, and the teaching of film appreciation at all education levels, including through Poland's vibrant circuit of state-sponsored film clubs. Administered by a socialist state, this was also an experimental media program, one that aimed to produce a population of "active and critical spectators who will eventually replace the passive mobs" (67, 99).

Socialist approaches to arts and media administration, and socialist aesthetic practices, affirmed Burtin's sense of culture as *programmable*, just as subject to the technical interventions and scientific management of expert planners as the future of the human environment itself.[85] Filmology's positivist dream of a scientific study of film in the postwar period had similarly technocratic tendencies; and Cohen-Séat was a natural choice to help provide an answer to one of Burtin's animating questions for Vision 67: "Is there one basic theory for film, television, graphic and architectural design?"[86] Although an overtly socialist theory of either media or the category of culture was a conceptual road not taken by Burtin, he was quite aware of this work. In his Vision 67 planning file, a handwritten note reads, "role of Marxist view of mass communication."[87] Even more strikingly, the planning documents include the full Second Report of the Birmingham Centre for Contemporary Cultural Studies (CCCS), prepared in October 1965 by its director, Richard Hoggart, and Stuart Hall, then the center's assistant director and research fellow.[88] When the Vision 65 conference proceedings were published—in part—in the *American Scholar*, one of the essays chosen to supplement the Vision 65 talks was Hoggart's "Literature and Society." Burtin thus not only knew about, but also likely welcomed, this alignment of two visionary interdisciplinary ventures on the frontier of knowledge work: the Vision conferences and the nascent CCCS.

Should this surprise us? Yes and no. As an intellectual movement and a political project institutionalized in the 1950s and 1960s alongside the rise of the British New Left, cultural studies in the socialist tradition of Raymond Williams and E. P. Thompson rethought culture as shaped by class, agency, experience, and value in ways frequently unacknowledged by the Vision conferees' often universalizing, liberal-international rhetoric.[89] But, as Richard Lee has shown, British cultural studies emerged alongside, and as a challenge to, the world liberal consensus in the midcentury of U.S. hegemony. Like Burtin's Vision conferences, cultural studies took up what Immanuel Wallerstein calls the "problem of how to regulate, speed up, slow down, or otherwise affect the normal process of change and evolution" in the 1960s.[90] Cultural studies, in other words, shared the liberal Burtin's contemporaneous aspiration in his "Live and Learn" talk to reform knowledge work as a cutting-edge communicative practice in times of epochal change. But Williams, like Hoggart and Hall's fledgling CCCS, had rather different attitudes toward this process of containment than those espoused at the Vision conferences. For them, the notion of culture as software or programming was a basically *political* act requiring revolutionary transformation. Beyond its methodological interest in the "sociology of communications," and the social scientific media theory behind it, the CCCS staked its claim for methodological distinction in its "critical-evaluative" approach to culture and media.[91] Practitioners of this method—of nascent ideology critique enacted in practices of critical reading or media analysis—were scant at the Vision conferences, where approaches to culture and communication rarely offered any sustained analysis of the categories of class, race, or gender fueling the new social movements of the 1960s.

Burtin, to be fair, did hope to include civil rights leaders and black nationalists in the Vision conferences, and he was especially preoccupied with the problem of the counterculture. Yet he was confronted with the vexing reality that the sense of mission and communicative passion fueling the new social movements did not sync with his own. And he sensed that the Vision conferences' calls for survival and growth were pitched in competition with other increasingly clamorous political demands and their dissenting takes on the problem of "development" and its others. He invited Dr. Martin Luther King Jr. to Vision 65, noting how the conference would deal in part with "morality in communication," and he used the prospect of King as a speaker to entice other conferees.[92] Stokely Carmichael, whom Burtin name-dropped at the center of an epochal change of youth cultural values in "Live and Learn," appears on an early program draft of Vision 67, and James Baldwin, described as a "prominent social critic," was also actively pursued as a speaker.[93] At Vision 67, an anonymous conference attendee slipped Burtin a note, retained in the archive, explaining how the conference mission faced a basic "problem of attention arousal" in a politicized environment where "events can no longer wait for patient approaches."[94] The writer named specifically an attention economy that included both Vision 67 and the "thousands demonstrating in Washington" that same day, October 21, in the march on the Pentagon—a massive antiwar demonstration drawing together radicals, black nationalists, veterans, women's groups, and hippies.

In fact, the apparent unhappiness of hippies was a real design problem for Burtin, a sign of the limits of growth. Like the American underground film, sphere of decadent sensations and twitchy imps like Taylor Mead, the hippies' dissenting pursuit of well-being and nonalienation demanded analysis, however skeptical. The young Stuart Hall at Birmingham's CCCS agreed, writing a detailed anatomy of the hippie "way of life, and the values and attitudes embodied in it," at precisely the same time.[95] Burtin's planning file for Vision 67 includes a document titled "Notes about Hippies: Related to the V67 Program," a typed list of "random thoughts" occurring during Burtin's viewing of a CBS special about Haight-Ashbury, *The Hippie Temptation,* broadcast on August 22.[96] As the products of a culture of affluence and "permissive" parents, "they demonstrate a self-centered, self-pitying behavior, which elevates unwillingness to accept responsibility (for themselves and others) to the level of WELTSCHMERZ."[97] Beginning with an animus toward a neoimperialist war and a bankrupt arena of "commercialized communications" shared by many of the Vision conferees, the hippie zone of bad feeling extended problematically toward what Burtin hailed as "the amazing material abundance of the West and the nature of people's needs around the world." It refused "political ideas and the organization of human resources," and it rebuffed the underlying project of the Vision conferences: "understanding through communication, and patient study of cause-effect relationships." Having abandoned the consensual, rational terrain through which the problem solving of environmental futurity would commence, hippies were a growth problem—a sign of lapsed social integration. "Where are we failing them?" he asked. "How large a symptom are they? How can we guide them to where?"

So, too, while "environment" was everywhere discussed at the Vision conferences, issues of environmental justice and ecology were largely sidestepped. Stories of environmental transformation and novelty abounded, and fears of ecocatastrophe were anxiously acknowledged. But rarely did stories about the radical transformation of categories such as "nature" and "environment" as a function of the developed world's hypertrophic growth turn into systematic indictments of capitalism, or the monolithic teleology of modernization theory that often intertwined with the ideology of design conference technique.[98] One notable exception here was the presence at Vision 67 of the industrial designer and artist Selby Mvusi, a black South African (of Bantu descent), then teaching in the Department of Fine Art at the University of Nairobi. Mvusi's talk turned the conference's abiding cybernetic idiom in the direction of radical ecology, and the design of the interface toward the reality of constitutive political antagonism. It insisted that Western humanism had produced not only materialism but also a war on nature itself as an object of continual violence, abetting an imperial and neoimperial ideology. Generally, however, as a technique of speculation, planning, and prediction, the Vision conferences sought to manage future growth rather than, as Mvusi suggested, to force the capitalist world system to a crisis point.

This is not to say that "environmental design," as approached at the Vision conferences was somehow apolitical. Rather, "environment" was everywhere conceptualized at the conferences as the social organism's very medium of change and potentially catastrophic development, and environmental design as a technical and political matter of species' evolution and growth. Survival and happiness were always at stake. Further, that developmental narrative was intrinsically connected to the vanguard potential and environmental reach of information and communications media. Although the currents of postwar futurology that joined Burtin's conference planning and, for example, Fuller and McHale's contemporaneous Geoscope experiments are often read as the bourgeois, technocratic appropriation of left futurism in the domains of military and industrial planning, their more liberal versions were often sympathetic to the antitechnocratic sentiments of new youth movements.[99] Like Fuller and McHale, Burtin turned to the counterculture and the avant-garde for models of experimental futurity, and his managerial project of growth management overlapped with a tradition of environmental futurology linked to the birth of the ecology movement and its attendant theses about the future. So much depends on what it meant, for Burtin, to survey the avant-garde of VanDerBeek, to scrutinize the negative affect of hippies, or to study the media program of the insurgent CCCS in the key of futurological planning. As the enactment of Burtin's own brand of interdisciplinary cultural studies, the Vision conferences couldn't help but confront the potential limits of liberal-capitalist growth, both in symptomatic manifestations such as the counterculture, or in critical conceptual alternatives, including socialist accounts of media, spectatorship, and the category of culture itself.

By the early 1970s, the assumptions underlining Burtin's happy prognostications of film's and the media's roles in projects of rationally managed growth—and the expanded purview of the designer in them—came under fire on a variety of fronts, and not just from the counterculture. The design world witnessed the publication of landmark calls for ecologically responsible design, for example, Victor Papanek's *Design for the Real World* (1971).[100] In environmental studies, as Jason W. Moore has recently argued, radical geographers like David Harvey began to advocate "a relational view of humanity-in-nature, and nature-in-humanity" that has now been confirmed in the age of the Anthropocene *as* the Capitalocene.[101] The assumptions of midcentury modernization theory and its cheery model of capitalist development were questioned in the increasing visibility of population politics in the work of Paul Ehrlich and Barry Commoner, and with the 1972 publication of the Club of Rome's *Limits to Growth,* an exemplary project of visualization. These developmental premises and politics were even more thoroughly dismantled in Wallerstein's anti-imperialist world-systems theory, hatched in the 1970s to extricate sociology from "the cul-de-sac known as modernization theory."[102] From what Wallerstein would call the peripheries of the world system, the film world of the 1960s saw the emergence of Third Cinema movements, "another kind of useful film," but one that now joined U.S. political hegemony to its forms of cultural imperialism (i.e., Hollywood), and thus began to break the link between film, mass communications media, and cultural projects of progress and modernization taken up at the Vision conferences.[103] And UNESCO, too, as it broadened its member nations, was increasingly attentive to structural inequities of power undergirding the doctrine of the free flow of information, helping to "create spaces for the cultural expression of postcolonial filmmakers."[104] In all these ways, the increasingly political contests over communications media, cultural programming, and critical spectatorship at Vision 67 spoke to a much broader and more pervasive unhappiness with those technical interventions in communication and human evolution that I've called environmental design.

5

designer film theory

Techniques of Happiness

AT DESIGN MEETINGS such as the IDCA and the Vision conferences, films and filmmaking were approached within the broader assemblage of interdisciplinary knowledge work and media practice that I've called midcentury conference technique. Will Burtin, for example, hoped that the conferees' vanguard perspectives on communications media would help answer one of Vision 67's animating questions: "Is there one basic theory for film, television, graphic and architectural design?"[1] The yield of the Vision conferences was less a medium-specific reckoning with film than a heterodox, survivalist theory of communications media as tools of environmental design and control. And it was Burtin's commitment to the educational potential of visual media in ministering to crises of capitalist development worldwide that allowed him to convene—under the rubrics of "visual communication" or "communications design"—far-flung figures like VanDerBeek, Horvat-Pintarić, and Dickinson, or Eco, Bense, and Toeplitz. Their work, and the trajectories of their careers, crossed disciplinary boundaries at precisely the moment when a category like "film theory" did not yet exist as the property of one discipline.

Film theory is also knowledge work. At midcentury, it was consolidated alongside a bid for the disciplinary integrity of "film studies" itself, whose academic institutionalization proceeded steadily over the course of the 1960s. This does not mean that the serious study of film hadn't breached the walls of the university until midcentury—indeed, film studies had made fascinating, erratic forays into academia in the Progressive Era. Rather, these "random ventures in film instruction," as Dana Polan has shown, "did not coalesce into a coherent field solidified around fixed questions and sets of practices."[2] If a retrospective canon of film theory emerged at a time of disciplinary formation for a nascent field, that midcentury period overlapped significantly with the boundary-crossing media experiments of designers, whose theories of film were often fomented as overt challenges to specialization and the fragmentation of knowledge regimes. Designer film theory understood and promoted the virtues of humanistic training in film and other media as holistic and interdisciplinary endeavors during precisely the moment that film studies became a humane discipline by purging itself of the methods of other disciplines that had helped to build it in the postwar period. And the "classical" film theory canonized or written at midcentury, and conscripted by film studies' proponents in a bid for academic legitimacy, was helpful to the cause of incipient disciplinarity largely because it explored questions of film's ontology: the problem of film's essence or specificity as a medium. In this way, the becoming classical of film theory dovetailed with the prestige and institutionalization of a Greenbergian account of modernism as a project of "hunting the arts back to their mediums," purifying media by "isolating, concentrating, and defining" them.[3]

As we've seen, designers such as the Eameses or Burtin were largely uninterested in issues of medial purity, though they were keenly attentive to the specific properties of media and materials. Their practice tended to fold questions of the properly filmic or cinematic into broader categories like "communication" and "information"; and it subordinated medium specificity to a larger concern with instrumental or managerial projects of visualization, visual presentation, or sensory training in which film is just one of many available tools, often part of a more expansive technical apparatus. Individual mediums, like the stuff of the mid century object world, were embedded in networked relationships and the technical systems that produced and sustained them. To ask after a designer film theory is thus to insist upon what was conceptually productive about its abiding medial promiscuity and interdisciplinarity at a time when film-theoretical classicism summoned a modernist purity of medium and sought to erect boundaries around a new discipline—film studies—and to define its proper objects and methods.

The year 1960 was crucial for that fledging discipline, which held the inaugural meeting of its first professional organization—the Society of Cinematologists—in April at the Faculty Club of New York University, following preliminary conversations among university film teachers convened at MoMA in 1957 and 1958. Despite this haughty title's nod to Cohen-Séat's scientistic filmology, the SoC worked to distinguish academic film studies as a humanistic, liberal-arts discipline, methodologically aligned with the New Criticism. They privileged close reading and the development of a specialized analytical vocabulary for the "exclusive language of cinema."[4] The society's founding president, NYU professor of English Robert Gessner, hoped the organization would end the college film teacher's "second-class citizenship in university classrooms."[5] This meant shifting the academic study of film from social scientific paradigms, thereby demarcating film studies' methods and objects from the domain of postwar communications research. But it also meant elevating film's special status as a humane art, and thus separating it from the deleterious effects of mass culture, a vigorously debated category in the 1950s, when practices of cultural legitimation were embedded in Cold War strategies of containment.

Designer film theory in the midcentury period was fueled by film studies *in statu nascendi*—still productively undisciplined and allowing for surprising interdisciplinary crossings. Because of the designer's central location in postwar cultures of liberal-democratic abundance and technocratic administration, as well as the profession's role in producing the very consumer culture of technical civilization that would be decried as mass culture, designer film theory was constitutively impure. In emphasizing this heterogeneity, I seek to extend here the previous two chapters' analysis of the broader organizational *dispositif* through which designers conceptualized film at midcentury design conferences. In chapters 5 and 6, I turn to the terrain of film theory proper, putting design theory and classical film theory into dialogue to draw out a midcentury design *dispositif* foundational to both. The concept of the dispositive ("apparatus," in its more familiar English translation) has its etymological roots in concepts of administration, in the designed instrumentality of a once-divine set of "practices, bodies of knowledge, measures, and institutions that aim to manage, govern, control, and orient—in a way that purports to be useful—the behaviors, gestures, and thoughts of human beings."[6] At the end of the midcentury period, one now-familiar film-theoretical model of "the apparatus" emerges, most famously in the work of Jean-Louis Baudry, and in the discourse of so-called political modernism in France and the United Kingdom. As recent returns to "apparatus theory" have reminded us, however, this account of the technical components of cinema as a technology and of its ideological work often considers the *dispositif* as a "homogeneous and closed whole" that "directly determines what a spectator experiences."[7] This chapter's turn to designer film theory, by contrast, follows the lead of film scholarship seeking a deeper history of the cinematic device, "characterized by multiple genealogies and variable structures."[8] The interdisciplinary terrain of modernist practice it reveals is similarly promiscuous and impure.

The heterogeneity of the modern design *dispositif* was fed from a range of social scientific disciplines (anthropology, sociology, psychology) that film studies would, for a time, abjure as it got itself disciplined. It drew heavily on the transdisciplinary aspirations of communication and information theory, cybernetics, and semiotics.[9] And it tended to understand film's epistemological and informatic capacities in tandem with overtly educational missions and institutions, from the Weimar-era Bauhaus and its wartime transplantation in the United States through the energies of Moholy-Nagy, to its postwar reemergence in Germany in the Ulm School of Design's experiments in humanistic, creative democratic education. Nourished by its interwar, avant-garde roots, designer film theory saw modern technical media such as film as inherently pedagogical. And conversely, it understood pedagogy as a fundamentally *technical* matter—an intervention in human development that required intermedial instruction and exploration. Designer film theory was thus strongly wedded to the practice and process of design, and design education. And design education was implicated in heated postwar debates about the relationship between human technique and technology. There, film itself became a harbinger of the potential and threat of modern technics to the self-evidence of categories such as nature and human nature.

The disciplinary errancy and theoretical eclecticism I model in this and the next chapter are inspired by the bibliography assembled by Millie and Morton Goldsholl for the IDCA 1959 conference, Communication: The Image Speaks. As a thought experiment, we might consider IDCA '59, held a year before the founding meeting of the cinematologists, as that professional organization's unheralded other, seeking to cross disciplinary boundaries under the master rubric of "communication" just when the SoC would circle the wagons around the specific disciplinary object of film by severing ties with postwar communications studies. The Goldsholls' list, which sought to provide conferees with "a reference" for the speakers on the "Film Image" panel, is divided into two sections, "Art & Design" and "Film." The former includes Laszlo Moholy-Nagy's *Vision in Motion* (1947), György Kepes's *Language of Vision* (1944) and *The New Landscape in Art and Science* (1956), Lancelot Hogben's *From Cave Painting to Comic Strip: A Kaleidoscope of Human Communication* (1949), Jurgen Ruesch and Weldon Kees's *Nonverbal Communication* (1956), and Rudolf Arnheim's *Art and Visual Perception: A Psychology of the Creative Eye* (1954). The film list includes four canonical works of film theory—Arnheim's *Film as Art* (1957; originally published as *Film als Kunst* in 1932), Sergei Eisenstein's *The Film Sense* (1942), Béla Balázs's *Theory of the Film* (1952), and *Grierson on Documentary*, edited by Forsyth Hardy (1947).

The Goldsholls' curious bibliography will serve as a conceptual touchstone for these two linked chapters, helping me fill a lacuna in the historiography of postwar film theory. By taking seriously the category of designer film theory, and by historicizing its lineaments in the new media environments and politics of the Cold War period in which designers like the Eameses and Will Burtin expanded their professional ambitions, I explore the anxious humanism that joined the work of Moholy-Nagy and Kepes to some of the more familiar figures of classical film theory, including Maya Deren, Siegfried Kracauer, and Rudolf Arnheim, the only figure whose work spans the IDCA list's two categories. Embracing the postwar vogue for communication, this was a different mode of humanism than the sort affirmed in the SoC's attempts to legitimate film study as a liberal art. It was technophilic, brokering inspired interdisciplinary crossings between art and science, but also worried about period-specific threats to the "human scale." Pragmatic and experimental, this humanism sought to understand the very status of "nature" as the newly malleable target of postwar technics and rational design. And it worked to define and defend forms of humane technique, identifying the role of film in the forms of creativity and interdisciplinary practice that designers deemed the special province of human agency and capacity. As medium and technology, as index of modern technics and their objects—both nature *and* human beings—film was conceptualized by designers and film theorists alike as an essential part of a broader technique of postwar happiness.

The key design theorists in what follows are Kepes and his mentor and colleague Moholy-Nagy, whose work intersected with some of classical film theory's more familiar figures in ways largely overlooked in film historiography. I place these designers' work in a genealogy linking Bauhaus understandings of film and photography in the interwar period with various postwar attempts to conceptualize film and filmmaking's mediating role in the senses' encounter with the new nature of the postwar period and the variants of humanism that would be happy in it. For Moholy and Kepes, film and moving-image technologies were the very media of postwar happiness; and happiness was a technical process and an ideological problem that needed film—that required it as a special kind of salve. At the high-water mark of what Mark Greif had dubbed the "age of the crisis of man," a pervasive humanist discourse at midcentury that arose in the historical shadow of fascism and totalitarianism, designers viewed the postwar human condition as both set in and beset by a world of technological saturation that demanded managerial technique, and fueled their media experimentation and pedagogy.[10] No

Figure 5.1. László Moholy-Nagy, *Self-Portrait with Hand,* 1925/29. Image courtesy of Moholy Nagy Foundation, copyright 2017 Estate of László Moholy-Nagy/Artists Rights Society (ARS), New York.

surprise, then, that designer theories of film and visual media doubled as reckonings with the fragile promise of the postwar happy life.

Like much classical film theory, designer film theory was always already media theory, and embedded in ancillary concepts of work and play, consumption and pedagogy, communication and knowledge production. Being happy demanded not just new things but also vanguard approaches to living, working, and learning in and through the technical media that had so radically transformed the concept of nature itself. Happiness would require a technophilic humanism capable of confronting new models of the sensorium shaped by period-specific approaches to communication, the psychology of the organized (or entropic) technical image, theories of information processing and data visualization, and the alien landscape of a new nature revealed by scientific imaging technologies.

Pursing this argument, the chapter begins with Moholy's film and media pedagogy as a technique of the happy. Working largely with his 1947 treatise *Vision in Motion,* I describe the contours of Moholy's holistic media practice at the Institute of Design in Chicago. My goal here is to demonstrate the abiding relationship in his work at the School of Design between technophilic media practice and media therapy, and to place his theories of film within a series of specific wartime experiments in physical and emotional rehabilitation. Moholy's notion of film as a means of "conditioning to creativity"—as an encounter with and rehabbing of humans' biological capacities—thus overlaps with a similarly therapeutic account of medial happiness in Maya Deren's *Anagram,* an anthropological account of film as a humane "form of man." Both Moholy and Deren embed film in a theory of organic design that is happy in a new, creatively transfigured postwar nature. I also describe the particular utility of Deren's account of "creative" cinematography in a few of Kepes's interdisciplinary attempts to bridge art and science through explorations into postwar visual culture. These ambitious projects, which directly take up theories of organization offered by communications theory, cybernetics, and systems theory, will serve as bridge between chapters 5 and 6. As we'll see, they brought Kepes into dialogue with Arnheim, whose encounter with information aesthetics I take up more directly in the next chapter.

Rehab Media: Moholy-Nagy and the New Bauhaus

Perhaps no designer better understood the high stakes of midcentury technics than László Moholy-Nagy, director of the Institute of Design. In 1943 the *Saturday Evening Post* chronicled the school's far-flung activities in an article titled "Are You Contemporary?" The author invites the reader of this bastion of middlebrow taste to "check your mind against Moholy-Nagy's, a modernist who is so far ahead that he's almost out of sight."[11] It's an admiring piece, but the author is clearly a bit baffled by this so-called painter who works in light, etches abstractions in something

16 THE SATURDAY EVENING POST July 3, 1943

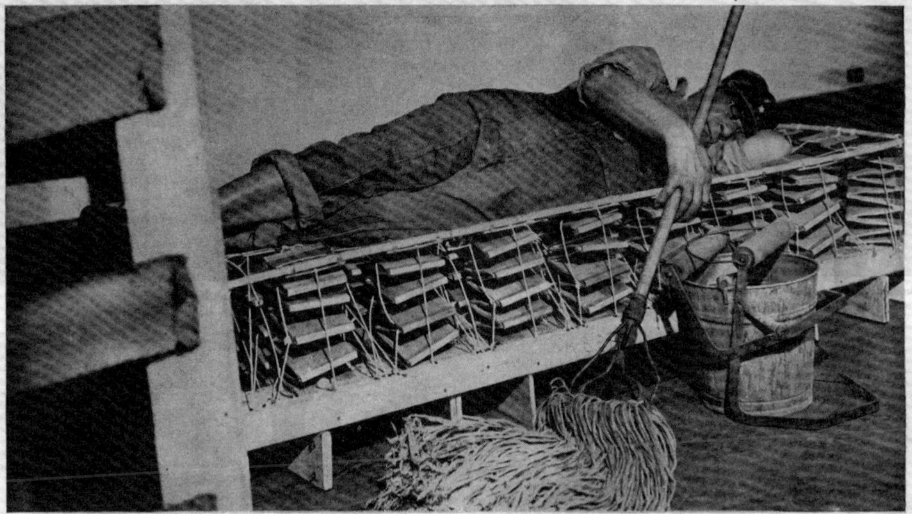

When war shortages of metal threatened our supply of bedsprings, Moholy-Nagy set his disciples to ersatzing springs of wood. After showing the photographer how these work, the janitor dozed, ceased to work himself.

ARE YOU CONTEMPORARY?

By ROBERT M. YODER

SHORTLY after the war began, there was talk that the United States might face a shortage of mattresses and bedsprings. This focused attention on a Chicago designer named Lazlo Moholy-Nagy, who, it was widely printed, had invented a fine set of bedsprings made of wood. Since then, the shortage has pretty successfully been met without the use of such expedients, but perhaps it would be interesting to set out Moholy-Nagy's own version of the case, which is a little more involved than the others

In the first place, he explains, he didn't design the springs himself. They were simply a project he suggested to the students in a remarkable school of de-

Check your mind against Moholy-Nagy's, a modernist who is so far ahead that he is almost out of sight.

signing he runs in a former Chicago bakery. In the second place, he says, wooden bedsprings are as old as the hills, and are described in many, many patents dated around 1800 to 1830, when there was actually some use for them. Then, in the third place, Moholy-Nagy is only incidentally a designer, and primarily a painter. A painter of the most advanced type—so far, far ahead of the rest of the class that he is working happily on a plan whereby it may not be necessary to paint at all.

The important thing about the wooden bedsprings, he continues, is that his students were using one of the new materials, plywood, and using it in ingenious ways, so as to take advantage of that material's fine springiness. They were practicing what Moholy-Nagy preaches—that modern times abound with fine new materials whose possibilities have not even been tapped. Thousands of fine opportunities go unseen because most of us look toward the past. "Most adults," says Moholy-Nagy gently, "never know what

With infra-red rays the Chicago modernists roasted a chicken in 23 minutes, ate it in less.

String hung in your doorway will keep visitors out, but let the breeze—and the flies—in.

A Moholy-Nagy student tests the resilience of wooden springs dreamed up at the school.

344

Figure 5.2. "Are You Contemporary?" promotion of László Moholy-Nagy's School of Design, Chicago. *Saturday Evening Post,* July 3, 1943.

Figure 5.3.
Cover, New Bauhaus catalog, 1937–38. Institute of Design collection, box 3, folder 53, IDC_0003_053_Coverfront. Special Collections and University Archives, Richard J. Daley Library, University of Illinois at Chicago.

called Plexiglas, and is generally "so far ahead of the rest of the class that he is working happily on a plan whereby it may not be necessary to paint at all."[12] As a chronicle of the ID's various wartime activities and investigations of materials, from its prototyping of wooden bedsprings, to its fashioning of a jerry-built oven, the article's mere existence affirms Moholy's skills as not just an artist but also an arts administrator, and a deft PR man packaging the school's animating interdisciplinary and intermedial ethos. "It is Moholy-Nagy's idea that we are anywhere from fifty to a thousand years behind the times, and among the causes, he blames the habit of learning one field of endeavor, one profession or one craft, and one alone. There are far too many specialists, he thinks."[13] Moholy's contemporaneity wedded modernism and communication in a shared mission to devise the basic equipment for everyday postwar life. As *Vision and Motion* attests, it was an interdisciplinary modernism of sweeping idealism. And it could roast a chicken in a garbage can with infrared light.

Film history and filmmaking played an essential role in Moholy-Nagy's practice of "emotional education" at the ID, and *Vision in Motion* laid out the medium's therapeutic role in a more ambitious theory of intermedial therapy, general education, and democratic happiness.[14] Written largely in 1944 and published the year following his early death from leukemia, the treatise revised and updated his previous works of media theory—chiefly *Painting, Photography, Film* (1925; revised in 1927) and *The New Vision: From Material to Architecture* (1930)—while framing them within an account of his research "laboratory for a new education," namely, the Institute of Design in Chicago. With Moholy as director, the ID was founded in 1937 as the "New Bauhaus" for "the training of artists, industrial designers, architects, photographers, and teachers" (*VM,* 63).[15] *Vision in Motion* is animated by a biosocial account of modernity as defined by the coevolution of media and the human sensorium. "The biological evolutionary progress of man," Moholy argued, "was possible only through the development and constructive use of all his senses, hands, and brains, through his creative ability and intuition to master his surroundings; through his perceptive power, conceptual thought, and articulated emotional life" (*VM,* 20). But as the industrial revolution "stabilized," it has led to the "disintegration" of human beings' most basic sensory capacities: "Man who is by nature able to express himself in different media allowed these most valuable biological potentialities to be amputated or paralyzed" (*VM,* 20).

Because Moholy-Nagy understood humanity's inherent multisensory facility with media as the motor of its evolutionary progress, widespread media illiteracy augured species decline. "The illiterate of the future," he declared, "will be the person who does not know how to use a camera." In *Vision in Motion,* Moholy's thoughts on species being bore the stamp of the "evolutionary humanism" of British biologist and ecologist Julian Huxley, an adviser to the ID and, as of 1946, UNESCO's first inspector general, whom Moholy met during his time in London's vanguard artistic and scientific circles in the mid-1930s.[16] Moholy's curriculum at the ID was thus designed to minister to primary human needs for media literacy, and to intervene in the "future of man" through "the development

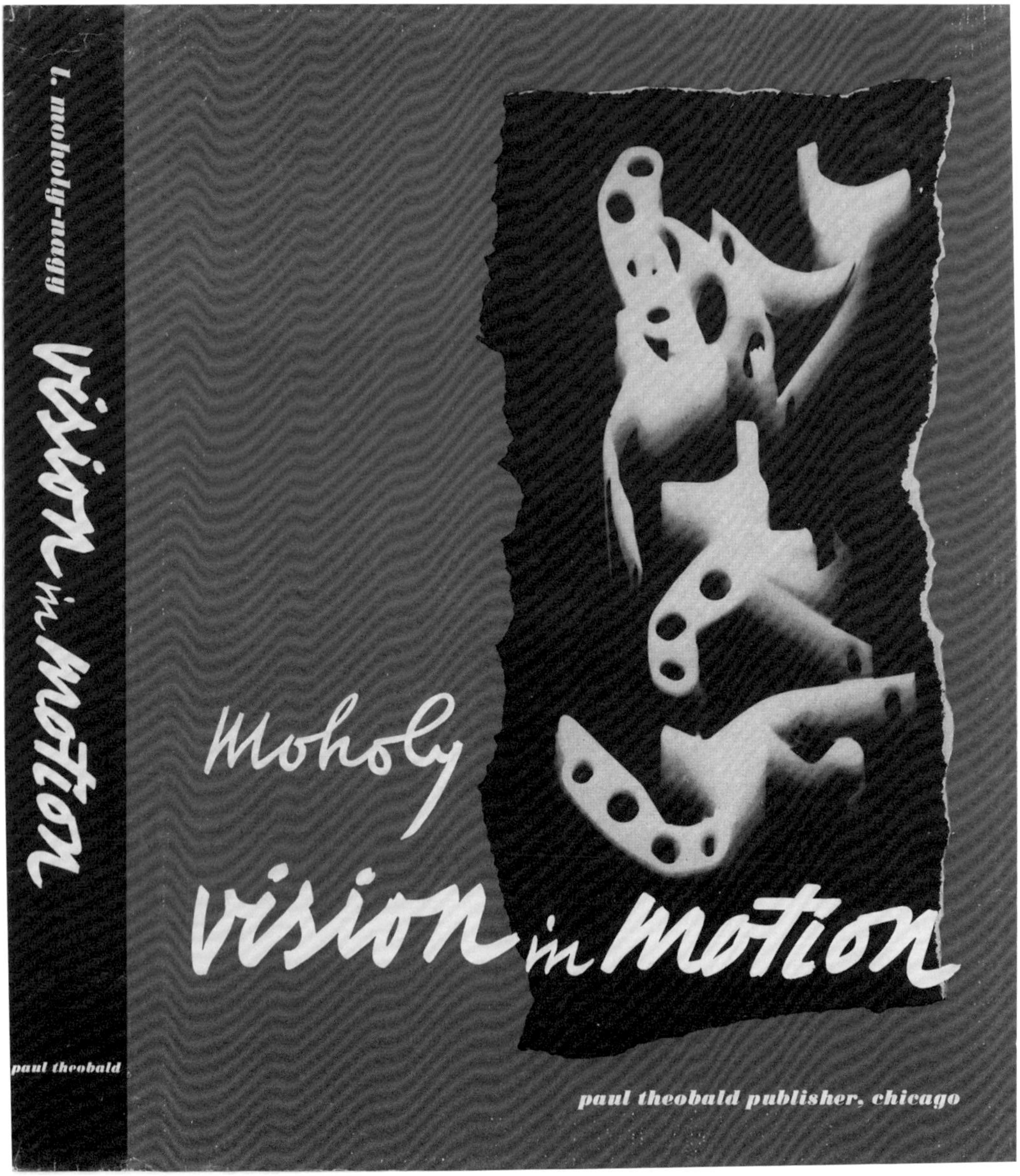

Figure 5.4. Cover, László Moholy-Nagy, *Vision in Motion* (Chicago: Paul Theobald, 1969 [1947]).

of man's capacities" (*VM*, 14). These prerequisites were at once biological and social, and their urgency was sharpened by the perils of war, as his corporeal idiom of amputation and paralysis suggests. In this sense, Moholy's design pedagogy at the New Bauhaus in the United States, specifically its attempts to "redirect human evolution by inscribing a technologically mediated new vision," extended and modified the "biocentric" approach to media Moholy developed in Berlin in the 1920s, embedded in utopian "life reform" (*Lebensreform*) practices of health, education, and communal living.[17] *Vision in Motion* transplanted and updated this interwar strategy, framing it within what Moholy dubbed an "organic approach" to education—both in a climate of wartime emergency and with a hopeful eye toward a new, postwar life (*VM*, 63).

Part of what is most remarkable about *Vision in Motion* today is just how much the book seeks to defend the role of the techno-savvy humanities themselves in producing happy, postwar citizens, and how forcefully this program of "integrated" education across media is pitched as a democratic technique honed in a present of conflict and total war. Overcome by modernity, humans have struggled to control their "dangerous antibiological and asocial dynamics," squandering in the process the human's "prodigious potentialities for healthy living" and "harmonious social relationships" (*VM*, 13). Moholy was not only making a general argument about managing modernity by absorbing or acclimating to its sensory demands, one familiar to readers of his Benjaminian *Painting, Photography, Film*.[18] Rather, he mounted a more specific brief against the workings of a global capitalist economy and a pervasive "social ethics based on economic superiority rather than on the principles of justice" (*VM*, 14). The critique is all the more plangent in the wartime context of its writing, which crystallized for Moholy how the "monopolistic and fascistic tendencies" of competitive capitalism, and its inability to address "smouldering class struggle," have precipitated "repeated world wars." The "blind dynamics of competition and profit," he argues, "automatically leads to conflicts on a world scale" (*VM*, 14). It is in the thick of wartime mobilization, then, that Moholy calls for a reinvestigation of "healthy living," and lays out a pedagogical program consistent with the "human values" and the inalienable rights of the American and French revolutions: "life, liberty, and the pursuit of happiness" (*VM*, 14).

As a European émigré with deep ties to a socialist design school shuttered by the Nazis in 1933, Moholy-Nagy's invocation of the Declaration of Independence a decade later is surely fraught. The FBI, we should recall, kept detailed files on Moholy, Mies, and Gropius for several years, and delayed Moholy's efforts at naturalization, which he was granted just months before his death.[19] While partly a rhetorical gambit to assimilate ideologically to a new nation whose government was suspicious of leftist Bauhauslers, Moholy's appeal to Jeffersonian happiness is also a sincere attempt to yoke the Institute of Design's view of "human values" to a defense of the value of the humanities as such.[20] As a technique of postwar well-being, Moholy's organic approach to the "new education" offers "a simultaneous affirmation of individual and social needs" and can, he predicts, "become the instrument of a happier and healthier life"

(*VM,* 24). While Moholy explains that the value of "harmonious social existence" is measured by "cooperation, social usefulness, and personal happiness," it is clear that happiness itself is understood as an effect of being knitted into social life, inextricable from projects of collective utility (*VM,* 25). For Moholy, in short, there really is no "personal" happiness as such without social integration, and no social integration without an abiding integrative *technique*: "a new methodology for approaching problems; a social mechanism of production and a creative education" (VM, 25).

Vanguard, democratic education is therefore the best tool for bringing out our biological capacity for creativity, and for acknowledging the ur-reality of the human as an "*integrator*" (*VM,* 64). "Everyone," Moholy-Nagy insists, "has a creative nature. Everyone is naturally equipped . . . to think and to feel. The schools must know the *technique* of developing this natural equipment in the most formative years of youth" (*VM,* 25). As in the Bauhaus pedagogy that it revises, *Vision in Motion* positions this technique as a response to modernity's tropism toward specialization, witnessed in the debilitating rise of "careerists" rather than sensitive "amateurs," and in a misguided emphasis on vocational rather than "cultural education" (*VM,* 20–21). But human creativity is also threatened by educational reformers' putative corrective to vocationalism: a " 'liberal' education" that, as Moholy's scare quotes indicate, is everywhere static and mechanical in its approach to "learning through quantitative verbal information" (*VM,* 22). The liberal arts, by largely discarding training in arts, crafts, and machine technology for the hoary wisdom of the "classics," furnish the "skill of verbalization" just when multimedia training and "the organic practice of self-experience and self-expression" are most urgently needed (*VM,* 20–21). Narrow vocational education is often technically outmoded, and requires "the brake of the newest technological innovation"; a liberal education based on "the classics" requires "the brake of social thought," and can otherwise lead to "worship of the past" that reinforces "petrified forms of class-determined thinking" (*VM,* 21). Avant-garde pedagogy at the ID therefore rejects the memorization of facts and rote repetition (what Moholy calls "phonographic mentalities"), which emphasizes the "process of receiving rather than producing" (*VM,* 22, 18). The experiences and cultural products of the past must be "assimilated" but "not literally, not without creative analysis. Tradition must be dynamic," animated through productive, creative practice (*VM,* 22).

To "better fulfill its revolutionary aims," then, progressive education must lead students not just to a "collection of data with the aim of a verbalized performance" but also to the possibility of arriving at a "simultaneous creative concept" by synthetic, integrative working across media:

painting, sculpture, poetry, music, drama, and film (*VM,* 23). Here, Moholy calls instead for the training of a "new" kind of specialist, both flexible and adaptable—one who "integrates his special subject with the social whole" and is equipped with faculty of "vision in motion" (*VM,* 21). By this, Moholy doesn't mean mere physiological vision but rather what he calls "simultaneous grasp," a basic biopropensity for "seeing, feeling and thinking in relationship and not as a series of isolated phenomena" (*VM,* 12). Such relationship or pattern seeing "instantaneously integrates and transmutes single elements into a coherent whole" (*VM,* 12).

Under Moholy-Nagy's leadership, the Institute of Design's curriculum cultivated "vision in motion" by extending the framework of the Weimar Bauhaus, whose core was the famed Foundation Course: a wide-ranging introduction to a variety of materials, processes, and experimental exercises and techniques that Moholy taught from 1923 to 1928. In *Vision in Motion,* he described the product of the Foundation Course as "a working union, a spirit of cooperation for social aims," as well as a "talent test" that allowed students first to "recover their all-embracing biological potency," and then discover their more specific aptitudes to be pursued in more advanced, specialized workshops (*VM,* 71–72). Here, the Institute of Design "changed the old Bauhaus tradition of segregated crafts (for metal, wood, glass, stone, fiber, etc.)" and set up only three departments: architecture, product design, and the "Light Workshop," where students were trained in film and photography alongside painting, sculpture, and weaving (*VM,* 84). First headed by Kepes, the Light Workshop allowed students a thorough "re-valuation" of the "elements of visual expression with emphasis on advertising art. Experiments are made in photography, the motion picture, and display, with emphasis on the investigation of light and the rich possibilities of colored light displays" (*VM,* 86).

Moholy-Nagy had been a staunch critic of the commercial film industry since the 1920s, a theorist of the biosocial and ideological potentialities of light as film's fundamental medium, and a dogged champion and practitioner of various modes of nonnarrative experimentation in the medium, from his "typophoto" film scripts and his "optophonetic" experiments in hand-drawn film sound, to his own abstract films.[21] While film had always been discussed at the ID, and conceptualized as part of its curriculum, Moholy first received funds ($7,500) for film production at the ID from the Rockefeller Foundation in 1942, with the support of his patron Walter Paepcke, chairman of the Container Corporation of America in Chicago and visionary developer of postwar Aspen as the site of humane culture, including the IDCA's administrative efforts.[22] A dynamic speaker with a showman's flair, Moholy also traveled with films of the ID students' wide-ranging activities during the war (collected as *Design Workshops*), using them to publicize and fundraise for the school in public appearances across the United States, from the corporate boardroom to the artist's branch of Chicago's local CIO union.[23] "Since we can't afford to advertise," he told his wife, Sibyl, "I have to be the advertisement."[24] Film production at the ID was a riposte to the commercial industry, both in its small scale and in its dedication to the innovation and holism of amateurs. As Amy Beste has shown, the ID's film program was "framed by Chicago's nontheatrical filmmaking industry," and resonated significantly with other pedagogical reform efforts in the city, including William Benton's work with *Encyclopedia Britannica* films.[25]

At an institution such as the ID, then, film was the utopian medium of luminous well-being, a way of training students for Chicago's flourishing nontheatrical film industry, and a pragmatic, rhetorically sophisticated PR tool. Maximizing what Moholy-Nagy saw as light's purely biological appeal, training in film and photography restored students to their basic human capacities for creativity, and it allowed them to hone more particular talents as they developed integrative expressive faculties—faculties whose holism was enacted and enhanced by group or collective processes.[26] In the context of Moholy's pedagogical program in *Vision and Motion* and elsewhere, the study and practice of film as a medium "with specific technical potentialities" was part of a broader agenda of humanist technique, sensory therapy, and collective process (Plate 19).[27] Experiments with light—in film and other media—were balm for the cognitive depredations of modern specialization and the stultifying sensory impoverishments of commercially driven aesthetic forms, including Hollywood.

For Moholy-Nagy, this multimedia training of vision in motion was a public good, and the humanistic program of education he constructs around it and defends in *Vision in Motion* is foundational to democratic life and the democratic polis. "Thus, why teach humanities, cultural subjects," he asks, "when the greater part of the pupils [in grade schools and high schools] will become workers, technicians, clerks?" (*VM*, 21). His answer—that the consequence "would be an educational and cultural monopoly of a minority" of U.S students privileged enough to attend college, "making an empty shell of democracy"—resonates with what Wendy Brown has critiqued as the hollowing out of the university's democratic value in the neoliberal present (*VM*, 21).[28] Near the close of a devastating world war, Moholy wrote *Vision in Motion* in response to the "dramatic thinning of key democratic values" of his own urgent moment, staking out his belief that "no democracy can exist without the most careful education of its citizens" (*VM*, 24).[29] For him, such values were imperiled by specialization, and market fundamentalism's premium on competition and profit accumulation—the stifling of educational reform by "the well-knit influence team of purely economic leadership" (*VM*, 22).

But he also envisioned his efforts to revive the tradition of "indivisible education" as stymied by the cultural power of "unofficial education": a "mighty propaganda machine run by intricately interwoven interest of lobbyists and pressure groups, monopolists and hired politicians from whose tentacles there is almost no escape" (*VM*, 18). Overlapping significantly with the thrust of Horkheimer and Adorno's contemporaneous "culture industry" thesis, Moholy-Nagy indicted unofficial education—"a widely organized advertising, publications, books, fairs, exhibitions, press and radio"—for fomenting an atmosphere of ideological mystification that "machine guns" its public "with half knowledge, conglomerations of significant and insignificant facts" (*VM*, 19). For Moholy, the culture industry of unofficial education produces a media environment "of a thousand details, but missing all fundamental relationships" (*VM*, 19). Without "the tools of integration, the individual is not able to relate all this casual and scattered information into a meaningful synthesis. He sees everything in clichés" (*VM*, 19). The Light Workshop that housed the film and media program at the Institute of Design was framed within this broader regime of sensory and medial therapy. In sum, it was a democratic rehab program to redress the ideological and biological impairments inflicted by corporate mass media and the seeming saturation of market values that threatened to swap *homo politicus* with *homo oeconomicus*.

Democratic rehabilitation was also, of course, an urgent response to the conditions of a nation at war, demands that impinged directly on the pedagogical program of the school following the United States' entry into the conflict after Pearl Harbor. The cover of a brochure for the school's 1942 summer sessions features a group of students staging an outdoor photography shoot—a still life, it seems—on the sunny, bucolic grounds of the school's farm in Somonauk, Illinois, a gift from the Paepckes. Inside, the brochure contextualizes the program of students' and teachers' working "together in close community" in the thick of "a country at war."[30] The School of Design, precisely "because of its past educational policy" of "integrated training of art, science, and technology," has "readily adapted to the present emergency."[31] War demanded the same kind of flexible, interdisciplinary, and intermedial creative capacities the school had always taught, and total mobilization thus spawned a number of pragmatic design projects for students. As they navigated wartime metal shortages, students prototyped plywood springs; they designed

Figure 5.5. School of Design, summer session catalog, 1942, cover. Institute of Design collection, box 3, folder 72, IDC_0003_072_Coverfront. Special Collections and University Archives, Richard J. Daley Library, University of Illinois at Chicago.

parachute clothes and new kinds of barbed wire, and experimented with shockproof helmets and portable runways for temporary airfields. The curriculum was also tweaked and new courses were developed: an art historical survey was reframed as "The Social Usefulness of Art and Its Relationship to a Nation at War"; and the school offered a "Visual Propaganda in Wartime" course in collaboration with the army, where graphic design abetted public education about air-raid procedures and wartime information campaigns such as the CCA's *Paperboard Goes to War* endeavor. Student work from the School of Design and the Illinois WPA Arts and Crafts Project was also featured in a special exhibition, *War Art*, held at the Renaissance Society of Chicago in April and May 1942, devoted to showcasing what Moholy called "new developments in art in their application to war activities" (Plate 20).[32]

The state of emergency yielded a wartime art of utility and an aesthetics of information and communication, but also, in the school's new "Principles of Camouflage" courses, a more direct application of the school's formalist investments in the laws of vision and the manipulation of light.[33] The courses were taught by Kepes under the auspices of the Office of Civilian Defense and promoted in the 1942 summer session brochure. Kepes, in fact, was trained for two weeks in the art and science of camouflage at the Army Engineer School at Fort Belvoir in Virginia, and some of his students would go on to work in the army's Camouflage Research Department, and in active camouflage battalions in the European theater.[34] In his introductory lecture for the camouflage course, Kepes described the subject as an ideal site of interdisciplinary activity and collaboration, requiring "the combined knowledge of people with a great variety of training—architects, engineers, painters, sculptors, graphic artists. They are finding a synchronization of their divergent knowledge in the fulfilment of this urgent task."[35] Moholy-Nagy,

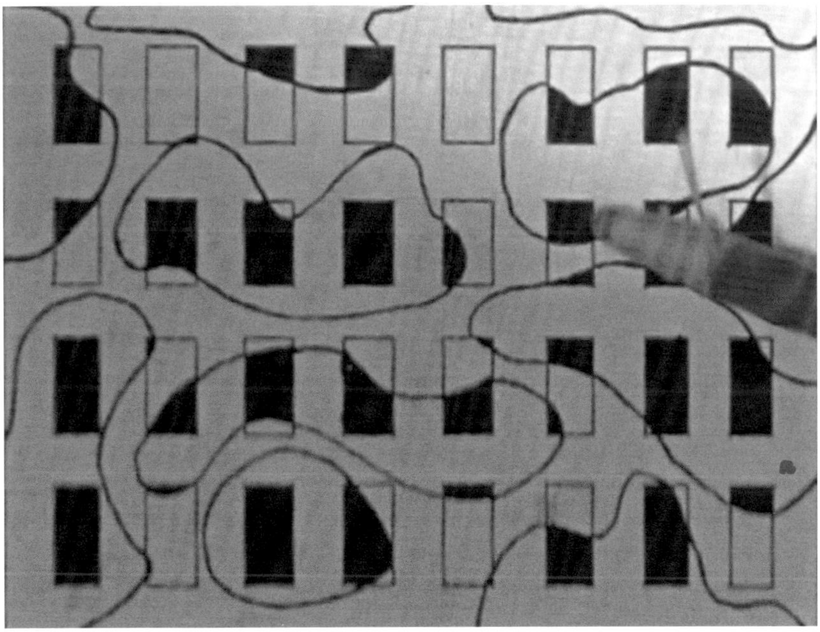

Figure 5.6. László Moholy-Nagy, "camouflage course," *Design Workshops*, 1944.

who had proposed the school as the site of a full-service camouflage "research laboratory," was himself appointed by the mayor of Chicago to its Civil Defense Commission. The team hatched a plan to camouflage the city—especially the Lake Michigan waterfront—against aerial bombardment, and Moholy reported to the *Chicago Daily News* on his proposed solutions, which included changing the contours of the city by constructing "dummy buildings" on barges on the lake, and devising a technique for blacking out the city by having janitors citywide choreographed to drop a chemical into boilers for smoke cover in response to a signal. As Robin Schuldenfrei has argued in her detailed account of the school's wartime activities, camouflage entailed "an almost seamless merger of important, originary Bauhaus ideals—the joining of the arts in work on a common goal, one that had aspects of both artistry and technology, and which could be undertaken only by working *as* a community and *within* a larger community."[36] Like Moholy's media pedagogy more broadly, the camouflage courses were integrative in both method and aim—a performative poetics of the group.

If camouflage courses required training in the art of concealment and illusion, an aesthetics of protection that doubled, in practice, as galvanizing group work, the school's experiments in media therapy also entailed an avant-garde aesthetics of rehabilitation. During the war, Moholy-Nagy proposed a "new plan for rehabilitation" based on "*contemporary* thinking and practices without traditional fixations": an Occupational Therapy program dedicated to demobilized and disabled servicemen, and sponsored by the deputy director of the Mental Hygiene Service of the Illinois Department of Public Welfare.[37] Moholy was particularly interested in the stress, fatigue, and psychological breakdowns suffered by soldiers both in training and in war, as well as by injured industrial workers. Operated in conjunction with veterans' hospitals, the program involved two ID courses—Rehabilitation I and Rehabilitation II—in "the training of the handicapped and of new personnel for rehabilitation work" such as doctors, nurses, therapists, and social workers.[38]

Moholy-Nagy insisted on an expansive definition of rehabilitation, including "psychological, social, recreational, and occupational therapy," a concept that would be "more scientific and more intuitive at the same time," and follow "new developments in education, psychological research, psychoanalysis, vocational guidance, and scientific motion studies."[39] Experts in these novel approaches, tackled more directly in Rehabilitation II, were featured in a series of accompanying guest lectures. Dr. Conrad Somner, deputy director of the Mental Hygiene Service, explained how the ID's "method of group therapy," aiming to "sail out into the sea of heart-brain-creative experience," can "be likened to psychoanalysis in that it reaches down into the unconscious."[40] The courses' basic aim was "conditioning to creativeness," not narrowly applied to art but rather to human capacities for "inventiveness, resourcefulness, and the ability to establish new relationships between given elements" that apply to "all types of work in the artistic, scientific, and technological spheres" (*VM*, 72). The curriculum promoted the "constructive rehabilitation" of the senses, achieved first through "tactile charts" and "hand-sculptures," and then through work in and across a gamut of materials and media: wood and paper cuts, metal work, plastics, weaving, drawing, "*volume and space division* and their further articulation; *photography; motion picture; group poetry; plays, music* and *dance,*" so that a "full coordination of potentialities can be accomplished." Rehabilitation I included workshop exercises *and* theory, in the form of eight lectures by Moholy "with a motion picture and lantern slide," including a broad survey of avant-garde medial practice: sculpture and "the new architecture," "Contemporary Painting (Cubism and Constructivism, etc.)," "New Ways in Photography," and "The Origins of Modern Literature (Dada, Surrealism, Joyce)."

The usefulness of film and media in the context of the wartime rehabilitation courses clarifies their therapeutic function in Moholy-Nagy's pedagogical theory and practice; media sought to create in patients "a happy dynamic feeling of potential usefulness for practical work."[41] As

Figure 5.7. László Moholy-Nagy, "Better Than Before," detail of therapy course. Institute of Design collection, box 6, folder 187, IDC_0006_0187_Better_P3_Detail. Special Collections and University Archives, Richard J. Daley Library, University of Illinois at Chicago.

technical and aesthetic interventions into the realm of the senses, modernism—he knew—was always both pedagogical and therapeutic. As a response to trauma, loss, and corporeal wounding on a vast scale, aesthetic modernism's understanding of human "ability" and "capability" followed from an encounter with the fragile myth of "normal," healthy bodies, and the stylistic or epistemological petrification of that humanist myth in conventions of perspective, narrative, or figuration. The novel epistemologies and regimes of perception that modernist art developed as so-called nature became second nature were, in their seeming "dehumanization," ways of grappling with a wider, stranger terrain of disability. In this way, the Bauhauslers' diagnosis of modernity's debilitating regimes of bureaucratic specialization and the abstraction of sense experience, like their restorative pedagogical program, anticipated a familiar, Jamesonian line of thought. To capitalist modernity's abstraction of sense experience through technological mediation, and rationalization's ruthless dismantling of *all* natural unities, including the sensorium, modernism responds with a sensory regime at once autonomous and fragmented, a symptom of modernity and its utopian compensation.[42] Much like Walter Benjamin, however, Moholy understood creative work in the technical media of film and photography as part of the cure for human nature transfigured—indeed, the evolutionary spur toward a state of being not restored to one's previous condition but rather "better than before."[43] And better precisely by virtue of having incorporated what seemed inhuman or unnatural about technical media into its most foundational human capacities.[44]

Humanism and New Nature: Plywood and Anagrams

Moholy-Nagy's organic approach to film at the ID was a technique of postwar well-being honed during the war. And the ID's broader program of intermedial, integrated education was the product of the designer's sustained thinking about the therapeutic dimensions of media, the biological capacities of students, and the shape and democratic value of a postwar humanities education. In short, this was an urgently humanist film and media theory, shaped by the rise of fascism and totalitarianism in "the age of the crisis of man." Everywhere at midcentury, as Greif argues, the nature and scale, the measure and making of "man" as a "majoritarian, unmarked human subject" were assessed and debated.[45] Film theory of the postwar period was acutely shaped by this idiom, for two good reasons: first, because theories of totalitarian man and "the authoritarian personality" as a new psychological type developed alongside investigations of the fascist uses of the media (i.e., propaganda); and second, because the crisis of man was powerfully marked by fears about technology and technics run amok, outstripping humane ends. The domain of technology included both technical objects like airplanes, bombs, and films, but also what Greif, following Lewis Mumford and others, calls "human techniques, especially the forms and techniques that organize men and women," whether in discourses of planning, machine control, or technical efficiency.[46] Professionally positioned between technology as material artifact and as technique—a process one conceives and executes with humans *as* media—designers and teachers like Moholy were uniquely situated to theorize film's humane and therapeutic value in a wider technical landscape, one requiring interdisciplinary assessment.

But not just designers, of course. A similarly therapeutic and holistic account of medial happiness pervades the work of Moholy-Nagy's modernist contemporary—filmmaker Maya Deren, especially her *Anagram of Ideas on Art, Form, and Film,* published late in 1946. As film theory, Deren's remarkable, idiosyncratic *Anagram* tends to be positioned in a familiar binary that separates the "realist" ontologies of Bazin and Kracauer and the "formative" or "creationist" tradition—with its largely anti-mimetic and thus "modernist" claims that film's value and specificity as a medium lie in its transcendence of mere mechanical reproduction. Deren's proscription in *Anagram* that film must "renounce the natural frame of reference" scans as a formative defense of the medium, along the lines of Rudolf Arnheim, Hugo Münsterberg, Béla Balázs, Sergei Eisenstein, and, of course, Moholy himself, whose account of film and photography, from as early as his essay "Production-Reproduction" (1922), insisted that the "creations" of photomechanical media like his own beloved photograms "only have value when they produce new, previously unknown relationships."[47] In *Anagram,* Deren's riff on this claim is her way of linking modernist filmmaking with the human's dedication to the "creative manipulation and transfiguration of all nature, including himself, through the exercise of his conscious, rational powers" (*A*, 41).

But the shopworn modernism-realism opposition fails to grapple with Moholy-Nagy's and Deren's shared commitments to versions of both modernism and realism, or with the extent to which neither of these terms, finally, are as pressing for their theory and practice as the status of the human itself. At stake is the very category of human nature and its perceptual capacities within a technical landscape demanding analysis and shaping the very future of human creativity. For Moholy and other Weimar-era artists and critics, when realist figuration first returns *after* modernism in the 1920s, it does so as nature denaturalized and "new." This "nature," like this post-modernist realism, already presumes the foundational presence of technical frameworks, what Devin Fore has called the human's "subcutaneous technicity."[48] Moholy's evolutionary theories, even in the 1920s, were consistent with strains of philosophical anthropology that understood the human as a "deficient being," whose essence was "prosthetic exteriorization": "adapting by incorporating the technical forms around him."[49] For Moholy, photomechanical media produced rather than reproduced nature, and generated perceptual forms of novelty "as a service to human development," because it "is a basic fact of the human condition that the functional apparatus craves for further new impressions every time a new exposure has taken place."[50] Deren's appeal in *Anagram* to film as one of many contemporary "forms of man" is similarly anthropological. It betrays a quasi-evolutionary interest in film as a humane technique in an era of humanism in crisis.

As crucial figures spanning the aesthetic politics of interwar modernisms and their postwar futures, Moholy-Nagy's and Deren's work crossed paths in a more direct way. In the summer of 1946, just months before his death, Moholy hired photographer Arthur Siegel to organize and lead a new, four-year photography program at the ID. Fresh from his work at the Office of War Information and the Army Air Corps, Siegel's first task was to convene in Chicago a six-week seminar, "New Vision in Photography," bringing together "outstanding pioneers and practitioners" in the history of photography to explore new avenues for experimentation in the "functional uses of photography in advertising, education, and science . . . in light of the postwar world."[51] Photography lectures were given by Moholy himself and visiting luminaries such as Paul Strand, Berenice Abbott, Weegee (Arthur Fellig), and fashion photographer Erwin Blumenfeld, and were accompanied by a robust film program assembled by Siegel. "Motion pictures," the seminar brochure noted, "will be shown and discussed with the aim of achieving a perspective on their future development."[52] The screening program kicked off with a series of Moholy's own films; classics of the 1920s European avant-garde (Hans Richter's *Rhythmus 21* [1921], Man Ray's *Anemic Cinema* [1926], and Luis Buñuel and Salvador Dalí's *Un chien andalou* [1929]); F. W. Murnau's first Hollywood feature, *Sunrise* (1927); and Julian Huxley's groundbreaking wildlife documentary *The Private Life of the Gannets* (1934).[53] And the first day of week three was devoted almost exclusively to the work of Maya Deren: *Meshes of the Afternoon* (1943), *At Land* (1944), *Study in Choreography for the Camera* (1945), and *Ritual in Transfigured Time* (1946). Almost. That program, oddly enough, concluded with a screening of Leni Riefenstahl's *Triumph of the Will* (1935).[54]

Jarring at first blush, the Deren-Riefenstahl double bill is actually quite telling—both of the historical matrix in which the "New Vision" seminar was offered and of Deren's changing fortunes in the summer

Figure 5.8. Cover, "New Vision in Photography" seminar brochure, 1946. Institute of Design collection, box 3, folder 98, IDC_0003_0098_cover1. Special Collections and University Archives, Richard J. Daley Library, University of Illinois at Chicago.

of 1946. She had just premiered in February a program of her work at Greenwich Village's Provincetown Playhouse titled "Three Abandoned Films." But, as its title suggests, the success of Deren's now-legendary show came after several years without institutional support. During that time, her work, and that of her partner, the Czech filmmaker Alexander Hackenschmied (changed to Hammid in 1947), was not so much abandoned as caught up in—like Moholy-Nagy and Kepes—modernism's encounter with the emergence of wartime communications research. After collaborating on *Meshes,* the couple had moved from Los Angeles to New York in 1943, when Hammid took a job with the Office of War Information, for which he made four documentary films for the OWI's Overseas Branch, promulgating abroad the American way of life.[55] Deren, meanwhile, was struggling for legitimacy at cultural institutions such as MoMA. Iris Barry, then curator of MoMA's Film Library, knew Hammid (because she oversaw the OWI's projects at MoMA), but, as Hammid later claimed, she "didn't dig *Meshes* or Maya."[56]

As Peter Decherney has argued, Barry's antipathy toward Deren was not just personal but part of the ideological drift of the Film Library during the war. It worked then under contract with John Marshall's communications research wing of the Rockefeller Foundation—a crucial source of funding for the burgeoning field of communication studies, then finding its disciplinary footing in the study of fascist propaganda. Under Barry's leadership, the Film Library tended to see avant-garde film as "antithetical both to commercial and documentary work she thought crucial to the fight against communism and fascism."[57] And the Rockefeller Foundation was then focused on sponsoring documentaries exclusively, what the Film Library promoted as "the film of fact."[58] MoMA's endorsement of "the film of fact" and the political potency of propaganda film, like the Film Library's framing of Hollywood as a quintessentially "American" art, exemplified what Decherney calls its "sociological" approach—its tendency to view films as expressive of national identity or character. During the war, in fact, MoMA owned the only print in the United States of *Triumph of the Will,* whose elaborate choreography of fascism was often adduced as factual footage of German life and national character.

In pairing Deren's modernism and Riefenstahl's propaganda, the "New Vision" seminar was shaped by the cultural politics of the MoMA Film Library, whose brochure for the 16mm collection is included with Siegel's planning documents for the film series. It also echoed Deren's and Hammid's way of pitting film as an expressive art against film as "communication," a position central to *Anagram.*[59] Moholy-Nagy's own relationship with MoMA was long-standing, from the museum's sponsorship of his own film *New Architecture and the London Zoo* (1933), to its landmark U.S. retrospective, *Bauhaus: 1919–1928* in 1938, to director Albert Barr Jr.'s consistent defense and support of Moholy's pedagogical efforts at the New Bauhaus, where he served on the board of trustees. In 1942 MoMA hosted an exhibition of student work from the School of Design, *The Making of a Photogram or Painting with Light,* which underscored the centrality of cameraless photography in Moholy's teaching: light as a plastic medium, but also light as a medium of creative development—of luminous well-being.[60] So, too, did the school's camouflage courses and its programs in occupational therapy for wounded veterans dovetail with MoMA's wartime mission. This spanned not just the work of the Film Library in "showing films designed for civilian defense" and "analyzing enemy propaganda films," as MoMA's bulletin "The Museum and the War" explained, but also the exhibition *Camouflage for Civilian Defense* (August–September, 1943), cosponsored with the Pratt Institute, and *The Arts in Therapy* (1943), an exhibition of prize-winning works in a sponsored competition devoted to both occupational and "creative therapy."[61] The latter section featured the use of "free media in art—painting,

Two coils of string and some tacks were placed on a sheet of sensitized paper. The whole was illuminated briefly with a small flashlight. The objects were then moved on the paper and another exposure was made.

Making Photographs WITHOUT A CAMERA

Producing "photograms" will give you an understanding of the basic principles of photography and composition.

by
L. MOHOLY-NAGY
Director, School of Design, Chicago

Two spoons and a napkin ring produced this photogram. The highly reflective, curved surfaces give interesting tone gradations. They were illuminated from a low angle.

IF you want to come to the most intimate understanding of how your camera operates, if you want to achieve a fresh approach to the art and science of photography, lay your camera aside for a while and try taking pictures without it. Get acquainted with the "photogram," which is produced by camera-less photography. "Photogram" is a term I applied in 1921 to the method of making designs on sensitized paper by direct exposure to a light source without the aid of a camera or negative. The shadows cast by objects placed between the sensitized paper and the light source prevent the full intensity of light from striking the paper in the affected areas thus producing gradations in tone which in turn produce a pattern determined by the shape of the shadow-casting objects used. Such pictures are also known as "shadowgraphs," "light-ray photographs," and "photogenic drawings."

30

Moholy-Nagy laid his head down on the projection paper to make the photogram shown above. He then turned his head on the paper and made a second exposure.

A circular piece of wire screen was placed on sensitized paper and then covered with an inverted, bell-topped glass vase. The light was placed slightly off vertical. This setup was then removed and replaced by a silver fruit basket for the second exposure.

You will find that it is the easiest and most direct method of learning basic photographic principles.

Then you begin to realize the importance of the three working factors with which you control your work:

1—*Light:* You can control its intensity, its duration, its direction, its color composition, etc.

2—*Light-sensitive emulsion:* You can control its speed of reaction, its color selectivity, and its gradation scale.

3—*The object:* You can control its size, shape, position, motion (if any), and color; and if you wish to, you may use a number of different objects in one photogram. Variations are almost endless.

The making of photograms does not require elaborate equipment. Some require only printing-out paper and access to sunlight, while others demand simple darkroom facilities. If you can use your darkroom for printing and developing, you can use it for making photograms. The only additional item will be a small flashlight. In the School of Design we use an ordinary fountain-pen flashlight with the tiniest kind of unfrosted bulb, and the result is that several persons can be working at once without disturbing each other.

I suggest that you use printing-out paper, in daylight, at first. Even in direct sunlight it is slow in action, so you can have plenty of time for experiment—and you will need it. There is the further advantage that you can see the results of what you are doing immediately, as they progress, without waiting for the developer to act. You see for yourself how much more slowly the paper darkens as you decrease the amount of light by moving the setup into the shade, or by moving it a foot or a yard away from the window. Also you can see how rapidly or slowly any type of reflected light acts on the emulsion.

Remember, these pictures are solely for your own information and not for any salon, so make sure you are getting the information they can give you. Select the objects you use for experiment with this in mind. You are not going to make mere silhouettes, so do not use any object with a large flat surface which, no matter how you light it, will make only a white image of its shape, with the rest of the paper dark. Pick out some object with plenty of curved surfaces, only a small part of which will actually rest on the paper. This will give you an opportunity to achieve a sweeping gradation from the white of the unexposed portion to the deepest color the emulsion will produce.

There are many such forms available, and I cannot know what might intrigue your fancy as the object of your first photogram. We will suppose it is a spoon. That would be excellent for the purpose. It is easy to identify because of its familiarity to everybody, and its shape offers numerous possibilities for interesting study.

Probably you will begin by laying the spoon, concave side up, on the sensitized paper. Place this setup so the sun shines directly down on it. Keep a record of how long it requires to build up the density of color you desire. Then take a fresh piece of paper, put the spoon in the same position, and hold the entire setup so the sun hits it at an angle of 45 degrees off the vertical. Again make a record

(*Continued on page 167*)

Upper right: Originally a paint brush and a wire grid were placed on the paper. When the design began to appear on the paper in the developer, the author placed his hand on the paper and made two more exposures. Right: Here a rose was laid on the paper and the illumination was concentrated in certain spots with a very small flashlight.

31

Figure 5.9. László Moholy-Nagy, "Making Photographs without a Camera," *Popular Photography* 5, no. 6 (December 1939): 30–31.

sculpture, drawing, etc.—employed both as a means of diagnosis and cure," and included the display of "a continuously projected motion picture illustrating the use of free media," and the projections of a Clavilux color organ.[62] Moholy would likely have admired this enactment of *projection as rehabilitation.*

Deren's anthropological theory of film in *Anagram* is equally therapeutic, its abiding humanism as powerfully shaped by the violence of war and the power and scale of midcentury technics as Moholy-Nagy's media pedagogy. She begins by summoning a global "spectacle of current anxiety" about the atomic bomb, whose awesome power Deren frames within a series of technoscientific "miracles"—electricity, radio, tanks, and airplanes (*A*, 38). Inaugurating her fascination with technical method and interdisciplinary process, which will redound to Anagram's own formalism, Deren observes how the "curtains of specialization descended on the methodology of science," keeping men from understanding the "detailed processes of such miracles" (*A*, 38). What we are limited to knowing, and evaluating, is not scientific process, which remains unfathomably specialized, but its final, and often disastrous, results: "cars can collide; airplanes can crash; tanks can explode" (*A*, 38). Deren's humanist film aesthetics are hatched to fill the epistemological gap embodied in dysfunctional technical objects, a breach in holistic knowledge produced by "modern specialization," which "has discouraged the idea of the whole man" (*A*, 37). This is why her own method in *Anagram* must be interdisciplinary and "comparative," why she has "found [herself] involved in fields and considerations which seem far from [her] original concern with film" (*A*, 37). The once remote, inviolate nature of a "desolate island" has become an airplane fueling station, an infrastructural node in a global technical network (*A*, 49). In a world transformed by technoscience, older notions of isolated integrity give way to the concept of things in relation, dynamically interconnected wholes that can only be seen and understood by abandoning disciplinary propriety or turf. This is *Anagram*'s early version of what Moholy calls the "new vision": relationship seeing.

In this relentlessly technical and dynamic world, Deren describes the kind of art that cinema might become as a special kind of humane "art instrument" (*A*, 54). The term "instrument" lies at the heart of Deren's consistent analogies between the experimental procedures of the artist and the scientist. Like Moholy-Nagy, she frames film's potential as a medium within an evolutionary account of specifically human capacities, "all that which makes him human": creativity, intelligence, imagination, and the "command and control of memory" (*A*, 44, 48). This last, telling phrase reflects Deren's awareness of the cybernetic idiom of the burgeoning military-industrial complex, a knowledge that would deepen over the course of her postwar correspondence with anthropologist Gregory Bateson.[63] The "memory of man," compared to the "complex instinctual patterns" of nonhuman animals, allows a human being to "access all his experience simultaneously," beyond "the natural chronology of experience" (*A*, 44). By contrast, for an animal like a cat (Deren's example), "all experience remains immediately personal" (*A*, 44). This anthropocentric distinction of human/animal consciousness through the capacity for abstract thought is familiar enough. Deren's more surprising move in *Anagram* is to link this humane capacity back to her preoccupation with finding a technical method suitable for perceiving and producing the kinds of dynamic, living wholes that now constitute life in the postwar world: horizontal memory allows humans "to perceive that a natural, chronological whole is not immutable, but that it is a dynamic relationship of functioning parts" (*A*, 44). Deren yokes her evolutionary account of human development to a defense of organic form—like Moholy-Nagy's, though, this is an organicism thoroughly permeated by technicity and technique.

"All of living nature," Deren argues, is constituted of "dynamic, living" wholes, "in which the interaction of the parts produces more than their sum total" (*A*, 47).[64] And humans strive to approximate these dynamic Gestalts: in "creating man's consciousness" through evolution, "nature created an impatience which will not wait the necessary aeons until a million conditions coincide to produce a miraculous mutation" (*A*, 47). The name for that impatience, for Deren, is the human imagination, whose powers lie in its capacity to "so accelerate real, natural processes that they become unreal and abstract" (*A*, 47). This, then, is how art and science are methodologically aligned: in their technical "violation of natural integrity," in their creative intervention upon and transfiguration of an "ostensible inviolate whole" in the "creation of a new contextual whole—a new, original style of matter and reality" (*A*, 46). The shared method of art and science lies in their strategic nonnaturalism, their way of submitting "to the rigors and disciplines" of their instrument to produce an "original, *artificial* reality" (*A*, 45). And this is where Deren indicts a "realism" devoted to the experience of describing reality as it objectively exists. Her point is not that modernist art should discard reality, but that *it has a better, more current version of it*. Realism's notion of reality, by contrast, is impoverished and outmoded. Deren's theory of modernist technique demands taking moral responsibility for a changeable and relativistic reality: a nature that "has, increasingly, *become itself a reality created by the manipulation of instruments*" (*A*, 54).[65] The modernist organicisms of Deren and Moholy-Nagy are happily at home in this

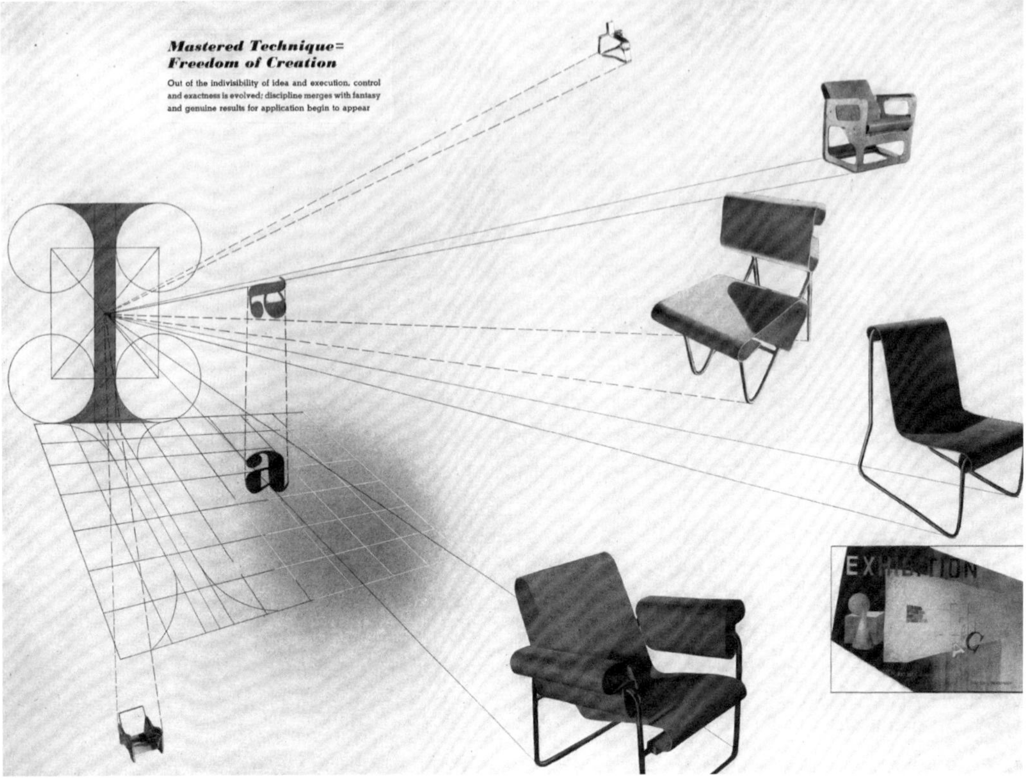

Figure 5.10. The "new nature" of plywood. School of Design catalog, 1941–42, interior page, "Mastered Technique = Freedom of Creation," Institute of Design collection, box 3, folder 63, IDC_0003_063_P21. Special Collections and University Archives, Richard J. Daley Library, University of Illinois at Chicago.

new, transfigured nature, shaped and reshaped by incessant technical interventions in media and in evolutionary processes themselves.

There are other organicisms, Deren acknowledges, with their own moral commitments and degrees of responsibility. Her privileged kind used film not as a "form of nature" that seeks—in the way of surrealism—to extend or exploit man "as a natural phenomenon," but as a "form of man" dedicated to the "creative manipulation and transfiguration of all nature, including himself, through the exercise of his conscious, rational powers" (*A*, 41). Forms of nature such as a mountain or a tree are "not intentionally designed, by nature, to serve any of the purposes to which man may put it" (*A*, 42). Indifferent to human design, they are also amoral. But forms of man "are much more explicitly and economically determined by the function for which they are intended," and are thus subject to "moral evaluations" (*A*, 42). Deren's account of organic form here recalls Moholy-Nagy's notion of biotechnique, which linked the evolutionary necessity of natural forms—their fit for their own, inhuman purpose—to the aspirations and aesthetics of modernist functionalism.[66] For both theorists, the inherent dynamism of human nature, and nature more broadly, is best enacted in formal, creative processes that yield "mysterious and miraculous" new natures—that *create* reality through the technical manipulation of media (*A*, 47). Such processes own up to mediation as a fundamental reality. Through them, media both become new and produce newness, no less novel or alive for being thoroughly artificial. For Moholy, such new media at the Institute of Design included the photogram, Plexiglas, and plywood, that Eamesian miracle of postwar new nature. In *Anagram*, the medium is ritual: a process-based technique for creating dynamic new relations, and the poetic instrument of a sphere of happy human being in common.

Deren's technoscientific design idiom in *Anagram* encourages us to think about ritual as a machine of impersonality, a special kind of "emergent whole" whose parts are "transformed in the process of functioning" (*A*, 47). Indebted in part to her encounter with theories of poetic impersonality in the work of T. E. Hulme and T. S. Eliot, Deren's account of "ritualistic form" is also an account of communitarian being produced through humane, scientific methods of instrumentation.[67] Depersonalization through ritual technique and dramaturgy "enlarges" the bourgeois individual "beyond the personal dimension and frees him from the specializations and confines of personality. He becomes part of a dynamic whole which, like all such creative relationships, in turn, endows its parts with a measure of its larger meaning" (*A*, 58–59). For Deren, ritual is a design method and yields a design product. In its "method—*a conscious manipulation designed to create effect*"—ritual poses a challenge to spontaneous expression (*A*, 59). Through its design product—"*the new, man-made reality*"—ritual becomes the "art equivalent of modern science," refusing a retrograde naturalism and opting instead "to create a form of life" (*A*, 59, 64). Ritual, for Deren, is a kind of artificial medium, as given to dynamic manipulation and susceptible to creative shaping as plywood was for Moholy-Nagy.

The final sections of *Anagram* work to connect Deren's critique of naturalism and defense of ritual techniques of natural transfiguration to the instrument of film and its photographic base. Film and ritual performance, for Deren, share a formal impulse toward depersonalization and abstraction—and the making of artificial, corporate bodies. A similar investment in the modern technology of film and modes of theatrical abstraction on the grounds of these mediums shared potential for nonnaturalism was also evident at the Bauhaus, whose dramaturgy was marked by a fascination with dolls and puppets of various kinds as indices of a broad repatterning of human subjectivity in the Weimar era, as Juliet Koss has shown.[68] Moholy-Nagy, for his part, insisted on nonnaturalistic theater as a way of coming to terms with technology, the reification of the body, and the reality of a technical world of serial production rather than expressive individuals. For Moholy and his Bauhaus colleague Oskar Schlemmer, the theatrical abstraction of the human body functioned both "to disconnect components from an existing whole . . . and, on the other, results in generalization and summation, to create a new whole in bold outline."[69] The technique of the doll, Schlemmer argued in 1930, "does *not* create a *natural human being,* but an *artificial* one; it creates a *metaphor,* a *symbol* of human form."[70] Bauhaus performance rituals reckoned with the absorption of modern technique and technology into the gestures and movements of bodies and their composition in abstract groups—those corporate bodies Kracauer would famously read as the ambivalent surface phenomenon of the "mass ornament." A well-known photograph by Erich Consemüller neatly captures the status of the human body under this regime of modern abstraction: seated in a tubular steel chair designed by Marcel Breuer, a fashionably dressed woman, her face turned toward the camera, dons a Schlemmer mask. The at-home-ness (and estrangement) of the human body in this world of technical abstraction is confirmed by the sitter's inhuman gaze, which mimes the camera's own look. Furniture and body, mask and

Figure 5.11. Erich Consemüller, photograph of woman wearing Oskar Schlemmer mask at the Dessau Bauhaus, 1925–26. Bauhaus-Archiv, Berlin.

Figure 5.12. Maya Deren, "Experimental Portraiture," 1945–46. Courtesy of Sarah Keller. Maya Deren Papers. Howard Gotlieb Archival Research Center, Boston University.

photograph are joined in their nonnature and in their semiotic function as new nature.

Deren defends a similar choreography for the camera when *Anagram* turns in its final third from the old machine of ritualistic form to the newer apparatus of cinema—both capable of sparking magic. Deren's early photography, we should remember, was also preoccupied with dolls and mannequins, forms of creative nonnaturalism in dynamic tension with the deictic recording of the camera. In *Anagram* this entails, first, casting photography that dispenses "with all but the most manual services of a human being" as yet another weak naturalism, because it excludes "conscious manipulation" (*A*, 74). Second, it demands a sustained discussion of the moral value of documentary film as a way of addressing war as a "social and political phenomenon" (*A*, 76). Insofar as wartime documentary depends upon "the accidents of reality" that it refuses to contextualize or imbue with value or a creative point of view—insofar as it refuses *to design*, it extends the amorality of naturalism (*A*, 77). But

Deren is equally bothered by the naive contemporary endorsement of so-called documentary objectivity, which effectively represses or forgets the interwar period's rich traditions of poetic, modernist documentaries of Alberto Cavalcanti, Basil Wright, Walter Ruttmann, and Dziga Vertov. These combined fact and feeling, actuality and construction. The "form proper of film is, for me, accomplished only when the elements, whatever their original context, are related according to the special character of the instrument of film itself—the camera and the editing—so that the reality that emerges is a new one" (*A,* 89). Wedding its medium-specific sensitivity to contingent reality to the force of creative design, film produces realities that are totally unnatural. Film form is a "special integrated complex" suited to the "relativistic relationships" that define the postwar period (*A,* 108, 109). Like those relationships, such integration must be designed. It requires the human faculty of what Moholy-Nagy called "vision in motion."

If we can consider Deren's midcentury treatise on film aesthetics as a theory of organic design in the age of the "crisis of man," we might also understand Moholy-Nagy's design pedagogy as a collective, ritual choreography of bodies, movements, and knowledge. We've seen how his best known kinetic object, *Light Prop for an Electric Stage* (1922–30), built for a Werkbund installation at the exposition of the Société des artistes décorateurs in Paris in 1930, was given filmic life in his abstract short *Lightplay: Black White Gray.* In the context of *Vision in Motion* and the curricular ambitions of the Institute of Design, the *Light Prop,* then called a "light-space modulator," became not just a utopian metaphor for a revolutionary, democratic lifestyle but the key example of the ID's intermedial method of happy, creative integration. Light modulators, Moholy explained, were at the heart of the institute's "interrelated training," fashioned to acquaint designers with "textures and structures" of all kinds, but especially with the principles of photography and cinema (*VM,* 202). A student's "sculpture, tactile chart, wire work, wood cut, etc. take on new meaning if he also understands them as light modulators" (*VM,* 202). And modulators could be sculpted in plastic, hand drawn, photographed, and filmed: "each different experiment is another end which literally constitutes the object anew" (*VM,* 202). The magic of the light modulator is its capacity to function as what Deren would call an impersonal, ritualistic machine. The processes it modeled were at once intermedial and socially instrumental. Within this pedagogical program, in which photographic technologies existed as part of other media practices and ensembles, the modulator made concrete Moholy's way of understanding media as an open and incomplete apparatus. The modulator was for him the very "frame of vision, the very condition of the perpetual field itself."[71] There is no position outside of this material field of mediation. One can only aim to be happy within it.

In *Vision in Motion*'s two concluding sections, Moholy-Nagy expanded the social dimensions of the light modulator to other group dynamics and communitarian visions. First, he extended their depersonalizing processes to the "technique of group poetry" (*VM*, 355). Modeled on Apollinaire's simultaneity procedures, the technique asked students to write, individually, single sentences on a "common theme such as 'War,' 'Cinema,' 'The Professions,'" and then assemble a collective poem from the unrelated sentences in small groups of five to ten people (*VM*, 355). Unlike the surrealist technique of the exquisite corpse, the collective body of the group poem at the ID came from collaboration and rational exchange, not the inhuman dynamism of the unconscious. Tellingly, Moholy called this "group poetry as word-modulator" because the technique of bringing students out of isolation and preparing them for common life (like the light modulator) did not end in one medium—here, language (*V*, 354). Rather, it would be performed by the groups and recorded on a phonograph, in multiple "channel[s] of self-expression" (*V*, 355). Further, this kind of "group activity of the future," leading to "happy participation," would be conceptually up-scaled to the level of national and global knowledge work in Moholy's concluding proposal for a "parliament of social design": "international cultural working assemblies" comprised of scientists and sociologists, artists and writers, musicians and technicians. Working together in studios and laboratories, these experts would model integrated knowledge production, publishing it "in reviews and books, motion pictures and broadcasts" (*V*, 358–61). As "the nucleus of a world-government, it could prepare new, collective forms of social life for a coming generation" (*VM*, 361). As such, the "parliament of social design" anticipated the communicative role of cinema in the interdisciplinary knowledge work of design conferences such as the IDCA and Vision, but also more specific crossings between arts and sciences in the 1960s. These also needed film theory.

Art, Science, and the Creative Image

The Moholy-Deren pairing was no one-off. In New York during the war, when surrealism was both in vogue and in exile, Deren befriended and collaborated with a number of modernist designers and architects. These encounters shaped her films' architectural manipulations of space and time, and her consistent defense of a humane, "creative" process that united technique, skilled instrumentation, and intervention in natural processes rendered new and strange by postwar technoscience. In a 1945 program note, she explained how her unfinished film *Witches*

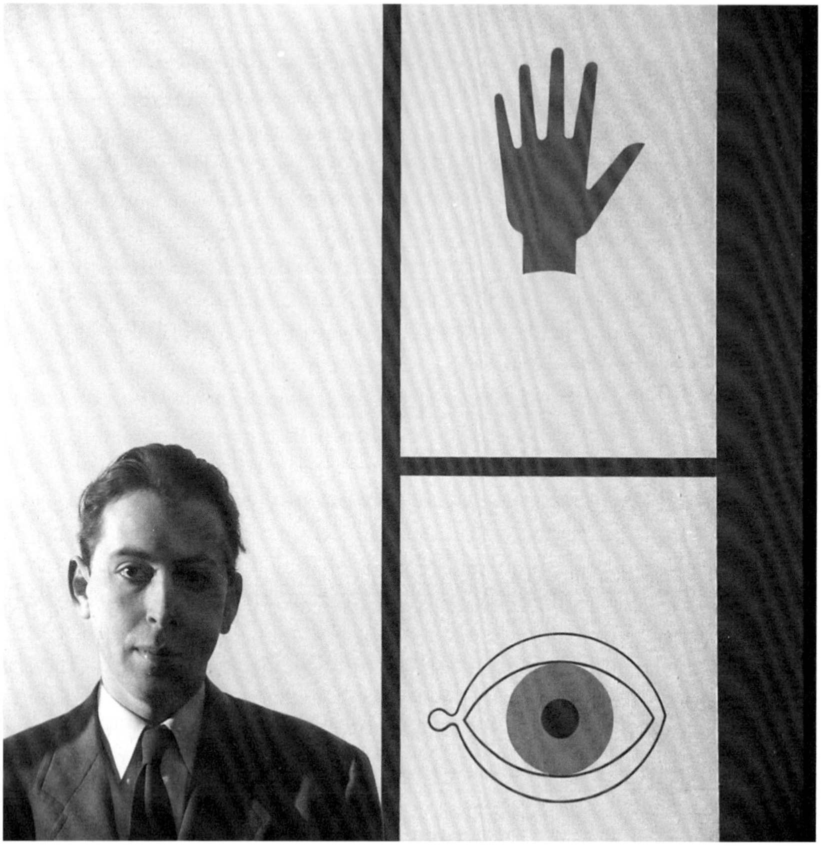

Figure 5.13. Maya Deren, portrait of Alvin Lustig, for Knoll International advertisement. Maya Deren Papers, Howard Gotlieb Archival Research Center, Boston University.

Cradle, shot in Peggy Guggenheim's "Art of This Century" gallery, was "inspired by the architectural structure and paintings and objects" in an exhibition designed by surrealist architect and set designer Frederick Kiesler, who became a close friend. Deren compared the émigré surrealist artists to "feudal magicians" in their "defiance of normal time . . . and normal space," and explained her sense that the "camera was peculiarly suited to delineate that kind of magic."[72] Rather than the outside of reason, "magic" was Deren's term for the mysterious, dynamic qualities of postwar nature in "the new age" that would be morally confronted by an equally unnatural, "creative" formalism.

In the same year, Deren received her first commission as a still photographer for a series on the vanguard office designs of Alvin Lustig, then director of visual research at *Look* magazine. These profiles, and Deren's photographs, appeared in *Architectural Forum* and *Interiors* in 1945. As Deren's camera took stock of the "experimental nature" of Lustig's multifunctional office layouts—combining display, work, and product testing—so did Lustig find his way into the vanguard interiors

DESIGNED BOTH FOR WORK AND FOR DISPLAY

LOOK MAGAZINE'S VISUAL RESEARCH OFFICES

THE fact that one picture is worth ten thousand words is no news to the guiding spirits of *Look* magazine. The rapid increase in circulation from nothing to two million in nine short years is largely the result of constant preoccupation with the persuasiveness of things that can be seen and understood with little assistance from the alphabet. During a comparatively short period, the business of telling, teaching, and explaining by means of drawings, diagrams, and other graphic devices has been developed into a highly skilled art and a highly complicated science.

For practical reasons *Look* regards this art and science so reverently that the organization maintains a department of Visual Research to study and extend the job that can be done with it.

Director of this department is a twenty-nine year old Westerner, Alvin Lustig, who grew up with the school of modern design which found such nourishing ground on the West Coast. It is pertinent to mention here that Mr. Lustig is at home in the fields of interior and architectural design, and that he created the typography and format of the distinctive *California Arts and Architecture* magazine.

On these pages are shown the offices which Mr. Lustig designed for himself and his department in *Look's* New

62

THE RECEPTION ROOM IS PRIMARILY A DISPLAY AREA, AS THESE STAGGERED, ANGLED BOARDS INDICATE. SPOTLIGHTS EMERGE THROUGH THE LOWERED CEILING OF WOOD STRIPS. OTHERS COME CLOSER TO THE DESK AND WRITING TABLES.

OTHER DISPLAY DEVICES IN THE RECEPTION ROOM INCLUDE A BACK-LIGHTED BOARD FOR KODACHROMES AND A SLANTED TABLE FOR LAYOUTS. KNOLL CHAIRS REST ON A PALE YELLOW COTTON RUG ISLAND IN FRONT OF YELLOW DRAPES.

Photos by Maya-Derren

63

of Deren's films, earning a role as a chess player in *At Land*.[73] Lustig, who had befriended Deren and Hammid in Los Angeles, recommended Deren to the influential impresario of modernism, James Laughlin, who solicited "suggestions for visual material" to be published in his journal *New Directions*. This resulted in the publication of Deren's first theoretical essay on the medium, "Cinema as an Art Form."[74] In it, she defined the work of film art as creative and organic—as an "independent, organized form" suited to the relativistic "dislocations of reality itself"—in terms she would refine and develop in *Anagram*.[75] And in 1960, an updated version of that inaugural blast of theory, "Cinematography: The Creative Use of Reality," was published in a special issue of the journal *Dœdalus* titled "The Visual Arts Today," edited by Moholy-Nagy's collaborator and former Institute of Design instructor György Kepes, then on the faculty of architecture at MIT.

Figure 5.14. Profile of Alvin Lustig's Visual Research Offices for *Look* magazine, photographs by Maya Deren. *Interiors*, June 1945.

To understand the appeal of Deren's "Cinematography" essay to the program of a designer like Kepes, and to defamiliarize it for film theorists, we should remember the journal's relationship to Kepes's own postwar intellectual agenda and editorial ambitions. The house organ of the American Academy of Arts and Sciences, *Dædalus* was launched in 1955 by John E. Burchard, dean of MIT's School of Arts and Sciences, to help the academy promote "various topics of cross-disciplinary interest."[76] Kepes had joined MIT's School of Architecture in 1945 as the first artist on the faculty. He did so as the curriculum was revised in keeping with a general education philosophy that would train broad-based, socially useful cognitive faculties rather than specific vocational skills. As Anna Vallye has explained, Kepes was hired to teach in this curriculum, in part, because of his insistence in *Language of Vision* (1944) on the image as a "visual technology of knowledge, oriented toward 'training the creative imagination for positive social action.'"[77] Amidst the institution's postwar absorption and reconfiguration of the liberal arts in a curriculum uniting science, technology, and art, visual pedagogy in architectural training provided "a sense of organic interrelatedness," integrating "structural, biological, technical, psychological, and intellectual frames of reference."[78]

"The Visual Arts Today" was one of Kepes's early ventures in interdisciplinary communication that began with a series of themed seminars at MIT assembling various specialists across the domains of art

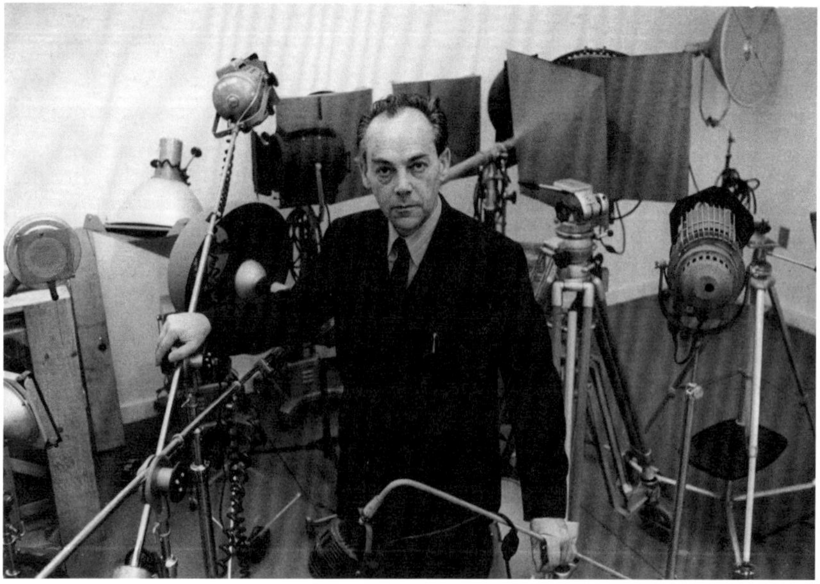

Figure 5.15. György Kepes with light equipment, MIT's Center for Advanced Visual Studies, 1967. Copyright MIT. Photo by Ivan Massar.

and science. Their knowledge work was featured in symposia and exhibitions, and gathered in the landmark six-volume Vision + Value book series, published by George Braziller between 1965 and 1966, and with book jackets designed by Quentin Fiore.[79] These publications overlapped with Kepes's ambitious plans for an "Expanded Visual Arts Program" at MIT that would teach and model the capacities for what he called "interfeeling" and "interthinking," thus sparking "creative achievement" through "the confluence of many types of creative personalities."[80] Conceptualized in the pages of *Dædalus* in 1965, this program, which Kepes called alternatively a "research laboratory" or a "small work community," was institutionally realized in 1967 with the foundation of MIT's Center for Advanced Visual Studies (CAVS), devoted to fostering collaboration between artists and MIT scientists. Its inaugural fellows included artists Jack Burnham, Otto Piene, Ted Kraynik, Takis Vassilakis, and Stan VanDerBeek.

We could think of CAVS as the Cold War realization of the integrated "cultural working centers" dreamed of in Moholy-Nagy's final call for a "social parliament" in *Vision in Motion* (*VM,* 359). Its aspirations and personnel also overlapped with the knowledge work of the IDCA and Will Burtin's Vision conferences. Like Moholy and Burtin, Kepes understood technology expansively, not just as the domain of inhuman machines, but as *human technique*—a "systematic, disciplined, collaborative approach to a chosen objective" that could be realized in a conference, a laboratory, or a research center.[81] CAVS and Kepes's Vision + Value series have been discussed by scholars within contemporaneous attempts to bridge art and postwar technoscience such as Experiments in Art and Technology (E.A.T.), and increasingly scrutinized for their fraught entanglement in the knowledge work of the military-industrial complex—what Pamela Lee has dubbed "think-tank modernism."[82] But scant attention has been paid to Kepes's contributions to the terrain of postwar film theory, despite the fact that he brought a number of film theorists and filmmakers into his interdisciplinary initiatives, including Deren, Arnheim, Richter, VanDerBeek, and Gessner.

"Cinematography" appeared in "The Visual Arts Today" between George Amberg's essay "The Ambivalence of Realism," and Kepes's "The New Landscape." This is a careful, intriguing sequence of theoretical positions on the technical image and its claims on "realism" and the new nature.[83] Amberg, the curator of the Department of Theatre Arts at MoMA, had managed to get *Meshes* screened in MoMA's auditorium for the first time in 1946, despite Barry's ambivalence about Deren, and he taught NYU's first course on experimental film, "New Frontiers in the Cinema," in 1950, before joining the Humanities Program at the University of Minnesota. "Ambivalence" was a brief excerpt from Amberg's work in progress, a theory and aesthetics of cinema titled *The Captive Eye.* Taking issue with the prevailing assumption that realism is "inherent in the medium of film," Amberg's essay quoted approvingly Deren's call for the "creative use of reality."[84] Amberg's essay thus set the table for Deren's sensitive parsing in "Cinematography" of the distinction between the impoverished realism of the graphic image and that of the photograph "as *a form of reality itself,*" one that demands the viewer's "recognition" of its "fidelity," its indexical claim on the real, and thus "exercises an authority comparable in weight only to the authority of reality itself."[85]

Kepes's "New Landscape" was not an essay but rather theory in the form of a series of eight images from *The New Landscape in Art and Science* (1956), including a Lichtenberg figure's elegant pattern of electric sparks, an electron micrograph of the growth patterns of crystals of silicon carbide (courtesy of the General Electric Research Laboratory), a photomicrograph of copper and calcium carbonate, an X-ray photograph of tulips (courtesy of the Eastman Kodak Research Laboratory), an image of cathode ray oscilloscope patterns, and an aerial photograph of ocean floors (courtesy of the Aero Service Corporation). In this context, Deren's "Cinematography" essay bridges Amberg's argument for a more nuanced understanding of cinematic "realism" in the service of the "imaginative extension of reality beyond physical reality" (*VA,* 152) and Kepes's defense of the technical image as an epistemological guide to a radically transformed sensorium. Recall that *The New Landscape*—recommended reading for IDCA 1959—emerged from Kepes's encounter with a new generation of scientific images developed at MIT's various research labs, many of which (especially the Instrumentation Laboratory and the Lincoln Laboratory) were involved in war and weapons research in increasingly controversial ways as the United States escalated its involvement in the Vietnam War. For Kepes, such pedagogical products of the new knowledge economy of MIT were "images of a new scale." This was also a claim to the image's capacity for realism, but one adequate to the transfigured nature of the postwar world. "Leading away from the system of fixed *things,* and toward the system of spatio-temporal patterns," Kepes argued in *The New Landscape,* "the newly revealed visible world brings us to the threshold of a new vision."[86]

Both Kepes and Deren, like Moholy-Nagy, shared a fascination with the scientific image as the site of an intervention in time, space, and natural processes—a manipulation they all deemed "creative." As Anna Vallye has argued, the images of the "new scale" in *The New Landscape,* for Kepes, were "records of experimental manipulations of

material conditions, enabled by imaging devices" (oscilloscope, stroboscope, inferometer, radar, radiograph, spectrograph) "developed for the purposes of tracing the effects of processes unfolding in time."[87] They were less images of static things or properties than what Vallye dubs "diagrams of *events*" in which natural processes and patterns were set into motion through experimental techniques, or what Deren would call creative instrumentation. In "Cinematography," Deren recalls the role of the camera in scientific films, where "its fidelity is applied to reality in conjunction with the revelatory functions of telescopic or microscopic lenses," and seeks to distinguish this use of the camera as "an instrument of discovery rather than of creativity" ("CU," 115). She argues that film becomes "creative" only in the delicate manipulation of "the controlled accident": when cinema incorporates "natural phenomen . . . into our own creativity, to yield an image where the reality of a tree confers its truth upon the events we cause to transpire beneath it." ("CU," 118, 119). Thus is contingency tempered by conscious human design, but without

Figure 5.16. György Kepes, *The New Landscape,* Uranium Metal under Polarized Light, and X-Ray Photograph, from *Visual Arts Today,* 1960. Courtesy of Juliet Kepes Stone.

sacrificing the power of indexicality to confer authority on the real. Kepes, for his part, would make similar comments about his contemporaneous kinetic art installations involving light manipulation, which involved a similar dialectic of natural contingency and human design, what he called "acceptance of randomness" and the "creative invocation of chance events."[88] Such is the creative activity of the "controlled accident," or what Deren calls the moral, rational purposiveness of humane "forms of man."

In fact, Kepes's company allows us to get a better purchase on what exactly Deren means by "creativity," a ubiquitous term in her film theory and practice. Her prescription in "Cinematography" for the "use of reality" entails Deren's defense of the "meaningful manipulation of sequence" ("CU," 126). She invokes the word in calling for "an order of creative action available only to the motion-picture medium," including reprinting frames, freeze frames, swing-pans and various forms of what she dubbed, in another essay, "creative cutting" ("CU," 126). Deren scholars tend to use the word "creative" synonymously with Deren's modernism in film theory's "formative tradition"—her insistence on the manipulation of reality "for the purpose of creating a new reality."[89] But viewed within the larger design idiom of *Anagram,* Deren's description of creativity as a conscious, rational action that produces an unnatural, novel nature is inseparable from the new landscape of postwar technoscience: its potential threat to human capacities, its perceptible violence to the human scale.

Deren's defense of creative action is not just modernist, then, but the ground of a technophilic and therapeutic liberal humanism that brought her into the ambit of designers like Kepes and Moholy-Nagy. Brokering a moral compromise between the disciplinary ambitions of art and science in both the postwar and Cold War contexts, her idiom of "creativity" needs to be approached within the midcentury's broader fascination with creative processes, minds, and personalities. As Jamie Cohen-Cole has argued, "creativity" emerged as a central term in Cold War social scientific attempts to describe and measure the kinds and qualities of persons that best exemplified liberal-democratic character and action.[90] Conceptualized against the specter of the authoritarian personality—intolerant, ideologically rigid, conformist in behavior and thought—creativity named a model of humane, socially oriented subjectivity that was defined by autonomy and rationality, flexibility and open-mindedness. The liberal discourse of creativity, for many U.S. intellectuals, would be the foundation of a postwar pluralist society, united in diversity across gender, race, religion, and class. It was evident in a surge in foundation-funded "creativity research" from the mid-1940s to the mid-1960s; in a host of general education curricular reforms taking aim at specialization and the fragmentation of knowledge, including Moholy's and Kepes's own efforts; in the corporate experiments in humanistic pedagogy and management training that sought to cultivate creative intellectual workers as a challenge to the "organization man," and intersected with the work of designers like the Eameses and Nelson; and, of course, in Walter Paepcke's Aspen initiatives. It involved the now-familiar enshrinement of certain modes of modernist abstraction as avatars of democratic freedom, but also the celebration of academic interdisciplinarity itself as a model for the kind of creative open-mindedness and propensity to happy, therapeutic talk that could be extended to American society, and through the communicative work of international organizations like the United Nations and UNESCO.

By folding Deren's "Cinematography" essay within his own interdisciplinary agenda, Kepes added Deren to his burgeoning collections of creative thinkers and theories of creativity.[91] Kepes believed in the role of the visual arts and in the perceptual training of knowledge workers' creative capacities, and had participated in a symposium on creativity at Cooper Union in 1958, as well as a series of radio broadcasts titled "The Creative Mind" and "The Creative Method," featuring distinguished artists and scientists, philosophers, anthropologists, educators, psychologists, and theologians, and published as an essay collection in 1960.[92] A number of the broadcast participants, including Deren's former mentor Margaret Mead, Edward Steichen, and Ben Shahn, also appear with Deren in "The Visual Arts Today," and a photograph of Steichen's (*The Maypole*, 1932) featuring the technique of multiple exposure is laid out as the recto to the verso of Deren's paean to the "space-time manipulations" constituting the "creative act." Mead's own essay for Kepes's volume, "Leisure, Work, and Creativity," reckons with various efforts, across cultures, to categorize creative activities. But it is also, like Deren's "Cinematography," an attempt to describe the production of novelty itself, what Mead calls the elusive "idea of something made new" in a postwar American landscape defined by a "glut" or "plethora" of mechanical reproductions (*VA*, 15).

In his introduction to the issue, Kepes clarifies the role of the "creative visual image" in a postwar modernity marked by a crisis of scale, and in terms that resonate with Deren's therapeutic diagnosis in *Anagram*. As "visions of a felt order," the creative image mediates between the inner world of subjectivity and the outer, "man-made world" that has "expanded so explosively in so many directions that we are unable to grasp its dimensions or assert authority over its dynamics" (*VA*, 7). The world of "new nature," harboring "strange forms, such as nuclear particles and radiation, none visible to our naked eyes, none relatable to our bodies," is "alien to our senses" (*VA*, 7). It demands sensory mapping through the shared creative activity of the artist and scientist to "reach beneath surface phenomenon to discover basic natural patterns and basic natural process" (*VA*, 6). Like Deren, Kepes is skeptical of the rising tide of irrationality in the arts, and its surrender to what Deren called "forms of nature." Both see this as a solipsistic withdrawal to the unconscious, and an abrogation of humanity's "common obligations." Kepes's organicism, like Deren's, is also a classicism, linked to a critique of the expressive self and modeled on the patterns and "living process" of new nature's dynamic equilibrium and its "symbols of order." Creative activity is a way of keeping step with a "common world that unites the thinking mind, the motivating heart, and the acting body" (*VA*, 11). Creativity entails autonomy, then, but is socially instrumental. It requires what Moholy-Nagy called "conditioning to creativeness" in group processes and collaboration, thinking across disciplines and modes of ritual depersonalization. Creativity is the process of being involved in an anagrammatic, "dynamic whole which, like all such creative relationships, in turn, endows its parts with a measure of its larger meaning" (*A*, 58–59).

We need to understand the conceptual work of Deren's "Cinematography" essay and its defense of creative process as situated at the heart of the "two cultures" debate. For Kepes and others, this meant arguing for technical media's role not just in the making of "creative images," but in the production of morality and citizenship—their capacity to serve as forms of "aesthetico-social regulation."[93] Indeed, the claims of the "Cinematography" essay's concluding section, "The Twentieth-Century Art Form" lead neatly into the image terrain of Kepes's "new landscape" that follows it. In terms that echo Kepes's insistence on a fluid, mobile "system of spatiotemporal patterns," Deren insists that "creative film form" is linked to a "new way of thought and a new way of life—one in which an appreciation of time, movement, energy, and dynamics is more immediately meaningful than the familiar concept of matter as a static solid anchored to a stable cosmos" ("CU," 127). This change, film's orientation toward Kepes's new scale, is evident in "every field of human endeavor," but Deren's telling example is "architecture, in which the mass-upon-mass structure has given way to the lean strengths of steel and the dynamics of cantilever balance" ("CU," 127).[94] Deren defends cinema on the grounds not merely of its unique potential as a medium of art but because it best expresses, "in terms of its own paradoxically intangible reality, the moral and metaphysical concepts of the citizen of this new age" ("CU," 127). And she ends by linking the terms of this new-age citizenship with questions of disciplinarity, insisting that cinema "must relinquish the narrative disciplines it has borrowed from literature," and instead "explore the new realms and dimensions" that owe their existence to the film instrument ("CU," 128). In sum, Deren's vocabulary of instrumentation, research, and discovery extends the design idiom of *Anagram,* and concludes with the aspiration that this quest to "determine the disciplines inherent in the medium" might "enrich our culture artistically as science has done in its own province" ("CU," 128). The pursuit of medium specificity, rather than purifying the specifically filmic, has brought Deren fully into the regimes of Cold War interdisciplinarity and their humanist enshrinement of creative design practices.

6

designer film theory II

Media Pedagogy and Modernist Information Aesthetics

AS A MODE OF ORGANIC DESIGN, Maya Deren's account of creative cinematography brought her film theory into dialogue with the therapeutic ambitions of artists such as György Kepes and László Moholy-Nagy. This proximity between classical film theory and postwar designer practice also defined the career of another famous formalist, Rudolf Arnheim. His Gestalt notions of perceptual organization intersected with postwar communications theory and cybernetics, and likewise found their way into Kepes's interdisciplinary projects. A number of Arnheim's key writings on film and technical media in the 1950s and 1960s can be productively rethought as encounters with the terrain of midcentury information theory: its account of organization (perceptual and social), its perceived challenges to human agency, and even its role in schemes of utopian social planning and their own designs on happiness.

While information had long been a central term mediating between the governance of states and the happy lives of their populations, or systemically joining individuals and corporations, the 1960s saw the entry of "informatics" into the English language as a new word to capture information's sprawling technical infrastructure. A crucial determinant of Eames-era modernism, the informatic turn transformed the media practices of the Eames Office in the 1950s and '60s, fomenting a range of pedagogical techniques that experimented with the scale and delivery of data, from Art-X and the Berkeley architecture courses to the Eameses' sponsored multiscreen propaganda work for IBM and the United States Information Agency. Midcentury design conferences such as the IDCA and Vision 65 and 67 were conceptualized as vital techniques of information processing and swift knowledge transmission. As venues for interdisciplinary knowledge work and international communication, the conferences proliferated a range of data-processing fantasies and models of informatic futurity, from Stan VanDerBeek's Movie-Drome, Bruce MacKenzie's global information stock exchange, or Will Burtin's *Brain* to the "open works" as theorized by Umberto Eco and Vera Horvat-Pintarić and designed by the New Tendencies movement, or the filmological program of Gilbert Cohen-Séat's Cité scientifique internationale.

As articulations of a modernist media practice at midcentury, these techniques of information design and visual communication were indebted to the pedagogical and propagandistic traditions of interwar exhibition design. They were refined by cybernetic models of communication at midcentury, and shaped by Cold War fantasies of environmental modeling and liberal-humanist projects of democratic governance and control. As the sine qua non of designer media experimentation, vanguard practices of information management abetted organizational processes of various kinds, and at multiple scales. They joined accounts of the systemic functioning, health, and future growth of organizations to their ways of being and staying informed. Information processing, and its expansive postwar aesthetics, were redefined at midcentury as essential to a peaceful geopolitical environment—a global well-being secured by the Pax Americana, and, as we'll see, through the curricular programs of postwar design institutions such as the School of Design (Hochschule für Gestaltung, or HfG), in Ulm, Germany.

But before we get there, we will return to Rudolf Arnheim, whose exemplary effort to define a humane midcentury film theory was forced to reckon with a seemingly inhuman aesthetics of information so decisive for a range of postwar designers. Another infamous formalist and defender of film's medium specificity, Arnheim encountered a new technical idiom of information with transdisciplinary aspirations that inspired his well-known critique of Siegfried Kracauer's *Theory of Film* (1960) and his fascinating late essay "Entropy in Art: An Essay on Order and Disorder" (1971). I then consider the place of classical film theory such as Arnheim's in the design theory and pedagogy of Tomás Maldonado, rector at the HfG during the school's tumultuous institutional life in the 1960s. Like Moholy's Institute of Design, the HfG was a crucial geopolitical site of media rehabilitation, and one programmatically devoted to considering film as a subspecies of information design, product design, and visual communication. Working backward from Maldonado's post-1968 treatise *Design, Nature, and Revolution: Toward a Critical Ecology* (1972), I describe how designer film theory was shaped by a modernist aesthetics and ideology of information that crossed a range of disciplines and institutional agendas, both at Ulm and in the contemporaneous intertwining of structuralist linguistics, semiotics, and Marxism that came to be called "apparatus theory" in film studies.

Turning to Arnheim, the HfG, and the domain of political modernism as it emerged in the late 1960s and early 1970s, this chapter explores three overlapping sites of film theory's formal and technical reckoning with the midcentury vogue for information and for new technologies of information management. The HfG's fate in the 1960s—in which film as a disciplinary object was caught between a rigorous, systems-conscious scientism and what I'll describe as a humane "organizational" auteurism—offers a unique window into designer film theory's role in programs for managing the "nature" of the human environment now conceptualized as the site of alienation and nascent ecological disaster. And it allows us to reconsider the discourse of political modernism as another such technical program—a related brand of vanguard formalism.

Arnheim, Kracauer, and the Image of Information

Like Deren, Arnheim was an unlikely contributor to Kepes's interdisciplinary knowledge work. The film and perceptual theorist's writings appeared in three of Kepes's Vision + Value volumes: *The Education of Vision* (1965), *Sign, Image, Symbol* (1966), and *Module, Proportion, Symmetry, Rhythm* (1966). The unsexy Arnheim has become a reliable whipping boy in accounts of film-theoretical formalism, or dismissed in a broader skepticism about cognitivist film theory's penchant for biological universals. So it may seem odd to consider his midcentury theories of visual perception in the company of Kepes's grand program of creative vision as a regulative technique, or to encounter his work strategically placed alongside the knowledge work of biologists and architects, cyberneticians and systems theorists, art and design educators, and experts in general education. And yet there Arnheim was, in the thick of it all, as the modernist commitments to form and medium he shared with Deren, Kepes, and Moholy-Nagy encountered the midcentury social sciences' fascination with communication and information across various medial forms.

The striking dust jacket of the landmark enunciation of those formal commitments, *Film als Kunst* (1932; published in English as *Film* [1933]), which depicts the sinuous curves of an unspooled roll of celluloid film stock, was designed by Kepes himself, then working at Moholy-Nagy's Berlin design studio. There is something unnatural and abstract about Kepes's film strip, threaded in suspension through a black void given graphic order by Kepes's tipped, rectilinear *L*. In its ghostliness, which

Figure 6.1.
Cover, Rudolf Arnheim, *Film als Kunst,* designed by György Kepes. Courtesy of Márton Orosz and Juliet Kepes Stone.

gestures toward the photogram technique, and in its insistence on material rather than mimesis, the image acknowledges the famous terms of Arnheim's defense of film art: its constitutive difference from perceptual reality, and thus its inherent capacity to transcend "mere reproduction" by exploiting the conditions of its materials to mold and shape human perception.

The cover image is an artifact of an early moment in a sustained friendship between these two theorists of perceptual organization. Its graphic crossing of Kepes's abstract design idiom and classical film theory may have been inspired by Arnheim's clear admiration for the organizing principles of modern design. In 1927 the young Arnheim wrote of his first visit to the Dessau Bauhaus in the pages of the left-wing journal *Die Weltbühne,* for which he had begun to write art and film reviews while completing his doctorate at the Institute of Psychology in the Friedrich Wilhelm University in Berlin. For Arnheim, the building was "a house of pure function," defined by a "will to cleanness, clarity, and boldness in design."[1] This was functionalism for the eye, given to sensuous perception. Its "constructivism produces visual gratification of its own," Arnheim argued, by finding the beautiful in the practical, and giving "the old theme of unity in diversity" a new meaning: "a house containing a thousand different things can be perceived as a structured totality."[2] In reading architectural form for its capacity to serve as a perceptual whole that exceeds its constituent parts, Arnheim quite literally saw the Bauhaus through the terms of Gestalt psychology.

The short essay affirms the abiding rapport between the disciplines of design and Gestalt psychology apparent also in Paul Klee's interwar investment in the research of Arnheim's mentor Max Wertheimer, and in the work of Kandinsky and Albers. At midcentury this disciplinary crossover was perhaps most apparent in the political aesthetics of Kepes himself, whose *Language of Vision* credited Arnheim's teachers and colleagues at the institute—Wertheimer, Kurt Koffka, and Wolfgang Köhler—for providing him with the "laws of visual organization."[3] Like Kepes, Arnheim—in *Film als Kunst* and elsewhere—was invested in theorizing perception as a mode of cognition, a creative power of organizing perceptual stimuli into meaningful units and ordered patterns. Film form, used artistically, was one way of setting into motion the humane processes of creative intelligence, and the formative powers of vision. Arnheim would further explore this "psychology of the creative eye" in his landmark midcentury work, *Art and Visual Perception* (1954). But already in 1941, Arnheim's Gestaltist principles had become what Anna Vallye calls "a key reference for Kepes's developing conception of the image."[4] They were set forth in Arnheim's 1943 essay, read by Kepes and titled "Gestalt and Art," which cast Gestalt theory as "a new style of science" that "revived in a strongly emotional way the feeling of the wonderful secrets of the organism" and "the creative powers of natural forces" as manifested by human cognition.[5] This fact is important for a genealogy of Kepes's aesthetics, but also for unsettling the terms of Arnheim's film-theoretical formalism. The theory of the image that Arnheim helped Kepes produce was, of course, formalist, but also socially instrumental and historically specific. It was part of a humanist reckoning with the broader wartime landscape and postwar utility of what Kepes in *Language of Vision* called "optical communication" or "visual communication" as "a potential means to reunite man and his knowledge and to re-form man into an integrated being" (*LV,* 13). The organized image was a medium of postwar happiness.

Language of Vision opens with a section on the "created image." It positions the formative processes of visual perception as conceptualized by Arnheim and other Gestaltists against a wartime terrain of "tragic formlessness," wasted human and material resources, and the horror of totalitarian aggression and its techniques of "obsolete organization" (*LV,* 12). Contemporaneity, as Kepes understands it, is defined by a "whirlwind of light qualities. From this whirling confusion we build unified entities, those forms of experience called visual images. To perceive an image is to participate in a forming process; it is a creative act. . . . Every experiencing of a visual image is a forming; a dynamic process of integration" (*LV,* 15). From visual chaos to homeostatic and happy integration: in *Language of Vision,* what might otherwise scan as mandarin formalist investigations into the laws of perceptual organization were set to the urgent task of "equilibrating our life in the contemporary dimension" through "integration, planning, and form" (*LV,* 12).

As we've seen, Kepes's interest in the "experience of the image as a creative activity of integration" (*LV,* 13) embedded him in a series of pedagogical reform efforts and interdisciplinary initiatives such as MIT's Center for Advanced Visual Studies (CAVS), as well as ideologically charged postwar debates about creativity and the growth of mass media, what he calls the "contemporary vehicles of visual communication": advertisements, movies, television. The same is true for the midcentury Arnheim, despite a recurring critical tendency to understand the revised, 1957 English-language publication of *Film as Art* as a sign of Arnheim's retreat from the social and the political in this period—a symptom of Red Scare quietism. In fact, Arnheim was a socially minded and politically astute critic and theorist of remarkable disciplinary range. His modernist formal investigations were consistently embedded in reckonings with a host of media forms, their institutions, and their ideological work. His early investigations into film and radio in Berlin were extended in the seven months he spent studying radio serials with Columbia University's Office of Radio Research, led by the Frankfurt School sociologist Paul Lazarsfeld. His modernist film theory, like Kepes's and Deren's, was thus formulated in the crucible of wartime communications research and in dialogue with social scientific approaches to the technical image.[6]

Further, like Deren, his thinking about the specifically "creative image" was similarly inflected by the postwar fascination with creative processes, and the role of art education in fostering creative citizens. In 1949 he appeared alongside Kepes and Robert J. Wolff, Kepes's former colleague at the Institute of Design, in a MoMA-sponsored symposium, "Art Education 1949: Focus for World Unity." In 1957, the year of *Film as Art*'s publication, he again joined Kepes in the "Creative Mind and Method" symposia, where he spoke in a roundtable with Margaret Mead, Lyman Bryson, and Milton Nahm. There, Arnheim insisted on the need to "avoid the departmentalization of creativity," and "the need for discipline . . . technical discipline in the field."[7] He also expressed an admiration for efforts by business to "train their executives in creativity," a "kind of alertness of mind" and "openness of response."[8] In the same year, Arnheim participated in a conference titled "Art and Communication," sponsored by the American Federation of Arts, where he joined a panel discussion titled "The Creative Act" with Gregory Bateson and Marcel Duchamp. While Bateson's talk theorized art as a form of metacommunication in cybernetic and ecological terms, Meyer Schapiro (on another panel) marshaled the increasingly common example of Jackson Pollock to defend a modernism of "noncommunication" against the sway of technocratic and cybernetic paradigms of communicative efficiency.[9] Arnheim, while famous for a theory of filmic medium specificity, was not only not immune to the prestige of communication and information theory that proved so influential to designers like Kepes, but also actively explored its potentials and limitations in a variety of essays and reviews. Arnheim's account of the technical image in the 1950s and 1960s was also, in important and unrecognized ways, an information aesthetics, and his defense of human creativity the product of an encounter with the conditions of superabundant data.

Consider the context in which his work appears in the Vision + Value volumes. In *Education of Vision* (1965), promoted as the inaugural volume in the series, Arnheim's "Visual Thinking" is the lead essay.[10] It follows an introduction by Kepes that, in large part, repeats the narrative of scalar crisis and sensory disequilibrium floated in both his "Visual Arts Today" introduction and his proposal for CAVS. Here, Kepes lauds

Arnheim's work for its insistence on vision "as a cognitive power in its own right," and one inspiring the book's sweeping rethinking of the techniques and technologies of visual education across a range of fields and debates: psychology, physics, sculpture, design education, art education in Africa, and general and liberal education in the United States (*EV*, v). The faculty of vision as cognition, the "fundamental interdependence between perception and conception, between the visual and the rational," as embodied in Arnheim's thought, thus animates the volume's survey of pedagogical techniques of information visualization. These include the models or diagrams of order of Will Burtin (whose

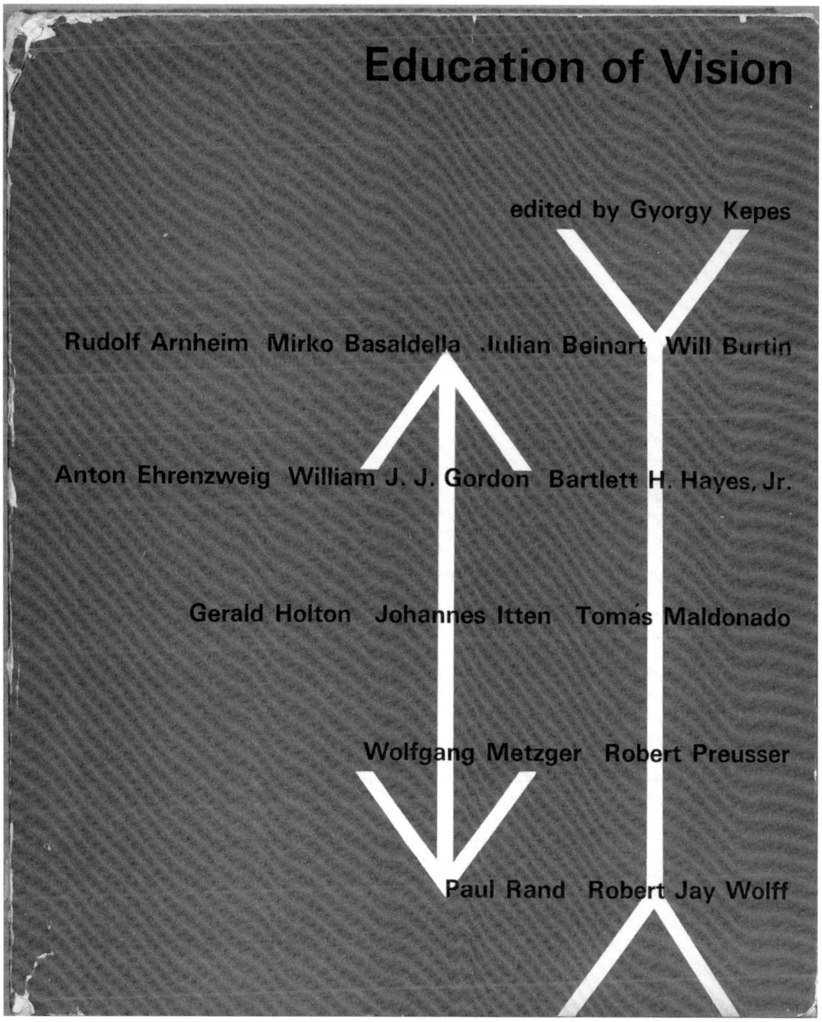

Figure 6.2. Cover, *The Education of Vision*, edited by György Kepes, in the Vision + Value series (New York: George Braziller, 1965).

essay "Design as Communication" appears in this volume), and physicist Gerald Horton's discussion of the potential of film and television in science education (*EV,* vii). Such cutting-edge approaches are then linked to the "concrete techniques of visual education" in the Bauhaus tradition, represented both by Johannes Itten and Tomás Maldonado, then director of the UfG, whose tactic of "assail[ing] his students with a wealth of information drawn from our scientific-technical society" is hailed as a "fresh" approach to design (*EV,* vi).

Similarly intriguing constellations of Arnheim's thought within Kepes's interdisciplinary networks and their abiding paradigms of communication emerge in other volumes in the series. In *Sign, Image, Symbol,* Arnheim's "Image and Thought" appears after the work of two prominent cyberneticians: psychologist Lawrence Frank's essay "The World as a Communication Network" and biophysicist Heinz von Foerster's account of the coevolution of "the maker and user of symbols and his environment."[11] Arnheim's approach to visual thinking is presented alongside the semiotics of Charles Morris, the perceptual theories of James J. Gibson, and a concluding essay by systems theorist Ludwig von Bertalanffy. And in *Module, Proportion, Symmetry, Rhythm,* Arnheim's "A Review of Proportion," a paean to the "harmony found in many products of nature and man," concludes the volume's interrogation of modularity as a principle of biological form, humane knowledge, and—for Kepes and Arnheim alike—an ideal of harmonious, patterned aesthetic organization that could be upscaled to social life writ large.[12]

This company encourages us to understand Arnheim's aesthetic commitments to perceptual organization in the 1950s and 1960s alongside Kepes's cybernetic approach to vision, communication, and information. While this may seem a fluke of shared publication venues, we should note, first, that Arnheim's formalism had already been framed this way in an earlier influential convergence of postwar science and vanguard aesthetics. In 1951 his essay "Gestalt Psychology and Aesthetic Form" was included in British biologist and IDCA regular Lancelot Law Whyte's landmark collection *Aspects of Form.* A key influence on Kepes's *The New Landscape in Art and Science,* Whyte's collection emerged from a symposium that accompanied Nigel Henderson and Richard Hamilton's famous *Growth and Form* exhibition at the Institute of Contemporary Art in London. In it Arnheim's account of "the formative processes of perception" followed British cybernetician W. Grey Walter's "Activity Patterns in the Human Brain." As Whyte argues in his introduction, from Walter's experimental investigations into the brain we are but a "small step" to Arnheim's interest in the "role of the visually-perceived configuration in determining aesthetic qualities."[13] In other words,

Arnheim's midcentury theory of organic form developed through interdisciplinary collaborations with scientists like Whyte and designers like Kepes, both eager to consider parallels between "the structures of natural phenomena and of authentic works of art."[14] And it reckoned with the prestige of cybernetics, information theory, and a waxing systems ethos in the art world in ways that bore directly on his reading of film theory and vanguard aesthetics.[15]

Take the curious place of information theory in Arnheim's important 1957 essay, "Accident and the Necessity of Art," which explores the tendency of modern artists, writers, and composers to "deliberately rely on accident for the production of their work," from surrealist practices of automatic writing and the *cadavres exquis* to "the scrap heap as a supplier of inspiration for sculptors, the adoption of nature's shapes and textures, the exploitation of chance effects of running paint, molten metal, etc."[16] Realism in the arts, Arnheim argues, develops through art's desire to navigate growing complexity, and find aesthetic patterns to suit it. As a result, realist technique will increasingly include accident into its subject matter, providing "less probable" aesthetic solutions to increasing complexity ("AN," 19). The language of probability here is crucial, pointing toward Arnheim's interest in more overtly statistical, machinic, and computational methods. Arnheim insists that realism's aesthetic "deviation[s] from prototype" only seem disorderly, contingent, or random, "rather than a necessary part of a new order" ("AN," 21, 20). Instead, realism often incorporates accident on purpose, as in Degas's *A Cotton Office in New Orleans* (1873), where "the lack of a common purpose, the atomization of society, is precisely the theme of these pictures" ("AN," 21).

There is a difference, however, between accident as subject matter and accident as a principle of formal composition, whereby "the phenomenal chaos of accident from which man seeks refuge in art, has entered art itself" ("AN," 24). At this point, the photographic image enters Arnheim's narrative to exemplify, in its indexical contingency, the artistic "encounter of natural accident and the human sense of form" ("AN," 24). No news to readers of *Film as Art*. More surprising is his immediate turn to the "'statistical' use of accidental patterns" in which "accidental agglomerations can acquire organization and meaning, namely, quantity" ("AN," 24). As an example of the law of large numbers, Arnheim adduces the experiments of psychologist Fred Attneave, "interested in the theory of visual information" ("AN," 25). Arnheim includes a pictorial image from Attneave, "a random field of 19,600 cells" generated by painting tiny squares in either black or white in an order based purely on random numbers ("AN," 25). As Arnheim summarizes the experiment, Attneave had associated visual homogeneity with redundancy, and so constructed his visual field to be completely nonredundant. He was thus surprised by the image's monotony, "which goes to show that piles of accidents add up to very little" ("AN," 25). Arnheim thus compares the monotonous "texture" of Attneave's experiment in the so-called informational aspects of visual perception to Pollock's technique in *Greyed Rainbow.* In both, units of visual information can be perceived "only as texture" because their "units do not fit more comprehensive shapes" ("AN," 26). We get textural qualities (prickliness, softness, viscosity), but "nothing happens." The "pattern itself is endless" ("AN," 26). There is structure, but at a very low level. Mere texture, for Arnheim, sacrifices the necessities of "diversity and hierarchy" that define the kind of order art produces to meet "the complexity of human existence," and to allow humans to recognize themselves in it ("AN," 26, 27).

Regarding the hierarchy of organisms by means of organized complexity, Arnheim's footnote refers readers to the fields of biology, but also to architecture and urban planning. He cites Kepes's MIT colleague Kevin Lynch on the formal differences between "primitive and advanced human settlements" based on the kinds of morphological distinctions revealed in aerial photographs—here, the "texture" of the village of Kano, Nigeria, as described in Lynch's essay "The Form of Cities" ("AN," 27). The essay appeared in *Scientific American* in 1954, and anticipated many of the claims of his influential study *The Image of the City* (1960).[17] Influenced by cybernetics, the cognitive sciences, computing, and Gestalt psychology, Lynch sought to identify what he called "the environmental image" of the city, an image rooted in our biological need to "recognize and pattern our surroundings."[18] The odd place of an urban planner like Lynch in Arnheim's essay demonstrates how the latter could understand photographs, despite their medium-specific penchant for accumulating accident, as capable of transmitting patterns of organized complexity of various levels. But it also underscores Arnheim's awareness of how Gestaltist notions of aesthetic form and perceptual clarity, structure, and organization extended into contemporaneous accounts of postwar cities as cybernetic environments. For Lynch and Kepes, the organized mental image was a bulwark against disorientation in sprawling cities, a key mode of emotional security within the communicative and informatic system of urban forms.

Referencing Attneave and Lynch on the "texture" of visual information, Arnheim thus imports into his account of aesthetic accident the yield of a special symposium called "Information Theory and the Arts" that he had chaired at the Convention of the American Psychological Association in New York City. Two of the papers presented there—one by Attneave titled "Stochastic Composition Processes," the other,

playmates (and the adults, fellow-sufferers), but it may be wrong to extend such an area beyond a square mile, forming a one-class section from which it is not easy to escape.

Shape

Besides size, density and grain, there is the matter of the shape of cities. Even the silhouette of a city tells us a great deal about its living quality. The old cities usually were roughly circular or rectangular in outline, with a sharp boundary commonly marked by a wall. Such is the medieval town of Lucca or a great city like Peking. The compelling motive was protection—the carving out of a special environment in an alien world. In the Etruscan ritual of city-founding, the first act after consulting the omens was to cut a furrow marking the new city boundary. For centuries towns were built first by throwing up a wall, then filling in with development.

Beyond its defensive value, the compact mass is a logical form when it is not too large. The center is close to all sectors of the periphery; the town has a solid, visible unity. It is particularly delightful when the countryside can readily be seen, giving the sense that it can be entered easily. The English city of Bath, ringed with green hills, is a fine example of this.

As the population grows, the compact shape begins to exhibit difficulties. Growth must occur by crowding within or by annular accretion, like the growth rings of a tree. Unlike a tree, however, the center cannot be left to die. It must continue to function, and its obsolescence is increasingly difficult to remedy. It becomes a critical problem to serve the spreading mass with transportation. The open country recedes farther and farther away.

A second city form is the long, narrow ribbon, usually lying along a road or river. The typical "street village" is a good example. The road or river is the primary fact, and the town has developed along it. Topography also may dictate this shape, as in coastal towns or in a settlement like Colle di Val d'Elsa, on a narrow ridge in Italian Umbria. The linear city rarely grows very large. An exception is Stalingrad, which developed this way partly because of the importance of river transport to it and partly for theoretical considerations. On a regional scale the ribbon form may take in a string of towns, such as the urban "corridor" running from Springfield, Mass., through New

GRAIN of a city refers to the texture of its functional differentiation. At the top is Kano in Nigeria; it has little differentiation. In the middle is a part of Akron, Ohio; the large factory is poorly differentiated from a residential section. At the bottom is Harlow in England; its residential section in the center is clearly differentiated from other areas.

60

© 1954 SCIENTIFIC AMERICAN, INC

Figure 6.3. Kevin Lynch, "The Form of Cities," *Scientific American,* 1954.

"Information as Measure of the Experience of Music," by David Kraehenbuehl and Edgar Coons—were published in the *Journal of Aesthetics and Art Criticism* in 1959, and the strengths and limitations of their methods were framed by Arnheim's brief essay "Information Theory: An Introductory Note."[19] The piece clarifies Arnheim's keen interest in information theory's incursion into the domains of psychology and the arts, and his skepticism about its approach to order and structure, which he perceives as a bypassing of human capacities for the finding and invention of patterns: the work shared by critical interpretation and by the artist as *homo faber*. Arnheim admires information theory's basic understanding of "art as a carrier of information," and he is drawn to the kinds of criteria applied by communications engineers to the information that interests them: "accuracy, lack of ambiguity, and economy" ("IT," 502). He also expresses sympathy for its "promise of quantification," likening its scientific approach to aesthetic measure to recent attempts "to measure the so-called goodness of a gestalt" ("IT," *501*, 502). Art criticism and interpretation, he concedes, begin with such formal ministrations to what is perceptibly *there* in a pattern, and given to quantification.

But counting and measurement are not enough. The humanist in Arnheim insists that such patterns and structures need to be analyzed—that "an inventory of structural elements is no analysis of structure" ("IT," 502). Moreover, even if Attneave could, as he proposes, turn Mozart's existing forty-one symphonies into a "huge assembly of samples," analyze their rules, and forecast from this vast combinatory "a nonexistent forty-second symphony as the structurally logical continuation," he would nonetheless bypass the "translation of experience into form," the "essence of the artistic process" ("IT," 502). Information theory's method, in other words, is indifferent to the humane process of "finding—and indeed inventing—the patterns that perceivably represent [the artist's] conception of life, existence, reality" ("IT," 502). It forgoes "meaning and ideas," which Arnheim insists are the "prime movers of creation" ("IT," 502). Artworks are peculiar because they "take the word 'in-formation' literally: they give shape rather than merely supply data" ("IT," 503). In this way, Arnheim's grappling with information theory has produced a recognizably humanist set of distinctions between shape-giving artistic form and "mere data," quality and quantity, meaning and counting, the human cognitive experience of pattern recognition and inhuman computation. These are the stakes of his distinction between "pattern" and "texture."

For the Arnheim of the late 1950s, questions of contingency and accident—as challenges to the aesthetic lawfulness of humane, organic form—were raised across media, and became part of his broader social diagnosis that also implicated the medium of film in the unfortunate repudiation of what Deren defended as "forms of man." The mereness of unshaped data that Arnheim critiques in the texture of Attneave's experiments, or Pollock's paintings, or Lynch's aerial photographs of Kano, Nigeria, was also a tropism of the technical media of photography and film, likewise tending dangerously toward textural shapelessness and informatic disorganization.

This is perhaps clearest in Arnheim's well-known review of Siegfried Kracauer's *Theory of Film* (1960), "Melancholy Unshaped," whose terms and conclusions we would now be wise to reconsider as an episode of Arnheim's encounter with information theory.[20] As some critics have noted, "Melancholy Unshaped" extends many of the claims of the "Accident" essay, especially its way of linking Kracauer's defense of filmic realism to "the medium's affinity with the 'flow of life' " ("MU," 293). But for Arnheim, this realist sense of reality as an "infinite, indeterminate, unfathomable reality" is only a partial view ("MU," 292). By piling up accidents and details, film, as Kracauer theorizes it, endorses a view of reality that, following Arnheim's critique of Attneave, we might call *textural*: a world of the endless, shapeless, irrational agglomeration of contingency. This is a world of mere data, without meaningful shape or pattern, absent what Arnheim, at the essay's end, dubs "significant form" ("MU," 297). Arnheim overtly links the perceptual work of this kind of filmic continuum to widespread forms of distraction. In fact, he positions film—and its photographic base—as a symptom of a larger social condition defined by informatic superabundance, overload:

> Do we observe that modern man, surfeited with photographs that crowd out the words in his reading matter and are the staple of his leisure time edification, is being led back to the highways? He is immensely better informed about the epidermis of the world at large, the appearance of what goes on; but is it unfair to call him less wise than was his equal in the pre-photographic era? The addicts of photography seem highly distracted. They think less well. . . . Photographic information, potentially a magnificent source of knowledge, seems to serve as a powerful distraction from insight. ("MU," 294–95)

Arnheim indicts the pervasive interest in "the irrationality of minutely scanned surfaces" as a kind of postwar modern decadence, the "late refinement of fatigued cultures" ("MU," 295). Film's automatism, accreting data about the world at the superficial, epidermal level, distracts from the mind's capacity to perceive general patterns, and becomes yet another index of an unhappy affective condition evident in the pervasive "melancholy" of visual art.

For Arnheim, Kracauer's melancholic realism was emblematic of a broader crisis in humanism and human agency evident across midcentury visual culture. Because the shift to texture is tantamount to a refusal "to permit the eye to organize the material presented," it is also apparent in the "aimless and endless roaming" of Michelangelo Antonioni's open form in *L'Avventura*; in the "embrace of nature at its most amorphous" in the work of Jean Dubuffet; and in the various modes of outsourcing the human's creative perception to the powers of what, in "Accident," Arnheim dubs an "ingenious agent," from the surrealist unconscious to the mainframe computer ("AN," 28). As he explains in "Accident," the human's biological propensity for organic form manages to defend it against textural disorganization and inorganic rigor, both of which threats are figured as machinic. The kind of nature such humane making abhors is, like Dubuffet's, "remote from the formative impact of man and equally remote from the formative powers of nature itself" ("MU," 296).

It is precisely these contested categories of "man" and "nature"—their innate capacities and limitations, their transformations within the new landscape of postwar technoscience, and their mediation by the redemptive medium of film—that I have been tracing across the terrain of designer film theory in the past two chapters. By locating Kracauer's account of film ontology and spectatorship in a broader shift in modern art from pattern to texture, Arnheim's "Melancholy Unshaped" essay casts the broader realistic tendency in Western art that this theory stands for as an antihumanist capitulation, an "increasing surrender of the formative capacity of the human mind to the raw material of experience" ("MU," 296). The category of "experience" was, of course, decisive for Kracauer's *Theory of Film,* and central to what Johannes von Moltke has identified as its implicit critique of a middlebrow liberal humanism bent on subsuming experiential particularity under the violent abstraction of some common humanity, some implacable "family of man."[21] In *Theory of Film*'s pivotal final section, "Film in Our Time," Kracauer described a postwar modernity defined by the "breakdown in binding norms," and by an overweening tendency toward scientific abstraction.[22] For Kracauer, this "mathematization of the traces of reality" was evident in the methodologies of the natural and social sciences, preoccupied with "measurable elements or units" to the neglect of the qualitative dimensions of material life, and also in the "technological-minded" sensibilities of audiences indifferent to the "quality of the communications themselves" (*TF,* 292–93). In his hostility to the quantitative, Kracauer was partially aligned with the terms of Arnheim's critique of information theory. But whereas Arnheim joined Kracauer's defense of filmic particularity to the inhuman disorder of unshaped data, Kracauer saw film's tropism to the material qualities of things as a mode of redemption, of confronting the human with its alienated essence.

In *Theory of Film*, Kracauer argued that film redeemed a form of modern experience defined by what Miriam Hansen—in her introduction—calls "discontinuity, fragmentation, and negation," and by forms of transience and indeterminacy (*TF*, xxvii). In other words, Kracauer's language in *Theory of Film*, like that of Kepes, Deren, and Moholy-Nagy, is also therapeutic. In fact, Kracauer credits Moholy for "emancipating the medium from the 'narrow rendering of nature,'" adjusting vision to "man's situation in a technological age," and relativizing ideological "absoluteness" by revising habits of seeing (*TF*, 10, 8, 9). Film would become a medium of rehabilitation, what Kracauer dubs a "remedy" for abstraction, by challenging the reification of experience, "blast[ing] the prison of conventional reality," and making the fortuitous or unforeseen in "the flow of life" available for perception—newly concrete, but mediated (*TF*, 296, 48). Film defamiliarizes our ossified perceptual habits while also decentering the human subject, revealing its location in an estranged, nonanthropocentric landscape. In this fashion, the "nature" of physical existence as revealed by film appears to Kracauer as an inhospitable ruin, what Jennifer Fay as called a "natural history of the photographic present" that only redeems the world in the ways it makes salient our alienation from it.[23] This is precisely the picture of nature—cold and unsentimental, hostile to human subjectivity—that Arnheim finds so objectionable, because it is so far removed from the human's formative powers of creative perception.

This picture of nature, of course, had found its scientific validation in the principle of entropy, the melancholic other to the cybernetic happy that would preoccupy Arnheim in his fascinating work *Entropy and Art: An Essay on Order and Disorder* (1971). The essay clarifies the extent of Arnheim's engagement with cybernetic accounts of communication, information, and systems functioning. As Pamela Lee has shown, by the end of the 1960s, such theories—and their abiding picture of time as endless, recursive, and ongoing—had infiltrated the visual arts, and became linked to a broader anxiety about the organic progression of historical and art-historical time.[24] Arnheim's *Essay* sought to challenge the prestige of the Second Law of Thermodynamics in information theory, and to lament its incursions into symptomatically chaotic aesthetic practices, from John Cage and Robert Smithson to minimalism. Because Arnheim believed organic and inorganic nature shared a "harmonious striving for order," he was disturbed, like many others before him, by the countervailing tendency of closed physical systems toward mechanical disorder.[25] And he was *still* annoyed by what he had, over a decade earlier, identified as "an appalling paradox to any friend of the arts": namely, information theory's belief "that complete disorder or chaos provides a maximum of information whereas a completely organized pattern yields no information at all" ("IT," 501). For Arnheim, both the physicists and the information theorists demonstrate "the absurd consequences of neglecting structure but using the concept of order" (*E*, 15). In *Essay* Arnheim sought to rehabilitate an idiom for talking about aesthetic order more sensibly, to rescue descriptive language itself from the "Babylonian muddle" of information theory (*E*, 15). To do so, he described organized form in both nature and art as a complex pattern of dynamic forces—the interplay of entropic, "catabolic" forces and the "anabolic" creation of structure and what Arnheim calls "structural themes" (*E*, 49).

In an analysis that seems so removed from history and conspicuously eschews references to the political upheavals of the late 1960s, Arnhem's account of entropy and information theory nevertheless brought him, late in the *Essay*, into a striking critique of the utopian aspirations of rational social planning and design. For in the *Essay*'s second part, Arnheim sketched various attempts to respond to the threat of an entropic universe, from the nineteenth century to the present, through the positing of what he calls "articulate structural 'themes'"—counterprinciples of structure and organization, from Darwin, Spencer, and Fechner to Freud (via David Riesman) (*E*, 38). Now dissenting a bit from the terms of Kepes's regulative organicism, Arnheim insists that any concept of aesthetic and social order based on a notion of natural "equilibrium" or "balance" is incomplete. "Homeostasis," he quips, "is not enough" (*E*, 47). It may enable survival, and establish a kind of static order, but it "contributes little to living well" (*E*, 48). In these ways, Arnheim's defense of structure and "structural themes" against the confusions of information theory entailed an account of happiness, one that extended from the cognitive domain of the aesthetic to the built environment and the domain of planning and politics. Such happiness, first, will not be based on "mere orderliness," which Arnheim linked to "the emptiness of homogeneity" evident in the contemporary taste for serial forms in suburbia and minimalism alike: "the monotonous rows of identical human dwellings in so-called subdivisions" and the "rows of identical boxes in art galleries" (*E*, 51, 52). Rather, he offered a picture of human existence defined by "fullness," "plenitude," and the forms of dynamic complexity and heterogeneity that inhere in "articulate structures," like works of art, and that are biologically preferred by creative people (*E*, 49, 55).

We can perhaps discern here an echo of Kepes's own insistence in *Language of Vision* and elsewhere on the mediating role of the ordered, creative image between the inner world of subjectivity and the "man-made"

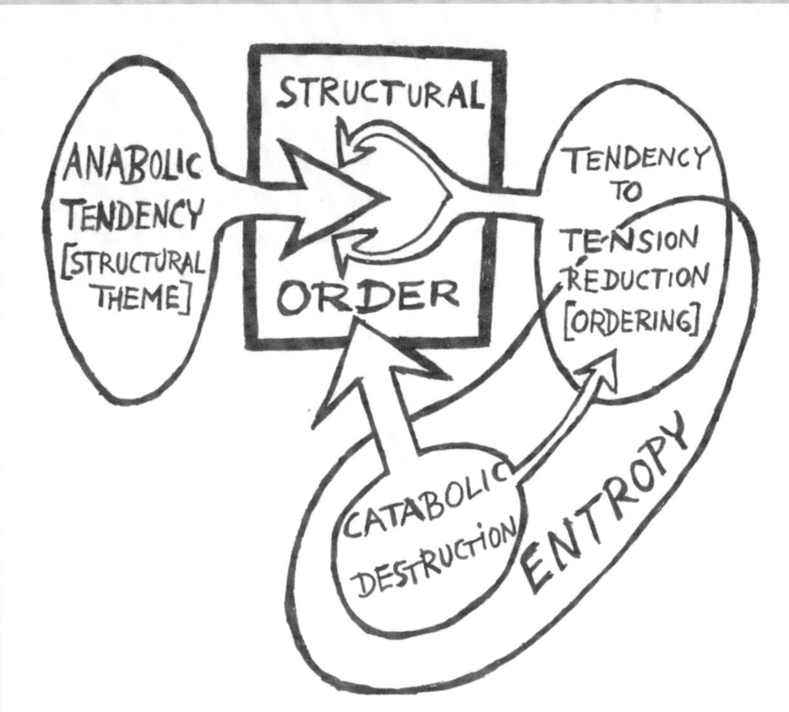

Figure 6.4. Rudolf Arnheim, diagram, from *Entropy and Art* (Berkeley: University of California Press, 1970).

world of the human environment. The value of the artwork's structural theme is derived from the quality of "the human condition" it makes visible or audible, and only deserves "to become a message" if it can offer a "genuine" view of life (*E*, 55). While Arnheim admits that fleshing out such a perspective is beyond the scope of the essay, he notes that it would be dynamic, and in keeping with the "stream of life" that understands history as largely progressive (*E*, 56). By contrast, homeostatic order, as foreseen by "philosophers, social reformers, therapists" is indicted as a kind of static perfection, the "definitive order of utopias and heavens" that "smacks inevitably of boredom" (*E*, 56). Underlying Arnheim's overlapping critique of information theory and entropic nature, in other words, is a repudiation of a moribund temporality joining utopian thought *and* the kinds of technocratic planning for world futures that would continue to preoccupy designers like Kepes.

Rehab Media II: Film Theory for the Human Environment at Ulm

By 1971 Arnheim seemed to have little truck with planned utopias, having lost confidence in the homeostatic principles of aesthetic and social organization that had inspired Kepes's organicist vision. Curiously, though, both Arnheim's and Kracauer's film theories managed to work their way into the opening pages of Argentine artist, designer, and teacher Tomás Maldonado's treatise *Design, Nature, and Revolution: Toward a Critical Ecology* (1972). Written at the peak of New Left and countercultural politics, the book—an endorsement of the future of rational design and planning in political life—opens with a sweeping discussion of the interlocked concepts of alienation, nature, and the "human environment."[26] Taking a conceptual inventory, Maldonado asked what resources were available for thinking "the human environment"—the idea of a "surrounding" that mediates between human consciousness and contingent reality (*DN*, 1).[27] He first named post-Hegelian philosophy, and then credited the "revolutionary contributions of ecological science" (*DN*, 5). But he also appealed to a more unlikely third source of environmental and ecological thinking: artistic descriptions of the "mediating membrane" provided by the modern literature of Fyodor Dostoevsky, Henry James, Marcel Proust, Italo Svevo, James Joyce, and in the "visual environmental material" accumulated in photography, television, and film (*DN*, 4–55).

Modernism, Maldonado intuited, styled ways of living in the forms of technological mediation that both constitute "the environment" and allow us to sense it and know it.[28] Modernist literature, for example, transforms "the human environment" from a philosophical concept to a "fact" of human sensibility and perception. But Maldonado was also interested in the usable past of film theory for design. Here Arnheim was lauded for joining film to a "psychology of aesthetic perception," and Kracauer celebrated for the value of his contributions to a "macrosociology" of film, along with Adorno, Paul Lazarsfeld, and Leo Handel (*DN*, 86). Though film theory had begun to make its semiotic and structuralist turn in the work of Metz, Mitry, Barthes, and Eco, what "we still lack," Maldonado argued, is an "'environmental microsociology of the cinema'—that is to say, a serious study of the contribution made by the film world to the determination of the behavior of men toward other men and towards their microenvironment" (*DN*, 86–87). Despite its increasing sophistication and scientism, film theory, circa 1970, was still struggling in its mission to "determine"—condition, understand, explain, even predict—human behavior, both interpersonally, and within that more intimate unit of sociological analysis Maldonado dubs "the microenvironment."

Let's reverse engineer this puzzling claim. In the wake of 1968, Maldonado's call for an "environmental microsociology of cinema" in a text chiefly concerned with the status of design and planning in utopian ecological thought reveals an obscured strand of modernist film theory. In Maldonado's case, this was not threaded directly through the consolidating discourse of so-called political modernism in France and the United Kingdom, but rather through the aesthetic politics and media pedagogy of a particular German institution: the Hochschule für Gestaltung at Ulm, West Germany's conflicted heir to the Bauhaus legacy, where Maldonado taught between 1954 and 1967 and served for several years as rector.[29] At the HfG, film—and calls for film theory—played a formative role in the school's ambitious media pedagogy, its sociological awareness, and its scientific approach to a "human environment" defined by flows of communication and information whose rational operations and enabling technical media required systematic study in a program of integrated design education. As I've argued, designer film theory at midcentury was primarily a reckoning with a built environment whose contours seemed perilous to the human scale, and whose alienating nature provoked anxious humanisms and spawned various technophilic approaches to film as a medium abetting more expansive techniques of postwar happiness. In what follows, I explore the film theory—and forms of film-theoretical modernism—implicated in the institutional matrix of the HfG, so tightly bound to the happy liberal-democratic, capitalist fortunes of West Germany itself. At stake was the

Figure 6.5. Tomás Maldonado, lecturing at the Hochschule für Gestaltung in Ulm, elementary course, March 15, 1956. Photograph by Hans G. Conrad. Copyright Dr. René Spitz.

very future of design in the context of dawning ecological catastrophe and a crisis of functionalism.

While Moholy-Nagy's wartime program of media rehabilitation at Chicago's Institute of Design anticipated the collective contours of postwar happy life, the HfG aimed to wed media training to cultural regeneration and overtly ideological rehab. Both design schools' media curricula aspired to the construction of liberal-democratic citizens. Conceived by Inge Scholl and Otl Aicher, family and friends of martyred members of a group that resisted the Nazis, the HfG became a crucial institution in the U.S.-sponsored program for the political reeducation of postwar Germany, and was funded in significant measure by the U.S. occupation government and the Rockefeller and Ford Foundations.[30] As Paul Betts has shown, Ulm's initial curricular scheme—designed by Scholl, Aicher, and former Bauhausler Max Bill—involved a holistic program of "universal education" that united media studies and art instruction as a remedy against "narrow-minded provincialism."[31] Intermedial training in photography, radio, and film—especially as film applied to the critical analysis of Nazi propaganda techniques—would cultivate the democratic consciousness of a new vanguard of postwar citizens and leaders.[32]

Under the founding rectorship of Bill, the school shifted its emphasis from political education through media studies to design instruction and practice. When the school opened its doors in 1955, now lauded as a center of antifascism and international modernism, the study of film and photography was folded into the program of general education, taught alongside graphics in the Department of Visual Design, one of three. Strategically downplaying the historical legacy of Hannes Mayer and other Bauhaus leftists, Scholl, Aicher, and Bill worked in consultation with U.S. authorities to implement a curriculum featuring "disciplines that supported liberal capitalist democracy across a spectrum of practices, ranging from the technologies of shaping public opinion to the design and promotion of objects of international mass consumption, a keystone of the U.S. Marshall Plan and its blueprint for political stability through economic prosperity."[33] As a mass medium, a technology of public opinion, and an informatic medium, film was initially approached alongside the liberal pedagogical work of the industrially produced design object itself. Film, Ulm's promotional materials explained, was part of "the field of industrial product design": "The term 'industrial products' is taken to cover objects designed for everyday use and for use in production, administration, and in science, as well as in the building industry, and also the visual and linguistic vehicles of information disseminated through the modern mass media."[34]

As the formal manifestation of the school's ideological agenda and its high-stakes geopolitical location, the curriculum was hotly contested, as were the philosophical terms of Bill's high-minded humanism. Bill enshrined the moral duty of the noncommercial designer as tasked with "reenchanting the forms of everyday life in a kind of grandiose *Gesamtkunstwerk*," aestheticizing everything from the scale of the spoon to the city.[35] Amidst this turmoil and debate between the "Maxists" and the "anti-Maxists," led by Maldonado, Bill resigned as rector in 1957, to be succeeded by Maldonado. Critical of Bill's mysticism, aestheticism, and distaste for industry and commerce, Maldonado presided over the reorientation of the Ulm curriculum beginning in 1958 in line with his rational, functionalistic approach to design and design pedagogy. Designed objects, Maldonado insisted, were neither commodity fetishes nor morally uplifting incarnations of "good form," but rather semiotic ensembles, technical objects, communicative products. Because the design object, as Betts puts it, "was nothing but material information and production coordination," and the designer a "coordinator" collaborating with other specialists in an efficient, automated system of mass production, design education needed more science, more sociology, and more

Figure 6.6. Josef Albers, Max Bill, and HfG students at HfG Ulm main railway station, July 1955. Photograph by Hans G. Conrad. Copyright Dr. René Spitz.

theory—specifically, semiotics and systems theory, information theory and cybernetics.[36] As Maldonado saw it, only if they were freed from metaphysics, expressionist aesthetics, and the history of *Kultur* would HfG students be equipped for their pressing role in technical civilization: designing as part of a rigorous "theory of needs." To Bill's eyes, this amounted to a "technoid degeneration of [the HfG's] once good idea."[37]

The terms of this dispute between Bill's quasi-mystical humanism and Maldonado's technical antihumanism shaped the film curriculum and film culture at the HfG as it matured throughout Maldonado's tenure. In 1958, the first year of Maldonado's co-rectorship, Charles Eames visited HfG to screen three of his films, and Maldonado delivered an important address on the changing function of the industrial designer at the Brussels World's Fair, published in the inaugural issue of the school's quarterly bulletin, *Ulm*. The issue clarifies film's institutional location in two closely related departments: Visual Communication and Information, both "devoted to the design of visual and verbal means of communication."[38] The former's purpose is to design information "in a way that corresponds to function," in keeping with how, "in many phases of social life, men are addressed, linked, and put into contact with one another."[39] It therefore handles "typography, graphic design, photography, exhibition, film, and television techniques" as "an homogeneous field."[40] And its methods draw on "knowledge which has been won in recent decades in the field of perception and meaning."[41]

The Department of Information, begun as the school's public relations arm, by 1958 had expanded its mission to the preparation of writers for careers in the press, radio, television, and film.[42] Here, in pedagogical theory if not practice, screenwriting would be taught. In fact, the department prided itself on an "experimental" writing program headed by former Stuttgart philosopher and pioneer of information aesthetics Max Bense, recruited by Bill in 1954.[43] Under Bense's leadership, the department "opts to look at texts—from 'simple' utilitarian copy to literature—in terms of the quantity of information they contain," and views "the social order [as] decisively influenced by the quality of information" purveyed by the communications media.[44] The department's "novelty," Bense explained, also lay "in its close collaboration with the Department of Visual Communication" and "the fact that general semantics and information theory are disciplines that underlie the work of both departments."[45] Bense's philosophical system aimed to free aesthetics and the social sciences from humanist values he saw as politically reactionary and technically outmoded; in an era of mass reproduction, the aura of the autonomous artwork or cultural artifact had disappeared, and with it, romantic notions of agency, authenticity, and originality. While the

Figure 6.7.
Max Bense and Max Bill, discussion during Bense's lecture at HfG Ulm, March 31, 1954. Photograph by Hans G. Conrad. Copyright Dr. René Spitz.

Department of Information's curriculum included literature and literary history, it didn't seek to teach "self-expression" or produce literary stylists, but technically proficient and semiotically savvy "information practitioners."[46] What counted, as a contemporaneous radio documentary explained, was "no longer a humanist education; nor is it art, but the mastering of technological methods in an industrial age marked by the phenomenon of cybernetics, automation, and function."[47]

While the inaugural issue of *Ulm* noted plans for a forthcoming "institute in communications," and described film on the books in these two departments, training in filmmaking didn't actually emerge until 1961–62, when the Department of Visual Communication split off a separate filmmaking sector.[48] And when it finally established itself institutionally, it appeared to eschew the antihumanist tenets of both of its sponsoring departments, devoted to the training of so-called information practitioners. Instead, this: "a creative filmmaker must be a passionate one," for whom "film is the medium that gives expression to his own individual free will."[49] Somehow, in the throes of Ulm's rational scientism, another, seemingly discrepant principle of film design emerged, one undergirded by an expressive, even romantic model of communication. This designer, taking their cue from the French, would be reborn as an auteur.

At the HfG, this movement toward a *cinéma des auteurs*—or a *Kino der Autoren*—transpired largely through efforts of the young Adornean Alexander Kluge, and alongside the now-legendary Oberhausen Group manifesto of 1962, hailed as providing the founding myth of the New German Cinema and its repudiation of a bankrupt commercial industry. A month after the Oberhausen salvo, Kluge published a brief article titled "What Does the Oberhausen Group Want?" in *Output*, the student journal at Ulm, where he had been teaching film as an adjunct to the Department of Visual Communication alongside Detten Schleiermacher, Edgar Reitz, and several other manifesto signatories. Declaring a state of crisis in filmmaking in the Federal Republic, despite insurgent, politically conscious, modernist art cinemas in France, Italy, Poland, and Czechoslovakia, Kluge's essay extended the Oberhausen polemic, calling for "a mental revolution" in German filmmaking and a "restructuring of the whole way in which the German motion picture industry is organized."[50]

Kluge's holistic language is crucial, because it gestures toward the systems-based approach to structure, organization, and mental labor taught at Ulm. For Kluge, what the moribund German film industry needed was not just technicians but the intellectual labor of theoretically sophisticated generalists, "as required by a doctrine of the *cinema des auteurs*."[51] They would be trained at Ulm, the "focal point for the brain workers of the motion picture industry."[52] Beginning in 1962, and until the institute's closing in 1968, that intellectual center was known as the Ulm Filmmaking Department.[53] It included a film school, a "development studio" where groups would work on "problems that arise in the field of filmmaking and film organization," and a third institution devoted to "commissioned research on the theory, technique, formal design, and history of motion pictures."[54]

This threefold mission for Ulm's short-lived Filmmaking Department, which balanced film training with creative, group-oriented problem solving and theoretical R and D for industry, begins to suggest how a *politique des autuers* familiar to film history and theory—with its romantic picture of agency—might have been imagined differently within the pedagogical aims of a design institution whose increasing scientism and enthusiastic functionalism seemed fundamentally allergic to expressivist myths. Rather than hostile to institutional life, Ulm-style auteurism was shaped by it—and by a model of agency conceptualized *inside* an institution increasingly devoted to teaching the cutting edge of how institutions theorized their own operations—namely, management theory and "operational philosophy," especially as they intersected with information theory, communication theory, and cybernetics.[55]

Writing in the same issue of *Output* in 1962, Schleiermacher explained that "the personal, i.e., organic principle of filmmaking stands in an apparent contradiction to the industrial methods of the motion picture industry."[56] For Schleiermacher, the point was not to pit iconoclastic personality against hidebound industry, but to critique the intellectual bankruptcy of a film industry so ignorant of the bleeding edge of postwar techniques of industrial coordination. Organic film training at the HfG, by contrast, does *not* take "the individual specialties as its point of departure, but produces a filmmaker who is a generalist," one who has "mastered the whole process of making films," and who possesses a "wider perspective . . . which goes beyond filmmaking to embrace a general restructuring of the whole motion picture business."[57] In other words, the HfG's institutional culture already understood "organic" film and media education as fully compatible with rational, industrial methods, corporate forms, and dynamic processes of organization. Notice here the echo of Moholy-Nagy's commitment to therapeutic group-oriented process, and the Bauhaus's broader hostility to specialization in the insistence that the Filmmaking Department is aiming at "a comprehensive motion picture education. . . . Basic to the whole is technical proficiency and organized thinking in every field."[58]

The kind of auteurism that emerged at Ulm bespoke less a commitment to unfettered originality or genius than an allegiance to tech-savvy, theory-heavy, socially embedded, process-driven holism: to comprehensive mastery of what Edgar Reitz called "the medium as a whole."[59] A film, Reitz noted in 1963, can be signed by one person, but authorship can also be "shared by a team" in which "the roles of the individual members of the team are not rigidly distinguished."[60] Ulm's Filmmaking

Department emerged within an institutional commitment to the training of information practitioners, so we not should be surprised to hear auteurist expressivity framed within a quasi-informatic idiom. See Reitz's explanation of film adaptation as a change of information content, or his attempts to square auteurism and communication theory: "the *auteur* theory embodies, firstly, the recognition that every medium of communication is a filter that blocks out particular contents (information) and favors others, and secondly, the conviction that motion pictures are a particularly well adapted means of communicating those ideas and forms that are characteristic of the present day."[61]

James Tweedie's powerful revisionist account of postwar modernist cinemas casts global new waves as, at base, responses to midcentury economic booms, and the commitment to mise-en-scène in auteur cinema as the material horizon of global capitalism's uneven modernization, making visible its "characteristic" forms.[62] Since Ulm designers were themselves producing what Tweedie calls the "mise-en-scène of modernization" within the Federal Republic's own economic miracle, we should understand Ulm auteurism alongside Maldonado's own arguments about the autonomy of the designer within Ulm's pedagogical program. As for the agency of the designer—his originality or expressivity, and their limits—so for the *auteur.* Both, at Ulm, would be trained in "organized thinking" and for "productive work in a society that is every day becoming more technicalized and where science plays from day-to-day a more decisive role."[63] Both are to be equipped with knowledge of the "well-adapted means of communicating those ideas and forms"—films and other industrially designed objects—that define postwar modernity.

Maldonado's essay "Design Education," published in 1965 in Kepes's *Education of Vision,* sets the terms of the designer's agency and the account of organized form it depends on. Disabusing readers of the notion that "education for creativity" in design education means "education for self-expression," or a "process of liberation from the inhibiting aspects of personality," Maldonado defines design education instead as "education for responsible creativity" ("DE," 122). In the process, he takes aim at several mistaken notions of the profession of the industrial designer. The first, an "illusio[n] of liberal economy," sees the designer as a salesperson whose goal is to stimulate consumption as part of a "marvelous 'roundabout of happiness'" ("DE," 129). The second, a moralizing or aesthetic view he associated with Bill, holds that designers are "the persons responsible for beauty and reason in a world ruled by ugliness and absurdity" and that the world's unhappiness can be ameliorated by "improving formally the objects of this world" ("DE," 130). Against these misconceptions, Maldonado defines design as a systemically situated, culturally enmeshed practice that aims to determine *"the formal properties of the objects produced by industry"* ("DE," 133). Form corresponds to an object's "innermost organization," and is the consequence of the integration of all the factors—"functional, cultural, technological, and economic"—that participate in this organization and development ("DE," 133). For Maldonado, the happiness that designers enjoy, and produce, follows from their proficiency in the coordinated complexity and brain work of technical civilization, whether the final product of that knowledge be a plate, a Braun radio, or a film.

In drawing out some overlaps in the technical aspirations of Maldonado's scientism and institutional emergence of Ulm-style auteurism, I don't want to collapse important distinctions between the modern functionalism of the HfG and the kind of cinematic modernism the early Kluge and Reitz promoted at Ulm. Indeed, their contemporaneous theoretical essay "Word and Film" (1965) called for a modernism defined by familiar models of vanguard linguistic complexity: a montage-based "sophisticated film language" disallowed by the clichés of the culture industry; an idiom marked by a Godardian "degree of indeterminacy" capable of producing an active spectator; and a "language at liberty" (inspired by Duras, Resnais, and Antonioni) exploring the unreasonable as the outside of a regime of technical reason whose "totalizing quest for meaning has itself become irrational."[64] At the same time, as Miriam Hansen reminds us, Kluge's "literarization of the cinema" was always wedded to a conceptualization of literature and cinema as culturally, socially, and politically embedded institutions, always part of a contested public sphere.[65] Kluge and Reisz insist on linguistic "complexity," then, not simply to describe the literariness of modern *film form*, but as the distinctive product of modern *institutional forms*. So their essay calls for "intellectual centers" such as the HfG: "We can already envision a complexity of expression that film could achieve and the kind of intellectual institution that would encourage such complexity."[66] But they can just as easily imagine another, failed "institutionalization of filmmaking" that would make "film a specialized branch of the mass media." Thus, they end by affirming the interdisciplinary holism of the HfG itself: "The worst that could happen to film would be to be banished to its own domain."[67] As an act of interdisciplinary brain work hatched in the HfG, "Word and Film" enacts the kind of institutional and expressive complexity it calls for. It is a metainstitutional modernist manifesto, extending calls for formal and methodological innovation into the domain of institutional life.

As an institution, though, the HfG did not survive the 1960s. After losing public confidence and state financing, and faced with an increasingly radicalized student body hostile to the school's rationalist ethos and complicity with consumer capitalism, it closed its doors in 1968; Maldonado himself departed in 1967 for the Princeton School of Architecture.[68] By that time, as Kenneth Frampton has argued, the "critical theory" of the HfG "had already reached the threshold of disputing by implication the viability of design schools *per se*."[69] It became impossible to ignore the broader crisis of functionalism in which the school's pedagogy was implicated, or to overlook how, as Gui Bonsiepe put it, "the "communications industry" in which Ulm students were trained was "a consciousness industry," and its revolutionary aesthetic idealism was now "harnessed by the agencies of power and thus used to acquire and maintain power."[70]

On the other side of the tumult of 1968, Maldonado's *Design, Nature, and Revolution* seeks to grapple systematically with the relationship between design and politics. As he saw it, humans' relationship to their "environment" had become increasingly alienating and ecologically unsound, but also pervaded by faulty, irresponsible managerial thinking: the inhuman "new utopian" systems thinking of technocrats like Robert McNamara, which purports to be anti-ideological, and the "old utopians," chiefly planners of ideal cities and "megastructures" inspired by Buckminster Fuller (*DN*, 21, 27). For Maldonado, these current forms of utopian thought are untenable because they sever management from the domain of politics, antagonism, and decision making. Nondesign—the belief that "disengagement from planning will contribute to the collapse" of capitalism—is also a nonstarter, a "subtle form of consent" masquerading as dissent (*DN*, 36, 30). Faced with a looming ecological crisis, there is no hope without planning, no planning without politics, and no "revolutionary sense of dissent" without human forms of "concrete projection" into our environment (*DN*, 30, 8). What Maldonado terms "utopia in action" is only possible if we "rebuild, on new foundations, our faith in the revolutionary function of applied rationality" (*DN*, 73).

One such foundation would be what he called a "critical ecological consciousness" attentive to the primary "scandal of society" and its centuries-long assault on nature (*DN*, 77). Only in the context of doubling down on rational planning and politics can we understand Maldonado's desire for "an environmental microsociology of cinema . . . a serious study of the contribution made by the film world to the determination of the behavior of men to other men and towards their microenvironment." The function of environmental design and planning is "ever that of bringing ordered complexity back to systems which are always by their very nature tending toward disordered complexity—that is, towards complication" (*DN*, 66). So, film's ability to observe and analyze on "microsociological" and "microenvironmental" levels might—or so Maldonado hoped—be wedded to a rational politics of design and planning. That demands techniques and technologies capable of subtle, rigorous accounting for the systems of ordered complexity that constitute the "human environment." *Design, Nature, and Revolution* dreams of a film theory that would follow sociology's own turn in the 1960s from a macroanalysis of the determinations of system and structure—increasingly seen as too abstract—toward microsociology's renewed attentiveness to the concrete and the habitual, the domains of the phenomenological and the everyday. Such were the scaled-down environments constitutive of human social and political life, and thus alienation and the promise of happiness.[71] Human microenvironments were not outside of power, but—as of 1970—where and how Maldonado understood power to materialize, and where its sociological effects and determinations might be most intimately registered and, through film, be most acutely observed. To wish for an "environmental microsociology of the cinema" was, for Maldonado, to aspire to a film theory best equipped to sharpen designers' sense of responsibility, which demands they "put every environment to the test" (*DN*, 71).

Political Modernism as Design Thinking

The case of the HfG and Maldonado's post-1968 assessment of film theory's role in a politics of the human environment presents a largely forgotten trajectory for modernist film theory from the postwar period through the early 1970s. In closing, I want to consider how the modernist design *dispostif* in film theory and its account of postwar nature described in these past two chapters aligns with the more familiar emergence in the early 1970s of so-called political modernism in France and the United Kingdom. For political modernism's anatomy of the cinematic *dispositif*, today dubbed "apparatus theory," had contemporaneous conceptual designs on the once-and-future shape of a human environment generating alienation, frustrating utopian futures, and precluding human satisfactions. Political modernism was deeply pedagogical, and demanded its own techniques of happiness.

This claim may seem curious at first glance, because apparatus theory has been increasingly cast as cold and unfeeling in the wake of film theory's pronounced affective turn over the last decade or so. Summoned as a regrettable episode in the film-theoretical forgetting of embodied sensation, the material, and the haptic, political modernism's interdisciplinary conjuncture of structural linguistics, psychoanalysis, and Marxism has been faulted for producing precisely the disembodied spectator—an abstract, textual subject *position*, rather than a fleshy, feeling *viewer*—about which so much contemporary film theory has been suspicious, whether from Deleuzian, or cognitivist, or phenomenological vantages. Dismissed today as a bad object arriving at the high-water mark of structuralism, semiotics, and the linguistic turn, apparatus theory has seemingly precluded the thinking of affect as a "general term for any resistance to systematicity, a promised recovering of contingency, surprise, play, pleasure, and possibility."[72] In this way, by extolling all manner of "formless feeling/what-is-not-structure," affect has today become what Eugenie Brinkema calls "the negative ontology of the humanities."[73]

We might note that by pitting affect against system, these contemporary debates replay a familiar set of oppositions in the midcentury period consistently belied by what I've called "happiness by design." These debates also tend to forget that apparatus theory of the early 1970s was primarily a radical modernist formalism, one worth returning to in our current moment of renewed attention to form. This formalism extended into the terrain of a then-vanguard film theory strains of the very technical thinking that, over the course of the 1960s, increasingly defined political modernism's adversary: the ideological work of capitalist technocracy, and its production of consensus and pseudo nature. Political modernism, in other words, had its own technical and pedagogical program, and its own revolutionary designs on the senses now understood to be the subject of an apparatus demanding a rigorous theoretical account. The interdisciplinary ambitions of its scientism and technicism, especially in its communicative and informatic ambitions, should be understood as a related species of design thinking at the end of the midcentury period.[74]

At first glance, political modernism would seem to be film theory's own most visible commitment to what I've called a modernism of noncommunication. In the writings of Roland Barthes, Philippe Sollers, Julia Kristeva, and Jean-Louis Baudry, and in the pages of a Maoist journal such as *Tel Quel*, this involved defending modernist *écriture* and what *Screen* critic Colin MacCabe identified as its "agonistic conception of textuality" as a mode of ideology critique defined against a Sartrean commitment to instrumental language and communicative clarity.[75] In the domain of English-language film study, this materialist notion of modernist textuality was at the heart of the rigorous reconceptualization of filmic signification in the British journal *Screen*, relaunched in 1971 under the editorship of Sam Rohdie. *Screen*'s extraordinarily influential conceptual agenda, supported by the British Film Institute and abetting the academic institutionalization of film studies in Anglophone universities in the 1970s, began with a sweeping rethinking of classical film theory's account of the relation of film to reality. *Screen,* in its critique of positivism, was a pivotal late-modernist intellectual enterprise. Because it approached the problem of cinematic realism in relationship to materialist questions of ideology and technology, it resuscitated the technophilic avant-gardes of the Russian formalists and futurists of the 1920s. It returned to the pages of *Lef* and *Novy Lef,* provided English-language translations of early Soviet texts, and in 1974, produced a landmark special issue on Brecht and revolutionary cinema.[76]

Although never overtly announced as a design idiom, *Screen*'s modernism consistently returned to constructivist models of aesthetic production and technical process. As Philip Rosen has argued, *Screen*'s radical materialism "often conceived of the artist as one producer among many, a specialist in perception who would help construct a new, revolutionary reality."[77] At *Screen,* filmic modernism, and a constructivist fidelity to technique, process, materialist demystification, and the production of nonbourgeois subjectivity, underwrote the journal's own editorial commitment to conceptual rigor and scientificity in film study. Such scientism sought to overcome the undisciplined mystifications of auteur criticism. It likely did not know that Ulm had already systematized auterist production. Returning to the utopian technical ambitions of modern design (here, via Eisenstein and Vertov, rather than Moholy-Nagy or Kepes), *Screen* created its own audience of specialists. In the process, it engineered a highly technical theoretical language for a vanguard cadre of university experts and pedagogues around a new disciplinary object—film studies.

To poach Moholy-Nagy's own interwar, constructivist idiom, *Screen*'s was a modernism of production, not reproduction. It grappled with cinema's crucial function in advanced industrial societies as a powerful technology with special designs on the real. But it understood that bourgeois illusionism was also, crucially, about textuality—which is to say, a technical matter of filmic signification, with its elaborate strategies and codes requiring expert analysis and new modes of disciplined close reading. Insofar as it took aim at the role of the classical-realist text in the naturalization of bourgeois subjectivity, it was in the basically modernist business of producing what Marcuse, in *One-Dimensional Man,* called the "unhappy conscience." In this sense, *Screen*'s film-theoretical scientism and rebooted Brechtianism were emphatically pedagogical, following a modernist commitment to the production of unfamiliar varieties of unpleasure, to engineering, through style and technique, different forms for feeling, and to disavowing the sorts of enjoyment offered by Hollywood.[78] Rosen has noted that many members of *Screen*'s reconstituted editorial board in the 1970s were associated with the Education

Department of the British Film Institute, and that its vision offered two rationales for a new film theory. The first, an "educationalist" one, aimed at reforming film education; the other made a radical materialist commitment to ideology critique.[79] But the traditions of interwar materialism *Screen* reanimated were always pedagogical in the first place. They aimed at a political retraining of spectators and their senses, what Laura Mulvey called "destruction of pleasure as a radical weapon," and the cultivation of spectators' tastes and capacities for novel kinds of pleasure.[80] In the pages of *Screen* and elsewhere, political modernism consolidated and disseminated a rigorous theoretical agenda and stumped for a program of oppositional countercinemas. This program, and the disciplined theory at its core, constituted *Screen*'s own technique of happiness. It was technophobic in its theory of the apparatus as a pervasive machine of bourgeois subject formation. It was technophilic in its embrace of the interwar constructivist promise and its sense that cinema's reality effects and manipulation of pleasure could only be overcome by more rigorous conceptual techniques, more stringent systematicity.

Such technophilia, we might say, was a happy side effect of a more widespread structuralist malady. Political modernism's methodological preoccupation with getting systematic as the means of diagnosing systemic ills in bourgeois nature was anticipated as early as Barthes's *Mythologies* (1957), an early merger of nascent structuralism and postwar design history. A kind of reverse ethnography of the object world and media culture of postwar France, then in the throes of rapid, state-sponsored modernization, *Mythologies* also bore the traces of French Marxism and structuralism's "shared concern with things" in the 1950s and 1960s, evident in Barthes's inspired "The New Citroën" and the miraculous new nature of postwar plastics.[81] As Kristin Ross has argued, Barthes's critical method in *Mythologies* aspired to the rigor of the engineer, and in this way, marked what contemporary analysts of the structuralist enterprise such as Henri Lefebvre critiqued as the widespread "infusion of technocratic thought into the intellectual field."[82] Even in an early work of protostructuralist Marxism like *Mythologies,* a critique of the ideological system of bourgeois nature was brought into a kind of mimetic relationship with its own object, doubling its bureaucratic method and its technocratic imperative to classify and taxonomize. In the discourse of political modernism, this Linnaean impulse appeared most famously in the seven categories of film, parsed *A* through *G* according to their ability to "show up cinema's so-called 'depiction of reality,'" delineated in Jean-Louis Comolli and Jean Narboni's "Cinema/Ideology/Criticism," published in a newly radicalized *Cahiers du cinéma* in the wake of May 1968, and translated in *Screen* in 1971.[83] But it was also apparent in the period's signature performances of structuralist method: Raymond Bellour's reading of the "Bodega Bay" sequence of *The Birds,* "System of a Fragment" (1969); Steven Heath's bravura analysis of *Touch of Evil,* "Film and System" (1975); Peter Wollen's "morphological breakdown" of *North by Northwest* (1976). Political modernism's regime of reading proliferated charts and graphs, tables and schemata. These were detailed systems of accounting for what Bellour called film's status as an "object of communication," and thus "a system of signs" that might "someday expect to attain the sanction of a codified formalization."[84] For apparatus theory, Hollywood itself was a textual and ideological system of what Maldonado might call "organized complexity." It demanded its own mapping, and yielded, in the pages of *Screen* elsewhere, a quasi-conceptualist "look of information."[85]

In France the close institutional relationship between the often technocratic ambitions of designer film theory and emergent apparatus theory, and their points of convergence during structuralism's postwar heyday, was most apparent in the journal *Communications,* the "flagship journal of the semiological enterprise."[86] In 1975, at the high-water mark of *Screen* theory, *Communications* published Baudry's "The Apparatus: Metapsychological Approaches to the Impression of Reality" in a special issue, "Psychoanalysis and Cinema," alongside essays by Metz, Kristeva, Barthes, Bellour, and Félix Guattari. But we need to remember that *Communications* began in 1961 as the house organ of the interdisciplinary Centre d'études des communications de mass (CECMAS) at the École pratique des haute études (EPHE). Founded in 1960, the EPHE would soon be the institutional heart of structuralism's interdisciplinary endeavor in France, employing Barthes, Lévi-Strauss, and A. J. Greimas. Established as "an institutional successor" to the recently closed Institute of Filmology, CECMAS epitomized the midcentury proximity of what David Rodowick has called the two "fundamental lines" that "converge in the 1960s to produce 'theory' as a discursive formation or genre: first, the directive idea of filmology that positivism guides every discipline applied to the 'scientific' study of art, and second, a transformation of the conceptual framework of the human sciences effected by the increasing dominance of structuralism."[87] All of the members of *Communications* editorial board in its early years, including Barthes, Claude Bremond, and Edgar Morin and Violette Morin, worked at the Institute of Filmology in the 1950s, although the journal would shift filmology's emphasis on experimental psychology toward the disciplines of sociology and anthropology.[88] Barthesian semiology, as announced in the *Communications* landmark "Semiological Research" issue of 1964, was framed as "contestatory and countercultural."[89] Its project of structuralist demystification seemed poised to challenge some conceptual continuities between the technocratic ambitions of filmology and the transdisciplinary gambit of postwar communications theory and its sponsoring institutions.

But structuralism itself was deeply entwined with what Bernard Dionysius Geoghegan has dubbed the "cybernetic apparatus," with its Cold War communicative politics and its "anti-Soviet political agendas."[90] Roman Jakobson developed his technicist approach to phonology in dialogue with a range of communications engineers, including Warren Weaver, and he received Rockefeller Foundation funding to draw up a survey of "worldwide linguistics" that would help the United States understand the Soviet mind. In his 1960 lecture "Linguistics and Poetics," Jakobson used elements of Claude Shannon and Warren Weaver's *The Mathematical Theory of Communication* to reframe some of Saussure's linguistic categories; in the process, "language itself became part of an economically distributed series of technical tasks within an assembly line of communications."[91] Lévi-Strauss, too, was convinced that information theory's models of communication were applicable to other forms of human activity and seemingly far-flung disciplines, including linguistics, economics, kinship systems, and geopolitics. Lecturing widely for UNESCO as director of its International Social Science Council, Lévi-Strauss lauded cybernetic techniques of communication for their capacity to "overcome the differences that divided scientific disciplines, ethnic groups, and the political sensibilities of capitalists and Communists."[92] He even proposed including passages from Wiener's *Cybernetics* into the UNESCO constitution, a move postwar designers such as Maldonado, Burtin, and the Eameses would surely have applauded.

Geoghegan's important analysis of structuralism's embeddedness in the rational agenda of postwar communications study helps us understand the intertwining of cybernetics and some of the crucial institutions and works of political modernism in film theory. Both *Tel Quel* and *Communications* "adapted elements of Jakobson's and Lévi-Strauss's cybernetic structuralism and merged it with French Marxist critiques" to produce a heterodox tradition of French semiotics.[93] Here, the projects of positivist science and a scientific critique of positivism overlapped in strange ways.[94] In Anglo-American film theory, Peter Wollen worked to prize them apart in the 1972 conclusion to his landmark *Signs and Meaning in the Cinema* (1969), a book commissioned by the BFI's Education Department for the influential Cinema One series. It is a well-known paean to Godardian modernism and its manner of "making things 'difficult' for the spectator."[95] But it requires Wollen to cast aesthetic modernism as an ideological and philosophical challenge

Figure 6.8. Cover, Peter Wollen, *Signs and Meaning in the Cinema* (Bloomington: Indiana University Press), 1972.

to a particular, "functionalist" model of communication in Western thought (*SM*, 157–59). This model, in which an individual "constructs a message in his mind, a complex of meaning," and then transfers the idea "from one mind to another" via the agency of a "common code or grammar," holds good—he observes—for "most contemporary linguistics and semiotic: Weaver and Shannon, Jakobson, Chomsky, Prieto, and their followers" (*SM*, 158). These thinkers assume that "language, or any other system of transmitted signals, is an instrument, a tool (*SM*, 158). For Wollen, this approach is not just functionalist but humanistic and theological—that is, logocentric: it "rests on the notion of the thinking mind or consciousness which controls the world," and "makes use of the material signal as a tool" (*SM,* 159).

Wollen's early poststructuralism reimagines modernism as foundationally hostile to this positivist transmission of messages, intentions, and content as what Barthes, in "The Death of the Author," would cast as a "theological activity." Instead, Wollen produces a genealogy of modernism committed to the text as a "material object," and to the semiological "interrogation of its own code" by creating "spaces within meaning, within the otherwise rigid straitjacket of the message" (*SM,* 162). As for Barthesian *écriture,* Metz's semiology involves the radical reconceptualization of the reader or spectator, "no longer outside the work as receiver, consumer, and judge," but one whose very consciousness is "at risk within the text itself," forced to "interrogate his own codes" in the act of reading—reading now as "an open process, existing in a topological rather than a flat space, controlled yet inconclusive" (*SM,* 162). As a reading *program,* Wollen's modernism is "centrifugal," "problematic," "difficult" (*SM,* 163). This technique of reading is "a challenge to the mystification that communication can exist. For inter-personal communication, it substitutes the idea of collective production" (*SM,* 163). The modernist text is processual, a constructivist "factory where thought is at work, rather than the transport system which conveys the finished product" (*SM,* 164). As design thinking, Wollen's book recasts modernist textuality as a material object, thought as a factory, and reading technique as a collective production remaking patterns of bourgeois consumption and spectatorship. The essay shows how the constructivist avant-garde could fuel a modernism of noncommunication and an antifunctionalist agenda.

But the constructivist legacy was contested in the early consolidation of political modernism, as Wollen knew, and could also be seen to abet the organizational ambitions and techniques of cybernetic structuralism. An eloquent example of this is Metz's essay "Le cinéma: Langue ou langage?," a groundbreaking attempt to articulate a semiology of cinema, published in Barthes's special issue of *Communications* in 1964. The essay begins with a fascinating history of film theory that bears out another trajectory of constructivist design idioms through a critical assessment of Eisenstein. For Metz, Eisenstein's "relentless, almost embarrassing" fidelity to montage, and its behaviorist psychological roots in Lev Kuleshov and Ivan Pavlov, is an example of a desire for "*all-powerful manipulation.*"[96] The problem is what Metz mockingly calls the "montage-or-bust" approach ("C," 32). Despite having lost prestige in the postwar period's ascendant realisms (the films of Rossellini and the writings of Bazin), the approach epitomizes a widespread "spirit of manipulation" characterizing postwar French modernity ("C," 34). As engineer, Eisenstein anticipates a contemporary "state of mind peculiar to 'structural man'" ("C," 38).

For Metz, this combinatory, instrumental tendency extends from the "erector sets" of children—what he calls "syntagmatic toys," much like the Eameses' own—to the "whole operational attitude" of "engineers, specialists in cybernetics, even ethnographers and linguists" ("C," 34). The cybernetic "theory of information," he continues, has "outdone even the most structuralist of linguistics" ("C," 35). It sees human language, "already fairly organized," as still unruly, in needed of organization ("C," 35). Metz's resulting characterization is striking:

> Thus the language we speak has become—very paradoxically if one thinks about it—what certain American logicians call "natural" or "ordinary" language, whereas no adjective is needed to describe the languages of machines, which are more perfectly binary than the best analyses of Roman Jakobson. The machine has ground up human language and dispenses it in clean slices, to which no flesh clings. Those "binary digits," perfect segments, have only to be assembled (programed) in the requisite order. The code triumphs and attains its perfection in the transmission of the *message*. It is a great feast for the syntagmatic mentality.
>
> There are other examples. An artificial limb is to the leg as the cybernetic message is to the human sentence. And why not mention—for amusement and a change from erector sets—powdered milk and instant coffee? And robots of all kinds? ("C," 35)

What these far-flung "*products*" share, for Metz, is an attitude that sees "the natural object (whether human language or cow's milk)" as "a simple point of departure for structuralist technique" ("C," 35). The natural object can be analyzed, as in a "*breakdown analysis*" in the cinema of the kind Bellour would soon perfect, and then—in the syntagmatic moment—reassembled as a technical "*model*," a "duplicate of the original object" ("C," 35–36). By reconstructing models from nature, this manipulative formalism is "neither *poiesis* nor *pseudo-physis*, but a simulation, a product of *techne*" ("C," 36). Thus Eisenstein's ethically dubious constructivism: "To Rossellini, who said, 'Things are. Why manipulate them? the Soviet film-maker might have replied, 'Things are. They must be manipulated'" ("C," 36). How far, Metz asks, will this modern "taste for manipulation, one of the three forms of what Roland Barthes calls 'sign imagination' (*l'imagination du signe*) go?" ("C," 37).

In framing the question this way, Metz's foundational essay in film semiotics returns us directly to the context of the HfG, and Ulm's own contemporaneous commitment to designer film theory in the context of a cutting-edge information aesthetics. For his first rhetorical question is followed by another: "Does not [Abraham] Moles anticipate a 'permutational art' in which poetry, discarding the chaste mystery of inspiration, will openly reveal the portion of manipulation it has always contained, and will finally address itself to computers?" ("C," 37). Indeed he did. And this kind of approach bothered humanists like Arnheim. Max Bense, Moles and Maldonado's colleague at the HfG, would present a paper describing the mathematical contours of such just a poetics at Will Burtin's Vision 67 conference.[97] Anxiously appraising the future of computational poetics as predicted by Moles in 1962, Metz adduces Moles's vision of a programmed poetry—"A utopia? Or prophecy?"—as an analogy to the techniques of organization in Eisenstein's "erector-set" approach to filmic constructivism. By confronting these symptoms of "the flood tide of the syntagmatic mind," Metz understands the shared orientation of Moles and Eisenstein, information aesthete and montageur, as "entirely consistent with a certain spirit of modernism, which, when called cybernetics or structural science, yields results that are much less questionable" ("C," 38). Cybernetic art, for Metz, is the dubious limit case for the ethical excesses of the constructivist passion, which never met a thing it didn't want to organize.

The essay is surprising for a range of reasons—not just because film theory of the 1970s tended to oppose Metz and Bazin, whereas here they're joined in a shared anxiety about abstracting, artificially modeling, and instrumentalizing the real, but also because Metz seems so critical of Lévi-Strauss and, implicitly, his own mentor at the EPHE, Roland Barthes. In his powerful reading of Metz's essay, Rodowick has helpfully proposed that we understand this ambivalence—this urgent stocktaking of structuralism from film theory's most famous semiologist—as a way of "contrasting two forms of life or modes of existence characteristic of his modernity: the structural and the phenomenological."[98] Metz's essay works to bridge the precision and rigor of structural linguistics with "the phenomenological richness of the analogical and aesthetic image."[99] The result is not a film-theoretical science like filmology, a constant reference point in Metz's essay, but what Rodowick calls a kind of "soft" structuralism. While the Wollen of *Signs and Meaning* is more optimistic than Metz about what the return to constructivism might mean for the design thinking we today call political modernism, he shares Metz's concern about semiology's proximity to positivist instrumentality and behaviorism. In fact, his 1968 essay "Cinema and Semiology: Some

Points of Contact," which takes up Metz's "Langue ou langage?" in some detail, opens by eschewing what he sees as the behaviorist trappings of semiology, following the Saussurean breakthrough: "Semiology was later explored in the United States, under the name of semiotic, by [Charles] Morris, who deflected it in the direction of Carnapian logic and behaviourist psychology: it is of no further interest to us in this Anglo-Saxon form."[100]

Of course, at design schools like the HfG, and before that, at Moholy-Nagy's Institute of Design in Chicago, this "Anglo-Saxon" branch of the Cold War semiosphere was very much on the media agenda, explored within a wildly capacious, interdisciplinary approach to the science of signs. As we've seen, at Ulm the semiotic curriculum included the study of film in the Departments of Visual Communication and Information, and, in 1958, it had no truck with Wollen's later desire to excise behaviorism from the program of a critical semiology.

Maldonado's "Communication and Semiotics," for example, a text "assembled from lectures on semiotics at the HfG" and published in the school's bulletin in July 1959, hails semiotics as a "promising interdiscipline" poised to "consolidate" various fields: Charles Morris's theory of signs; Ferdinand de Saussure's general linguistics; the "pragmatism-instrumentalism" of Charles Sanders Peirce, John Dewey, and William James; the behaviorism of John Watson and Edward Tolman; the social behaviorism of George Herbert Mead, Morris's teacher and mentor; the philosophical anthropology of Ernst Cassirer; the "philosophy of symbolism" of C. K. Odgen, I. A. Richards, and Susanne Langer; and the logical positivism of Rudolf Carnap and Otto Neurath.[101] And, Maldonado continued, there is "nothing to prevent [semiotic theory] from drawing to itself new disciplines such as, for example, engineering psychology, functional and social perceptual theory, information theory, structural and statistical linguistics, and rhetoric and aesthetics."[102] The extensive bibliography appended as the "most important reference material" for Maldonado's HfG seminars in semiotics includes, in addition to multiple works from all of the preceding scholars, a number of key texts of the New Criticism in literary theory. This is telling, underscoring how the New Critics helped make literary studies itself a specialist, technical enterprise in the midcentury administration of culture, and one with its own deep connections both to behaviorist psychology and the communications paradigm.[103]

Taking in all manner of communications theory and theorists, the list also included a fairly substantial dose of Marxist critiques of communication: Lefebvre's *Marxism and the Theory of Information* (1958), Lukács's *The Destruction of Reason* (1954), and Horkheimer and Adorno's *The*

Dialectic of Enlightenment (1947). It's a sign of Maldonado's late-1950s confidence in the positivist program of semiotics that he is willing to take on board some of the midcentury's most trenchant critiques of instrumental reason and capitalist technocracy. As he framed it retrospectively in 1987, positivism at the HfG "was never conformist, but also critical."[104] Further, he confessed to being "particularly receptive to some of the thinking of the Frankfurt School," noting that the "presence of Adorno in Frankfurt represented for me, as it were, a contradictory intellectual stimulus."[105] Maldonado himself acknowledged that Adorno's noncommunicative modernism, "his complicated and cryptic way of writing," exerted "a fascination on me that was anything but rational. 'The useless is eroded, aesthetically inadequate. But the merely useful lays waste to the world,' he once said to me."[106] Adorno's attempt to "cool [his] enthusiasm for an industrial culture of usefulness" in his 1965 lecture on functionalism at the Werkbund in Berlin, Maldonado explained, fueled his examination of "the relationship between industrial culture and the culture industry," and sparked his desire to "undertake a critical investigation of the role played by 'design' in between these two realities."[107] Such are the paradoxes of the functionalist malady.

Maldonado's *Design, Nature, and Revolution* was one such investigation of design's capacity to mediate between commitment to rational technique, and sympathy with some of the midcentury's most trenchant critiques of positivism and mass culture. The contemporary critical discourse of political modernism was another. It was film theory's own post-1968 reckoning with the role of the "cinematic apparatus" in producing the very mediating membrane Maldonado called "the human environment." This *dispositif* divided man from nature, producing pseudo nature. It cleaved the human from himself, producing alienation. And it capitalized on cinema's technological capacity to simulate, and reify, bourgeois reality. Apparatus theory's critical semiology, its pedagogical commitment to a materialist, modernist design program, constituted its own kind of applied rationality. Such rationality understood textuality—and special techniques of reading and writing—as the collective scene of work, of new forms of disciplined unpleasure, and of open-ended process. Acknowledging the semiotic aesthetics of Barthes, Metz, and Eco, Maldonado called for an "environmental microsociology of cinema" that would scale down into ever-more-intimate units of psychological analysis, in the textual model of James and Proust, to better understand the operations of power, and the behavior of humans to each other and their environment. Political modernism, having learned the structuralist lesson of codes at all levels, scaled both up and down. It scaled up through its model of subject positioning, because it understood the apparatus as the abstract scene of ideological formation and naturalization, indifferent to phenomenological specificity. It scaled down in its scientistic model of reading, attentive to the nuances of textual detail and coding, and to the minutiae of an organized, complex system of variations and differences, unfolding dynamically, shot-by-shot, and frame-by-frame. As modes of design thinking, neither, finally, could do without models or the highly technical, pedagogical programs that accompanied their radical formalisms.

CODA

the norton chair, circa 1970

Trilling or Eames?

IN THE FALL OF 1970, as the fate of the HfG had thrown into question the future credibility of design education, Charles Eames accepted the august post of Charles Eliot Norton Professor of Poetry at Harvard University. Established in 1925 to honor the school's former president, the Norton Lectures feature speakers deemed to have made landmark contributions to literature, music, and the fine arts, and they have become a reliable barometer of celebrity in the humanities. This appointment was Harvard's institutional acknowledgement of the reality of the Eames era. And it came as the heroism of the midcentury's designs on happiness was increasingly besieged and coming to an end.

For designers of the Eameses' stature, the writing was on the wall a few months before, at IDCA '70: "Environment by Design." During the conference's final session, presided over by a flummoxed Reyner Banham, San Francisco activist and founder of the Environment Workshop Michael Doyle read eleven resolutions in recognition of "the major issues of our natural-social-physical environment." The list included the immediate withdrawal of U.S. troops from Southeast Asia and an end to the draft; a moratorium on all extractive industries; the U.S. government's recognition of the land claims of American Indians; the state's enforcement of the right of various people to "live in various lifestyles that do not necessarily reflect the mainstream of American society"; the legalization of abortion; and the wholesale abandonment of design for profit.[1] The most sweeping indictment of conference technique came from the "French delegation," who read a statement—titled "the Environmental Witch-Hunt" and penned by Jean Baudrillard—that critiqued the conference's failure to consider "the social and political status of Design."[2] The French denounced the "mystique of environment" as a conspiracy of "overdeveloped countries."[3] The threat of environmental apocalypse, as they saw it, was a way of rallying rich nations in a false interdependence that denied the realities of class conflict, political antagonism, and what Alain Touraine diagnosed as the "dependent participation" of underdeveloped nations in the capitalist world system.[4]

At IDCA '70, the communicative technique of the lecture itself was subjected to intense ideological scrutiny by Sim Van Der Ryn, then an assistant professor of architecture at UC Berkeley, who had served as the university's student negotiator during the 1969 People's Park protests. Titled "The Persistence of Form," Van Der Ryn's talk embedded conference technique in a broad survey of six thousand years of human history. This period, he argued, had evolved three basic "cultural forms"—the tribe, bureaucratic empire, and capitalist democracy—each accompanied by its own modes of participation, living together, decision making, and communication.[5] He described the present as a period of transition, a dysfunctional formal merger of empire and democracy resulting in the decline of common beliefs, alienation from life, and the "design for death," with the Vietnam War as the United States' most exemplary design object. He analyzed the various formal "settings" (family, work, school) in which "culture is imprinted" through the distribution of space and objects. By describing "settings" as disciplinary forms regulating bodily comportment and speech in keeping with the ideological work of the institutions housing them, Van Der Ryn implicated his own function as IDCA conference speaker, playing an outmoded, hierarchal role in which "I talk and you listen," and positioned IDCA technique at the center of a series of obsolete, meaningless rituals. Such desiccated forms, and "culture as a collection of behavior settings," persist through self-sustaining modes of communication best exemplified, for Van Der Ryn, by the corporate form itself: "in the corporation, communication only exists to extend the form; it has no intrinsic value." These institutionalized forms could not be reformed, but only scrapped and supplanted by new, living cultural forms—his example was the "enclave"—always "evolving and growing" in time, and devoted to increasing experience and awareness. Bringing novel social forms into being required "a conscious mutation," an avowedly utopian becoming of "new kinds of people."

The stakes of the Norton Lectures, circa 1970, were high for Charles Eames. Although he was not the first architect or designer appointed as Norton lecturer, Eames's appointment was framed in the press as a significant break with form.[6] Under a large photo of the Eames lounge chair, the headline of the *Harvard Crimson* announced, “Eames to Use Multi-Media in ’70–’71 Norton Lectures,” and the Eameses’ long-standing strategies of multimedia communication, beginning with “Sample Lesson,” were cast as potentially transformative of the Norton Chair in a career distinguished chiefly by a series of revolutionary takes on the chair. “The question,” the *Crimson* reporter explained, is “not what he will do *to* it, it is what Charles Eames will do *with* it.”[7] The university lecture hall will again be tested as an Eamesian medium: “In the same way that Eames has transformed the ottoman into a voluptuous and functional medley, he has transformed the lecture into a multi-image, multi-media environment.”[8] Eames also sensed the novelty of the gig, and put himself in a genealogy of chairs beginning with a famous fellow St. Louisan. “Well,” he remarked to the *Crimson* reporter, “there was T. S. Eliot, Ben Shahn, and now me. I don’t know what that will do to it.”[9]

There was also Lionel Trilling, a fellow liberal Cold Warrior whose lectures in 1969–70 immediately preceded Eames’s own, and would be shortly published as *Sincerity and Authenticity.* By way of a conclusion, I want to linger on this movement from Trilling to Eames as successive Norton Chairs at the end of the 1960s, and consider the assumptions about happiness underlying their media poetics, at once liberal-humanist and modernist. In both content and form, the Trilling-Eames sequence epitomized a movement from an expressivist, unhappy modernism preoccupied with the moral value and attraction of subjective authenticity—what Trilling called “the downward movement through all the cultural superstructures to some place where all movement ends, and begins”—toward a designer modernism concerned with creative problem solving, communication, and informatic dexterity in networked environments.[10] In this way, Eames’s multimedia series, “Problems Related to Visual Communication and the Visual Environment,” clarifies the pedagogical stakes of a humanities mission reoriented at the end of the 1960s toward the training of knowledge workers at a moment when, as Alan Liu argues, “all culture is increasingly the culture of information.”[11]

Coming near the end of a career spent describing the moral force of literature for the liberal imagination, Trilling’s sweeping lectures took up the intertwined ideas of sincerity and authenticity in the West, from Shakespeare, Diderot, and Rousseau, to Freud and his contemporary interpreters R. D. Laing and Herbert Marcuse. He aimed to show that an earlier preoccupation with sincerity had been devalued—drowned out by a pervasive rhetoric of authenticity suggesting a “more strenuous moral experience than ‘sincerity’ does, a more exigent concept of the self and what being true to it consists in” (*SA*, 11). While the lectures make no specific references to political events, they are consistently

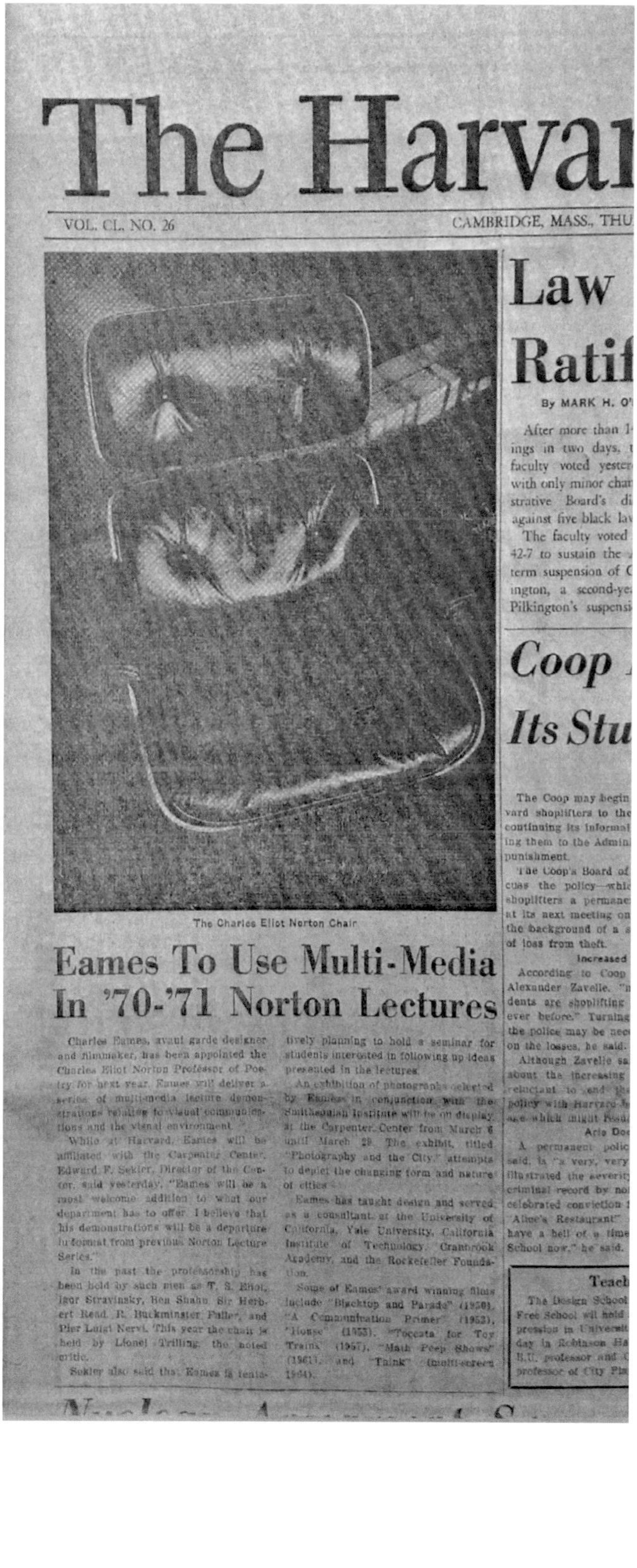

The Harvar

VOL. CL. NO. 26 CAMBRIDGE, MASS., THU

Law Ratif

Coop Its Stu

The Charles Eliot Norton Chair

Eames To Use Multi-Media In '70-'71 Norton Lectures

Charles Eames, avant garde designer and filmmaker, has been appointed the Charles Eliot Norton Professor of Poetry for next year. Eames will deliver a series of multi-media lecture demonstrations relating to visual communications and the visual environment.

While at Harvard, Eames will be affiliated with the Carpenter Center. Edward F. Sekler, Director of the Center, said yesterday, "Eames will be a most welcome addition to what our department has to offer. I believe that his demonstrations will be a departure in format from previous Norton Lecture Series."

In the past the professorship has been held by such men as T. S. Eliot, Igor Stravinsky, Ben Shahn, Sir Herbert Read, R. Buckminster Fuller, and Pier Luigi Nervi. This year the chair is held by Lionel Trilling, the noted critic.

Sekler also said that Eames is tentatively planning to hold a seminar for students interested in following up ideas presented in the lectures.

An exhibition of photographs selected by Eames in conjunction with the Smithsonian Institute will be on display at the Carpenter Center from March 6 until March 29. The exhibit, titled "Photography and the City," attempts to depict the changing form and nature of cities.

Eames has taught design and served as a consultant at the University of California, Yale University, California Institute of Technology, Cranbrook Academy, and the Rockefeller Foundation.

Some of Eames' award winning films include "Blacktop and Parade" (1950), "A Communication Primer" (1953), "House" (1955), "Toccata for Toy Trains" (1957), "Math Peep Shows" (1961), and "Think" (multi-screen 1964).

Figure C.1.
"Eames to Use Multi-Media in '70-'71 Norton Lectures," *Harvard Crimson,* March 5, 1970.

preoccupied with their central dyad's capacity to illuminate a suite of contemporary affective states: alienation and the problem of happiness itself in a basically coercive and estranging social order. In this sense, *Sincerity and Authenticity* is Trilling's attempt to reckon with the counterculture's account of unfreedom, and its specific hostility to coercion and encumbrances on autonomy as indices of repression and control. For Trilling, the social and the historical must nonetheless limit or place some constrains on any self that is worth fashioning in the first place. On this, he and the Eameses would agree. Even Marcuse, in his critique of repressive sublimation in *One-Dimensional Man,* would defend sublimation as an enabling constraint, one that "preserves the consciousness of the renunciations which the repressive society inflicts upon the individual" (*ODM,* 75). This, Trilling argued, was to be admired. It amounted to a defense of a "character-structure" strengthened by the demands of a traditional society, and set Marcuse "apart from, and at odds with, the prevailing tendency of radical speculation about personal authenticity" (*SA,* 167).

Emerging in the sixteenth century, the idea of sincerity was bound to the concept of society, the rise of the bourgeois individual, and to a theatrical and public-oriented notion of the self as capable of *not* dissembling, of not being false *to others.* But for Trilling, it was Hegel's account of the "Spirit in Self-Estrangement" in the *Phenomenology of Mind* that precipitated a new idea in the West—namely, that the truth of the self consists "in its being *not* true to itself" (*SA,* 34, 44). Hegel's historical anthropology limned the evolution of the spirit's self-realization from a "noble," happy accord with society to an insurgent, "base" self, one that understands its relationship with the social as the ground of alienation, and is increasingly antagonistic to "the authoritative power of the state" (*SA,* 36). The base self would reject the noble condition of being at the center of the European educated middle class. This ideal, Trilling explains, "went by the name of happiness" (*SA,* 40).

Trilling draws out a genealogy of the contemporary prestige of alienated authenticity stretching from Hegel's account of the unhappy consciousness to "the literature of our own day (*SA,* 40, 41). "As *readers,* he insisted, "as participants in the conscious, formulating part of our life in society, we incline to the antagonistic position" (*SA,* 41). Literature, for Trilling, is a medium of antagonism and unhappiness, and a regulative technique of liberalism itself.

It will come as no surprise to those familiar with Trilling's work that modernism enters his historical account as part of this broader shift over the course of the nineteenth century. In modernism, art's capacity to produce "the sentiment of being, of being strong, is increasingly subsumed under the conception of personal authenticity" (*SA*, 99). Just as "the work of art is itself authentic by reason of its entire self-definition," existing "wholly by the laws of its own being," painful and unhappy and socially fractious as they may be, so the artist "seeks his personal authenticity in his entire autonomousness—his goal is to be as self-defining as the art-object he creates" (*SA*, 99–100). Like Marcuse, whose work *Eros and Civilization* he turns to in the book's conclusion, Trilling enshrines a modernism that communicates by noncommunication. Or, to use Michael Fried's terminology in "Art and Objecthood" (1967), Trilling insists on a version of the modernist aesthetic object that does not require its beholder to complete it—that has the Friedian quality of presentness. Its job is to model its own autonomy: "As for the audience, its expectation is that through its communication with the work of art, which may be resistant, unpleasant, even hostile, it acquires the authenticity of which the object itself is the model and the artist the personal example" (*SA*, 100).

Sincerity and Authenticity therefore positioned modernist unhappiness in a special relationship to the thickening of what Tomás Maldonado, in his contemporaneous treatise *Design, Nature, and Revolution,* called "the mediating membrane" between human consciousness and contingent reality. For both thinkers, the problem of alienation and the "revolutionary revolt of the young" could not be understood without the interlocking concepts of "nature" and the "human environment." And they shared the sense that diagnosing contemporary political antagonism required the vanguard aesthetic and pedagogical resources of modernist aesthetics. For Maldonado, as chapter 6 argues, modernism helped transform "the environment" from a philosophical abstraction to a fact of sensibility and perception. This, in part, was why Trilling also loved modernism: it limned a human surround defined by what he called "variousness, possibility, complexity, and difficulty."[12]

Trilling was an erudite man, but he was not, to my knowledge, reading Maldonado. He was, however, reading Reyner Banham, whom he most likely met in Walter Paepcke's Aspen. They were both there in the summer of 1963: Banham, a featured speaker at the IDCA's "Design and the American Image Abroad" conference, with robust representation by the USIA, and Trilling, the keynote speaker at the inaugural Aspen Film Conference, "The American Film: Its Makers and Its Audience." And Trilling would return in 1974 for the Aspen Institute's conference titled The Educated Person in the Contemporary World, delivering a paper titled "The Uncertain Future of the Humanistic Educational Ideal." This should not surprise us, since Trilling, with Aspen regular Mortimer Adler, had taught in the groundbreaking Great Books curriculum at

Columbia University under John Erskine and was committed to *Bildung* as "the making of a human being."[13] Trilling's early work at the *Partisan Review* was embedded in the same postwar network of philanthropic support for communications studies and research, under the auspices of the Rockefeller Foundation, that fueled the interdisciplinary humanist media endeavors of Paepcke, Moholy-Nagy, and the Eameses described in this book.[14] The sweeping postwar communications complex that forced literary criticism to justify itself as a special domain of technical expertise in the New Criticism, and that pushed film studies to discipline itself as a humanistic enterprise also—in Aspen and elsewhere—facilitated a new, humane interdisciplinary media practice under the rubric of design.

A minor consequence of this practice, Trilling's reference to Banham's *Theory and Design in the First Machine Age* (1960) appears in the lectures' most sustained account of modernism. After a discussion of Joseph Conrad's *Heart of Darkness* as the paradigmatic expression of a modern concern with authenticity, and a jag to the role of masks and ironic detachment in Nietzsche and Wilde's principled objection to sincerity, Trilling turns to the "idea of the machine" in the deep history of modern alienation. It's the only moment in the book's capacious intellectual history that takes up either design theory or the history of technology. Trilling traces the anxiety-producing influence of "the idea of the machine" on the "conduct of life, imposing habits and modes of thought which make it ever less possible to assume that man is man," from Emerson through the young, humanist Marx, to John Ruskin's unwavering belief in the organic—his conviction that the machine could only make "inauthentic things, dead things" (*SA*, 126, 127). While acknowledging modernism's partisanship with the organic (in D. H. Lawrence, E. M. Forster, Henry Miller, and Samuel Beckett), Trilling invokes Banham to isolate the strains of another, technophilic modernism antagonistic to Ruskin's organicism, beginning with Marinetti and Italian futurism, and leading to Banham's own technofuturist present in the thick of the Eames era.

Trilling's point is not to take sides between mechanism and organicism, or modernist technophilia and technophobia. Nor will he entrench their contemporary apportioning on either side of some epochal cultural schism. He had no truck with any facile "two cultures" distinction, a point he sharpened to a cutting edge in his earlier essay "Science, Literature, and Culture: A Comment on the Leavis-Snow Controversy." We might suspect that Trilling, who wrote his first book on Matthew Arnold, would be swayed by the good Victorian's warnings on the limits of merely technical education, and side with Leavis against Snow on these terms. We would be wrong. The essay instead followed from

Trilling's umbrage at Snow's twinned claims about literary culture as a failed *managerial* project.

To Trilling's astonishment, and despite the vast power of postwar technoscience, Snow claimed, first, that "it is traditional culture . . . which manages the Western world," and second, that it has done a lousy job of it.[15] Exhibit A: Auschwitz. For Snow, this management error was a problem, since scientists had "the future in their bones," and "literary men," especially modernists, did not ("SLC," 15). Orwell's *1984,* Snow argued, expressed "the strongest possible wish that the future shall not exist" ("SLC," 16). Trilling saw this as a horrible but telling misreading of Orwell's novel, and of modernism itself. In fact, it's the capacity of the literary past to challenge optimism about the future, especially Snow's vision of a "future made happier by science," which Trilling feels obliged to clarify ("SLC," 29). Trilling was bothered by Leavis's ill-mannered tone, but he was more upset by his failure to defend literature in its proper political capacity as a criticism of life. In suggesting that a united front of scientists in the United States and the Soviet Union might join the world in peace, what Snow really wanted, Trilling surmised, was to grant scientists "the right to go their own way *with no questions asked*" ("SLC," 20). Literature's job, especially in the unruly depths of antisocial feeling plumbed in modernism, was to get in the way—to make politics, and society, the objects of moral judgment.

By asking what directing influence in the West its literary culture might possibly lay claim to, and by framing the two-cultures debate as a managerial discourse, Trilling extended his early discussion of liberalism and literature as co-implicated in a broader organizational project in *The Liberal Imagination* (1950). Liberalism's politics, he insisted, were the "politics of culture, the organization of human life towards some end or other, toward modification of sentiments, which is to say the quality of human life" ("P," xvii). As such, liberalism was marked by a crucial affective paradox around the problem of happiness. "It is concerned with the emotions above all else, as proof of which the word happiness stands at the very center of [liberal] thought" ("P," xviii). But insofar as liberalism is "active and positive, so far, that is, as it moves towards organization, it tends to select the emotions and qualities that are most susceptible of organization," and thus develops theories and principles about the human mind that limit it, that denies emotions their full possibility ("P," xix). Liberalism envisions a "general enlargement, and freedom, and rational direction of human life," but it drifts toward various forms of emotional simplification and technocratic management: "agencies, and bureaus, and technicians" ("P," xix, xx). As Trilling saw it, the urgent task of literature, especially its unhappier modern variants, was to criticize the liberal imagination's organizational tropism. Literature was liberalism's moral servomechanism, reminding it of the "largeness and modulation and complexity" of emotion and imagination and the "lively sense of contingency and possibility" in human life it tends to sacrifice in its very reasonableness and progressive optimism ("P," xx–xxi).

Modernism thus helped Trilling and other Cold War liberals define what Amanda Anderson has dubbed a "bleak liberalism," oscillating between pessimism and hope, and everywhere marked by the midcentury "crisis of man."[16] Trilling rejected a misguided or idealizing progressivism, he was skeptical about the rational agenda of liberal happiness, and he insisted, in Eamesian fashion, on the necessity of conceptualizing freedom with a sense of subjective limits and restraints. Modernism's zone of unhappy feeling helped him gauge both the value of liberalism's "organizational impulse" and its manifest and ongoing failures in the wake of the political upheavals of the late 1960s, with their competing utopian visions and designs on happiness ("P," xx). Like Banham or Bass or Noyes at IDCA 70, Trilling had been confronted with the affective rupture of "the sixties" rather directly—in his case, during the student occupation of Columbia University in 1968. As his former student Louis Menand tells the story, Trilling was stunned to find scrawled on the wall of his office, "evidently by a student who had failed French, the words 'Fuck Bourgeoisie Culture' and 'Lionel Trilling you pig.' "[17] His collaborator and spouse, Diana, recalled another student "zealot" posting about campus a photo of the professor, with the legend beneath it: "WANTED, DEAD OR ALIVE. FOR CRIMES AGAINST HUMANITY."[18]

Trilling's turn to Ruskin, Banham, and the question of technology through the discourse of organic design in *Sincerity and Authenticity*, allowed him to extend his own skepticism about liberal management toward nature and the environment itself as objects of liberal responsibility and anxiety. Despite divergent authenticating sources, modernist organicism and vanguard technophilia alike understand nature and principled antagonism to organic unity as having a moral status. Trilling recognized the "imperious" energies of the modern movement as often hostile to natural integrities, engineering technical interventions into nature à la Moholy-Nagy or Maya Deren, or with the craft of Joyce's famous artificer Dedalus. The natural universe was noticed, but modernism "refused to be submissive or dutiful to it. In the spirit of vanguard play, "the universe might be taken apart and put together in a new way," like the Dymaxion map a young Kenner would cut from the pages of *Life* at the dawn of the Eames era (*SA*, 131). But Trilling also acknowledged the violence at work in modernism's principled hostility to nature and the organic, violence explicit "in the Greek ancestry of the world 'authentic': *Authenteo*: to have full power over; also, to commit a murder" (*SA*, 131).

The problem of organic design—as both a historical response to alienation deepened by the development of modern technics and a contemporary reckoning with environmental devastation—seems to force Trilling's Norton lectures into a bracing encounter with the dilemmas and confusions of agency defining the present:

> The belief that the organic is the chief criterion of what is authentic in art and life continues, it need hardly be said, to have great force with us, the more as we become alarmed by the deterioration of the organic environment. The sense of something intervening between man and his own organic endowment is a powerful element in the modern consciousness, an overt and exigent issue in our culture. In an increasingly urban and technological society, the natural processes of human existence have acquired a moral status in the degree that they are thwarted. It is the common feeling that some inhuman force has possessed our ground and air, our men and women and our thought, a machine more terrible than any that Emerson imagined. (*SA*, 127–28)

Organic natural processes, Trilling insists, have a moral claim on our attention the more they are interfered with. And the sheer extent of that intervention, that quasi-modernist violence to natural integrity that Deren called "instrumentation" in *Anagram* in 1946, now, in 1970, seemed to produce a threatening sense of man-made nature's inhuman agency. As a nascent premonition of the Anthropocene, Trilling's remarks brought his long-standing doubts about liberal management and instrumental reason into the domain of ecological thought, and its anxiety about the fearful boomerang return of modernity's so-called goods.

Following Trilling, Eames's turn in the Norton Chair was equally preoccupied with the organizational impulses of liberalism and the problem of happiness, though neither was directly named as such. Rather, their contours were modeled, in content—as lectures *about* models—and, in form, as multimedia environments. As Franklin F. Ford, dean of the Faculty of Arts and Sciences at Harvard noted in his letter of invitation to Eames, " 'poetry' is interpreted as all forms of poetic communication," and the intention of the foundation was to offer the Norton post to "men actively engaged in creation."[19] So, while Eames took with him to Harvard the works of previous Norton chairs (E. E. Cummings's *Six Nonlectures* and Jorge Luis Borges's *Labyrinths*), and cribbed some notes on Octavio Paz from a review in the *New Yorker*, his lectures were made up primarily of slide shows and films representing a broad cross section of the Eameses' work and conceptual preoccupations to date. Eames spoke from loose notes rather than a formal text, and topics included the problems of making choices and decisions; the need to find beauty and pleasure in the experience of everyday life; the cultivation of a respect for things; the role of discipline and restraint in expression and problem solving; the reality of changing social needs; the nature of work and the "professional environment"; and the overlapping interest of designer, client, and society. Two key ideas ran as leitmotivs threaded throughout the lectures: the centrality of models and modeling in the Eameses' media practice, and the use of visual material, including film, as a means of structuring and disseminating information and knowledge.

These were perennial Eamesian concerns, but we can see them in a different light following Trilling, and through his lectures' central dyad. Trilling's etymology of sincerity begins by reminding his audience that the earliest use of that word referred "not to persons but things"—the soundness or purity or integral values of unadulterated material objects (*SA*, 12). In the Eameses' filmography, the paean to sincerity in this sense is *Toccata for Toy Trains*, which opens with Charles explaining why the film features "real" and "old" toys, and not scale models. "In a good, old toy," his gentle narration explained, "there is apt to be nothing

Figure C.2.
"Tin as tin." Sincere trains in *Toccata for Toy Trains*, 1957, directed by Charles and Ray Eames.

self-conscious about the use of materials. What is wood is wood. What is tin is tin. What is cast is beautifully cast." Celebrating the trains' "direct and unembarrassed manner," the voice-over asks viewers to take pleasure in the sincerity of toys, but of course the Eameses became famous for the bravura of their experimental technical interventions into wood and plastic, for the seeming insincerity of plywood and fiberglass. The Eameses' chairs showed how the serialized mass production of the postwar period's new nature could achieve the sincerity of old tin, an honest "plastic as plastic" aesthetic rather than polymers' dissembling, pretending to be wood. As I've argued, this was part of their compensatory media function as happy furniture.

As we've seen, their furniture's materiality, manufacture, and distribution always had a crucial moral dimension for the Eameses. This was the morality of a system of production and consumption, and the systemic "goodness" of performance factors "all the way down the line," as Charles explained in 1952 ("DD"). We should also note that the Eameses' own iconic designs had, by 1970, become subject to a plague of imperfect copies. As Charles noted, "The first imitations of the molded plastic shell that appeared in this country horrified the Herman Miller Furniture Company. They soon found it in their hearts not to be completely outraged, because each time a copy appeared, the sales of the original went up!"[20] When asked how they felt about fake Eames chairs, Charles answered by framing them not as things but as models or ideas in a circuit of knowledge production and dissemination: "In any work, whether it's film or furniture design, you hope that somebody will come along and take the central idea and improve upon it."[21] He wished only that the good ideas would be copied, not the bad ones. Underlying this generous notion of intellectual property is a modernist theory of style predicated on the impersonal. As Charles once said of the beauty of an ax handle, "It has no style because it has no mistakes. Style reflects one's idiosyncrasies. Your personality is more apt to show the degree that you did not solve the problem than to the degree that you did."[22]

In comments like these, Eames revives the modernist theories of impersonality of one-time Norton chair T. S. Eliot, and blends them with Corbusier's notion of the industrial *objet-type*. Trilling saw modernist impersonality as a repudiation of sincerity, and a declaration of the kind of autonomy he linked to the waxing regime of authenticity. Eamesian modernism, by contrast, is utterly unconcerned with any authenticity welling from subjective depths. Instead, it idealized an informatic model of originality: the persistence and continuity of an original idea, or any other unit of information, in a channel of transmission threatened by noise and entropic degeneration. As Todd Cronan has framed

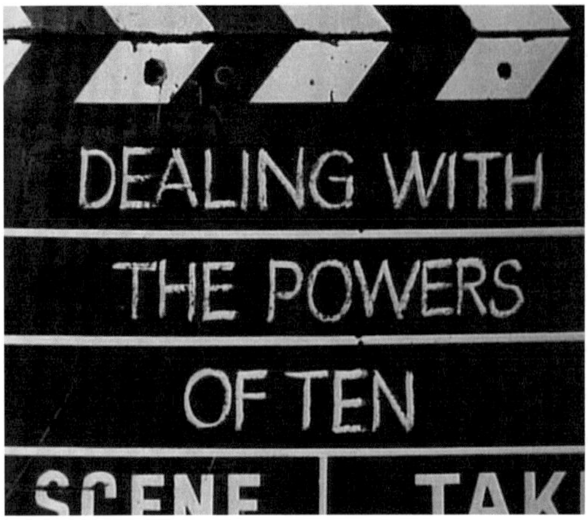

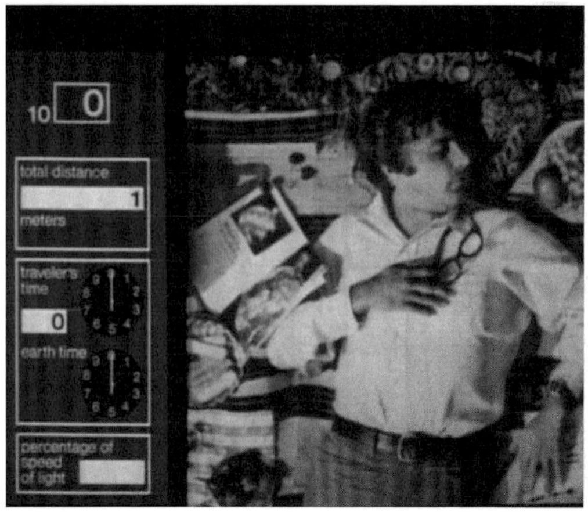

the Eameses' modernist morality, every object of design, no matter the size or scale, was mired in noise and "swamped in the density of responsibilities."[23] What mattered, finally, was the extent to which ideas (and the ideas incarnated in things) could be modeled and put into an efficient and organized network of distribution that fueled more problem solving, and thus more knowledge production. In these terms, as Will Burtin knew well, information design was always a moral matter.

As Trilling did in his lectures, Eames too found himself confronting a vexing transformation of social values and designs on the limits of the "good life," and forced to speak to—and model—the present liberal politics of organization and administration. In Lecture Four, Eames offered a slide show called "Goods." As a moral parable, it was animated by a recent break-in to Ray's car, parked outside 901. Stuffed with a range of objects—flowers, gifts for the grandchildren, objects for a picnic at the office—the car, Charles joked, "invited" breaking in. To Charles's shock, the thief had left most of the stuff there, strewn on the street, including a "magnificent bolt of cloth."[24] This object and the series of things then shown in the slide show (a hank of rope, a ball of twine, a keg of nails) were modeled as capital-*G* "Goods, the kinds of goods that people lay great store in, the kind of things you have a tremendous security about." Consensus about what constitutes Goods, evidently, had changed. And this shift led Charles to propose a theory of what he called "The New Covetables." These were special kinds of desired goods that, "if shared and broken like the fishes and the loaves . . . will not diminish in value; they will not degenerate no matter how much you spread them around."[25] Such covetables were not really things at all but "concepts," "applicable models," actionable principles. The New Covetables were the Goods of endlessly transmissible information, organized and conveyed in models that could preserve the idea without decay.

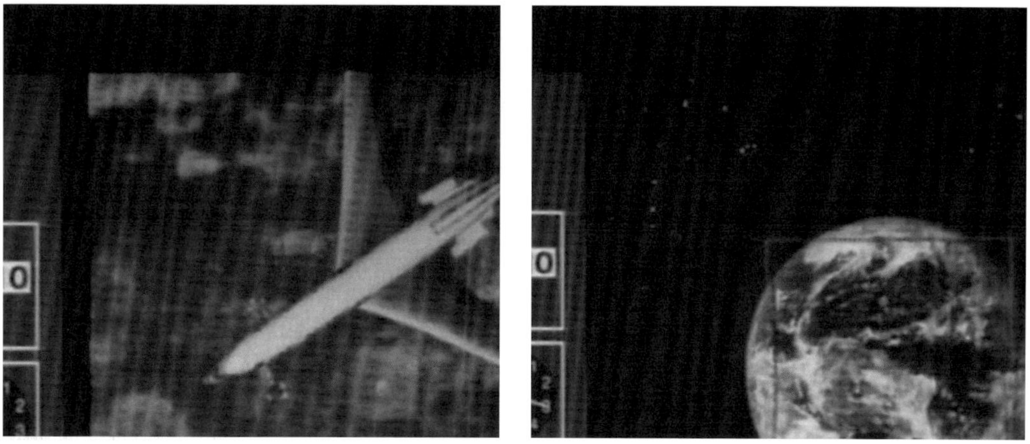

Figure C.3. "Perspectiveless space." Ecological perception in *Powers of Ten: A Rough Sketch for a Proposed Film Dealing with the Powers of Ten and the Relative Size of Things in the Universe*, 1968, directed by Charles and Ray Eames.

Eames's Norton lectures returned reflexively to the idea that the lecture's medium was the message, and they began and ended with some of the Eameses' most famous models, in films and slide shows. Lecture one opened with *Powers of Ten: A Rough Sketch for a Proposed Film Dealing with the Powers of Ten and the Relative Size of Things in the Universe* (1968). It is, of course, the culmination of the fluidity in the Eameses' work between the scales connecting the private and the geopolitical, the domestic and the national, the human and the cosmic—scales united, as I've argued through the book, by the dream of communication. First produced for the Commission on College Physics, the iconic film consists of one long and exponentially timed zoom linking an unnamed man, enjoying a nap on a golf course in Florida, in networks of teeming matter that vastly exceed him on both macroscopic and microscopic scales. An instrument panel at frame left measures the spectator's spatial movement exponentially, in distance traveled, the traveler's time, earth time, and percentage of speed of light, and these measurements are doubled in the cold monotone of the film's narrator (Judith Bronowski) that accompanies the journey into outer and inner space, and back. In his essay on the Eameses published in *Film Quarterly* just a few months prior to the Norton Lectures, film critic Paul Schrader called this the experience of "perspectiveless space; from which there is no one place where the viewer can objectively judge another space."[26] He was primed to read it as a model of an idea about an ecological perception, the point of view of a "citizen of the universe, an unbounded territory."[27] For Schrader, *Powers* made concrete a concept true to contemporary experience. "And that idea is covetable."[28] As a sign of that idea's contemporaneity, remember, Hugh Kenner simultaneously hailed Fuller and Pound as "world men," and in the chapter of *The Pound Era* titled "Space Craft."

Eames, for his part, framed *Powers* not just as an ecological film but as an account of the unforsakable terrain of liberal responsibility and security amidst epochal change. He prefaced the screening by acknowledging ecological catastrophe, and asking about the limits of responsibility:

> Or rather, there are no innocents. Is it Con Edison or General Motors? Who is General Motors? General Motors are all the stockholders, it's Harvard University, it's the Rockefeller Foundation and then something happens. You've got to think; people, trustees of institutions, begin to take Trusteeship seriously.[29]

These prefatory remarks cast the zooming anthropocentric view of *Powers,* rigorously oriented on a straight line through universes large and small, as a call to a distributed, networked responsibility for the planet. The university, the corporation, the foundation: these crucial enabling institutions of the Eames era's media experimentation, are all positioned as liberal agents, potential trustees of the universe whose survival must involve them all. As such, they are in positions to choose, and manage, the future. *Power*'s viewer is hailed to take the mobile and impossibly vast scale of his responsibility seriously. For the Eameses, the expansive network of liberal choice and decisionism involves individuals *and* collectives *and* corporate entities equally. In so doing, this terrain of responsibility for happy life risks collapsing crucial asymmetries of power and interest between and among these various actants. Instead, it aligns the needs of the designer, the client (whether corporate or state), and society itself in a zone of overlapping, nonconflictual "areas of interest," as in a well-known topological diagram designed by Ray. With *Powers* as lecture one's inaugural pedagogical model, Eames then drew an analogy between the anthropocentric security of the slumbering space voyager and the aquatic life of pelagic fish, the flexible marine protagonists of his film *Tanks* (screened in lecture five), surviving in constantly changing environments, before screening the *Circus* slide show, debuted in 1952 at UC Berkeley. If *Powers* enshrines a cosmopolitan perception of organized responsibility, and *Tanks* recasts fish as icons of liberal security, thriving in unnatural environments, *Circus* models an efficient, communal coordination of energies. An embodied poem of collective discipline, it rebukes the excesses of self-expression in ways Trilling might well admire.

As the apex of this modeling of modeling, Eames's sixth and final Norton lecture clarified, and defended, the organizational tropism of the Eames era. The problem with administration, his lecture notes indicated, is "centralization," and a centripetal concentration of decision-making power.[30] This could be combated, the Eameses hoped, by distributing the technical, infrastructural, and institutional resources for informed decision making, and by the unimpeded transmission of covetable ideas, as democratically as possible.[31] The problem facing society was "not so much a lack of scientific, or technical, or sociological knowledge," but a lack of "ways of transmitting existing knowledge to people as they need it, in forms they can readily grasp and use."[32] Similarly, the challenge to liberal-democratic happiness in the late 1960s was not "a lack of values" but rather a vexing excess of conflicting ones. Indeed, Eames continued, "our present discontents, our consciousness of a multifarious predicament, shows that we do have quite a range of values and that we still feel strongly about them. The difficulty is in accepting that we have no choice but to choose!"[33] At the end of the day, then, values had to be chosen, preferences made, distinctions of quality asserted. This, for the Eameses, was the basic ontology of liberal political life. It acknowledged the ongoing necessity of life's organization: "If human nature is viewed as changeable, then armies, police, and *administration* will be seen as interim necessities, not immutable requirements."[34]

The final lecture began with the slide show *Movie Sets,* featuring on-location photographs of the Eameses' friend Billy Wilder in the studio, at work, on various films. The film studio's technical environment, Eames submitted, was a "model of the environment of the professional process" in a presentation about the role of such models in democratic knowledge work, and the capacities of the computer as a tool of modeling and political decision making. The slide show was followed by some of the Eameses' more famous films about the computer: the recent *A Computer Glossary* (1968) and the earlier *Information Machine.* About the latter, then twenty-one years old, Eames felt obliged to note its age and its "impossibility naïve/wide-eyed" attempt to describe the possibilities of a once-alien technology.[35] But as "a rhetorical case, to push things in a different direction by presenting them in a favored light," he would still defend the film. A drawing by Ray mapping out the sixth lecture's

Figure C.4. Billy Wilder at work, *Movie Sets* slide show, Charles Eames, lecture six, Charles Eliot Norton Lectures, Harvard University, 1970–71.

themes connected the Eameses' rhetorical work of modeling, and issues of "machine use," to the ongoing task of meeting the "universal sense of expectation" ushered in by World War II. That devastating war made people aware of "the promises, and powers, of technology." And the long postwar boom offered "immediate exposure to different ways of living, and a catalog of possessed and possessable objects," producing the widespread "feeling that he could, even should, have all those things he has seen the others have." Can the world, Eames asked, still "be arranged so as to fulfill" these universal expectations? The Eameses' career-long answer to this question was a resounding yes. But not without organizational tools and media such as the computer. And not without understanding—as Ray's diagram put it—that the use of such technology is a "political choice," one not up to manufacturers but redounding rather to that broader administrative unit of society, as "the real test of Jeffersonian democracy."[36]

And not, of course, without films. Ray's drawing also included a quotation by Lillian Gish that "films are the mind and heartbeat of this technical century."[37] *Happiness by Design* has endeavored to examine how the demands of that American century helped the Eameses, and other designers in their orbit, invent new uses for that medium within a broader technical, and often technocratic agenda of postwar, liberal well-being and *Bildung.* As I've shown, they transformed modernism in the process. Schrader sensed this when he compared the futurity of Snow's scientists with the Eamesian filmmaker, poised to challenge "the hegemony of pessimism in the contemporary arts."[38] Unsurprisingly, Charles's Norton lectures thus ended on a note of sincerity, with *Tocatta for Toy Trains.* This seems like a nostalgic choice, a way of looking back at one of the couple's first filmic experiments near the close of the high-tech Eames era. But as I've argued, the scale of the toy, like all modes of Eamesian work and play, pedagogy and interdisciplinary practice, was the potentially threatening scale of the world of modern technics at midcentury and its many organizational challenges. In the context of Eames's lectures at Harvard, the studio environment of 901 materialized in that early toy film—stuffed with playthings and plywood and all manner of technologies and Goods—was a final model of the technical and informatic environments that constituted the abiding subject of Eames's Norton lectures. In these environments, so the Eameses believed, happiness would be produced. With a pragmatic optimism that seems embarrassing today, all the factors and the responsibilities and the choices such designers faced in meeting the midcentury's universal sense of expectation would be calculated, endlessly. The challenge of happiness would be administered with ever more efficient tools and techniques, but never, thankfully, overcome.

acknowledgments

THIS BOOK HAS BEEN A JOY to research and write from start to finish. For that, I'm grateful to my intellectual home, the Department of English and the Film Studies Program at Michigan State University. Thanks to chairpersons Pat O'Donnell, David Stowe, and Cara Cilano for the research leaves, course releases, and resources needed to complete this project. Early on, this book was supported by a Humanities and Arts Research Program (HARP) development grant from the Office of the Vice President for Research and Graduate Studies at Michigan State University, and its final form as an object was shaped by a generous HARP production grant.

My friends, colleagues, and students at MSU contributed enormously to this book. Thanks to Karl Schoonover for his initial enthusiasm about the project and for keeping me thinking hard about midcentury material culture. To the members of our faculty writing group (Josh Yumibe, David Bering-Porter, Pat O'Donnell, Ken Harrow, Ellen McCallum, Scott Michaelsen, Lily Woodruff, and Matt Handelman), thanks for the encouragement and critique and for suffering some early chapter drafts. I'm lucky to have you all as colleagues. Thanks to Kaveh Askari, Amrutha Kunapulli, and the members of the Moving Images Research Workshop for their smart feedback and questions about the book's Introduction. It has been a privilege to test the ideas in the book in the classroom during the past few years, and I'm grateful to the students in my Midcentury Media Environments and Film and Architecture seminars for their energy and intelligence, especially Laura McGrath, Anna Green, Sarah Panuska, Cameron Clark, Lance Conley, Josh Wucher, Pat Bird, Nate Paolasso, and Simon Tessmer.

This project has benefited from the expertise, generosity, and patience of various archivists. First, my thanks to Margaret McAleer at the Library of Congress, who answered my every query and was very welcoming during my first, well-timed trip to the Eames Papers. She encouraged me to see the vastness of the Eameses' designs on communication. I'm indebted to Genevieve Fong and David Hertsgaard at the Eames Office for their support of the project, for their willingness to make available hard-to-see films and other archival material, and for their kindness with the image permissions essential to this book. Thanks also to Eames Demetrios for a helpful conversation at the Michigan Modern Symposium at Cranbrook. At Herman Miller's Corporate Archives in Zeeland, thanks to Linda Baron and Amy Auscherman, as well as the hospitable Mark Schurman. I'm grateful to John Berry, former director of corporate communications at Herman Miller, for talking with me about the contexts in which the Eameses' films were screened for clients. At the Graphic Design Archives at the Rochester Institute of Technology, Amelia Hugill-Fontenel made space and time for me, sometimes in the middle of her own classes. Kari Horowicz sent me corrected versions of several of Will Burtin's writings. Thanks also to Carol Burtin Fripp for allowing me access to rare recordings of her father and to Erica Stoller, who shared kind memories of her own father's friendship with Will Burtin. At the Special Collections and University Archives at the University of Illinois–Chicago's Daley Library, thanks to Val Harris, who also assisted with image permissions, and Kellee E. Warren. At the Illinois Institute of Technology archive, thanks to Ralph Pugh. At the Getty Research Institute, thanks to Aimee Calfin. At the University of Chicago's Special Collections Research Center, thanks to Christine Colburn. At the Ryerson and Burnham Archives at the Art Institute of Chicago, thanks to Nathaniel Parks. At the Southern Illinois University Library, thanks to Matt Gorzalski. At the Chicago Film Archive, thanks to Anne Wells, Michelle Puetz, and Brian Belak. At the Cranbrook Academy of Art, thanks to Gina Tecos and especially Leslie Edwards, who asked sharp questions and steered me in the right direction.

Colleagues at various institutions invited me to share portions of this book in progress, and I'm indebted to the smart, engaged audiences for the work. At Vanderbilt University, thanks to Jen Fay and Mark Wollaeger for including me in the Modernist Jamboree; to Laura Doyle, for the conversation; and to everyone at the Robert Penn Warren Center. Thanks to Jennifer Wild and James Rosenow at the University of Chicago for inviting me to the Chicago Film Seminar. I'm grateful to Lynda Zwinger at the University of Arizona for asking me to speak at the *Arizona Quarterly* Symposium, and to the stimulating questions I received there from Scott

Selisker, Lee Medevoi, Lauren Mason, Paul Hurh, and John J. Melillo. Thanks to Elsa Högberg and Jane Goldman for bringing me to Uppsala University for the Intimate Modernisms Symposium; to Aaron Jaffe for including me in his terrific Paleofuturisms Symposium, sponsored by the University of Louisville; and to Sara Blair at the University of Michigan for inviting me to participate in the Visual Cultures Workshop. It was a special treat to discuss portions of the project while consulting on the "Up Is Down" exhibition at Northwestern University's Block Museum. Great thanks to Amy Beste and Corinne Granof for their curatorial vision and for including me in the exhibition catalogue, and to Lynn Spigel, Michael Golec, Michael Dyja, Tom Gunning, Dan Bashara, Jan Tischy, and Talia Shabtay for an inspiriting conversation around our shared interests. It was also a pleasure to talk about this project with graduate students in Jeff Menne's "Postwar Media Artists" seminar at Oklahoma State University, Haidee Wasson's "Film and Media Historiography" seminar at Concordia University, and Todd Cronan's "Midcentury Modern" seminar at Emory University.

I am grateful for the incisive, formative feedback I received on this project from many friends and colleagues over the years, whether in conference panels, symposia, electronic exchanges, or in more intangible acts of generosity. Thanks to Lisa Akervall, Jennifer Buckley, Robert Burgoyne, J. D. Connor, Mark Garrett Cooper, Todd Cronan, Laura Frahm, Oliver Gaycken, Marsha Gordon, Corinne Granof, Jonathan Greenberg, Katie Greulich, Josh Guilford, Juliet Guzzetta, Orit Halpern, John Harwood, Pete Johnston, Dimitrios Latsis, Erica Levin, Akira Mizuta Lippit, Benjamin Mangrum, Kate Marshall, John Marx, James McFarland, Laura McGrath, Johannes von Moltke, Omri Moses, Julian Murphet, Jennifer Peterson, John David Rhodes, Scott Richmond, Merrill Schleier, Lisa Siraganian, Matthew Solomon, Noa Steimatsky, Judith Stoddart, Sarah Street, Juan A. Suárez, Julie Taylor, Joyce Tsai, Charles Tung, and James Tweedie. Many colleagues generously made available access to their own archival research or shared their own work in progress, including Amy Beste, Colin Gunkel, Corrine Granof, Kylie Rae Escudero, Henning Engelke, Jan-Christopher Horak, Mark Garrett Cooper and John Marx, Bernard Dionysius Geoghegan, Sarah Keller, Margaret Re, John R. Blakinger, Dr. René Spitz, Gloria Sutton, Lynn Spigel, David Wittenberg, and Neil Verma. I'm especially indebted to friends who read and commented on drafts of the book's chapters and provided invaluable insight and advice, including Erika Balsom, Brian R. Jacobson, Josh Lam, Jeff Menne, and Peter Lurie. A special thanks to Haidee Wasson, for her consistent encouragement about this project and for her always sharp feedback on the writing. Mark Goble, too, has been a terrific reader and a model of generosity and kindness. For their early enthusiasm about this project, I owe a special debt of gratitude to Douglas Mao, Matt McAdam, Mark Wollaeger, Kevin Dettmar, Allan Hepburn, and Lindsey Stonebridge.

At the University of Minnesota Press, it's been a real pleasure to work with Danielle Kasprzak, who was excited about the project from the jump. Dani has always welcomed the book's interdisciplinarity and its various audiences. I'm very grateful for her expert advocacy. I was also fortunate to have smart, substantial readers' reports on the manuscript in its early stages. These readers decisively shaped the book's final form. Thanks also to Doug Armato for his support for the book. Anne Carter has been a delight—uber-professional, with crazy-fast replies to my queries. I'm also grateful to Mary Byers, a terrific copy editor, and to Shelby Connelly, Rachel Moeller, and Laura Westlund. Special thanks to Elizabeth Elsas Mandel, who designed this book as an object that makes me very happy indeed.

There are a few people to whom I owe a special debt. Pat O'Donnell has been a champion of my work and career throughout my time at MSU and has always given me the best advice. I'm grateful for the countless conversations we've had about this project over the years and for Pat's constant friendship and guidance. Josh Yumibe is the Platonic ideal of colleagues, in the flesh. He arrived at MSU to direct our Film Studies Program just as I was beginning this project, and it's been an enormous privilege to have him as a most-valued interlocutor and friend. It was a special treat to work on this project while Josh was also thinking and writing about design, and his careful readings helped to sharpen the argument of the book. Jen Fay and Scott Juengel are the dearest and closest of readers and friends. Thanks for hosting the Wohlford–Nieland crew in Nashville over the past few years and for the patient and inspired readings of this book from the beginning. You guys are the best.

My family sustains me and makes everything possible. Thanks to Andrew, Morgan, Leif, and Jus, for all your Chicago hospitality, and to James for your commitment. This book is dedicated to my parents, Sue Erickson Nieland and Maurice B. Nieland. They have always supported their sons in their work: they want it to be rewarding, and they know why it matters for us also to be happy in it. My ongoing happiness is not a product of design at all but rather the sheer good fortune of being married to Sarah Elizabeth Wohlford. We share the pleasure of raising two wonderful daughters, Lila and Iris, who were much younger when this book began. Sarah, Lila, and Iris—thanks for helping me see what a good life is all about. We live it together every day.

notes

The following abbreviations are used throughout the notes.

A	Maya Deren, "An Anagram of Ideas on Art, Form, and Film." In *Essential Deren: Collected Writings on Film by Maya Deren,* edited by Bruce R. McPherson. Kingston, N.Y.: Documentext, 2005.
"AN"	Rudolf Arnheim, "Accident and the Necessity of Art." *Journal of Aesthetics and Art Criticism* 16, no. 1 (September 1957).
"AYFM"	Amos Vogel, "The Angry Young Film Makers." In *Cinema 16: Documents toward a History of the Film Society,* edited by Scott MacDonald. Philadelphia: Temple University Press, 2002.
"C"	Christian Metz, "The Cinema: Language or Language System?" In *Film Language: A Semiotics of the Cinema,* translated by Michael Taylor. Chicago: University of Chicago Press, 1974.
"CI"	Stan VanDerBeek, "Culture: Intercom and Expanded Cinema. A Proposal and Manifesto." *Film Culture* 40 (Spring 1966): 15–18.
"DD"	Charles Eames, "Design, Designer, Industry." In *An Eames Anthology: Articles, Film Scripts, Interviews, Letters, Notes, and Speeches,* edited by Daniel Ostroff. New Haven, Conn.: Yale University Press, 2015.
"DE"	Tomás Maldonado, "Design Education." In *Education of Vision.* Edited by György Kepes. New York: George Braziller, 1965.
"DM"	George Nelson, "The Designer in the Modern World." In *Problems of Design.* New York: Whitney Publications, 1957.
DNR	Tomás Maldonado, *Design, Nature, and Revolution: Toward a Critical Ecology.* New York: Harper & Row, 1972.
E	Rudolf Arnheim, *Entropy and Art: An Essay on Order and Disorder.* Berkeley: University of California Press, 1971.
EC	Gene Youngblood, *Expanded Cinema.* New York: E. P. Dutton, 1970.
ED	John Neuhart and Marilyn Neuhart, with Ray Eames, *Eames Design: The Work of the Office of Charles and Ray Eames.*
EP	Charles and Ray Eames Papers, Manuscripts Division, Library of Congress, Washington, D.C.

ER John McHale, *The Expendable Reader: Articles on Art, Architecture, Design, and Media (1951–79),* edited by Alex Kitnick. New York: GSAPP Books, 2011.

"EV" George Nelson, "The Enlargement of Vision." In *Problems of Design*. New York: Whitney Publications, 1957.

FCP Lancelot Hogben, *From Cave Painting to Comic Strip: A Kaleidoscope of Human Communication*. New York: Chanticleer Press, 1949.

HC Hannah Arendt,*The Human Condition,* 2nd ed. Chicago: University of Chicago Press, 1998.

HU Norbert Wiener, *The Human Use of Human Beings: Cybernetics and Society*. New York: Avon Books, 1967.

"I" Will Burtin and Laurence Lessing, "Interrelations." *Graphis* no. 22 (January 9, 1948): 108–22.

IDCAUIC International Design Conference in Aspen Papers, Special Collections and University Archives Department, University of Illinois at Chicago.

"IE" Margaret Mead, "The Information Explosion." *New York Times,* May 23, 1965.

IG *The Independent Group: Postwar Britain and the Aesthetics of Plenty,* edited by David Robbins. Cambridge, Mass.: MIT Press, 1991.

"IT" Rudolf Arnheim, "Information Theory: An Introductory Note." *Journal of Aesthetics and Art Criticism* 17, no. 4 (June 1959): 501–3.

"LL" Will Burtin, "Live and Learn: Communication in Transition and Changing Functions of Design." *Art Education* 21, no. 6 (June 1968): 5–9.

"MM" C. Wright Mills, "Man in the Middle: The Designer." In *Politics, Power, and People: The Collected Essays of C. Wright Mills,* edited by Irving Louis Horotitz. New York: Oxford University Press, 1963.

"MU" Rudolf Arnheim, "Melancholy Unshaped," *Journal of Aesthetics and Art Criticism* 21, no. 3 (Spring 1963): 291–97.

"NS" George Nelson, "Notes on the New Subscape." In *Problems of Design*. New York: Whitney Publications, 1957.

"OC" Susan Sontag, "One Culture and the New Sensibility." In *Against Interpretation and Other Essays*. New York: Delta, 1966.

ODM Herbert Marcuse, *One-Dimensional Man: Studies in the Ideology of Advanced Industrial Society*. Boston: Beacon Press, 1964.

"P" Lionel Trilling, Preface to *The Liberal Imagination*. New York: New York Review of Books, 2008.

PH Howard Mumford Jones, *The Pursuit of Happiness*. Cambridge, Mass.: Harvard University Press, 1953.

SA Lionel Trilling. *Sincerity and Authenticity*. Cambridge, Mass.: Harvard University Press, 1971.

SC Margaret Mead and Paul Byers, *The Small Conference: An Innovation in Communication*. Paris and The Hague: Mouton, 1968.

65 *Vision 65: World Congress on New Challenges to the Human Communications.*

67 *Papers. Vision 67: Survival and Growth.* N.p.: International Center for the Communication Arts and Sciences, 1967.

"SLC" Lionel Trilling, "Science, Literature, and Culture: A Comment on the Leavis-Snow Controversy." *Higher Education Quarterly* 17, no. 1 (1962).

SM Peter Wollen, *Signs and Meaning in the Cinema.* Bloomington: Indiana University Press, 1972.

TI John Harwood, *The Interface: IBM and the Transformation of Corporate Design, 1946–1976.* Minneapolis: University of Minnesota Press, 2011.

TF Siegfried Kracauer, *Theory of Film: The Redemption of Physical Reality.* Princeton, N.J.: Princeton University Press, 1997).

VA György Kepes, ed., *The Visual Arts Today.* Middletown, Conn.: Wesleyan University Press, 1960.

VM László Moholy-Nagy, *Vision in Motion.* Chicago: Paul Theobald, 1969.

WBP Will Burtin Papers. RIT Libraries: Graphic Design Archives, Rochester Institute of Technology.

WPP Walter Paepcke Papers. Special Collections Research Center, University of Chicago Library.

Introduction

1. Alexandra Lange, "This Year's Model: Representing Modernism to the Post-War American Corporation," *Journal of Design History* 19, no. 3 (2006): 244.

2. On the contemporary science of happiness, and its modes of measuring happiness through "hedonimeters" and "happiness indicators," see Sara Ahmed, "The Happiness Turn," *New Formations* 63 (Winter 2007/2008): 7–14. For a longer history, see William Davies, *The Happiness Industry: How the Government and Big Business Sold Us Well Being* (London: Verso, 2015).

3. For more recent work that complicates this declension narrative from different disciplinary vantages, see Lynn Spigel, *TV by Design: Modern Art and the Rise of Network Television* (Chicago: University of Chicago Press, 2009); Greg Barnhisel, *Cold War Modernists: Art, Literature, and American Cultural Diplomacy* (New York: Columbia University Press, 2015).

4. *The World of Charles and Ray Eames,* ed. Catherine Ince with Lotte Johnson (New York: Rizzoli, 2016), 34.

5. On the broader relationship between wartime and domestic applications for novel postwar materials, see Beatriz Colomina, *Domesticity at War* (Cambridge, Mass.: MIT Press, 2007); *Cold War Hothouses: Inventing Postwar Culture from Cockpit to Playboy,* ed. Beatriz Colomina, Annmarie Brennan, and Jeannie Kim (New York: Princeton Architectural Press, 2004); and *Atomic Dwelling: Anxiety, Domesticity, and Postwar Architecture,* ed. Robin Schuldenfrei (London: Routledge, 2012).

6. Hugh Kenner, *Bucky: A Guided Tour of Buckminster Fuller* (New York: William Morrow, 1973), 4.

7. Kenner, 11.

8. Hugh Kenner, *The Pound Era* (Berkeley: University of California Press, 1971), 560.

9. Fuller's knot, a model of "patterned integrity," was adduced by Kenner to explain Pound's theory of the poetic image as Vortex; the poet's notions of growth were likened to the designer's description of the spherical bubble. Joyce, too, was credited with "synergism." Kenner, *The Pound Era*, 148, 163, 231.

10. Mark Goble, *Beautiful Circuits: Modernism and the Mediated Life* (New York: Columbia University Press, 2010), 3.

11. Goble, 4.

12. For two superb accounts of designers' role in shaping a midcentury sensorium, see Orit Halpern, *Beautiful Data: A History of Vision and Reason since 1945* (Durham, N.C.: Duke University Press, 2014); and Fred Turner, *The Democratic Surround: Multimedia and American Liberalism from World War II to the Psychedelic Sixties* (Chicago: University of Chicago Press, 2013). For an overview of the Eameses' films in the context of their design practice, see Eric Schuldenfrei, *The Films of Charles and Ray Eames: A Universal Sense of Expectation* (New York: Routledge, 2015), and the indispensable John Neuhart and Marilyn Neuhart, with Ray Eames, *Eames Design: The Work of the Office of Charles and Ray Eames* (New York: Harry N. Abrams, 1989).

13. See Reinhold Martin, "The Dialectic of the University: His Master's Voice," *Grey Room* 60 (Summer 2015): 109; and Friedrich Kittler, "Universities: Wet, Hard, Soft, and Harder," *Critical Inquiry* 31 (Autumn 2004): 244–55.

14. See my discussion of this revisionist work, "Infrastructures of Being: Modernism as Media Theory," *Modernism/modernity* 23, no. 1 (January 2016): 233–42.

15. See Haidee Wasson, *Museum Movies: The Museum of Modern Art and the Birth of Art Cinema* (Berkeley: University of California Press, 2005); Peter Decherney, *Hollywood and the Culture Elite: How the Movies Became American* (New York: Columbia University Press, 2005); *Films That Work: Industrial Film and the Productivity of Media*, ed. Vinzenz Hediger and Patrick Vonderau (Amsterdam: Amsterdam University Press, 2009); *Useful Cinema*, ed. Charles R. Acland and Haidee Wasson (Durham, N.C.: Duke University Press, 2011).

16. See Acland and Wasson, *Useful Cinema*.

17. See Spigel, *TV by Design*; Amy Beste, "All Roads Lead to Chicago: Encyclopedia Britannica Films, the Institute of Design, and Nontheatrical Film" (Ph.D. diss., Northwestern University, 2011); Olivier Lugon, "Dynamic Paths of Thought: Exhibition Design, Photography, and Circulation in the Work of Herbert Bayer," in *Cinema Beyond Film: Media Epistemology in the Modern Era*, ed. François Albera and Maria Tortajada (Amsterdam: Amsterdam University Press, 2010), 117–44; *G: An Avant-Garde Journal of Art, Architecture, Design, and Film, 1923–1926*, ed. Detlef Mertens and Michael W. Jennings (Los Angeles: Getty Research Institute, 2010); Jan-Christopher Horak, *Saul Bass: Anatomy of Film Design* (Lexington: University Press of Kentucky, 2014); Michael Cowan, "Absolute Advertising: Walter Ruttmann and the Weimar Advertising Film," *Cinema Journal* 52, no. 4 (Summer 2013): 49–73; Stephen J. Phillips, *Elastic Architecture: Frederick Kiesler and Design Research in the First Age of Robotic Culture* (Cambridge, Mass.: MIT Press, 2017); Daniel Bashara, *Cartoon Vision: UPA Animation and Postwar Aesthetics* (Oakland: University of California Press, 2019).

18. On the cinematic model as a category of modern experience central to interwar exhibition design, see Lugon, "Dynamic Paths of Thought," 128. Haidee Wasson, "Cinema and Industrial Design: New Media Ecologies and the Exhibition Film," in *Films That Work Harder*, ed. Vinzenz Hediger and Patrick Vonderau (Amsterdam: Amsterdam University Press, forthcoming).

19. Bayer, "Aspects of Design of Exhibitions and Museums," *Curator: The Museum Journal* 14, no. 3 (1961): 257-58; Mary Anne Stanizewski, *The Power of Display: A History of Exhibition Installations at the Museum of Modern Art* (Cambridge, Mass.: MIT Press, 1998), 3.

20. See the introductory essay of Douglas Mao and Rebecca Walkowitz's collection *Bad Modernisms* (Durham, N.C.: Duke University Press, 2006); Fredric Jameson's discussion of late modernism in *A Singular Modernity: An Essay on the Ontology of the Present* (London: Verso, 2001); Serge Guilbaut's *How New York Stole the Idea of Modern Art: Abstract Expressionism, Freedom, and the Cold War,* trans. Arthur Goldhammer (Chicago: University of Chicago Press, 1983); and Barnhisel, *Cold War Modernists.*

21. For an excellent discussion of the Communications Group, see Brett Gary, *The Nervous Liberals: Propaganda Anxieties from World War I to the Cold War* (New York: Columbia University Press, 1999), 85–130. On Siegfried Kracauer's work at MoMA, and its relationship to the Communications Group, see Decherney, *Hollywood and the Culture Elite*; and Johannes von Moltke, *The Curious Humanist: Siegfried Kracauer in America* (Oakland: University of California Press, 2016). On Theodor Adorno's relationship to the Communication Group's Paul Lazarsfeld, see David Jenneman, *Adorno in America* (Minneapolis: University of Minnesota Press, 2007).

22. Von Moltke, *The Curious Humanist,* 49.

23. Christopher Simpson, *Science of Coercion: Communications Research and Psychological Warfare, 1945–1960* (New York: Oxford University Press, 1997), 52.

24. John Durham Peters, *Speaking into the Air: A History of the Idea of Communication* (Chicago: University of Chicago Press, 1999), 28–29.

25. Herbert Marcuse, *One-Dimensional Man: Studies in the Ideology of Advanced Industrial Society* (Boston: Beacon Press, 1964), 66. Hereafter cited parenthetically as *ODM.*

26. Mark Wollaeger, *Modernism, Media, and Propaganda: British Narrative from 1900 to 1945* (Princeton, N.J.: Princeton University Press, 2006), 30.

27. Sven Spieker, *The Big Archive: Art from Bureaucracy* (Cambridge, Mass.: MIT Press, 2008), 6.

28. Reinhold Martin, *The Organizational Complex: Architecture, Media, Corporate Space* (Cambridge, Mass.: MIT Press, 2003), 8.

29. Meyer Schapiro, "The Liberating Quality of Avant-Garde Art," *ARTnews* 56, no. 4 (1957): 40.

30. Schapiro, "The Liberating Quality of Avant-Garde Art."

31. On the role of modernism in the Rockefeller Foundation's funding of literary criticism, see Evan Kindley, "Big Criticism," *Critical Inquiry* 38, no. 1 (Autumn 2011): 71–85. On the expansion of the postwar university as a media project, see Mark Garrett Cooper and John Marx, "Crisis, Crisis, Crisis: Big Media and the Humanities Workforce," *differences* 24, no. 3 (2014): 127–59, and Mark Garrett Cooper and John Marx, *Media U: How the Need to Win Audiences Has Shaped Higher Education* (New York: Columbia University Press, 2018).

32. Most directly associated with Alfred Korzybski in the 1930s, the general semantics movement—like the Vienna Circle—was a philosophical outgrowth of pragmatism and analytical philosophy. It promoted a rational, transparent, and often therapeutic approach to language that would challenge the mystifications of propaganda. General semantics was taught at the New Bauhaus in Chicago, and key members of the movement such as S. I. Hayakawa—then affiliated with the University of Chicago—shaped the theories of mass communication of designers like György Kepes and Moholy-Nagy. See Anna Vallye, "Design and the Politics of Knowledge in America, 1937–1967: Walter Gropius, György Kepes" (Ph.D. diss., Columbia University, 2011), 215–18; and Peter Galison, "Aufbau/Bauhaus: Logical Positivism and Architectural Modernism," *Critical Inquiry* 16, no. 4 (Summer 1990): 709–52.

33. On Burke's challenge to the elite formalist and romantic strains of modernism, see Robert Genter, *Late Modernism: Art, Culture, and Politics in Cold War America* (Philadelphia: University of Pennsylvania Press, 2010).

34. George Nelson, "Design as Communication," in *Problems of Design* (New York: Whitney Publications, 1957), 4.

35. Reyner Banham, "Design by Choice," in *Design by Choice: Ideas in Architecture,* ed. Penny Sparke (New York: Rizzoli, 1981), 103; Pamela M. Lee, "Aesthetic Strategist: Albert Wohlstetter, the Cold War, and a Theory of Mid-Century Modernism," *October* 138 (Fall 2011): 15–36.

36. Mark Jarzombek, "Good-Life Modernism and Beyond: The American House in the 1950s and 1960s. A Commentary," *Cornell School of Architecture* 4 (Fall 1990): 78.

37. Gay McDonald, "Selling the American Dream: MoMA, Industrial Design and Post-War France," *Journal of Design History* 17, no. 4 (2004): 399; Terrence Riley and Edward Eigen, "Between the Museum and the Marketplace: Selling Good Design," in *The Museum of Modern Art at Mid-Century: At Home and Abroad,* ed. John Elderfield, Studies in Modern Art 4 (New York: Museum of Modern Art, 1995), 150–79.

38. Edgar Kaufmann Jr., *What Is Modern Design?* (New York: Simon and Schuster, 1950), 8.

39. Greg Castillo, *Cold War on the Home Front: The Soft Power of Midcentury Design* (Minneapolis: University of Minnesota Press, 2010), xi.

40. Sara Ahmed, *The Promise of Happiness* (Durham, N.C.: Duke University Press, 2010), 24, 32.

41. Sara Ahmed, "Happy Objects," in *The Affect Theory Reader,* ed. Melissa Gregg and Gregory J. Seigworth (Durham, N.C.: Duke University Press, 2010), 35.

42. Ahmed, *The Promise of Happiness,* 33.

43. On postwar, systems-based organicism, see Martin, *The Organizational Complex,* and John Harwood, *The Interface: IBM and the Transformation of Corporate Design, 1946–1976* (Minneapolis: University of Minnesota Press, 2011). Hereafter cited parenthetically as *TI.*

44. Douglas Mao, *Solid Objects: Modernism and the Test of Production* (Princeton, N.J.: Princeton University Press, 1998).

45. Theodor Adorno, "Culture and Administration," in *The Culture Industry Reconsidered,* ed. J. M. Bernstein (London: Routledge, 2001), 107.

46. C. Wright Mills, "Man in the Middle: The Designer," in *Politics, Power, and People: The Collected Essays of C. Wright Mills,* ed. Irving Louis Horowitz (New York: Oxford University Press, 1963). Hereafter cited parenthetically as "MM."

47. Part II, box 190, folder: "*Discovery* television program (1953)," Charles and Ray Eames Papers, Manuscript Division, Library of Congress, Washington, D.C. Hereafter cited as EP.

48. John Harwood, "Imagining the Computer: Eliot Noyes, the Eames and the IBM Pavilion," in *Cold War Modern: Design 1945–1970,* ed. David Crowley and Jane Pavitt (London: V & A Publishing, 2008). Harwood, *The Interface,* 193.

49. Decherney, *Hollywood and the Culture Elite,* 146.

50. Decherney, 146.

51. Part II, box 189, folder: "Brochure and Printed Announcement," EP.

52. Part II, box 189, folder: "Brochure and Printed Announcement," EP.

53. Mark Greif, *The Age of the Crisis of Man: Thought and Fiction in America, 1933–1973* (Princeton, N.J.: Princeton University Press, 2015), 4.

54. Greif, 11.

55. Part II, box 173, folder: "*Omnibus* television series," EP.

56. Banham, "Design by Choice," 103.

57. Banham, 101.

58. Banham, 97.

59. David Riesman, "Abundance for What?," in *Abundance for What? and Other Essays* (New York: Doubleday, 1964), 305, 304.

60. Riesman, 307, 308.

61. Hannah Arendt, *The Human Condition,* 2nd ed. (Chicago: University of Chicago Press, 1958), 4. Hereafter cited parenthetically as *HC.*

62. Riesman, "Leisure and Work in Postindustrial Society," in *Abundance for What?,* 166.

63. Riesman, 168–69.

64. Riesman, 171, 173.

65. Riesman, "Abundance for What?," 305. Education was also central to Machlup's definition of "knowledge work," and he devoted a lengthy chapter to it ("the largest of the knowledge industries") in his influential parsing of the period's "increasing degree of division of labor between knowledge production and physical production." See Fritz Machlup, *The Production and Distribution of Knowledge in the United States* (Princeton, N.J.: Princeton University Press, 1962), 6.

66. See Cooper and Marx, *Media U,* especially chapter 3.

67. On postwar creativity research, see Jamie Cohen-Cole, *The Open Mind: Cold War Politics and the Sciences of Human Nature* (Chicago: University of Chicago Press, 2014); Amy F. Ogata, *Designing the Creative Child: Playthings and Places in Midcentury America* (Minneapolis: University of Minnesota Press, 2013); Pierluigi Serraino, *The Creative Architect: Inside the Great Midcentury Personality Study* (New York: Monacelli Press, 2016).

68. Part II, box 189, folder: "Rough Sketch for a Sample Lesson for a Hypothetical Course, Correspondence, 1952–53," EP.

69. Howard Mumford Jones, *The Pursuit of Happiness* (Cambridge, Mass.: Harvard University Press, 1953), 146. Hereafter cited parenthetically as *PH.* I'm indebted to Mary Esteve's excellent work on happiness in midcentury literature for alerting me to Jones's work. See, for example, Mary Esteve, "Postwar Pastoral: The Art of Happiness in Philip Roth," in *American Literature's Aesthetic Dimensions,* ed. Cindy Weinstein and Christopher Looby (New York: Columbia University Press, 2012), 328–48.

70. Steve Joshua Heims, *The Cybernetics Group* (Cambridge, Mass.: MIT Press, 1991), 164.

71. Rappleye, quoted in Heims, 169.

72. Rappleye, quoted in Heims, 161.

73. Horkheimer, quoted in Heims, 172.

74. Mead, "A Meta-Conference: Eastborne, 1956," *ETC: A Review of General Semantics* 15, no. 2 (Winter 1957): 151.

75. Charles Eames, "Design, Designer, Industry," in *An Eames Anthology,* ed. Daniel Ostroff (New Haven, Conn.: Yale University Press, 2015), 97. Hereafter cited parenthetically as "DD."

76. See Eames's related speech from later in 1951, "The Relation of Artist to Industry," in Ostroff, *Eames Anthology,* 96.

77. Daniel Bell, "Notes on the Post-Industrial Society (1)," *Public Interest,* Winter 1967, 27.

78. Bell, 25.

79. Nils Gilman, *Mandarins of the Future: Modernization Theory in Cold War America* (Baltimore: Johns Hopkins University Press, 2003), 9.

80. Gilman, 3, 7.

81. Gilman, 17.

82. Pheng Cheah, "World against Globe: Toward a Normative Concept of World Literature," *New Literary History* 45, no. 3 (Summer 2014): 303–29.

83. See Paul N. Edwards, *The Closed World: Computers and the Politics of Discourse in Cold War America* (Cambridge, Mass.: MIT Press, 1996). My analysis is indebted to the groundbreaking work of Beatriz Colomina and John Harwood. See especially Harwood's *The Interface,* 161–215, and Colomina's "Enclosed by Images: The Eameses' Multimedia Architecture," *Grey Room* 2 (Winter 2001): 5–29.

84. Theodore Roszak, *The Making of a Counter-Culture: Reflections on the Technocratic Society and Its Youthful Opposition* (Berkeley: University of California Press, 1968), 10.

85. Ulrich Beck, *Risk Society: Towards a New Modernity* (London: Sage, 1992), 96.

86. Beck, 19–20.

87. Nelson, interview with Studs Terkel, "Oral Histories," Herman Miller Corporate Archives, Zeeland, Michigan.

88. J. R. McNeill and Peter Engelke, *The Great Acceleration: An Environmental History of the Anthropocene since 1945* (Cambridge, Mass.: Belknap Press of Harvard University Press, 2014).

89. Lauren Berlant, *Cruel Optimism* (Durham, N.C.: Duke University Press, 2011), 2.

90. Berlant, 15.

91. Berlant, 11.

92. Jodi Dean, *Democracy and Other Neoliberal Fantasies: Communicative Capitalism and Left Politics* (Durham, N.C.: Duke University Press, 2009), 23.

93. Dean, 23.

94. Jonathan Crary, *24/7: Late Capitalism and the Ends of Sleep* (London: Verso, 2013), 76.

95. Crary, 70.

96. Crary, 67, 68.

1. Happy Furniture

1. On postwar material culture's movement between wartime violence and domestic ease, see especially Colomina, *Domesticity at War.*

2. Larry Busbea, "Metadesign: Object and Environment in France, c. 1970," *Design Issues* 25, no. 4 (Autumn 2009): 103; Jean Baudrillard, *The System of Objects,* trans. James Benedict (London: Verso, 1996).

3. On the Eameses' turn from objects to "situations," see Ralph Caplan, *Connections: The Work of Charles and Ray Eames* (Los Angeles: UCLA Art Council/Frederick S. Wright Art Gallery, 1977), 32; on the network of the Eameses' design process, see Harwood, *The Interface,* 219–20.

4. Acland and Wasson, *Useful Cinema.*

5. *Organic Design in Home Furnishings* (New York: Museum of Modern Art, 1941).

6. Walter Benjamin, "The Work of Art in the Age of Its Technological Reproducibility: The Second Version," in *Walter Benjamin: Selected Writings,* vol. 3, *1935–1938,* ed. Michael W. Jennings, Howard Eiland, and Gary Smith; trans. Rodney Livingston et al. (Cambridge, Mass.: Harvard University Press, 2002), 108.

7. Part I: box 282, folder 4: "Ray Eames, Notes, Miscellaneous, ca. 1930–39," EP.

8. Part I: box 282, folder 4: "Ray Eames, Notes, Miscellaneous, ca. 1930–39," EP.

9. The 1941 annual report notes that the academy has had a series of small exhibitions from MoMA, as well as a program of films from the museum "every other Monday night." Cranbrook Foundation RG 1: Office Records, box 18, folder 4, Cranbrook Archives, Bloomfield Hills, Michigan.

10. The same issue of the school's *Academy News* that announces the arrival of Charles Eames describes "Academy Film": "As it shows the processes involved in the production of paintings, sculpture, ceramics, etc., the film is quite educational, and of interest to most groups." Cranbrook Academy of Art Publications, *Academy News,* May 1939. Cranbrook Foundation RG 1: Office Records, box 27, folder 15, Cranbrook Archives. The foundation's annual report from 1940 notes that revisions have been made to the academy film, which "has been shown in many cities from coast to coast and is a potent force for publicity." Cranbrook Foundation RG 1: Office Records, box 18, folder 4, Cranbrook Archives. The 1941 *Academy News* that announces Eames and Saarinen's MoMA win also notes that the Eames-directed "new Academy movie will be ready for circulation in the fall." Cranbrook Foundation RG 1: Office Records, box 27, folder 17, Cranbrook Archives.

11. Tamblyn and Tamblyn's statement for Cranbrook Foundation trustees describes their plan to "proceed in such matters as booklets, motion pictures, and receptions in a way that will present the schools continuously to the public as part of one great cultural center," as "not only good schools, but good schools *plus.*" Cranbrook Foundation RG 1: Office Records, box 41, folder 4, Cranbrook Archives.

12. Nelson, "Notes on the New Subscape," in *Problems of Design,* 194–95. Hereafter cited parenthetically as "NS."

13. Nelson, "The Enlargement of Vision," in *Problems of Design,* 65. Hereafter cited parenthetically as "EV."

14. School of Design, "Course and program descriptions, 1938–1944," Institute of Design collection, box 3, folder 64, Special Collections and University Archives, Richard J. Daley Library, University of Illinois at Chicago.

15. Barbara Goldstein, introduction to *Arts & Architecture: The Entenza Years,* ed. Barbara Goldstein (Cambridge, Mass.: MIT Press, 1990), 8.

16. Eric Smoodin, introduction to *Hollywood Quarterly: Film Culture in Postwar America, 1945–1957* (Berkeley: University of California Press, 2002), xiv.

17. *Arts & Architecture,* September 1943, 16. Alvin Lustig designed the first cover of the reboot. Ray Eames designed ten covers that year, and another eight in 1944.

18. Eliot Noyes, "Charles Eames," *Arts & Architecture,* September 1946, 26.

19. "The Germans See Their Concentration Camps," *Arts & Architecture,* September 1946, 14. Michael Leja, *Reframing Abstract Expressionism: Subjectivity and Painting in the 1940s* (New Haven, Conn.: Yale University Press, 1993).

20. John Harwood, "R and D: The Eames Office at Work," in *Explorations in Architecture: Teaching, Design, Research,* ed. Reto Geiser (Basel: Birkhäuser Architecture, 2008), 200.

21. See Peter Galison and Caroline Jones, "Factory, Laboratory, Studio: Dispersing Sites of Production," in *The Architecture of Science,* ed. Peter Galison and Emily Thompson (Cambridge, Mass.: MIT Press, 1999), 497–540.

22. Catherine Ince, "Something about the World of Charles and Ray Eames," in Ince, *The World of Charles and Ray Eames,* 13.

23. For a more detailed discussion of 901, see my "Postindustrial Studio Lifestyle: The Eameses in the Environment of 901," in *In the Studio: Visual Creation and its Material Environments,* ed. Brian R. Jacobson (Oakland: University of California Press, forthcoming).

24. Quoted in Jeffrey Meikle, *American Plastic: A Cultural History* (New Brunswick, N.J.: Rutgers University Press, 1995), 202–3.

25. John Neuhart and Marilyn Neuhart, with Ray Eames, *Eames Design: The Work of the Office of Charles and Ray Eames* (New York: Harry N. Abrams, 1989), 142.

26. Part II, box 7, folder: "Ford, Henry," EP.

27. Beatriz Colomina, "Introduction," in *Cold War Hothouses: Inventing Postwar Culture, from Cockpit to Playboy,* ed. Beatriz Colomina, Annmarie Brennan, and Jeannie Kim (New York: Princeton Architectural Press, 2004), 19.

28. Baudrillard, *The System of Objects,* 29.

29. So concludes Charles's letter to Ford Jr.

30. Lee Grieveson, "The Work of Film in the Age of Fordist Mechanization," *Cinema Journal* 51, no. 3 (Spring 2012): 37.

31. Grieveson, "The Work of Film."

32. Part II, box 190, folder: "*Discovery* Television Program" (1953), EP.

33. Part II, box 190, folder: "*Discovery.*"

34. Lynn Spigel, *TV by Design: Modern Art and the Rise of Network Television* (Chicago: University of Chicago Press, 2008), 164.

35. Part II, box 4, folder: "CBS Television Network, 1953–54," EP.

36. Part II, box 190, folder: "San Francisco Museum of Art, San Francisco, Calif., *Discovery* television program, 1953–54," EP.

37. Part II, box 173, folder: "*Omnibus,* CBS television series, notes and storyline for a program on the Eameses' work, 1955–56," EP.

38. Spigel, *TV by Design,* 4.

39. Part II, box 173, folder: "*Omnibus,*" EP.

40. Part II, box 173, folder: "*Omnibus,*" EP.

41. Part II, box 173, folder: "*Omnibus,*" EP.

42. Part II, box 173, folder: "*Omnibus,*" EP.

43. These works include *S-73/Sofa Compact* (1954), *Eames Lounge Chair* (1956), *Kaleidoscope Jazz Chair* (1960), *ECS/Eames Contract Storage* (1961), *Soft Pad* (1970), and *The Fiberglass Chairs: Something of How They Got the Way They Are* (1970), as well as two films about Herman Miller furniture displayed at the World's Fairs in Brussels and Seattle: *HMI at the Brussels Fair* (1958) and *Before the Fair* (1962). These last two were made not to explain the furniture to dealers and clients but as gifts to Herman Miller.

44. Ralph Caplan, "The Messages of Industry on the Screen," *Business Screen,* April 1960, 48–64.

45. Acland and Wasson, *Useful Cinema,* 4.

46. John Durham Peters, *The Marvelous Clouds: Toward an Elemental Philosophy of Media* (Chicago: University of Chicago Press, 2015); Alexander Klose, *The Container Principle: How a Box Changes the Way We Think,* trans. Charles Marcrum II (Cambridge, Mass.: MIT Press, 2015).

47. *The Eames Lounge Chair: An Icon of Modern Design* (London: Merrell, 2006), 154. On Wilder's Mies chair, see Pat Kirkham, *Charles and Ray Eames: Designers of the Twentieth Century* (Cambridge, Mass.: MIT Press, 1995).

48. "A Designer's Home of His Own: Charles Eames Builds a House of Steel and Glass," *Life,* September 11, 1950, 342.

49. See Lynn Spigel, *Make Room for TV: Television and the Family Ideal in Postwar America* (Chicago: University of Chicago Press, 1992).

50. Neuhart and Neuhart, *Eames Design,* 208.

51. The Eameses' film and media practice transpired within what Jesse LeCavalier calls "the logistics revolution," starting after World War II and "maturing in the 1970s," and enabling "coordination at new scales, speeds, and efficiencies with new attendant forms." The Eames chair, *S-73* suggests, is one such midcentury form. Jesse LeCavalier, *The Rule of Logistics: Walmart and the Architecture of Fulfillment* (Minneapolis: University of Minnesota Press, 2016), 54.

52. Reinhold Martin, *The Organizational Complex: Architecture, Media, Corporate Space* (Cambridge, Mass.: MIT Press, 2003).

53. Reinhold Martin, *The Organizational Complex,* 62.

54. Jonathan Crary, *Techniques of the Observer: On Vision and Modernity in the Nineteenth Century* (Cambridge, Mass.: MIT Press, 1992), 116.

55. Kirkham, *Charles and Ray Eames,* 338.

56. David E. James, *Allegories of Cinema: American Film in the Sixties* (Princeton, N.J.: Princeton University Press, 1989).

57. Peter Smithson, "Just a Few Chairs and a House: An Essay on the Eames Aesthetic," *Architectural Design* 36 (September 1966).

58. Smithson, 14.

59. Beatriz Colomina, "Reflections on the Eames House," in *The World of Charles and Ray Eames: A Legacy of Invention* (New York: Harry N. Abrams in association with the Library of Congress and the Vitra Design Museum, 1997), 134.

60. *Arts & Architecture: The Entenza Years,* ed. Barbara Goldstein (London: MIT Press, 1990), 35.

61. *Arts & Architecture,* 35.

62. *Arts & Architecture,* 46.

63. Eames and Saarinen, quoted in Kirkham, *Charles and Ray Eames,* 107.

64. Eames and Saarinen.

65. Eames and Saarinen.

66. Eames and Saarinen.

67. On the mediatic conditions of the Eames house, see Colomina, "Reflections on the Eames House."

68. Eames, quoted in Kirkham, *Charles and Ray Eames,* 186.

69. Caplan, *Connections,* 63; Kirkham, *Charles and Ray Eames,* 186.

70. Victoria de Grazia, *Irresistible Empire: America's Advance Through Twentieth-Century Europe* (Cambridge, Mass.: Belknap Harvard, 2006).

71. Fred Turner, *The Democratic Surround: Multimedia & American Liberalism from World War II to the Psychedelic Sixties (Chicago: University of Chicago Press, 2013).*

72. Fred Turner, "*The Family of Man* and the Politics of Attention in Cold War America," *Public Culture* 24, no. 1 (2012), 67.

73. Neuhart and Neuhart, *Eames Design,* 199.

74. Likewise, on *Omnibus* in 1956, Charles explained that the couple approached the design of their home in the same way as they approached the design of the chair; thus, "before talking about the design of the chair, it might be good to show you a little bit more of the house."

75. Part II, box 215, folder: "1953–1954 University of California, Berkeley, Calif. lectures," EP.

76. The book would appear on the list of recommended readings for the International Design Conference in Aspen in 1959.

77. Jurgen Ruesch and Weldon Kees, *Nonverbal Communication: Notes on the Visual Perception of Human Relations* (Berkeley: University of California Press, 1956), 135.

78. "People," Ruesch and Kees note, "have their preferred ways of storing: through piling, shelving, dumping, aligning, or through exposing or hiding." *Nonverbal Communication,* 135.

79. Fred Turner, "*The Family of Man* and the Politics of Attention in Cold War America," *Public Culture* 24, no. 1 (2012): 58.

80. Venturi, quoted in Kirkham, *Charles and Ray Eames,* 167.

81. Part II, box 190, folder: "*Discovery* Television Program" (1953), EP.

82. See Baudrillard on the "pseudo-functionality" of the gizmo in his chapter "The Metafunctional and Dysfunctional System," *The System of Objects,* 114.

83. Paul Schrader, "Poetry of Ideas: The Films of Charles Eames," *Film Quarterly* 23, no. 3 (Spring 1970): 2–16.

84. Lawrence Alloway, "Eames' World," *Architectural Association Journal* 72 (1956): 54.

85. Tamar Zinguer, "Toy," in Colomina, Brennan, and Kim, *Cold War Hothouses,* 144. On the Eameses' "toy" films as a subset of their interest in "object films," see Schrader, "Poetry of Ideas," and Kirkham, *Charles and Ray Eames,* 333–44.

86. Zinguer, "Toy," 146.

87. Ogata, *Designing the Creative Child.*

88. "A Twirling Toy Run by Sun: Gadget Is Forerunner of Future Solar-Power Machine," *Life,* March 24, 1958, 22–23.

89. Hannah Arendt, *The Human Condition,* 2nd ed. (Chicago: University of Chicago Press, 1998), 1. Hereafter cited parenthetically as *HC*.

90. Daniel A. Barber, "The World Solar Energy Project, c. 1954," *Grey Room* 51 (Spring 2013): 66.

91. Andrew Uroksie, *Between the Black Box and the White Cube: Expanded Cinema and Postwar Art* (Chicago: University of Chicago Press, 2014), 101.

92. László Moholy-Nagy, *Vision in Motion* (Chicago: Paul Theobald, 1969), 241.

93. Hal Foster, "The Bauhaus Idea in America," *Albers and Moholy-Nagy: From the Bauhaus to the New World,* ed. Achim Borchardt-Hume (New Haven, Conn.: Yale University Press, 2006), 92–102; see also Benjamin H. D. Buchloh's discussion of Greenberg's two versions of his essay "The New Sculpture" (1948, 1958), in "Cold War Constructivism," in *Reconstructing Modernism: Art in New York, Paris, and Montreal, 1945–1964,* ed. Serge Guilbaut (Cambridge, Mass.: MIT Press, 1991), 103.

94. Larry Busbea, "Kineticism-Spectacle-Environment," *October* 144 (Spring 2013): 92–114.

95. Guy Habasque, "Notes on a New Trend: Multidimensional Animated Works," *Yale French Studies* 19/20 (1957): 35–44.

96. *CYSP 1* also was an early incarnation of Schöffer's ever more ambitious attempts to dynamize public space by integrating kinetic indeterminism into the urban environment.

See Larry Busbea, *Topologies: The Urban Utopia in France, 1960–1970* (Cambridge, Mass.: MIT Press, 2007), 54.

97. See Baudrillard, "Structures of Atmosphere," in *System of Objects,* 30–62.

98. Sianne Ngai, "Merely Interesting," *Critical Inquiry* 24 (Summer 2008): 786.

99. Joshua Shannon, *The Disappearance of Objects: New York Art and the Rise of the Postmodern City* (New Haven, Conn.: Yale University Press, 2009).

100. Caplan, *Connections,* 52.

101. John Chandler and Lucy R. Lippard, "The Dematerialization of Art," *Art International* 12, no. 2 (February 1968): 31–36; John Chandler and Lucy R. Lippard, "Visual Art and the Invisible World," *Art International* 11, no. 5 (1967): 28.

102. Chandler and Lippard, "Visual Art and the Invisible World," 28, 29.

103. Chandler and Lippard, 28.

104. Michael Fried, "Art and Objecthood," in *Art and Objecthood: Essays and Reviews* (Chicago: University of Chicago Press, 1998), 148–72. Ngai links the aesthetic object's capacity for recursive, systemic complexity to the minor aesthetic category of *the interesting* itself. For Ngai, the interesting—which came to dominate the art of the 1960s—is a specifically modern aesthetic response to "the experience of novelty and change in capitalist society." Ngai, "Merely Interesting," 786.

105. Smithson, "Just a Few Chairs and a House: An Essay on the Eames Aesthetic," in *Eames Celebration,* reprinted from *Architectural Design* 9 (1966) by Herman Miller, 15.

106. Liz Kotz, *Words to Be Looked At: Language in 1960s Art* (Cambridge, Mass.: MIT Press, 2007), 177.

107. Julie H. Reiss, *From Margin to Center: The Spaces of Installation Art* (Cambridge, Mass.: MIT Press, 1999).

108. Alex Potts, "Tactility: The Interrogation of Medium in the Art of the '60s," *Art History* 27, no. 2 (April 2004): 299.

109. Benjamin H. D. Buchloh, "Conceptual Art, 1962–1969: From the Aesthetic of Administration to Critique of Institutions," *October* 55 (Winter 1990): 107.

110. Kotz, *Words to Be Looked At,* 184.

111. See Greenberg, "The Presentness of Sculpture" (1967), reprinted in *Design and Art,* ed. Alex Coles (Cambridge, Mass.: MIT Press, 2007), 26, 28.

112. Banham, "Design by Choice," 101.

113. Banham, 101.

114. Banham, 103, 101.

115. Alison Smithson, "And Now Dharmas Are Dying Out in Japan," in "Eames Celebration," ed. Peter Smithson and Alison Smithson, *Architectural Design* 37 (September 1966), 17.

116. Hamilton's *Interior II* bears out Banham's desire to advance what Hal Foster calls "imaging of technology as the principal criterion for design—for design of the second machine age or the first pop age as well." Hal Foster, "Notes on the First Pop Age," in *Richard Hamilton,* ed. Hal Foster (Cambridge, Mass.: MIT Press, 2010), 46.

117. Foster, "Notes on the First Pop Age," 91. The Eames chairs are consistent points of reference in Hamilton's essays on design, as are Nelson's own writings. See especially "Persuading Image," "Artificial Obsolescence," and "Popular Culture and Personal Responsibility." Hamilton also takes up the Eameses' and Nelson's multiscreen experiments in his striking lecture on widescreen technologies of the midcentury, "Glorious Technicolor, Breathtaking Cinemascope and Stereophonic Sound." The essays are anthologized in Richard Hamilton, *Collected Words, 1953–1982* (London: Thames and Hudson, 1982).

118. William R. Kaizen, "Richard Hamilton's Tabular Image," *October* 94 (Autumn 2000): 118.

119. Neuhart and Neuhart, *Eames Design,* 223.

120. Hamilton, quoted in Foster, "Notes on the First Pop Age," 59.

2. The Scale Is the World

1. Saloni Mathur, "Charles and Ray Eames in India," *Art Journal,* May 2011, 34–53.

2. Part II, box 189, folder: "Rough Sketch for a Sample Lesson for a Hypothetical Course, Brochure and printed announcement," EP.

3. See Halpern on designers' reshaping of perception "as the capacity to consume bandwidth," in *Beautiful Data.*

4. For excellent recent work on the history of modern design education, see Zeynep Çelik Alexander, "The Core That Wasn't," *Harvard Design Magazine* 35 (2012): 84–89; "Jugendstil Visions: Occultism, Gender, and Modern Design Pedagogy," *Journal of Design History* 22, no. 3 (2009): 203–26; and *Kinaesthetic Knowing: Aesthetics, Epistemology, Modern Design* (Chicago: University of Chicago Press, 2017). In film studies, see Acland and Wasson's *Useful Cinema;* Lee Grieveson and Haidee Wasson, eds., *Inventing Film Studies* (Durham, N.C.: Duke University Press, 2008); Dana Polan, *Scenes of Instruction: The Beginnings of the U.S. Study of Film* (Berkeley: University of California Press, 2007); and *Learning with the Lights Off: Educational Film in the U.S.,* ed. Devin Orgeron, Marsha Orgeron, and Dan Streible (New York: Oxford University Press, 2012). On the university as a project to "manage populations by managing media," see Mark Garrett Cooper and John Marx's "Crisis, Crisis, Crisis! Big Media and the Humanities Workforce," *differences* 24, no. 3 (2013): 129, and *Media U.* My thanks to Cooper and Marx for providing me with an advance copy of this book. On the university as a technical apparatus, see Martin, "The Dialectic of the University," and Kittler, "Universities."

5. See Martin, *The Organizational Complex,* and Halpern, *Beautiful Data.*

6. Charles Olsen, quoted in Mary Emma Harris, *The Arts at Black Mountain College* (Cambridge, Mass.: MIT Press, 1987).

7. Part II, box 3, folder: "Black Mountain College, Black Mountain, N.C., 1952," EP.

8. I borrow this double-pronged sense of "world" from Eric Hayot, *On Literary Worlds* (New York: Oxford University Press, 2012), 26.

9. Gilman, *Mandarins of the Future.*

10. Gilman, 7.

11. IBM press release, cited in Ben Highmore, "Machinic Magic: IBM at the 1964–1965 New York World's Fair," *New Formations* 51 (2004): 134.

12. Cited in Highmore, 134.

13. Andrew Uroskie, *Between the Black Box and the White Cube: Expanded Cinema and Postwar Art* (Chicago: University of Chicago Press, 2014), 19–26.

14. Uroskie, 26.

15. Uroskie, 22, 24.

16. Liz Kotz, "Disciplining Expanded Cinema," in *X-Screen: Film Installations and Actions in the 1960s and 1970s* (Cologne, Germany: Walter König, 2004), 44–57; Highmore, "Machinic Magic"; Branden W. Joseph, "'My Mind Split Open': Andy Warhol's Exploding Plastic Inevitable," *Grey Room* 8 (Summer 2002): 80–107.

17. Joseph, "'My Mind Split Open,'" 93–94.

18. See, respectively, Kotz, "Disciplining Expanded Cinema," 51; Highmore, "Machinic Magic"; and Joseph, "'My Mind Split Open.'"

19. D. N. Rodowick, *The Crisis of Political Modernism: Criticism and Ideology in Contemporary Film Theory* (Berkeley: University of California Press, 1994).

20. Laura Frost, *The Problem with Pleasure: Modernism and Its Discontents* (New York: Columbia University Press, 2013).

21. On a similar challenge to the expressionist rhetoric of spontaneity and immediacy in vogue at Black Mountain, see Eva Díaz's account of the experimental processes of Fuller, John Cage, and Josef Albers, *The Experimenters: Chance and Design at Black Mountain College* (Chicago: University of Chicago Press, 2015).

22. Dodd had also considered bringing in Henry Francis Taylor of the Metropolitan, Buckminster Fuller, and visionary architect Frederick Kiesler, but he decided to call Nelson first.

23. Nelson, "Art-X," *Problems of Design*, 16.

24. Nelson, "High Time to Experiment," *Problems of Design*, 81. Hereafter cited parenthetically as "HT."

25. Nelson, "Art-X," 16.

26. Nelson, 16.

27. Eames, for his part, always referred to the performance as "A Rough Sketch for a Sample Lesson for a Hypothetical Course" (or "Sample Lesson," for short), which reflected his lifelong investment in the provisionality of models, and anticipated the title of the first version of his best-known film *Powers of Ten*: "A Rough Sketch for a Proposed Film Dealing with the Powers of Ten and the Size of the Universe."

28. See Jamie Cohen-Cole, *The Open Mind: Cold War Politics and the Sciences of Human Nature* (Chicago: University of Chicago Press, 2014).

29. Harpham, quoted in Cooper and Marx, "Crisis, Crisis, Crisis," 138.

30. Red Book, quoted in Cooper and Marx, 38, 54. On the Red Book's approach to new instructional media, see Cooper and Marx, *Media U*, 107–20.

31. Cohen-Cole, *Open Mind*, 22.

32. Cohen-Cole, 26; Red Book, quoted in Cohen-Cole, *Open Mind*, 25–26.

33. Cohen-Cole, 33.

34. Cohen-Cole, 33, 34.

35. Red Book, 259, 266, quoted in Cooper and Marx, "Crisis, Crisis, Crisis," 139.

36. Nelson, "The Enlargement of Vision," in *Problems of Design*, 60. Hereafter cited parenthetically as "EV."

37. For a superb discussion of Nelson's often despairing design vision, see John Harwood, "The Wound Man and the 'End of Architecture,'" *Grey Room* 31 (Spring 2008): 90–115.

38. Nelson, "The Designer in the Modern World," *Problems of Design*, 75. Hereafter cited parenthetically as "DM."

39. Vallye, "Design and the Politics of Knowledge in America, 1937–1967," 262.

40. Vallye, 261. As a category of labor, "knowledge worker," whose elusive definition would preoccupy sociologists and management theorists for decades, was simultaneously coined by both Peter Drucker and Fritz Machlup in 1962. See Alan Liu, *The Laws of Cool: Knowledge Work and the Culture of Information* (Chicago: University of Chicago Press, 2004).

41. Part II, box 215, file: "The Relation of the Artist to Industry," EP.

42. Mark D. Bowles, "The Organization Man Goes to College: AT&T's Experiments in Humanistic Education, 1953–1960," *Historian* 61, no. 1 (September 1998): 15–32.

43. Part II, box 5, file: "The Container Corporation of America," EP.

44. Morse Peckham, *Humanistic Education for Business Executives: An Essay in General Education* (Philadelphia: University of Pennsylvania Press, 1960), 29, 16. Beyond the Aspen and the AT&T Institutes, liberal arts programs tailored to business in the 1950s included the New England Experiment at Clark University, the University of Akron's Liberal Education Program for Executives, the Institute for Executive Leadership at Southwestern University, and the University of Denver's Program in Liberal Education for Business Leadership. For an overview of the most influential of these programs, see Peter E. Siegle, *New Directions in Liberal Education for Executives* (Syracuse, N.Y.: Center for the Study of Liberal Education for Adults, 1958). On the AT&T experiment and curriculum, see the fascinating account by Bell vice president of personnel John Markel II, "Widening the Scope of Management Development: The Institute of Humanistic Studies for Executives," in *Strengthening Management for the New Technology: Organization, Automation, Management Development*, General Management Series no. 178 (New York, 1955), 15–31. See also Mark Wollaeger's "Reframing Modernism: The Corporation, the University, and the Cold War," *affirmations: of the modern* 3, no. 1 (Autumn 2015): 49–77; and Mark D. Bowles, "The Organization Man Goes to College: AT&T's Experiment in Humanistic Education, 1953–1960," *Historian* 61, no. 1 (1998): 15–31.

45. Peckham, *Humanistic Education for Business Executives*, 17, 18.

46. Part II, box 216, file: "Printed Matter Accompanying the Fragments, 1950–57," EP.

47. Charles Eames, "Language of Vision: The Nuts and Bolts," *Bulletin of the American Academy of Arts and Sciences* 28, no. 1 (October 1974): 14.

48. Eames, 14.

49. Vallye, "Design and the Politics of Knowledge in America," 251.

50. Peter Galison, "The Americanization of Unity," *Dœdalus* 127, no. 1 (Winter 1998): 45–71.

51. Martin, *The Organizational Complex*, 61.

52. György Kepes, introduction to "The Visual Arts Today," special issue, *Dœdalus* 89, no. 1 (Winter 1960): 7. Hereafter cited parenthetically as "VA."

53. Pepper Stetler, "'The New Visual Literature': László Moholy-Nagy's *Painting, Photography, Film*," *Grey Room* 32 (Summer 2008): 88–113.

54. See also Susan Sontag's "One Culture and the New Sensibility," in *Against Interpretation and Other Essays* (New York: Delta, 1966), 45. Hereafter cited parenthetically as "OC."

55. On the relationship between the aesthetics of UPA animation and midcentury designers like Eames and Kepes, see Bashara, *Cartoon Vision*.

56. Nelson, quoted in George Abercrombie, *George Nelson: The Design of Modern Design* (Cambridge, Mass.: MIT Press, 2000), 144.

57. Part II, box 189, folder: "Brochure and Printed Announcement," EP.

58. Peter Galison, "Ontology of the Enemy: Norbert Wiener and the Cybernetic Vision," *Critical Inquiry* 21, no. 1 (1994): 228–66.

59. On cybernetics as a Foucauldian *dispositif* (apparatus) allying "researchers and institutions across disciplinary, political, and national borders," see Bernard Dionysius Geoghegan, "From Information Theory to French Theory: Jakobson, Lévi-Strauss, and the Cybernetic Apparatus," *Critical Inquiry* 38, no. 1 (Autumn 2011): 98. On cybernetics' transdisciplinary aspirations, see Geof Bowker, "How to Be Universal: Some Cybernetic Strategies, 1943–70," *Social Studies of Science* 23 (February 1993): 107–27.

60. See Fred Turner, *From Cyberculture to Counterculture: Stewart Brand, the Whole Earth Network, and the Rise of Digital Utopianism* (Chicago: University of Chicago Press, 2006), 23–24.

61. Norbert Wiener, *The Human Use of Human Beings: Cybernetics and Society* (New York: Avon Books, 1967), 50, 49. Hereafter cited parenthetically as *HU.*

62. Nelson, *Problems of Design*, 6.

63. Nelson, 6.

64. For a careful elaboration of structural linguistics' encounter with cybernetics, see Geoghegan, "From Information Theory to French Theory."

65. Part II, box 215, EP. The citations from the lectures that follow come from a typed, unpaginated transcript of the lecture content. Over the course of two semesters, the Eameses screened their own films (*Parade, Blacktop, A Communications Primer, Chair Story, Wilder at Work*) and slideshows; Norman McLaren's *Fiddle-de-Dee* (1947) and *Hen Hop* (1942); UPA films like *The Four Poster* (1952), *Flat Hatting* (1944), *The Near-Sighted Mr. Magoo* (1950), *Magoo's Masterpiece* (1953), *Rooty Toot Toot* (1951), and *The Unicorn in the Garden* (1953); a French film on calligraphy called *La lettre*; a Jean Mitry film on the French National Railways; *Maya*, described in the transcript as an "archaeological film" by Giles Healey; portions from a film about Michelangelo called *The Titan*; *The Brotherhood of Man* (1946); *The Family Circus* (1951); *Madeline* (1950); *Christopher Crumpet* (1953); *Man on the Land* (for CBS); and what the transcripts call a "[György] Kepes film giving his introductory remarks before a speech." I have been unable to locate the title of this last film.

66. In his reply to the Eameses, Kaufmann described the proposal for the "scapes" as exemplary of the appeal of the Eames Office when it joins how it "produces things" and "sees things" to the larger "philosophy and insight" that "inheres in [their] products." Part II, box 14, folder: "Edgar Kaufmann, Jr.," EP.

67. The MIT experiment in the pedagogical appropriation of science fiction and Cold War speculation was called Arcturus IV, and conceptualized by John E. Arnold, associate professor of mechanical engineering. See Hartley E. Howe, "Space Men Make College Men Think," *Popular Science*, October 1952, 124–27, 266–68. John McHale discusses the project in "Marginalia" (1957), in *The Expendable Reader: Articles on Art, Architecture, Design, and Media (1951–79)*, ed. Alex Kitnick (New York: GSAPP Books, 2011), 140. Hereafter cited parenthetically as *ER.*

68. On Fuller's "autonomous dwelling unit" in the context of his Chicago-based pedagogy, see Tricia Van Eck, "Buckminster Fuller in Chicago: A Modern Individual Experiment," in *Chicago Makes Modern: How Creative Minds Changed Society*, ed. Mary Jane Jacob and Jacquelyn Baas (Chicago: University of Chicago Press, 2012), 11–47.

69. Vallye, "Design and the Politics of Knowledge in America," 262.

70. Harpham, quoted in Cooper and Marx, "Crisis, Crisis, Crisis," 138; the Harvard Red Book, quoted in Vallye, "Design and the Politics of Knowledge in America," 266.

71. Kepes, "The Education of Vision," unpublished manuscript, quoted in Vallye, "Design and the Politics of Knowledge in America," 266.

72. On Moholy-Nagy's and Kepes's "language of vision" see Martin, *The Organizational Complex*, 42–79; Turner, *The Democratic Surround*; and Charles Eames, "The Language of Vision: Nuts and Bolts," *Bulletin of the American Academy of Arts and Sciences* 28, no. 1 (October 1974): 13–25.

73. David Mellor, "The Pleasures and Sorrows of Modernity: Vision, Space, and the Social Body in Richard Hamilton," *Richard Hamilton*, 18.

74. IG member and architect Geoffrey Holroyd, for example, visited Charles and Ray Eames at their already famous Case Study home in Santa Monica in 1953, and would, like his colleagues Peter Smithson and Alison Smithson, pen tributes to the Eameses' achievement in a 1966 special issue of the British journal *Architectural Design,* which began publishing the writings of the IG in 1956.

75. Richard Hamilton, "Man, Machine, and Motion," *Collected Words,* 19.

76. Richard Hamilton, "Glorious Technicolor, Breathtaking Cinemascope and Stereophonic Sound," *Collected Words,* 112–31.

77. Alloway, quoted in Nigel Whiteley, *Reyner Banham: Historian of the Immediate Future* (Cambridge, Mass.: MIT Press, 2002), 113.

78. Lawrence Alloway, "Eames' World," *Architectural Association Journal* 72, no. 7–8 (1956): 54.

79. Alloway, 54.

80. Hamilton, quoted in Foster, "Notes on the First Pop Age," 59.

81. *The Independent Group: Postwar Britain and the Aesthetics of Plenty,* ed. David Robbins (Cambridge, Mass.: MIT Press, 1991), 135. Hereafter cited parenthetically as *IG.*

82. McHale, quoted in John-Paul Stonard, "Pop in the Age of Boom: Richard Hamilton's 'Just What Is It That Makes Today's Homes So Different, So Appealing?'" *Burlington Magazine* 149 (September 2007), 611.

83. Stonard, 611–12.

84. See John McHale, "The Expendable Ikon 1," in Kitnick, *The Expendable Reader,* 48.

85. On "imageability" as a crucial IG criterion of value, see Whiteley, *Reyner Banham,* 138–39; on the world's relationship to problems of aesthetic totality, see Hayot, *On Literary Worlds,* 15.

86. McHale called this "the multi-ordinal character of the pictorial structure in much ikon material—the ways in which enormous close-ups, serial, X-ray, micro- and macroscopical views are used, and the fragmentary, blurred, and out-of focus qualities which give ambivalence to the image" (*ER,* 63).

87. See especially McHale's essays "Buckminster Fuller" (1956) and "World Dwelling" (1967), in Kitnick, *The Expendable Reader,* 104–23, 143–70.

88. On the resurgence of interest in Fuller, see Anthony Vidler, "What Ever Happened to Ecology? John McHale and the Bucky Fuller Revival," *Architectural Design* 80, no. 6 (November–December 2010): 24–33; and the superb exhibition catalog for the Whitney Museum's 2008 Fuller retrospective, *Buckminster Fuller: Starting with the Universe,* ed. K. Michael Hays and Dana Miller (New Haven, Conn.: Yale University Press, 2009).

89. See Fred Turner, "R. Buckminster Fuller: A Technocrat for the Counterculture," in *New Views on R. Buckminster Fuller,* ed. Hsaio-Yun Chu and Roberto G. Trujillo (Stanford, Calif.: Stanford University Press, 2009), 146–59; and Felicity D. Scott, *Architecture or Techno-utopia: Politics after Modernism* (Cambridge, Mass.: MIT Press, 2007), especially 185–206.

90. See Peder Anker, "Buckminster Fuller as Captain of Spaceship Earth," in *From Bauhaus to Ecohouse: A History of Ecological Design* (Baton Rouge: Louisiana State University Press, 2010), 68–90; Jonathan Massey, "Buckminster Fuller's Reflexive Modernism," *Design and Culture* 4, no. 3 (2012): 325–44.

91. See Mark Wigley, *Buckminster Fuller Inc.: Architecture in the Age of Radio* (Zurich: Lars Müller Publishers, 2015).

92. Fuller, quoted in Mark Wigley, "Planetary Homeboy," *ANY: Architecture New York* 17 (1997): 16–23.

93. K. Michael Hays, "Fuller's Geological Engagement with Architecture," in *Buckminster Fuller: Starting with the Universe,* 9.

94. R. Buckminster Fuller, *Critical Path,* adjuvant Kiyoshi Kuromiya (New York: St. Martin's Press, 1981), 400.

95. On the problematic elimination of the political as a site of constitutive antagonism in Fuller's postsovereign thinking, see Felicity D. Scott, "Fluid Geographies: Politics and the Revolution by Design," in *New Views on R. Buckminster Fuller,* 161.

96. Alloway, "Eames' World," 54–55.

97. Wigley, "Planetary Homeboy," 20.

98. Wigley, 20.

99. Fuller, "Keynote Address at Vision '65," in *Utopia or Oblivion: The Prospects for Humanity* (New York: Bantam Books, 1969), 115.

100. Fuller, 117.

101. Uroskie, *Between the Black Box and the White Cube,* 9.

102. Uroskie, 10.

103. Gene Youngblood, *Expanded Cinema* (New York: Dutton, 1970), 42. Hereafter cited parenthetically as *EC.*

104. See, for example, artist and critic Jack Burnham's essays "System Aesthetics" and "Real-Time Systems," as well as his *Beyond Modern Sculpture: The Effects of Technology and Sculpture on the Art of This Century* (New York: Braziller, 1968); Jim Burns, *Arthopods: New Design Futures* (New York: Praeger, 1971); as well as the postminimalist and conceptual art practices on view at groundbreaking exhibitions such as the London ICA's *Cybernetic Serendipity* (1968), and MoMA's *The Machine as Seen at the End of the Mechanical Age* (1968) and *Information* (1970). On these tendencies, see Pamela M. Lee, *Chronophobia: On Time in the Art of the 1960s* (Cambridge, Mass.: MIT Press, 2006), and Edward R. Shanken, "Art in the Information Age: Technology and Conceptual Art," in *Conceptual Art: Theory, Myth, and Practice,* ed. Michael Corris (Cambridge: Cambridge University Press, 2003).

105. Youngblood draws liberally on McHale's work, including "Information Explosion–Knowledge Explosion" (1968), "Education for Real" (1968), "The Plastic Parthenon" (1967), and *The Future of the Future* (1969).

106. For an important step here, see Turner, *The Democratic Surround.*

3. Management Cinema

1.On the "great acceleration" as marking the second stage of the Anthropocene, beginning in 1945 with the explosion of global-scale human enterprise spawned by a new postwar regime of international institutions abetting capitalist production, see Will Steffen, Paul J. Crutzen, and John R. McNeill, "The Anthropocene: Are Humans Now Overwhelming the Great Forces of Nature?" *Ambio* 36, no. 8 (December 2007): 614–21.

2. The medium, of course, has a long history of being wedded to the instrumental work of industry, the optimization of industrial operations through training and education films, and the theory and practice of scientific management. JoAnne Yates, *Control through Communication: The Rise of System in American Management* (Baltimore: Johns Hopkins University Press, 1989). Media, and communications technologies in particular, are, as Vinzenz Hediger and Patrick Vondreau remind us, the technical a priori of modern organizations. See "Record, Rhetoric, Rationalization: Industrial Organization and Film," in *Films That Work: Industrial Film and the Productivity of Media*, ed. Vinzenz Hediger and Patrick Vonderau (Amsterdam: Amsterdam University Press, 2009).

3. See Felicity Scott's groundbreaking discussion of IDCA 1970 in *Architecture or Techno-Utopia: Politics after Modernism* (Cambridge, Mass.: MIT Press, 2007), 234; and Alice Twemlow, "'I Can't Talk to You If You Say That': An Ideological Collision at the International Design Conference in Aspen, 1970," *Design and Culture* 1, no. 1 (2009): 23–50. The speaker was Walter Wilding; box 11, folder 579, International Design Conference in Aspen Papers, Special Collections and University Archives Department, Richard J. Daley Library, University of Illinois at Chicago.

4. At IDCA 1970, this critique of the mise-en-scène of the conference within a theory of various scenes in which "culture is imprinted" was most forceful in the talk titled "The Persistence of Form," by Sim Van Der Ryn, then an assistant professor at UC Berkeley. By describing "settings" as disciplinary forms regulating bodily comportment and speech in keeping with the ideological work of the institutions housing them, Van Der Ryn implicated his own "setting" as IDCA conference speaker, playing an outmoded, hierarchal role in which "I talk and you listen," and positioned IDCA technique at the center of a series of obsolete social forms—meaningless rituals. Box 11, folder 573, International Design Conference in Aspen Papers, Special Collections and University Archives Department, Richard J. Daley Library, University of Illinois at Chicago.

5. The term was coined by William H. Whyte Jr. in his essay "Groupthink" in *Fortune* magazine in 1952, which originally appeared as part of the publication's "communication" series.

6. On the history of the modernism and the avant-garde in Aspen, see James Sloan Allen, *The Romance of Commerce and Culture: Capitalism, Modernism, and the Chicago-Aspen Crusade for Cultural Reform* (Chicago: University of Chicago Press, 1983); Dean Sobel, *One Hour Ahead: The Avant-Garde in Aspen, 1945–2004* (Aspen: Aspen Art Museum, 2004); and Gwen Allen, "The Magazine as Medium: *Aspen*, 1965–71," in *Artists' Magazines: An Alternative Space for Art* (Cambridge, Mass.: MIT Press, 2011), 43–67.

7. Adorno, "Culture and Administration," 107.

8. Cooper and Marx, "Crisis, Crisis, Crisis," 129.

9. Peters, *Speaking into the Air*, 25.

10. Turner, *The Democratic Surround*, 163.

11. Peters, *Speaking into the Air*, 26.

12. Margaret Mead and Paul Byers, *The Small Conference: An Innovation in Communication* (Paris and The Hague: Mouton, 1968), v. Hereafter cited parenthetically as *SC*.

13. The Delos Symposia were the brainchild of Greek architect and urban planner Constantinos Doxiadis, and the first eight-day boat trip, in 1963, which included Mead, also provided the first meeting between two key theorists of the midcentury network, Buckminster Fuller and Marshall McLuhan. See Mark Wigley, "Network Fever," *Grey Room* 4 (Summer 2001): 82–122.

14. Margaret Mead, "A Meta-Conference: Eastbourne, 1956," *ETC: A Review of General Semantics* 15, no. 2 (Winter 1957): 151.

15. In "A Meta-Conference," Mead describes her fellow conferees as "veterans of conferences, of the heyday of rural committees generated by the New Deal, of the early days of UNESCO when 'feedback' became, not an engineer's phrase for cybernetic effects, but rather a word for certain good small group procedures" (148).

16. S. I. Hayakawa, "How to Attend a Conference," in *The Use and Misuse of Language* (Greenwich, Conn: Fawcett, 1962), 73.

17. For a helpful overview of the rise of the human relations school of management in organizational thought and practice, and its paradigmatic shift of attention from technical to social-psychological aspects of work, see Mauro F. Guillén, *Models of Management: Work, Authority, and Organization in a Comparative Perspective* (Chicago: University of Chicago Press, 1994), especially 30–90.

18. On Aspen's postwar development, see William Philpott, *Vacationland: Tourism and Environment in the Colorado High Country* (Seattle: University of Washington Press, 2013).

19. Sidney Hyman, *The Aspen Idea* (Norman: University of Oklahoma Press, 1975), 95.

20. Herbert Bayer, "Goethe and the Contemporary Artist," part of a panel from the festival titled "Goethe and Art Today," *College Art Journal* 11, no. 1 (Autumn 1951): 39.

21. Shaped in part by Adler's *How to Think about War and Peace* (1945) and Borgese's indictments of Italian fascism, Hutchins would in 1946 serve with Adler and Borgese on the Committee to Frame a World Constitution, and publish the *Preliminary Draft of a World Constitution* in 1948 in *Common Cause*, a journal (1947–51) dedicated to promoting and debating world government ideals.

22. Pheng Cheah, "World against Globe," 318.

23. Cheah, 319.

24. "Goethe and the Unity of Mankind: A Report on the Goethe Bicentennial Convocation in Aspen, Colorado," in *Common Cause: A Journal of One World* 3, no. 3 (October 1949): 113.

25. "Goethe and the Unity of Mankind," 130, 131.

26. "Goethe and the Unity of Mankind," 131.

27. C. Wright Mills, *The Power Elite* (New York: Oxford University Press, 1956), 380.

28. Walter Paepcke, "Notes for Speech, University of Colorado, November 1, 1951," box 104, folder 5, Walter Paepcke Papers, Special Collections Research Center, University of Chicago Library. Hereafter WPP.

29. Walter Paepcke, "Industry in the Arts," box 104, folder 5, WPP.

30. Paepcke, "Industry in the Arts."

31. In his April 16, 1953, correspondence with Francis W. Brush of the University of Denver, Paepcke wrote, "Don't you agree that the contemporary problems, important as they seem to us at the time, are more or less of a passing nature? . . . And in the last analysis, they all stem from unresolved age-old questions. The present disagreements and misunderstandings between Russia and its satellites and the U.S.A. and its NATO allies is substantially the same as the struggle between Athens and Sparta and their respective allies. . . . Should we not confine ourselves to universals rather than particulars?" Box 104, folder 12, WPP.

32. Allen, *The Romance of Commerce and Culture*, 103.

33. Martin, "His Master's Voice," 95.

34. Adler to Robert Craig, December 2 1957, box 105, folder 13,WPP; Martin, "His Master's Voice," 95.

35. "Happiness," in *The Great Ideas*, vol. 1, *A Syntopicon of Great Books of the Western World*, ed. Mortimer Adler and William Gorman (Chicago: Encyclopedia Britannica, 1952), 694.

36. Quoted in Allen, *The Romance of Commerce and Culture*, 269. Jacobson helped Paepcke bring good design to the CCA's factories, offices, advertising campaigns, and internal communications.

37. Banham, "Design by Choice," 101.

38. Drucker was a speaker at the 1952 Aspen Institute devoted to the topic "Human Freedom," in a section of the festival titled "Economic Freedom: Free vs. Planned Economy." His talk, "Can Prosperity Be Planned?," announced that the United States was a "warfare state" and likely would be for another twenty years, a state of emergency that led to restricted individual freedoms for the social whole—freedoms whose return must be demanded when the emergency has passed. "Aspen Festival and Conference, Week of July 28, 1952," box 104, folder 7, WPP.

39. Peter F. Drucker, *Landmarks of Tomorrow* (New York: Harper & Row, 1957), 4.

40. Drucker, 10.

41. Hyman, *The Aspen Idea,* 163.

42. See "The Aspen Institute Milestones," https://asssets.aspeninstitute.org.

43. Stan Phillips, "Film Makers Share Concepts at This Forum: Aspen's Second Film Conference," *Business Screen* 6, no. 25 (1964): 64.

44. Phillips, 64.

45. Arthur Knight, "Film: A Matter of Survival," *Journal of Popular Film,* Fall 1972, 327.

46. Polan, *Scenes of Instruction,* 367.

47. Polan, 354.

48. Adler, "Some Philosophical Questions about Design," part II, box 13, folder: "International Design Conference, Aspen, 1955–1956," EP.

49. Aspen Institute for Humanistic Studies brochure, "Executives Program 1957," box 104, folder 9, WPP.

50. Part II, box 12, folder: "International Design Conference, Aspen, 1951–1953," EP.

51. On the couple's conference program, Charles has jotted down the name and Park Avenue address of the conference's "guide to art film," one Otto Spaeth—businessman, art patron, and, like MoMA director René d'Harnoncourt (who led Friday's roundtable session "The Designer and the Social Climate"), a champion of modern art's role in mid-century cultural diplomacy efforts. "International Design Conference, Aspen, 1951–1953."

52. Part II, box 12, folder: "International Design Conference, Aspen, 1951–1953," EP.

53. In the early 1950s, Schawinsky's groundbreaking multimedia investigations into concepts of seeing and hearing through music, movement, and projected light were being compared to nonnarrative improvisational works such as John Cage's proto-"happening," *Theater Piece No. 1,* staged at Black Mountain in the summer of 1952. Harris, *The Arts at Black Mountain College,* 40.

54. Vallye, "Design and the Politics of Knowledge."

55. The graphic potential of new imaging technologies and their surpassing of human vision were explored in contemporaneous design trade journals read by IDCA conferees. See Herbert W. Franke's "Beyond Human Vision," *Graphis* 16, no. 81 (1960): 76–81; 86–87.

56. György Kepes, *The New Landscape in Art and Science* (Chicago: Paul Theobald, 1956), 206.

57. Part II, box 13, folder: "International Design Conference, Aspen, 1955–1956," EP. That year, for the first time, the Aspen conference would be preceded in May by a "prelude" in the form of a special symposium in Los Angeles sponsored by the Association of Graphic Designers. Titled "The Common Basis of the Arts," the symposium was promoted as an "introduction to a major event in the visual arts," namely, the Fifth International Aspen Conference, and featured graphic designer and filmmaker Saul Bass, architect and planner Victor Gruen, and painter Rico le Brun.

58. The director of the famous modernist film *A Page of Madness* had just won the Palme d'or at Cannes for *Gates of Hell.* Part II, box 13, folder: "International Design Conference, Aspen, 1955–1956," EP.

59. Part II, box 13, folder: "International Design Conference, Aspen, 1955–1956," EP.

60. On Cornberg's experiments in television as an educational medium, see John Harwood, "TV University, ca. 1964," *Art Papers Magazine*, January/February 2015, 24–37.

61. Part II, box 13, folder: "International Design Conference, Aspen, 1955–1956," EP. The memo was written by Will Burtin, program chairman, and R. Hunter Middleton.

62. John Houseman, "How Does a Movie Communicate?," in *The Aspen Papers: Twenty Years of Design Theory from the International Design Conference in Aspen*, ed. Reyner Banham (New York: Praeger, 1974), 23–30. Hereafter cited parenthetically as "MC."

63. A similar atomic metaphor for auteurist genius appears in André Bazin's famous 1957 essay, "On the politique des auteurs," in *Cahiers du Cinéma: The 1950s; Neo-Realism, Hollywood, the New Wave*, ed. Jim Hillier (Cambridge, Mass.: Harvard University Press, 1985), 248–59.

64. Film's and design's overlapping roles as ideological tools in propaganda for the West, and the "soft power" and cultural diplomacy efforts of the USIA, would be taken up directly at the 1963 IDCA, "Design and the American Image Abroad." See Greg Castillo, "Establishment Modernism and Its Discontents: IDCA in the 'Long Sixties,'" in *Design for the Corporate World, 1950–75*, ed. Wim De Wit (London: Lund Humphries in association with the Iris and B. Gerald Cantor Center for Visual Arts at Stanford University, 2017), 40–49.

65. "1955 5th IDCA Crossroads: What Are the Directions of the Arts?," box 101, folder 3, Will Burtin Papers, RIT Libraries: Graphic Design Archives, Rochester Institute of Technology. Hereafter WBP.

66. "1955 5th IDCA Crossroads: What Are the Directions of the Arts?," WBP.

67. A small, independent studio that worked across a variety of media, the Goldsholls' firm quickly established a reputation for its "designs in film" as advertising agencies began to create in-house filmmaking units in the 1960s, and would hire ID alums like Wayne Boyer and Lawrence Janiak to assist with their film projects.

68. Rhodes Patterson, "Millie and Morton Goldsholl: Designs for Film," *Print* 16, no. 7 (1962): 34. As Amy Beste has argued, the Goldsholls attempted to use the medium of film to "find a middle path between the social ideals of their Bauhaus training and the rapidly growing multinational corporate environment" in which they worked. See Beste, "All Roads Lead to Chicago," 247.

69. Millie Goldsholl, quoted in Rhodes Patterson, "Morton Goldsholl & Associates," *Communication Arts* 5 (July–August 1963): 46.

70. Patterson, 46.

71. Patterson, 46.

72. *Report: 9th International Design Conference in Aspen*, International Design Conference in Aspen papers, box 1, folder 5, Richard J. Daley Library Special Collections and Archives, University of Illinois at Chicago. Hereafter IDCAUIC.

73. Box 1, folder 2: "IDCA Executive Committee Meeting, January 18, 1958," IDCAUIC. All of Goldsholl's quoted remarks on the "Design and Obsolescence" conference come from these minutes.

74. Goldsholl and Burtin had championed plans for a 1958 "East-West conference," in which "Japan invites countries from the Eastern countries, such as India, Burma, Ceylon, and Indonesia, while IDCA handles Western participation." The plan was first pushed back to 1959 due to lack of advanced planning, then voted down by the IDCA executive committee. Goldsholl and Burtin were furious. In a memo to Burtin and the IDCA board, Goldsholl expressed his frustration at IDCA members' inability to understand that

"international means going beyond our borders," and speculated that the "idea of design flourishing in other countries makes some of our corporate members fearful of growing competition overseas." For Burtin, the board's cowardice betrayed the values of a nation that "purports to be a leader in international affairs," and reflected a disturbing "lack of reciprocity," whereby the U.S. design community imports, and is enriched by, "visitors from elsewhere." Box 103, folder 8: "IDCA/Japan Conference Correspondence, 1956–1958," WBP.

75. IDCA Executive Committee Meeting, January 18, 1958, IDCAUIC.

76. IDCA Executive Committee Meeting, January 18, 1958, IDCAUIC.

77. Millie Goldsholl had also been involved in film programming in Chicago in the 1950s, both for the Magic Lantern group of the Society for Typographic Arts (with programs combining art film, documentary, animation, experimental film, dance film, and science films) and for the North Shore Film Society, based in Highland Park. Thanks to Amy Beste for sharing her research on these programs.

78. Sarah Nilsen notes that the major film events at the Brussels World's Fair included an Experimental Film Competition (April 21–27); World Film Festival (May 30–June 13); Festival of Children's Films (September 19–21); and a contest for the "best film of all time" (October 12–18). See Sarah Nilsen, *Projecting America, 1958: Film and Cultural Diplomacy at the Brussels World's Fair* (New York: McFarland, 2011), 115–16.

79. Goldsholl's list of distributors is divided between "commercial" and those providing "gratis films." Commercial distributors include Cinema 16, Brandon Films, Creative Film Society, International Film Bureau, Maya Deren, Contemporary Films, Pictura, the Museum of Modern Art, Yeshiva University, Rembrandt Films, Audio Film Center, and Transworld Films. "Gratis" films were provided by Modern Talking Pictures, Ford, Shell Oil, Standard Oil, American Cancer Society, U.P.A., Terrytoons, Storyboard Inc., Coronet Films, the National Film Board of Canada, the Canadian Broadcasting Company, Cinéma et Publicité, Churchill-Wexler, Air France, Shirley Clarke, René Blas, Lewis Jacobs, the British Film Institute, CBS, Stanley Kubrick, Saul Bass, Eastman Kodak, Horizons of Science, and the Netherlands Information Service. See "Film Program Report, June 1959," box 1, folder 7, IDCAUIC.

80. Dudley Andrew, "Time Zones and Jet Lags: The Flows and Phases of World Cinema," in *World Cinemas, Transnational Perspectives,* ed. Nataša Ďurovičová and Kathleen Newman (New Brunswick, N.J.: Rutgers University Press, 2010), 71.

81. From Czechoslovakia, Goldsholl included Jiří Brdečka's *Love in a Dirigible* (1948); from Denmark, Henning Carlsen's *The Bicyclist* (1958); from Sweden, Arne Sucksdorff's *Shadows over Snow* (1946); from Israel, Yoram Gross's animated *Song without Words* (1958); and from Romania, Ion Popescu-Gopo's animated *The Seven Arts* (1958).

82. Turner, *The Democratic Surround,* 232.

83. Reisz, "Experiment at Brussels," *Sight and Sound,* Summer 1958, 231.

84. An early program outline for the "Film Image cycle" suggests a more expansive program under the rubric "The International Film": "Italian film, Japanese film, French film, English film, USSR film, Polish film, US film." It also suggests a plan to study the "Effect of Social Climate on Film Making," including "War, Tensions, Prosperity, Political Upheaval, Industrialization." International Design Conference in Aspen records, "Aspen Program Plan/1959," box 5, folder 1, Getty Research Institute.

85. Also included on the list are Orson Welles, John Huston, Marie Seaton, Vittorio De Sica, Federico Fellini, Stanley Kubrick, Akira Kurosawa, Jan Lenica and Walerian Borowczyk, Hans Richter, John Hubley, Siegfried Kracauer, Maya Deren, Lindsay Anderson, Rudolf Arnheim, Fred Zinnemann, and George Stevens. International

Design Conference in Aspen records, "Aspen Program Plan/1959," box 5, folder 1, Getty Research Institute.

86. See *The Grierson Effect: Tracing Documentary's International Movement,* ed. Zoë Druick and Deane Williams (London: BFI/Palgrave Macmillan, 2014).

87. Thanks to Amy Beste for alerting me to Grierson's role in the "New Visions" seminar.

88. Moholy-Nagy, *Vision in Motion,* 273.

89. First developed in theory in Grierson's Rockefeller Foundation–funded fellowship at the University of Chicago in the 1920s, where he studied the role of mass communications in the shaping of public opinion, this approach was famously instrumentalized in his work first at the Empire Marketing Board and then at the GPO. There, film became the crucial medium of imperial communications, at the heart of Grierson's ambitious campaign to wed film, propaganda, and citizenship formation in an interwar period marked by the explosive growth of Britain's media infrastructure.

90. Lee Grieveson, *Cinema and the Wealth of Nations: Media, Capital, and the Liberal World System* (Oakland: University of California Press, 2018), 160.

91. Grieveson, *Cinema and the Wealth of Nations,* 181. Grierson was particularly interested in film as an "ideal matter for all manner of suggestion," a concept that came from his interest in the "social psychology of popular media." See Grierson's "Notes for English Producers," quoted in Grieveson, 181.

92. Bill Nichols, "Documentary Film and the Modernist Avant-Garde," *Critical Inquiry* 27, no. 4 (Summer 2001): 605.

93. See Greg S. Faller, "Unquiet Years: Experimental Cinema in the 1950s," in *Transforming the Screen, 1950–1959,* ed. Peter Lev (Berkeley: University of California Press, 2003), 279–302. The jury for the Brussels Experimental Film Festival, we should note, consisted not just of Norman McLaren, Man Ray, Pierre Prévert, and Edgard Varese, but also Grierson himself. Grierson left Brussels two weeks later for Montevideo, Uruguay, to attend the Third International Documentary and Experimental Film Festival—where the tradition of the Griersonian documentary would be yoked to Latin American articulations of national cinemas over and against Hollywood models.

94. Amos Vogel, "The Angry Young Film Makers," reprinted in *Cinema 16: Documents toward a History of the Film Society,* ed. Scott MacDonald (Philadelphia: Temple University Press, 2002), 336. Hereafter cited parenthetically as "AYFM."

95. Schapiro, "Liberating Quality of the Avant-Garde."

96. Schapiro, 40.

97. "Communication: The Image Speaks," n. p., Conference Program and Papers, IDCAUIC.

98. "Communication: The Image Speaks."

99. "Communication: The Image Speaks."

100. Vishniac's and Lye's comments appear in "Communication: The Image Speaks."

101. During an evening film session, Cohen-Séat projected three "simple situations, each involving two or more people," without sound or titles, then asked the audience "specific questions related to the scene just shown." See *Report: 9th International Design Conference in Aspen,* 34, IDCAUIC. For an excellent overview of filmology's various perceptual experiments, many published in the *Revue Internationale de Filmologie,* see the chapter "Psychology of Cinema," in Francesco Casetti, *Theories of Cinema, 1945–1995* (Austin: University of Texas Press, 1999).

102. During the "Film Image" roundtable, Lancelot Law Whyte translated "rather freely" a paragraph from *Essay* headed "The Intervention of the Cinema in Contemporary Civilization," which described the changing meaning of the cinematic image's "popularity" in terms of the space it traverses or conquers, and the "number of people it touches across the world." International Design Conference in Aspen records, box 272, R 10–11, Getty Research Institute, Los Angeles.

103. Cohen-Séat, *Essai,* quoted in Edward Lowry, *The Filmology Movement and Film Study in France* (Ann Arbor: UMI Research Press, 1985), 34.

104. In fact, the French government secretly funded the Institute of Filmology throughout the 1950s (until 1959) because it shared Cohen-Séat's sense of the potential threat of cinema as an archaic mass medium in need of democratic discipline and the supervision of a technocratic state. See D. N. Rodowick, *Elegy for Theory* (Cambridge, Mass.: Harvard University Press, 2014), 120.

105. See Timothy Boon, *Films of Fact: A History of Science in Documentary Films and Television* (London: Wallflower Press, 2008). In a 1936 issue of *Sight and Sound,* Hogben reviewed both Rotha's book *The Documentary Film* and Grierson's essay "The Cinema Today." He cast them as "custodians of a new social culture" in which cinema "will be the university of the future," one whose goal is "to bring the new world of citizenship into the imagination." See Hogben, "The New Visual Culture," *Sight and Sound* (Spring 1936): 7, 8. Hogben was a patron of London's Scientific Film Society, and would advise Paul Rotha's Associated Realist Film Producers, serving as consultant on two of Rotha's films: *Science and War* (planned for 1942) and *Land of Promise* (1946). In conceptualizing this last film, an astonishing, dialectical, and formally adventurous polemic on the need for planning in postwar Britain, Rotha described Hogben as "one of the few people qualified to talk about social planning for human needs." See Rotha, quoted in Boon, *Films of Fact,* 147.

106. Lancelot Hogben, *From Cave Painting to Comic Strip: A Kaleidoscope of Human Communication* (New York: Chanticleer Press, 1949), 11. Hereafter cited parenthetically as *FCP.*

107. As Hogben argued in *From Cave Painting,* educational film's potential universality not only models "the minimal vocabulary of world-wide communication" available "in the world-wide vocabulary of science," but also delivers on the rationalist interwar dream of an international picture language formalized by Otto Neurath, whose Isotypes liberally illustrate Hogben's book and in whose memory the book is offered in tribute (*FCP,* 280, 183).

108. Lancelot Hogben, "Biography," n.p., "Communication: The Image Speaks," Conference Program and Papers, IDCAUIC.

109. *Report: 9th International Design Conference in Aspen,* 47, IDCAUIC.

110. "Communication: The Image Speaks."

111. On the tight discursive connections among the Bauhaus, the logical positivism of the Vienna Circle, and the constructivist impulses of Neurath's program of visual education, as well as its reemergence in Moholy-Nagy's New Bauhaus in Chicago in the late 1930s, see Peter Galison, "Aufbau/Bauhaus."

112. Maya Deren, "An Anagram of Ideas on Art, Form, and Film," in *Essential Deren: Collected Writings on Film by Maya Deren,* ed. Bruce R. McPherson (Kingston, N.Y.: Documentext, 2005), 46. Hereafter cited parenthetically as *A.*

113. See Maya Deren, "Cinematography: Or, the Creative Uses of Reality" (1960), in McPherson, *Essential Deren,* 127; and Deren, "Anagram."

114. Deren, "Cinematography," 126.

115. Bruno Latour, "Agency at the Time of the Anthropocene," *New Literary History* 45, no. 1 (Winter 2014): 1–18.

116. Acland and Wasson, *Useful Cinema*, 6.

117. Jack C. Ellis, "Ruminations of an Ex-Cinematologist," *Cinema Journal* 24, no. 2 (Winter 1985): 49.

118. Lee Grieveson, "Discipline and Publish: The Birth of Cinematology," *Cinema Journal* 49, no. 1 (Fall 2009): 174.

119. Jacques Derrida, "The Ends of Man," *Philosophy and Phenomenological Research* 30, no. 1 (1969): 31–57.

4. Memories of Overdevelopment

1. Letter from Burtin to Amos Vogel, September 5, 1967, "Vision 67 Correspondence, 1966–68," box 106, folder 6, WBP.

2. Burtin to Toeplitz, box 106, folder 6, WBP.

3. Burtin to Toeplitz, box 106, folder 6, WBP.

4. R. Roger Remington and Robert S. P. Fripp, *Design and Science: The Life and Work of Will Burtin* (London: Lund Humphries, 2007), 96.

5. Remington and Fripp, 45–46.

6. VanDerBeek had coined the term "underground film" a few years before, in "The Cinema Delimina: Films from the Underground," *Film Quarterly* 14, no. 4 (Summer 1961): 5–16. VanDerBeek's talk was interspersed with screenings of *Vision III #2* (5 min.), *Science Friction* (10 min.), *Wheeeeels #2* (5 min.), *Mankinda* (10 min.), *Breathdeath* (15 min.), and *The Human Face Is a Monument* (10 min.).

7. Vogel to Burtin, box 104, folder 5, WBP.

8. Burtin to Vogel, box 106, folder 6, WBP.

9. Donna M. Binkiewicz, *Federalizing the Muse: United States Arts Policy and the National Endowment for the Arts, 1965–1980* (Chapel Hill: University of North Carolina Press, 2004).

10. *Vision 65: World Congress on New Challenges to Human Communication* (New York: International Center for the Typographic Arts, 1966), 8. Hereafter cited parenthetically as *65*.

11. Scott, *Architecture or Techno-Utopia*, 90.

12. McLuhan's essay was published late in 1967 in *Perspecta: The Yale Architecture Journal* as "The Invisible Environment: The Future of an Erosion."

13. "Tentative Outline" of Vision 65 hardcover publication, box 104, folder 5, WBP.

14. Gloria Sutton, *The Experience Machine: Stan VanDerBeek's Movie-Drome and Expanded Cinema* (Cambridge, Mass.: MIT Press, 2015), 53.

15. Sutton included images of the sketches in *The Experience Machine*, and graciously provided them to me so that I could reproduce them here.

16. Sutton, *The Experience Machine*, 53.

17. Reinhold Martin, "Organicism's Other," *Grey Room* 4 (Summer 2001): 40.

18. Kepes, "Art and Ecological Consciousness," in *Arts of the Environment* (New York: George Braziller, 1970), 4.

19. Stan VanDerBeek, "Culture: Intercom and Expanded Cinema; A Proposal and Manifesto," *Film Culture* 40 (Spring 1966): 15–16. Hereafter cited parenthetically as "CI." The essay was also published in the *Tulane Drama Review* 11, no. 1 (Autumn 1966): 38–48, and *Motive*, November 1966, a magazine published by the Methodist Church's Division of Higher Education. It was delivered during VanDerBeek's talk at the IDCA's Order or Disorder conference in 1967, and anthologized that same year in Gregory Battcock's important *New American Cinema: A Critical Anthology.* The essay was reprinted for the Cross Talk Intermedia Festival in Osaka, Japan, 1969.

20. Burtin mentions the essay, and de Jouvenel's call for a "1985 Work Group," in his letter of invitation to the philosopher, box 103, folder 12, WBP; Bertrand de Jouvenel, "Letter from France: The Technocratic Age," *Bulletin of the Atomic Scientists,* October 1964, 27–29.

21. On postwar futurology, see Andrew Ross, "Getting the Future We Deserve," in *Strange Weather: Culture, Science, and Technology in the Age of Limits* (London: Verso, 1991), 169–92. Fuller's collaborator John McHale is the first expert quoted in a 1966 *Time* magazine piece titled "The Futurists: Looking toward A.D. 2000." McHale's work with Fuller at the Inventory of World Resources, Human Trends, and Needs—housed at Southern Illinois University—is listed alongside the RAND Corporation, Herman Kahn's Hudson Institute, and the Commission on the Year 2000, headed by Daniel Bell. Burtin's research files for Vision 65 include reports on Fuller and McHale's futurological Inventory and on their famous data and resource visualization project, the Geoscope. Box 105, folder 6, WBP.

22. Will Burtin, "Live and Learn: Communication in Transition and Changing Functions of Design," *Art Education* 21, no. 6 (June 1968): 6. Hereafter cited parenthetically as "LL."

23. Acknowledging the influence of Vision 65 on VanDerBeek's practice in her recent study of the Movie-Drome, Gloria Sutton has noted the artist's avid interest in McLuhan's writings, and his adulation of Fuller, which dates back to their time at Black Mountain College. Sutton, *The Experience Machine.*

24. VanDerBeek's name first appears as an "addition" to the Vision 65 roster of speakers dated August 12, box 104, folder 4, WBP. A second draft of a memo dated August 1965 lists him, describing him as a "film designer and producer" who will show both his films and "films made by a rising avant-garde of painters, dancers, sound composers, and poets. While details of his integrated program are still forthcoming, it can be stated now already that Mr. VanDerBeek's performance will reflect the questioning and socially-concerned attitude of new creative generation." Box 104, folder 4, WBP. A number of his films are listed in the New York Film-Makers Cooperative catalog included in Burtin's "V65 Research Material," box 105, folder 5, WBP.

25. In the design world, the fallout of such debates was perhaps most apparent at IDCA 1970, Environment by Design.

26. Johanna Drucker, *Graphesis: Visual Forms of Knowledge Production* (Cambridge, Mass.: Harvard University Press, 2014).

27. In his Vision 65 address, for example, the Dutch designer Wim Crouwel proclaimed, "A new method, called *visual communication*—a term which is so fashionable at the moment that it is already threatening to grow into a problem—is replacing earlier concepts and trends. It deals with the transmission of a message by visual means, and with concrete presentation of complex ideas. It embraces many aspects of design, such as typography, book design, advertisement, film, exhibitions, book design, etc." (*65,* 191).

28. Burtin, "Design and Communication," in *The Education of Vision,* ed. György Kepes (New York: George Braziller, 1965), 78.

29. See Remington and Fripp, *Design and Science,* 13–23.

30. The Visual Presentation Branch included designers Walter Dorwin Teague, Henry Dreyfuss, Raymond Loewy, and Norman Bel Geddes. By the end of the war, it had 114 members, among them "architects, industrial designers, artists, editors, illustrators, engineers, machinists, photographers, filmmakers, composers, economists, cartographers, psychologists, and even a historian." Barry Katz, "The Arts of War: 'Visual Presentation' and National Intelligence," *Design Issues* 12, no. 2 (Summer 1996): 9.

31. Katz, "The Arts of War," 12.

32. Will Burtin and Lawrence Lessing, "Interrelations," *Graphis*, no. 22 (1948): 108. Hereafter cited parenthetically as "I."

33. Will Burtin, "Integration: The New Discipline in Design," *Graphis*, no. 27 (1949): 232.

34. Burtin, 232.

35. Burtin, 232.

36. Box 124, folders 1–2, WBP. My thanks to Carol Burtin Fripp for granting me access to this recording.

37. Remington and Fripp, *Design and Science*, 77.

38. Roszak, *The Making of a Counter-Culture.*

39. Box 103, folder 7, WBP.

40. Box 103, folder 7, WBP.

41. Box 103, folder 7, WBP.

42. Herbert Schiller, "Genesis of the Free Flow of Information Principles," in *Communication and Class Struggle*, vol. 1, *Capitalism and Imperialism*, ed. Armand Mattelart and Seth Siegelaub (New York: International General, 1979), 349; *Yearbook on Human Rights for 1947* (Lake Success, N.Y: United Nations, 1949), 439, quoted in Schiller, 350. In its early years, UNESCO established a special section on the free flow of information in its Department of Mass Communications. See Schiller, 349. On UNESCO's early studies of national and communicational infrastructures worldwide, see Zoë Druick, "UNESCO, Film, and Education. Mediating Postwar Paradigms of Communication," in Acland and Wasson, *Useful Cinema*, 85.

43. Sean MacBride and Colleen Roach, "The New International Information Order," in *The Global Media Debate: Its Rise, Fall, and Renewal*, ed. George Gerbner, Hamid Mowlana, and Kaarle Nordenstreng (New York: Praeger, 1993).

44. Burtin to Mead, box 104, folder 2, WBP.

45. Margaret Mead, "The Information Explosion," in "The Information Revolution," *New York Times*, May 23, 1965, 18. Hereafter cited parenthetically as "IE."

46. Burtin to Mead, box 104, folder 2, WBP.

47. "Manifesto," dated January 10, 1963, box 103, folder 7, WBP.

48. "Draft proposal for first call for a 'working' conference, VISION '64," "Vision 64, 1963," box 103, folder 7, WBP.

49. "Draft proposal for first call for a 'working' conference, VISION '64."

50. Geoghegan, "From Information Theory to French Theory."

51. "Draft proposal for first call for a 'working' conference, VISION '64."

52. On the role of communications media in the emergent category of knowledge work, see Machlup's chapter "The Media of Communication," in *The Production and Distribution of Knowledge in the United States*, 207–94.

53. Burtin describes satellites in his letter to Max Bill, box 103, folder 12, WBP.

54. Burtin to Singer, box 103, folder 7, WBP.

55. Burtin to Grey Walter, box 103, folder 12, WBP.

56. Burtin to Grey Walter, box 103, folder 12, WBP.

57. Burtin to Bill, box 103, folder 12, WBP.

58. Burtin to MacKenzie, box 103, folder 12, WBP.

59. "Vision 65: Work-in-Progress Report Meeting: 28 July," box 104, folder 3, WBP.

60. "Contents and sequences of Vision 65 trailer," box 106, folder 1, WBP.

61. Burtin to Fuller, box 103, folder 12, WBP.

62. Burtin to McLuhan, box 103, folder 12, WBP.

63. Jeffrey T. Schnapp and Adam Michaels, *The Electric Information Age Book: McLuhan/Agel/Fiore and the Experimental Paperback* (New York: Princeton Architectural Press, 2012), 48.

64. "Draft proposal for first call for a 'working' conference, VISION '64," "Vision 64, 1963," box 103, folder 7, WBP.

65. "I cannot think of a better person than Satyajit Ray to represent India at the 'Vision '65' Congress," Sarabhai wrote to Burtin. "Before he became a film director, he was Art Director of an advertising agency in Calcutta. He is therefore fully conversant with problems of visual communication." Box 103, folder 12, WBP.

66. At the suggestion of his friend Bruce MacKenzie, a linguist and data-processing theorist then working for IBM-Europe, Burtin had invited Senegalese president Léopold Senghor. Burtin to MacKenzie, box 103, folder 12, WBP.

67. Burtin may have heard a version of it at IDCA 67: Order and Disorder, when VanDerBeek read substantial portions of it in his talk. Box 10, folder 541, IDCAUIC.

68. The "Triple Revolution" manifesto is included in the research file as it was reprinted in the trade magazine *Advertising Age* on April 6, 1964. Box 105, folder 5, WBP.

69. "The Triple Revolution," www.marxists.org. Last accessed on August 20, 2017.

70. The writings of Alice Mary Hilton, and her two "Conferences on the Cybercultural Revolution" in 1964 and 1965, are documented extensively in Burtin's research file. Box 105, folder 5, WBP.

71. Burtin to Ferry, box 104, folder 3, WBP.

72. Burtin to Herbert Roan, box 104, folder 2,WBP.

73. Thorold Dickinson, "The Maturing Cinema," *Journal of the Society of Cinematologists* 4/5 (1964/65): 10.

74. Dickinson, "The Maturing Cinema," 16.

75. Dickinson, 16.

76. See Ješa Denegri, "Inside or Outside 'Socialist Modernism'?: Radical Views on the Yugoslav Art Scene, 1950–70," in *Impossible Histories: Historical Avant-Gardes, Neo-Avant-Gardes, and Post-Avant-Gardes in Yugoslavia, 1918–1991,* ed. Dubravka Djurić and Miško Šuvaković (Cambridge, Mass.: MIT Press, 2003), 170–208.

77. On the New Tendencies, see *A Little-Known Story about a Movement, a Magazine, and the Computer's Arrival in Art: New Tendencies and Bit International, 1961–1973,* ed. Margit Rosen et al. (Cambridge, Mass.: MIT Press, 2011), and Margit Rosen's "'They Have All Dreamt of the Machines—and Now the Machines Have Arrived': New Tendencies—Computers and Visual Research, Zagreb, 1968–69," in *Mainframe Experimentalism: Early Computing and the Foundations of the Digital Arts,* ed. Hannah B. Higgins and Douglas Kahn (Berkeley: University of California Press, 2012), 90–111.

78. Burtin to Horvat-Pintarić, box 104, folder 1, WBP.

79. In a letter from Burtin to Bruce MacKenzie, Tinguely is described as a "sculptor of philosophical machines"; box 106, folder 2, WBP. The program describes his work as "sculptured communications." Bense provided Vision 67 with a conceptual link between the computational aesthetics of the New Tendencies and the pedagogical work of Bauhausian rationalism. A philosopher of technology and mathematical logic, Bense developed the information programming department at the Hochschule für Gestaltung, where he served as a lecturer from 1954 to 1958. In 1962 Eco wrote the introduction to the catalog for an important touring exhibition of kinetic art, *arte programmata* (programmed art), sponsored by the Olivetti Corporation, and held in 1963 in the Olivetti sales rooms in Milan before traveling in Europe and the United States. See Margit Rosen, "The Art of Programming: The New Tendencies and the Arrival of the Computer as a Means of Artistic Research," in Rosen, *A Little-Known Story,* 35.

80. Eco's talk was part of a panel devoted to "new perspectives for communications in a technologically and socially transformed environment," *Papers. Vision 67: Survival and Growth* (n.p.: International Center for the Communication Arts and Sciences, 1967), 54. Hereafter cited parenthetically as *67.*

81. Rodowick, *The Crisis of Political Modernism,* 120.

82. Cohen-Séat, "Methodical Utilization of Visual Processes toward Development," box 106, folder 2, WBP.

83. The goal of this program of modern visual training was the "development of human resources," by which Cohen-Séat meant the increased productivity of labor, and thus, the increased income of an "active population," which "economists agree is the key to social and economic progress." Cohen-Séat, "Project for the Creation of an International Scientific and Technical Center for the Utilization of Modern Visual Techniques," in "Appendix: Aspects of Educational Problems in Developing Countries," box 106, folder 2, WBP.

84. Toeplitz to Burtin, "Vision 67 Correspondence, 1966–68," box 106, folder 6, WBP.

85. A letter to Toeplitz from Burtin's colleague Larry Creshkoff notes approvingly that his description of the state-sponsored Polish film clubs would provide a "striking" contrast "with the laissez faire system of the West . . . and could be the subject of considerable discussion—without descending to the level of ideological polemics"; box 106, folder 2, WBP. The term "programming" also recalls the prestige at the Vision conferences of the cybernetic analogy that joined men and machines to their capacity for environmental programming and control. At Vision 67, this analogy was discussed by British cybernetician Gordon Pask, whose talk defined "society [as] a class of programmes" run in a computing machine ("a community of people and artifacts") itself "organized by a software configuration usually called a culture" (*67,* 42).

86. "V 67: Proofs, 1967," box 107, folder 2, WBP.

87. The radical German poet and media theorist Hans Magnus Enzensberger was proposed to Burtin as a speaker, and his Hamburg address appears in Burtin's handwritten notes; box 107, folder 6. WBP. A German-language copy of Enzensberger's essay collection *Details 1: The Consciousness Industry* (1962) is included with Burtin's speech; box 96, folder 2, WBP.

88. "Centre for Contemporary Culture Studies, Second Report, University of Birmingham, October 1965," box 107, folder 6, WBP.

89. Lawrence Grossberg and Janice Radway, quoted in Richard E. Lee, *Life and Times of Cultural Studies: The Politics and Transformation of Structures of Knowledge* (Durham, N.C.: Duke University Press, 2003), 2.

90. Wallerstein, quoted in Lee, *Life and Times of Cultural Studies,* 5.

91. "Centre for Contemporary Culture Studies, Second Report, University of Birmingham, October 1965," WBP.

92. Burtin to Martin Luther King Jr., box 104, folder 1, WBP. King referenced the "triple revolution" thesis in the last speech before his assassination in 1968, and took up the promises and threats of technology for global oppression and revolutionary liberation in "The World House," the last chapter of his book *Where Do We Go from Here?* (Boston: Beacon Press, 1967).

93. "V67 Notes," box 107, folder 1, WBP. On Burtin's efforts to secure Baldwin as a speaker, see the letter from Arline Legis, box 104, folder 3, WBP. In his polite letter of decline to Burtin, King noted that he was "spending more time on the Civil Rights struggle," and not able to accept every attractive offer that crossed his desk. King to Burtin, box 104, folder 1, WBP.

94. "V67 Notes," box 107, folder 1, WBP.

95. Stuart Hall, "The Hippies: An American 'Moment,'" in *Student Power,* ed. Julian Nagel (London: Merlin Press, 1969), 170–202.

96. See Aniko Bodroghkozy, *Groove Tube: Sixties Television and the Youth Rebellion* (Durham, N.C.: Duke University Press, 2001).

97. "Notes about Hippies," box 107, folder 1, WBP.

98. A political activist and exiled ANC member, Mvusi introduced the first university program in industrial design in Africa, and in the 1960s was often the sole representative of the Global South at international design conferences. Burtin planned to include Mvusi's talk "Problem Growth or Growth Problem" in a proposed final session with Fuller, and was in discussions with the Canadian Broadcasting Company to air this as a live "tele-address," linked to McLuhan and Hayakawa's concurrent speeches at McGill University, as part of Expo 67. Burtin to Fuller, box 106, folder 6, WBP.

99. See Ross, "Getting the Future We Deserve."

100. Victor Papanek, *Design for the Real World: Human Ecology and Social Change,* 2nd ed. (Chicago: Academy Chicago Publishers, 1971).

101. Jason W. Moore, ed., *Anthropocene or Capitalocene? Nature, History, and the Crisis of Capitalism* (Oakland, Calif.: PM Press, 2016), 4.

102. Wallerstein, quoted in Gilman, *Mandarins of the Future,* 238.

103. Druick, "UNESCO, Film, and Education," 96.

104. Druick, 99.

5. Designer Film Theory

1. "V 67: Proofs 1967," box 107, folder 1, WBP.

2. Polan, *Scenes of Instruction,* 6.

3. Clement Greenberg, "Towards a Newer Laocoön," *Partisan Review* 4, no. 7 (July–August 1940).

4. Grieveson, "Discipline and Publish," 169.

5. Gessner, quoted in Grieveson, 168.

6. Giorgio Agamben, *What Is an Apparatus? and Other Essays,* trans. David Kishik and Stefan Pedatella (Stanford, Calif.: Stanford University Press, 2009), 12.

7. Francesco Casetti, *The Lumière Galaxy: Seven Key Words for the Cinema to Come* (New York: Columbia University Press, 2015), 77.

8. Casetti, 78.

9. In this way, the design dispositive intersected in various moments with what Geoghegan has dubbed the "cybernetic apparatus."

10. Greif, *The Age of the Crisis of Man,* 4.

11. Robert M. Yoder, "Are You Contemporary?" *Saturday Evening Post,* July 3, 1943, 16.

12. Yoder, 16.

13. Yoder, 89.

14. Moholy-Nagy, *Vision in Motion,* 11. Hereafter cited parenthetically as *VM.*

15. From 1939 to 1944, the Institute was named the School of Design. On the origins of the New Bauhaus, see Lloyd C. Engelbrecht, "The Association of Art and Industries Background and Origins of the Bauhaus Movement in Chicago" (Ph.D. diss., University of Chicago, 1973). On Bauhaus pedagogy's specific approach to nondiscursive, embodied knowledge, and Moholy's relationship to German experimental psychology, see Alexander, *Kinaesthetic Knowing.*

16. For a detailed discussion of the Bauhaus's "London interlude," see Peder Anker, "The Bauhaus of Nature," *Modernism/modernity* 12, no. 2 (2005): 229–51.

17. Martin, *Organizational Complex,* 54. See also Oliver A. I. Botar, "Prolegomena to the Study of Biomorphic Modernism: Biocentrism, László Moholy-Nagy's 'New Vision' and Ernö Kállai's Bioromantik" (Ph.D. diss., University of Toronto, 1998); and Oliver Botar, *Sensing the Future: Moholy-Nagy, Media, and the Arts* (Berlin: Lars Müller, 2016), especially "Sensory Training," 17–39.

18. On this remarkable work as a kind of training manual for Weimar urban modernity's new kind of reader—an overstimulated scanner of information—in the form of a new kind of book, see Pepper Stetler, " 'The New Visual Literature': László Moholy-Nagy's Painting, Photography, Film," *Grey Room* 32 (Summer 2008): 88–113.

19. Moholy's naturalization papers were apparently delayed owing to his involvement while in the United States with the Hungarian Democratic Council, an organization "which sought to foster democracy in Hungary." On the FBI's investigations of the Bauhauslers, see Robin Schuldenfrei, "Assimilating Unease: Moholy-Nagy and the Wartime/Postwar Bauhaus in Chicago," in *Atomic Dwelling,* 90–91, 120. The FBI documents are also reproduced and discussed in Margaret Kentgens-Craig, *The Bauhaus and America: First Contacts, 1919–1936* (Cambridge, Mass.: MIT Press, 1999), 238–40, and the appendix.

20. Drafted simultaneously with *Vision in Motion,* the Harvard "Red Book," *General Education in a Free Society* (1945), would do something very similar. A document outlining the "Philosophy and Method" of the Institute of Design's foundation course quotes from the Red Book to link the problem of the education of the designer and architect to "a general educational approach," and cites from two passages in the Red Book recommending design and architecture training for a rethinking of fine arts education within a general education program. Box 4, folder 108, "ID Text for Catalog: Desc. of ID Foundation Course, ca. 1946," IDUIC.

21. Botar, *Sensing the Future,* 54.

22. Box 61, folder 1, WPP.

23. For more on the *Design Workshop* films, see Justus Nieland, "Color Communications: László Moholy-Nagy, Walter Paepcke, and the Humanities Program of *Design Workshops,*" *Cinéma & Cie* 19, no. 32 (Spring 2019): 79–84.

24. Sibyl Moholy-Nagy, *Moholy-Nagy: Experiment in Totality* (Cambridge, Mass.: MIT Press, 1969), 213.

25. Beste, "All Roads Lead to Chicago," 196. After Moholy-Nagy's death, film production at the ID expanded significantly as the school merged with the Illinois Institute of Technology; filmmaking was taught alongside film history, photography, and visual design and understood as an indispensable technical preparation for careers in visual communication and media production of all kinds.

26. László Moholy-Nagy, "Problems of the Modern Film," in *Moholy-Nagy: An Anthology,* ed. Richard Kostelanetz (New York: Da Capo, 1970), 133.

27. Moholy-Nagy, 131.

28. Wendy Brown, *Undoing the Demos: Neoliberalism's Stealth Revolution* (New York: Zone Books, 2015), 182–83; see especially chapter 6, "Educating Human Capital."

29. Brown, 179.

30. Course catalog, "Two Summer Sessions of the School of Design in Chicago," box 3, folder 72, IDUIC.

31. Course catalog, "Two Summer Sessions."

32. Moholy, quoted in Schuldenfrei, "Assimilating Unease," 109.

33. Course catalog, "Principles of Camouflage Course," box 3, folder 76, IDUIC.

34. On Kepes's camouflage aesthetics, see John R. Blakinger, "Camouflage Aesthetics," from *Un camouflage New Bauhaus: György Kepes et le militarisation de l'image* (Paris: Editions B2, 2014). I'm grateful to John Blakinger for providing me with the original English version of a portion of this work, from his Ph.D. dissertation. See also John R. Blakinger, "Camouflage 1942: Artists, Architects, and Designers at Ft. Belvoir, Virginia," in *Conflict, Identity, and Protest in American Art*, ed. Miguel de Baca and Makeda Best (Newcastle upon Tyne, England: Cambridge Scholars Publishing, 2015), 35–56.

35. Kepes, quoted in Schuldenfrei, "Assimilating Unease," 106.

36. Schuldenfrei, 109.

37. Box 3, folder 64, "Courses in Rehabilitation, Orientation Course in Occupational Therapy," IDUIC.

38. "Courses in Rehabilitation, Orientation Course in Occupational Therapy."

39. "Courses in Rehabilitation, Orientation Course in Occupational Therapy."

40. Moholy-Nagy includes Somner's comments on the ID's technique in *Vision in Motion*, 72.

41. Moholy-Nagy, "Better than Before," *Technology Review* 46, no. 1 (November 1943): 8.

42. Fredric Jameson, *A Singular Modernity: An Essay on the Ontology of the Present* (London: Verso, 2001), 215.

43. Moholy-Nagy, "Better than Before," 21–23, 44–48.

44. See Marin Tova Linett, *Bodies of Modernism: Physical Disability in Transatlantic Modernist Literature* (Ann Arbor: University of Michigan Press, 2017); Janet Lyon, "On the Asylum Road with Woolf and Mew," *Modernism/modernity* 3 (September 2011): 551–74; Michael Davidson, *Concerto for the Left Hand: Disability and the Defamiliar Body* (Ann Arbor: University of Michigan Press, 2008).

45. Greif, *The Age of the Crisis of Man*, 4.

46. Greif, 11.

47. Deren, *An Anagram of Ideas on Art, Form, and Film* (Yonkers, N.Y.: Alicat Book Shop Press, 1946), 64. Moholy-Nagy, "Production-Reproduction," in *Painting, Photography, Film*, trans. Janet Seligman (Cambridge, Mass.: MIT Press, 1969), 30.

48. Devin Fore, *Realism after Modernism: The Rehumanization of Art and Literature* (Cambridge, Mass.: MIT Press, 2012), 6.

49. Fore, 7, 70.

50. Moholy-Nagy, "Production-Reproduction," 30.

51. "New Visions in Photography" brochure, box 3, folder 98, IDUIC.

52. "New Visions in Photography" brochure.

53. "Photographic Summer Seminar Program," Arthur Siegel Papers, box 18, folder 4, Ryerson and Burnham Libraries, Art Institute of Chicago.

54. "Photographic Summer Seminar Program."

55. Hammid's OWI films included *Valley of the Tennessee* (1944), *Toscanini: Hymn of the Nations* (1945), *A Better Tomorrow* (1945), and *Library of Congress* (1945). See Thomas E.

Valasek, "Alexander Hammid: A Survey of His Filmmaking Career," *Film Culture* 67–69 (1979): 250–322.

56. Hammid, quoted in Decherney, *Hollywood and the Culture Elite,* 170.

57. Decherney, 173.

58. Iris Barry and Richard Griffith, *The Films of Fact* (New York: Museum of Modern Art Film Library, 1942).

59. See also Hammid's essay "New Fields, New Techniques," *Screenwriter,* May 1946, 21–27.

60. On the pedagogical program of Moholy-Nagy's photograms, see Emma Stein, "László Moholy-Nagy and Chicago's War Industry: Photographic Pedagogy at the New Bauhaus," *History of Photography* 38, no. 4 (November 2014): 398–417; Elizabeth Siegel, "The Modern Artist's New Tools," in *Moholy-Nagy: Future Present,* ed. Matthew S. Witkovsky et al. (New Haven, Conn.: Yale University Press, 2016), 224–34.

61. "The Museum and the War," *Bulletin of the Museum of Modern Art* 10, no. 1 (October–November 1942): 3–19.

62. "Museum of Modern Art Opens Exhibition of Arts in Therapy for Disabled Soldiers and Sailors," 43201-8, accessed via MoMA online.

63. Deren corresponded with Gregory Bateson and Margaret Mead in 1946–47 regarding her plans for an unfinished film comparing ritual practices across cultures, and she credited Bateson with teaching her to see "what distinguishes culture from culture" in *Divine Horseman,* her study of Haitian voudoun practices. On the relationship between Bateson and Mead, see Catrina Neiman, "An Introduction to the Notebook of Maya Deren, 1947," *October* 14 (Autumn 1980): 3–15; and Orit Halpern, "Anagram, Gestalt, and Game in Maya Deren: Reconfiguring the Image in Post-War Cinema," *Postmodern Culture* 19, no. 3 (2009).

64. Deren studied Gestalt psychology with Kurt Koffka while completing her M.A. in English literature at Smith College. For more on Deren's relationship to Gestalt psychology, its postwar function as a "lingua franca for rethinking perception and human cognition" across the fields of art history, psychology, and the social sciences, see Halpern, "Anagram."

65. Deren's phrasing here recalls Walter Benjamin's argument in the "Artwork" essay about the film studio as an allegory for technically mediated existence.

66. Moholy-Nagy was especially influenced by the naturalization of technology in the work of Austro-Hungarian biologist Raoul Heinrich Francé, who understood the functional forms of human technology and culture as the result of the same forces that produced the elemental forms of nature.

67. Annette Michelson has compared Deren's investment in ritualistic form to Eisenstein's interest in epic form via their shared interest in "the meaning of community in its most absorbing and fulfilling instance, of collective enterprise grounded in the mythic." See "Poetics and Savage Thought: About *Anagram,*" in *Maya Deren and the American Avant-Garde,* ed. Bill Nichols (Berkeley: University of California Press, 2001), 36.

68. Juliet Koss, "Bauhaus Theater of Human Dolls," in *Bauhaus Culture: From Weimar to the Cold War,* ed. Kathleen James-Chakraborty (Minneapolis: University of Minnesota Press, 2006), 91.

69. Schlemmer, quoted in Koss, 98.

70. Koss, 98.

71. Fore, "The Myth Reversed," 40. Fore observes that Moholy-Nagy's choice, in the film *Modulator,* never to provide a long shot of the object itself, affirms his commitment to a materialist approach to technical media, his way of insisting—like Vertov—that "the eye is in things."

72. *The Legend of Maya Deren: A Documentary Biography and Collected Works,* vol. 1, part 2, *Chambers (1942–47),* ed. VèVè A. Clark et al. (New York: Anthology Film Archives, 2006), 149.

73. "Designed Both for Work and Display: *Look* Magazine's Visual Research Offices," *Interiors,* June 1945, 65. See also "About the Career of a Young Man with an Inquiring Mind: Alvin Lustig, Designer," *Interiors,* September 1946, 68–75.

74. *Legend of Maya Deren,* vol. 1, part 2, *Chambers,* 311.

75. "Cinema as an Art Form," 25, 32, in McPherson, *Essential Deren.*

76. Vallye, "Design and the Politics of Knowledge in America," 303, 317.

77. Vallye, 279.

78. Kepes, quoted in Vallye, 280.

79. The volumes were titled *The Education of Vision; Structure in Art and Science; The Nature and Art of Motion; Module, Proportion, Symmetry, Rhythm; The Man-Made Object;* and *Sign, Image, Symbol.*

80. Kepes, quoted in Vallye, "Design and the Politics of Knowledge in America," 299.

81. György Kepes, interviewed by Douglas M. Davis, "Art & Technology—Conversations," *Art in America* 56, no. 1 (January–February 1968): 40.

82. See John R. Blakinger, "The Aesthetics of Collaboration: Complicity and Conversion at MIT's Center for Advanced Visual Studies," *Tate Papers,* no. 25 (Spring 2016), http://www.tate.org.uk/research/publications/tate-papers/25/aesthetics-of-collaboration, accessed November 1, 2016. See also Pamela M. Lee, "Aesthetic Strategist: Albert Wohlstetter, the Cold War, and a Theory of Mid-Century Modernism," *October* 138 (Fall 2011): 15–36.

83. Vilém Flusser, *Into the Universe of Technical Images,* trans. Nancy Ann Roth (Minneapolis: University of Minnesota Press, 2011).

84. *The Visual Arts Today,* ed. György Kepes (Middletown, Conn.: Wesleyan University Press, 1960), 150. Hereafter cited parenthetically as *VA.*

85. Deren, "Cinematography: The Creative Use of Reality," in McPherson, *Essential Deren,* 116–17. Hereafter cited parenthetically as "CU."

86. Kepes, *The New Landscape in Art and Science,* 206.

87. Vallye, "Design and the Politics of Knowledge in America," 292.

88. Kepes, *Kinetic Light as a Creative Medium,* 26. Vallye has discussed Kepes's site-specific *Kinetic Light Mural* (1959), commissioned for KLM Royal Dutch Airlines' New York offices, as positioned between "natural contingency and human purpose." Vallye, "Design and the Politics of Knowledge in America," 295.

89. See, for example, Sarah Keller's excellent *Maya Deren: Incomplete Control* (New York: Columbia University Press, 2015), 41.

90. Cohen-Cole, *The Open Mind.*

91. Another was psychologist Abraham H. Maslow, who appeared in Kepes's *Sign Image Symbol* volume. On Maslow's role in the psychology of creativity in the postwar period, and the appeal of his account of the creative personality for management theory, see Sarah Brouillette, *Literature and the Creative Economy* (Stanford, Calif.: Stanford

University Press, 2014), and Jamie Cohen-Cole, "The Creative American: Cold War Salons, Social Science, and the Cure for Modern Society," *Isis* 100 (2009): 219–62. On the privileged role of the architect and designer in midcentury studies of creativity, see Serraino, *The Creative Architect*.

92. *The Creative Mind and Method: Exploring the Nature of Creativeness in American Arts, Sciences, and Professions*, ed. Jack D. Summerfield and Lorlyn Thatcher (Austin: University of Texas Press, 1960).

93. Martin, *The Organizational Complex*, 67.

94. Deren's language echoes George Nelson's on characteristic architectural forms of the "new subscape," described in chapter 1.

6. Designer Film Theory II

1. Rudolf Arnheim, "The Bauhaus in Dessau," in *The Weimar Republic Sourcebook*, ed. Anton Kaes, Martin Jay, and Edward Dimendberg (Berkeley: University of California Press, 1995), 450.

2. Arnheim, 450–51.

3. György Kepes, *The Language of Vision: Painting, Photography, Advertising-Design* (Chicago: Paul Theobald, 1969). Hereafter cited parenthetically as *LV*.

4. Vallye, "Design and the Politics of Knowledge in America," 213.

5. Rudolf Arnheim, "Gestalt and Art," *Journal of Aesthetics and Art Criticism* 2, no. 8 (Autumn 1943): 71.

6. Jürgen Wilke, "Cinematography as a Medium of Communication: The Promotion of Research by the League of Nations and the Role of Rudolf Arnheim," *European Journal of Communications* 6 (1991): 337–53.

7. Rudolf Arnheim, "The Conditions for Creativity," in Summerfield and Thatcher, *The Creative Mind and Method*, 107.

8. Arnheim, 108.

9. Schapiro, "The Liberating Quality of Avant-Garde Art," 40.

10. *The Education of Vision*, ed. György Kepes (New York: George Braziller, 1965). Hereafter cited parenthetically as *EV*.

11. *Sign, Image, Symbol*, ed. György Kepes (New York: George Braziller, 1966), 42.

12. *Module, Proportion, Symmetry, Rhythm*, ed. György Kepes (New York: George Braziller, 1966), 218.

13. *Aspects of Form: A Symposium on Form in Nature and Art*, ed. Lancelot Law Whtye (Bloomington: Indiana University Press, 1961), 6.

14. Herbert Read, preface to *Aspects of Form*, n.p.

15. For a sustained account of the role of Gestalt psychologists at the Macy Conferences on cybernetics (1946–1953), see Heims, *The Cybernetics Group*, especially chapters 9 and 10.

16. Rudolf Arnheim, "Accident and the Necessity of Art," *Journal of Aesthetics and Art Criticism* 16, no. 1 (September 1957): 18. Hereafter cited parenthetically as "AN."

17. Kevin Lynch, "The Form of Cities," *Scientific American*, April 1954, 55–63.

18. Kevin Lynch, *The Image of the City* (Cambridge, Mass.: MIT Press, 1960), 4. For a helpful account of Lynch's rethinking of planning as a linking of "perception and cognition without recourse to utopian forms," see Orit Halpern, *Beautiful Data*, 120.

19. Rudolf Arnheim, "Information Theory: An Introductory Note," *Journal of Aesthetics and Art Criticism* 17, no. 4 (June 1959): 501–3. Hereafter cited parenthetically as "IT."

20. Rudolf Arnheim, "Melancholy Unshaped," *Journal of Aesthetics and Art Criticism* 21, no. 3 (Spring 1963): 291-97. Hereafter cited parenthetically as "MU."

21. Von Moltke, *The Curious Humanist.*

22. Siegfried Kracauer, *Theory of Film: The Redemption of Physical Reality,* intro. Miriam Bratu Hansen (Princeton, N.J.: Princeton University Press, 1997), 287. Hereafter cited parenthetically as *TF.*

23. Jennifer Fay, "Antarctica and Siegfried Kracaeur's Cold Love," *Discourse* 33, no. 3 (Fall 2011): 297.

24. See Lee's discussion of the role of entropy in the cybernetic model or temporality joining the work of Robert Smithson, art historian George Kubler, and Norbert Wiener in chapter 4 of Lee, *Chronophobia,* "Ultramoderne: Or, How George Kubler Stole the Time in Sixties Art," 218–56. In linking entropy to the boredom and homogeneity of serial and minimal art, Arnheim directly takes up Smithson's own reading of the serialized objects of Ronald Bladen and Sol LeWitt in "Entropy and the New Monuments."

25. Rudolf Arnheim, *Entropy and Art: An Essay on Order and Disorder* (Berkeley: University of California Press, 1971), 7. Hereafter cited parenthetically as *E.*

26. Tomás Maldonado, *Design, Nature, and Revolution: Toward a Critical Ecology,* trans. Mario Domandi (New York: Harper & Row, 1972), 1. Hereafter cited parenthetically as *DNR.*

27. His answers discussed the role of language and images in mediating between inner and outer, human subjectivity and its man-made environment, in terms that echo Kepes and Arnheim.

28. Modernism, as scholars have recently argued, had a persuasive account of the nature of the "mediated life"; it was also given to ecological, "eco-technical" thought. On the former, see Goble, *Beautiful Circuits;* Julian Murphet, *Multimedia Modernism: Literature and the Anglo-American Avant-Garde* (Cambridge: Cambridge University Press, 2009); and David Trotter, *Literature in the First Media Age: Britain between the Wars* (Cambridge, Mass.: Harvard University Press, 2013). On eco-modernism, see Joshua Schuster, *The Ecology of Modernism: American Environments and Avant-Garde Poetics* (Tuscaloosa: University of Alabama Press, 2015); and in the context of Bauhaus modernism, Peder Anker's "The Bauhaus of Nature" and *From Bauhaus to Eco-House.*

29. Maldonado, quoted in Kenneth Frampton, "Apropos Ulm: Curriculum and Critical Theory," *Oppositions* 3 (May 1974): 35; *Ulm: Quarterly Bulletin of the Hochschule für Gestaltung* 1 (October 1958): 1.

30. Paul Betts, *The Authority of Everyday Objects: A Cultural History of West German Industrial Design* (Berkeley: University of California Press, 2004).

31. Scholl and Aicher, quoted in Betts, *Authority of Everyday Objects,* 142.

32. Scholl and Aicher, 142.

33. Greg Castillo, "The Bauhaus in Cold War Germany," in James-Chakraborty, *Bauhaus Culture,* 183–84.

34. *Ulm Design: The Morality of Objects; Hochschule für Gestaltung Ulm, 1953–1968,* ed. Herbert Lindinger, trans. David Britt (Cambridge, Mass.: MIT Press, 1991), 30.

35. Betts, *Authority of Everyday Objects,* 152–53.

36. Betts, 156.

37. Betts, 167.

38. *Ulm: Quarterly Bulletin of the Hochschule für Gestaltung* 1 (October 1958): 1.

39. *Ulm: Quarterly Bulletin of the Hochschule für Gestaltung* 1 (October 1958): 20.

40. *Ulm: Quarterly Bulletin of the Hochschule für Gestaltung* 1 (October 1958): 20.

41. The list of "theoretical and practical courses" offered in the Department of Visual Communication offers a sense of the curriculum's interdisciplinary training: in addition to technology (typesetting, process reproduction, printing, paper), visual communicators would take classes in semiotics, such as a "modern theory of signs" with a "social psychological basis"; sociology (of "industrial society," advertising and propaganda, and public opinion); theory of science; operational theory (group theory, set theory, statistics, linear programming, standardization); copyright; and a "Seminar on the History of Typography, Exhibition Design, and Film in the 20th Century." *Ulm: Quarterly Bulletin of the Hochschule für Gestaltung* 1 (October 1958): 21.

42. *Ulm: Quarterly Bulletin of the Hochschule für Gestaltung* 1 (October 1958): 21.

43. Theoretical courses listed in the Information Department also included semiotics, operational research, sociology, theory of science, but also linguistics (general structural and statistical linguistics), information theory, typography, history and organization of means of communication (press, broadcasting, television, film), photo, film, sound (available forms), and history of modern literature. *Ulm: Quarterly Bulletin of the Hochschule für Gestaltung* 1 (October 1958): 23.

44. *HfG-Info, 1955–56*, quoted in Lindinger, *Ulm Design*, 171.

45. Max Bense, *Texte und Zeichen*, 8, 1956, quoted in *Ulm Design*, 170.

46. Bernhard Rübenach, "Der rechte Winkel von Ulm," radio documentary, 1959, quoted in *Ulm Design*, 175.

47. Rübenach, 175.

48. *Ulm: Quarterly Bulletin of the Hochschule für Gestaltung* 1 (October 1958): 2.

49. "Expansion of the Motion Picture and Television Sector (Oberhausen Group)," quoted in *Ulm Design*, 24.

50. Alexander Kluge, quoted in *Ulm Design*, 183–84.

51. Kluge, *Ulm: Quarterly Bulletin* 10/11 (1964), quoted in *Ulm Design*, 190.

52. Kluge, 190.

53. Kluge later explained that the idea for the center came from Fritz Lang, who, with his colleague and partner Lilly Latté, "had been very frustrated by Artur Brauner and the production style in the Federal Republic." Latté visited Ulm and discussed with Otl Aicher the possibility of a film training and theory center in Ulm, with Lang as director. The plan was scrapped owing to Lang's poor health and the fact that, according to Kluge, Aicher "didn't like Lang." See Kluge, "The Early Days of the Ulm Institute for Film Design," in *West German Film-Makers on Film: Visions and Voices*, ed. Eric Rentscher (London: Holmes and Meier, 1988), 111–12.

54. Detten Schleiermacher, "Operation 'Oberhausen Group,' Ulm," *Output* 14 (1962), quoted in *Ulm Design*, 183.

55. Especially relevant here was the prestige at Ulm of Anatol Rapoport's "operational philosophy," a philosophical system that combined Dewey's pragmatism and Korzybski's general semantics in a rational, scientific approach to ethics, communication, and knowledge-based action. See Rapoport, *Operational Philosophy: Integrating Knowledge and Action* (New York: Harper & Brothers, 1953). For a superb rethinking of auteurism in New Hollywood cinema as a reckoning with the force of institutions, see Jeff Menne,

"The Cinema of Defection: Auteur Theory and Institutional Life," *Representations* 114, no. 1 (Spring 2011): 36–64.

56. Schleiermacher, quoted in *Ulm Design*, 182.

57. Schleiermacher, quoted in *Ulm Design*, 182.

58. Schleiermacher, quoted in *Ulm Design*, 182.

59. Reitz, "The Filmmaker as Auteur," *Output* 15 (1963), quoted in *Ulm Design*, 186.

60. Reitz, 185–86.

61. Reitz, 185.

62. James Tweedie, *The Age of New Waves: Art Cinema and the Staging of Globalization* (Oxford: Oxford University Press, 2013).

63. Tomás Maldonado, "Design Education," in *Education of Vision*, ed. György Kepes (New York: George Braziller, 1965), 134. Hereafter cited parenthetically as "DE."

64. Alexander Kluge, Edgar Reitz, and Wilfried Reinke, "Word and Film," trans. Miriam Hansen, *October* 46 (Autumn 1988): 86, 88, 91–92.

65. Miriam Hansen, "Space of History, Language of Time: Kluge's *Yesterday Girl* (1966)," in *German Film and Literature: Adaptations and Transformations*, ed. Eric Rentschler (London: Methuen, 1986), 194.

66. Kluge, Reitz, and Reinke, "Word and Film," 95.

67. Kluge, Reitz, and Reinke, 95.

68. Although it was a private school, funded by the Scholl Foundation, the school was dependent on subsidies from federal, state, and city governments throughout its life. For a detailed discussion of the school's closing, and the eventual withdrawal of state funding by the Baden-Württemberg government, see René Spitz, *hfg ulm: The View behind the Foreground; The Political History of the Ulm School of Design, 1953–1968* (Stuttgart/London: Edition Axel Menges, 2002).

69. Kenneth Frampton, "Apropos Ulm: Curriculum and Critical Theory," *Oppositions* 3 (May 1974): 32.

70. Gui Bonsiepe, "Communication and Power," *Ulm* 21 (1968), quoted in Frampton, "Apropos Ulm," 34.

71. For a helpful overview of an observation-based microsociology's relationship to the dominance in the United States of "macro" theories such as Talcott Parson's structural functionalism, see George Ritzer, "The Rise of Micro-Sociology Theory," *Sociological Theory* 3, no. 1 (Spring 1985): 88–98. "Microenvironment," we should note, was the term of art of sociologist and information theorist Abraham Moles, Maldonado's colleague at the HfG. Moles proposed the word in *Sociodynamique de la culture* (1963) as part of his cybernetic, feedback-driven model of culture as operating through mass-communications media. As an instance of the relevance of Moles's cybernetic thinking for theories of mass communications, and its overlap with both Birmingham cultural studies and documentary film practice, see Edgar Morin's discussion of Moles in his contribution to a UNESCO roundtable on mass media, *New Trends in the Study of Mass Media* (Birmingham, England: University of Birmingham Centre for Contemporary Cultural Studies, 1968), 8–9. Moles, who also began teaching at the University of Strasbourg at the invitation of Henri Lefebvre in 1961, trained his attention as well on the intimate dimensions of modern urban space in what he dubbed "micropsychology," a "sociologically informed phenomenology . . . that embraced the ostensibly incompatible methods of structuralism, cybernetics, information theory, behavioral psychology, and avant-garde art, music, and spectacle." For more on Moles's approach to urban space, see Larry Busbea, *Topologies*, 21.

72. Eugenie Brinkema, *The Forms of the Affects* (Durham, N.C.: Duke University Press, 2014), 30.

73. Brinkema, 30, 31.

74. For a helpful overview of the movement of "design thinking" from the methods of professional designers into the domains of contemporary business, consulting, and management, see Lucy Kimbell, "Rethinking Design Thinking, Part I," *Design and Culture* 3, no. 3 (2011): 285–306. For a more recent critique, see Lee Vinsel, "Design Thinking Is a Boondoggle," *Chronicle of Higher Education*, May 21, 2018.

75. Rodowick, *The Crisis of Political Modernism*, 32; Rodowick is drawing on MacCabe's "Class of '68: Elements of an Intellectual Autobiography 1967–81," in *Tracking the Signifier: Theoretical Essays* (Minneapolis: University of Minnesota Press, 1985).

76. Philip Rosen, "*Screen* and 1970s Film Theory," in Grieveson and Wasson, *Inventing Film Studies*.

77. Rosen, 271.

78. *Screen*'s asceticism, and its way of taking aim at the pleasures of Hollywood's classical-realist text, thus replays in film theory what Laura Frost has called modernism's "ways of managing different kinds of pleasure," with "unpleasure" not as pleasure's opposite, but its "modification," across the great divide. See Frost, *The Problem with Pleasure*, 5, 6.

79. Rosen, "*Screen* and 1970s Film Theory," 267.

80. Laura Mulvey, "Visual Pleasure and Narrative Cinema," *Screen* 16, no. 3 (Autumn 1975): 6–18.

81. Kristin Ross, *Fast Cars, Clean Bodies: Decolonization and the Reordering of French Culture* (Cambridge, Mass.: MIT Press, 1996), 180.

82. Ross, 176.

83. Jean-Luc Comolli and Paul Narboni, "Cinema/Ideology/Criticism," *Screen* 12, no. 1 (1971): 27–38.

84. Raymond Bellour, "*The Birds*: Analysis of a Sequence," trans. Ben Brewster; mimeograph (London: British Film Institute, 1972), 28; Stephen Heath, "Film and System: Terms of Analysis Part 1," *Screen* 16, no. 1 (Spring 1975), 7–77; Peter Wollen, "*North by Northwest*: A Morphological Analysis," *Film Form* 1, no. 1 (1976): 19–34.

85. See Eve Meltzer, *Systems We Have Loved: Conceptual Art, Affect, and the Antihumanist Turn* (Chicago: University of Chicago Press, 2013), 34; and Ngai, "Merely Interesting."

86. Rodowick, *Elegy for Theory*, 184.

87. Rodowick, 133–34, 112.

88. Edward Lowry, *The Filmology Movement and Film Study in France* (Ann Arbor: UMI Research Press, 1982).

89. Rodowick, *Elegy for Theory*, 136.

90. Geoghegan, "From Information Theory to French Theory," 111.

91. Geoghegan, 115.

92. Geoghegan, 117.

93. Geoghegan, 124.

94. See Julia Kristeva, "Semiotics: A Critical Science and/or a Critique of Science," in *The Kristeva Reader*, ed. Toril Moi (New York: Columbia University Press, 1986), 74–89.

95. Peter Wollen, *Signs and Meaning in the Cinema* (Bloomington: Indiana University Press, 1972), 165. Hereafter cited parenthetically as *SM*.

96. Christian Metz, "The Cinema: Language or Language System?," in *Film Language: A Semiotics of the Cinema,* trans. Michael Taylor (Chicago: University of Chicago Press, 1974), 32–33, 31. Hereafter cited parenthetically as "C."

97. Max Bense's precirculated paper for Vision 67 was titled "Aesthetics and Programming." On Bense's ambitious antihumanist program to measure the quantity and quality of information in aesthetic objects, see Christoph Klütsch, "Information Aesthetics and the Stuttgart School," in *Mainframe Experimentalism: Early Computing and the Foundations of the Digital Arts,* ed. Hannah B. Higgins and Douglas Kahn (Berkeley: University of California Press, 2012), 65–89.

98. Rodowick, *Elegy for Theory,* 181.

99. Rodowick, 190.

100. Peter Wollen, "Cinema and Semiology: Some Points of Contact," in *Working Papers on the Cinema: Sociology and Semiology* (London: BFI Education Department, 1968), 17.

101. Tomás Maldonado, "Communication and Semiotics," in *Ulm: The Quarterly Bulletin of the Hochschule für Gestaltung* 5 (July 1959): 69–78.

102. Maldonado, 75.

103. R. P. Blackmur's *Language as Gesture* (1952) appears near the general systems theory of von Bertalanffy and the information aesthetics of Bense; three works by Richards, including *Principles of Literary Criticism,* appear just after Anatol Rapoport's *Operational Philosophy*; W. K. Wimsatt's *The Verbal Icon* (1952) follows Norbert Wiener's *Cybernetics* (1948). See Evan Kindley, *Poet-Critics and the Administration of Culture* (Cambridge, Mass.: Harvard University Press, 2017).

104. Tomás Maldonado, "Looking Back at Ulm," in *Ulm Design,* 223.

105. Maldonado, 223.

106. Maldonado, 223.

107. Maldonado, 223. See Theodor Adorno, "Functionalism Today," in *Rethinking Architecture: A Reader in Cultural Theory,* ed. Neil Leach (New York and London: Routledge, 1997), 4–19.

Coda

1. Box 11, folder 577, International Design Conference in Aspen Papers, Special Collections and University Archives, Richard J. Daley Library, University of Illinois at Chicago.

2. "Statement by the French Group: The Environmental Witch Hunt," in Banham, *The Aspen Papers,* 208.

3. "Statement by the French Group," 209.

4. Alain Touraine, *The Post-Industrial Society: Tomorrow's Social History; Classes, Conflicts, and Culture in the Programmed Society,* trans. Leonard F. X. Mayhew (London: Wildwood House, 1971), 9–10.

5. Sim Van Der Ryn, "The Persistence of Form," box 11, folder 573, International Design Conference in Aspen Papers, Special Collections and University Archives, Richard J. Daley Library, University of Illinois at Chicago.

6. The 1960–61 season featured Buckminster Fuller, and the Italian and Mexican virtuosos of concrete, Pier Luigi Nervi and Félix Candela.

7. "Eames to Use Multi-Media in '70-'71 Norton Lectures," *Harvard Crimson,* March 5, 1970, www.thecrimson.com, accessed September 1, 2017.

8. Meredith A. Pahmer, "Art Is a Chair, a Test Tube, a Loaf of Bread," *Harvard Crimson*, May 8, 1970, www.thecrimson.com, accessed September 1, 2017.

9. Pahmer, "Art Is a Chair."

10. Lionel Trilling, *Sincerity and Authenticity* (Cambridge, Mass.: Harvard University Press, 1971), 12. Hereafter cited parenthetically as *SA*.

11. Liu, *The Laws of Cool*, 1.

12. Lionel Trilling, preface to *The Liberal Imagination* (New York: New York Review of Books, 2008), xxi. Hereafter cited parenthetically as "P."

13. Trilling argued, in Eamesian fashion, that the humanistic ideal of the past was unlikely to continue because *Bildung* was increasingly seen as a check on "autonomy," an unacceptable limit on the self and the life you choose to form: "Such limitation, once acceptable, now goes against the cultural grain—it is almost as if the fluidity of the contemporary world demands an analogous limitlessness in our personal perspective." See "The Uncertain Future of the Humanistic Educational Ideal," in *Lionel Trilling: The Last Decade; Essays and Reviews, 1965–75*, ed. Diana Trilling (Oxford: Oxford University Press, 1982), 175.

14. For an account of Trilling's role in Rockefeller Foundation postwar subsidizing of literary culture, especially of modernist little magazines, see Kindley, "Big Criticism."

15. Lionel Trilling, "Science, Literature, and Culture: A Comment on the Leavis-Snow Controversy," *Higher Education Quarterly* 17, no. 1 (1962): 12. Hereafter cited parenthetically as "SLC."

16. Amanda Anderson, "Character and Ideology: The Case of Cold War Liberalism," *New Literary History* 42, no. 2 (Spring 2011): 209–29.

17. Louis Menand, "Regrets Only: Lionel Trilling and His Discontents," *New Yorker*, September 29, 2008, www.newyorker.com, accessed September 2, 2017.

18. Diana Trilling, quoted in Adam Kirsch, *Why Trilling Matters* (New Haven, Conn.: Yale University Press, 2011), 154.

19. Part II, box 217, folder: "1970–1971 Charles Eliot Norton Lectures, Miscellany," EP.

20. Owen Gingerich, "A Conversation with Charles Eames," *American Scholar* 46, no. 3 (Summer 1977): 328.

21. Eames, quoted in Eric Schuldenfrei, *The Films of Charles and Ray Eames*, 134.

22. Schuldenfrei, 134.

23. Todd Cronan, "Architects in the Hands of an Angry God," *Los Angeles Review of Books*, May 25, 2016.

24. Part II, box 217, folder: "1970–1971 Charles Eliot Norton Lectures, Miscellany," EP.

25. Part II, box 217, folder: "1970–1971 Charles Eliot Norton Lectures, Miscellany," EP.

26. Paul Schrader, "Poetry of Ideas: The Films of Charles Eames," *Film Quarterly* 23, no. 3 (Spring 1970): 11.

27. Schrader, 11.

28. Schrader, 12.

29. Eames, quoted in Schuldenfrei, *The Films of Charles and Ray Eames*, 139.

30. Part II, box 217, folder: "1970–1971 Charles Eliot Norton Lectures, Notes, Lecture 6," EP.

31. This aspiration joined a range of roughly contemporaneous projects, from their 1969 report for the MIT Arts Commission recommending that departments produce in-house filmmakers to generate "packets of information" to combat disciplinary discontinuity and inform the community outside the university; to their film *Cable: The Immediate*

Future (1971), made for the Corporation for Public Broadcasting and extolling cable's future as a two-way, participatory system of information transmission in which "wired schools and universities" were "linked directly to the wired cities." See Schuldenfrei, *The Films of Charles and Ray Eames*, 199.

32. Eames, "Smithsonian Lecture Notes," quoted in Schuldenfrei, 202.

33. Part II, box 217, folder: "1970–1971 Charles Eliot Norton Lectures, Notes, Lecture 6," EP.

34. Part II, box 217, folder: "1970–1971 Charles Eliot Norton Lectures, Notes, Lecture 6."

35. Part II, box 217, folder: "1970–1971 Charles Eliot Norton Lectures, Notes, Lecture 6."

36. Part II, box 217, folder: "1970–1971 Charles Eliot Norton Lectures, Notes, Lecture 6."

37. Part II, box 217, folder: "1970–1971 Charles Eliot Norton Lectures, Notes, Lecture 6."

38. Schrader, "Poetry of Ideas," 6.

index

JUSTUS NIELAND is professor of English and film studies at Michigan State University. He is the author of *Feeling Modern: The Eccentricities of Public Life*, *David Lynch*, and, with Jennifer Fay, *Film Noir: Hard-Boiled Modernity and the Cultures of Globalization*. He is coeditor of the Contemporary Film Directors book series.